D1384899

THE SPANISH INQUISITION

JEAN PLAIDY

THE SPANISH INQUISITION

ITS RISE, GROWTH, AND END

32098

NEW YORK
THE CITADEL PRESS

FIRST AMERICAN EDITION, 1967

The Rise of the Spanish Inquisition copyright © 1959 by Jean Plaidy.
The Growth of the Spanish Inquisition copyright © 1960 by Jean Plaidy.
The End of the Spanish Inquisition copyright © 1961 by Jean Plaidy.
All rights reserved. This one-volume edition published by The Citadel
Press, 222 Park Avenue South, New York, N. Y. 10003. Printed in the
United States of America by Book Printers, Inc., Mamaroneck, N. Y.

Library of Congress Catalog Card Number: 67-12374

This volume contains

THE RISE OF THE SPANISH INQUISITION
THE GROWTH OF THE SPANISH INQUISITION
THE END OF THE SPANISH INQUISITION

An index will be found at the end of each book

THE RISE OF THE
SPANISH INQUISITION

NOTE

In order to avoid footnotes, sources and references are given in the text.

My very special thanks are due to the librarians of Kensington Public Library who have worked so hard and patiently to procure rare books for me, and thus have aided me considerably in my research.

CONTENTS

7

LIST OF ILLUSTRATIONS

BIBLIOGRAPHY

Acton, John Emerich Edward Dalberg, First Baron Acton, D.C.L.,
LL.D., Edited with an introduction by John Neville Figgis,
M.A., and Reginald Vere Laurence, M.A. *The History of
Freedom* and *Other Essays*. (1907)
Aradi, Zsolt. *The Popes*. (1956)
Aubrey, William Hickman Smith. *The National and Domestic
History of England*.
Bainton, Roland H. *The Reformation of the 16th Century*.
(1953)
Bainton, Roland H. *The Travail of Religious Liberty*. (1953)
Baker, The Rev. J., M.A. (Compiled and Translated by). *The
History of the Inquisition as it subsists in the Kingdoms of
Spain, Portugal, etc., and in both the Indies to this day*. (1734)
Berdyaev, Nicolas. With a Commentary and Notes by Alan A.
Spears. Translated by Alan A. Spears and Victor B. Kanter.
Christianity and Anti-Semitism. (1952)
Bertrand, Louis and Sir Charles Petrie, M.A., F.R.Hist.S. *The
History of Spain*. (1934)
Bury, J. B. with an Epilogue by H. J. Blackham. *A History of
Freedom of Thought*. (1952)
Butterfield, Herbert. *Christianity in European History*. (1951)
Cary-Elwes, Columbia, Monk of Ampleforth. With a preface by
Professor Arnold Toynbee. *Law, Liberty and Love*. (1949)
Creighton, M., D.D. Oxon. and Cam. *Persecution and Tolerance*.
(1895)
Dawson, Christopher. *Religion and the Rise of Western Culture*.
(1950)
Deanesly, M., M.A. *A History of the Medieval Church, 590-1500*.
(1925)
Gifford, William Alva. *The Story of the Faith*. (1946)
Gordon, Janet. *The Spanish Inquisition*. (1898)
Gowen, Herbert H., D.D., F.R.A.S. *A History of Religion*. (1934)
Guizot, M. Translated by Robert Black, M.A. *The History of
France*. (1881)
Hope, Thomas. *Torquemada, Scourge of the Jews*. (1939)
Hume, Martin A. S. *Spain, Its Greatness and Decay (1479-1788)
Cambridge Historical Series*. (1931)
Lea, Henry Charles, LL.D. *A History of the Inquisition of the
Middle Ages*. 3 Volumes. (1887)
Lea, Henry Charles, LL.D. *A History of the Inquisition of Spain*.
4 Volumes. (1908)

Lea, Henry Charles, LL.D. *Chapters from the Religious History of Spain connected with the Inquisition.* (1890)

Lea, Henry Charles, LL.D. *Superstition and Force.* (1892)

Lea, Henry Charles, LL.D. *The Inquisition in the Spanish Dependencies.* (1908)

Limborch, Philip. *The History of the Inquisition.* (1816)

Marchant, John and others. *A Review of the Bloody Tribunal; or the Horrid Cruelties of the Inquisition as practised in Spain, Portugal, Italy and the East and West Indies.* (1770)

Maycock, A. L., M.A. With an Introduction by Father Ronald Knox. *The Inquisition from its Establishment to the Great Schism.* (1926)

McKinnon, James, Ph.D., D.D., D.Th., LL.D. *Calvin and the Reformation.* (1936)

McKnight, John P. *The Papacy.* (1953)

Mortimer, R. C., M.A., B.D. *The Elements of Moral Theology.* (1947)

Nickerson, Hoffman. With a Preface by Hilaire Belloc. *The Inquisition, A Political and Military Study of its Establishment.* (1923)

Poole, Reginald Lane. *Illustrations of the History of Medieval Thought and Learning.* (1880)

Prescott, William H. *History of the Reign of Ferdinand and Isabella the Catholic.* 2 Volumes.

Prescott, William H. *The History of the Reign of Philip the Second, King of Spain.* 3 Volumes. (1873)

Robertson, John M. *A Short History of Freethought Ancient and Modern.* 2 Volumes. (1915)

Roth, Cecil. *The Spanish Inquisition.* (1937)

Rule, William Harris, D.D. *History of the Inquisition.* 2 Volumes. (1874)

Sabatini, Rafael. *Torquemada and the Spanish Inquisition.* (1928)

Shewring, Walter (Translated and Introduced by). *Rich and Poor in Christian Tradition.* Writings of many centuries. (1947)

Simon, Dr. Paul. Translated from the German by Meyrick Booth, Ph.D. *The Human Element in the Church of Christ.* (1953)

Stephen, James Fitzjames, Q.C. *Liberty, Equality, Fraternity.* (1873)

Swain, John. *The Pleasures of the Torture Chamber.* (1931)

Turberville, A. S., M.C., M.A., B.Litt. *The Spanish Inquisition.* (1932)

Turberville, A. S., M.C., M.A., B.Litt. *Medieval Heresy and the Inquisition.* (1920)

Wiseman, F. J., M.A. *Roman Spain. An Introduction to the Roman Antiquities of Spain and Portugal.* (1956)

Essays by

Amado, Ramón Ruiz. *Isabella the Catholic.*
Amado, Ramón Ruiz. *Spain.*
Bihl, Michael. *Elizabeth of Hungary called Saint Elizabeth.*
Blötzer, Joseph. *The Inquisition.*
Burton, Edwin. *Simon de Montfort.*
Callan, Charles J. *Rainerio Sacchoni.*
Kirsch, J. P. *Conrad of Marburg.*
O'Connor, John B. *Saint Dominic.*
O'Kane, Michael. *Raymond de Penaforte.*
Ott, Michael. *Innocent III.*
Ott, Michael. *Gregory IX.*
Ott, Michael. *Honorius III.*
Wilhelm, J. *Hus.*

All from *The Catholic Encyclopedia* Edited by Charles G. Herbermann, Ph.D., LL.D.; Edward A. Pace, Ph.D., D.D.; Condé B. Pallen, Ph.D., LL.D.; Thomas J. Shahan, D.D.; John J. Wynne, S.J. Assisted by numerous collaborators. (1907)

1

INTRODUCTION

I T I S sad and sobering to contemplate the torture which has
been inflicted, the blood which has been shed in the name of
Christ; and out of this contemplation arises an inevitable
question: If the good and evil which have grown out of the
Christian Religion could be weighed against one another, which
would tip the scales?

It is important, I submit, to remember that Christianity and
the Church do not always walk in step. In fact the simple
doctrines, founded on the teachings of Jesus Christ, have too
rarely been followed. They are too simple to appeal to men
who love power and wealth—but mostly power—and how can
men acquire power by following the doctrines of Christ? What
temporal glory could they find in taking staff and scrip, divesting
themselves of their worldly goods, and going forth to preach the
simple doctrine: "Love one another"?

Where in such a life were to be found the pomp and splendour,
the ceremonial robes, the swaying censer, the fat incomes and the
splendid palaces? Yet these were the signs of rank and importance necessary to induce that hypnotic state in which men might
worship themselves whilst feigning to worship God.

Christ's doctrine was easy to teach, though by no means easy
to carry out; and what was wanted by these seekers after power
was a way of life difficult to teach and easy to live. Such a
doctrine must therefore be attended by legends to make men's
flesh creep; fear was necessary to a religion which was to bring
power to its leaders, for fear is the complement of power. Men
seek power to gain their objectives and to overawe their fellows;
and simplicity must be disguised by mysticism for the glorification of the high priests of power.

Thus, the simple doctrine was wrapped round and round with
dogma so involved that the seed which had been planted by
Jesus Christ was hidden and forgotten; taking the place of the
wandering teacher who had given up all his worldly goods to
the poor and followed in his Master's footsteps, there were the
powerful men of the Church.

15

But the men of the Church could not agree, and since the dogmas and doctrines were of greater importance to them than the words of Jesus Christ, they fought amongst themselves, seeking to enforce their rule upon each other. Yet they did not altogether forget their Master for constantly they invoked His Name. Thousands were submitted to the cruellest torture these men could devise; the flesh of their victims was torn with red hot pincers, and molten lead poured into the wounds; many suffered the agonies of the hoist and the water torture; some were racked to death; some were burned at the stake; every means of dealing pain and indignity to the human body was explored; and all this was done in the name of One who had commanded his followers to love one another.

There must have been many—Jews and Moslems—who fervently wished that Jesus Christ had never made His appearance on Earth, when contemplating all the misery which would have been spared them, their families and friends, but for this, to them, calamitous event. This will be considered a shocking statement—and indeed it is. But it is a true one and therein lies the horror of it.

The Inquisition was surely one of the most cruel institutions ever set up by man, and it is interesting to study it in relation to the history of that country which embraced it most fervently. It was an evil thing and from it grew evil. The comparative religious tolerance displayed by Spain's great rival—England—was in some measure the cause of that rival's success, to the detriment of Spain. The known world was too small to contain two mighty seafaring colonizers; and it was those whose main intention was to trade, who scored over those who went to extend the Catholic world with the help of instruments of torture.

No great Empire has yet achieved permanence, and we who are witnessing the dissolution of one of the greatest, are unable at this stage to understand exactly where it failed. History is like a picture that must be looked at from a distance; it is like a vast oil painting; and the brilliant figures, which seem to dominate it when we stand close to it, in the long view may appear to be of lesser importance.

It is nearly five hundred years since Isabella and Ferdinand brought the Inquisition into their territory; so that the picture on which we can look back is a clear one. We can see the conquistadors going forth with patriotic valour in their hearts and the rack and the bilboes in their ships; we can see the expulsion of the Jewish race from Spain; we can see the folly of trying to force an unwanted religion on natives who were less inclined to hate the explorer if he came to trade and not to destroy their gods; we can see the even greater folly of expelling those men who, throughout the ages, have made rich the countries they inhabit. Thus, the Inquisition abroad brought bloodshed and misery to thousands and sowed the seeds of hatred instead of love, while the Inquisition in Spain robbed the country of the men who made it rich. Persecution of the Jews has always been one of the most foolish policies any country can pursue. Not only is persecution an evil thing, but also a very stupid one.

It may be said that the greatest disaster Spain suffered was in the year 1588 off the coast of Britain; although it is fashionable now to state that it was not the genius of Drake, Effingham, and the English sailors, which defeated the " Invincible Armada ", but the inclemency of the English climate. Quite clearly it was the fine fighting spirit of the English sailors and the English people which defeated the Armada although the storms came after the battle and completed the victory. But the determination to hold off the invader was surely the fiercer because it was known throughout the land that with the fighting ships, came also the ships of the Inquisition, and that it was Philip's intention to set up the dreaded monster in our islands. Therefore, this major defeat of a country, which was until that time the mightiest in the world, was in some measure due to the Inquisition.

My plan is to study this hideous monster, to expose it in all its horror, to try to understand the motives of those who installed it and those who fought against it. For this purpose I want to look at the country which embraced it so wholeheartedly, at the origins, the ignoble existence and the end of this institution which called itself the " Holy Office " and operated in the name of Jesus Christ who had commanded His followers to love one another.

2

BEGINNINGS

WHEN IN the twelfth century Pope Innocent III commanded members of the Church to persecute suspected heretics, he heralded the birth of the Inquisition, although this was not firmly established as such until the reign of Pope Gregory IX. The term *inquisitio* was already known; but before the twelfth century heretics were rarely burned to death for refusing to adopt the doctrines of the Catholic Church, and were usually punished by confiscation of their property.

Deanesly, in his *A History of the Medieval Church 590-1500*, recalls one instance in 1075 of a Catharist's being put into a shed which was set on fire; and another which took place in 1114, when an enraged mob took heretics from a prison and burned them alive; but it was only when the Catholic Church began to see danger in allowing men to live who supported a doctrine different from their own, that the great Inquisition was founded.

It has been said that the zealots of the Inquisition, even in their acts of greatest cruelty, believed themselves to be justified in what they did. We are asked to accept as a fact that they were deeply religious men who honestly and sincerely believed that they were serving God in what they did. We are told that they believed heretics were destined for eternal damnation, and that it was their duty to save them from that, no matter what pain they inflicted on the bodies of these heretics here on Earth. Those who would have us believe that the Inquisition was in itself evil, but kept the Catholic Church in existence despite those who sought to destroy it, tell us that the Inquisitors believed that while the bodies of unrepentant heretics were being consumed by the flames, they would be given—as nothing else could give them—a taste of what perpetual hellfire would be like. Thus, declared the supporters of the Inquisition, in their last moments of life on Earth, might these lost men and women save their souls for God—saved 'yet as by fire'.

It is a plausible excuse; but we must remember that it was fear of the heretic which inspired the foundation of the Inquisition; and that its victims were more likely to be rich men, whose goods were worthy of confiscation, than men whose worldly goods were few.

There may have been some who believed that they were obeying the Divine Will by spreading fear throughout the land and torturing their fellow men; but if we excuse these men their simple-mindedness, we must condemn their stupid arrogance, for it is surely the height of stupidity to persecute those who do not think as ourselves; and when this is a matter of 'Faith', surely the condemnation is doubly arrogant.

The very word heresy, derived as it is from the Greek *Hairesis*, 'choice', might—had these persecutors been possessed of one little streak of that humility, without which real wisdom cannot be acquired—have made them pause to ask themselves how they dared interfere in such a brutal way with the considered conclusions to which other men had come. But these persecutors had placed themselves outside the world of logic, as all who possess blind faith, and believe there is virtue in possessing this, must be; they were not even prepared to pity those who lacked it; they were going to castigate them; they submitted them to the most acute mental and physical torture they could contrive; and all because they did not accept the dogma which they in their blind faith accepted.

Persecution there has always been but, in the early history of religion when men might be expected to be less civilized, there was never any persecution to compare with the horrors of the Inquisition. A great deal has been written about Roman persecution of the Christian martyrs, but it is said that the number of victims sacrificed to the Inquisition in the reign of Philip II of Spain exceeded by many thousands those who died at the order of the Emperors of Rome. Moreover, the Roman Emperors worshipped Pagan gods; they had not been commanded to love one another.

It has often been stated that the early Christians might have lived in peace, pursuing their own religious beliefs, had they been inclined to do so; yet it seems that these men and women were so zealous, so determined to convert all those with whom they came into contact, or denounce them as heathen, that they brought upon themselves the ire of the Roman community; they refused to serve in the armies, declaring that it was forbidden for a Christian to kill his fellow men. (What a pity Christians did not remember this in the centuries to come!) Such conduct was certain to bring trouble upon them and may have been one of the reasons why they were thrown to the lions for the entertainment of the Romans.

Claudius expelled them as undesirables; Nero and Domitian were less lenient but, when the wife of the latter arranged for his removal in the year 96 and the just Nerva was elected by the

Senate, a new age of tolerance began, and this wise Emperor made Christians welcome in Rome and forbade persecution on the ground of religion.   Marcus Ulpius Trajan, who became Nerva's successor was, perhaps, less tolerant; he declared the Christians to be a political danger, yet he did not allow them to be persecuted on account of their beliefs, but with the coming of Marcus Aurelius Antoninus, the Stoic and philosopher, came a new era of persecution for the Christians which was in its turn to be replaced by a more tolerant one.

It seems possible that, had the early Christians been content to obey the Master's simple instructions, they would not have suffered so intensely as martyrs.   Had they been content to love each other, would they have been prevented from doing so? Perhaps, had they carried out the simple instructions, those about them would have noticed the admirable example they set, and have wished to emulate them.   This might have resulted in a spreading of real Christianity, as no amount of preaching or martyrdom could do.   But the creed was too simply stated, too difficult to follow.   They must have their meetings, their little pomps, their rites; and since they would, during the years of persecution, have been forced to meet in secret, they were naturally suspected and marked as dangerous political enemies of Romans.   They were brave men and women; but perhaps it was less difficult to live as they did—dangerously, excitingly— than to live the life of self-denial, loving their neighbours as they loved themselves.

Did these beginnings give them a contempt for life in general? If they risked their own they would surely be more ready to jeopardize the lives of others.   The Christian Faith had been spread by many who had died the martyr's death.   Was that why the Christian Faith imposed the martyr's death on others?

Intolerance appeared to be embodied in the Faith.   Indeed, all those who sought to mould it and direct it were determined to cultivate and preserve intolerance.   St. Augustine who, I suppose more than any other man of the Church, directed it in the way it was to go, set the pattern for the future when he demanded: *Quid est enim pejor, mors animae quam libertas erroris?*   He firmly believed that heretics should die, as their presence among the believers was a danger.   It is a pity that this Bishop of Hippo, the most important of all the Fathers of the Church, should have taken as his mentor—as so many others did—St. Paul rather than Jesus.

His predilection for the apostle rather than the Master was probably due to the fact that in his youth he had led a dissolute life.   He was converted to the faith of his mother (St. Monica) on reading in the Epistle of Paul the Apostle to the Romans:

"Let us walk honestly, as in the day; not in rioting and drunkenness, not in chambering and wantonness, not in strife and envying.

But put ye on the Lord Jesus Christ, and make not provision for the flesh, to fulfil the lusts thereof."

Do those who have to subdue the lusts of the flesh, as did St. Augustine and St. Paul, in doing so suppress their finer feelings, their sensitivity? Are they conscious of a burning resentment against that which makes its demands on them, and while they are determined not to fall into temptation—and indeed succeed with a resolution which is admirable—do they feel a great desire to see others share their suffering, their frustration and their triumphs? These are the hard men; the men who build with determination, with fire, with zeal, but with bitterness, with stoical determination which leads them to say: "I have suffered; so shall others suffer."

Perhaps there would have been fewer blots on the Christian story if it had continued in the style of the Master instead of in the bitter pioneering one of the Master's brave, religious but human followers.

From the fifth century—when the barbarian hordes put an end to the great Roman Empire—to the twelfth, while there had been few religious persecutions there had been men to question certain tenets of the Church, putting forward their own ideas and—as they considered—improvements. Among these were the Arians, the Catharists, the Gnostics, the Manichaeans, and the Waldenses.

Arius, who founded Arianism, was a priest of Alexandria who lived in the fourth century. The main tenet of Arianism was the denial of the consubstantiality of the Son with the Father in the Trinity. His theories were condemned in 325 and he was banished to Illyricum; his writings were destroyed and it was forbidden for any to possess them. However, the Emperor Constantine, who was later baptized as a Christian, relented and recalled Arius, who would have been taken back into the Church had he not died before this could be done. But his theories did not die with him, and a sect grew up which called itself Arian.

The Catharists or Cathari were puritanical in outlook; they were confirmed in the belief that all fleshly desire was sinful and sought to suppress these desires and mortify the flesh in order to cultivate purity.

The Gnostics believed that knowledge was more important than blind faith; and thus they began to question Christianity itself, expressing doubts as to whether Christ was God manifest in the flesh.

The Manichaeans believed that the world had been created not by God alone, but by two opposing influences: God which is spirit, and the Devil which is evil and matter. This idea was put forth by Manes who was a Persian and who died in the year A.D. 274; but it seems that it was not original since it was obviously borrowed from the theories set out by Zoroaster who founded the Parsee religion about 800 B.C.

The Waldenses were of much later origin, being founded in 1170 by Peter Waldo (or Pierre de Vaux) whose idea was to purge the Church of much which had been added during the past centuries and return to the original primitive doctrines. This sect was also known as the Vaudois; and naturally suffered great persecution.

It was the activities of these various sects in France which attracted the attention of Rome in the twelfth century.

France, habitually leading the world in intellectual matters, had for some years been casting about for ways to reform the Church. The North and the South were as different as if they had been two separate countries. North of the Loire, and the Rhone, the people were faithful to the orthodox Church, however much they craved for reform.

Peter Abélard was thundering forth from the Mount St. Geneviève and at the Paraclete, posing his scientific-religious questions for the Church to answer. These questions produced a certain amount of trepidation, for they threatened the simple faith which so far had been followed.

But there was that pillar of the Church, the Abbot of Clairvaux, St. Bernard himself, to pit his wits against those of the fiery philosopher and to remind the people of this man's scandalous passion for Hélöise, the prioress of Argenteuil and Abbess of the Paraclete. St. Bernard was the victor in this verbal duel and the teachings of Abélard were condemned at the Councils of Soissons and Sens, as a result of which Abélard was forbidden to lecture and forced to retire to the Abbey of St. Marcellus, not far from Châlon-sur-Saône, that he might cause no more disturbance. The Holy Office had not yet been set up and there was no question of Abélard's burning at the stake because his opinions diverged from those of the Church. He was, on the contrary, received with great kindness by Peter the Venerable, Abbot of Cluni, and there he stayed until his death in 1142.

In the north of France the battle between Abélard and the Church had been won by the Church. It was a different matter in the south.

The people of the south were of very mixed blood. There had been constant invasions over the centuries and mingling with the blood of Gaul was that of Rome; and there had been Arab, Visigothic and Asiatic infiltration. These people then had been made aware of many faiths; they were a highly civilized people accustomed to thinking for themselves; and it was in the south of France that the various sects were more numerous than in any other part of Europe.

These people were pleasure-loving and cultured. From such districts as Provence and Aquitaine came the troubadours and the poets. These were bold men and not of a temper to accept any faith blindly. Their rulers, lords of a district, such as the Count of Toulouse, were well satisfied with their way of life and made no attempt to interfere with the manner in which their subjects worshipped God. Indeed, they were accused of listening to those who sought to spread their different sects; and so interesting were these, and such favour did they find with so many people, that it came to the ears of the Pope Eugenius III that heresy was growing in the south of France and spreading beyond its borders.

St. Bernard, fresh from his triumphs over Peter Abélard, decided to go to the south of France in order to turn the heretics from their evil ways; and taking with him Cardinal Albéric, the Papal legate, he set out. He was appalled by what he found. "Churches without flocks, flocks without priests," as he wrote; and he sought to harangue these pleasure-loving people of the south to achieve greater piety. He found them indifferent and when he preached in the church at Vertfeuil, many of the most important people of the district walked out; moreover when the more humble saw what their lords were doing, they did the same. St. Bernard followed them into the streets, continuing with his sermon; but the people had determined not to be preached to; those who could disappear, did so; others knocked on the doors of the houses in unison, and there was such a clamour that St. Bernard could not hear his own voice.

The incensed saint cursed the place, shouting in a far from saintly manner: "Vertfeuil, God wither thee!"

Then he departed; but that was not the end of the campaign against the bold men of the south.

In the year 1165 the Council of Lombers was called together in the diocese of Albi, and the heretics of the south of France were publicly condemned; and from that time they were all known—whether they were Arians or Gnostics, Manichaeans or Catharists—as Albigenses, after the town of Albi in which the Council had met.

Persecutions were carried out but feebly during the next thirty years; the old Count of Toulouse, Raymond V, had died and his son, Raymond VI, was said to be even more lenient than his father had been. News of what was happening in the south of France filtered through to Rome, but nothing was done; and the Albigenses continued to live their pleasant lives, assembling to discuss religion, putting forward their newest theories, all under the benign protection of Raymond who was, according to Rome, infected with the new ideas.

In the year 1198 a new Pope was elected. This was Lotario de' Conti, who became Innocent III. Innocent was determined to stamp out heresy and spread the Holy Catholic Faith throughout the world. He had long been aware of how matters stood south of the Loire and he was determined to put an end to the *laissez-aller* policy of the last thirty years. He began by despatching missionaries to France. Before persecuting, he meant to persuade.

This, as in the case of St. Bernard, met with little success. The rulers of the various districts, when asked why they allowed heretics to remain in their terrain, replied that these people whom the Pope's missionaries called heretics were those for whom they had great affection; they had been brought up with them; they had married into their families and they had discovered that their divergence from orthodox Christianity had in no way impaired their honesty. It was impossible to turn them out.

Meeting with what seemed to be indestructible opposition, the missionaries lost heart and asked to be allowed to give up the work. Among these was Peter de Castelnau, a man who had worked with great enthusiasm in an endeavour to drive heresy from the south of France.

Two Spanish priests who were travelling in France met the Papal missionaries in Montpellier, and they discussed at great length the difficulty of bringing about reform among the heretics; and the Spanish priests were appalled by the despondency of the missionaries.

One of these Spaniards was the Bishop of Osma, Diego d'Azevedo, and the other his sub-prior, a nobleman of Spain named Domingo de Guzman, who was afterwards to achieve great fame as St. Dominic, the founder of the Dominicans who were to control the Inquisition.

During the discussions the Spaniards suggested that if the missionaries went among the heretics simply clad and on foot, as their Master had, they might make more impression on these people than by travelling, as they did at present, with all the pomp and splendour of Papal emissaries.

The weary missionaries were so discouraged by failure, that they were ready to try anything which might bring them success; but they insisted that they could not diverge so extraordinarily from custom unless they had the authority of a person of importance.

The Bishop of Osma remained in France with his sub-prior, de Guzman, sending his retinue back to Spain; and this matter of founding a mendicant order was discussed among priests and

Papal missionaries until it so fired the young Domingo de Guzman that he determined to make the founding of such an order his life's work.

Dominic and Diego d'Azevedo worked among the Albigenses with great fervour, casting aside all splendour and going among them simply clad; but the Albigenses loved their troubadours and their poetry, their intellectual discussions, and they were no more impressed by the humble preachers than they had been by those who had come in splendour. All they desired was to be allowed to live in freedom, to give their minds full range. This was a state of affairs which had existed in the south of France for many years; they were determined that it should remain so.

Raymond VI was not a bold man; he was a lover of peace. He could not welcome the officials of the Church in his domain because he knew that they wished him to imprison and torture those who followed beliefs diverging from the Catholic Faith as set out by the Church. All Raymond asked was that life should go on pleasantly as it had in the last years.

When Peter de Castelnau found Raymond evasive, twisting words and arguments in such a manner that it became clear that he would not introduce stern measures against heretics in his domains, he was angry and demanded Raymond's excommunication. Innocent excommunicated Raymond and let him know that other dire penalties awaited him if he did not conform.

Raymond was now afraid; he prevaricated, sought for time; he made promises which he knew he would not keep, and indeed he did soon afterwards revoke them.

Castelnau, furious at this treatment, decided to return to Rome to assure the Pope that the only way in which Raymond could be dealt with was by fire and sword.

In January of the year 1208 the Legates, with Castelnau at their head, set out for Rome. They rested for a night at an inn on the banks of the Rhône and early next morning, as they were leaving, two men who had stayed the night at the same inn came towards them as though to speak in a friendly fashion; then one of them drew his sword and plunged it into the body of Peter de Castelnau.

Castelnau fell to the ground, crying out that he hoped God would forgive his murderer as he himself did. Then he died.

This was one of the greatest calamities which could have befallen the Albigenses and freedom of thought.

The Papal Legate had been murdered. This was a blow at the Pope, at the Church itself. It could not be ignored; and through it Innocent saw a way of rallying the whole Catholic world against the Albigenses of the south of France.

The man who was blamed for this outrage was Raymond VI

of Toulouse, although he had not been present at the murder.

An event, which had taken place in England thirty years before in 1170, was recalled.   Then the Archbishop of Canterbury, Thomas a'Becket, had fallen into a difference of opinion with his King, Henry II, because Becket was eager to preserve the independence of the Church.   The King, it was believed, had been heard to murmur that he wished someone would rid him of this man; consequently the Archbishop had been murdered by four knights on the steps of the altar of Canterbury Cathedral. The point was that, although the King had not been present at the murder, it had been committed at his instigation; he realized his guilt and had done penance for the deed.   As Henry II of England had been guilty of the murder of Thomas a'Becket, so was Raymond VI of Toulouse guilty of the murder of Peter de Castelnau.

This gave Innocent the excuse he needed.   The Crusades, those holy wars under the banner of the Cross, the purpose of which was to recover the Holy Land from the Saracens, were still being carried on.   In fact at this time the fourth Crusade (there were eight in all), which had been organized by Innocent himself, had just terminated.   If, declared Innocent, good Christians made war on the Infidel in the Holy Land and received the blessing of God for so doing, how much more necessary was it to do God's work nearer home?   These people in the south of France were even worse than the Infidel; for the Infidel was ignorant and had had no chance of coming to the true faith.   It was therefore the duty of all lovers of the Church to act against them; and he commanded the King of France, Philip II (Philip-Augustus), with the nobles and clergy, to put on the cross and begin a crusade against the heretics of the South.   Raymond of Toulouse was a greater scoundrel than Saladin, said Innocent, and the Albigenses more worthy of extermination than the Saracens.

Innocent was more than a religious fanatic; he was a good politician.   While he called forth the wrath of Christianity against the Albigenses, he did not forget to offer their lands and other possessions to any who would conquer them.   So he was sure of raising a large army.

Thus in the year 1208 began the war against the Albigenses which was to drag on for fifteen years and bring great misery to people who had asked for nothing but to be allowed to use their minds and state their opinions.

It was more than a wasteful, stupid war; for out of its misery and horror was born that monster: the Inquisition.

The man whose name is linked with that of Innocent III in the war of the Church against the Albigenses is Simon, Count of Montfort-l'Amaury, the father of the famous Simon de Montfort

who married the sister of Henry III of England and came into
notorious conflict with that monarch.   Simon the father was a
French count, whose ancestor, the first Lord of Montfort, had
possessed nothing but a little castle, situated between Paris and
Chartres.

The family, however, prospered, and one of the lords of Montfort married the daughter of the Earl of Leicester, thus giving
the family a stake in England.   The fourth Earl of Leicester on
his death left the Honour of Leicester to this daughter who had
married the de Montfort and who was the mother of that Simon
who distinguished himself in the war against the Albigenses.
King John reluctantly recognized Simon as the Earl of Leicester,
but later took an opportunity of seizing his estates; which were
after a while restored but again confiscated.

It evidently became apparent to Simon that he would be wiser
to throw in his lot with France than England, for this is what he
did; and he took up residence among his Norman estates under
Philip II of France (Philip-Augustus).

Simon took part in the Fourth Crusade against the Infidel and
during this achieved great renown as a fine soldier and leader,
a man entirely devoted to the establishing of the Catholic Faith
among the Infidels.

With the death of Castelnau, Innocent, determined to carry
war into the Albigenses' stronghold, saw in the return of Simon
an opportunity too good to be missed; so he called upon the
returning hero to take part in a new crusade, this time nearer
home, in his own France against a people who, declared Innocent,
needed the scourge even more than did the Infidels.

Thus in the year 1208 Simon de Montfort became Captain
General of the army which waged war against the heretics.

His experience of battle, his fervour and his confidence that
right was on his side, soon gained the victories he desired; and
one by one the towns which the Albigenses defended fell into the
hands of de Montfort.

In the battles against the Saracens the holy warriors had
believed that no cruelty or indignity was too extreme to be
indulged in; they were able to assure themselves that whatever
they did was for the glory of God; and since they had made God
in their own image, it was easy to imagine Him, sitting on His
throne above, watching with approval their cruelty because it
was all perpetrated in His honour.   Simon was no exception,
and in the towns of Carcassonne, Béziers, Toulouse and countless
others, fanatical cruelty was carried out.

But the Albigenses were stubborn folk.   Moreover there was
more than freedom of thought to fight for; there was their property which the Pope had declared should be forfeited to the
conquerors, and many of these towns which fell to the invading

armies were won back and lost again; and so the war was to drag on, causing great misery to this beautiful country.

Simon, a true fanatic of his day, believed that the just punishment of heretics should be death by fire, and he did not fail to inflict this.

There is a story told of him that, after the battle of Castres, two heretics were brought forward for his judgment. One of these men, terrified at the prospect of the torture and terrible death which he knew awaited those who fell into the hands of de Montfort, declared his willingness to be converted. The other, however, was a braver man and he definitely said that the tormentors could do what they would with his body; he would remain true to his beliefs.

De Montfort's reply was: "Take them both to the stake and there let them suffer death by burning. If this man who declares his willingness to reform his ways speaks the truth, his fiery death will expiate the sin against God which he has committed by falling into heresy; and if he is lying, he will suffer the penalty for his deceit."

No doubt he was busy, but one wonders how Catholic historians can write so fulsomely of a man who could lightly condemn, to one of the most horrible deaths conceived by man, a victim who expressed his willingness for conversion. The answer may be that, like so many such stories, this one is apocryphal. It may be so; but there is the terrible cruelty of the campaign against the Albigenses and the pillaging of that land of the Rhône, the Garonne and the Pyrenees with all the attendant horror and massacre, to bear witness to this bloody war which was carried on in the name of Holy Church.

When the Church's forces conquered the town of Béziers, Arnauld, Abbot of Cîteaux, was so eager for the extirpation of the heretics that, on being told that many good Catholics resided in the city and asked how the soldiers should be able to differentiate between the faithful and traitors to the Church, he replied in his fanatical zeal: "Slay all, for God will certainly know His own."

So great was this man's desire to stamp out heresy that it seemed unimportant that a few of the faithful should be sacrificed in the attempt.

It is said that on that occasion twenty thousand men, women and children of the town of Béziers were killed.

Pierre de Vaulx-Cernay tells another story which throws a light on the manner in which the holy campaign was carried out, and this seems the place to relate it.

The siege of the Château de Lavaur had been broken in the year 1211, and the seigneur of the château was made a prisoner with about eighty of his followers and, probably because he was pressed for time, Simon de Montfort decided that they should be hanged on one gibbet. The seigneur was hanged, but the poles of the gallows, which had been erected in a hurry, broke; thereupon de Montfort, eager to go on to fresh conquests, ordered that the rest of the knights should be decapitated on the spot immediately. This was done. But the lady of the castle, who happened to be the sister of the seigneur, was noted for her heresy, and had committed the heinous crime, not only of practising it herself, but of spreading it; and it was decided that a very memorable example must be made of her. She was thrown into a well, and the holy men then showed their zeal for their faith by seeking as many large boulders as they could find and throwing them down the well after the lady.

The War of the Albigenses, in which the seeds of the Inquisition were first planted, soon ceased to be a war of religion; conquest under the cloak of religion was the aim of those who waged war in the name of the Church against the Albigenses. How often in the history of the Inquisition were rich men seized because they were rich men rather than because they were heretics? Was the fury of the Holy Office directed against those Jews because they, having been forced to accept Christianity, were accused of reverting to their own faith, or because they were rich men whose goods could be confiscated by the Inquisition? There can be no clear-cut answer to this, for human motives were then, as always, mixed. But there can be no doubt that Simon de Montfort, while being a zealous follower of the faith, was also a very ambitious man. Even his apologists must admit that he lost few opportunities of enriching himself while he worked for the glory of the Church; and while he showed a great hatred of the heretic he could not hide an equally great love for their possessions.

It is interesting to remember that after the fall of Béziers and Carcassonne, when the land and treasure of Raymond Roger were to be shared among the conquerors, these were offered to the Duke of Burgundy, the Count of Nevers and the Count of St. Paul. Now these Frenchmen must have felt some shame in robbing one of their own countrymen of his possessions, for they all declined the offer, declaring that they had lands enough of their own.

There was one, however, who did not share their delicate feelings. This was Simon de Montfort who lost no time in adding the title of Viscount of Béziers and Carcassonne to those he already possessed.

Raymond Roger was imprisoned in Carcassonne and three months later he was dead. It has been said that he was murdered, but it is by no means certain that this crime was committed by de Montfort.

The war against the Albigenses continued to drag on and it was still in progress in the summer of 1216 when Innocent died. Honorius III, his successor, lacked his reforming skill; much of the fire which had spurred on the crusaders in the beginning was lost, and the men of the south of France took fresh hope. It was then that the towns which they had lost fell into their hands once again; and two years after the death of Innocent, Simon de Montfort found himself outside the walls of Toulouse, making an attempt to recapture it. A shower of stones from the city's ramparts descended on him, unhorsing him and killing him.

So neither he nor Innocent saw the end of the war which they had begun. But when they had made war against the Albigenses, they had laid the foundations for the establishment of the Inquisition.

Innocent III has been called the greatest of the medieval Popes. He was 37 at the time of his election, and we are told that he accepted the tiara with reluctance; though why this should have been so is hard to understand since he was clearly a very ambitious man and, as he had entered the Church, it seems unlikely that he would have been reluctant to achieve its highest office.

I think this reluctance, which is referred to again and again by Catholic writers (not only in the case of Innocent III, but in that of almost every Pope with the exception of those such as Alexander VI—Roderigo Borgia—whom it is impossible for the most determined recorder to whitewash) was a matter of lip-service paid to the high office. Of course it may have been a point of etiquette to feign reluctance; but one is reminded of the case of Julius Caesar who was offered the crown three times, and who put it from him although he was ' very loth to lay his fingers off it.'

Innocent, then Lotario de' Conti, was the son of Count Trasimund of Segni; and Clement III was his uncle; so it may well have been that from childhood he was destined for high office in the Church. He prospered during the four brief reigns of Lucius III, Urban III, Gregory VIII and Clement III; but when Celestine III was elected to the Papal throne, it was necessary for Lotario to retire into obscurity, for Celestine was of the House of Orsini, and the Orsinis were enemies of the Counts of Segni; so for seven years there was no hope of advancement for Lotario.

But on the death of Celestine he was elected Pope.

He was very young, and it is surprising that he should have been elected, for youth was certainly no asset in an election. There were many Cardinals who, although had the offer of the tiara been made to them would no doubt have shown the usual reluctance to take it, were very loth to lay their fingers off it. If these Cardinals failed to be elected it was always a matter of consolation to contemplate that before long there would be another Conclave and consequently another chance. That was why aged Popes were usually elected. The strength of Innocent's character must have been marked at this time, for it was a great achievement to be elected Pope at the age of 37. He died at 56, so he had a long session.

He was possessed of three great ambitions: to capture the Holy Land for Christendom, to make the Papacy supreme in Europe, and to wipe out heresy.

He could be said to have achieved some success in two of these desires. He very soon subdued the Italian peninsula which was at the time of his accession in the hands of German overlords; and before his death there were few countries in Europe which did not come under Papal influence. As for the last of his ambitions: on him falls the shame of having laid the foundation of the Inquisition. It was he who, during the first year of his reign, despatched the two Cistercian monks, Rainer and Guido, into the south of France, there to hunt out heresy, commanding all lords in the neighbourhood to give these 'inquisitors' all the help they should need. The failure of his emissaries was to result in the war against the Albigenses.

In 1209 he set up the Council of Avignon at which every bishop was ordered to gather together men of authority in his diocese and force them to swear that they would do all in their power to exterminate heretics.

Some five years later, in November of 1215, the Fourth Lateran Council took place. This is referred to by Michael Ott in his essay in the *Catholic Encyclopedia* as " the culminating point in the glorious reign," and " the most important conference of the Middle Ages." Its glory is doubtful; its importance is not disputed. At this gathering of Churchmen it was decided to launch a further Crusade to the Holy Land, and so further Innocent's great ambition to extirpate the Saracen and bring the Holy Land under Christian domination. This did not give the conference its significance in history; there had been other crusades. But during this meeting seventy decrees of a reformatory nature were issued. Among these was the creed *Firmiter Credimus*, and all those in authority were commanded, if they would be considered faithful to the Church (and it was becoming more and more clear that it was very dangerous for any man to be otherwise) to swear publicly that they would with all their might and with all their strength drive heresy from the face of the Earth.

This was not all; and here was that menace which was such an integral part of the Inquisition. A Bull was issued which informed the faithful that it was a crime *not* to extirpate heretics, and any discovered to be guilty of this crime would not only be excommunicated, but would himself be suspected of heresy.

Thus men were instructed to be not only faithful Catholics, not only haters of all those who held different views from their own; they must also become spies to carry tales of their neighbours, and perhaps—if there were nothing to report—to invent them; because a man who had nothing to tell might lay himself open to suspicion.

Thus the Lateran Council.

It is natural, looking back over the centuries, to view with repulsion any who could have had a hand in establishing the terrible Inquisition, but it would not be fair to dismiss Innocent as a cruel man because of the part he played in its establishment. Innocent is called, by Catholics who make light of the sufferings of heretics and often refer to the 'much maligned Inquisition', the greatest Pope of the Middle Ages; and from one point of view this was so.

Innocent was energetic; there is no doubt that he acted in accordance with his lights. He believed that suffering was the just punishment of all who did not agree in the smallest detail with the laws as set down by the Church, for they were weakening the foundations of that great Body of which he was the Head. He worshipped the Church, its ceremonies and its doctrines; and as the teaching of Christ was hidden far beneath the many wrappings of creeds and dogmas about that Body, he had lost sight of it; therefore he had no more compunction in commanding that the utmost brutality be administered to those who threatened that Body than we have in attacking the virus of diseases which threaten the human body.

The Church was all-important; and he left the Papacy stronger than he found it.

His character is displayed by his actions with regard to Frederick II of Sicily. When Emperor Henry VI died leaving little Frederick, who was only four years old, as King of Sicily, Constance, the mother of Frederick, in terror of those who she knew would seek to snatch the throne from a helpless child, called upon Innocent to help her. Innocent was benign; he was sorry for this poor woman and her little child. He therefore took them under the apostolic mantle and looked after their interests. It was a kindly action; but Innocent, conscious of the need to strengthen the Papacy, could not resist adding common sense to kindness. Therefore, while being kind to Constance and her baby son, he did not omit to increase Papal influence in Sicily; and later, he acknowledged Frederick as King only when greater privileges were surrendered to the Papacy. Yet when Constance died and left her son in the Pope's charge, he cared for him assiduously and arranged a marriage for him; and there is no

S. DOMINICVS

Calarogæ, è nobili Gusmannorum
familia natus, de Canonico Regulari
Fundator Ordinis Fratrum Prædicatorum,
sub regula S. Augustini, ab Honorio III.
anno 1216. confirmati, Obijt aᵒ. 1221.

C. Galle sculp.   T. Galle exc. cum priuilegio.

St Dominic

Tomás de Torquemada

doubt that the boy, alone in a harsh world, had a great deal for which to thank Innocent. But Innocent, being Innocent, did not omit to demand his dues.

It was during his reign as Pope that the Mendicant Orders, founded by St. Francis and St. Dominic, were brought into being. Here were two Orders built on the best possible foundation, two communities which would live humbly and go among the people to preach the gospel even as had Christ Himself.

It is a pity that both have been tainted by their association with the Inquisition.

The Franciscans, after the death of their founder, forgot the original intention, accumulated great wealth and instituted ceremonies calculated to appeal to sensationalism rather than piety. With the Dominicans they went among the people to seek out heresy and stamp on it. The Franciscans however were simpler men than the Dominicans who were noted for their intellectual powers and theological education. It was the Dominicans who set out to teach men how to think; and their name has been more closely associated with the Inquisition than that of the followers of St. Francis.

In fact when one visualizes the horror of that monstrous institution pictures of the Dominicans must inevitably rise to the mind. When one thinks of that knock on a door in the night which called men and women from their beds to the prisons of the Inquisition, when one recalls the dank gloom of the torture chambers, one sees always in the background of these piteous scenes the sinister cowled figures—the followers of Domingo de Guzman whom Gregory IX canonized in the year 1234, and who then became St. Dominic.

St. Dominic, son of Felix Guzman and Joanna of Aza, belonged to a noble Spanish House; and, it appears, was the most pious member of a pious family, for his brothers, Antonio and Manes, were both of a highly religious nature. Indeed, there was a saintliness about these brothers which almost matched that of St. Dominic particularly in the case of Antonio who, after he had given his fortune to the poor, became a secular priest and spent his life working in a hospital.

There can be no doubt that the Guzman brothers wished to follow Christ's teaching.

Their uncle was Gumiel d'Izan, an archpriest; so it is not surprising that the family of brothers were imbued with religious instincts.

Dominic was as saintly in his habits as was Antonio. In the year 1184, when at the age of fourteen he was put to study in Palencia University, he distinguished himself by going among the poor and relieving their misery as far as was in his power.

There is a story that he sold his books that he might have money
to buy food for them; and Bartholomew of Trent, who was his
contemporary, assures us that on two occasions he would have
sold himself into slavery in order to raise ransom money
demanded by the Moors for certain men whom they had taken
captive. This may well be apocryphal, but at the same time it
seems certain, from these remarks of one who lived close to him,
that St. Dominic was noted for his unselfish and saintly way of
life.

It is to be regretted that he was called to help in the extirpation
of the heretic; and it seems incredible that a man, such as St.
Dominic is presented to be, could be capable of giving himself
so wholeheartedly—as he undoubtedly did—to this cruel task.

But Dominic was at heart a reformer concerned with reforming the masses, and like most of his kind lacked the gentleness,
the concern for the feelings and comfort of *individuals*, which is
often felt and shown by people who are otherwise less admirable.

His friend Francesco Bernardone, the son of a rich merchant
of Assisi, was of a different nature. It is difficult to imagine that
St. Francis dedicated himself so fiercely to the destruction of his
fellow men. The characters of the two saints must have been
entirely opposite, although they both, at one time in their lives,
appeared to be setting out on a similar path.

Dominic's life is dramatic, for he might so well have spent it
in obscurity and be no better known than his brothers, Antonio
and Manes, but for the fact that he happened to be in France at
that time when Innocent had despatched his Legates to preach
the wisdom of bringing back the rebellious Albigenses to the
Church.

When Dominic was a student his piety had been observed, and
he had been called by Don Martin de Bazan, who was the Bishop
of Osma, to the Cathedral Chapter; and when Don Diego
d'Azevedo became Bishop he made Dominic the Superior of the
Chapter. He was known as the Prior, and there followed nine
pleasant years of meditation and great sanctity in the Chapter
House.

Here it seemed that he would remain for the rest of his life,
but events forced him out of his obscurity. This happened when
the Bishop was sent on an embassy by Alfonso IX, the King of
Castile. Bishop Diego d'Azevedo decided that Dominic should
accompany him, and thus it was that the Prior found himself in
Toulouse when the discouraged Legates were in that town.

Dominic, surveying the pomp of the Legates, then expressed
his belief that if these emissaries of the Pope had come in the
manner of Christ, their Master, they might have made a deeper
impression on the heretics; and thus in the brain of Dominic
was born the idea of founding an Order which should consist of

mendicant friars who set out to preach the gospel in the steps of the Master.

This was indeed a worthy idea, and characteristic of St. Dominic at this stage; but he was by nature a reformer, a military general, rather than a loving Shepherd.

The embassy on which he and Diego d'Azevedo had set out was to arrange a marriage for Ferdinand, the son of Alfonso IX, King of Castile, and having successfully accomplished this they were sent on a second journey to bring home the bride. The young Princess however died before they could set out on the return journey and, finding themselves far from home, with no duties to perform, the two priests decided that they would visit the Pope.

Their travels had roused fervent desires within them both; they had seen the heretic in Southern France, and they both longed to go into the world and bring back to the true fold those who were straying.

Innocent was unimpressed; he told them that if they wished to work among the heretics, they could join the Cistercians, whom he had sent to France, and work with them. There was nothing the two could do but obey, and so fervent were they that they did prevail upon the Cistercians to give up their love of luxury and live simply.

Indefatigably did Dominic work; he was the true fanatic. With the assassination of Castelnau and the war against the Albigenses, he became a close friend of Simon de Montfort.

Catholic historians, eager to exonerate their Saint from the charge of cruelty, tell us that we are wrong to label him " The First Inquisitor ". They are at pains to insist that the charges of cruelty and fierce zealotry are unfounded. He was a good man, they insist; and we must agree that in part he was a good man. Oh, but that blind spot, that assumption that " I am right, and you who do not agree with me are wrong "—how often has that tainted the character of the best of men!

Dominic was obviously a man who *wished* to do good. He was sincere; no one doubts it. He lived a life of piety and saintliness in his Chapter House. But at the same time this man was a friend of Simon de Montfort and was present during the siege of many towns; he must have witnessed hideous cruelty, approving of this because the men, women and the children who were being tortured, tormented and subjected to hideous and humiliating death were only heretics, whom his God (made in his own image) would commit to eternal damnation because they had failed to believe in the dogma accepted by the Roman Catholic Church. As if these people could really believe at will! The arrogance in assuming that his particular sect and that only had the right answer cannot surely be reconciled with the humility which must be an essential part of saintliness. What is the use of walking about the Earth, in a plain robe, with bare feet and in all humility, when the mind is as arrogant as all those possessed by religious persecutors must be.

St. Dominic, like most of us, had a character which was partly good and partly bad. There is no doubt though that he *wished* to be good; and because he wished to be good his blindness in dealing with heretics must perhaps be forgiven. But what a pity that he did not continue in his Chapter House, living his quiet life in the manner of Brother Antonio; what a pity that, wherever his name and that of his foundation is mentioned, the first feelings they arouse in the minds of all those who do not see the Inquisition as a 'much maligned institution' is one of horror and revulsion.

In an apology for the Inquisition in the *Catholic Encyclopedia*, Joseph Blötzer, writing round about the year 1909, tries to explain why the Inquisition arouses such horror among people of this century. It is worth quoting.

"Moderns experience difficulty in understanding this institution because they have to some extent lost sight of two facts. On the one hand they have ceased to grasp religious belief as something objective, as the gift of God, and therefore outside the realm of private judgments; on the other hand they no longer see in the Church a society perfect and sovereign based substantially on a pure and authentic revelation whose first and most important duty must naturally be to retain unsullied this original deposit of faith."

All one can say to this is: What a happy state of affairs that 'moderns' cannot condone this institution. May the moderns of the centuries to come regard it in the disgust with which it is largely regarded to-day—and more also.

It was in 1214 when St. Dominic founded his Order. In this he was helped by Foulques, the Bishop of Toulouse, who made him Chaplain of Fanjeaux that he might have some property and funds for the use of the Order. From the first the main aim of the Dominicans was the extirpation of heresy.

Thereafter St. Dominic travelled widely and established his monasteries in various countries, making his way to those districts which were most infected by heresy.

There are many stories of his virtues. We hear that when terrible pillage was being carried out in the streets of St. Béziers, St. Dominic walked bravely among the soldiers, holding his cross high, imploring them to show mercy to the women and the children and those who were old or sick. We are told that in his role of First Inquisitor he was merciful and forbearing. Yet he spent a great deal of time with the armies which were waging such hideous war against the Albigenses; the victory for the

Church at Muret is said to have been a miracle due to his intercession, for, while the battle was in progress he had knelt in
prayer before the altar at the Church of St. Jacques, and the
battle had gone against the heretics.

All the stories of his virtues, all the tales of his saintliness cannot compensate for the zeal he displayed in hounding the heretic.
He, St. Dominic, will be remembered as the first Inquisitor, the
founder of the Dominicans, that order which was responsible for
the development of the Inquisition, and the coming to power of
men such as Tomás de Torquemada.

St. Dominic died in the year 1221. Pope Innocent III was
already dead and had been followed in 1216 'most reluctantly'
by Honorius III, who was very old. He was eager, even as his
predecessor had been, that heresy should be stamped out, but he
lacked the vigour of Innocent, and it was not until the election
of Ugolino, Count of Segni, as Gregory IX, that the Inquisition
was firmly established.

Gregory was also a very old man at the time of his election;
this was probably why he was elected. He was about eighty
(there is some doubt as to his actual birth date and he may even
have been eighty-two). He had been Papal chaplain, Archpriest
of St. Peter's and Cardinal Deacon of Sant' Eustachio under
Innocent III, and was awarded more honours under Honorius
III.

Honorius died in March 1227, and when the Cardinals
assembled to elect a new Pope they agreed to do this by compromise, choosing three among them to decide who should
follow Honorius to the Papal throne. One of the three was
Conrad of Urach, and he was chosen; but Conrad, fearing that it
might be thought that he had been responsible for his own election, refused the honour. A conclave was then held with the
result that Ugolino, Count of Segni, was elected. So old was he
that it seemed certain there would be another election before
long; but Ugolino surprised everybody by living until he was
almost a hundred, and because of his actions he has become the
most notorious Pope of the Middle Ages.

When he took the tiara with the usual reluctance and became
Gregory IX, he followed in the footsteps of Innocent III inasmuch
as he was a fervent persecutor of heretics and greatly desirous of
winning the Holy Land from the Saracen.

He had been in office only a few days when he began harangu-
ing the Emperor Frederick II to set out on a crusade to the
Holy Land. He believed that Frederick was the man in Europe
best equipped to go into battle against the Infidel; but Frederick,
in spite of a vow he had made, was in no hurry to embark.

He found however that the new Pope was less inclined to

leniency than Honorius III had been, and Gregory very quickly made it plain that, unless Frederick was ready to set out at once on the Holy campaign, he might discover something to his disadvantage.

Innocent III had empowered the Papacy to such an extent that Frederick realized he would be wise to act, and he forthwith set out in the September of 1227 for the Holy Land; but after three days he made an excuse to return to his dominions: one of his companions, the Landgrave of Thuringia, had contracted an illness which, Frederick declared, might prove fatal if he continued the journey.

Furious, Gregory excommunicated the Emperor. This gives an indication of the fierce fanaticism of Gregory, the determination to force those in his power to serve his God in the way he thought best, ignoring their desires and their beliefs.

He immediately turned his attention to the extirpation of heretics and was delighted with the work which was being done by those two mendicant orders founded by Francesco Bernardone and Domingo de Guzman. These two men had been great friends of his and Gregory had, before his election, often delighted to go among their followers, simply garbed as they were, and discuss with them matters of theology and the great need to wipe heresy from the face of the Earth. Gregory canonized Francesco, who became St. Francis of Assisi on July 16th, 1228; and the same honour was accorded to Domingo on 13th July, 1234.

He showered honours on these two orders—the Franciscans and the Dominicans—and quickly realized what good work they were doing in the fight against heresy.

In 1229, Gregory called an ecclesiastical council in Toulouse. The decree which came out of this was that heretics and their abettors (having been discovered by the Inquisitors) should be handed to the magistrates and nobles—in other words the secular arm—for punishment. This was, in what were called 'cases of obstinacy', death by burning at the stake. A death which, it is pointed out by apologists for the Inquisition, was recognized as the just punishment of traitors to the state; traitors to the rulers of the country, so goes on the apology, were guilty of *lèse-majestè* and therefore were considered deserving of this horrible death; how much greater then was the sin of treason against God! Therefore it is argued these death sentences grew out of a love of justice, not cruelty towards mankind!

While Gregory was absent from Rome during the years 1228 to 1231, heretics in that city made the most of his absence and, as a result, on his return he found many people questioning the dogma of the Church. He thereupon set about cleansing his own city; arrests were numerous; and those who insisted on their right to their own opinions were publicly burned that all might take warning; those who were prepared to admit their fault were imprisoned, and monasteries—Monte Cassino, Cava and Benedictine—were full of those who must be 'persuaded' to confess to their evil ways or, having repented, expiate that greatest of all sins—falling into heresy.

The monster was about to grow to maturity; in the previous centuries he had been but a sickly infant compared with what he was now to become.

Excommunication was threatened to those who concealed, defended or in any way abetted heretics; and the threat lay over all those lands under Papal jurisdiction like a threatening cloud which would, at the smallest false step or through ill-luck, break about the heads of its victims.

It might be wondered why people should have so feared excommunication; but when the meaning of the Ban of the Church is understood it is easy to see why it should have been so dreaded. Those who were excommunicated from the Church could hold no office; they had no rights as citizens; if they were ill or in any trouble no one was allowed to help them. They were completely shut off from human charity. Perhaps one of the most evil aspects of the ban was that anyone who showed charity to an excommunicated person became himself a candidate for excommunication.

It is extraordinary that these men calling themselves Christians could have set up laws which were in so many ways the complete reverse of Christian teaching.

". . . faith, hope and charity, these three, and the greatest of these is charity."

What did these men think when they read words such as those? The fact is that they ignored them. They had rejected the simple faith, and had set up their own in its place. The only resemblance to Christianity it appeared to have was in the name.

At this time the Spanish Dominican, Raymond of Peñaforte, had come to the notice of the Pope. Raymond, canonized by Clement VIII in 1601, was an ardent believer in the duty of all Catholics to persecute the heretic.

He was born at Villafranca de Benadis near Barcelona and had studied canon law so assiduously that he had become a professor in this subject. After some years he left Spain for Italy, and while occupying a chair of canon law in the university of Bologna, he wrote a treatise dealing with ecclesiastical legislation which attracted a great deal of attention.

He had listened to the preaching of the Dominicans, had become interested in the order and eventually returned to Spain to become a Dominican. There he was so concerned with the conversion of Jews and Moslems to the Christian Faith that he set up institutes where oriental languages were studied by those who would go among Jews and Infidels and preach the gospel.

Such a man was certain to draw attention to himself, and in the year 1230 Gregory summoned him to Rome. So impressed was the Pope by the writings of this man (Raymond had at this time produced his *Summa Casuum*) that he gave him the task of reconstructing the canons of the Church.

This brought to Raymond the chance he had been waiting for, and when his work was completed Gregory gave orders that it, and it alone, should be considered the true authority and none other should be used in schools.

Thus Raymond of Peñaforte takes his place among the personalities who were concerned with the building of the Inquisition, and it is for this work that he is remembered in history.

It was in the year 1232 that Gregory established the Inquisition. In his Bull he declared that all heretics should suffer excommunication. Those who were condemned should not suffer their punishment at the hands of the Church but be handed over to the secular arm that sentence might be given and carried out by that body. The punishment for the unrepentant was burning at the stake; and even those who, having been found guilty of heresy, wished to repent, must suffer punishment, though not that of death. They should be condemned to perpetual imprisonment. All those who helped heretics in any way should suffer excommunication; and any who showed friendship for the excommunicated should themselves suffer excommunication. Those who were in such circumstances excommunicated would be given one year in which to prove they were not tainted with heresy; if they failed to do this, then they would fall into the hands of the Inquisition. Anyone discovered giving an excommunicated person Christian burial, should immediately be excommunicated and he should suffer under the ban until he took the offending corpse from its place of burial and arranged that, ever after, no one of the faith should be buried therein.

Any persons, knowing that heresy existed, were bound in duty to the Church to inform on this; failing to do so they would incur excommunication, and suspicion of being themselves involved in heresy.

Children of heretics, and of any who were found guilty of helping heretics, should lose their right to any public office, to the second generation.

These were the rules; in the name of Christianity had been established the Inquisition which was to bring misery and death to tens of thousands in the centuries to come.

The Inquisitors, those cowled figures, who were to strike terror wherever they appeared, were to be the Dominicans and the Franciscans—those two orders which had been founded by two saintly men, who had become imbued with the desire to serve Christ: St. Dominic and St. Francis.

It seems ironical that these monks should have been the first of the Inquisitors. But more ironical still is the appalling truth that the Inquisition itself was set up in the name of Jesus Christ.

3

THE INQUISITION IN SOME
EUROPEAN COUNTRIES

I T I S interesting to follow the spread of the Inquisition in various European countries, and to see how it was largely rejected, mostly through popular feeling.

Conrad of Marburg made a great effort to establish it in Germany.

He was a very earnest persecutor of heretics; and certainly he had his worries in a land such as Germany, where there were men who were interested in new ideas and ready to brave dangers to express and discuss them.

By some historians Conrad is said to have belonged to a monastic order (Henke says a Franciscan, Hausrath a Dominican), but J. P. Kirsch in the *Catholic Encyclopedia* writes that ' according to the Thuringian court chaplain Berthold and Caesarius Heisterbach he was probably a secular priest.'

In any case none could have been more ardent in his pursuit of the heretic and the various sects which were, in the first half of the thirteenth century, becoming very numerous in Germany.

Conrad's determination to fight heretics, and his manner of preaching, soon attracted the attention of Ludwig, the Landgrave of Thuringia.

The Landgravine was a very pious lady, Elizabeth, who was the daughter of André II of Hungary. It had in the first place been arranged that Elizabeth should marry the eldest son of Landgrave Hermann I of Thuringia, and she had accordingly been brought from Hungary to the Court of Thuringia at a very early age. This Court was reputed to be licentious, and it was said that the little girl was jeered at for her piety. Hermann however died and, like so many princesses in similar circumstances, little Elizabeth was passed on to Ludwig who was the second son. She was only fourteen at the time of the marriage, Ludwig being twenty-one; and she was very fortunate in having a husband who was almost as strongly attracted by piety as she was herself.

It was to the Court of Thuringia that Conrad was called because Elizabeth's confessor had left her; and, considering all he knew of

Conrad, Ludwig believed that Elizabeth could not have a better mentor than the saintly but energetic man.

Conrad was in his element, for Elizabeth was not only eager to be corrected, she wished to be corrected with harshness so that she might subdue her body and live the life of a saint. We are told that even Conrad had to forbid her to punish herself too drastically, though often corporal punishment was applied.

To us today there appear to be so many ways of doing good in the world and living a really Christian life that it seems a somewhat pointless gesture to flagellate the body and torment it with hair-shirt and privation. We might even ask if these self-inflicted tortures are not the result of pride—a pride in the ability to suffer. Is, somewhere in the mind, the thought: "See how good I am! See how I inflict torment on my body!" We might ask: "But how, in torturing your flesh, are you carrying out the commands of Christ to love your neighbour? Of what use this to your fellow men? That they may follow your example and torture *their* bodies? But for what purpose?" But perhaps it is simpler to mortify the flesh in the heroic manner than to lead a simple Christian life which asks too much when it demands forgetfulness of self.

However, this was Elizabeth's way of living a saintly life and there can be no doubt of her sincerity.

In 1227, six years after her marriage, Ludwig who had gone off on a Crusade with the Emperor Frederick II died at Otranto. Elizabeth's third child had just been born and, being heart-broken when she heard the news, she declared that her life was over; but she became more pious than ever. When she died four years later there was great talk of her saintliness; and miracles, it was said, were performed on her grave.

Conrad, who had known her so well, and could vouch for the truth of the life she had led, was asked to bear witness as to her saintliness; and in 1235, four years after her death, she was canonized.

Meanwhile heresy had spread rapidly throughout Germany and Conrad received orders from Rome. He was to be the Papal Inquisitor of Germany.

This task delighted Conrad; he now put all his vigour into smelling out heretics, and this he set about doing with the help of a Dominican, Conrad Dorso, a Franciscan, Gerhard Lutzelkolb, and his servant John. These last were not learned men, but they had enough fanaticism to make up for that; and there began a reign of terror. A careless word, a look, conversation with one whose views might smack of heresy, were enough to bring a man before the Papal Inquisitor; and once there it was very difficult for him to escape.

Conrad believed that the more violent the persecution, the

more easily could he destroy heresy. German though he was, he did not understand the Germans. They were a quiet people but a determined one. They watched men whom they had loved and respected being burned at the stake; they said little, but a strong determination was forming in their hearts; and in spite of the seeming quiet there was unrest in Germany, and the most hated of men was the Papal Inquisitor.

Conrad either was unaware of this unrest or did not care. He continued on his way and, when one of the most powerful and influential noblemen of the land acted carelessly, he did not hesitate to summon him to appear before the tribunal. This was the Count of Sayn.

The Count was very angry and demanded a fair hearing. Conrad was soon to appreciate not only the temper of the German people but that he was far from Rome. A fair trial was demanded for the Count and he got it, with the result that the charge of heresy broke down. The Count was released; and the spirits of the Germans rose accordingly.

Conrad, however, continued as violent as ever in his persecution, but the people had taken courage from the affair of Count Sayn and, one evening when Conrad and Lutzelkolb were returning to Marburg, they were set upon by a group of men who were determined to take revenge for all the misery Conrad had brought to their friends and relations.

After that encounter Conrad and his henchmen were left lying dead on the ground.

In Rome Gregory might rage; he might determine to have the murderers of his faithful servants punished with the utmost severity; but whatever he did, he had received an indication of what Germany's answer to the Inquisition was likely to be; and all through the thirteenth century, although the Holy Office was still represented in Germany, after the murder of Conrad it did not establish itself with any real firmness.

Urban V, a Pope noted for his ascetic nature, who occupied the Papal throne from 1362 to 1370, dissatisfied with the state of affairs in Germany, despatched two Dominican monks to that country with threats to the prelates there of excommunication if they did not give full support to his emissaries; nor was the Emperor Charles IV spared the Pope's reproaches.

There had now arisen several new sects among whom were the Flagellants from Italy. They believed that the end of the world was in sight and that God would forgive their sins and those of the world if they scourged their bodies.

Charles IV, afraid, as so many had been before and would be henceforward, of the dreaded threat of excommunication, received the newly-appointed Inquisitors with honours; he sanctioned the censorship of literature, which censorship soon began to have its effect: the dissenters began to move out of Germany to other parts of Europe.

Kerlinger, the new chief Inquisitor, went to work with an enthusiasm and harshness common to his kind, and there was great suffering in certain towns; but the bishops, who believed that they had been slighted by the coming of the Inquisitors, were not always inclined to work with them; and on the death of Urban V and the election of Gregory XI, the bishops informed the new Pope that Inquisitorial conduct had not always been exemplary.

Gregory ordered an investigation, and when the bishops' statements were proved to be correct, the Pope gave the bishops new powers over the rival Inquisitors. This lack of unity was a further blow to the Inquisition.

With the coming of the fifteenth and sixteenth centuries the Inquisition suffered further setbacks. Germany during those centuries brought forth men of great intellectual power, such as Johann Wessel, and, most important of all, Martin Luther.

Wessel who lived from 1420 to 1489, was a great reformer, a John the Baptist of the Reformation; he was a teacher and known to thousands as *Lux Mundi*.

There was Desiderius Erasmus, born in Rotterdam in 1466, who was to exercise a tremendous influence over European thought, and particularly in Germany, for it was often said that Erasmus was the man to lay the egg, although Martin Luther was the one to hatch it.

Erasmus started life under the cloud of illegitimacy, but he soon overcame this and during a six years' sojourn in a monastery he studied the manners and habits of monks and was not inclined to admire what he saw. He then began that series of writings which were to be the prelude to the Reformation; and books such as *Praise of Folly* must have caused a great deal of apprehension in Inquisitorial circles. He died in 1536, ten years before the death of Martin Luther. In his sixty-nine years he had left a significant mark on the world.

Then came the great reformer himself. He was born in the year 1483 at Eisleben, Prussian Saxony. His childhood was one of great hardship, for he was born into poverty; but from earliest days he displayed great intellectual powers and was put to the study of law. However he was more interested in theology, and it was when he entered an Augustine order that he made the discovery that men could not expect salvation merely by the singing of masses.

His views attracted the attention of the Elector of Saxony who gave him an appointment at Wittenburg. Here he might have continued in moderate obscurity had not John Tetzel, a Dominican, arrived from Rome with indulgences for sale, the object being to raise money to rebuild St. Peter's which, dating back to 306, was falling into decay. Luther's anger at the selling of indulgences was aroused and there followed the famous gesture of denunciation.

Retaliation came from Rome: Luther's writings were to be burned; he himself was summoned to the Diet of Worms. But the Inquisition which had grown feeble with the years was powerless against him.

He continued with his writings, and when he died in 1546 he had created a powerful rival to the Catholic Church; and it had become clear that in Germany the Holy Office was no longer effective, no longer to be feared.

In France the Inquisition began with a firmer start. The Albigensian war had made the way easy. Yet when Guillem Arnaud came with his pioneering spirit and the might of Gregory IX behind him, his cruelty aroused such anger among the people that he and his assistants received the same treatment as Conrad and Lutzelkolb, and were murdered.

However the Pope was determined that the Inquisition should be established in France; and there began that long struggle between the Kings of France and the Popes for the right to stand supreme in that country.

This came to its climax when Philip IV, known as the Fair, ascended the throne in 1285. No sooner had he done so than he announced his determination to prevent the spread of the Church's power in his dominions; moreover he meant to curtail that which already existed. This attitude of Philip's resulted in the famous struggle between himself and Boniface VIII. Philip had, before the election of Boniface, already taken from the clergy certain judicial powers and placed them in civic hands; and Boniface was, even on his accession, in a weak position because in the great family of Colonnas he had enemies in his own city; for this reason he had no intention at this stage of raising an issue with the King of France whose friendship he could not afford to lose.

But in the year 1296, when Philip the Fair was at war with the English and the Flemish, he imposed fresh taxes on the clergy, who took their grievances to Boniface. Boniface, two years in office, immediately came to the rescue of his suffering prelates, and declared that clerics could not pay further taxes without the consent of the Pope; at the same time he implied that, although Kings and Emperors might be the rulers of their lands, there was one who was above them all and to whom they owed allegiance: the Holy Father himself. Failure to recognize this vital fact, Boniface pointed out, could result in excommunication.

Philip was furious; but he was at war, and he decided to wait awhile before taking action. However he commanded his merchants to cease the export of gold and silver which had been previously sent to Rome; and thus a large source of revenue was prevented from entering that city.

Boniface now began to realize that he had a formidable enemy in the King of France; and weakly he issued a Bull which allowed the French King to collect taxes from his clergy provided there was great need to do so. To show his appreciation, Philip, who had previously limited the power of the Inquisitors in France, now relaxed his veto.

However, when there was a dispute between Philip and the Bishop of Narbonne on account of certain monies which each declared should have come to him, the Pope took the side of the Bishop against the King, and Boniface wrote sternly to Philip: " If, my son, you tolerate such actions against the Churches of your kingdom, you should tremble lest God, author of judgments and King of Kings, take vengeance on you."

Philip's fury at such words was great; but the Pope did not content himself with words only; he sent to Paris as his Legate the newly appointed Bishop of Pamiers, Bernard de Saisset.

This was an unhappy move because Bernard was a Languedocian and a natural enemy of Philip; the domination of the north over the south of France, which had followed the war against the Albigenses, rankled in the heart of Bernard; moreover he was a descendant of the Counts of Toulouse, and no sooner had he arrived in Paris than he became rather abusive and even went so far as to declare that Philip could only be said to descend from Charlemagne through an illegitimate line.

The incensed Philip summoned Bernard to Senlis to answer a charge of plotting against the King and State; Philip's two faithful servants, Pierre Flotte who was his Chancellor, and Guillaume de Nogaret who was judge-major at Beaucaire, had always been determined to withstand the domination of the Church. As a result of the investigation at Senlis Bernard was arrested, and Philip despatched the Chancellor and the judge-major to Rome with a letter to Boniface in which he asked that Bernard be divested of his orders and privilege.

Boniface's answer was to ask that Bernard be sent back to him. His note was somewhat threatening, for he warned Philip of the displeasure of God if the possessions of the Bishop of Pamiers were seized by the King of France. He pointed out to the King's emissaries that the power of the Pope was spiritual, and that it embraced the temporal power of kings, which was included in the spiritual power of the Holy See.

Pierre Flotte retorted boldly that this might be so, but the power of the Pope over events in France was merely nominal; whereas in France the power of the King was very real indeed.

This angered Boniface who was given to violent outbreaks of temper; whereupon he demanded that Philip the Fair acknowledge the all-embracing power of the Holy See.

The result was an exchange of acrimonious notes; one of which coming from the Pope, the King burned ceremoniously before a crowd of his subjects in Paris. Afterwards Philip called to the capital an assembly which was to consist of the most important people from all over the country—two or three men representing each of the cities. They met in Notre-Dame, and this meeting has often been called the first States General of France.

Philip then proclaimed his desire to reform the existing laws between Church and State; and, as a result of the meeting, letters were sent to Rome deploring the Pope's interference in temporal matters.

Although most of the country stood for the King there was opposition from forty-five Bishops who insisted that both temporal and spiritual power lay in the hands of the Church; and that temporal power was held by kings only with the consent of the sovereign of them all: the Pope. All people, they declared, were subject to the Pontiff; moreover only those who believed this could enjoy salvation.

Philip's retort was to put the Bishops under restraint and to forbid them to leave his kingdom; while Boniface ordered them to come at once to Rome.

The conflict between King and Pope was drawing to its climax. Philip held a Council at the Louvre during which one of his most trusted advisers, Guillaume de Plasian, set forth an accusation against the Pope, and there was a demand that a new Pope should be elected who could be a true Defender of the Faith.

Boniface's reply was that if the King of France did not mend his ways he would have to be chastised and treated as a little boy; and he added that unless the Bishops whom he had commanded to come to Rome were allowed to leave French territory at once, the King of France would be excommunicated.

Philip was a little alarmed at this, for the threat of excommunication had always carried dread with it; he was afraid that his subjects, who had for so many generations blindly obeyed the rules of the Church, might feel it their duty, once the Ban was laid upon their King, to desert him. He therefore demanded the support of the churches and universities insomuch that they should make it known that all those who came within their sway should ignore the Pope's orders and obey only their King.

A few refused; among these was the Abbot of Cîteaux and the Templars. The latter were very soon to pay dearly for this.

Statue of Ferdinand of Spain in Malaga Cathedral
(from the drawing by Otto Bacher)

Wooden statue of Isabella the Catholic in Granada Cathedral
(from the drawing by Otto Bacher)

The King, feeling that he had the support of his country behind him, sent Guillaume de Nogaret to interview the Pope who was staying at the little town of Anagni where he had been born. News had reached Philip that Boniface had been received by the people of Anagni with the utmost respect and affection; moreover they had, in their eagerness to show their support for the Pope, insulted his enemy by taking the banner of France and dragging the sacred lilies in the dust.

Before going to Anagni, Guillaume de Nogaret sought out the old enemies of Boniface in Rome, the Colonnas, and by paying them handsomely had secured their services.

One of the family, Sciarra Colonna, hated the Pope more than most. He was a harsh man who had been captured by pirates at one time of his life and worked as a galley slave. Had he revealed the fact that he was a Colonna, there would have been no doubt that the corsairs would have asked the Pope to pay a ransom for his freedom; but the proud Colonna, determined to ask no favours of an enemy, preferred to endure the life of a slave for a year before escaping.

Sciarra was only too willing to accompany Nogaret to Anagni; and with their few followers they rode into the town shouting "Death to Boniface! Long Life to Philip the Fair and the Lilies of France! "

The simple people of that little town were terrified when they heard the shouts, for they thought that the armies of France were coming against them. They ran into their houses and barricaded themselves in, forgetting that they had promised to protect the Holy Father. Thus was the Pope left alone to face his enemies.

Sciarra Colonna demanded that he abdicate immediately.

This Boniface refused to do. "I am betrayed," he said bravely, "as Jesus was betrayed. I may die, but I shall die Pope." He had great dignity in that moment, for he was seventy-five, yet he faced them appearing unafraid, magnificently dressed— he had prepared himself to meet them—in the cloak of St. Peter and the crown of Constantine, the cross and the keys in his hands.

The Colonna would have killed him on the spot, and it is said that he actually did strike the Pope across the face with his mailed hand, which must have been very painful for the old man. However, the courage of Boniface persisted and Guillaume de Nogaret, realizing that it would be unwise deliberately to murder the Pope, prevented the Colonna from going farther.

"Caitiff Pope," we are told he said, "confess and enjoy the mercy of my sovereign, the King of France, who, though far away, watches over you and defends you through my hands."

Thereupon the Frenchman took the Pope into custody where he remained for three days; but by that time the townspeople, ashamed of their desertion, gathered together and, assuring themselves that it was not an army which had come against them but only a few foreigners, went in a body to the house in which he was held prisoner and secured his release.

When they brought him out into the streets his plight was pitiful. He was hungry and thirsty, and the kind people of Anagni brought him bread and wine and sustained him, not only with food and drink, but shouts of " Long Live His Holiness! "

He set out for Rome, and the crowds went with him; but the ordeal through which he had passed had proved too much for him.

He did reach the city but immediately became very ill. Some say that he was overcome by fever; others declare that he fell into such a mad rage that he lost his reason. There is probably no truth in this latter; it may well be a statement circulated by his contemporary enemies and preserved by others who came after. There is no doubt that Boniface was a fanatic, but so were many other people; and there is a distinction between fanaticism and madness. It may be true that he was subject to fits of rage which left him blind to the views of others and stubbornly determined to cling to his own; but this is a common enough human weakness. Boniface was ambitious, cunning and proud; it was unfortunate for him that he had been called upon to do battle with an enemy who was more ambitious, more proud, more cunning—and perhaps infinitely more cruel.

He died in Rome on 11th October, 1303. He had tried to follow in the footsteps of Innocent III who had extended the Papal authority throughout Europe; he had failed to see that since the reign of Innocent, nearly a hundred years before, great changes had come about, and power was passing from the Papacy to the secular rulers. In fighting to retain what had become impossible to hold, he had not only come to his own unfortunate end, but had done nothing to uphold the prestige of the Holy See.

Philip was determined to make the most of the advantage he had secured and when, shortly after the death of Boniface, Benedict XI was elected, he sent his congratulations through Guillaume de Plasian together with an intimation that he would expect the new Pope to profit from the lesson of the old and understand that if he would remain secure he must not forget the power of the King of France.

Benedict did realize the need to placate the most powerful monarch in Europe and immediately lifted the ban of excommunication against the King and the French nobles; however, he did not feel that he could show the same leniency towards Guillaume de Nogaret and those Frenchmen who had actually gone to Anagni and confronted the Pope there in such a manner as to be the indirect cause of his death; nor could he, as Philip wished him to, denounce his predecessor.

In June of 1304 he showed his growing strength by issuing a fresh Bull of excommunication against those who had dared commit a crime against the good memory of Pope Boniface.

Philip received this news in silence, but a month after the launching of that Bull a basket of fresh figs was brought to Benedict; they were so delectable that the Pope ate several of them. Almost immediately afterwards he was dead.

We cannot be sure who poisoned the figs. The name of the Colonnas and Guillaume de Nogaret have been put forward with that of Philip. It seems more likely that Philip—particularly in view of what followed—was the poisoner, for the removal of Benedict was so necessary to his plans and he immediately set about finding a Pope who would give him complete obedience.

This he found in Bertrand de Goth, the Archbishop of Bordeaux who, though known to be no friend of France, was possessed of limitless ambitions; and Philip believed he knew enough of ambition—possessing it in such a degree himself—that he had no doubt of the lengths to which it could carry a man.

De Goth had little chance of rising above the rank of Archbishop without the help of powerful friends. Philip decided to offer that help—at a price.

He sent for the Archbishop and promised that he would make him Pope if he would grant certain requests of the King. De Goth, overcome with delight at the power which he saw within his grasp, promised the King anything he should ask. Philip smiled, and put forward some of his requests which were simple enough for a Pope to grant. One of Philip's demands was however that the memory of Boniface should be desecrated—which was not a very easy task for the new Pope; the remaining request Philip declared he would not yet divulge, but would demand the granting of it when the time came. Then, keeping the brother and two nephews of de Goth as hostages, he dismissed the Pope-to-be; and a few weeks after his encounter with the King, de Goth became Clement V.

Now Philip knew himself to be the most powerful man in Europe. The only other who might have challenged him was his creature, bound to do his service. One of the first actions of the new Pope under the influence of the King was to move the Papal residence from Rome to Avignon, which was however owned by the Papacy though situated among the dominions of the King of France; this meant that the Pope was under the eye of his master. The period which elapsed before the return of the Papacy to Rome (sixty years) has been called the ' Babylonish captivity'.

It was not long before the King of France made known to
Clement the last of his demands. This was the destruction of
the Knights Templar.

That he should demand this came as a shock to the Pope, for
it was not known that Philip had felt towards them any particular
rancour. It was true that they had not supported him against
Boniface, but this was an extremely severe punishment for such
a small affront.

Philip had other reasons. He needed money, and the Templars
were very wealthy. Philip had always been friendly towards this
group and had borrowed money from them; but during the year
1306 there had been riots in Paris and it had been necessary for
the King to take shelter. This had been offered him in the
Temple Palace, the stronghold of the Templars, and while
he was in hiding there Philip had discovered the immense
value of the treasures which were in the possession of this
Order.

Philip was now in great need of money. His wars had impoverished his coffers and he saw a way of replenishing them.
He was determined to have the wealth of the Templars.

The Order of the Knights Templar (which had been started,
it will be remembered, by nine knights who had made it their
duty to conduct pilgrims through the Holy Land, and had become
known as the Templars because Baldwin II of Jerusalem had
granted them a residence in his palace built on the site of the
Temple of Solomon) had changed a great deal since its inception.
Founded in 1119 it had grown rapidly; before the end of the
twelfth century it had acquired land and wealth all over the
Christian world; by the end of the thirteenth century the order
had multiplied and become more affluent.

As was probably true regarding most such orders, the original
intention was lost—as instance the Franciscans and Dominicans
—and with the passing of the years what was intended to be a
virtuous and self-sacrificing life became one of luxury and
acquisitiveness.

However, now that the Templars had become very rich indeed
Philip was bent on acquiring those riches; and Pope Clement,
who knew who was his master, could do nothing but acquiesce
in view of the promise he made to the King as the price of his
election.

Consequently, Jacques de Molai, Grand Master of the
Templars, a nobleman of Burgundy who was at the time living in
Cyprus, was summoned to Paris by the Pope as well as by the
King.

No hint was immediately given of the King's intention, Philip
explaining to de Molai that he wished to discuss a new crusade
with him. While de Molai was in Paris Philip arranged for

the spreading of rumours concerning the evil manner of living into which the Templars were reputed to have fallen. True to his character he gave no hint that he had even heard the rumours, and de Molai imagined himself to be basking in royal favour since he was godfather to one of the King's children and played an important part at the funeral of another member of the royal family.

Philip cunningly allowed some time to pass; then he summoned Clement to meet him at Poitiers; there they discussed the disturbing rumours, and the King declared his desire that there should be an enquiry into them.

It was a simple matter to get the required evidence, and the outcome of the investigation was the arrest of Jacques de Molai and all leading Templars throughout France. The torturing and burning began. Clement might have been ashamed of this treatment of men who, even if they had been guilty of acquiring riches and loving luxury, were certainly innocent of the ridiculous charges brought against them, and in any case had never shown themselves to be enemies of the Holy See.

De Molai and two companions, both high in the Order, were burned to death on March 11th, 1314 in Ile de la Cité where the Place Dauphine was later to stand. They had been hideously tortured and under torture had made the required confessions; but later, confronted by the fire, they recanted these confessions, and before he died the Grand Master declared that woe would come to those who had condemned the Templars without a cause. "God," he said, "will avenge our deaths."

This gave rise to a rumour that de Molai had cursed those who had been responsible for the terrible tragedy which had befallen the Templars and, because the Pope died in April, a month after the Grand Master had perished at the stake, and Philip only eight months later in November, their deaths gave weight to the rumour.

Philip had received the wealth of the Templars; more important still, he had established for ever in France the power of the Kings over the Papacy.

In 1334 Philip VI allowed the Inquisitors to continue in their privileges, providing they understood that all their power came to them through the crown. The strength of the French monarchy had relegated the Inquisition to that of an organization to be employed when the State needed it, as in the case of the Templars.

That is not to say that hideous persecution was no longer practised in France. In the reign of François Premier the culmination of these horrors was in the notorious massacre of the Vaudois; but even before this melancholy event, those who diverged from the views of the Catholic Church were very severely dealt with; and between November 1534 and May 1535 twenty-four people were burned alive in Paris, and many others were sentenced to slightly less terrible fates.   The methods used in France were similar to those already being employed by the Inquisition in Spain; victims were chained to planks which were lowered into fires, then raised and lowered again; this was continued until the agonized sufferer became completely unconscious and so afforded little satisfaction to the bestial observers.

François however was no moralist, and his cruelty was a matter of policy; and there were times when he seemed to repent of that cruelty, with the result that persecution was sporadic. His action against the Vaudois will always be recalled with particular disgust.

The Vaudois (or the Waldenses) had settled in the valleys between the Alps and the Juras; and in Dauphiné, Provence and the valleys of the Piedmontese Alps they lived peaceably—quiet people, farmers and shepherds who asked nothing but to be left alone to work and follow their own religion.

Lutherism had spread to their neighbourhood, and this seemed to them a faith of great possibilities.

Pope Paul III, calling François' attention to these people, declared them to be a danger to the Catholic world, and demanded that they should be treated as heretics.   As a result many of them were arrested and, on a March day in 1536, thirteen of them were burned alive.

Guillaume du Bellay was sent by François to ascertain what manner of people were these Vaudois whom the Pope was so eager to destroy, and his report disclosed them to be hard-working, conscientious and good neighbours to one another; they did not of course conform to the laws of the Church.

François then ordered that any of the Vaudois who, during the following three months, abjured his religion and accepted that of the Orthodox Church should be forgiven past sins.

The result of this edict was that the Vaudois drew up a manifesto, which explained fully their beliefs, and sent the documents to the King and two Bishops, John Durandi, Bishop of Cavaillon, and Cardinal Sadolet, Bishop of Capentras.   The latter discussed their beliefs with them, telling them how they must conform; but the sturdy Vaudois pointed out that it was impossible for them to declare their belief in things in which they could not believe.

After this, there followed a period of peace for these persecuted people, the reason being that François was at that time concerned with winning the friendship of the German Protestants; but later, when that need no longer existed, a certain Jean de Maynier, Baron d'Oppède, a cruel and bigoted man of power in Rome, brought accusations, not only of heresy but of a political nature, against the Vaudois. He declared that they were plotting to bring foreign reformers into France with the motive of making Provence an independent state.

This was at the beginning of the year 1545, and François was already becoming exhausted by ill-health brought on by excesses —he was to die two years later—so that when an edict against the Vaudois was presented to him for his signature, he signed it, it is said, without reading it.

The result was the massacre.

Unfortunately for the Vaudois the command of this shameful affair was placed in the cruel hands of Baron d'Oppède.

The Vaudois were without self-defence when the troops descended on them; and these troops were the most brutal of men. The mob followed the army, scenting spoil and loot. None was spared. Women were violated in the most hideous manner the maddened mob and bestial soldiers could devise; they were submitted to every indignity and were continuously raped before their bodies were thrown over cliffs. Men and children were tortured and submitted to lingering or speedy death, according to the mood of the tormentors.

Three thousand people were murdered, and two hundred and fifty-five given a mock trial and later executed; between six and seven hundred were condemned to the galleys, and as many children were sold into slavery. Three towns and twenty-two villages were laid waste.

This was the terrible massacre of the Vaudois, those people who had taken refuge together that they might think and act as their consciences bade them.

Two years later, the cynical François on his death-bed recalled this great crime and deeply repented it; he implored his son, Henri Deux, to have an enquiry made into the matter; and in the year 1550, when the massacre was still vividly remembered, Madame de Cental, who had estates in Provence, brought a complaint against the men who had led the assault on her subjects.

D'Oppède, who was accused with Guérin, a man who had been advocate-general in 1545, declared that he had carried out the orders of François Premier and if they condemned him they should condemn Saul who had obeyed God's commands to slay the Amalekites. The powerful Duke of Guise was his friend, and d'Oppède was therefore released. Not so Guérin. The King remembered his father's death-bed wish, and there had to be a scapegoat; Guérin supplied the need and was condemned to death.

But even the massacre of the Vaudois pales beside the horror of that of August 1572—the massacre of the St. Bartholomew—

when Catholics rose against Huguenots and slaughtered them in their thousands, committing a crime which can never be forgotten.

Persecution there certainly was in France, hideous bigotry, and the foulest murder; but it was not done by the Inquisition.

The *chambre ardente* was instituted, but that was set up by the state. France rejected the Holy Office when Philip IV entered into a struggle with the Papacy, and from that time the Inquisition had no real foothold in France.

The Inquisition started with great strength in Italy. Rome—naturally—and Florence being its strongholds. There was no lack of fervent men to carry on the task of extirpating the heretic; and two of the most well known are the Dominicans, Peter Martyr and Rainerio Sacchoni.

In the early days of the Inquisition the persecuted seemed more determined to oppose tyranny—perhaps they had greater opportunity of doing so than those who came later—for Peter Martyr met the same fate as had Conrad of Marburg in Germany and Guillem Arnaud in France.

Peter Martyr worked fanatically against heretics in Milan and Florence; and it was in Florence that the people, unable to tolerate his cruelty, rose against him. But the conflict in Italy at this time was bound up in the rivalry between two political parties and was therefore more than merely a struggle to establish the Catholic Faith firmly in Italian territory. These two parties were the Ghibellines and the Guelphs. The Ghibellines wished to uphold the supremacy of the German Emperors over the Italian States, whereas the Guelphs wished to free Italy from German domination, to proclaim the independence of Italy and accept the supremacy of the Holy See.

Peter Martyr was so successful that it was not long before he made the Guelphs triumphant in Florence; this meant that the Inquisition began to flourish freely there.

So zealously did he work however that in the year 1252 he was attacked and murdered by the maddened crowd, according to some accounts at Milan, to others at Como. Thereupon he was nominated the patron saint of the Inquisition.

Rainerio Sacchoni, born at Piacenza, was in his youth a Catharist and even became one of their bishops. For seventeen years he remained with this sect and then, we are told, on hearing the preaching of Peter Martyr he deserted the Catharists and became a Dominican.

Like most converts he was an enthusiast, and when Peter Martyr was murdered he stepped into his shoes and became Inquisitor for Lombardy.

It was not long before he, like Peter, was arousing murderous feelings among the people. They failed to kill him; but so unpopular did he become that it was felt advisable to send him into exile. But before this, Pope Alexander IV had sent forces against two Ghibelline overlords, Uberto da Pallavicino and Eccelin da Romano, and defeated them, with the result that the Inquisition was then set up in the territories of these two lords.

The Inquisition was at the height of its power in Italy at this time; there was of course opposition such as the murder of Martyr, the exile of Rainerio Sacchoni and the burning of one of the Dominican monasteries in Parma in the year 1279.

Venice refused to accept the Inquisition, and as a result the persecuted began to make their way to that refuge; but Papal authority soon put a stop to this state of affairs, and Venice realized that it would be unwise to hold out against such a power. However, the city was in a position to bargain and although Inquisitors were admitted, the laws of the Inquisition were not incorporated with those of the city, and Venice took to herself those goods which were confiscated from heretics. This of course had the result of slackening the desire of the Inquisition for persecutions in that city.

When Charles of Anjou took over Naples he established the Inquisition there, but he made it clear that it was under the control of the head of the State to whom it must look for orders; and this in turn robbed the Papacy of its power.

Yet the Inquisition in Italy was more firmly established and of longer duration than in France; and as late as 1448 there was a crusade against heretics. This however was defeated, and the Waldenses continued to flourish in the mountain areas; and because of the fight put up against the Inquisitors by the people of Italy, because of the frequent flights from those areas which were in the thraldom of the Inquisition, and because of the attitude of such states as Naples and Venice, the Inquisition became considerably weakened throughout the peninsula.

The farther the area from Rome, the more difficult was it to establish the power of the Inquisition, and very little headway was made in those countries situated east of Italy.

Boniface VIII, in 1298, four years after his election to the Papal throne, did his utmost to establish the Inquisition there but without success; and the Dominicans made a further attempt in 1336; but the Catharists were very strong in these countries, and the secular rulers, realizing that these men were good subjects, were very loth to persecute them for heresy.

In 1432 Eugenius IV despatched Giacomo della Marca to Slavonia, for della Marca had distinguished himself as a fiery persecutor of Italian heretics; he had some success but when trouble broke out nearer Rome he was recalled to quell that, and afterwards the futility of sending Inquisitors into Slavonia was realized.

Eventually the Inquisition endeavoured to penetrate into Bohemia, and the first Inquisitors appeared about 1318; but after the treatment accorded to Hus and Jerome the Inquisition was looked upon with great suspicion by the Bohemians; and because they were so far from its centre they were able to prevent its spreading in their country.

Jan Hus was born at Husinetz in South Bohemia in 1369. Having passed through the University of Prague he was ordained and appointed Rector of the University.

He became absorbed in the writings of John Wyclif, Master of Balliol College, Oxford, who had taken upon himself the task of reforming the Church. He had translated the Bible into English and was fearless in his denunciation of certain tenets of the Church.

Wyclif became known later as the Morning Star of the Reformation, and he had become greatly admired throughout his University for his attacks on the Mendicant Friars who, while outwardly going among the people in their coarse garments and with a humble air, really possessed great wealth and lived in stately mansions. They were hypocrites, he declared; they flattered the people and granted absolution through the sale of indulgences.

Fortunately for Wyclif he lived in England.

Jan Hus, however, was a very brave man. He translated the works of Wyclif and circulated them.

Innocent VII, hearing what was going on in Prague, fulminated in Rome and ordered the Archbishop Sbinco to take action against Hus. Sbinco obeyed the Pope as best he could, but Prague was far away from Rome and he knew the temper of the Czech people; so although Hus was warned by the Archbishop he continued to state his views from his pulpit where he could be sure of a big and appreciative audience.

By 1408 Gregory XII was on the Papal throne and determined to put a stop to the spread of heresy. He made overtures to the King, Wenceslaus, implying that he was not unaware of the royal tolerance towards the new ideas; and when there were hints of the dreaded excommunication, Wenceslaus stirred himself to action and declared that, since the University of Prague was suspected of permitting heresy in its midst, it must clear itself from that charge.

Hus continued with his preaching, and it was not until 1409, when there was another Pope at the Vatican, Alexander V (Gregory XII's reign had been of only three years' duration), that the Archbishop was ordered to forbid preaching except in cathedrals, or collegiate and parish churches.

Hus, however, no doubt spurred on by the persistence of his hero Wyclif in Oxford, was not to be subdued; he continued to state his views and his supporters grew in number. They even went so far as to send a protest to the Pope. The Papacy had changed hands again (Alexander V only held office for a year) and the retort of the new Pope, John XXIII, was to excommunicate Hus and all those who agreed with him. This however made little impression, for the supporters of Hus continued loyal.

John XXIII was eager to send forth a new Crusade against the Holy Land and, anxious to raise money for this, he declared that all who supplied funds for the Crusade should be forgiven their sins.

This sale of indulgences was one of the main grievances against the Catholic Church, and was of course, later stressed vigorously by Martin Luther; now Hus and Jerome of Prague went into their pulpits and declaimed against such practices.

Furious, John ordered Hus to be imprisoned and his church burned. But John was far away and the Papacy had little influence in Prague. Hus remained free; however, he was prevailed upon to leave Prague; and he retired for a while to the country, where he wrote *Dé ecclesiâ* and prepared his treatise *Dé sex erroribus*.

Afterwards he returned to Prague and the treatise was posted on the walls of his church; heresy was discovered in the treatise and he was invited to appear at the Council of Constance to instruct the Council in his doctrines.

Hus, having lived in comparative security at Prague, felt few qualms about making the journey to the city in south Germany; but on arriving he found he had walked into a trap. They had not asked him to state his doctrine; they had brought him from Prague to try, and condemn him. This they did. He was burned at the stake on the 6th July, 1415.

Jerome of Prague met the same fate a year later.

The people of Bohemia were horrified by these burnings; and when other members of the Husite group were invited, as their leader had been, to appear before the Council, very wisely they refused to leave Prague.

There was little chance therefore of installing the Inquisition with any firmness in a land where there were so many people of fierce independent spirit; and although preachers were sent among the heretics and efforts were made to bring in the Inquisitors, the people of Bohemia kept the Inquisition from their land.

There is one instance of the Inquisition's working in England. This was when Clement V, on instructions from his master, Philip

IV of France, issued a proclamation throughout Christendom that there was to be an enquiry into the habits and customs of the Knights Templar.

Action against them had already started in France, and in the year 1309 *plumbea bulla bullatæ* was brought to England and read to the Bishop of London and other members of the clergy in the episcopal hall. In this Bull the Pope informed the Bishop that the Knights Templar had adopted evil habits, and he had been unwilling to believe this until Philip IV of France had brought the matter to his notice and the charge had been proved. He ordered that all Knights Templar in England should be arrested and that a careful examination of these men take place.

Edward II, the English King, who had married the daughter of Philip IV, was ready to obey his father-in-law and the Pope; and forthwith all English Templars were arrested and put in prison at London, York and Lincoln.

The Papal Commissioners visited England to conduct the enquiry, but it was very difficult to prove a case against the Templars, who all firmly protested their innocence of the charges brought against them.

Torture in such circumstances was not applied in England, and without this the Inquisitors realized that they could make little progress. In France they were getting wonderful results; in England there was deadlock.

Clement, with the King of France behind him, thundered forth his instructions that Edward must do his duty, and the weak King forthwith gave orders that the Inquisitors should be allowed to do what they wished with the bodies of the prisoners as that was the ecclesiastical law.

This brought better results; moreover witnesses were found— very unreliable ones—to testify against the Templars; but when the latter were condemned, the sentence passed on them was by no means as barbaric as that which their fellows had suffered in France.

They were to be imprisoned for the rest of their lives in monasteries, and their goods were to be confiscated and delivered into the King's hands.

The King, however, who was himself to come to a very unhappy end in Berkeley Castle, was inclined to be lenient with the Templars, and even allowed them a little money with which to support themselves in their prisons: two shillings a day for the Grand Master, and fourpence a day for his Knights.

Edward then distributed their property among his favourites.

The Inquisitors while in England were aware of the hostility of the people. The English did not like the Inquisition. It was surprising how important a strip of water could be; England was divided from Europe by the sea; and public opinion was hostile to the setting up of Inquisitors in their land.

The trial of the Templars was the only occasion when the Inquisition worked in England. That is not to say that there was not persecution in England; but it rarely reached such fanatical heights as on the Continent.

One of the earliest instances of religious persecution occurred in the year 1159 in the reign of Henry II. This was when a very small community, not more than thirty men and women, appeared in England. We do not know who they were because records are sparse and only monks pass down the account to us, and they were, naturally, very prejudiced. Yet the story comes to us that this little community attracted attention to itself because it did not worship God after the manner of the majority.

These people spoke German, so presumably they were refugees from religious persecution on the Continent. It was thought necessary to bring them before the clergy at Oxford, and there it was discovered that their leader was a man named Gerard; he told the Council that he and his followers were Christians but that they denied certain doctrines of the orthodox Church; for instance, they did not believe in purgatory, nor that the saints should be invoked when praying for the dead. This seemed to be the extent of the differences but they were judged heretics, and therefore deemed worthy of punishment.

The people who had witnessed their demeanour at the Council of Clergy, and who knew them in their daily life, found them modest and good citizens. But the clergy would not allow them to go unpunished; therefore the King was obliged, in obedience to the Church, to offer judgment and pronounce sentence.

First, all these people were to be branded on their foreheads with hot irons that all might know them for heretics. They were to be stripped to the waist and whipped through the streets of Oxford; and afterwards their clothes were to be cut short and they themselves turned into the fields just as they were. Anyone who dared show a little Christian spirit and a wish to help these people in distress would, of course, be committing a grievous sin against the Church, and in their turn would suffer similar penalties.

It was winter when these poor people, half naked, without food, their wounds bleeding, were turned into the fields to die.

They are said to be the first who suffered as heretics in England; it is sad that they should not have been the last. There is also a terrible story of the persecution of the Jews in England.

Intolerance towards Jews increased rapidly in the reign of Henry III, and they continued to live in this land uneasily until 1292 in the reign of Edward I.

The Jews were marked out for persecution because they were for the most part rich; and lest they should not be recognized immediately they were required to wear on their breasts, pieces of white linen or parchment attached to their outer garment. This in itself was not enough, and the Archbishop of Canterbury, assisted by the Bishop of Lincoln, forbade any person to buy of Jews or sell to them any of those commodities which were necessary to the preservation of life. They were, declared these men of God, excommunicated by the Church, not only because they practised usury, but because they were not Christians.

Henry III was more lenient than his clergy and, when the Jews appealed to him, had sent forth a proclamation that all people who refused to sell goods to Jews, as the Church had commanded, should themselves be imprisoned.

It must have been very galling to the Church to see how these monarchs set themselves against it and insisted on ruling. However, the strip of water set the obstinate little island apart from other European countries, and the edict of the King was obeyed, with the result that the Jews lived peacefully in England for seven years.

Unfortunately for them, when unmolested they grew richer, and Henry began to think that he would like some of their wealth for himself; so a new law was made which proclaimed that one third of the wealth of every Jew must pass to the crown.

Nor was this all. Henry had given permission for the Jews to build a very splendid synagogue and, no sooner was the building completed, than he took possession of it, that it might be converted into a Christian Church.

Then in the year 1230 began a series of extortions which increased yearly to immense proportions; so that from 1265 to 1273 they paid over a sum of four hundred and twenty thousand pounds—worth a great many times the value of that sum today.

The Jews naturally protested at being thus penalized for their talents in making money, but the more complaints they made the more were taxes raised; and, when they began to find life in the country intolerable and thought of emigrating, they were, since they provided the exchequer with such a big source of income, forbidden to do so.

The people, seeing with what ease the King extracted money, looked about them for similar means of enriching themselves. It was a simple matter to fabricate tales about the Jews which would provide excuses for looting their houses and robbing them of their wealth. There were stories of Christian children being kidnapped and circumcised; worse still some of these children, it was alleged, had been crucified as an insult to the beliefs of Christians. Violence broke out and the Jews, bowed down by taxation, forbidden to leave the country and subjected to brutalities by the people, lived in great fear.

With the coming of the next King, Edward I, there was a big step towards modern times which was perhaps more discernible in England than in any other country. The English people began to show those characteristics which have been their strongest through the ages: a love of liberty and a determination to make their rulers feel the power of public opinion. But for this, Mary I, when she married Philip of Spain, might have established the Inquisition in these islands. Thanks to the spirit of the English, although her reign is darkened by the terrible fires of Smithfield, and those of other places in England, she was unable to do so.

With the coming of the strong Edward I to replace weak Henry III, it appeared that the Jews might expect better treatment. Edward, however, soon showed himself to be even harsher than his father. During his reign taxes continued to be levied, the Jews were confined to certain areas, and officers were appointed to assess the value of their possessions and tax them accordingly.

As if this were not enough, after he had been King for seven years, Edward brought in the death penalty for any Jew who was heard to question the divinity of Christ. This naturally struck at the root of their religion; and how easy it was for any who bore a grudge to bear witness against them!

Certain Dominican friars, no doubt in an endeavour to bring the Inquisition into the land, went among the Jews in the hope, they declared, of converting them to Christianity; and, under pain of punishment, they were forced to attend the sermons given by the monks.

A new law proclaimed that any Jew who became a Christian should immediately relinquish all his worldly goods to the crown; thus if a Jew sought to live in safety he must forfeit his goods. Jews apparently loved their possessions as much as the gentiles coveted them, and there were few converts; and no doubt because the wily King hoped for conversions and the accompanying benefits to his coffers, he relaxed the law a little and declared that converted Jews should not be compelled to abandon *all* their possessions.

Jews were continually being accused of crimes; and a favourite one was clipping coins, which was punishable by death. Many Jews suffered. Not only were they subjected to the excessive and unfair taxation by the state, but private people, we are told, made a great profit by extorting large sums as payment for *not* accusing them of some crime.

Further measures were taken against them. One night, in all cities, officers of the law were sent into the Jewish quarters and many Jews were arrested and put into prison; they were only released on payment of a large ransom.

It may have been that so impoverished had the Jews become that they could no longer provide the great source of income which they had hitherto, for by the year 1290 the country was clamouring for their expulsion.

This Edward agreed to; he even allowed them to take a few of their possessions with them, although their houses and lands were seized by the crown; he also arranged that they should have protection from the mob.

They suffered greatly and must have been glad to leave a country which had treated them so badly; yet they would have known that they were unlikely to be received with any hospitality wherever they settled.

Holinshead tells a story of the exodus of the Jews which gives an idea of the attitude of the people towards them.

A party of very rich Jews on their departure hired a big ship to carry them away from England. They loaded it with the possessions which they could take with them and sailed down the Thames with it. The Captain of the ship cast anchor on pretext of waiting for a wind, and as the tide ebbed the ship grounded on the dry sand. As they must stay there some time, said the Captain, a little exercise would be good for them, and he invited the Jews to leave the ship and walk with him on the sand. He must have commiserated with them and made them believe he was their friend; but the crafty man had his eyes on the tide and, at a certain moment when he knew the ship could be refloated, was hauled up by a rope. The Jews, attempting to follow him, were too late to do so; and the Captain, from the safety of his ship, asked them why they did not call on their God, as Moses had done, to divide the water.

The Jews now unable to return to the land, where hostile people waited for them, made an effort to reach the ship which contained their treasure, but all were drowned in the attempt.

The Captain, Holinshead tells us, returned with the treasure to the King, and for this he was thanked and rewarded.

However, the historian does add that many others who behaved in such a manner were by no means rewarded and "more truly as should seem" were hanged for their fraudulent conduct.

Thus the Jews were expelled from England and were not allowed to return until the days of Oliver Cromwell.

There are, to our shame, many cases of religious persecution in England but in later years nothing so terrible as that which occurred during the reign of Bloody Mary.

The times were violent; life was not held in the same respect as it is today; and we can be proud that public opinion played a big part in keeping the Inquisition—apart from that one instance of the persecution of the Knights Templar—from our shores.

In Norway and Sweden the Inquisition, happily, never appeared, but there was one country where it was received and flourished to such an extent that it was to become known throughout the world as The Spanish Inquisition.

4

SPAIN—BEFORE THE RECONQUEST

W HY SHOULD Spain have been the country to embrace the Inquisition so wholeheartedly? Perhaps the answer is to be found by looking back to the very beginning of its recorded history.

Spain was a much-conquered country; from earliest times it had been the prey of invaders. It might have been that Ferdinand and Isabella, and those who came after, never lost sight of this, and that it was for this very reason that they nourished the Inquisition in their land that it might be a means of upholding not only the Catholic religion but the State.

The population, it appears, were originally Iberians and Tartesians; the Iberians living in the north, the Tartesians in the south. There was in these very early days some infiltration from the Celtic race which drifted in from France in the north, and from Great Britain in the west; thus before the appearance of the first conquerors there was probably a population of Iberians in the east, Celts in the north and west, with a Celtic influence on the Iberians in the centre of the country who were called Celtiberians.

Spain's geographical position made her vulnerable. She could be reached by land from the east; and Africa was within easy striking distance in the south. This no doubt accounts for the advent of so many colonizers and conquerors.

The Phoenicians were obviously a very adventurous people far in advance of their times, for not only were they enterprising traders but peaceful ones. They were fortunate in being in possession of a country which was rich in natural resources. This land on the eastern shore of the Levant was a very small one, and no doubt it was for this reason that the Phoenicians decided on colonization.

They were Semitic in origin—traders, not fighters; they made glass, metal goods and dyes which must have seemed miraculous to the primitive peoples to whom they determined to sell their wares.

The Phoenicians were clearly of a civilization far in advance of their times, for not only did they sail the seas with a skill which was as remarkable as that which they displayed in the manufacture of their goods, but they produced an alphabet. This, it is said, was not an original one, but possibly adapted from the Egyptian; yet it is clear that these people had a great effect on the world.

They brought knowledge with their goods; and what is so remarkable is the picture of those primitive peoples gathering on the shore at the approach of a Phoenician vessel with something like the feelings that people in the last century, living in remote places, felt at the sight of the pedlar: pleasure and excitement devoid of fear.

Such an enterprising race could not be expected to remain in one small country; colonization was inevitable and, as those into whose lands they penetrated had learned that they had nothing to fear and much to gain from these peaceful traders, colonization continued on peaceful lines.

All along the Mediterranean coast they settled, bringing prosperity to their adopted lands, teaching the manufacture of glass and the making of their famous Tyrian purple dye, named after their city, Tyre, which was captured in 332 B.C. by Alexander the Great. In 850 B.C. they founded Carthage, which was their most important colony; it grew to such strength and power that it became more important than the homeland. Situated in North Africa on a peninsula not far from Tunis, Carthage was in a position to dominate Mediterranean shipping; and so important did it eventually become that it threatened Rome itself in the Punic wars until it was destroyed by Scipio in 146 B.C.

In Spain the Phoenicians settled in Malaga, Cadiz, Calpë (Gibraltar) and other towns in the south; and the Phoenicians were followed in this peaceful colonization by the Greeks.

Peace however did not continue, and the Tartesians of the south sought to drive the Phoenicians, who had settled in Cadiz, from that town. The Phoenicians called in the help of those who had settled in Carthage, with the result that the Tartesians were driven back; but the Carthaginians, who had suffered heavy losses in the first of the Punic wars, decided that they would make up for these by the conquest of Spain.

The Spaniards, however, while they had been willing to receive the peaceful Phoenicians and Greeks, were determined not to surrender their land to the ambitious men of Carthage. The struggle to keep the invader out of Spain had begun.

Hamilcar Barca, the great Carthaginian general, who had fought in Sicily, led the invaders and defeated two chieftains, one Celtic, the other Celtiberian; Hamilcar's intention was to invade Italy by way of the Alps. However, no sooner had Hamilcar firmly planted his feet in Spain than another Iberian chief gathered together an army and, at Elche, Hamilcar's men were defeated and he himself killed in battle.

With Hamilcar in Spain was his son, the famous Hannibal, another son Hasdrubal, and his son-in-law also named Hasdrubal, all of whom were to play a part in Spain's history.

Hasdrubal, son of Hamilcar, won great victories in Spain in the year 212 B.C. and later commanded the Carthaginian army in Italy; he was killed at the battle of Metaurus in 207; the second Hasdrubal, Hamilcar's son-in-law who, on the death of Hamilcar, became the administrator of Spain and established Carthaginian power in the south of the peninsula, was murdered by one of his slaves in the year 221 B.C.

Hannibal, determined on the subjugation of the whole of Spain, laid seige to Saguntum, that city which destroyed itself rather than fall to the enemy; and the result of the battle for it led to the second Punic war and the famous march across the Pyrenees and the Alps into Italy. Hannibal's adventurous life terminated when he poisoned himself in 183 B.C. rather than fall into the hands of his enemies.

His failure in the second Punic war brought the Romans into Spain; and once again the natives of the troubled country were subject to an invader.

They were no more willing to accept the Romans than the Carthaginians, and in the first years they put up great resistance. But the highly civilized Romans soon proved themselves more than a match for the people of the Iberian peninsula, and, as they had no wish to spoil the country by fire and pillage, and antagonize the people by cruelty, a compromise was quickly reached. The people of Spain began to acquire the culture of their conquerors, as had other invaded peoples before them.

While Spain was under Roman control, Christianity was brought to the country, and this the Spaniards assimilated with Roman culture; as the years passed they produced poets, philosophers and statesmen to compare with the Romans.

There is the case of the poet Martial (Marcus Valerius Martialis) who was born in Bilbilis and went to Rome to become the favourite of both Nero and Domitian, who admired his poems and witty, if somewhat risqué, epigrams. There is also Lucan of Cordova who in Rome proved himself to be such a good poet that Nero was jealous of him and caused him to be banished; his life was a short one and he did not reach his thirtieth year, for, joining in a conspiracy against Nero he was caught and, rather than fall into the hands of the tyrant, caused his veins to be opened and bled to death in his bath. Had he not been as good a poet as he was he might have lived longer; but his existence is proof of the acceptance of Roman culture by the people of Spain.

And if more evidence is needed, there is Lucius Annaeus Seneca himself, uncle of Lucan; brought from his native Cordova when he was a child, the philosopher was given the dangerous post of tutor to Nero, and although he accumulated great riches during the course of his duties he, like his nephew, was accused of conspiracy, ordered to kill himself and ended as Lucan did by opening his veins that he might bleed to death. There was also his father, Marcus Annaeus Seneca, who became a tutor of rhetoric in Rome.

Rome was even governed by an emperor who was of Spanish birth. This was Marcus Ulpius Trajan, given the succession by Nerva on account of his calm wisdom. Trajan was a persecutor of Christians, but he did not pursue this policy with the fanaticism of the Dominicans; he believed the Christians to be politically dangerous, and for that reason only did he persecute them.

It is obvious therefore that the Roman conquerors were acknowledged by the people of Spain to have brought them many advantages, and that there was no discrimination in Rome against Spaniards.

The Huns, that breed of barbarians who had invaded Europe in the fourth century, now came again in the fifth under their leader Attila. They were Mongolians, noted for their cruelty, and the Germanic peoples fled before them, invading Italy and Spain.

The Romans had become effete, and disaster overtook their once mighty Empire.

The Vandals swept on to Spain destroying the treasures of Rome and those of every town through which they passed. They established themselves in Baetica which was renamed Vandalusia —the Andalusia of today—but after a while they left Spain for Africa.

Then came the Visigoths—Western Goths—led by their King, Alaric, who had passed through Greece and Rome on his triumphant way.

The Visigoths settled in north-east Spain which was then called Gotha-landia, later to become Catalonia; those other invaders, the Suevians, were forced, on account of their fierce neighbours, to remain more or less shut up in Galicia.

Attila, called the Scourge of God because he inspired great terror wherever he appeared, was, after he had over-run the Roman Empire from which he had demanded enormous tribute, eventually defeated near Châlons-sur-Marne in a battle in which Goths, under Theodoric, joined with the Romans. Attila died in 453 on the day of his marriage; he was buried with great secrecy, so we are told, in a golden coffin in which had been placed fabulous treasures; and the slaves who had dug his grave were afterwards murdered lest they should disclose the secret. But with Attila dead and Euric, the King of the Visigoths reigning over the land, the kingdom of Visigothic Spain had begun.

Religious differences arose within the kingdom, for the Hispano-Romans were Catholics and determined to cling to their faith.

Meanwhile the Franks had settled in Gaul, but thirty years after the famous battle of Châlons-sur-Marne, they still consisted of a nation of tribes, two of the principal of which were the Salian Franks and the Ripuarian Franks.

Meroveus was the principal chieftain of the Salian Franks; and his son Childéric was father of Clovis I who became the founder of the Kingdom of France.

Clovis proved himself to be a stalwart warrior whom his followers could both fear and respect. When he decided that he wished to marry, his choice fell on Clotilde who was a niece of Gondebaud the King of Burgundy. She was reputed to be of great beauty and wisdom, but it might have been that the chivalry of Clovis was aroused by the peril in which she lived.

Her uncle the King, jealous of his brother Chilpéric, had had him and his two sons put to death. Agrippina, the wife of Chilpéric, had had a stone tied about her neck and been thrown into the Rhône; but Clotilde and her sister Chrona had escaped; Chrona had entered a nunnery, but Clotilde had fled to Geneva where she lived a very pious life.

There is a romantic story of how Clovis, unable to approach Clotilde on account of the jealous anger of her uncle Gondebaud, sent the Roman, Aurelian, in rags as a beggar, to her with a ring and a message that he, Clovis, wished to make her his wife.

Clotilde was delighted, and advised the Roman to return with all speed to Clovis and bid him demand her hand from her uncle.

This was done and Gondebaud, who dared not refuse such a powerful man as Clovis had become, sent for his niece and, after a marriage by proxy, she was allowed to leave with much treasure for Clovis's domain.

Clotilde, who was undoubtedly as wise as she was reputed to be, begged those who were taking her to her husband to make all speed as she feared her uncle might repent his benevolence. She was right in this because when Aridius, adviser of Gondebaud, returned from a journey which he had made to Marseilles and heard what had been done, he advised Gondebaud to set out after his niece and bring her back. Gondebaud retorted that he was delighted that a bond of friendship had been made by this marriage between him and the Franks; but he was then reminded of the murder of Clotilde's father, mother and brothers and warned that she would avenge them.

Gondebaud, seeing the wisdom in this, despatched troops to bring her back, but he was too late; and Clotilde, determined to avenge her family, had already instructed her escorts to burn and pillage Gondebaud's land as they passed through it.

The romantic story however is frowned on by the more sober historians. They suggest that Clovis asked Gonbebaud for the hand of his niece Clotilde and Gondebaud agreed, not daring to offend the powerful Franks.

The marriage though was important historically because the Franks were pagans and Clotilde was Christian.

When their first son was born, Clotilde, who like most Christians, was burning with the desire to make all those about her accept her faith—and what was more natural than that she should desire her husband to do so more than any other?—wanted the boy to be baptized. There was evidently some controversy about this, for although Clovis was lenient concerning his wife's religion he was eager that his son should have the best gods working on his behalf.

Clotilde must have been very persuasive for she won, and the boy was baptized. Unfortunately for Clotilde the child died almost immediately. This brought forth reproaches from Clovis who was certain that if the boy had been dedicated to *his* gods he would have lived.

Another son was born, and again Clotilde prevailed on her husband to allow the child to have Christian baptism. Almost immediately the child fell sick. Clovis raged. This was *her* god, he cried. Such a god was clearly powerless.

Clotilde, however, prayed fervently and watched over the child, determined that he should live; and he did. Clovis was impressed for the little boy had been very ill indeed; but he still remained aloof from Christianity in spite of Clotilde's urgent pleas that he should accept it.

In 496 the Allemannians, a race of Germanic origin from the Rhine, invaded the territory of the Franks. These Allemannians had the reputation of being fierce fighters and, according to the romantic chroniclers, before setting out to do battle, Clovis, who was certainly uneasy, told his wife that if he beat the Allemannians, he would accept her religion.

The point was that Clovis was eager not to be off with the old gods before he was on with the new, and he was very uncertain during the battle at Tolbiac near Cologne.

Aurelian, the Roman who had been his messenger and who

was a Christian, was at his side; and when the battle was going against the Franks, he urged Clovis to become a Christian before it was too late.

Clovis is reputed to have cried: "Jesus Christ, Thou who art the God of my wife Clotilde, I have prayed to my own gods and they have withdrawn from me. I invoke Thee. If Thou wilt give me the victory over my foes and if I find Thee to be as powerful as I have heard Thou art, then will I believe in Thee and be baptized in Thy name."

The battle turned in Clovis's favour; the Allemannians were thoroughly beaten and their King slain.

As in Clovis's view the God of Clotilde had so clearly proved His mettle, he no longer put off his conversion; he was baptized by St. Remi, Bishop of Rheims; and there was great rejoicing throughout the Catholic community.

The conversion of a powerful leader such as Clovis had its effect throughout his kingdom. His sisters, Alboflède and Lanté-childe, were baptized, and three thousand men in Clovis' army were also received into the Catholic Church. Pope Anastasius II was delighted and sent his congratulations.

Clovis, however, had lost none of his ambition; after all he had chosen what he believed to be the more powerful God on the battlefield. He thereupon turned to Burgundy and, defeating Gondebaud and setting up his rule there, he looked for fresh conquests; and his plans included the kingdom of Alaric II the Visigoth whose possessions, as well as those he held in Spain, included Aquitaine.

So Clovis set out to do battle with the Visigoths, but as he marched he did not forget his new religion, and he forbade his troops to pillage the country through which they passed; they might take only grass and water. There is a story that one of his soldiers, coming upon a poor man among his hay, stole his hay, declaring that hay was grass; but when Clovis heard of what happened, he drew his sword and cut off the head of the man who had taken the hay. "What hope have we of victory," he demanded, "if we offend the saints?"

The battle took place at Poitiers where the Visigoths were at a disadvantage from the first, because they had only missiles with which to fight; and the Franks mowed through them with their swords. Clovis with his own hands slew Alaric; and the Visigoths retreated.

Clovis probably dreamed of taking his conquests south into Spain, but Theodoric of Italy had sent men to the aid of Alaric, who was his son-in-law; and Clovis was too wise to hazard all he had gained by taking his armies too far afield. So he made his way to Paris (taking Angoulême on his way) and set up his capital there.

He became the first King of France and established the Christian Faith in that land. He died in the year 511 and was buried in the church which had been built by his wife Clotilde (then called the Church of St. Peter and St. Paul, and later to be known as St. Généviève).

The Christians in Spain were strengthened by the advent of a Christian neighbour, and during the troublous years to come the Kings of France were the allies of the Catholics in Spain; it may well have been that the knowledge of a powerful Christian neighbour kept the Christian Faith alive, in spite of the overwhelming presence of the Visigoths with their Arianism, and so prepared that flame which was, ten centuries later, to flare into the intolerance and bigotry which nourished the Inquisition.

Christianity in the Visigoth kingdom spread to the royal family and provoked a civil war. Leovigild, the King, had united the country and made it politically stronger than it had ever been; but his son Hermengild, afterwards St. Hermengild, became a Christian and when, during the conflict between the Christians and the Arians he put himself at the head of the Christian army, he was defeated in battle; he suffered the martyr's death when he refused to accept the Arian belief.

When his brother Recared became King, he in his turn accepted Christianity at Toledo in 589. Recared was a strong man and the result of his conversion was that the Catholic clergy began to rise to a position of importance in the country. Recared grew rich; he loved comfort and learning; and it was during his reign that seats of culture were established in Toledo and Seville.

In the early part of the seventh century Isidore, Bishop of Seville, distinguished himself with his preaching and writings; and this man, in addition to his philosophical and theological work, wrote a history of the Visigothic kingdom.

The Christians were fast becoming a strong force within Spain; and eventually marriages between Latins and Goths were permitted. There were however many Jews in Spain, and their presence caused a great deal of friction, for wherever they appeared they seemed to be the victims of persecution.

They were accused of allying themselves with the enemies of the country and given a year to leave or become converts to Christianity. Many of them were baptized (some records say as many as 90,000) but it was inevitable that, with such an alternative before them, there were many pretended conversions to Christianity, while the rites of Judaism were practised in secret. And who can blame them for that?

The Visigothic kingdom, designed on Roman lines, appeared

to follow the Roman pattern. After years of struggle within the kingdom a peaceful state of living had been attained; there was culture and prosperity; but it seemed, as in the Roman Empire before them, that this state of affairs produced a lethargy, a carelessness, an overfondness for a luxurious and easy way of life.

Meanwhile Carthage was "blotted out" and every Christian stronghold in Africa was lost. Triumphant Islam was now very close to the Visigothic kingdom. The rulers of Spain seemed unaware that they might find it impossible to go on with their easy mode of living; they continued blindly in splendid palaces which included their harems. Everywhere was luxury and comfort calculated to appeal to the senses.

Sisebut, one of the Kings who had taken the extreme methods against the Jews, had expelled many of them, and these had settled among the Berbers of Africa; Sisebut's cruelty to this much persecuted race brought its reward, for the expelled Jews became the allies of the Berbers and naturally could give to a potential enemy information about the land they had vacated.

Soon after the fall of Carthage those Jews who remained in Spain, finding their position there intolerable and being fully aware of the lethargy into which the state had fallen, staged a rising which, if successful, was to be the means of bringing back to Spain their exiled brethren.

It is thought that the expatriated Jews in Africa may have persuaded the Berber tribesmen to give them their aid.

This plot was discovered before the Jews had time to carry it out; the result was, naturally, increased harshness towards the Jewish population within the kingdom.

Discontent continued; but the rulers did not modify their manner of living; and all about them their enemies were alert.

There is a romantic story concerning the cause of the Arab invasion and the crumbling of the Visigothic kingdom.

There may be some truth in it, but it is certainly not the only cause of the invasion. The stage was set; and the forces of destruction had been creeping nearer for many years; yet it may have been that disruption within the kingdom supplied the match which started the blaze.

The story goes that a high official of the land, a certain Count Julian, had a very beautiful daughter named Florinda.

It was the custom in Visigothic Spain—and it was to continue in the centuries to come—to send the sons and daughters of noblemen to the Court, there to learn the manners and habits of the nobility.

Roderic, the King, who was luxury-loving as all Visigothic

kings had become, and who doubtless had his harem in the palace, no sooner became aware of the growing charms of Florinda than he longed to add her to his collection of women.

It seems that Florinda was a virtuous girl, who had no intention of submitting. She therefore held out against the importunate King, which of course only increased his ardour.

One day when Florinda went down to bathe in the Tagus, Roderic found her there, and raped her.

This may have seemed a trivial incident in the life of a sybarite king, but Florinda had no intention of accepting such treatment without protest and she hurried to her father, Count Julian, to tell him what had taken place.

Julian, incensed at the deflowering of his daughter, swore he would revenge himself upon the King; so he went to Tangiers where Tarik governed for the Moslems in the name of the great ruler Mousa. Julian told Tarik that although the plans for the attack on Spain had previously failed, if Tarik tried again he might be successful. King Roderic was weakened by luxurious and riotous living, and he, Julian, would place himself on the side of Tarik and give him all the information at his disposal. He would help him bring about the downfall of Roderic's kingdom because, since Roderic had violated his daughter, he was determined on his destruction.

Tarik, delighted to have secured the cooperation of Julian, immediately began making plans, and with the help of the angry Count many Arab soldiers were smuggled into Spain to await and assist the landing of the invading forces when they should arrive.

Many historians, however, refuse to accept the story. It is too melodramatic. Is it possible, they ask, that the rape of a girl could be responsible for the domination of Christian Spain by the Mussulman for more than seven centuries?

But the legend was preserved and at Toledo on the Tagus there are ruins which are known as the Baths of Florinda and it is at this spot that the rape is said to have taken place. There seems to be little doubt, moreover, that there was a Count Julian and that he betrayed his country.

Mousa must have been a cautious man for, in spite of the help offered by Count Julian, he decided first to send a small force to Spain to spy out the land; and this he did under the command of one of his freedmen, Tarif.

This happened in the year 710. Tarif landed opposite Tangiers, and the spot where he first set foot in Spain was thenceforth known as Tarifa. Tarif came with a very small force but he managed to penetrate as far as Algeciras; the expedition was meant to be only a raid, and Tarif contented himself with looting the houses of the inhabitants. He was able to show Mousa the sort of treasures and women which would be won if they carried an offensive war into Spain.

The treasures—and chiefly the women—so delighted Mousa that he determined to make further investigations, and this time they should be on a more ambitious scale.

Tarik was commanded to set out for Spain, not to make a raid as Tarif had done, but to establish a foothold that the Arabs might pour into the country.

He established his troops on a rock which was called the Gebel-Tarik (The mountain of Tarik) and which was to become known in the centuries to come as Gibraltar.

Hearing that the enemy had a foothold in his country, Roderic prepared to do battle; but he and his men had wasted a great deal of time in luxurious living and it was not easy to prepare themselves for the fierce Arabs in the time left to them. The army might be superior in numbers, but it lacked the fighting fervour of the Arabs. Moreover, now that a bridgehead had been established, it was possible for Tarik to add to his forces; he had Count Julian to advise him; and when the battle took place, it was so fierce that there were thousands of casualties in the Visigoth King's supporters, and Roderic himself must have been among them, for he disappeared and the manner of his dying was never discovered.

The battle won, the King dead, the Arabs lost no time in marching forward. They had not only the help of the enraged Julian, but also the active support of the Jews, who made it easy for them to take possession of the main cities of the south.

Mousa came to Spain to consolidate Tarik's triumphs; and gradually the south of Spain fell under the domination of the Mussulman.

Some of the Christians remained in their cities and accepted the Arab rule. They became known as Mozarabs—which meant that they, although retaining their Christian religion, were subjects of the Moorish Kings; but many left their homes for the mountains of the north. Here they remained aloof from the conquerors—in such areas as Navarre, Aragon, Catalonia and the Asturias; here they lived through the centuries, waiting for the day when they would drive the Infidel from their country.

Having completed the conquest of southern Spain, Mousa and his lieutenant Tarik would have preferred to return to Africa, for the Arabs were never lovers of the sea and were always apprehensive when it divided them from their homeland. However, Caliph Walid refused to allow them to do this. The Arab Empire was growing and it was the intention of the Arabs to enlarge it still further. What point was there in capturing land, plundering and then abandoning it? Southern Spain had become part of the Arab Empire and Mousa and his men must remain there. He and his soldiers were therefore given lands and property in the country and were told it was their duty to stay there, to govern the people, and keep this new acquisition within the Empire.

In the beginning there was tolerance towards the Christians, but there was naturally the usual strife and suspicions.

The Mozarabs were contemptuous of those who had become converted to Islam; and the Mussulmans were suspicious of them both.

Heavy taxes were imposed on Christians, who might find these relieved if they gave up their religion for that of the conquerors. It was the beginning of persecution, and a violent people such as the Arabs, to whom life was cheap, wasted little time in arguing.

Tarik was a conqueror; it was he and his forces who had made possible the successful occupation; he was however involved in a suspicion of having kept to himself certain monies and properties which by right belonged to his masters; and when Mousa and he met, instead of being received with the honours which a successful general might have expected, Mousa flourished a whip with which he began to beat Tarik; and when the astonished general was bleeding from the lashes, Mousa roared to his men to take Tarik away and shave his head so that all might know of his shame.

It was then that the conquered people must have realized the violence and cruelty of their conquerors. But the Arabs were not consciously cruel. They were barbaric and brutal by upbringing. Cutting off the heads from the bodies of enemies had seemed a reasonable act; and crucifixion was the recognized punishment meted out to those who had offended against their laws.

Arab chroniclers tell us that so eager were they for peace in the land they had conquered that Abd el Aziz, the son of Mousa, married the daughter (some say widow) of the defeated Roderic. She was a Christian and, if this actually happened, it must have had a very soothing effect on the conquered people.

It was not long before there was trouble, for the conquerors were made up of numerous tribes among whom there were perpetual rivalries. The Berbers, who had first come to Spain under Tarik, considered they had not had their fair shares of the spoils and, since they had done the hardest part of the work of conquest, they quickly grew dissatisfied. The haughty Arabs were contemptuous of them and determined to flaunt their own superiority. This gave rise to internal quarrels and, as they were by no means a gentle people, violent atrocities were committed on both sides. For instance, when a quarrel broke out between the ninety-year-old Abd el Malik and the Syrian Baldj, Abd el Malik was seized by Baldj's soldiers, beaten, cut with swords and crucified. As was the custom with crucifixion, animals were treated in the same manner at the same time, and on either side of the old man a pig and a dog were also crucified.

Meanwhile the Christians in the north were waiting, and between them and the Mussulman territory of the south was a no-man's-land, a desert to divide them. Each side was alert, unsure of the other; the Christians determined that some day they would regain their lost territory, the Arabs determined to hold what they had won.

It may have been that the continual quarrels would have brought disaster to Arab Spain but for the first of their great rulers, Abd er Rhaman.

The Arabs were a people who believed in destiny, and prophecy played a great part in their lives. In fact it may have been Abd er Rhaman's conviction that he was destined to be the saviour of Spain, that made him so; for when he was a very young child it was prophesied that he was destined to conquer Spain, and this was believed by his family, and he himself was soon made aware of it.

His grandfather was the Caliph Hisham whose family were defeated and replaced by the Abbasides. Young Abd er Rhaman, who was in the palace when it was being looted, escaped with his young brother and hid in a nearby village; but the boys were betrayed, and soldiers came in pursuit of them with orders to kill them if they should be found.

Abd er Rhaman ran with his brother to the river's edge, the soldiers of their family's enemies close behind them. If they were to escape they must swim across the river, and they plunged in. Abd er Rhaman swam strongly, shouting encouragement to his brother who, unable to swim fast enough was caught by the soldiers who waded in after him.

From the other side of the river, where he stood in safety, young Abd er Rhaman saw the soldiers cut off the head of his brother.

This must have been a distressing sight, but Abd er Rhaman was an Arab; he believed in destiny; and as "it was written" that he should rule Spain, so, he would have told himself, was it that his brother would fall into the hands of their enemies and perish, as had so many of his relations. After that the boy lived a wandering life, learning a great deal, suffering much hardship, never forgetting his destiny. In Kairouan he encountered the suspicions of Ibn Habib who had himself great ambitions and, doubtless hearing of the great destiny in store for Abd er Rhaman, was determined to remove him. Abd er Rhaman escaped with his life and arrived in Ceuta where he lived for a while among the Berbers (his mother was a Berber slave girl).

Across the straits were Gibraltar and Spain; it is certain that he had not forgotten his brilliant destiny, and it was not long before Abd er Rhaman was sending his spies into the country across the water to discover how he would be received if he should appear among them.

He discovered that the people were ready for him. Somail, leader of the Kaishites who had conquered the Yemenites and beheaded their chiefs in the Cathedral Square of Saint Vincent, was universally hated for his cruelty; and the Yemenites were ready to receive Abd er Rhaman as their new leader.

Abd er Rhaman knew however that it would not be a matter of defeating Somail only; there was the latter's powerful ally, Yousouf, and before attempting to land in Spain he tried to separate these two; failing to do this, yet so sure of himself, he arrived, ready to do battle, and he defeated the combined forces of Somail and Yousouf on the banks of the Guadalquivir.

Abd er Rhaman, as the outcome of that battle, became Emir of Spain. This took place in the year 756.

Determined to fulfil his destiny he set out to be completely independent of Bagdad; but it was not long before Yousouf rose against him. Yousouf was beaten, however, and *pour encourager les autres* Abd er Rhaman placed his head and that of his son on the bridge at Cordova.

Somail, who had also revolted, was captured and imprisoned. But Abd er Rhaman had no intention of letting this enemy live, so he was strangled in his prison.

This however was not the end of Abd er Rhaman's troubles. The Yemenites, who had supported him because they hated Somail and Yousouf, now considered that they had been denied their full share of the spoils of conquest; therefore when urged to revolt by the Caliph El Mansour, one of the Abbasides who had taken the Caliphate from Abd er Rhaman's family, they were willing to do so. As a result Abd er Rhaman was besieged in Carmona. However his certainty in his destiny seemed to inspire him with great vigour, for he defeated the rebels, had their leaders beheaded and sent their heads salted and stuffed with myrrh to El Mansour.

Other rebels were stripped of their clothes which were replaced by rags, their heads were shaved, and they were made to ride on donkeys through the city of Cordova to a hill whereon crosses had been set up. There, to provide a spectacle for the citizens which was meant to be both an entertainment and a lesson, they were crucified.

Abd er Rhaman fulfilled his destiny; he had established the Caliphate in Spain; he was triumphant over all his enemies, although it was necessary for him to fight against them all his life. Tall, fair, something of a poet, he who had been driven from his own kingdom had succeeded in planting his dynasty in a new one. He was the father of only twenty children—not many according to Arab standards—and this was probably due to the fact that he spent a great deal of time in war instead of with his harem. He must have been a somewhat cultured man, and it is unfortunate that he was forced to spend so much of his time in fighting. It was during his reign that culture began to flower; and in 786 he began to build the mosque in Cordova which was to become the cathedral and is one of the most magnificent examples of Arab architecture.

The Emirs and Caliphs at first respected the religion of the Mozarab Christians, but with the reigns of Abd er Rhaman II and his son Mohammed I persecution set in.

There were many Catholics in Cordova, and in the neighbourhood there was no lack of churches and monasteries; it may have been that the sight of the Christians' growing numbers alarmed the Arabs, for they began to look about them for Christian martyrs.

The Christians appeared to make no attempt to avoid martyrdom; in fact they seemed to seek it, and Abd er Rhaman II was so annoyed by this that he declared that those Christians who sought martyrdom should be denied it; and as a result the persecution ceased temporarily. However, Abd er Rhaman's son, Mohammed I, determined to renew it; and he did.

Meanwhile, with a long sojourn in an alien land, the character of the Arabs was undergoing a change. They had been hard fighters, nomads, unaccustomed to luxury; but the climate of Southern Spain sapped their vitality; they began to crave for luxury, and lived in idleness, surrounded by their harems.

They lived dangerously. There were the Hispano-Visigoths, who had been driven into the north, for ever ready to descend upon them and win back what they had lost; but perhaps most dangerous were the warring elements in their own midst.

There were many risings against the Caliphate, and one of the most terrible and the most typical was that which occurred on the accession of Hakam I.

Hakam's father was the serious-minded Hisham I who had followed Abd er Rhaman I in 788; and during the reign of Hisham I a Berber *faquis*, Yahya ben Yahya, had risen to prominence, and on the death of Emir Hisham, this man stated that Hakam was unfit to rule. He was not, declared Yahya ben Yahya, serious enough to follow the pious Hisham, being too fond of the pleasures of bed and board.

Hakam quickly discovered the plot, arrested about seventy of those concerned, and had them publicly crucified. Yahya ben Yahya escaped to Toledo where he was given refuge.

The people of Toledo had always sought to hold themselves aloof from the Arabs, and there were many Christians living in the city.

Hakam, not wishing to make war on Toledo, was yet determined to show the city that he intended to be its master. He appointed a new governor to the town, who was not an Arab; this delighted the people of Toledo, for they did not know that Hakam had arranged with the new governor that all the most important people of the town should be murdered.

The new governor, on secret instructions from Hakam, had an alcázar built in the town; it was proposed to use it for troops who would protect the city.

When it was built, a great feast was given in it to all the notable people of Toledo. To reach the alcázar it was necessary to cross the courtyard in which a ditch had been dug while the building was being erected; there was chalk and clay in this ditch.

Seven hundred of the town's most important citizens were invited, so say some Arab sources (others declared it was not more than 500) and as they were admitted, one by one they were escorted across the courtyard to the building. Soldiers were standing at attention beside the ditch and, as each guest passed, a soldier would raise his sword and cut off the guest's head. Bodies and heads were then thrown into the ditch.

It was an Arab custom to pile up in heaps the heads and sometimes the bodies of their victims; this was their method of assessing the size of a victory.

The affair of the ditch subdued the Toledans and the agitator, Yahya ben Yahya, but the latter continued to preach against Hakam, and the citizens of Toledo did not forget the affair of the ditch.

Six years later there was another rising, this time in the suburb of Secunda on the bank of the Guadalquivir, and Hakam was determined to sow fear in the hearts of all rebels this time. So he made up his mind that he would burn the suburb of Secunda.

First, however, three hundred of the suburb's most important people, who were suspected of being leaders of the revolt, were arrested and crucified heads downwards; the crosses had been set up along the river bank opposite the Bridge of Cordova.

The people of Secunda were forced to witness the slow death agonies of the three hundred before they were driven from their homes and banished from Spain. Hakam then set fire to every house.

Surely that must have been one of the most terrible scenes in history: three hundred men dying in lingering agony, watched by those who were being driven with whips from their burning homes.

The change in the character of the Arabs of Spain began to show itself in the tenth century. Their palaces were becoming more luxurious and Abd er Rhaman II went so far as to have water brought to his palace.

Abd er Rhaman III, who came nearly a hundred years later, was also a great builder, and spent much time, when he was not fighting, in producing mosques and palaces, or embellishing those he already had. His most spectacular achievement was the palace of Medina az Zahara which was built for his favourite, Zahara, and named after her.

Meanwhile the Christians in the country were living very precarious and dangerous lives.

Those who had remained in Arab territory were obliged to live together in certain quarters, as the Jews did in their ghetto; it may have been that they preferred this to living free of Arab domination in the north, for life there was one of poverty and uncertainty. There was continual war because, fearful of attacks from the north, the Arabs perpetually attacked; and twice yearly an army was sent north to harry the Christians, to destroy their churches, to burn their crops and to steal their women and children that they might be sold as slaves.

The Christians were on the defensive for centuries, but Alfonso III, King of the Asturias, who came to the throne in 866 secured many victories over the enemy. This was a sign. The Christians, living their hard lives in the north, were growing stronger; the Arabs were growing weaker through excesses in their grand palaces. Alfonso died in 910, but although he had shown that it was possible to win victories over the Moors, this merely produced a stirring of resentment against the oppressor; and with the coming of strong rulers such as El Mansour, the usurper of the Caliphate, the Christians lost any advantage they had gained. This man, who had one of his own sons whipped to death in his presence for some misdemeanour, was unlikely to show leniency towards his enemies.

It was El Mansour who, after a battle which brought him thirty thousand Christian prisoners, ordered them all to be decapitated, their heads and bodies piled high; and from the top of this great human mound the muezzin chanted his call to prayer. On another occasion after a victory he returned to Cordova with thousands of Christian prisoners carrying the spoils of the battle through the streets, and those spoils were the treasures of their own churches.

But in the year 1043 there was born the man who was to show

that what could be done by the conquerors could be done by the conquered; and it was this man who has a place of honour in Spanish history, because he roused the conquered people from their lethargy. I refer to Roderigo de Vivar who is better known as the Cid Campeador.

He was born in Vivar, that little village not far from Burgos, which in the days of the Cid's childhood was on the border and in danger of being ravaged each spring and autumn by the Caliph's punitive forces.

The Cid was left an orphan when he was in his early teens and, because his mother was a member of a noble Asturian family, he was sent to the court of the Infante Don Sancho to be given the upbringing which was accorded to children of the nobility.

He proved himself to be more interested in the art of war than in culture, but he was by no means illiterate; the young boy, who would doubtless have witnessed the cruelty meted out to his people by the Arabs, may have been fired then by a determination to dedicate his life to the deliverance of those people.

There have, of course, been many romantic stories concerning this man; and it is difficult to discover what he was really like. Those who would depreciate him tell us that he was a rough soldier, unlettered, almost barbaric; in the Spanish poems and plays which have been written about him he emerges as a romantic lover, handsome and cultured, almost a saint.

It may be true that, when he took prisoners at the siege of Valencia, some of those prisoners were torn to pieces by hungry dogs and others burned alive. Even so, it is necessary to consider the amount of barbaric cruelty the Cid must have witnessed. It must also be borne in mind that whatever else he was, he was a man of his times, that he was fighting a great battle against the oppressor, and that he, even as Ferdinand and Isabella, is responsible for the reconquest of Spain.

He fought with the Infante Sancho at Graus and later was made *Alférez* of Castile when Sancho was King; this meant that he was in command of Sancho's army, so it is clear that his military genius was apparent at an early age.

A melodramatic legend about his marriage to Jimena tells how he killed her father in a duel because he opposed the match; this may well be false and the marriage purely one of convenience.

Sancho had been killed by his brother Alfonso at the time the marriage took place; and, probably because Sancho's friends would not find much favour with the brother who had supplanted him, the Cid lost his post of *Alférez*. But Alfonso would have realized the merits of this man and, not wishing to offend him, arranged the marriage which, from the Cid's point of view, was a good one. For he, although his mother was of a noble house of the Asturias, was the son of a humble father, and Jimena Díaz was the daughter of Count Oviedo and Alfonso's niece.

For ten years the Cid remained in obscurity; then began his life as a warrior.

His genius was apparent from the first and resulted in victory for the side on which he fought; his name became a legend; but Alfonso had always been suspicious of him, particularly as the Cid knew that it was Alfonso who had been responsible for the murder of Sancho; and he seized an opportunity of sending the Cid into exile, although he did not confiscate his goods.

So the Cid was forced to leave Jimena and his children at Vivar while he moved on with his followers. He was a soldier by profession and, presenting himself to the ruler of Barcelona, he offered to fight for him; when the offer was refused he made another to Moctadir who, though a Moor and King of Saragossa, was an ally of Alfonso; for there were occasions when Moors and Christians were allies against a common enemy.

Moctadir was quick to discover the worth of the Cid; and so the Cid stayed at his court for several years, an honoured companion and adviser.

So famous did the Cid become, hailed everywhere as El Campeador, that he desired a kingdom of his own and eventually won Valencia for himself.

Valencia, it is said, was the great love of his life. He loved it, it is said, ' as lovers love the place where they have tasted the delights of love '. Jimena and his children joined him there and for four years, until he died, he was lord of the place.

When he died at the age of fifty-six, Jimena could not long hold Valencia, and it was recaptured by the Mussulmans. It might have seemed then that all the victories which the Cid had won were of no account, since it was left to Ferdinand and Isabella four hundred years later to expel the Moors from Spain.

But the example of the Cid was to shine through the ages of oppression to come. He had proved that there *were* Spaniards from the north who could fight in such a manner as to subdue the conquerors. Even though the results of his conquests had been lost, his example remained.

The reconquest was certainly delayed by two further invasions, those of the Almoravides and the Almohades; and these invasions were entirely due to the people of Spain themselves. Afraid of the growing triumphs of Alfonso VI, which had been so advanced by the triumphs of the Cid, Christians and Moslems alike, determined not to fall under the sway of the "Emperor of the Christians", called in the help of the Almoravides, a Moslem dynasty which ruled from 1055 to 1147.

They must soon have realized the folly of this, for as the

Almoravides swept over the country they behaved as conquerors. Motamid, the ruler of Seville, was taken prisoner and others were slain. The whole of the south was under one rule and the Christians in the north were more unhappy than they had previously been.

The Almoravides reigned until a new dynasty appeared in Africa; the Almohades, who in their turn invaded Spain and took possession of the southern land from 1129 to 1273.

It may have been that these two invasions, following on the vigorous example set by the Cid, made the Spaniards of the north realize that, unless they expelled the invader from their country for ever, they would be constantly subject to similar invasions; and that they themselves might one day be driven from their northern settlements. Surely it occurred to them then that there was only one course open to them. They must, if they were to enjoy any security, turn the invader from their country.

The Almohades were devotees of their faith, and they were greatly influenced by their *faquis*; they went into battle with the belief that it was the will of Allah that they should do so.

The Christians too had their belief. They had been long oppressed; but they had the glowing example of the Cid to guide them.

In July of 1212 they met the enemy at Las Navas de Tolosa; and the battle resulted in a victory for the Christians.

This was a significant date in the history of Spain, for it was a beginning.

Progress was slow, and it was not until 1236 that Ferdinand III captured Cordova; later Malaga and Seville fell into his hands; and his son, Alfonso X, continued with the conquests.

Saragossa was recovered, Valencia won back; and of the utmost strategic importance—Algeciras.

By the end of the fourteenth century the only part of Spain occupied by the Moors was the kingdom of Granada; and it seems incredible that Granada should have been allowed to remain in Moorish hands.

Granada, it was true, was well protected by the sierras; many of those who were antagonistic to the Christians had fled to Granada and settled there; hatred of the Christians had been brought to a higher pitch than ever; moreover, the rulers of this last stronghold were ready to call in help from Africa if they were attacked in any force.

Strife among the Christian kingdoms no doubt delayed the reconquest. Castile and Aragon were rivals for power; and while civil wars persisted the Moors remained secure in Granada.

It was not until Isabella of Castile and Ferdinand of Aragon united that the Moors were conquered. To these two sovereigns goes the credit of freeing Spain from the invader and uniting the country. To them also is attached the stigma of introducing the Inquisition into Spain.

It is, I feel, only by looking back over the early history of Spain that it is possible to understand why the Inquisition prospered there as in no other country. The Catholic sovereigns were determined to have a united country, and they did not believe this ambition could be achieved unless all their subjects accepted one religion. This they were determined to bring about through persuasion, if possible, and if not, by force.

Spain under Isabella and Ferdinand was ripe for the Inquisition; that was why the cruel institution was embraced so heartily and continued to survive until the nineteenth century.

5

ISABELLA AND FERDINAND

WHEN THE early days of Isabella the Catholic are considered one understands why such a woman, of virtue and stern devotion to duty, was eventually persuaded to set up the Inquisition and use it as a means of strengthening the state.

Isabella was born on the 22nd April in the year 1451 in the town of Madrigal de las Altas Torres, into a world of uncertainty and conflict.

Her father's reign had been far from peaceful and she was not quite four years old when he died. John II had proved himself to be a weak King, and during his reign lawlessness had spread throughout Castile. The nobility were arrogant in the extreme and, since robbery and rape went unpunished, the goods and families of humble citizens were unsafe; and in many of the towns the honest men and women gathered together to try to discover a means of bringing law and order to the land.

John was completely in the hands of one of his favourites, Alvaro de Luna who, though illegitimate, belonged to one of the noble houses of Aragon. He was handsome, charming, fond of music, and a writer of poetry—all of which greatly appealed to the King, who made him Grand Master of St. James and Constable of Castile.

Alvaro de Luna, insatiably ambitious, began to accumulate great treasure as he usurped the power from under the King's very nose. The nobles of Castile, who prided themselves on their aristocratic connections, were infuriated to witness the arrogance of this man and as a result there was continual strife throughout the kingdom, in which John's son, Henry, did not hesitate to join against his own father.

De Luna, believing himself to be above reproof, not only imposed heavy taxes but withdrew from the people all the privileges which had been won during the preceding years. Such a state of affairs could not go on indefinitely, and de Luna eventually met his death on the scaffold.

But in the meantime a great deal of harm had been done and, although King John supported the arts and had made his court

a place of culture, because he was weak in matters of government and because he had placed himself in the hands of the
scheming, if attractive, de Luna, his kingdom was in a state of
anarchy at the time of his death.

His first wife was Maria of Aragon, and by her he had one
son, Henry, who was heir to the throne. His second wife was the
Princess Isabella, who was a granddaughter of John I of Portugal,
and by her he had two children; one of these was Alfonso; the
other Isabella.

On his death-bed King John begged his son Henry to take
great care of his young sister and brother, and this Henry swore
he would do.

These two young children were taken from the Court to the
little town of Arevalo in the care of their mother who guarded
them and personally superintended their religious instruction.
It was a very pious upbringing which fell to the lot of
Isabella.

Their elder brother Henry was far from pious.

He was acclaimed with delight by his people who had long
wearied of the futility of his father. The fact that Henry had
placed himself among those who had stood in opposition to John
gave the people great hope. Here was a young King, a man with
new ideas, one who was known to have disapproved of the
follies of his father.

Only a short period elapsed before the long-suffering people
of Castile began to see that John had been slightly more
admirable than his son.

Henry was determined to win popularity; he was of an equable
temper and declared his determination to lead campaign after
campaign against the Moors until they were driven out of
Granada. He loved luxury; but he differed from his father
inasmuch as he had no love for music or poetry.

He began his reign by delving deep into the royal coffers, and
to all protests replied that Kings must be liberal; generosity
ensured popularity for it was necessary to turn enemies into
friends by the means of gifts, and to offer gifts to friends to keep
them friendly. He enjoyed splendour and so increased his household. As for the promised forays against the Moors, he spent
a great deal of money on these, but he liked the pomp and show
of soldiering more than fighting; and, although he and his armies
set out with shouting and fanfares of trumpets, they showed little
desire for real fighting and would return after the briefest
encounter with the enemy, which had cost his subjects much in
taxes and had brought nothing but derisive contempt from the
Moors.

It was useless for him to say that he did not care to risk the lives of his men, since one Christian was worth a thousand Mussulmans. He had gathered together an army to fight, and that army consisted of nothing but men in fancy dress performing a masque for the King's entertainment.

It was at this time that the people began to ask themselves whether they had not been better ruled by King John II than by his son King Henry IV.

Henry who had indulged in sensual orgies from an early age, repudiated his wife, Blanche of Aragon, after they had been married for twelve years. There were no children of the marriage, and the excuse for rendering the marriage void was "*Por impotencia respectiva*, owing to some malign influence." So was this woman turned from her husband's household to tragic fate, for Henry, if he was foolish, if he was a voluptuary, was at least of a benign temper, and the years she spent in Castile must have been some of the most bearable of her life.

Having rid himself of Blanche, Henry took a new wife. She was Joanna of Portugal who was sister of Alfonso V.

Joanna lacked the graceful manners which were considered so important in Castile; she was lighthearted and coquettish; and it was not long before she brought scandal into the court.

One of the handsomest men about her husband's throne was Beltran de la Cueva, and it soon became apparent that the new Queen found his company enthralling.

Henry, not to be outdone by his wife in providing scandal, had already shown a preference for one of the maids of honour whom she had brought in her train. This girl quickly made her influence felt at court, and the Queen, although she did not object to the girl's sharing her husband's attention, was determined to maintain her own power.

Thus very shortly after the arrival of the new Queen there was gossip, scandal and friction.

Money was needed to pay for the luxurious court, and more taxes were extorted; great sums were raised ostensibly for the campaigns against Granada, but were in reality used to satisfy the whims of the favourites of both King and Queen.

And while this was going on young Isabella was leading a quiet existence, with her brother Alfonso, praying at her mother's knee, being prepared for future greatness—which it must have occurred to Isabella's mother and those loyal supporters in her household —was not impossible, for who should take the throne on the King's death, if he died childless, but his brother Alfonso; or should he fail to reach maturity: Isabella.

Then the astonishing thing happened. Queen Joanna was pregnant.

From the beginning nobody believed that the father was Henry, and when the girl was born, because all were certain that she was the fruit of the passion between her mother and the favourite, Beltran de la Cueva, she was known (although named Joanna) as La Beltraneja. Henry, all believed, was impotent; and therefore could not be the father of the girl.

This gave rise to great scandal, for the unfortunate child, since she was the only one Henry possessed, was heir to the throne of Castile. Henry, in his easy-going manner taking the simplest way out of the difficulty, insisted that an oath of fealty be sworn to her and she be accepted as heir to the throne.

It was at this point that the young Alfonso, until now living quietly in the care of his mother, found interest focused upon him. Revolution was in the air; and although warned by his advisers to take sharp action, Henry procrastinated; he had no wish to shed blood over this matter. It might have been that he wanted to hush up the scandal which surrounded his court, and felt that the best way of doing this was to accept the little Beltraneja as his own.

Henry now summoned his sister Isabella and their brother Alfonso to court, on the pretext of supervising their education; but he must have done this because he realized that with the nobles in a state of ferment it was dangerous to allow the children to be anywhere but in his own court.

The scandal of Henry's private life was fast earning him contempt; but there was one other factor which was making him very unpopular, and that was his easy-going nature which allowed him to be led by those of his favourites on whom he doted.

Henry, realizing that his throne was in danger and that he must make some concession to the nobles, named Alfonso as his heir on condition that he married La Beltraneja.

One important nobleman who was responsible for making a great deal of trouble was Juan Pacheco, Marquis of Villena. The Marquis had originally been a page in the household of the favourite, Alvaro de Luna, and when Henry was young Villena had been put into his service. Wily and ambitious Villena had quickly begun to dominate his master; and he was therefore furious when he saw new favourites ousting him from the King's regard.

So Villena determined to depose Henry and put Alfonso in his place.

Thus in the year 1465 the boy Alfonso was taken to a field near Avila where a platform had been set up; and on this was placed a chair in which was set an effigy of Henry in all his regalia. Alfonso Carillo, the Archbishop of Toledo, an uncle and ardent supporter of Villena, then mounted the platform and removed the crown from the effigy; Villena and his adherents took away the remains of the kingly splendour, and the effigy was thrown from the platform to the spectators, who with great pleasure rolled it in the dust.

Then eleven-year-old Alfonso was required to mount the platform and induced to be seated; the crown was placed on his head; homage was paid to him, and the people shouted that he was the new King.

Although this dramatic display was received with vociferous delight by the spectators, it was not regarded with approval by the rest of the country. Much as the conduct of Henry was deplored, he was still the King and could at that time have rallied his army about him and defeated the opposing party; but he was a lover of peace, and he sought to make conciliatory terms.

In the meantime there appeared to be two Kings of Castile—Henry and little Alfonso.

Characteristically Henry, realizing that the powerful Villena was his enemy, sought to make him his friend; and, as Henry's idea of making friendship was to offer gifts, he now decided to win Villena to his side by a gift of such importance that he could not fail to proffer friendship in return for it.

Villena had a brother, Don Pedro Giron, Grand Master of the order of Calatrava; and to this brother was offered the hand of Isabella, who was at this time sixteen years old.

Henry believed that by such a marriage Villena must become his ally, and as his other enemy, the Archbishop of Toledo, was the uncle of the proposed bridegroom, he too would welcome the honours such a marriage would bring and replace with friendship 'the enmity he bore Henry.

Isabella had already been promised in marriage to three suitors—Ferdinand of Aragon, his elder brother Carlos and Alfonso of Portugal, and when the proposition was made to Isabella that she would marry the Grand Master she haughtily declined.

The marriage seemed to her most unsuitable; she had already made up her mind that alliance with Aragon would unite the kingdoms, and she was determined not to marry merely for a whim of her rather feeble-minded brother, Henry.

Imbued with the dignity and piety with which she had been surrounded in the quiet retreat of Arevalo, she replied that the nobles of Castile must be consulted before their infanta could be given in marriage.

However, she realized that she was powerless in the hands of the King. She was fully aware that the Grand Master, many years her senior, had during his lifetime indulged in the licentious behaviour which was characteristic of the court; and she is reputed to have retired to her apartments in deepest gloom, to have spent hours on her knees imploring the saints to save her from the marriage, going without sleep and food in her fear and grief, and declaring to her attendant, Beatriz de Bobadilla, that she would plunge a dagger into the heart of the Grand Master if he approached her.

All her entreaties were ignored and the bridegroom and his relations, delighted at the prospect of being connected with the royal family, set about preparations of such magnificence as had rarely been seen at the court before.

The bridegroom left his home in Almagro for Madrid where the wedding was to take place, and the first night of the journey was spent at Villarubia, where the bridegroom was suddenly attacked with a violent illness which it was difficult to diagnose. He became so ill that within four days he was dead.

It is not certain what or who brought about this timely death, but it seems very likely that the merry bridegroom had taken a dose of poison. He must have had many enemies, and Isabella many friends. There has never been any suggestion that the pious Isabella played a part in the removal of the man whom she had threatened to kill should he approach her.

Isabella was then free to make that other most important and most famous marriage and to earn for herself the distinction of bringing the Inquisition into Spain.

With the death of the Grand Master all the hopes of Villena and the Archbishop of glorification through marriage with the royal house were lost, and since there was nothing to be gained, they once more showed their enmity towards the King. Civil war broke out, and at the head of the rebels side by side with the Archbishop of Toledo, rode young Alfonso. A battle took place, and although it lasted throughout one day it resulted in stalemate.

There was anarchy throughout the country and people were fighting one another on the slightest pretext, or perhaps no pretext at all. And on the 5th July, 1468, young Alfonso was discovered dead in his bed. The reason for his death remains a mystery; although we hear of certain trout of which he had partaken rather freely on the night before. Poison was naturally suspected and probably was used; although plague was raging at the time and may have been the cause of the young boy's death.

The death of her young brother brought a dramatic change in the life of Isabella for, since the legitimacy of La Beltraneja was in doubt, she found herself in the direct line of succession. She was seventeen, and serious for her years; fully understanding the dangerous turmoil within the country and her own position with regard to it, she very wisely retired to a nunnery at Avila, there to live in obscurity until it was safe for her to emerge.

She was visited at the nunnery by the Archbishop of Toledo who declared that he and his faction considered her to be the Queen of Castile on the death of her young brother Alfonso.

Isabella again showed her wisdom by declaring that she did not consider she had any right to the crown while her brother Henry lived. She also expressed doubts of heavenly approval, since Henry still lived and Alfonso had been the one to die. Her great desire, she added, was to see peace between the opposing factions, although she sincerely hoped that the licentious conduct of the court and the abuses which were carried on there, would be rectified.

As a result of Isabella's calm wisdom in the face of the glittering proposals which were laid before her, peace was restored on certain conditions. Henry was to divorce his Queen and send her back to Portugal; Isabella was to inherit the Asturias and become the heir of Castile and Leon; and she should not be forced to marry against her will, but at the same time she was not to enter into marriage without the consent of Henry.

Isabella was now a brilliant *partie* and was sought in marriage by many great personages, among them the brother of Edward IV of England, the Duke of Gloucester who was to become Richard III. There was also an offer from the brother of Louis XI (the Duke of Guienne). But Isabella had long dreamed of union between Aragon and Castile, and the suitor she favoured was Ferdinand of Aragon.

Chance seems to have played a great part in the lives of both Ferdinand and Isabella. At the time of their births it did not appear that they were destined to unite and rule Spain; yet in both cases all who stood between them and the crown were eliminated.

But for this marriage, but for the union of the states of Aragon and Castile, but for the piety of Isabella and the cupidity of Ferdinand, would the Inquisition have wilted away in Spain as it did in other countries? Had Henry been a strong man, had Alfonso not eaten trout or suffered from the plague, Isabella would have lived her life in comparative obscurity. And so easily Ferdinand might have done the same.

Yet they married; they became great rulers; they strengthened the Inquisition in Spain; and because of this thousands were to die the fiery death, thousands were to be humiliated and tortured. Isabella and Ferdinand united Spain; they drove the Moors from their last stronghold; it was under Isabella's aegis that Christopher Columbus discovered America; but all their achievements are darkened by the grim shadow of pain and death which they caused to be inflicted on so many people.

When Ferdinand came into the world, his father already had three children—Carlos, Blanche and Leonora—so his prospects were not very bright; perhaps this was why his ambitions were limitless.

In Aragon Alfonso V had followed his father, Ferdinand I, after the latter's brief reign; but Alfonso V spent little time in Aragon; he had conquered Naples and had set up his kingdom there, and finding the place to his liking, he appointed his brother John as Regent in Aragon.

John had married Blanche who was the daughter of Martin, King of Sicily; they had three children, all of whom lived tragic lives. The first was Carlos who was Prince of Viana; the second was Blanche who was the unfortunate wife of Henry of Castile and who was put aside by him in the humiliating manner already mentioned; and the third, Leonora, married Gaston de Foix. When John's wife Blanche died she left the kingdom of Navarre to her son Carlos (Blanche was the daughter of Charles III of Navarre) and according to the terms of her marriage contract this kingdom would, should her son die without heirs, pass to her other children even if they should be female.

John took a second wife. This was Joanna Henriquez who was a Castilian of royal blood, and the son she bore her husband was that Ferdinand who, with Isabella, was to rule Spain and foster the Inquisition in that unhappy land.

When Joanna's son was born she was obviously filled with ambitious longings to place him above his half brothers and sisters; and as she was a very strong-minded woman—and clearly a very clever one—she very soon set about gaining her desires.

The first thing she did was to set out for Navarre with the object of taking that kingdom from Carlos.

In Navarre there were two families of the Montague and Capulet type. These were the Beaumonts and the Agramonts. Their feud was of long standing and, if no one was quite sure what it was about, the enmity was not allowed to die away.

These two families seized every opportunity of taking sides against each other and, when Joanna showed her intention of taking Navarre from Carlos, the Beaumonts rose against her while the Agramonts took her side.

The Beaumonts surrounded the castle in which the Queen was staying and kept her besieged there. John came to her rescue, and the result was that as brother and brother fought against each other in Castile, so in Aragon the opponents were father and son.

The result of the battle was victory for John; and Carlos was taken prisoner.

John, under the influence of the strong-minded Joanna, was ready to be harsh with Carlos, while he doted on baby Ferdinand who at this time was only a few months old, having been born in March of that year, 1452.

Carlos was obviously a charming young man; he was gentle, and his manners were courteous. On being released—perhaps

deploring the discord in his family and sensing the hatred which
he, merely because he was his father's eldest son, inspired in his
stepmother—he went to Naples to put himself under the care
of his uncle Alfonso V in the hope that the powerful Alfonso
would be able to bring about a reconciliation between him and
his father.

Carlos was unfortunate, for Alfonso died, and when he did so
John became King of Aragon, and an illegitimate son of Alfonso's
(another Ferdinand) was left the Kingdom of Naples.

Carlos then went to Sicily which his father had inherited with
Aragon, and there entered a monastery, such a life suiting his
temperament.

The charm of Carlos was admired by the people of Sicily and
the reports of his popularity reached John in Aragon. No doubt
the Queen at his elbow, planning furiously for baby Ferdinand,
was afraid that the Sicilians might elect Carlos as their ruler; and
as Joanna had determined that her precious son should inherit
his father's dominions, she wanted no sentimental preferences
shown by any portion of those dominions, however small or
remote.

It was not long before Carlos was recalled to Aragon. It was
wrong for quarrels to persist in any family, John implied; and
in royal families it was more than foolish; it was highly dangerous.

Carlos was advised by his Sicilian friends that he would be
most unwise to return to Aragon; Carlos may have known this,
but so gentle was his nature, and so did he abhor the friction
in his family, that he decided to take a chance and return to his
father.

It was now expected that John would name Carlos as his
heir. Joanna, of course, was not going to allow this. Ferdinand
was at this time eight years old—bright, intelligent, already aware
of his mother's overpowering ambition on his behalf.

Joanna had so worked on the King that the only one of his
children whose future seemed of real importance to him was
Ferdinand.

Carlos now realized his folly in hoping to obtain a reconciliation with his father while John was under the influence of
Joanna, who was determined to misconstrue all his actions and
never lost the smallest opportunity of denigrating him for the
advancement of her son.

Carlos looked about him for a way of escape, and asked for
the hand of Isabella of Castile in marriage.

This enraged Joanna, for she had already been making plans
for a marriage between Isabella and her own Ferdinand. It was
acting under Joanna's advice that John had summoned his son
Carlos to the Cortes; and when Carlos arrived he was arrested
and put in prison.

The people of Aragon disliked the Queen and, like the Sicilians, they had been charmed by the personality and character of Carlos. There was an immediate reaction following the unfair imprisonment of Carlos, and a demand from the people to be told why John had imprisoned his son.

John's reply to this was that Carlos had plotted against his life, and he declared that even though he was his son, he should suffer the penalty for such an offence. As John had not yet left Lerida, the town in which the Cortes had taken place, the infuriated people rose in a body determined to make *him* their prisoner. However, he managed to escape, and the mob had the satisfaction of looting the palace in which he had been staying.

This, however, was the signal for revolution. The people of Navarre rose in revolt against the King, and the Beaumont family, at the head of their followers, marched on Aragon.

Both John and Joanna were afraid, and both realized that it was the Queen in particular who had aroused the hatred of the people. Therefore, John, to save his face and to bring some favour back to the Queen at the same time, declared that he would release his son because his wife had implored him to do so. The Prince was released, and he was acclaimed with great affection by the people, who insisted that the King immediately accept him as his heir.

John had no alternative but to do this, and he complied with an air, not of resignation, but of pleasure as though the trouble had been the result of misunderstandings and it had always been his intention to do what now might seem to have been forced upon him.

Carlos, acclaimed, popular, now hoped to settle down to a life of peace among the people whose affection he had won. Unfortunately he was suddenly taken ill, and another of those mysterious deaths occurred at an opportune moment.

The kingdom of Navarre now passed to Blanche, that sister of Carlos who had been repudiated by her husband, Henry IV of Castile. On the death of Blanche, Navarre would go to her father, and on his death to his daughter Leonora, the Countess of Foix.

Leonora and her family cast covetous eyes on Navarre. Her son Gaston had married a sister of Louis XI, King of France, and this son was very eager to rule Navarre; nor was the King of France averse to his possessing it, owing to Gaston's connection with the royal family.

Poor Blanche, who had suffered so much in Castile, now realized, as she considered the fate of her brother Carlos whom she had loved and supported wholeheartedly, that her life was in danger. She was very suspicious therefore when John suggested that she should go to France to stay with her sister Leonora because he believed it was possible to make a very good marriage for her there; he even suggested the King's brother, the Duc de Berri.

The terrified Blanche refused to go, but her father had her forcibly removed from her own estate; she was taken to her castle of Ortes in Béarn where, after two years, during which she was treated like a prisoner, in the care of Leonora and the Comte de Foix, terrified at the sound of every footstep, cautious of all she ate, she was poisoned.

It is gratifying to record that Leonora, who had caused her sister to be poisoned in order to obtain this kingdom, did not long enjoy it. When it eventually came to her after her father's death, Ferdinand was already stretching his greedy hands towards the family's possessions, and after Navarre had been but three weeks in the hands of Leonora, her half-brother seized it and Navarre became part of Ferdinand's kingdom.

Civil war continued to rage in Aragon, and the troubles of John came thick and fast in his old age. Leonora, impatient for his death, threatened to rise against him; and worst of all his eyesight began to fail him.

Queen Joanna emerges in all the vigour of her strong character at this time. She was determined to fight for the heritage of her son. She had made up her mind that Ferdinand should be king of Aragon and that his dominion should extend as far as she could possibly make it.

Accordingly she put herself at the head of the armies and, with the help of Ferdinand, prevented the utter defeat of King John.

But in the year 1468 she died and without her help the King was in despair. However, his luck seemed to change, for a Jewish doctor—miraculously it seemed at the time—operated on his eyes and saved his sight; and the Duke of Lorraine, who was his most formidable enemy and had put himself at the head of the Barcelonians, died suddenly leaving no heirs to lead the armies which had risen in revolt. So ended the civil war, with the King in possession of his kingdom and none to stand between Ferdinand and his inheritance.

Ferdinand was handsome and young—in fact a year younger than Isabella—and it was not only because of his future possessions that, of all the suitors who had been proposed, Isabella favoured Ferdinand.

Nevertheless there was great opposition to the match in Castile, and a faction, headed by Villena who was bitterly disappointed because the death of his brother prevented the family's connection with royalty, declared their support for La Beltraneja.

Henry, who had proclaimed Isabella as his heiress, was in a quandary and tried to marry La Beltraneja to Alfonso, the heir to the throne of Portugal.

He dared not explain his intentions, and as a blind the hand of Isabella was offered to Alfonso, son of the King of Portugal, who sent an embassy to Ocaña where Isabella was staying at that time. Isabella refused to consider the match, still determined on marrying Ferdinand of Aragon, and the people supported Isabella and made great efforts to show their support for the match by parading the streets with banners on which were displayed the combined arms of Aragon and Castile.

The King, however, abetted by Villena, was determined that Isabella should marry as they wished, and they continued to oppose the match with Aragon. Fortunately for Isabella war was raging in the south, and the presence of Henry and Villena was needed there; this gave Isabella her opportunity; she left Ocaña for Madrigal in the company of her mother, and they endeavoured to speed up the negotiations with Aragon concerning the marriage.

At Madrigal she found herself surrounded by the spies of Villena and her brother; and these men and women immediately began to bribe her personal servants to keep them informed of her actions that they might convey the news to Villena and her brother, Henry.

As a result Villena sent troops to Madrigal to secure Isabella, and make her a prisoner; however, the Admiral of Castile was Don Frederick Henriquez, who was the father of Ferdinand's mother and, since he saw the advantages to Ferdinand of a match with the heiress of Castile, he was ready to do all in his power to bring this about. The Archbishop of Toledo was also prepared to work for the marriage of Isabella and Ferdinand; and when these two men knew that troops were on the way to make Isabella a prisoner, they went with all speed to her palace and arranged for her to leave immediately. This she did, so that when the troops arrived they found she had escaped.

Isabella then came to Valladolid where the people turned out in their hundreds to greet her and to assure her that they were on her side.

Envoys were then despatched with all speed to Aragon that King John and Ferdinand might realize the difficult position of Isabella and speed up plans for the marriage.

John was at that time fighting for his kingdom against the Catalans, and consequently had no money to give Ferdinand for a wedding journey to Castile. It was arranged therefore that Ferdinand should enter Castile in disguise. His men would be dressed as merchants, and he as one of their servants. This ruse would not only excuse his arriving without the pomp and splendour expected; it was also necessary as there was so much opposition to the match from the King and Villena.

What chance at every turn attended this important union! Ferdinand might so easily have been killed before he was able to enter into it. On arriving at a castle where one of Isabella's adherents was waiting to give the party shelter, he and his friends were mistaken for enemies, and soldiers threw down great boulders from the battlements, one of which narrowly missed alighting on Ferdinand's head.

Isabella was delighted with her bridegroom. He was eighteen, fair and tanned by the weather; he excelled at sport; and Isabella must have recognized at once a strong man in this bridegroom of hers.

As for Isabella herself, we are told that she was very beautiful, although it is difficult to believe this when one studies her portraits. It may have been that she possessed those mild charms which, when accompanied by royal blood, are called, by contemporary courtiers, beauty. But at least she was young—nineteen years old; and Ferdinand, who had inherited his ambition from his mother, would have seen, in addition to a very presentable young girl, the kingdom of Castile.

After that first meeting there was no need to wait—indeed it was unwise to wait. Neither party had enough money to pay for the wedding, so it was necessary to borrow, and this they did.

So, on the 19th October, 1469, in the palace of John de Vivero, where Isabella had been staying since her arrival in Valladolid, the marriage took place.

As soon as the ceremony was over the married couple sent an announcement to Isabella's brother Henry, telling him the news.

Henry sent no congratulations; he replied merely that he would find it necessary to consult his ministers.

One result of the marriage was an immediate move by Villena and the King to make a match between Princess Joanna (La Beltraneja) and the Duke of Guienne (brother of Louis XI) who had been declined, in favour of Ferdinand, by Isabella.

Henry then issued a public proclamation that La Beltraneja was legitimate, and the Queen, her mother, joined him in swearing that the Princess Joanna was the daughter of Henry.

This made Isabella's hopes seem rather dark for, if the French marriage took place La Beltraneja, on the death of Henry, would have the French supporting her claim to the throne.

During all these alarms Isabella remained calm, and her serenity made a great impression on all those who witnessed it; so much so that people began to hope that if Isabella continued

as she had begun they could, under her rule, expect an end to
the anarchy in which the kingdom had been plunged for so long
and a return to sober living and piety.

The young couple lived in great poverty, relying on the
generosity of their friends (who no doubt took the long view and
looked upon this generosity as an insurance for the future).

Five dangerous years passed while the whole of Castile was
plagued by the barbarous behaviour of its people. Robbery and
murder were commonplace and amid all its attendant suffering
the court pursued its licentious and most frivolous course.

Meanwhile Isabella lived a life of the utmost piety, serenely
waiting.

In the December of 1473 there was a reconciliation between
her and Henry who received her at his court and gave a series of
fêtes in her honour. Unfortunately after a banquet Henry was
taken ill, and it was not difficult for Isabella's enemies to suggest
that there had been an attempt to poison him.

Henry's new friendship for his sister faded then, and he decided
that she should become his prisoner, and once more his schemes
were frustrated.

Villena died the following year, and Isabella no doubt believed
that once his baleful influence was removed she might have a
chance of again becoming friendly with her brother. This was
not to be, for Henry, who had been suffering from an incurable
disease for some time, himself died in December 1474.

The kingdom was weakened by civil wars, by the lack of
administration and the anarchy which had been allowed to spread
throughout the land.

There was scarcely any money in the treasury, and the state
of the country had rarely been so low. There were two rivals
for the throne, Henry's daughter (if she was his daughter) and
his sister, Isabella.

To all appearances it seemed that the terrible wars which
had ravaged the country during the last ill-fated reign would be
continued in the years to come.

On the death of her brother, Isabella was proclaimed Queen.
Ferdinand, who was at the time in Aragon, came hurrying to
join her. They discussed the government and Ferdinand immediately stated his desire to take precedence over Isabella. Serene
and peace-loving as Isabella undoubtedly was, she was also a
woman who was determined to insist on her rights. Their
adherents gathered about them and took sides; and after long
discussions and arguments it was agreed that Isabella was the true
heiress of Castile and Ferdinand must therefore derive his
authority from her.

Ferdinand, chroniclers record, was somewhat piqued by this

decision and haughtily declared that since he was of so little importance in Castile he would return to Aragon.

Isabella, however, was able to make him see reason and not show his petty pique at a time of their lives which might well be a very dangerous one. What did it matter in whose name the power was invested? They were husband and wife; their interests were similar. They had their daughter to think of. At this time they had only one child (called Isabella after her mother) who had been born in 1470 at Dueñas. Thus Isabella managed to soothe the wounded vanity of her young husband and keep him at her side in this most perilous time of their lives; and presumably Ferdinand learned wisdom, for in the future they worked together and, to show that they held equal authority, they made their device *Tanto monta, monta tanto—Isabel como Fernando.*

However they had difficulties to face before they were able to consolidate their kingdom; and Ferdinand had quickly to recover from his pique because it was not long before the supporters of La Beltraneja began to gather together and declare her to be the rightful heir to the throne. One of the chief of these was the Marquis of Villena, son of the old enemy, who was accounted to be one of the finest soldiers in the land. The Archbishop of Toledo, who had once stood so staunchly beside Isabella, treacherously joined her enemies. It was the old story of dissatisfaction with the power which had come his way. If he could not be Isabella's sole adviser, the Archbishop was ready to make a complete *volte-face* and be her enemy.

But there was one more powerful than either of these. This was Alfonso V of Portugal. Alfonso had several reasons for supporting the cause of La Beltraneja. The prospect of adding Castile to his dominions was inviting; moreover, Isabella had insulted him when she had shown so clearly her revulsion to marriage with him and her eagerness to marry Ferdinand.

Alfonso's idea was to take Castile and, in order to soothe the conquered Castilians, to marry La Beltraneja. There were two reasons which made this a little difficult; one was that the girl was only thirteen years old, but that could easily be ignored; the other was that she was his niece, her mother being Alfonso's sister. However, an obliging Pope would surely give the necessary dispensation to a monarch of Alfonso's importance. So, with this idea in view, Alfonso set forth to make war on Isabella and Ferdinand.

In May of 1475 he entered Castile, was welcomed by Villena and affianced to La Beltraneja, while a messenger was despatched to Rome for the dispensation. He and his bride-to-be were then declared the rightful sovereigns of Castile.

There then began the War of the Succession which was to last for four years, and in which Isabella and Ferdinand were eventually to be triumphant.

The Portuguese were decisively beaten near Toro, on that occasion when the Portuguese standard-bearer, Edward de Almeyda, continued to hold the flag with his left hand after his right arm had been cut away, and held it in his teeth when he had lost both arms, until his body was hacked to pieces. But individual bravery could not win the battle for Alfonso, and his army was eventually in disordered retreat.

Alfonso himself so humiliated, declared his intention of going on a pilgrimage to the Holy Land and resigning his crown to his son John. However he was deterred from this project and advised to return to Portugal; which he did, arriving in time to prevent the coronation of John who gave up the crown to his father.

However, no sooner was Alfonso back on his throne than he began once more to cast envious eyes towards Castile and planned another expedition against Isabella. But Doña Beatriz of Portugal, who was an aunt of Isabella and sister-in-law to Alfonso, begged to be allowed to mediate, and as a result she and Isabella met at the frontier and a treaty was drawn up.

This laid down that Alfonso should give up the arms with which he had invested himself as King of Castile and that he should break his engagement to La Beltraneja who should no longer claim the throne of Castile. She must either leave Portugal or agree to marry the son of Isabella and Ferdinand (Don John who had recently been born) or go into a convent. Alonso, the Prince of Portugal, should be affianced to Isabella, the daughter of Isabella and Ferdinand.

This treaty was signed, and it put an end to the strife.

La Beltraneja, realizing that she had been deserted and doubting whether she would ever be allowed to marry the boy who was now but a baby, decided that she was tired of the world and would accept the alternative of a convent. She retired to Santa Clara of Coimbra where she took her vows.

Alfonso then declared that since he had lost his bride he would follow her example, for he too was tired of the world. He would enter the monastery of Varatojo. He died before he could carry out this intention.

Ferdinand's father had meanwhile died, and to Ferdinand fell the crown of Aragon.

Aragon and Castile were now as one state. The two sovereigns determined to unite Spain as she had never in her history been united. They determined to bring law and order into the land, so their thoughts naturally turned to the Kingdom of Granada.

Under Isabella and Ferdinand order was restored. They were

determined to put an end to anarchy, and in this they were successful. Isabella had established the *Santa Hermandad* or the Holy Brotherhood which was in some respects a military force for protecting lives and property, and the *quadrilleros* (its officers) dealt with highway robbery, house-breaking, rape and other serious crimes. Taxes were levied on householders to maintain this service which proved to be efficient for, when a criminal was being hunted, bells were rung in those towns through which he was supposed to have passed and this resulted in many being brought to justice.

The laws were reformed; and after a few years the people were relieved of the great cost of the *Santa Hermandad,* for with the cessation of a great deal of the violence which had characterized the reign of Henry IV there was no longer need for such an elaborate institution; and in its place there was a police force to guard the safety of the people.

Naturally life was not all serenity; Isabella, as ruler of Castile, often had her difficulties to face; but it was quickly realized that the new respect for law and order was to the advantage of all worthy men and women, and that they had good reason to be thankful for their Queen Isabella and her husband Ferdinand.

Isabella was seeing her plans materialize. She was becoming the Good Queen she had always wanted to be.

She was a woman of great piety; and it is said that she had once made a vow to her confessor, Tomás de Torquemada, that if she should come to the throne she would devote her life to the extirpation of heresy for the glory of God and the Catholic Faith.

Before Isabella had been many years on the throne there were those to remind her of this vow.

6

PERSECUTION OF THE JEWS

I T I S not possible to say when the Jews first came to Spain; they appear to have inhabited the country from earliest times. Ancient historians tell us that Japhet, one of the sons of Noah, was given Europe as his inheritance, and that his son Tubal and his adherents settled in Spain. Nebuchadnezzar II is reputed to have brought several tribes of Jews with him and settled in the peninsula. Consequently many synagogues were set up throughout the land and Judaism spread. St. James came in A.D. 37 to instruct the Iberians in Christianity, to the consternation of the already large Jewish population.

Naturally enough on such a point there cannot be complete agreement between historians, and others tell us that the Jews did not arrive in Spain until after the Visigothic invasion.

It is inevitable that there has been disagreement between Jews and Christians: The Christians hating the Jews on account of the Crucifixion; the Jews contemptuous of a sect which had taken their old religion and grafted a new one on to it. They were natural enemies; but the Jews were ready to live side by side in peace with those whose opinions differed from their own; their great desires seemed to be to raise large families and become rich; the Christians, pioneers of a comparatively new religion, burned with the desire to convert.

The Jews, unfortunately for them, were a people who not only wished to make fortunes but to flaunt their wealth. They were lovers of flashing jewels and richly coloured garments. Had they lacked this love of ostentation they might have enjoyed a more peaceful existence. As it was, not only did they rouse the righteous indignation of Christians on account of the murder of Jesus Christ, but the envy of those Christians who were less successful. It may also have been that envy was a more dangerous emotion than righteous anger.

There had always been persecutions, but in the early centuries the persecutions were not severe and were generally confined to certain localities. As late as the reign of Alfonso VIII, who came to the throne in the year 1158, Jews were holding high positions at court; one was the King's treasurer, another his mistress. There appeared to be two types of Jew; the moneymaker, with his love of ostentation, and the intellectual who excelled in the arts, medicine, surgery and such professions. Both types had a great deal to offer the country they inhabited, and for a time the little irritations which the national character aroused could be forgotten.

But envy persisted and about the middle of the thirteenth century this envy grew into a menace against the Jews. Christians declared that the Jews made a mockery of the Crucifixion; and there was a rumour that a boy singer from Saragossa named Domingo de Val was kidnapped by Jews, who first whipped him, crowned him with thorns and then crucified him.

The Dominicans, ever ready to convert the peoples of the world to Christianity, had little tolerance to spare for those who remained outside their sphere. In the middle of the fourteenth century, when the Black Death swept over Europe with such devastating results, the Dominicans even blamed the Jews for that; and the people, whipped to fury against them by their own envy and the eloquence of the Dominicans, began to massacre them and rob them of their possessions. Taxes were levied against them, and Henry II who became King of Leon and Castile in 1369 demanded such large sums of them that it was often necessary for Jews to sell themselves into slavery to pay them as the only alternative to death.

This paved the way for the fanatic, Fernando Martinez. Martinez was a Dominican, and he was determined to arouse the violence of the people against the Jews. He confirmed the theory that the Jews were responsible for the Black Death; his reasons for this may have been the anger of Christ towards those who continually denied Him, or the habits of the Jews which were not considered to be as clean as those of Christians. For instance, they cooked their food with an abundance of oil and their persons were reputed to be malodorous. The first reason is more likely to carry weight than the second, for the people were more inclined to believe in the alleged cruel vindictiveness of Jesus Christ than in the virtue of cleanliness.

The preaching of Fernando Martinez resulted in pogroms in Catalonia, Aragon and Castile.

The Archbishop of Seville was appealed to by the terrified Jews, and the Archbishop, not insensible to the advantages brought to the country by the Jews, warned Martinez that he must desist.

Martinez however was a fanatic and therefore unafraid of the warnings of the Archbishop; and when the Pope, Boniface IX himself, added his voice to that of the Archbishop, still Martinez refused to stop his fulminations.

There were other occasions when Popes saw the folly of attacking the Jews. Clement VI, who took the Papal crown in 1342, intervened on their behalf when in Germany a choice between death and acceptance of the Christian Faith was offered them; and he even excommunicated those who attacked the Jews. Alexander VI, Roderigo Borgia, who reigned at the Vatican from 1492 to 1503, allowed them to live peaceably in Rome after they had been expelled from Spain. (It seems possible that the latter —a wily man always on the alert to seize an advantage, realized the affluence the persecuted race could bring to those lands in which they settled; and Alexander was almost as notorious for his love of wealth as for his scandalous personal life.)

Martinez, when reproached, declared that God put the words into his mouth and he personally had no power with which to thwart God's will even if he wished to.

The Archbishop of Seville, who naturally could not allow his authority and that of the Pope to be so flouted, brought Martinez for trial before an ecclesiastical court. An unfortunate incident happened at that stage. A few days before the examination of Martinez was due to take place, the Archbishop died.

The superstitious inclination of the people, always ready to read Divine interference in affairs of chance, led them to believe that the Archbishop had been struck dead by that vindictive monster whom they looked to in fear as their god, and that Martinez had really been speaking the truth when he said he merely uttered the words which had been put into his mouth.

Alas for the Jews! Martinez was awarded a position of high responsibility in the diocese, and no restraint was put upon his preaching.

Throughout Seville the riots started. Jews were robbed and murdered; their houses and synagogues put to the flames.

The Jews were ordered to live in their own quarters called *juderías* apart from Christians. This they did; but Martinez was not satisfied; he wanted blood as well as humiliation. The *juderías* or ghettos were attacked, and in Seville alone four thousand people were murdered.

Other towns, hearing of the excitement and realizing the richness of the spoils, were smitten with equal fervour to destroy those who denied the divinity of Jesus Christ. The cry was: "Baptism or Death."

The numbers of the slain mounted to fifty thousand; and many Jews naturally chose to accept the Christian Faith in preference to a horrible death.

Those who were baptized were known as New Christians, *conversos*. More often though, the term *marranos* was applied to them as a form of abuse. Derived from the Hebrew *Maran-*

atha (The Lord is coming) it was said by the Christians to mean
' accursed '; and is now come to mean in Spanish ' sow '.

New decrees had been made against Jews. They were obliged
to wear badges on their clothing in order that they might be
immediately recognized as Jews; they were forbidden to shave
or to ride on horseback; they must not be addressed as Don.
They might not marry Christians nor indulge in sexual intercourse with Christians—even prostitutes—and if discovered doing
any of these things suffered severe penalties. They were not
allowed to hold any office in the state and were debarred from
becoming innkeepers or apothecaries, surgeons or doctors.

But if they were baptized these restrictions were automatically
lifted for the Jews as a race were not objected to; it was only
their religion which gave offence. It is therefore not surprising
that they accepted baptism in their tens of thousands.

Immediately they were released from the restrictions placed
upon them their resilience was phenomenal. In a few years'
time the persecuted ones, fresh from the *judería*, were becoming
the wealthiest section of the population and, what is more
amazing, finding their way into government posts. Some married
into the nobility, for many noble families had become impoverished through periods of unrest in the country and were
glad of the money which a Jewish marriage could bring. They
even found their way into the Church.

The authorities might accept the *marranos*, but the masses
murmured as they watched the growing prosperity of these people
who, but a few years before, had been shivering in the *judería*.

The murmuring grew to a roar. Envy was abroad again, and
the riots began. Now they were directed not towards the Jews
who had remained Jews, but towards the new Christians who,
declared the people, were Christians in name only and in the
secrecy of their houses practised the rites of Judaism.

In 1449, when taxes were levied on the town of Toledo, it was
discovered that many of the tax-collectors were Jews turned
Christian. This incensed the people; and there was a rising
against *marranos*.

Three years later a story was set in motion that a boy had
been kidnapped and crucified at Valladolid. This was a rumour
which appeared from time to time and could always be relied
upon to inflame the people against Jews.

Two years after that, in 1454, there was another rumour. This
concerned a Christian boy, kidnapped as the others had been,
crucified, his heart cut from his body and burned.

Then in 1460 Alonso de Spina, a Franciscan, published a document in which he called attention to the wickedness of *conversos*.
He was very violent, perhaps more so because he himself was a
converso; perhaps he saw the growing anger of the people and

was afraid that it would be turned on all *conversos* even if they should be holy Franciscans; he was determined to show that he was on the right side, by his venomous attacks on his own people. He made that demand—which was always flowing from the lips and pens of Dominicans and Franciscans: he wanted the Inquisition to be set up in Castile that it might deal adequately with these men and women who had outwardly accepted Christianity and secretly practised Judaism.

The Inquisition had not been established in Castile, although in 1474 Sixtus IV had ordered it to be introduced into Spain. As a result of this command Inquisitors had made their appearance in Catalonia, Valencia, Aragon and Navarre. Castile had remained outside the orbit of the organization as charges of heresy had been brought against so few people living there, and it had been decided that the bishops could deal adequately with these.

However Alonso de Spina thought otherwise. He assured his readers that Jews were the enemies of Christians; that they brought about the plague; that the reason people often fell into a mysterious illness was because it was a Jewish custom to poison wells; and if previously they had doubted the rumours that it was a Jewish custom to kidnap boys and crucify them, as they had years ago crucified the founder of the Christian religion, they had only to recall the crucifixions of Valladolid and Zamora. These had been brought to light; how many more did they imagine had remained undiscovered?

He begged them to consider the Jews. They ate kosher food and cooked in oils. They ate too much, and consequently they stank. They were immoral and they had no respect for virginity; all they thought about was increasing the race.

Moreover they jeered at the holy rites of Christianity; and they had merely embraced the Faith for their material good. In secret they followed their own religion. They were guilty of the worst kind of heresy.

Not only did De Spina write; he set out on a tour which took him through Spain. Wherever he went he demanded action against the Jews and the introduction of the Inquisition into Castile to deal with them.

The Inquisition of course was a tribunal against heresy and could not deal with Jews unless they had become Christians, for only then could they be said to be guilty of heresy.

In 1468 there was another rumour of a crucifixion. On the Thursday of Holy Week, so the story goes, at Sepulveda a boy was kidnapped, crowned with thorns, whipped and crucified. This time there was an enquiry, and the result was that a party of men were arrested, found guilty and condemned to death.

Whether there were Jewish communities who were guilty of this ritual murder it is difficult to say. It may have been that these crucifixions actually took place. Jews had suffered a great deal from the hands of Christians; they may have used this cruel method of retaliation.

However, popular opinion was becoming so inflamed that it was obvious that some action against the *marranos* was inevitable.

Isabella was not eager to establish the Inquisition on Castilian soil, and had made it clear from the beginning of her reign that she—not even Ferdinand—was ruler of Castile. Isabella's reasons were that she had no wish to put herself under the influence of Rome.

The reigning pope was Sixtus IV, and Isabella had already been involved in a disagreement with him.

Sixtus had been elected to the Papal chair in 1471. He was the son of a fisherman, and it has been said that he never could adjust himself to the splendour of the Vatican; extremely clever —he must have been to have risen so high from such humble beginnings—he was an excellent administrator; he was however noted for that besetting sin of medieval Popes: nepotism. He lost no time in making sure that all relations and friends were well set up in life, and this brought him occasional difficulties.

Isabella had asked that her chaplain, Alonso de Burgos, be given the bishopric of Cuenca which had fallen vacant. Sixtus would have been pleased to grant her wish, but it so happened that his nephew Raffaele Riario, Cardinal of San Sisto, had cast acquisitive eyes on Cuenca. Naturally the post went to the nephew of Sixtus.

Isabella and Ferdinand were very angry. As a matter of fact it was not the first time their suggestions had been ignored, for when Isabella had sought the Bishopric of Tarragona and the Archbishopric of Saragossa for two of her protégés, the Pope had been unable to grant her wishes because he had two dear friends on whom he wished to bestow these benefices.

To be set aside on three occasions was more than Ferdinand and Isabella could be expected to endure; they therefore asked the Pope (first gently and then less gently) to cancel the appointment he had given to his nephew and bestow it on Alonso de Burgos.

This sent up the Papal eyebrows. Sixtus explained, with as much patience as he could muster at such an affront to his dignity, that God had given him his power and none but God could take it from him.

Not for the first time in the history of Rome there was coldness between reigning Pope and sovereigns. Isabella and Ferdinand recalled their ambassador from the Vatican and ordered Spanish subjects to leave Rome.

This was not all. Ferdinand and Isabella informed the Pope that they proposed to call a council that the powers of the Papacy might be discussed, and Sixtus, knowing that there had been considerable dissatisfaction throughout Rome on account of his flagrant nepotism, could not face the findings of such a council.

He therefore—wise man that he undoubtedly was—humbled himself, withdrew the nominations, not only from his own nephew but from the other two which had brought him into conflict with the Spanish rulers, and bestowed those honours on the candidates nominated by Ferdinand and Isabella.

This was a great victory for Ferdinand and Isabella, and particularly for Isabella as, in matters appertaining to Castile, she always took the lead; and she was firm in her decision that she would not allow the Vatican to encroach on her domain.

There were many people about the throne to urge the introduction of the Inquisition. Isabella, aware of Papal influence among the clergy, was wary; but there was one person whom she trusted. This was Tomás de Torquemada, who had been her confessor.

Isabella listened to him but, still afraid of the infiltration of too much Papal influence, turned again and again from the suggestion of bringing the Inquisitors into Castile.

Alonso de Ojeda, the Prior of the Dominicans of Seville, was a zealous fanatic, and he sought an audience with the Queen, for Ferdinand had left for Estremadura to review the fortifications on the frontiers of Portugal. With great fervour Ojeda pointed out to Isabella that she must put a stop to the spread of Judaism. He assured her that the only way to do this effectively was to establish the Inquisition.

The Queen listened in her gentle, courteous manner; she herself had established several *conversos* in her entourage and was fond of them; she was fully aware that the outcry against the *marranos* was very often caused by envy of their possessions. Isabella sincerely wished to maintain justice in Castile. She had received a poem written by a *converso* in which he vividly described the terrible injustice which was so often the lot of his fellows, and she had been deeply moved by the poem and the sufferings of this section of her subjects.

She was supported in her attitude by Don Pedro Gonzalez de Mendoza who was the Cardinal of Spain and Archbishop of Seville. He appears to have been a humane man. He was an aristocrat and lover of luxury; he wished to live comfortably himself and liked to see others do the same. He had entered the Church, not perhaps so much because he had a vocation for it, but because through the Church he saw a means of living the intellectual life of a nobleman. Besides being a priest he was a writer and enjoyed translating Latin verse.   Such a man lacked all the zeal of men like St. Dominic, St. Francis and Torquemada, but made life much more comfortable and pleasant for his fellows than did these zealous men.

The Archbishop had no desire to see the Inquisition installed in Castile; and strongly he advised Isabella against allowing its entry.   The Queen accepted the Archbishop's advice, much to the chagrin of Ojeda.

At this time there arrived in Spain the chief Inquisitor of Sicily: Filippo de' Barberi.   He added his voice to Ojeda's; and when they both realized that it was almost impossible to convince Isabella, they determined to work on Ferdinand.

Ferdinand lacked the finer qualities of his wife.   He was a man of deep sensual desires and he had never seriously sought to restrain these.   He was anxious however to prove himself a true follower of the Faith, and any way of doing this which did not interfere with his pleasures was agreeable to him.   There was one characteristic which he possessed to a large degree; this was acquisitiveness.   It may have been that his mother, when she had fought so hard to make him his father's heir, had imbued him with the cupidity and love of self-aggrandizement which he possessed.   However it became clear to those whose desire it was to instal the Inquisition in Spain that it was this cupidity of Ferdinand's which must be played upon.

Isabella was still determined to be mistress in her own kingdom and no matter who attempted to influence her—even Ferdinand himself—it must be she who had the last word.

Pious as she was, determined to see Christianity firmly established, she called to her the Archbishop of Seville and commanded him to prevent the spread of Judaizing among *conversos*.

This move incensed those who had been working to establish the Inquisition, for they were aware of the leniency of the Archbishop and they felt that all their work, all their importuning, had brought them nowhere.

The Archbishop applied himself assiduously to his task, compiled an *instrucción* in the manner of a catechism, and this was taught in schools and by priests in the churches.

There the matter might have rested for some time.   Isabella was satisfied that she had done her duty by placing the correction in the hands of the Archbishop whom she knew to be a just man. But a certain incident occurred; this, though trivial in itself, was to change the situation and make the way clear for the introduction of the Inquisition into Castile.

A young man, said to be of the noble house of Guzman, had a mistress who belonged to a *converso* family.   It was this young man's custom to visit the girl in her father's house in the *judería*.

These visits were secret from the girl's family who doubtless would have frowned on her receiving a lover in her rooms.

The young man was paying one of these visits to the girl on March 18th in the year 1478. This happened to be Holy Week; it was also the eve of the Jewish Passover which, of course, was celebrated for eight days in April. During his love-making the Guzman grew uneasy when he became aware of comings and goings below and evidence of excitement in the house.

The girl, terrified that she and her lover would be discovered, led him quietly downstairs, hoping to let him out of the house. She was frustrated in this by the sound of voices and presumably shut him into a cupboard or in some place where he was concealed.

While the young man was waiting to make his escape, the girl's father and her friends came and stood close to his place of concealment and the Guzman heard their conversation.

He understood that they, who were supposed to be New Christians, were in reality assembled together to celebrate the Passover.

The young man was horrified. It is extraordinary that these people, who were merely practising their own religion after having been forced to adopt another, should seem to him to be committing a major sin, whereas he himself, having entered this man's house in order to seduce his daughter and being forced to hide in an undignified manner for fear of discovery, would seem to be committing a minor one.

This attitude was typical of the times. And this young man, in spite of the fact that he had professed to be in love with the daughter of the house, lost no time, after making his escape, in informing against her family.

Ojeda, to whom he went with the story, was delighted; and as a result those who had assembled at the home of the Guzman's mistress were arrested.

Confessions were made, and the offenders implored that their sins might be forgiven and they themselves restored to the Church.

Fortunately for them the Inquisition had not been introduced into Castile, and their request was granted, after a penance had been performed.

Ojeda made all haste to Cordova where Isabella had been joined by Ferdinand.

But before seeking an audience with them he obtained one with Tomás de Torquemada and told him the story of the lovers and the *conversos* who had been practising Judaism in secret. Torquemada, deeply shocked—not by the behaviour of the Guzman but by that of the *conversos*—went with Ojeda into the presence of their sovereigns and joined his pleading with that of

Ojeda, assuring them that for the glory of the Catholic Church and the good of Spain the Inquisition must be introduced without further delay.

Ferdinand, visualizing the financial gain which could ensue from the establishment of the Inquisition, and weighing this against the probable strengthening of Papal influence, was eventually won over. Isabella followed her husband, but reluctantly, and at last they asked Sixtus IV to allow them to set up the Inquisition in Castile.

Sixtus granted their request in November, 1478. Yet, although the sovereigns had obtained this permission, they made no use of it for two years.

There is a difference of opinion as to why Isabella was so dilatory in making use of the Inquisition. Catholic historians tell us that she was a pious woman, reluctant to bring suffering to her subjects, eager to give those who offended against the laws of the Catholic Church an opportunity to repent. Her reluctance to set up the Inquisition is pronounced to be due to these qualities. There is however another opinion, which is that Isabella was determined to establish Catholicism throughout her country and was in complete agreement with the methods used by Tomás de Torquemada; and that the reason for the delay had nothing to do with the delicacy of her feelings, but was due to a disagreement with the Pope—Isabella demanding that the Inquisition should be appointed by the sovereigns of Spain, that the confiscated goods of heretics should be their concern only, and that Rome should have no voice in the disposal of such property.

It would seem that neither of these opinions is clear cut. Since the Bull of 1478 gave Isabella and Ferdinand what they asked, this would explain the delay in setting up the Inquisition in the first place; and Isabella was undoubtedly endowed with the gifts of Statescraft. On the other hand, when the Bull was in her possession and all her conditions were granted, still there was the two years' delay before she took extreme measures.

Isabella, I believe, wanted peace in her country; she had learned a great deal from the disastrous rule of her father and brother. She was determined to make her country uniformly Catholic, but it does appear that she would have preferred to do this without cruelty.

Moreover when the Bull was received from the Pope, Torquemada had returned to his convent and Cardinal Mendoza was with the Queen, no doubt urging her to continue with the methods he had put into force.

Torquemada at this time was dealing with the affairs of Hernan Nuñez Arnalt who had left a great deal of money for the founding of a monastery at Avila; he had assigned to Torquemada the right to supervise all the necessary arrangements, and this project, very dear to the heart of Torquemada, absorbed him, even to the exclusion of the persecution of heretics.

Both sovereigns were very busy with political matters, for Ferdinand had only that year taken the crown of Aragon; but in the spring of 1480 Isabella and Ferdinand went to Toledo where the Cortes had assembled. The object of this visit was to accept the oath of allegiance to Isabella's little son, Juan, the Prince of the Asturias, who was nearly two years old.

During the Cortes, the old laws regarding *marranos* were discussed, and it was agreed that these had been allowed to lapse. Thereupon it was decided that they should be enforced once more; that all Jews should not be seen abroad without the red badge on their shoulders; that they should not emerge from their *juderias* after dusk, and that none of them should enter a profession which had been denied to them.

Catholic historians declare that this is yet another example of Isabella's reluctance to introduce the Inquisition, another attempt to banish heresy through humane methods.

The Jews, who had been gradually emerging once more from their bondage, were very bitter at being thrust back, and one of them was misguided enough to write a pamphlet, and even more misguided to publish it. Unfortunately in expressing himself with great fervour he had fallen into heresy, and this was pointed out by Hernando de Talavera, the monk who was later to become Archbishop of Granada.

The publication of this pamphlet is said to have destroyed the last of the Queen's patience. It is also said that Ferdinand, thinking of the rich possessions of heretics which would fall to the state, was urging her to take action. The fact is that in September of that year (1480) Isabella commanded Cardinal Mendoza and Tomás de Torquemada to nominate Inquisitors; and as there was reputed to be more heresy rampant in the town of Seville than in any other, the Dominicans, Miguel Morillo and Juan de San Martino, were appointed Inquisitors.

In October, Ferdinand and Isabella issued a command that it was the duty of all citizens to make the work of Inquisitors easy by giving them all the help they needed.

The Inquisition arrived in Seville in a procession. The Inquisitors, in their white robes and black hoods, accompanied by friars and familiars, must have struck a note of awe and terror in all who beheld them. The Dominicans, after their custom, were barefoot and their robes were coarse; at the head of the procession marched a Dominican monk carrying the cross. Through the streets they walked on their way to the Convent of St. Paul where they would begin their hideous work. The people, we are told, watched them in silence and—most certainly—apprehension. There was good reason for this.

Meanwhile many of the *conversos* had made their escape from Seville and taken refuge on the estates of certain great nobles, such as the Duke of Medina Sidonia, who they believed would give them protection.

This they were to discover was a foolish action to have taken. If, the officers of the Inquisition declared, people felt it necessary to escape, they must be guilty. Suspicion was aroused in the Inquisitorial breast; this was a shadow of things to come, suspicion being often all that the Inquisition needed to condemn.

Commands were sent to the Duke of Medina Sidonia, the Marquis of Cadiz and others who had given shelter to the *conversos*. The Inquisitors must be supplied with the names of all those who had fled to them for shelter; moreover these people must be arrested and brought to the offices of the Inquisition for questioning. Anyone who did not obey the wishes of the Inquisitors would himself be immediately suspected of heresy; for was it not an offence against Holy Church to harbour heretics? The dreaded threat of excommunication was mentioned.

So, very soon after the dreary procession had passed through the streets of Seville, the prisons of the Inquisition were filled and the bloody work was about to begin.

It was very difficult for some people who had been living in Seville to realize what was happening. The rules had been lax for some time, and it was easy to forget the years of persecution when a period of comparative ease had been enjoyed.

Some of the *marranos* of Seville had prospered and, as was the habit of their race, given a few years of peace, had become rich.

There was one man living in Seville who was reputed to be possessed of great wealth—ten million *maravedis*. He was Diego de Susan, a man of great importance in the town; he had also been to the fore in municipal matters; and when he saw the grim procession parading the streets, it did not occur to him that those pale hard-faced men with their monks' robes and bare feet could not be prevented from changing the way of life in Seville.

Therefore he called together other important men of the town, and in his house there took place a meeting during which measures were discussed to turn out these intruders, that the life of Seville might go on in the pleasant, prosperous way of the past.

Diego de Susan reminded his friends that they themselves were doing no harm to anyone; that they were popular in the town, for the people realized they made it prosperous; they were rich; they had many servants; if they stood together they could fight the Inquisitors and make it impossible for them to remain in Seville.

He was evidently a man of forceful personality, for he drew many prominent men into his scheme; moreover he convinced them that they, with their men and money, could overcome the monks and turn the Inquisition out of Seville.

They might easily have done so, but luck was against them.

Diego de Susan had a daughter. She was so beautiful that she was known throughout Seville as *la hermosa hembra*. This girl had a Christian lover, and to him she betrayed the conspiracy.

No one knows why the girl behaved thus. Some say she did it in a moment of weakness; others that she was pregnant, and therefore unaccountable for her actions. The fact remains that the conspirators were betrayed, and by the daughter of the chief of them.

Nothing could have given the Inquisitors more pleasure. They had an excuse to arrest all the principal citizens of Seville on suspicion. These men were taken to the Convent of St. Paul for questioning, and there were tried on a charge of heresy.

Six of them were found guilty, and the citizens of Seville experienced the horror of watching the grim procession through the streets. This was not to be compared with the horrific pomp which was to be a feature of the *autos de fé* of the future.

The six were compelled to wear the horrible yellow garment of shame, and carry lighted candles in their hands; halberdiers marched beside them to prevent any attempt, on their part, to escape, or among the spectators to rescue them. At the head of the procession walked a Dominican, with coarse robe and bare feet, holding the banner of the Inquisition; he was followed by the familiars of the institution walking in pairs; after them were the condemned men and the guards, followed by the Inquisitors and a party of Dominicans led by Alonso de Ojeda.

From the convent to the Cathedral went the procession, there to halt for Mass and a sermon by Ojeda. Garcia Roderigo, that firm defender of the Inquisition, declares that Ojeda had done all in his power to urge the men to reform, as he hoped to save them. But as these men had in reality been arrested and condemned, not for their lack of faith, but for their conspiracy against the installation of the Inquisition in Seville, this can scarcely be believed.

Eventually the procession left the Cathedral for the fields of Tablada, and there the first *auto de fé* of Castile took place.

Even Andérs Bernaldez, a stern upholder of the Inquisition, does not deny that Diego de Susan met his death as a brave man and a Christian; and if he is right and Susan died in the Chris-

tian Faith, nonsense is made of Garcia Roderigo's statement that
Ojeda laboured long to save him from the fiery death. In any
case such labours do not fit in with what we know of Ojeda.

This *auto de fé* took place on February 6th, 1481. It was the
first of many.

As for La Susanna, *la hermosa hembra,* legend has it that she
was overcome with remorse when she realized what she had done,
and that the Bishop of Tiberiades arranged that she should be
given shelter in a convent and there take the veil. The girl,
however, was unable to settle down to convent life and, escaping
from it, became a prostitute. In the course of this profession
she bore several children, and when her beauty was lost and the
nobility were no longer interested in her she found a home with
a humble grocer. By the time of her death the daughter of the
millionaire of Seville was in abject poverty; and as she lay dying
she asked that her skull should be placed over the doorway of
that house where she had lived whilst pursuing her immoral
life.

This was meant to be an example to all of the fate which had
overtaken her, whether on account of the evil life she led or
because of the great betrayal, one is not quite sure. There grew
of course the usual legends surrounding the skull, and there were
many to declare that they had heard cries of remorse coming
from it in the dead of night.

The skull remained there however for centuries, and the story
has been remembered—if not because of La Susanna—because
her father was the man who tried to stage a rising against the
Inquisition and consequently became one of its first victims in
Seville.

The sight of those human bodies writhing in the flames, the
sound of their groans, inspired the Inquisitors to greater efforts.
They wanted more burnings, more human sacrifices.

Ojeda was urging the people of Seville to provide him with
heretics; if they did not produce them, they themselves would
very soon come under suspicion, for heretics he must have. At
this time however the plague which had been raging through
Spain came to Seville, and in the streets men, women and children
who had been struck down were unable to reach their homes and
lay dying. One of the first victims was Ojeda himself. He was
dead within a few days. He had witnessed the first *auto de fé*
and had planned many, much more impressive, to follow; but the
first was his last; and with the plague came a respite for Seville,
for it was impossible to carry on the work of the Inquisition in
such a stricken city, and it became necessary for the Inquisitors
to move out of the town. They set up their headquarters temporarily at the village of Aracena. Alas for Aracena! The
zealous Dominicans could not rest from their labours, and the

result of their sojourn in that village was an *auto de fé*, for which they managed to find twenty-three victims.

The plague in Seville was replaced by a worse enemy; the Inquisition returned. Now a state of terror reigned in the town. It had been seen how useless it was to protest. There was the example of Diego de Susan who had been one of the town's most powerful men. *Autos de fé* were now being held at the rate of about one a month, and the Inquisitors were indefatigable in their search for victims. The dungeons of the convent were full and no more could be kept there; many were taken to the Castle of Triana close to the city. There were vast dungeons in the castle, but these too were very soon filled to their capacity.

Not content with burning the living, the Inquisitors brought charges of heresy and apostasy against the dead whose bodies were dug up and publicly burned.

Victims were needed so new edicts were issued. All those who were guilty of heresy or apostasy were urged to come forward and confess. A time limit was given for them to do this; if any failed to do so and were discovered in their sin they would, they were warned, meet with little mercy.

Twenty thousand *conversos* came forward, trembling with terror, to admit that they had at times practised Jewish rites.

Confession must be sincere, was the answer to these poor people; and their sincerity could only be credited if they informed against those of their acquaintances who had been equally guilty.

The twenty thousand were faced with two alternatives. If they did not name some they suspected were guilty, their own repentance could not be relied upon; therefore it was the stake for them and ignominy and poverty for their children, because the law of the Inquisition was, as they knew, confiscation of property. On the other hand if they betrayed others their repentance would be accepted.

These poor people were in a terrible dilemma. It is true that many betrayed their friends. Thus were many human sacrifices provided for the fire, which, says a Catholic recorder who was also a priest (Andérs Bernaldez), was a glorious affair, for not only were these sinners brought back to the Church but they exposed those more guilty men and women who had not answered the call to repent.

Those fiends, Morillo and San Martino (against whose cruelty even the Pope protested) then issued a second edict. In this it was commanded that every citizen must search for those practising Judaism in their midst and, if they were *conversos*, the attention of the Inquisition must be called to them. Any failing to do his duty was himself in danger of being accused of heresy and must be prepared not only for excommunication but examination by the Inquisitors.

It would be no use their declaring innocence of the vile practises in which Jews indulged. To prevent this a list of all Jewish rites was to be published that all might know for what they had to look.

The whole of the population was panic-stricken: the Jews who were almost all *conversos* (for it had been necessary to receive baptism in order to live in Spain), and the Christians who could be accused of knowing that Jewish rites were practised, yet failing to report this.

The people must listen to the conversation about them, and if they heard any man, woman or child say that they were waiting for the coming of the Messiah, then that person did not believe that the Messiah had already come and had thereby committed an offence against Christianity. He must be reported at once to the Inquisition.

Naturally any who they knew had returned to Judaism after baptism must be reported. But this was a matter which all guilty of such sin would keep to themselves, so it would be necessary for those who wished to be considered good Christians to be very alert. They must watch for any who kept the Jewish Sabbath: Did they light no fires in their houses on Friday night and remain in their homes, doing no work? Did they put on clean clothing?

The manner in which they slaughtered animals for their food must be observed. Did they cut the throats of the animals including poultry and bleed them? Did they eat meat in Lent? Did they celebrate the Jewish feasts and fasts? They would of course do this in secret but it was the duty of all good men of the Church to detect them. Did they bless their children by laying hands on their heads without making the sign of the Cross? The law of Moses declared that women should not enter churches for forty days after bearing children. Let the Christians watch for those who respected this law. Let them report any child which had been circumcised or given a Hebrew name. Let them watch for any who took the *Ruaya*, that ceremonial supper before starting on a journey. If in any house a person died with his face turned to the wall, or had had his face turned to the wall by any present at his death-bed, then that house was suspect. If a corpse was washed and shaved and dressed for the tomb, if water was sprayed in houses of the dead, if while mourning there was abstention from the eating of meat, then those who behaved in this way were suspect, because this was in compliance with the Mosaic law.

No one who had been a Jew and become a Christian was safe. The historian, Juan Antonio Llorente, declares that the Inquisitors were determined to condemn thousands in the town of Seville because they wished to show the Queen how rife was heresy in that town, so that she, who had been so reluctant to establish the Inquisition, should recognize the need for it.

Llorente was clearly a man of great integrity, and Rafael Sabatini, who quotes him frequently in his *Torquemada and the Spanish Inquisition,* writes that he is an historian of 'unimpugned honesty and authority'. He also gives a brief biography of this extraordinary man, to the effect that he was born at Logroño in 1756 and twenty-three years later was an ordained priest, after taking a University course in Roman and Canon law. These qualifications brought him a seat on the Supreme Council of Seville, which was of course the Council of the Inquisition. He became the Commissary of the Holy Office in his birth-place, when it was necessary to give definite proof that he had no Jewish or Moorish blood in his veins.

He was a man of an enquiring mind however, a man who determined to think for himself—a quality likely to be frowned upon in the circles in which he moved. As a result of these ideas of his he was sent to a monastery to do a penance; and it was necessary for him to find a new occupation.

When Napoleon came to Spain and the Inquisition was abolished (temporarily) Llorente had an opportunity of going through the massive archives of the Institution.

He was eventually expelled from Spain, and while in Paris he wrote his book *Historia Critica de la Inquisicion de España.*

No one could have been better equipped to write such a book, and naturally enough he was reviled both by the Spanish Government and the Church. He was unfrocked and forbidden to teach in schools. However, disgraced in the eyes of the Church though he might be, before he died at the age of sixty-six he had given the world valuable information concerning the crimes of the Inquisition; and given it in a manner which inspired confidence —as the excuses for and glorification of the Holy Office by such writers as Garcia Roderigo on the Catholic side, and the venomous attacks on it by William Harris Rule, D.D. on the Protestant side, could not do.

What an unhappy city Seville must have been at this time with the dismal incantations of the monks which filled the streets during the hideous processions, the smell of the burning flesh of martyrs, and perhaps worst of all that atmosphere of suspicion, the feeling that no one was safe from friend, neighbour or even family. Children were encouraged to inform against parents, husbands against wives, wives against husbands. A similar situation existed and still exists, we know, in some countries in this twentieth century. Repellent as this practice must always be, to spy and to incriminate falsely for the State seems less

culpable than to do so in the name of Christ. The first is un-
natural and shocking; so is the second, but when added to these
unhealthy qualities there is hypocrisy and the hope of salvation
in the world to come, the shame is surely doubled.

None was more assiduous in discovering heretics than the
friars. There is the case of the friar who early on Saturday
mornings climbed onto the roof of the Convent of St. Paul's to
make a note of those houses from whose chimneys no smoke was
rising.

Smokeless chimneys meant no fire. Who were these people who
had omitted to light a fire on a Saturday? Surely they must be
conversos who had reverted to Judaism.

A smokeless chimney was enough to drag a man or woman
before the Inquisitors; and once in their hands it was a short
step to the torture chamber and the stake.

The first *auto de fé*, on February 6th, when Susan and his
friends had perished, was speedily followed by another, on March
26th; and before the end of the year—Llorente tells us, and he
should know, having access to the archives—298 people had been
burned alive in the town of Seville alone, and 79, repenting in
time, were sent to life-long imprisonment. Many corpses of
dead suspects were dug up and given public burnings, all of which
took place in the meadows of Tablada where a stone platform
had been built. This spot was called the *Quemadero*, the Burning Place.

Many of the *conversos* had managed to escape from Spain, and
some of them had actually gone to Rome to protest to Sixtus IV.
They assured him that they were good Christians but that in
spite of this they were unsafe in Seville where one's enemies only
had to make a lying statement to the authorities for a man or
woman to have no chance of redress.

Sixtus, who in any case was displeased with Isabella and
Ferdinand on account of the conditions they had forced him to
accept at the time when the Inquisition was established in Castile,
declared that the Inquisitors were not behaving in accordance
with the rules laid down by the Inquisition, and he sent a protest
to the two sovereigns. They themselves he pointed out, had
wished to appoint the Inquisitors, and it appeared that the two
who had been appointed were not satisfactory. He therefore
withdrew the permission he had given them to elect their own
Inquisitors, and declared that, should he receive more complaints,
he would make use of his powers to remove from those posts these
men nominated by the two sovereigns.

Isabella and Ferdinand made no protest. It may have been
that the appointing of Inquisitors did not concern them so deeply
as that other concession which they had wrung from Sixtus:

that which gave the two sovereigns the right to take the con-fiscated goods of the condemned.

Was it coincidence that so many of the condemned people had been very rich? Ferdinand's eyes must have glistened with joy when he saw the money which was being provided to equip the army he wanted to lead against the Moors of Granada. Isabella's very likely glistened also, even though she might have pressed her palms together and knelt in prayer asking the saints to inter-cede for Christ's help in giving her an all-Catholic kingdom.

Sixtus then appointed eight Dominicans as a council to direct the affairs of the Inquisition; at their head was Alonso de Cebrian, and among them was Tomás de Torquemada.

At the Pope's decree a court of appeal was set up in Spain; and Bulls were prepared that they might be sent to the Archbishops, reminding them that the utmost integrity must be employed within the Inquisition; but when refugees continued to arrive in Rome with their complaints, the Pope decreed that any man or woman who was ready to be reconciled to the Church should be given the chance to be so.

Sixtus however did not send these Bulls. He withheld them to reconsider certain points; and unfortunately for thousands, they were never despatched.

Isabella and Ferdinand, realizing that the Inquisition had grown to be the most powerful force in Spain and that it was partly governed by Rome, implored Sixtus to put a man at its head who could stabilize it and control those who displeased the Pope.

They had a suggestion to make as to who could best fill this role. The Pope concurred with their selection and Tomás de Torquemada was appointed to preside over the Supreme Council of the Inquisition (the Suprema).

On October 2nd, 1483, Torquemada was made Inquisitor-General for Castile, and fifteen days later Aragon was joined with Castile under his jurisdiction.

7

TORQUEMADA AND HIS "INSTRUCTIONS"

No NAME has been more closely connected with the Spanish Inquisition than that of Tomás de Torquemada, and there must be few people who have never heard of it. It is strange that this man, who for the first fifty-eight years of his life lived in comparative obscurity, should in his remaining twenty years have left such a mark on the world; and it is characteristic of human judgment that in some that name should arouse horror and in others admiration, in some disgust and in others something like adoration. Tomás de Torquemada has been called a cruel bigot; he has also been called the light of Spain, the saviour of his country and the honour of his Order.

Tomás was born in the year 1420 in a small town close to Valladolid; and the name of that small town was, of course, Torquemada. And how apt it proved to be!

He came of a good stock; they were petty nobles; the family having received its distinction in the fourteenth century under Alfonso XI when he had knighted Lope Alonso de Torquemada.

Tomás's uncle, Juan de Torquemada, was the famous theologian and writer. Juan had delighted the Vatican by his firm defence of Papal infallibility, and his reward had been the bestowal of the purple and the office of Cardinal of San Sisto.

The great Cardinal's brother was Pero Fernandez; Tomás was the latter's son.

From his early childhood Tomás showed his bent, and his love of piety of the most austere type was remarkable. He was very studious, distinguished himself as a scholar, and at a very early age received his doctor's degree in divinity and philosophy.

He was however aware of a vocation and after this brilliant scholastic career he made it clear to his family that he wished to enter the order of the Dominicans.

This must surely have been a blow to Pero Fernandez, for Tomás was an only son and the family must have hoped he would marry and continue the line. However, so firm was Tomás's determination that, young as he was, he entered the Order and was given the appointment of Prior in the Monastery of Santa Cruz at Segovia.

From the beginning Tomás showed his austere nature, submitting himself to all possible hardship, refusing to eat meat at all and living on a meagre diet; he refused to wear linen next his skin and this must have been a great discomfort, for the Dominican habit was of very coarse material. To make himself more uncomfortable still he often wore a hair shirt. He went bare-foot, and many marvelled at the humility of this nobleman who chose the life of a humble friar.

The news of his piety spread and, when Isabella was brought under the care of her brother Henry IV, it was Tomás de Torquemada for whom she asked, to be her confessor.

This was not seen at that time to be the post of importance which it turned out to be, for Isabella was then merely the King's sister and there appeared to be little likelihood of her reaching the throne.

There is however a story which is probably false and which may have been concocted afterwards in the light of what followed: Torquemada, while Isabella's confessor, is reputed to have extracted a promise from her that if ever she became Queen she would bring back the Inquisition to Spain.

Of course she did bring it back, and one of the people who had urged her to this course and who helped to strengthen it and make it the dreaded thing it became was Tomás de Torquemada. In any case Isabella had the highest possible opinion of her confessor and it was to him she turned again and again for advice.

During the time he spent with Isabella as her confessor Torquemada undoubtedly won her confidence, for when she became Queen she made him one of her most trusted advisers.

There seems to be little doubt that Torquemada was sincere. He was not, as so many of the Church, a seeker after wealth, and if he wanted power he appears to have won it in order to establish the Catholic Faith throughout the land. He wanted to force all men to share the austerity which he himself was prepared to practise. To some of us today his confidence that he and he alone was right smacks of a conceit so great that it belongs to that Pride included in the deadly sins. However there were many—and still are many—to construe this trait as a virtue bordering on sanctity.

If we examine the character of Torquemada in the light of modern knowledge we find something which is far from saintly in his attitude towards the Jews whom he hated with a fanaticism beyond even that which he had for relapsed *Moriscos* and Protestants.

Why did Torquemada earn for himself the title of Scourge of the Jews? Why was he even more fanatically inhuman towards them than towards others who did not share his religious views?

Some historians believe that Tomás's grandfather, Alvar Fernandez de Torquemada, had introduced a " Jewish taint " into the family when he married a Jewess. This was towards the end of the fourteenth century when the Jews were enjoying a respite from persecution. It was perfectly logical for this small noble-man, who may well have been financially embarrassed, to have brought money into the family by marrying the daughter of a rich Jew. He may have fallen in love with the Jewess. How-ever, there is this suggestion that Alvar Fernandez brought Jewish blood into the family, and in Castile where, more than in other places, men and women were proud of their nobility and the purity of their blood, this was a deviation which would have its repercussions in the years to come.

A Castilian should be able to trace his ancestry back through the centuries; he should be able to boast of his *limpieza*—the purity of his blood.

Alvar Fernandez and his Jewish wife may have lived happily enough, but with the coming of Fernando Martinez and his wild preaching against the persecuted peoples, and with the mob risings and the rumours of Christian boys being crucified, it was not only an embarrassment to have Jewish blood in one's veins, it was also dangerous.

It will be remembered that Alonso de Spina, the Franciscan who had demanded that the Inquisition be established in Seville, was a *converso*, and that there were few more eager for the perse-cution of those Jews who, having been forced to accept baptism, had reverted to the practice of Judaism. There must have been an element of fear in de Spina's fanatical attack against his own people. Can the same judgment be applied to Tomás de Torque-mada?

One imagines that knowledge ever present in his mind: in the blood of this fervent Catholic was that of the Jew. It may have been that in the days of his youth, before he was such an important man whom none would dare offend, he had been subjected to the sneers, the jeers, the humiliation which, for years, has been the burden of the Jewish race. It may have been that he sought to keep this a secret, that he lived in terror of its being discovered. Whatever the reason, if Torquemada really had this streak of Jewish blood in his veins, there can be no doubt that it does to some extent explain his fanatical hatred.

It is the writer, Hernando del Pulgar, Isabella's secretary, who tells of the Jewish blood in Torquemada; but his word is doubted by some historians who put forward the suggestion that Pulgar, himself a Jew and a New Christian, wished to bring into his own category a man who had proved himself the most zealous of all

Catholics—and for this reason wrote as he did about Torquemada.

Geronimo Zurita writing later is insistent that Tomás de Torquemada was the possessor of 'clean blood', which meant that his veins had been uncontaminated, for it was believed that Jewish blood was dark, and pure Christian blood bright red!

It seems however that there is a good case for Pulgar's assertion, as the name of Tomás's grandmother is discreetly omitted by most Catholic writers.

When Sixtus IV, at the request of Isabella, called together a conference of Spanish Cardinals, certain rules were decided upon and briefs were sent to the Spanish Archbishops, instructing them to conduct the affairs of the Inquisition with integrity; and, should there be any Bishops of Jewish blood, these should not be allowed to deal personally with those affairs appertaining to the Inquisition, but should at all councils be represented by other prelates of high rank in their dioceses, always of course providing these men had no Jewish blood whatsoever in their veins.

Sabatini in *Torquemada and the Spanish Inquisition* states that this decree entirely contradicts Pulgar's assertion that Torquemada was of Jewish extraction. Yet it seems possible that a man as powerful as Torquemada would not have allowed himself to be pushed aside by such a decree; and as the Jewish grandmother is not mentioned by Catholic writers it may surely have been that, if Torquemada was eager to forget the Jewish strain, those about him were equally ready to help him.

As for Isabella herself, she was not averse to *conversos* as such; it was only when she heard stories of their reverting to their own faith that she was horrified. She kept many *conversos* in her own personal service. She would therefore have felt no revulsion towards Torquemada who was such a zealous Catholic, merely because he had a Jewish grandmother.

Moreover, although the Pope sent his instructions, Isabella and Ferdinand were determined that in Spain the Inquisition should be ordered by themselves with as little Papal interference as possible. Therefore I do not think that, because there was this clause in the Pope's instructions and because Torquemada was appointed by his sovereigns and accepted by the Pope as Grand Inquisitor of Castile and Aragon, this is a proof that he had no Jewish blood.

Such fanatical hatred as Torquemada's could be at the very root of his determination to destroy the Jews. His pride would have been deeply wounded by the knowledge that he was in part —however small—Jewish; and make no mistake about this: all the refusals of great offices, all the sleeping on planks, the privations and irritations pressed upon the human body, the hair shirt and the white wool of the Dominican robe under the black hood, the bare feet—all these were the outward signs of a man steeped in pride. But the simple people did not look within; they saw the ascetic face; they heard of the great renunciation of worldly goods, they saw the humble Dominican whose one desire was to serve the Faith. They did not see the cruel thirster after blood, the proud man who, terrified of what he considered the taint in himself, was determined to show the world how he would scourge those who were similarly tainted. The taint in Torquemada was nothing to do with the state of his blood; it was in the state of his proud and arrogant mind.

Yet had he lived in different times, had he been educated to tolerance, he might have been a good man. Intellectual he undoubtedly was, but how many intellects of the past—and the present—have been and are cursed with that blind spot, of which intolerance of other men's views is the outward sign?

Torquemada's great interest in life was in architecture, and it is said that, when he was with the simple workmen who carried out the projects in which he was interested, he cast off his fierce burning fanaticism and became a pleasant and kindly man. When money came to him, as it inevitably did, in his position of influence and importance, he used it, either for what he would call the glory of God, which was seeking those who did not agree with him and torturing and burning them at the stake, or for erecting great buildings such as the Church in Torquemada and the bridge over the River Pisuerga. The great achievement of his architectural ambitions was of course the Monastery of St. Thomas at Avila, which took him ten years to complete; and after that it was his delight to use all the money, which he could spare from the expense of ferreting out heretics and apostates, in beautifying this magnificent monastery. It is significant that this beautiful building was used, not only as his residence, but also as the prison for his victims. Thereby it satisfied two ambitions. He had built one of the most magnificent monasteries in the country; and in its dungeons those accused of heresy were tortured.

There can be little doubt that when he was very young he yearned to lead a good life. It is interesting to speculate on the part chance played in his life. What if grandfather Alvar Fernandez had not married his Jewess? Would that fierce hatred never have existed? What if Tomás had never been called forth from his cloister to become the Queen's confessor? Would he have lived in quiet obscurity, pious, truly humble, happy in the quadrangles and cloisters of the Convent of Santa Cruz? Who can say?

When Torquemada was made Inquisitor-General he immediately began reforming the existing laws of the Inquisition and produced his "Instructions" which consisted of twenty-eight articles.

In the first of these articles he explained the mode of procedure when the Inquisition was to be set up in a place where hitherto it had not been. All the people must be summoned to the church, and the day chosen must be either a Sunday or a holiday. A sermon must be preached by the most eloquent preacher available or by one of the Inquisitors. When the sermon came to an end an announcement should be made that all faithful Christians must come forward to swear upon the Cross and the Gospels that they would favour the Inquisition and those who worked for it, and place no impediment in their way.

Then it should be announced that a period of grace was being allowed—it might be thirty or forty days—for all people who had committed heresy or apostasy, or who had practised Judaism, to come to the Inquisitors and confess. If they did this within the given time they would be charitably dealt with, providing their repentance was sincere and they told not only of their own sins but those of their neighbours.

There would, of course, be some punishment, for no one could offend against God's laws without punishment. (It seems strange that these men should have called themselves followers of the gentle Jesus and such haters of the Mosaic law, when thundering Jehovah would surely have been a God more suited to their needs and tastes.) But this penance should be light; that meant it would not be death at the stake, imprisonment, or confiscation of property and the impoverishment of the offender's family.

Those who confessed must write their confessions, and when they had performed their penances they must remember that although they were reconciled to the Church they had offended against the law of the land and that for this relapse they would not be allowed to wear ornaments of gold, silver, pearls or precious stones, nor dress in fine materials, nor ride on horseback, nor carry arms, for the whole of their lives. Moreover they must not forget that they had sinned against Jesus Christ and, although, most mercifully, they were escaping their just due ('the fire') and they were being allowed to keep their property, they could be called upon to give up a portion of it. This would be used for a holy purpose—such as the war which Queen Isabella and King Ferdinand were pursuing against the Infidels of Granada, who, as all knew, were enemies of the Holy Catholic Church. These penances would be decided on by the local Inquisitors, but they would depend on a guide which had been given them by the Reverend Father Prior of Holy Cross, Tomás de Torquemada.

Should a man or woman, who had fallen into heresy, fail to come forward during the period of grace, but offer his confession

Costumes worn by a woman and a man relapse or impenitent
condemned to death

Costumes worn by men and women penitents who confessed
after trial by the Inquisition

(*Above*) Costumes worn by men and women penitents who confessed before trial. The woman shown here belongs to a religious order. The term "sanbenito" (from St Benedict) was applied to the penitent's costume

(*Left*) The banner of the Inquisition in Spain

voluntarily afterwards, he would still be treated mercifully. That is, he would not be condemned to the fiery death. He would not be asked to give a portion of his estate because the *entire* estate would become forfeit to the Inquisition. He would suffer heavier penalties than those who had come forward earlier; and if the case were a bad one he might be awarded life imprisonment. But because he had come forward voluntarily he should not die by fire.

Children who had become heretics through the teaching of their parents should be treated leniently. If they were under twenty years of age and came forward voluntarily and informed the Inquisitors of the evil practices of their parents, they should be given very light penances and taught the true faith, for the merciful Inquisition excused them because they were young and had been led astray.

Any guilty of heresy and apostasy must lose all property, counting from the day of the first offence; so that, if a rich man knowing the Inquisition was about to arrest him decided to pass his property on to someone else, it could be confiscated by the Inquisition because it was the sinner's property at the time he committed heresy.

Heretics or Apostates who were arrested because of information given against them could ask for reconciliation to the Church, which might be allowed them provided they were sincere; this meant that they must inform against their friends. If it should be discovered that their confessions were not sincere, they would be immediately handed over to the secular arm for the death sentence.

If heresy or apostasy were not completely proved against a victim, the Inquisitors would be allowed to put the prisoner to torture. If, while being tortured, the heretic confessed his sins, he must repeat his confession during the next three days.

The publication of the names of witnesses was forbidden because, the instructions suggested, there had been cases of witnesses who, coming forward to the assistance of the Inquisition, had been wounded or killed by heretics. When the victim of the investigation had been proved guilty, an account of the evidence against him might be published as long as the names of the witnesses were withheld, together with any information which might lead to their identification. Suspects would be allowed to have their advocates who must however swear that, when they considered the prisoner guilty they would withdraw from the case. (It would have been a very brave advocate indeed who continued with the defence of a victim in the face of opposition from the Inquisition; he would need to be a man who was ready to brave examination, torture and the fire itself.)

If a suspected heretic, hearing of his impending capture, had managed to escape, an edict should be put on the church doors all through the district, ordering him to present himself to the Inquisitors within thirty days. If he did not do so his guilt was considered proved.

When heresy was proved against a dead man, there should be a trial and, if there was proof of guilt, his body should be dug up and committed to the flames, and his property should be confiscated. His family might defend him, but if they failed to prove him innocent they would suffer the penalties which fell to the children of condemned heretics.

The Inquisitors were to penetrate the small domains of petty overlords and there be treated as they were in lands belonging to the crown. Should such petty lords who ruled their lands decline to admit the Inquisition, then they should be considered guilty of aiding and abetting heresy.

Young people who were minors or unmarried and whose parents had been executed for heresy were to pass into the hands of the Inquisitors, that they might be instructed in the Faith and brought up as good Catholics. The royal bounty alms would provide for these, and girls should be given a small dowry that they might marry or go into convents. (Llorente states that in his perusal of the archives of the Inquisition he sought in vain for a case of a child of a condemned parent who had been so cared for.)

Although the property of a man or woman, who had been guilty of heresy and had become reconciled to the Church, would be confiscated, any they should inherit *after* their repentance they might keep.

Slaves of heretics might gain their freedom. (Was this an invitation to slaves to inform against their masters?) And even if a reconciled heretic were allowed to keep a part of his property he should not keep his slaves.

No officers connected with the Inquisition must receive gifts from the suspected. If they did so they might suffer excommunication; they would be required to forfeit twice the value of any gifts they had received. (Clearly a precaution against bribery.)

Any difference of opinion arising between Inquisitors must be submitted to Torquemada for his judgment.

Should any Inquisitor be found guilty of misdemeanour, he must be judged mercifully; and if he persisted in his ill conduct, then should Torquemada be informed and the offender should be replaced.

If any matter arose which was not provided for by the articles of the Instruction, the Inquisitors should themselves decide what must be done in the service of their Royal Highnesses and for the glory of God and the Faith.

This is the gist of the twenty-eight articles set out by Torquemada, which he was to amend and adjust during his years of office, and which were to be made use of by Inquisitors in the centuries to come.

Austere, self-righteous, determined to mould men in his own image, ever eager to deal out fearful punishment to those who had failed to embrace the privations which he forced on himself, Torquemada would have desired to see the methods employed by the Inquisitors used for other purposes besides the condemnation of heretics and apostates.

In the case of bigamy he declared that this should be a matter for the Inquisitors, for marriage was a sacrament and any who defiled it had offended against the laws of God. Sodomy should also be dealt with by the Inquisition, and those who were found guilty should suffer death by burning.

Thus new fears were growing within that land over which Torquemada held great power.

It was only natural that, while Torquemada dealt out terrible punishments for those who had been guilty of immorality, there should be whispers of the conduct of certain priests; and these murmurs caused a great deal of sorrow to Torquemada.

He knew that it was true that the reputation of the clergy was not as pure as it should be. Torquemada would have liked to sweep through the Church in the guise of an avenging angel and, discovering those who had sullied the name of Holy Church, deal with them as he dealt with heretics.

There was one offence which was looked upon with particular distaste. This was a habit—not infrequent—of priests, who lured attractive young women to the confessional where they did all in their power to seduce them. At this time priest and penitent were together during the confession, not separated as they were after the sixteenth century—a custom which was very probably introduced because of the licentious habits of the priests.

It was somewhat difficult for Torquemada to expose this habit, for to do so would bring great shame on the Church; and another reason was that instructions for the clergy must come from Rome, and the Pope at this time, Innocent VIII, was a man who had presumably made no great effort to subdue the lusts of the flesh. He was a family man, with his children about him in the Vatican; he delighted in them and showered great honours upon them. So, if the Pope himself indulged in amorous conduct, it would be rather cynical and hypocritical for him to condemn some poor priest for a little waywardness while listening to an account of the sins of some attractive penitent.

However so rampant was this crime of the confessional—*solicitatio ad turpia*—that something had to be done about it, and the conduct of several priests was examined, found to be at fault, and sentences passed.

These however were very slight—necessarily so if the Church was not going to be brought into ill repute.

John Marchant cites one case in which Joseph Peralta, Friar of the Order of St. Jerome, committed sodomy with John Romeo, a young boy of fourteen who was in his care. This crime being discovered, it was necessary to pass judgment. The Friar was therefore sentenced to a year's confinement in his monastery, but was allowed to celebrate Mass. The young boy, however, not being a priest, must be treated more severely. He was led through the streets and, at the corner of each, five lashes were administered. On the child's head was placed a mitre covered in feathers, which was to all who watched an indication of the nature of his crime. The boy, we are told, died after the whipping; the priest —presumably because he *was* a priest—resumed his merry life, ready, no doubt, after a sentence which was by no means a real punishment, to seduce any suitable young boy who came under his care.

Marchant also quotes the case of Father Pueyo, who was made Father Confessor to the Nuns of Our Mother St. Monica. Pueyo promptly seduced five of the nuns, and when this was discovered, even though he was a priest, it was agreed that this was a sin which could not be lightly passed over. When he was brought before the Inquisitors and asked to explain his sinful conduct, he replied that he had been sent to the Nuns that he might take care of them. He had done so as a faithful servant and said to the Inquisitors: *" Domine quinque talenta tradidisti mihi me, ecce alia quinque super lucratus sum."* To which the Inquisitors, highly amused, replied: *" Peccata tua remittuntur tibi, nunc vade in pace, et noli amplius peccare."*

His response, which had so amused the Inquisitors, had brought him freedom even from the light penance which he would otherwise have been expected to do.

It seems that the only punishment bestowed on the priests who had misconducted themselves was an order to abstain from hearing confessions and a short confinement in a monastery.

There is no doubt though that Torquemada abhorred the loose behaviour of the priests and probably realized the need to repress it, but had he been as stern with the priests as he was with those he suspected of heresy, Martin Luther would not have had such a good case to lay before his audiences in the century to come. But, of course, Torquemada's real venom was reserved for heretics and the Jews whom he hated with such a fierce passion.

He had already given Isabella and Ferdinand good proof of his hatred of the Moors. When Ferdinand had been making an assault on Granada, and had been in difficulties (his men were smitten with fever and he had no money with which to carry on the campaign), news of the King's troubles reached Torquemada, who at that time was deeply engrossed in the building of St. Thomas's monastery at Avila. Torquemada thereupon called his mule-driver to him and filled the water-jugs, which were on the backs of the twelve mules, with gold which he had intended to spend on the building of the monastery. These he sent in the charge of the muleteer, to Isabella, with a message explaining that the money was for the continuance of the war against the Moors.

It was true that the money proved useless, for Ferdinand's armies were too sick to fight, whatever weapons were put at their disposal, and Ferdinand was obliged to raise the siege of Loja. But the gesture was an indication to the Catholic sovereigns of what an ardent supporter they had in the austere Dominican.

Here was a man, they believed, whom they could trust. Doubtless this incident was one of many which influenced them when the question of setting up the Supreme Council arose, and again when the time came to elect the Inquisitor-General of Castile and Aragon.

8

THE HOLY HOUSE AND TORTURE

WHEN A MAN or woman was suspected of heresy, he or she was brought to a special chamber, reserved for this purpose, in the building which was used as the headquarters of the Inquisition. This building would be called the Casa Santa, the Holy House or the Holy Office.

The word of two witnesses, providing the evidence they gave was not substantially divergent, was enough to condemn, but instructions had been laid down, by Torquemada and those who had come before him, as to the treatment of *suspected* heretics.

The method of treating these unfortunate people was grossly unjust and exactly what would be expected, for the great desire of the Inquisitors was to bring as many victims as possible into their clutches; and the great desire of the sovereigns was to establish a country which was entirely Catholic, and at the same time receive confiscated goods into the state exchequer. Therefore men and women who were proved to be innocent were of little use.

Each victim, when he received the dread summons, must have known that he had very little chance of going free. His main hope would surely have been to escape torture and painful death. When faced with these horrors, perhaps the loss of his worldly goods and a life of imprisonment seemed bearable.

It often happened that victims were arrested at night. There would be the sudden knock on the door, and when this was opened, the *alguazils* or familiars of the Inquisition would demand entrance; and if there was any resistance force their way in.

The victim would then be told to dress and prepare to leave immediately. Some European countries in the twentieth century imitated the methods of the Inquisitors, and there can surely be no method more calculated to arouse terror in peaceful citizens. The sudden knock in the night, for which, after this inhuman method had become a custom, all men and women must have listened, would have been as alarming as an air-raid warning of the 1939-1945 war—only more so, because with the latter there was merely the possibility of pain and death, whereas with the former there was the certainty of the first, even if it should prove possible to escape the second.

The *alguazils* were very eager that the arrest should be made silently. Perhaps it was all part of the mental torture they had contrived. A man would be seen by his family, friends, and neighbours one day; the next he would have disappeared into the grim prisons of the Inquisition, perhaps only to emerge in the ghastly procession to the *auto de fé,* or at best to return robbed of his possessions, his body doubtless mangled and mutilated by their hideous torture machines.

The swift and silent removal was certainly sinister; should the victim cry out and threaten to wake the neighbourhood, he was gagged. There was in existence a very painful gag for recalcitrant victims. This was an instrument which when it was shut was shaped like a pear. It could be enlarged by means of screws, and was forced into the mouth, then extended so that the victim was obliged to keep his mouth open, being quite unable to move his jaws. It was, as can be imagined, very painful and effective.

Once inside the Casa Santa, the prisoner would be "tried". Every effort was made to strike him with terror so that he was in a state of such nervousness as would make him ready to admit all the charges which were brought against him.

The room into which he was taken was hung with black, presumably to remind him that he was already in the presence of death—and, poor man, it might have been happier for him if he had come immediately to that state. No light came through the windows; but on a table, which was set at one end of the room and covered with black velvet, there was an image of Christ on the cross, and six lighted candles. There was also a copy of the Bible on this table. Beside the table was a pulpit on which stood another candle; and at this pulpit sat a secretary who would read out the crimes of which the victim was accused.

The Inquisitors would be seated at the table in their white habits and black hoods; and the guards who had brought the prisoner from his house would be ranged behind him when he had been brought to stand before the table.

The Inquisitor-in-chief would take no notice whatever of the prisoner for some minutes, during which time he would pretend to be absorbed in the papers which lay before him. This was according to the "instructions" and was calculated to increase the prisoner's fear, which it assuredly did, for he must wonder what those papers contained to make the Inquisitor interested in them to such an extent that he appeared to be quite oblivious of the poor creature who was waiting, in a state of terror, for his attention.

Eventually the Inquisitor would put aside the papers, and the secretary would ask the prisoner for his name, address and other particulars.

Then the cold eyes of the Inquisitor would be turned upon him. Did he know why he had been arrested? he would be asked.

The poor bewildered man—who, it was very likely, had not the faintest notion why he had been arrested—would declare his innocence, at which the Inquisitor—again acting on "instructions"—would turn to the papers on the table and appear to study them significantly.

Had the man any enemies? Did he attend confession regularly?

The victim would know that he must answer truthfully, for the Inquisitor would then quickly fire a series of questions. What was his diocese? Who was his confessor? When did he last go to confession?

The Inquisitors were warned not to be moved by the terror of the prisoner. Should the man break down and weep, tell heartrending stories about his family, assure the Inquisitors that he was a good Catholic, they must not allow themselves to be moved. Heretics, they were reminded, were crafty. Had they not pretended to follow the Catholic Faith and practised heresy in secret? Again and again Inquisitors were reminded that the condemnation of one might be the salvation of thousands, for there were plausible heretics who not only sinned against the Church themselves, but inveigled others into doing likewise.

The aim of these interviews was to make the victim break down and confess and, in confessing, incriminate as many of his family and neighbours as possible.

If however the prisoner was a stubborn man, a bold man, who refused to be intimidated by the guards, the Inquisitor and the gloomy solemnity of the chamber, then other tactics must be used.

Then the Inquisitor should allow his expression to soften, he should speak to the prisoners as though for their own good, tell them that he wished them no harm, that he felt towards them as a father who sees his child straying into evil ways. What would a father's feelings be in such circumstances? Regret! Eagerness to lead the straying child back to holy paths! That was how the Inquisitors felt. A confession could do so much. It could ease the soul of its burden of sin, it could bring pardon, sudden release. What should the Inquisition say to one who was truly penitent but: "Come back to the Church. You are forgiven"?

True penitents naturally abhorred heresy, and in their commission of this great sin they could not have been alone. There must be others who were secretly sinful. Those who were regretful of past sins would wish to give others a chance of penitence.

Therefore, when they gave to the Inquisitors the names of those who had shared their sin, then and only then could there be no doubt of their true penitence.

This method was very successful. Many fell into the trap laid for them; and thus more and more victims were brought into the prisons of the Inquisition.

If however a man persisted in his innocence, insisting that he knew none who was heretic, he would be taken away to a cell and brought back again. There would be hours of questions, threats and cajoling, and if at the end of them he remained obdurate, the Inquisitor would shrug his shoulders and tell him that he had been called away and could question him no more for some little time. As he had not proved his innocence he would remain a prisoner until the Inquisitor's return.

If the prisoner continued to remain firm, more cunning methods would be tried. He would be told that he appeared to be innocent after all but, because his jailors were not entirely convinced, they must still keep him a prisoner. He would be removed to a more comfortable cell, and certain selected visitors would be allowed to see him. Thus his confidence would return and those who visited him would be instructed to encourage him to be careless in his talk. A stray word on which a certain meaning could be placed, and the Inquisitors might have what they sought. These visitors would invariably implore the prisoner to make his confession, assuring him that if he did so he would be discharged with a light penance.

What the prisoner did not know was that one of the officers of the Inquisition, in a place of concealment, was taking down all that was said during the interview.

Sometimes even this plan did not work, for the prisoner might be entirely innocent of heresy. Then a little trick was employed. The prisoner would share his cell with another who the prisoner would think was in the same position as himself but who was in actuality an agent of the Inquisition. The task of this man would be to talk to the prisoner during the long hours they were alone, to discuss his own pretended heresy, talk of his beliefs and trap the prisoner into damning admissions.

If however all these methods failed, the prisoner was brought once more into the chamber to stand before the table on which stood the cross, the candles and the gospels. Questions were fired at him at great speed; and this went on for a very long time, until at last the weary prisoner was bewildered into contradicting himself.

He was lying, he would be told. Then he would be taken away. His next journey would be to the torture chamber.

It was during the rule of Torquemada that torture became

such an important part of the work of the Inquisition. Earlier there had been reluctance to employ it; and there is mention, in a letter written by Philip IV of France (1268-1314), of the torturing of heretics, which method had been newly introduced by the Inquisition. Philip did protest against the harshness of the torture, although certainly he had no objection to its being used when he so desired it, as in the case of the Templars.

Clement V arranged that there should be an enquiry into the methods used by the Inquisitors, when he received protests that men and women were so severely tortured that they confessed to heresy knowing that if they did not they would die under torture.

These were the beginnings, and between this time (early fourteenth century) and the establishment of the Inquisition in Castile (in the late fifteenth century) there are not a great many records of torture; although of course it is very possible that many cases were not recorded.

According to Article 15 in Torquemada's instructions, the Inquisitors are given permission to torture where heresy is 'half-proven'. They were warned however that there must be no shedding of blood, because it was against the laws of the Church for a priest to shed the blood of another human being. It might seem that a little true Christianity was finding its way into the Inquisition, but this was not so. There was a hasty proviso: If, under torture, a victim died, the Inquisitor responsible must seek immediate absolution through his fellow priest. Each priest had the absolute right bestowed by Torquemada to absolve the murderer of his sin.

Thus it appears that whenever there is a hint of leniency or justice shining through these cruel laws, there always follows the quick adjustment, the sleight-of-hand as it were, to turn justice into mockery and kindness into fiendish cruelty.

There were several stages of torture. This was characteristically referred to by the pious Inquisitors, not as torture which was a harsh word, but as The Question.

The uses of torture had been laid down by Nicolaus Eymeric, who had been Grand Inquisitor of Aragon in the fourteenth century; and he had been inspired in the work he compiled by that of Bernard Gui written in the early part of that century.

Torquemada must have agreed with a great deal that these two had written, for he allowed much of it to stand and form a basis for his Instructions.

Eymeric had advised Inquisitors that there should be five stages of torture and each was important, for even during the early stages a confession might be wrung from the victim.

The first of the five stages was the Threat. This was delivered to the prisoner who, having heard a great deal about this terrible weapon of the cruel men into whose hands he had fallen, might become weak with horror when he was told that he was in danger of experiencing it.

The second was the journey to the torture chamber. Slowly, ceremonially, he would be led to that dismal room, lighted by candles and the glow of braziers which held their own hideous and significant meaning; he would be given time to glance round the room of pain, at the instruments ready for use, perhaps at one or two of the victims who were already receiving the attention of the black-robed fiends (their appearance was calculated to inspire terror; they wore black cowls over their heads and in these small holes had been cut that they might peer through them at their victims), perhaps hear groans of misery and screams of agony. A very important one, this second stage.

The third was even more terrifying (for these stages by their very nature grew more alarming as they followed one another). The prisoner was seized and stripped of his clothes, in readiness for the torture.

And the fourth—that was showing him the instrument which was to be used, strapping his naked body upon it and giving him time to savour the terrible knowledge that his time of agony was at hand.

If he had passed this fourth stage without confessing and giving the names of other sinners, then he was indeed a bold man; and there was nothing to delay passing on to the fifth and last stage. The pulley was hoisted; the rack turned. The physical torture had begun.

By law it was forbidden to *repeat* torture, so that a sufferer, having once endured the Question and maintained his or her innocence, must not be put to the test again. The Inquisitors found this an easy hurdle. Instead of *repeating* the torture, they *continued* it day after day, and any interval was a mere *suspension*.

The three tortures used more frequently than others in the dungeons of the Inquisition were the rack, the hoist and the water torture.

The method of the rack is well known, for it was in universal use.

The hoist was perhaps more commonly used in the dungeons of the Inquisition than any other torture, no doubt because it was the easiest to inflict, yet as painful as others.

The sufferer on the hoist had his arms tied behind his back, and the rope which bound them was passed over a pulley fixed to the ceiling. The victim was slowly drawn upwards so that his arms had to support the whole weight of his body. The pain was excruciating, and the victim would be lowered after a few minutes and told to confess. If he failed to do this he was pulled upwards once more, and so violently that his joints might be dislocated. Thus did he suffer a new and more exquisite torture. Again he was invited to confess and, if once more he failed to do so, weights were tied to his feet and the jerks began again. If after this he persisted in his refusal to confess to heresy and implicate others, he was left hanging in such pain as it is not easy to imagine.

When he became unconscious he was taken down, but the torture was not ended; it was merely suspended. The Inquisitors must remember the law (no man or woman must be tortured twice); it had merely been necessary to call a halt in the proceedings which would be continued as soon as the victim was able to feel pain once more.

The water torture was very popular with the Inquisitors, no doubt because it was particularly cruel. In this the victim was tied to a ladder, which was placed in a slightly sloping position, the feet higher than the head. Wrists and ankles were very tightly tied so that the rope cut into the flesh when the victim moved them. The head was held firmly in position by a band of metal, and the mouth opened forcibly by a piece of iron; pieces of wood were thrust into the nostrils, and over the mouth was placed a long piece of linen. When the victim was thus secured, jars of water were brought forward and slowly poured down his throat. The water carried the linen with it. The poor creature would automatically swallow and by so doing take the linen down his gullet; and as he struggled the cord would cut into his body where it bound him. Not until he was half dead from asphyxia would the linen be hauled back and the treatment be 'suspended', to be 'continued later'.

Although the rack, the hoist and the water torture were the main methods used by the Inquisitors, there were others equally diabolical.

One of these was the Spanish Chair. This consisted of an iron chair with rests for the arms. The sufferer must sit in this chair with an iron band about his neck and arms to keep them in one position. His bare feet were placed in stocks very close to a brazier. Then the feet were coated with fat and slowly allowed to roast; and so that the flesh might not burn too quickly, fat was continually applied.

Flogging was practised, as was the cutting off of toes and fingers by a gradual process, perhaps one each day. People were hung in the torture chamber, suspended by their thumbs, with weights attached to their feet.

Limborch, in his *History of the Inquisition*, tells a piteous story of a Jew (a new Christian) who was brought before the

Inquisition having been betrayed by a servant whom he had whipped for theft.

He was arrested and, when he refused to admit that he was a heretic, was told that he would be taken to the torture chamber. This was the first stage of the Torture: The Threat. He insisted that he spoke truthfully and the Inquisitors answered that, since he was so obstinate, he clearly chose to suffer torture, and in this case the Inquisition could not be held guilty if his blood was shed or he died while it was being applied. The Inquisitors were as dexterous with words and as expert at handling their own consciences as they were with the terrible machines they used.

The first of the tortures in this case was to put him in a linen bag and tie this so tightly about him that he was almost suffocated, but not quite. Then the bag was untied and he was freed, and once more asked to confess. Refusing to do so, his thumbs were bound with cords so tightly that the blood spurted up from under the nails. Still he refused. He was then made to stand with his back to the wall on which were several pulleys fitted with ropes. These ropes were fastened about his legs, arms and other parts of his tormented body; then the ropes were violently jerked so that his joints were dislocated; and finally, still not confessing, he was left suspended by the ropes.

Remaining, as these men would say, 'obstinate', he was struck with a ladder-like instrument on the shins with such force that he fainted with the pain. He was then bound with ropes which were pulled so tight that they cut into the flesh, making wounds; tighter and tighter were the ropes drawn; and the torture only stopped because much of the man's blood was shed and he was close to death. The Inquisitors, knowing that should a victim die whilst in their hands they would be exonerated, yet did not wish to let too many victims die. Their intention was to preserve them that they might be handed over to the secular arm which would then pronounce sentence of death; for it was convenient that these holy men should not be said to have caused the death of anyone.

This particular Jew was eventually released, made to wear the garment of shame—the *Sanbenito*—for two years, and then banished from Seville. Surely, but for their love of inflicting pain, the sentence of banishment would have been given in the first place.

Accounts of torture suffered by men and women who fell into the hands of Inquisitors is so harrowing to write and to read that one is tempted to slur over details, and to make the account of them as brief as possible, to leave to the imagination the terrible suffering which was inflicted on unfortunate people who were not being punished for doing harm to anyone, but merely for using their brains. But there again, in using the word punishment, I may be told by some supporters of this evil institution, that I am wrong. Torture was not inflicted as a punishment. Heretics were tortured that they might confess their sins, that they might betray their friends, and that thus these holy men who set themselves up in their arrogance to teach the world, might lead them to salvation.

Yet, if we are going to examine the Inquisition, how is it possible to overlook this shocking cruelty which was at its very roots?

In *The History of the Inquisition as it Subsists in the Kingdoms of Spain and Portugal to this Day,* compiled and translated by the Reverend J. Baker, M.A. in 1734, there are some horrifying accounts of cruelties inflicted by the Inquisition. One account tells of William Lithgow, a Scotsman, who was arrested in Malaga, accused of being a spy. Since he was a Protestant he was immediately pressed to become a Catholic. Refusing to change his religion he was loaded with irons, and his legs were extended by means of an iron bar, a yard long, of such weight that he was unable either to stand or to sit and could only lie flat on his back. He was given only a pint of water every other day, and had no bed, pillow or blanket; the window in his room was closed up with lime and stone and the orders were that he was to have nothing that ' bears any likeness to comfort'.

Forty-seven days after his imprisonment he heard a coach draw up outside his prison; officials of the Inquisition entered and took him away to a place where he was to be tortured. Unable to walk, he had to be carried; and when the irons were knocked off, so clumsy were his tormentors that they took away an inch of his heel with the iron. He was racked for five hours and taken back to his prison. It was arranged that every morning at a certain hour a coach should drive up and stop close to his window so that he might suffer the additional torment of believing that once more he was to be taken away to be tortured.

He was left in his noisome prison where he became ' over-run with vermin which crawled in clusters about his beard, lips and eyebrows so that he could scarce open his eyes'. With a great show of magnanimity it was ordered that he was to be swept free of vermin twice every eight days.

Furious because they could not shake this man's belief in his version of the gospels, he was kicked in the face by an Inquisitor and sentenced to undergo eleven different tortures. These he survived and was then condemned to be carried to Granada to be burned alive.

A Turkish slave and a Negress, also a slave, who had been charged to look after him that he might be preserved for the fire, showed him great kindness; and another servant, a Flemish boy, was so struck with the amazing courage of this man that he carried the story of his sufferings to some Englishmen who were in the town; because of this the case was taken before Sir Walter Afton, the English Ambassador.   Thus Mr. Lithgow's return to England was made possible.   He was carried on a feather bed to the King, James I, to whom he told his story, and we have yet another account of the inhumanity of the Inquisition, not only towards the Spanish, but towards foreigners who ventured into their country.

Another account (this comes from the same J. Baker and John Marchant) is of an event which took place in the eighteenth century when the French, reaching Aragon, are said to have rescued several young girls who had been taken up by the Inquisitors. These girls, we are told, were taken from their homes during the night—not because of their religious beliefs, but because of their physical attractions.   They were shown various instruments of torture and told that, unless they complied with the desires of their captors, these instruments would be used upon them.

One girl is reputed to have stated that she was shown a large brass pan with a cover which was placed on an oven.   In the oven a fire burned.   She was told that heretics were put in the pan and the cover placed over them, when a slow fire was kept going in the oven until the contents of the pan were reduced to ashes.   The girl also tells of a wheel, from the inside circumference of which protruded sharp knives.   Those who spoke against the Pope and priests were put on the wheel which was turned until they were cut to pieces.   A pit full of snakes was also shown to her; this was for people who did not pay proper respect to holy images.   The girl was told that unless she submitted to the will of the Inquisitor it would be the pan over the oven for her.

This is the wildest story of all, but there is no doubt that the Inquisitors had power over the life and death of a great many people, and such power inevitably corrupts.   There were lascivious priests—there always have been—and the laws of celibacy which were imposed doubtless increased that lasciviousness; and while Popes openly flaunted their families in the Vatican itself, how could continence be expected of priests?

One of the instruments of torture, which was discovered in the prison of the Inquisition in Toledo by the invading French, was a statue built to resemble the Virgin Mary.   The front of this statue was covered with sharp nails and knives.   Levers were pulled, and the arms of the statue would embrace its victim who would be crushed tighter and tighter, while the knives and nails pierced the naked flesh.   How ironic, and yet how apt, to have made this statue in the form of the Virgin Mary! What a commentary on the mockery these men had made of the Christian Faith!

The case of a certain Elvira del Campo, who was the wife of a scrivener, is quoted at length by Henry Charles Lea (*A History of the Spanish Inquisition* Vol. III), who takes it from the records of the Toledo Inquisition; it is again quoted by Cecil Roth in his book *The Spanish Inquisition*; but it is so shocking and at the same time so revealing that I feel it should be briefly cited here.

Elvira was arrested because she had put on clean linen on a Saturday and refused to eat pork. This happened in the middle of the sixteenth century, almost a hundred years after Torquemada had established the Inquisition in Spain.

She had no intention to commit heresy, she declared; but her tormentors showed her the dreaded instruments in their foul chamber, and the poor woman, falling to her knees in terror, begged them to tell her what they wished her to do; she declared she would do anything rather than suffer the torment.

She was told to tell the truth, and demanded piteously what they wished her to say, for she had told the truth. Cords were tied to her arms and twisted; and between her screams of pain she cried out: "Señors, tell me what I have to say. I do not know what I have done. Loosen me, and I will tell the truth. I do not know what you wish me to say, but only tell me, and I will say it." Again and again the cords were tightened; again she was commanded to tell the truth, and she continued to assure them that, if only they would tell her what to say, she would say it.

She was clearly a woman of little education, and it seems to have been sheer brutality in this case which goaded those fiends to continue.

She had not eaten pork, she said, because pork made her sick; she did not like pork. "I have done nothing," she continued. "Release me and I will tell you the truth. I don't know what I have to tell, but loosen me . . . tell me what I have to tell, and I will tell it. Say. Say."

And still they continued to torture her.

What had she done which was contrary to the Holy Catholic Church? they demanded.

"Release me," she moaned. "Take me from here. Only tell me what I have to say. Oh . . . wretched me! I will tell you all that is wanted. Señors, you are breaking my arms. Loosen me . . ."

She must tell in detail what she really had done.

"What am I wanted to tell? I did everything. Oh, loosen me, for I don't remember what I have to tell. I am a weak

Some forms of physical persuasion used by the Inquisition on heretics
(from the engraving by B. Picart, 1742)

The chamber of the Inquisition

An auto-de-fé for the burning of condemned heretics

woman and my arms are breaking. Have you no pity for a weak woman?"

They told her they would have pity for her if she would tell the truth. "Señors," she cried then, "tell me, tell me it . . ." Again the torture was applied. "I don't know how to tell it, Señor," she wailed. "I don't know."

The account goes on with the continual repetition which is so heartrending. Again and again she professes her willingness to say whatever they want her to say, but she does not know what it is. She has not eaten pork. Pork makes her sick, and she does not like pork. She has changed her linen on a Saturday. But then her linen needed to be changed. She had meant no harm; and she does not know what they want of her.

It was impossible for her to satisfy them, for they were taking what they wanted; they wished to torture her; they placed her naked body on the frame and she was given the water torture (not the torture of the same name which has already been described, but the more modern form, during which the body was painfully stretched, a funnel placed in the throat and jars of water poured into the mouth).

The account is punctuated by the agonized pleas of this woman. Always it is: "*Remind* me what I have to say, for I do not know. I do not know how to tell it. I pray you tell me how to tell it. I say I did it—whatever you wish me to have done—but, my God, how can I tell it?"

Eventually they 'suspended' the torture, but they renewed it after a lapse of four days. Again she begged to be told what to say, and it may have been that her tormentors conveyed this to the poor dazed mind, for she admitted that she had practised Judaism, declared she was penitent and begged for reconciliation to the Holy Catholic Church. This was granted at an *auto de fé*. And although many suffered even greater torment than Elvira del Campo, the detailed description of what took place in the torture chamber when all her remarks were recorded gives one of the clearest—and for that very reason most horrible—pictures of the Inquisition at work.

One of the most nauseating tortures of all was that in which a large dish was turned upside-down on the naked stomach of the victim. In the dish were placed several mice, and a fire was lighted on top of the dish. This caused panic among the mice, and as the dish grew hotter they burrowed into the flesh of the sufferer. This was similar to that of the ant torture which is said to be carried out by some natives in Africa.

The most terrible of tortures, such as that just described and burying alive, were used by the Inquisitors in the Netherlands when the savage attempt was made to turn that Protestant nation into a Catholic one.

Many of the stories which have been recorded cannot be accepted as truth in their entirety; but even allowing for exaggerations there can be no doubt that one of the most unhappy fates which could have befallen a man during any age was to have been taken—a suspected heretic—into the building which was known as Casa Santa, the Holy House.

9

THE SECULAR ARM AND THE
AUTO DE FÉ

I F O N E did not burn with indignation at the plight of tens of thousands, one could laugh at the method of passing sentence on them.

The holy men of the Church, who had been torturing the bodies of these most unfortunate men and women, were unable to deliver the death sentence, for a Christian must not shed the blood of a fellow creature! So the Inquisitors, determined as they were that the mutilated bodies of their victims should be consigned to the flames, made sure of their salvation by allowing someone else to condemn them to it. They could then piously wash their hands of the whole affair, turn their eyes to heaven and murmur: "We have done our duty; we have tried all means within our power to bring these men and women back to Holy Church. We have failed, so there is nothing we can do but abandon them to the secular arm."

They *abandoned* them; they did not *send* them. These men had to be very careful of their choice of words. It was the same deceitfulness as *suspending* not *repeating* the torture. Their image of their God, it seems, was of a potentate more powerful than themselves, equally vindictive, arrogant and vain, but slightly less intelligent since He could be so easily hoodwinked. The hasty absolution of a priest could exonerate a fellow prac-titioner if he had committed murder in the torture chamber—and God, it appeared, would be deceived by a hastily murmured penance. Thus they who had persecuted their victims, tricked them, tortured them, and determined on their death, were not guilty of murder because they merely murmured: "The Church can help you no more. The Church casts you out and you are abandoned to the secular arm. This we do beseeching it at the same time to deal moderately with you without shedding your blood and putting you to death."

They had one eye on Heaven as they uttered those words; they were for the ears of the recording angel. But woe betide any member of the secular arm who showed that mercy which they " beseeched ". He should know better—and very quickly all secular officers did learn the rule; the plea for mercy was for their *sleeping* God's ear. It meant " It was not we who did this murder. We are Christian priests. Our hands are clean. It is the secular arm which has felt it its duty to sentence to death these enemies of the state."

As for the officers of the secular arm, what were they to do? Act leniently towards those who were abandoned by the Inquisition? And be themselves brought before the tribunal to answer a charge of heresy!

But even the Inquisitors had to admit that it was possible for a true Catholic to be accused of heresy, to be submitted to the torture and perhaps be unjustly condemned to death. They consoled themselves. What a glorious death! To die for the Faith and in the Faith. They would go straight to paradise. Of what had they to complain?

Many prisoners who had been urged to repent and promised mercy if they did so, learned that they had not escaped the death penalty. The only mercy they would be shown was strangulation before their bodies were burned—which they had to agree would be a far less painful death than that of being burned alive. They were told that it was God who would have mercy on them; the secular arm must punish them in accordance with the law, and the punishment for heretics was death. This had been so since the Bull of Innocent IV, issued as far back as the fourteenth century, which compelled the officers of the secular arm to execute heretics or themselves suffer excommunication and trial for heresy.

Sentence on heretics—relapsed or reconciled—was to take place in public so that the scene might be witnessed by a large number of people. The ceremony, religious, barbaric, and a ritual massacre, was called an Act of Faith—*auto de fé* in Spanish but perhaps more commonly known as the Portuguese *auto da fé*. Sunday was considered quite the best day for this hideous spectacle to take place, because Sunday was a holy day; moreover more people were free to see the sights. It was good for the people to see what happened to those who sinned against the laws of Holy Church; it filled them with fear and determination that they would not stand among those wretched men and women. It was looked upon as a rehearsal for Judgment Day.

The Inquisitor was a person of great power. He was given the right to grant Indulgences, and there can be no doubt that many used this power to extract the information they desired. What a weapon to place in the hands of these men whose mission in life was to bring heretics to, what they would call, justice! How simple to say to those who felt the burden of their sins heavy upon them: "Come, tell me what you know of these men and women. Give me a good case against them, and in exchange you shall receive the indulgence you crave." Naturally the superstitious were ready to comply, and if they had no real information, how could they resist fabricating it, and perhaps so deluding themselves as to believe it was the truth?

Inquisitors, in their privileged position, could be excommunicated only by the Pope himself; and the Popes, who regarded the Inquisitors as their servants, in spite of the continual struggle with the various monarchs who were constantly on the alert to free their countries from Papal influence, naturally gave them their protection.

This protection was extended to all those who served, even in a less significant degree, under the Inquisitors. Each Inquisitor had many helpers. There were vicars, *socii*, familiars, notaries, and many others who performed the less important tasks necessary to deal with heretics, from the arrest to the *auto de fé*.

The vicars, or delegates as they were sometimes called, were really the understudies of the Inquisitor. When he was not available, or engaged with some very important victim, these vicars would take over his duties; and a great deal of the preliminaries which were simply routine were conducted by them. They were, in effect, Inquisitors in embryo.

The *socii* who accompanied the Inquisitor on his journeys, had no special official duty, but having followed the case as closely as had the Inquisitor himself, their function was to discuss the case with the Inquisitor and occasionally offer an opinion.

The familiars formed the Inquisitor's guard—a very personal guard. They were not necessarily priests, but usually came from more worldly callings, although, once having become a familiar, a man automatically became part of a half-religious order. Some of these familiars carried arms, for Inquisitors were naturally not beloved by the people, and must constantly be on the alert for attack from those who sought revenge on behalf of some loved one. Familiars were frequently in the prisons of the Inquisition; they visited prisoners and urged them to repent. It was generally a familiar who was used to visit a prisoner in the guise of a kindly friend, offering advice, luring the prisoner to make some careless remark which could be used against him. There was no need for them to be of high social standing; and it was of no importance what work they had done before joining the community. It was for this reason that they made such good spies. They could appear to be ordinary men of the work-a-day world so much more easily than could those who had spent years in seclusion. Of all the community concerned with the torturing and burning of mankind, next to the Inquisitors themselves, the familiars seem the most sinister.

The notary's was a position not so easy to fill, for there were few, humble enough to want it, who were sufficiently educated. The duties of the notary were to keep records of the examinations and questions and answers, given under torture; moreover records had to be kept so that those reconciled heretics who relapsed later should not be able to escape the stake. The records had to be written in Latin, which seems to have given the notaries unnecessary trouble, for the questions and answers were naturally spoken in the language of the people concerned. We owe a great deal to these notaries and their records; but for them, Llorente would never have had an opportunity of going through the archives and discovering so much of what happened.

Other servants of the Inquisition were bishops, abbés and sometimes lawyers. But the bishops and the Inquisitors from the earliest days had been on uneasy terms. The bishop had at one time been the arbiter of religious conduct, and never did he happily accept the power of the Inquisitor.

The Inquisition was devoted to formality; it was very eager to show the world that a great deal of thought had gone into the compilation of its laws. Again there is a hint of that hypocrisy which overshadows everything that was done. The Inquisition, on the surface, was a well-organized institution, the laws of which had been studied and adjusted during the centuries and in the light of experience. It was very important that it should appear to be an efficient organization, far above petty malice or love of cruelty for its own sake. The brutality must appear to be for the good of all concerned—only thus could men, even such as these, convince themselves that they were not inhuman monsters. It is all in line with their talk of 'suspended' not 'repeated' torture, and keeping the stain of murder from their souls by 'abandoning' their victims to the secular arm.

They had decided that there were several grades of heresy. *Affirmative* heretics were those who announced quite openly their divergence from the rigid line laid down by the Church, or their belief in another religion. *Negative* heretics were those who denied their heresy and, if they were forced to admit it, declared they had committed it in innocence. There were also *suspected* heretics who had shown evidence of conduct which might lead them to heresy, such as indulging in conversation with heretics or expressing pity for those who had been robbed of their goods or burned at the stake. Any man or woman suspected of heresy must make a formal announcement that he or she had no heretical tendency, and would in future remain outside the sphere of heretical influence.

Those who put obstacles in the path of the Inquisitors were

also guilty of offence. There were—and this revives one's belief in human nature—many who were in this class. People who performed the smallest kindness to a heretic fell into it. How could this attitude be reconciled with the teachings of Christ? In the gospel according to St. John, XIII, 34 and 35, it is written that Jesus said:

"A new commandment I give unto you, That ye love one another; as I have loved you, that ye also love one another. By this shall all men know that ye are my disciples, if ye have love one to another."

It is ironical that it should have been a definite sin against the Church to show Christian charity to those in distress. Surely this is an indication of the wide divergence between the Church and the teachings of Jesus. For to obey this commandment of Jesus Christ was a sin according to the Church. What, therefore could that Church possibly have in common with Christ, but the name?

The Inquisitors made themselves responsible for dealing with certain offences outside heresy, but they were much more lenient with regard to these. They would always arrange that the sin they dealt with could be construed as a sin against the Church, thus coming under their jurisdiction.

The cells in the prisons of the Inquisition were of varying degrees of comfort; the best were relegated to those guilty of offences such as bigamy. The second class of cell was slightly less comfortable, and into these were sent the servants of the Inquisition who had failed to carry out their duties in accordance with the commands of their masters; the third type—foul, dank dungeons in which rats and other vermin abounded—were reserved for heretics.

Bigamy was not in itself a sin which the Inquisition wished to punish with any degree of severity. A bigamist who confessed what he had done would be given a very light sentence; if he declared that he had been overcome by passion and so led to marry more than once, that was well enough; it was only if he expressed contempt for marriage itself—which was one of the Church's sacraments—that he came dangerously near to heresy, and a more severe sentence was inflicted.

Adultery and fornication presented difficulties. These were sins in which Popes and priests had indulged riotously. Adultery and fornication, declared the Inquisition, did not come under its jurisdiction unless the adulterers and fornicators expressed the belief that there was no sin in committing them; then, of course, they were setting themselves in opposition to the laws of Holy Church—thus being guilty of heresy.

The laws of the Inquisition had been worked out with the utmost care, and it was as though excuses for brutal conduct were continually drawn over the truth by obscure methods of expression and formal procedure.

Ludovico à Paramo declares that God was the first Inquisitor and that in the Book of Genesis He set an example to the Inquisitors to come. Adam and Eve ate of the fruit of the tree of knowledge and thus were guilty of heresy; their punishment was to be turned out of the garden. They lost the Garden of Eden, and clearly, says Ludovico à Paramo, God sets the example of confiscation of worldly goods. They wore skins and these were equivalent to the *sanbenito*, that hideous dress which proclaimed man or woman heretic. It was comforting to cite this example, to reassure themselves: We are brutal, we torture our fellow men and women although we fall short of shedding their blood—leaving that to the secular arm—but we are merely following the example laid down for us by God Himself.

The fiery Jehovah of the Old Testament seems to be a God after their own hearts, whereas the teaching of the gentle Jesus of the New, although they called themselves his followers, appeared to be ignored by them. It therefore seems extraordinarily illogical that they should have had such a contempt for the Jewish religion (which Jesus and his family followed devoutly) and looked with loathing on those who reverted to it after being baptized as Christians. Religion, to these people, was largely a matter of eating or not eating pork, sprinkling water or not sprinkling water in mourning chambers, circumcision and such rites. The real teaching of Christ had been choked out of existence in their churches by dogma and ritual.

The *sanbenito* was the garment of shame. Those who wore it did so as a sign that they had sinned, and that they were doing penance for those sins. It had first been brought into existence by St. Dominic, but the garment worn by penitents in his day was different from that with which Tomás de Torquemada burdened those whom he ordained should be punished. Its name derives from *saco bendito*, which quickly became *sanbenito* and was often called in Spain the *zamarra*, the sheep-skin jacket of today.

St. Dominic decreed that the garment of shame should be of sackcloth and dismal in colour. During the Albigensian war, those who were fighting for the Church wore crosses stitched on their tunics; the cross was the sign of a good Catholic. St. Dominic decided however that in order that a penitent should be recognized he should wear two crosses on his garment.

After the war men no longer displayed the crosses, and it was

decided that two yellow crosses should be used on the *sanbenito*
—one on each breast.

Before the days of Torquemada the *sanbenito* was simply a
tunic, very similar to those worn by the members of religious
orders; but the zealous Inquisitor-General had been quick to see
how this garment could provide an additional torture, and
decided to use it more frequently than hitherto. The ordinary
tunic with the cross was too similar to those worn by holy men.
Therefore its shape was changed. It became a loose-fitting
garment with a hole in the top that it might be slipped over the
head and hung on the body like a tabard. It reached the knees,
and was made of yellow sackcloth; the crosses which were sewn
to it were blood-red in colour.

The type of *sanbenito* worn by the victim depended on the
nature of his sin, and those condemned to wear them were
obliged to do so at certain times, according to their sins. Some
wore them on Sundays and holy days. Others dared not be seen
without them. People began to shrink from contamination with
them, for they quickly came to believe that there was evil in the
hideous yellow garment.

For the man or woman who was merely suspected of being
a heretic there was the *sanbenito* without cross, providing he or
she was a suspect *leviter*. If the person were a suspect *vehemen-
ter*, the *sanbenito* which was worn was decorated with only one
arm of the cross and this was on both back and front of the
garment; the suspect *violenter* wore the complete cross.

Men and women were sentenced to wear the *sanbenito* for
several years, some sentences including periodic flogging at the
church door.

But for those who were found guilty of heresy and condemned
to the stake there were the most hideous *sanbenitos* of all. These
bore grotesque figures painted on them, and these figures were
symbolic of the fate which awaited their wearers. Those who
had repented and were attending the *auto de fé* to hear a sentence passed which would be severe enough (such as life imprisonment and confiscation of all worldly goods) wore a *sanbenito*
with a cross on back and front, and in addition to this was a tall
cap, like a mitre, which was worn by all who had been found
guilty of heresy. This was called the *coroza*, and on this would
be a complete cross.

The relapsed heretic—who had repented and was condemned
to be burned but, as an act of mercy because of his repentance,
was to be strangled before the fire touched his body—wore a
sanbenito decorated with flames and devils with pitchforks prodding these fires; but the flames on this garment pointed downwards, as an indication that the wearer was not to die by the
fire but was to be strangled before burning.

The heretic who remained true to his beliefs to the last, and was condemned to be burned alive, wore a *sanbenito* decorated with flames and devils, but flames in his case pointed upwards, which indicated his fate.

Any who confessed their guilt and asked for reconciliation, even when the faggots were about to be lighted, were—in the great mercy of the Church—granted it, and strangled before burning.

It was this *sanbenito* which, the subtle mind of Torquemada enabled him to judge, would be of great benefit in his campaign against the heretic.

Many men and women were condemned to the *vergüenza*: that is 'the shame'. This was the sentence passed on those who had been found guilty of heresy and had requested to be reconciled to the Church. Their pleas had been granted but they must of course perform their penance, and this was the one allotted to them.

They must join a procession of similar offenders and in fine weather or foul parade the streets naked from the waist up. At the head of the procession walked the familiars of the Inquisition.

Each penitent carried a green candle, which was unlit; this was another of those affectations so beloved by the members of the Inquisition. It signified that these miserable wretches had not yet "seen the light", but they were not utterly damned since they were given candles to carry hopefully. When the Church received them they would be allowed to light their candles.

At the Cathedral the procession would halt and, as the half naked men and women passed into the church, two priests would be standing at the doors to mark the sign of the cross on their foreheads, bidding them, as they did so, receive the cross which they had rejected and lost.

In the Cathedral the Inquisitors would be waiting for the penitents, the green cross, symbol of the Inquisition having been hoisted above the altar. The notary would read out the names of the men and women who had come to hear their sentences, and what penance they were to perform.

For this offence it was decreed that for six Fridays in succession, stripped to the waist, their heads and feet bare, they were to walk in procession through the streets as they had on this day. As they walked they would be whipped; and even when this penance was over they would never be allowed to hold any honourable office, nor wear jewels or fine clothes; and they must give one fifth of their possessions into the keeping of the Inquisition, that some grace might come to them, since what was taken from them would be used in the holy war against the Moors of Granada.

There was one grim warning which was always issued. If any of these men and women fell again into error there was no hope for them. Whatever confessions they made they would not be believed; and the Holy Inquisition would have but one alternative in dealing with them. They would be abandoned to the secular law.

Every man or woman who had known the shame of walking almost naked through the streets, who had felt the whip across his or her shoulders, who had felt the press of eager sightseers avid for sensation yet never daring to show pity even if they felt it, also knew that one more slip, one more disgruntled enemy, and theirs would be the fiery death.

An *auto de fé!* The words must have caused a thrill of horror, yet hideous fascination, even among the most insensitive. Those days on which the *autos* were held were the gala days and attracted as many people and produced even more excitement than the traditional bull-fight.

The people must be made to understand the nature of these occasions. They were not entertainments merely, they were religious ceremonies. It was for this reason that they were always held on Sundays or the holy days of the Church.

It was not intended that the day should be marred by riotous revelling. The Inquisitors shuddered to think what might take place if the ceremonies were prolonged into the night. They had visions of men and women, intoxicated by excitement, giving way to sinful acts, and they, who were about to bring to numbers of people the most acute suffering that can be imagined, could not tolerate the thought of the occasions being desecrated by Sin.

Thus it was decided that *autos de fé* should begin in the early morning that they might be over before dusk and so the opportunity to sin would not be given to the spectators, and the Inquisitors and their adherents would have nothing on their immaculate consciences.

On the evening before an *auto de fé* was to take place relaxed heretics were brought to the palace of the Inquisition, and there they were told that the next day they were to be burned alive. In their 'mercy' the Inquisitors allotted each of them two priests who would be their companions throughout the night and who would do their utmost to save their souls; as for their bodies they were past saving; but if they should confess their heresy and declare their great desire for reconciliation with the Church, although they must die for their sins, they should be granted the privilege of strangulation before the flames consumed their bodies.

The next morning they were brought forth from the prison of the Inquisition, all the prisoners arrayed in their *sanbenitos*

which denoted their crime, about their necks ropes, which also
pinioned them. The procession was now ready to begin.

First came the bearers of the green cross which was draped
with black material, and immediately behind it were the company
of familiars.

The priest who was to celebrate Mass came next, and over
him, borne by four men, was a canopy of scarlet and gold. He
carried the Host and, as he passed through the crowds, all men,
women and children were expected to fall to their knees. With
so many members of the Inquisition close at hand none would
dare remain standing at such a time, for it was certain that such
behaviour would put the culprit into the class of 'suspected
heretic'.

More familiars followed, and then came the prisoners in varying degrees of misery—some having the marks of torture upon
them, others suffering only shame. With each of the prisoners
who was doomed to die by burning were two Dominicans—
penguin-like in their white vestments and flowing black hoods.
The people in the crowds must be shown how merciful were the
Inquisitors, and how even at this late hour it was their urgent
desire to save these wretched creatures from being burned alive.

Following the prisoners, and fastened to long green poles, were
effigies of people who had been found guilty of heresy and had
had the good fortune to escape from Spain. Their faces were
painted with hideous grimaces, and the yellow *sanbenitos* (flames,
fanned by devils, pointing upwards) had been on the figures
together with the *crozas*. Here also were the bodies, which had
been dug up from the graves, of those who had been condemned
as heretics after they had died. This must have been the most
ghastly if not the most pitiable section of the procession.

Now came the Inquisitors, banners of red sarcenet carried
before them; on one side of the banners were emblazoned the
Papal arms entwined with those of Ferdinand and Isabella, and
on the other the arms of the Inquisition.

The *alguazils* and minor officials followed and on either side
of the procession marched soldiers with halberds on their
shoulders.

Straggling in the rear came the sightseers all making their
way to the Cathedral Square (some eager to view the spectacle,
some afraid to stay away) to await the supreme excitement which
would culminate on the *quemadero*.

The Inquisition had always worked with the utmost formality,
and although the sentences of these poor people had already been
decided on, each must be called before a tribunal and listen to
the list of his crimes; and as there was a sermon to be preached,
and often several hundred victims to be individually accused, the
ceremony continued for many hours. There were occasions when

an *auto de fé* began at six in the morning of a summer's day and lasted until dusk. As the final scene was the burning, this meant that, in addition to the exquisite agony of the torture chamber, the sufferers were given the mental torture which such an occasion must have inflicted.

In a great square of the town in which the *auto* was being held—usually the Cathedral Square—platforms were set up and decorated with black crêpe. On these platforms benches had been arranged, tier on tier; and here the prisoners were forced to sit so that the crowds might see them and, to show what good Catholics they were, shout insults at them, and inflict minor indignities and pain, such as setting fire to their beards—a pastime which was lightheartedly called by the mob 'Shaving the New Christians'. On the benches with the prisoners were the friars, who continued to exhort them to confess . . . an outward sign of the merciful nature of the Inquisition; and all about the platform were set up the long poles with the grotesque straw figures in *sanbenitos* and the desecrated decomposing bodies dragged from their graves.

On a second platform the Inquisitors and their servants took their seats; on this platform a black-draped green cross stood, with an altar lighted by candles. Incense burned on this platform and no doubt it was necessary.

Mass was thus celebrated and the sermon was preached; this was usually of great length and, when it was over, the Grand Inquisitor rose and lifting his arms declaimed the oath of allegiance to the Inquisition; this the crowd must repeat after him; they must fall to their knees and swear that they would defend the Holy Office against all who came against it; they swore they would be faithful to it in life and in death; they would not flinch, whatever it should ask of them; they would pluck out their right eye or cut off their right hand and give their life itself if the Inquisition demanded it of them.

When the sovereigns were present at this ceremony they refrained from repeating the oath, for Isabella and Ferdinand had always determined that Spain should not rest under the domination of the Papacy; and it would never be forgotten that this organization had its roots in Rome, for its purpose was to maintain the Catholic Faith, the headquarters of which was the Vatican. The Emperor Charles never swore the oath of allegiance to the Inquisition; it was Charles's son, Philip II, who was the first sovereign to do so. Philip, the strange and morose hermit, the fervent and zealous Catholic, took the oath often and was seen by his subjects rising to his feet, his sword held high, swearing to serve the Inquisition.

Now came the farce of abandoning the prisoners to the secular arm. The Church had done all she could; she could not save their souls, and that was her only concern. There was nothing for her to do but hand them over to the law, that the punishment for heresy might be carried out.

This was followed by reading a detailed account of the crimes of each person condemned—from those who were to receive the lightest penance to those who were to be burned alive. The latter of course were kept to the last—the *pièce de résistance*.

From the altar a spurious appeal was made to the secular arm to show mercy: surely the most despicable moment of the whole wicked proceedings. Let the secular arm deal with them in such a manner that blood would not be shed. Well, if they were burned alive, blood would not be shed. And even if anyone put a different construction on the phrase, the Inquisition was blameless; it had merely despaired of saving their obstinate souls; it was not concerned with what happened to their bodies.

In a field was the *quemadero*—the place of fire. The stakes were set up, and at the foot of these the faggots were piled.

Those who had become reconciled to the Church, although they were relapsed heretics, were given the benefit of strangulation as the faggots were lighted. Many at that last dreadful moment naturally cried out that they wished for reconciliation, the quick death of strangulation being so much more preferable to the hideous pain of being burned alive.

The people shout their approval; the Inquisitors sit, hands folded, deeply shocked by all the wickedness in the world, serene in their own virtue, in bringing about justice, so clever that—although they have brought those groaning, fainting men and women to this horror—because they abandoned them in time to the secular arm, there is no blood on their hands. A pall of smoke hangs over the *quemadero*; the air is filled with the smell of roasting human flesh.

It is more exciting than a bull-fight, for it is much more thrilling to see a human being suffer than an animal; the long ceremony, the chanting of monks, the tolling of bells, the smell of incense, the holiness of the proceedings has a comforting effect. All has been sanctified by these things.

There would be a feeling too of exultation, and because it was vaguely tinged with apprehension it would be the more exciting for that. The Inquisitors were indefatigable. This *auto* was at an end, but before long there would be another. Scarcely four weeks separated one *auto* from another.

When would the next pall of smoke rise above the field which had become the *quemadero*? When would they again have such fun, throwing refuse at the prisoners and burning their beards? When would they hear again those cries of anguish? And who would be the next victims?

These were the questions which made the spectators pause and shiver. Who could tell? The Inquisition was more than two centuries old; but until now it had been as an infant struggling for life.

This was the new Inquisition. The Spanish Inquisition. Torquemada's Inquisition.

That was why many in the crowd, even those as humble and insignificant as muleteers or water-carriers, asked themselves: Who next?

10

THE MYSTERIOUS AFFAIR AT LA GUARDIA

THE FOREMOST ambition of Ferdinand—if not of Isabella—was to conquer the whole of Spain and demolish the last Moorish stronghold. The Moors were a warlike people and a desperate one for during the 1480's their position was growing more and more precarious.

It may have been due to this rooted preoccupation of the sovereigns that Torquemada was allowed to continue in such power. Next to the sovereigns themselves he was the most powerful man in Spain, and because of his fiery eloquence and his aura of sanctity he was on occasions able to dominate even them.

In addition to making war on the Moors the sovereigns had anxieties within their own kingdom. In 1484 a marriage was proposed between Catharine, the young Queen of Navarre and Jean d'Albret, a nobleman of France. The sovereigns naturally saw the danger to Spain of such a union for the d'Albret estates were on the border of Navarre, and the French had long been casting covetous eyes on the province. A French King of Navarre naturally would cause some anxiety to Isabella and Ferdinand.

Unfortunately for them, Catharine's mother was a Frenchwoman determined to further the match with Jean d'Albret, and in spite of their efforts to prevent it, the marriage took place.

However all was not peace in Navarre for a large proportion of the people had no wish to be overpowered by French influence; and Ferdinand, with sly diplomacy, came to an understanding with the discontented Navarrese that, should the French seek advantage from the situation, he and they would prevent its being taken.

This created an uneasy situation on the borders of Aragon, and here was at least one trouble spot to occupy the thoughts of the Spanish sovereigns, so that they were obliged to leave the management of certain home affairs to those ministers whom they considered trustworthy. And who, in the eyes of Isabella and Ferdinand, could be more worthy than Tomás de Torquemada? They knew that the Dominican had the interests of Spain at heart, yet at the same time the very nature of his office meant that he must be influenced by Rome.

Isabella, sternly insisting that she would dominate in Castile, had brought law and order to her dominion in a manner which was admirable. It had been no easy matter to subdue her unruly subjects who, accustomed to the anarchy which had prevailed during the reigns of her father and brother, at first were very reluctant to tolerate restraint. She insisted that the nobles, who had in the past settled their disputes with one another by force of arms, must submit to legal arbitration; and she was rapidly eliminating the bandits of the country by making great efforts to capture them, and, when they were in her hands, inflicting severe punishment.

Although she would always listen to Torquemada and paid him the utmost respect, she adhered to her determination to remain supreme ruler even if this meant coming into conflict with the Church. This is clearly shown by an incident which occurred in Truxillo in the year 1486. A priest of the town had been found guilty of a minor offence and sent to prison by the secular authorities. The ecclesiastical community, always jealous of their authority, were incensed that the civil law should take the judgment out of their hands. The misconduct of a priest, they maintained, was their affair, even if the priest had committed some offence which was in no way connected with his ecclesiastical duties. They therefore demanded that the priest be handed over to the Church that they might deal with him. This request was refused by the civic magistrate.

It was very easy for priests in the various pulpits to inflame the people; and it is not difficult to understand that, living in the grim shadow of the Inquisition, they were always more than eager to show their respect for the Church. Moreover, the mob was always ready to be inflamed. Raiding and pillaging were profitable, particularly when the approval of the Church and the Inquisition could be gained by indulging in them.

As a result of the promptings of the priests, the mob of Truxillo rose in a body, stormed the jail in which the priest was being held, and freed not only him but the other prisoners.

The ecclesiastical community folded its hands and smiled. This would be a lesson to the secular law, to leave churchmen to be dealt with by the Church. But the strong-minded Isabella was not to be intimidated. She had her own views on what was right or wrong, and devout supporter of the Church though she might be, she was determined to maintain the authority of civil law. She therefore sent her soldiers to Truxillo, where they were to restore order and arrest the ringleaders of the mob which had stormed the prison.

These were sentenced to death and the priests whose preaching had incited the mob were banished from Spain. This was Isabella's answer to the Church. It had her support within limits but the state was supreme.

The establishment of the Inquisition in Castile under the guidance of Tomás de Torquemada was proving very successful and Ferdinand was delighted. Much wealth was pouring into the exchequer, and he was sure that Torquemada's zeal would be one of the principal means of bringing about the downfall of the Moors.

The Inquisition in Aragon on the other hand was a feeble institution compared with that of Castile. It was a hundred years or so since it had been established in Aragon and the people there had never greatly objected to it, the reason being that its rule was slack; it was even tolerant, following the same course as in other countries where it was dying a lingering death.

Ferdinand needed money for his war; Isabella wished to see all Spain united under Catholic sway, and quite clearly there was one way of attaining both objects. Torquemada's instructions must be obeyed in Aragon as in Castile; Torquemada's Inquisition must replace the lackadaisical method of the last hundred years.

In April of the year 1484 the Cortes assembled at Taraçona, and Ferdinand, who presided over it, had taken Torquemada with him. He announced his intention of adjusting the Inquisition of Aragon that it might fall into line with that of Castile, and he introduced Tomás de Torquemada as the Inquisitor-General of Aragon.

The Aragonese were dismayed, for stories of the terrible sights to be seen at the Castilian *autos de fé* had travelled as far as Aragon. The New Christians trembled; and the richer they were, the more they trembled. They knew that Ferdinand's greedy hands were itching to seize their treasures, and when they looked at the gaunt, pitiless face of the Prior of the Holy Cross, Tomás de Torquemada, they would have known—even if his reputation had not travelled before him—that they could hope for little mercy.

But they did not altogether despair. They had *heard* of the horrors which had been taking place in Castile, and that was different from seeing them actually taking place; they must have thought that the Castilians were a little foolish to be as meek as they were, and that they, the Aragonese, would in such dire emergency show a little more spirit.

The usual orders were issued to the populace, the formula taking the same shape as so recently in Castile. Everyone was to help the officers of the Inquisition or be suspected of heresy; and Torquemada lost no time in appointing two Inquisitors—

Pedro Arbués de Epila, who was a Canon of the Metropolitan Church of Saragossa, and Fray Gaspar Juglar, a Dominican monk.

Even when these two men had been appointed, the wealthy New Christians of Aragon still did not believe that they could be forced to live under the same reign of terror as that which prevailed in Castile, and two deputations were despatched—one to the Pope, one to Ferdinand. They asked that they might continue with the old customs and that the new instructions of Torquemada might not immediately apply to Aragon. These two requests were ignored; and the new Inquisitors went to work with a zeal worthy of their master.

The results of their labours were the *autos de fé* of May and June 1485; and when the despairing people of Saragossa saw their friends in the hideous *sanbenitos* taking part in the grim processions, and witnessed the burning alive of several people, they grew sullen.

Before the second of the *autos* had taken place Inquisitor Gaspar Juglar was stricken by a mysterious illness; he died of this during May, and it was generally believed that he had been poisoned.

One consequence of this was an increase in the activities of the Inquisitors, but a certain note of fear had been struck, and Pedro Arbués was nervous. He carefully tested all he ate and drank, never moved without a bodyguard and wore armour beneath his habit; he even wore a steel cap hidden by his hood.

When Leonardo Eli, one of the richest New Christians in Saragossa, was arrested, those who had believed that through their wealth and influence they could, by presenting petitions, put a stop to the reign of terror, realized that they had been mistaken. However they did not mean to give up easily, and one of the wealthiest and most influential of the community, a *converso* named Juan Pedro Sanchez, called together a little group of men in similar position to his own (including his four brothers who held important government posts) and a plan was formulated.

The meetings were held at the house of a certain Luis de Santangel who held a high position under Ferdinand, and here they agreed that there was one way—and one way only—of making known their determination to turn Torquemada's Inquisition out of Aragon. They had witnessed the horrible deaths of certain of their friends; they must employ drastic remedies; nothing could be effective but the death of the Inquisitor Pedro Arbués. If he were assassinated, another would be reluctant to take his place and it would be realized that the people of Aragon could not be treated as the Castilians had been.

One of their number must perform the deed and as a reward the slayer would receive 500 florins. Six men offered themselves for the task; one of these was Juan de Esperandeu who had special reasons for wishing to strike the blow. His father had been arrested and was, at the time of the conspiracy, in the prison of the Inquisition, and so far as the son knew, suffering in the torture chambers.

Pedro Arbués, if he had no knowledge of the conspiracy, was aware of his unpopularity; after the death of his fellow Inquisitor he took so many precautions against assassination that again and again the conspirators found themselves foiled.

They grew more and more restive and at length decided on a daring plan. They knew that Arbués must visit the Metropolitan Church for midnight service, and they decided that, since they could catch him nowhere else, they would do so there. They hid themselves in the church and waited.

It was not difficult to conceal themselves in the dimly lighted church. They knew that Arbués would enter from the cloisters and had to traverse the dim church to reach the Dominicans in the choir. Even for that short journey he came armed. He carried a stout stick in his hand, beneath his robes was the suit of armour, and his cap was lined with steel. In his other hand was a lantern, and as he came he peered anxiously about him. Before joining the choir however he must kneel in prayer, and to do this it was necessary to set down his stick and lantern. This was what the conspirators had waited for. The singing of the choir was an advantage since they were able to creep up on the kneeling figure without being heard. Esperandeu, no doubt allowing his anguish for his father to blind his judgment, used his sword wildly, and merely wounded Arbués in the arm. But his friends came into the attack. Arbués was struck on the head with such force that the steel cap was dented, and a sword pierced a vein in his neck. Arbués struggled to his feet, but Esperandeu, not to be robbed of his revenge, found a vulnerable spot in the armour and drove his sword through the Dominican's body.

The assassins made their escape, for now those who had been singing in the choir realized that all was not well and came running to the fallen man to discover what had happened.

Arbués lived two more days and nights, and died on 17th September 1485.

The day following the attack, when the news of it had spread through the town, the people gathered in the streets shouting for reprisals on the New Christians. The affair had had the opposite effect to that which had been intended. Instead of arousing the people against the Inquisition it aroused them against that old whipping boy: Jewry.

It was apparent that serious riots were imminent; this is what would have occurred had not Ferdinand's natural son, a young man of seventeen whom his father had already made Archbishop

of Saragossa, happened to be in Saragossa at this time. Taking
the high officials of his retinue with him he rode into the streets
and faced the mob. He advised them against riots, which might
not bring retribution to the true perpetrators of the crime and
could result in disaster to themselves; let them go quietly to their
homes; he would promise them that justice should be done.

Torquemada at once sent three new Inquisitors (Fr. Juan
Colvera, Pedro de Monterubio, and Alonso de Alarcon) to the
town to replace Arbués and Juglar; and the officers of the Inquisition left their old building and established themselves in the
royal alcazar, the Castle of Aljaferia, where they were protected
by guards. Not that they were in need of this protection; but,
although Torquemada was pleased that Ferdinand's young son
had prevented rioting, he wished to sustain the anger of the
people of Saragossa against the New Christians.

Arrests were made; the torturers were soon working full time
in the dismal chambers; it was not long before men and women
were being brought in to testify against those who had conspired
to kill the Inquisitors of Saragossa.

Juan Pedro Sanchez was fortunate enough to escape from
Spain. His effigy was burned at an *auto de fé* with the live bodies
of others who had taken part in the plot. Esperandeu was caught;
his punishment was to be put on a hurdle and dragged through
the streets to the Cathedral, on the steps of which he was taken
from the hurdle that the hands which had struck the blows at
Arbués might be cut off. After that he was hanged, taken down
alive, castrated and quartered.

The hopes of the conspirators had failed to materialize. The
people of Saragossa, out of hatred of the New Christians, or perhaps in the hope of a little loot, had given their approval to the
setting-up of the Inquisition in Aragon.

Autos de fé began to take place regularly in Aragon as they
had in Castile; and determined to show the people that they must
submit to its decrees, the Inquisitors increased their harshness.
They wished the people to understand the power of this organization, and when one, a New Christian, realizing that none of his
sect was safe in Aragon, escaped and took refuge in Navarre with
the Infante Jaime, the latter, though he was the son of the
Queen of Navarre, was arrested and brought before the Inquisitors.

He was accused of hindering the activities of the Holy Office
and, as all knew, any who did this were suspected of heresy.
Jaime was found guilty of this sin against the Church; he was
put in prison and sentenced to be whipped, not through the
streets—this might have been too much for the royal family
to overlook—but round the church; and as an additional
insult, his bastard cousin (Alfonso of Aragon who had been

responsible for quelling the mob) should witness his discomfiture.

This should show the power of the Inquisition; this should warn the people against the folly of attempting to subdue the mighty Holy Office.

Nor were they satisfied with the humiliation of the·Infante Jaime. Another of the conspirators, Gaspar de Santa Cruz, who escaped to Toulouse and whose effigy was burned at the *auto de fé*, died before the Inquisitors could bring him back to Spain. His son who had helped him escape, was arrested, and his penance was to go at once to Toulouse, dig up the remains of his father, and there, arrayed in *sanbenito*, burn in public his father's body. To avoid being burned alive himself the young man did this.

As for Pedro Arbués, he was now regarded as a saint, and legends sprang up regarding him. The bells were said to have rung of their own accord the moment he died, and twelve days after his blood had been shed it was said (after it was too late to put this to the test) that it was still warm and wet on the stones of the church, and a handkerchief dipped therein would be stained red and provide a holy relic. He was buried in the church beneath that very spot where he had been struck down, and a monument was erected to him. He was beatified in the 17th century by Alexander VII, and canonized in the 19th by Pius IX. But perhaps his chief claim to notice (among those who see the Inquisition as a blot on civilization and an Institution which did great disservice to Christianity) is that his death was of significance in the history of the Inquisition. Had the people of Aragon forgotten their enmity towards the Jews, had they stood with them against the Inquisition, they could at that time have prevented its growth; they could have asserted their own right to freedom of thought. And if Aragon had taken that turning at that precise time, Castile would surely have followed; and the Inquisition could have become a feeble plant which struggled for a while and withered away, as it had in other European countries.

The great persecution came to a climax in the year 1490, the beginning of that decade which surely was the most momentous in Spanish history: the year 1492 stands out as of greatest significance, for during it Christopher Columbus discovered America, Torquemada expelled the Jews from Spain, and Ferdinand·and Isabella drove the Moors from Granada and the reconquest of Spain was completed.

It was in the year 1490 that an event took place which undoubtedly hastened the completion of one of these events; that is the expulsion of the Jews.

This began without apparent significance when a New Christian named Benito Garcia made a journey in the course of his business. As he was a woolcomber his trade made it necessary for him to travel from place to place in order to buy and sell his goods; and on one of these journeys he had the misfortune to stay the night at a small inn in the village of Astorga.

There were a great many people staying at the inn that night, and Garcia could not be given a room to himself; so he was forced to share one with a party of men.

These men were far from honest and, noticing the good clothes of their room-mate, they conspired to rob him while he slept.

As soon as he was asleep they took his knapsack, opened it and began quarrelling over its contents. However they were quickly subdued by a discovery they made. In the knapsack was a wafer, and the fact that it was in the possession of a layman, who being a Jew must have stolen it, meant that a great sin had been committed against the Church.

Like the Guzman who had entered the house of a New Christian in order to seduce his daughter, these robbers at once forgot their own crime in the immensity of the one they believed they had uncovered. They fell upon Garcia and insisted that he accompany them without delay to the magistrate.

This magistrate was Dr. Pedro de Villada who had worked often with the Inquisition and had, unluckily for Garcia, been promised that before long he would be raised to the position of Inquisitor. He was therefore determined to show his mettle, and Benito Garcia seemed to offer him a good opportunity of doing this.

He demanded that Garcia admit he was guilty of practising the rites of Judaism, and that he had stolen the wafer for an evil purpose.

Garcia was terrified. He guessed of what he would be accused, for there had been circulated in recent years many stories of Jewish practices, and again and again they were accused of partaking in ritual murder. This, it was alleged, usually took the form of kidnapping a Christian boy and crucifying him; and for this ceremony consecrated Hosts were said to be stolen from the Christian churches.

He insisted on his innocence, whereupon Pedro de Villada ordered that he be given two hundred lashes as a beginning, and when Garcia continued to protest his innocence, the water torture was applied.

During his terrible suffering the poor man broke down and admitted all that was required of him. Yes, he had been baptized; he was a New Christian; and he had relapsed into Judaism. That was not enough; he must incriminate others.

He thereupon explained that, five years before, he had met a New Christian named Juan de Ocaña; this man practised Judaism and advised Garcia to do the same, but to do so with craft; and in this Garcia had followed the advice of Ocaña; he had returned to Judaism in secret although he had forced his children to go to the Christian church lest by not doing so they should call suspicion on to himself. He had fabricated 'confessions' which he made to the priest, and he made a mockery of the communion; in secret he spat on the Viaticum.

In addition to Ocaña he mentioned the names of Mosé and Yucé Franco and their father Ça Franco. He visited this family in the course of business and he knew them to be Judaizers because he ate meat on Fridays at their home.

Villada immediately arrested Ocaña, Ça Franco, who was eighty, and his son Yucé who was only twenty. Fortunately for Mosé he died before he could be arrested.

They were then taken to the prison at Segovia which had at one time been the residence of the Queen's lady-in-waiting and intimate friend, Beatriz de Bobadilla; while they were there Yucé fell ill, and as he did not expect to live to stand further trial and condemnation he boldly asked for a Jewish physician to be sent to him that he might talk to him in his own language, and a Rabbi to pray with him.

This was an opportunity too good to be missed. The Inquisitors declared they could not refuse the request of a dying man. They therefore sent one of their spies with instructions to show great sympathy for the young man and at the same time make him divulge the names of others who had shared in his heretical practices.

The physician arrived, and with him came the Dominican, Alonso Enriquez, disguised as the Rabbi Abraham. He showered sympathy on the young man, and Yucé completely duped was greatly comforted.

It would do him good to talk, he was told; his comforter would like to know for what reason he had been arrested.

Yucé, who must have heard that the wafer had been discovered, replied that he had been arrested for being concerned in the ritual murder of a Christian boy.

This was a startling revelation, for although it was the sight of the wafer in Garcia's knapsack which had in the first place made the robbers drag him before Villada, this was the first time ritual murder had been mentioned.

Villada immediately realized the importance of the case on his hands. It was clearly no ordinary affair of New Christians turning back to their own religion. He sent Enriquez once more to talk to Yucé, but the young man had recovered his health a little and with it his sense. He refused to say any more.

The case was then taken to the highest authority—to Torquemada himself. Torquemada was delighted. He had long been seeking an excuse to drive all Jews out of Spain, and a case of ritual murder, which could actually be substantiated to the satisfaction of the excitable and superstitious people of Spain, was exactly what he needed. If he could make Ferdinand and Isabella realize the harm the Jews were doing in Spain and at the same time rouse the wrath of the people, he had no doubt that before long he could bring about that for which he had been working during the greater part of his life.

He therefore decided that the case should have his personal supervision.

Meanwhile Yucé, under examination, had admitted that he had gone to La Guardia three years before to buy wheat from a family of millers there. There were four brothers in this family. (It is rather confusing that they should have the same name as Yucé, but although they were Francos they were not related.) It was easy to understand how during the business deal the conversation turned to the making of unleavened bread and the passover. They also, Yucé continued, talked of other Jewish customs, and the brothers told him that one Good Friday they had stolen a young Christian boy and crucified him in the way Jesus of Nazareth had been crucified.

After making this extraordinary announcement, Yucé was left alone for three months. The suspense he endured during that time—when he would have realized the extent to which he had incriminated himself and others—must have been unnerving. It was exactly the effect the Inquisitors wished to create.

Yucé was not brought for trial until the following December. The year was 1490.

The first accusation brought against Yucé was that he had believed Christianity to be false and had tried to attract Christians to his religion.

Then came the important charge. He was accused of associating with men who had crucified a young Christian boy on a certain Good Friday.

He was also charged with having stolen a consecrated Host that it might be used for sorcery and mockery of Jesus Christ, and with other offences against the law of the Inquisition, which would be dealt with at a later date.

Yucé, who at this time had no idea that the man to whom he had talked of the crucifixion was any but the Rabbi Abraham, declared that the accusation was the greatest of falsehoods.

He was allowed a counsel for the defence and the lawyer Bachelor Sanc and the advocate Juan de Pantigoso were allowed to plead for him.

Sanc enthusiastically defended his client, declaring that the accusations were quite vague and, before they could condemn him on such flimsy evidence, the prosecution must be more precise concerning the people who had shared in his so-called guilt and the time when the offences were committed. Such vagueness might be permissible when the Inquisition was dealing with heretics, but Yucé Franco was not a heretic. He was a Jew who, as such, could not be treated as a heretic. Moreover Yucé was an uneducated boy, a cobbler by trade. How could one so lacking in education attempt to convert people to Judaism? Sanc demanded that his client be given his freedom.

The court then declared that thirty days should be allowed to the prosecution to prove the charges against Yucé. But in thirty days the prosecution had been unable to prove its case, yet Yucé was kept in prison.

The young boy was nearly driven insane by solitary confinement and ignorance as to what was going on. There was one thing for which he was grateful, and that was the kindness of his jailor, who brought him a guitar that he might strum on it to make the long hours pass more quickly.

One day, about three months after his appearance in court, he was playing the guitar when he heard a voice. It was that of Benito, who had been placed in the cell below him. There was a crack in the floor, which had been made by the jailors for this very purpose, but Yucé had no idea of this.

It was necessary for the two men to talk rather loudly to make themselves heard by one another; and notaries were outside the doors of their cells taking down all that was said.

So they talked together, Benito telling Yucé that his father had been arrested, how he had been tortured and during the process had given enough away to send him to the stake. Benito asked if Yucé had a needle—or a knife would do. He wished to destroy evidence of his circumcision. Yucé replied that he would die if he tried such a trick, to which Benito retorted that he would prefer to die that way than to be burned alive.

Yucé's great concern was about the wafer because he, as a Jew, could not be tried for heresy. He asked Benito about his arrest and that of his own father; then he wanted to know how much had been discovered about the wafer.

Benito could tell him little about that; he went on to curse the day when he had abandoned the law of Moses for the Christian Faith. He had not only been baptized and accepted Christianity, he complained, but had given a water font to the church; his reward had been to be given the water torture. He would die a Jew, he declared; they could burn him alive but he would be true to the old faith.

Having recorded all these remarks which had passed between the two prisoners, the Inquisitors had Yucé brought once more before them.

Under the fatigue of continual questioning Yucé told them

that he had heard from a Jewish physician that Benito Garcia had been commanded by his brethren to steal a consecrated Host, and that he had got possession of the keys of the Church of La Guardia and had stolen the Host. He had been suspected and sent to prison for two days, but as nothing was proved against him he was released. Yucé believed that Benito's friends wished to use the Host for some Jewish rite.

The Inquisitors felt that they were making some progress, and again Yucé was brought up for questioning, and again after some weary hours he was communicative.

From consecrated Hosts, Jews could make charms which could protect them from Christians. Thus spoke Yucé. His brother Mosé, who had since died, had together with the four millers procured a Host and made this charm.

Again there was a session of questioning and Yucé remembered that the spell had been created in a cave outside the village of La Guardia. Later he admitted that the spell was made with something besides the Host. This was a heart—the heart of a Christian boy.

There were long intervals between the examination of Yucé, and there is no doubt that in this the Inquisitors were adhering to the rules set out by Eymeric and acknowledged to be good by Torquemada. They were submitting the boy to the agony of suspense, for all this time he had no notion as to what was happening to his fellow conspirators.

At length he declared he would tell all he knew, on one condition. They had imprisoned his father; and his condition was that he and the old man should be pardoned.

He should be pardoned, said the Inquisitors, providing Yucé told everything he knew. Yucé then said that he had not confessed before owing to a pact he had made with the others not to confess anything until a year had passed.

All those who were now prisoners, he went on, had met one night in the cave of which he had already told them; and he saw there a Host and a human heart. A spell was made which was supposed to protect them against the Inquisition.

Whose was the heart? asked the Inquisitors.

He had been told, Yucé replied, that it had been taken from a Christian boy whom the others had crucified.

The Inquisitors were delighted. This was exactly what, for all these months, they had been working so hard to get.

They then decided that they would bring the old man Ça Franco up for questioning, letting him know that his son had betrayed the conspirators.

The old man, terrified by the subtle threats of torture, began to talk, telling them even more that Yucé had betrayed. Yes, there had been a stolen Host; there had been a human heart;

the boy had been whipped and crowned with thorns and crucified there in the cave before the eyes of them all, although he, Ça, had done nothing but look on; as for Yucé, all he had done was to give the boy a little push.

Both Yucé and his father sought to protect each other. Yucé reminded the Inquisitors that his father was a very old man whose sight was failing, and could not have seen clearly what was going on in the cave.

Now the Inquisitors had a case of ritual murder to present to Torquemada, and the Prior of the Holy Cross could lay these facts before the Queen and the country, and so make every Christian rise in fury against the Jews.

It had taken nine months—not thirty days—to collect the evidence, but it had been well worth the trouble.

The court re-opened in October. Sanc put up a good defence and the trial was conducted with the utmost fairness, for Torquemada believed that he had the evidence now to condemn all these men as guilty of the brutal murder of a Christian boy, and he wanted no slur cast on the proceedings. Yucé, however, refused to confirm the confession he had made and, as a result of this, he was taken to the torture chamber where it was planned to give him the water torture.

Seeing the terrible instrument waiting for him, feeling the cords cutting into his wrists and ankles, Yucé shouted that he would confess all.

He then explained that the child had been kidnapped by Juan Franco, who had offered him sweetmeats and taken him to the cave. He confirmed his confession later, so terrified was he of being taken once more to the torture chamber.

Yucé's eighty-year-old father was tortured at the same time as Juan Franco, and they both made confessions which were similar to that of Yucé.

Sanc now saw that he dared not remain in the case, so withdrew. The men were found guilty and were to be abandoned to the secular law.

An *auto de fé* was held, and they all appeared in their *san-benitos*. Three of the *conversos*, Juan Franco, Juan de Ocaña and Benito Garcia, declared their desire to return to the Catholic Faith when they saw the faggots under them; and before the fires were lighted they were strangled.

Ça and Yucé, however, showed great courage. They were Jews, they declared, and had never been anything else; they would remain faithful to the laws of Moses until they breathed their last.

These two were then bound to the stake and the flesh of their arms and thighs was torn with red hot pincers, for it was felt that they were too evil to be allowed the comparatively quick death by fire. Then, as they writhed in their agony, the faggots were dampened that they might not burn too quickly.

So the old man of eighty and his young son were roasted alive over slow fires.

Thus the famous La Guardia trial which was to have such repercussions throughout Spain.

There are many people who think that the murder of the child never took place at all, and that the confessions extorted under torture or threat were put into the mouths of the sufferers by those men who saw the possibilities which such a case could provide.

It is a fact that one of the men under torture said that the child had been buried in a certain spot, yet when a search was made there no body or remains were found.

A legend naturally grew around the child. This was that a party of Jews had determined on the destruction of Christianity and that the Law of Moses should be set up in its place. To bring about this state of affairs they needed to make a spell, and for this spell they needed two ingredients: a consecrated Host and the heart of a Christian child. These were to be burned to ashes which, when thrown into wells and rivers, would poison the water, with the result that all Christians who drank of it would die insane.

These Jews approached some Christian parents who were very poor and had a great many children; they offered a large sum of money for the heart of one of the children. The mother came to terms with the Jews but, instead of giving the heart of one of her children, handed over a pig's heart.

The Jews proceeded with their experiment, which proved useless. Therefore they determined that next time they would make sure they had the right ingredient by kidnapping a boy and, to ensure that the spell would be effective, crucifying him after the manner in which Jesus Christ had been crucified.

They found a beautiful four-year-old boy in the doorway of a church, gave him sweets and kidnapped him. He was taken to a cave by night and given five thousand strokes with a whip. The little boy, runs the legend, bore the beating with great serenity, but suddenly began to cry. This was when the number of strokes had reached five thousand.

He was asked why he cried, and astonishingly answered that he cried because they had given him five more lashes than His Saviour had received.

He was crowned with thorns and a knife thrust into his side to enable the Jews to fumble for his heart. They had some difficulty in finding this and the child calmly told them how to extract it!

He was then nailed to a cross.

He was known to Christians as Santo Niño; it was said that he was a holy child who was taken straight up to Heaven (for the body of the child, as already mentioned, could not be found) and miracles began to be performed which were credited to him.

It was also said that he had a blind mother who miraculously recovered her sight at the very moment when Santo Niño died.

Whether or not a young boy was crucified in the cave outside La Guardia must remain a mystery, but there is no doubt of the effect of the story on the persecuted people.

Torquemada had the material he needed. His instructions were that an account of the case, in all its hideous detail, should be read from every pulpit in the country. This was done.

Torquemada now awaited results.

He was not disappointed. All over the country the people stirred to action. The worst anti-Jewish riots of the century were threatened.

Torquemada knew that the time had come to put into action his great plan for the expulsion of the Jews.

11

THE *MORISCOS*

MEANWHILE FERDINAND AND ISABELLA were deeply concerned with operations against the Moors.

In 1487 Ferdinand had left the city of Cordova to launch an attack against Velez Malaga, a town which stood guarding the greater prize of Malaga—and Malaga was only second in importance to Granada, the capital.

The Moors were fierce warriors and, seeing such an array of Christian forces preparing to swoop on them, were determined to put up a brave fight; but foolishly they were quarrelling among themselves, and Boabdil (Abdallah) was on uneasy terms with his father Muley Abul Hacen and his uncle (also named Abdallah but known as El Zagal, or The Valiant).

Ferdinand was full of energy, and behaved with what was considered by his followers as reckless bravery; they often implored him not to endanger his person, to which he made the remark: "I cannot pause to consider my chances when my subjects are risking their lives for my sake." His bravery, his determination to lead his men into battle, sharing their risks, made him very popular in the army. And eventually Velez fell to him, and Malaga lay before him, the next goal.

This was one of the richest cities in Moorish Spain. Oranges, pomegranates and olives grew in profusion there and, open to the sea as it was, it enjoyed a brisk trade; the wealth of the inhabitants was apparent in the buildings they had erected; the beautiful gardens were full of flowers and decorated with sparkling fountains.

It was no easy matter to take Malaga, for the Moors had determined at all costs to defend such a prize. Its natural position, protected as it was by the Sierras, was formidable enough, but the Moors had built a great citadel which was connected by a covered passage with another fortress; and a great wall encircled the city except where it sloped to the sea.

News however reached Ferdinand that the rich merchants of Malaga favoured immediate surrender in order to preserve their property, and the King decided to open negotiations with the commander, Hamet Zeli. Hamet Zeli rejected the offer, declaring that he had been commanded by his King to protect Malaga at all cost, and that he was going to do so.

The siege of Malaga had begun. It was to last more than three months, during which the armies of Ferdinand were to undergo many hardships. There were difficulties in transporting water, and plague broke out in nearby villages, which sent a shiver of alarm through the armies. Isabella joined Ferdinand in the camp; a clever move, as the presence of the Queen brought new enthusiasm to the flagging spirits of the soldiers and, instead of grumbling among themselves, the men sought to outdo each other in acts of bravery that they might win the commendation of Isabella and her ladies.

At this time it was debatable whether the armies of Ferdinand and Isabella could take the port of Malaga which was all-important to Granada; the Moors were fanatical in their determination to hold the city for they had lived so long in Spain that they were fighting for their homeland. However the city was lost not so much by force of arms as through those dissensions within the Moorish stronghold; Aragon and Castile, Ferdinand and Isabella, stood together, united.

Muley Hacen and his son Boabdil were quarrelling; while Muley and his brother El Zagal stood together against the young man. Boabdil did all in his power to frustrate his uncle El Zagal, and it is rumoured that he was guilty of poisoning Muley Hacen, his own father. This discord was at the root of the collapse at Malaga and, in conjunction with Ferdinand's armies, brought disaster.

On his side Ferdinand had the wonderful works of his master of ordnance, Francisco Ramirez, whose skill no doubt helped to shorten the siege of Malaga. Ferdinand evidently thought so, for he knighted Francisco. It is said that in this siege gunpowder was used for the first time in European warfare; and under the direction of the clever Ramirez it was very effective.

Meanwhile in the city people were dying in the streets from starvation; and Hamet Zeli, who realized they could no longer hold out, withdrew his soldiers and left the citizens to make the best terms they could with the conquerors.

One of the most important of the merchants, Ali Dordux, sought to make terms of surrender, but at this request Ferdinand merely laughed, remarking that it was a little late in the day for such a conference; it should have taken place three months earlier; now it was for him to dictate terms, not discuss them.

Terror then reigned in Malaga, for the citizens understood that they could expect little mercy. Desperate, they sent a second deputation to Ferdinand's camp, through whom they suggested that the city should be surrendered to the conqueror with all its riches in exchange for the assurance that no harm should come to the citizens. Unless Ferdinand granted their request, they threatened, they would hang all the Christian slaves they possessed, and there were as many as six hundred of these in Malaga. They would also set fire to the town so that there would be no rich pickings for the invaders.

Ferdinand, however, was not inclined to bargain. If the Christian slaves were harmed, he replied, every inhabitant of Malaga would be put to the sword.

There remained nothing after that but for Ferdinand to force his way into the city. First he took the citadel, and above the city, for the first time for more than seven centuries floated the banner of Christian Spain.

The dead, who had been left to putrefy in the town, were then removed, the finest of the mosques was dedicated to Santa Maria de la Encarnacion, and Ferdinand with Isabella made their formal entry into the city.

Christian slaves were released from the dungeons, and when they came tottering forward to pay homage to the sovereigns Isabella wept and Ferdinand embraced them. The chains which bound them were removed, and a feast was ordered to be set before them. They were promised money and land.

Ferdinand then ordered the conquered commander, Hamet Zeli, to be brought to him. Before him stood the great chieftain, manacled and in chains, his head held high, his eyes flashing. "You were foolish," Ferdinand told him, "to hold out against us. It would have gone easier for you and these people had you surrendered three months ago." To which the brave Hamet Zeli cried out that his King had commanded him to defend Malaga, and if he had been supported he would have died before he surrendered.

Ferdinand shrugged him aside and declared he was ready to announce to the anxious people the punishment he had decided to inflict upon them. The entire population was to assemble in the great courtyard of the Alcazaba. There they were told their fate. All were condemned to slavery. One third was to go to Africa in exchange for Christian slaves held there. Of the remaining two thirds, half were the property of the state, which would use them as payment for the cost of the war; and the other half were to be given as presents to foreign friends, in Naples, Portugal and Rome.

The most fortunate were those who were sent to Rome—which seems ironical. Rome was the centre of the Catholic Faith, yet it is from Rome that we hear of leniency towards the Infidels. Innocent VIII put his slaves into the army and in a very short time, so we are told by the Curate of Los Palacios, made not only good soldiers, but good Christians of them. A comparison can be drawn between an *auto de fé* which took place in Rome under Alexander VI, and those hideous ceremonies which were becoming a commonplace in Spain. In July 1498 one hundred and eighty heretics (who had come from Spain after the great expulsion) were required to expiate their lapse into Judaism. Alexander watched the scene from St. Peter's. The victims paraded in their *sanbenitos*, went through the formal ceremony of reconciliation to the Church, entered Santa Maria della Minerva, where they took off their *sanbenitos*, and afterwards went home to lead the lives of ordinary citizens, no further penance having been demanded of them.

This makes one pause to consider the difference in two men— Roderigo Borgia, Pope Alexander VI, and Torquemada. Alexander was a sensualist and a murderer, we know; he, with perhaps the exception of his son Cesare Borgia, is the most notorious figure of his age; it has been said that he spent half his time performing his sacred duties as the Pope, and the other half with his mistresses in those orgies suited to his tastes. It is odd that he should have shown more kindness to the oppressed than did the saintly Torquemada. But it may have been because the worldly Alexander was a brilliant diplomatist, and Torquemada, for all his fervent devotion to Spain, a little foolish. When Torquemada banished the Jews from Spain, many of them found their way to Rome. They were the most fortunate section of the expelled community, for in Rome they were received with warmth. Alexander was clever enough to realize that they would help to enrich his domain.

The terrible fate of Malaga set panic raging throughout the Moorish kingdom. A whole town condemned to slavery! This was how the Christians treated their prisoners. And Malaga was the port of Granada. How could the Moorish kingdom continue to exist without it?

The doom of the Mussulmans was close.

They knew it, and perhaps it helped to hasten their surrender.

But although Malaga was conquered in 1487 there was a great deal to do before the last battle was won. There followed the siege of Baza, which was ruled by El Zagal; and whilst this was in progress the Sultan of Egypt sent threatening messages to Ferdinand, warning him of Egypt's intervention if Christian persecution of the Moors did not cease. El Zagal was not so fortunate nearer home. Arms and men from Boabdil in Granada would have been more effective than threats from the Sultan of Egypt. But Boabdil was not a great fighter; he was a lover of peace and had already made certain terms with Ferdinand which aroused the wrath of his mother and many of the people, who declared he was a Christian in secret and that, for favours he had received from Ferdinand and Isabella, he was aiding their campaign against his own brethren.

Great hardship was suffered by Ferdinand's armies, and Isabella was constantly with the soldiers, caring for the sick, raising money to carry on the war, rousing the men to fresh enthusiasm, so that her presence in the camp was a necessity; and with her inspiration, Ferdinand's bravery, and the determination of both of them to succeed, they were, as they had said, one as important as the other.

Baza fell, after a five months' siege, and the way lay open to Granada.

In 1490, the Infanta Isabella was married to Alonso, heir to the throne of Portugal, and the war against the Moors was suspended for a short while during which festivities took place. Isabella graced the fêtes and tourneys, and Ferdinand showed his dexterity with a lance; but Isabella mourned the loss of her daughter. She loved all her children dearly and, although she would not have dreamed of standing between them and the glory they could bring to their country, she suffered as a mother. But when the revelries were over, the sovereigns turned their attention to Granada; they sent for Boabdil, whose previous conduct had made him almost a vassal, to come to them and discuss terms.

Boabdil, however, showed unusual spirit. He had returned to Granada and was now among his people. He declared that he was not his own master and could not come when summoned by Ferdinand and Isabella.

Moreover the people of Granada now seemed to have taken heart. They had their backs to the wall and that knowledge seemed to infuse them with greater valour, greater determination to make the enemy pay for all he took.

There were skirmishes between the armies from which the Christians did not always emerge triumphant. Ferdinand marched against Granada then and, although he could not at that stage take the city, he destroyed all the crops surrounding it; and it was during these operations that he bestowed knighthood on his little son, the Infante Juan, who was then twelve years old.

Granada itself was strongly defended. On the east was the defence of the Sierra Nevada; and where there were not natural barriers, the Moors had built great walls and fortifications to defend their capital city.

Ferdinand and Isabella were prepared for a prolonged resistance at the last stronghold, and they undertook the enormous task of building a town close to Granada in case they should be forced to stay in front of the city for some time. The armies had suffered hardship before Malaga and Baza; this should not be the case before Granada. It seems incredible nowadays to imagine the scene: soldiers turned into workmen, building busily in the midst of a war. The new town had two wide avenues made in the form of a cross; and when it was completed it was called Santa Fé on Isabella's request, although it had been suggested that the town should be named after her.

The sight of Santa Fé had a devastating effect on the morale of the Moors; they realized that the Christians had determined to blockade them out of existence.

Unfortunately for the Moors they had not a strong leader in Boabdil who, convinced that it would be impossible to hold out against the massing Christian armies, and no doubt eager to avoid for Granada the fate which had befallen Malaga, offered to negotiate for peace. This offer was accepted, although the people of Granada were unaware of it, as all communications between Boadbil and Ferdinand were conducted in secrecy. Meanwhile the people of Granada continued to prepare themselves for a long siege and were in high spirits, for they did not believe their friends in Africa would allow the last Moorish dominions to fall into the hands of the Christians; and daily they waited for the arrival of their allies.

Boabdil no doubt believed that by negotiation he could get the best for his people; and he was right in this, as was seen by the stubborn stand taken by the people of Malaga, the reward of which had been slavery. Boabdil asked that his people should be allowed to worship as they wished, and that their mosques in the city of Granada should be left to them; that, although they would be subjects of Isabella and Ferdinand, they should have their own *cadis* to administer laws which should be Moorish laws. They were not to be robbed of their property, but allowed to wear their traditional dress, use their own language and keep their customs. Boabdil would naturally be deposed, but he was to be given a small dominion in the Alpujarras which he would rule as a vassal of the Catholic Sovereigns.

When the citizens of Granada knew what Boabdil had arranged for them they rose against him, and such was his jeopardy that Ferdinand decided he would take immediate possession of the town and not wait until the date specified in the agreement.

The Spaniards were at this time mourning the death of Alonso of Portugal who had fallen from his horse; he was closely connected with the royal family since, a few months before, he had married the Infanta Isabella. But mourning was set aside and a glittering Spanish cavalcade accompanied Isabella and Ferdinand into Granada on the 2nd January, 1492.

This was the finest hour in Spanish history. It must have been a splendid and moving occasion when the Christian standard was placed on the towers of the Alhambra.

As for sad Boabdil, he made his way to the Alpujarras and from a rocky point—a spot which is still called The Last Sigh of the Moor—he looked back on Granada. It is said that he wept with great bitterness and that his mother, disgusted because he had bargained with the conquerors, made that often quoted remark: "You do well to weep like a woman for what you could not defend like a man."

One feels a little sorry for Boabdil who after all would have brought misery on his people had he fought bravely to retain what it was impossible to hold. He lived for a brief year in his poor little kingdom of the Alpujarras, and then, being unable to remain so near Granada and yet so far from it, he crossed the sea to Fez and very soon afterwards, helping an African kinsman in battle, he was killed. "Wretched Boabdil!" it has been written of him. "He lost his life in another's cause though he did not dare to die in his own."

It was while they were in Granada that Ferdinand and Isabella signed the Edict which was to force to leave Spain all Jews who would not receive baptism.

For several years Torquemada had been urging the sovereigns to sign this Edict, but both Ferdinand and Isabella, deeply immersed in the war against the Moors, had hesitated. The Inquisition had disappointed them a little because of the amount of money it had produced. It was true that the confiscations brought in a great deal, but there were so many officers of the Inquisition, so many formalities, that a large proportion of the spoils was used up in the maintenance of the institution.

The Jews continued to grow richer, and it appeared that most of the wealth of the kingdom was in their possession. They had an uncanny instinct for attracting wealth, and Isabella and Ferdinand were beginning to realize that to turn them out of the country could mean destroying that source of revenue which, in spite of centuries of persecution, seemed inexhaustible.

For this reason the sovereigns had so far refused to listen to the importuning of Torquemada and his adherents. But now they changed their minds. The La Guardia trial had sent a wave of hysteria through the country. Scandalous stories were circulated concerning the Jews: Their doctors carried poison under their fingernails, it was said, that they might kill the sick whom they were called to attend; the old story of the poisoned wells was revived. Torquemada came to the Alhambra to see his sovereigns. The greatest event in Spanish history had recently taken place. The sovereigns had won the holy war, and as a result they had a chance of making all Spain Catholic. Yet they allowed these Jews to live in their midst.

Eloquent as ever, Torquemada raged against the Jews, nor did he spare his sovereigns. They must do their duty. They must expel the Jews.

As a result of his activities, the Edict was signed on the 31st March of the same year in which Granada had fallen.

The blow to the Jews was, as can be imagined, catastrophic. They had suffered great cruelties for many years, but to be expelled from the only land which they could call home, to be forced to give up their property (for that was what it amounted to, as they, having to sell so quickly what they possessed, could be sure they would be paid very little for it; and in any case they were not allowed to take gold or silver out of the country) was the greatest misery, short of death, that could befall them.

Torquemada sent Dominicans into the *juderías*. He was very eager that it should be known that he did not wish so much to expel Jews as to convert them. If they were baptized they might stay in Spain. The dread Inquisition would naturally be a great shadow over their lives, for New Christians were constantly suspected of reverting to their old Faith; but at least they would not have to sell their houses for an ass or their vineyards for a strip of cloth.

Against the Dominicans were the Rabbis, who urged their flock to remain true to the Law of Moses, reminding the people of how the children of Israel had been led from the land of Egypt. Thus appealed to many decided to go rather than be forced to pretend to believe what was outside their belief.

But the Jews knew that Ferdinand needed money, and it occurred to them that, if they offered a large enough sum, they might ask in exchange for permission to stay in their homes.

So they sent a deputation to Ferdinand telling him that if the Edict could be destroyed the Jews would collect thirty thousand ducats and present them to Ferdinand as a donation towards the cost of the war.

When Ferdinand heard this his eyes glistened. Thirty thousand ducats was a sum not to be despised, and the wars had indeed been costly. Isabella was also attracted by the offer. She knew that the Jewish population was not only clever but hardworking, and she would be glad of an excuse to let them remain.

They were about to accept the offer when Torquemada, who had heard of the arrival of the deputation, burst in upon them.

He strode towards the King and Queen and with a dramatic gesture held up the crucifix which he always carried.

"Judas Iscariot sold his Master for thirty pieces of silver," he cried. "Your Highnesses are ready to sell Him anew for thirty thousand." He threw the crucifix on the table and continued: "Here He is. Take Him and barter Him. But do not think that I will have any share in such an odious transaction."

Then he strode out of the room.

One might have thought that the two mighty sovereigns would have been angered by his insolence, but such was the power of Torquemada, such his fire and eloquence, that both Ferdinand and Isabella thrust aside the tempting ducats.

The Edict should go forth.

The time for leaving arrived, and what a pitiful sight it must have been! Men, women and children—babies in arms among them—huddled together like a great army in retreat. Some had horses or asses on which to ride; but a great many must travel on foot.

Many of those who had shortly before called for riots against them were moved by pity at this terrible sight of so many homeless people, robbed of their possessions—for there was little they could take with them—wandering towards the coast, uncertain to what new land they would go.

It was however forbidden to help them. The Grand Inquisitor, Torquemada himself, had laid down a rule that any performing an act of neighbourliness towards these suffering people, would have committed an offence against the Church.

Some made their way to Portugal, for the King, John II, had, at a price, offered them a safe passage on their way to Africa. Some went to Italy, and those who arrived in Naples took the plague with them which decimated many of their numbers besides countless members of the existing population. Others landed at Genoa where they were not allowed to stay for, according to the law, no Jewish traveller must rest there for more than three days; but they were allowed to refit and replenish their ships, and when they went it was discovered that they had left the plague behind them.

Others found their way to Turkey and the Levant. Some went to France and a few to England.

Many found their way to Ercilla, a Christian Settlement in Africa, hoping to make their way to Fez; but desert tribes, hearing of their arrival and believing that Jews were always rich, came to meet them. Not content with robbing them, they violated the women and cut off the head of any person who attempted to stop them. Some, believing that the travellers might have swallowed their valuables at the approach of danger, ripped up their bodies in the hope of finding them.

Those who were left struggled on without adequate clothing (for they had been robbed of all the good things they possessed), without food. They lived on the very small amount of grass which grew in the arid district; many died and the rest turned back to Ercilla, willing now to have the Christian Faith forced upon them for the sake of a little food.

There surely can be nothing more sad than to imagine these

people who had bravely refused to swerve from their Faith and had undertaken the hazardous journey into the unknown. We are told that they waited at Cadiz and Santa Maria for the sea to divide for them as, so their scriptures told them, it had divided for their ancestors.

The only fortunate Jews were those who went to Rome where, oddly enough, that old sinner Roderigo Borgia, Alexander VI (not out of his goodness of heart, but out of his wisdom), gave them a refuge.

So the Jews were expelled from Spain, and the Inquisition grew mightier yet. The fall of Granada was to bring it new victims. There would be those Moors who, as the Jews before them, would be forced to accept Christianity; and these *Moriscos* would very soon be found guilty of reverting to their traditional faith.

There were also the Protestants.

INDEX

Abd el Aziz, 77
Abd el Malik, 78
Abd er Rhaman I, origins, 78; Emir of Spain, 79; achievements, 80
Abd er Rhaman II, 80, 82
Abd er Rhaman III, 82
Abélard, Peter, theories, 22, 23
Abraham, Rabbi, 168, 169
Afton, Sir Walter, 143
Agramonts, 94
Agrippina, Wife of Chilpéric, 70
Alarcon, Alonso de, Inquisitor of Aragon, 165
Alaric II, Visigothic King, slain by Clovis I, 72
Albéric, Cardinal, goes to South of France with St. Bernard, 23
Albigenses, 23, 25, 26, 27, 28, 29, 30, 31, 34, 35, 36, 47
Alboflède, sister of Clovis I, 72
Albret, Jean d', 160
Alexander IV, Pope, 57
Alexander V, Pope, 58, 59
Alexander VI, Pope, 30; leniency to Jews, 106, 178, 184
Alexander VII, Pope, beatified Arbués, 166
Alfonso III, King of Asturias, 82
Alfonso V of Aragon, 94, 95
Alfonso V of Portugal, 89; suitor to Isabella, 91, 98; supports La Beltraneja, 101; death, 102
Alfonso VI of Leon and Castile arranges Cid's marriage 83, sends Cid into exile, 84
Alfonso VIII of Castile, 104
Alfonso IX of Castile, 34, 35
Alfonso X of Leon and Castile, 85
Alfonso XI of Leon and Castile, knights Lope Alonso de Torquemada, 123
Alfonso, brother of Isabella, 88, 89; set up as King 90, 91; death, 92, 93
Alfonso, natural son of Ferdinand, 164, 165

Almeyda, Edward de, bravery on battlefield, 102
Almohades, 84, 85
Almoravides, 84, 85
Alonso of Portugal, affianced to Infanta Isabella, 102; married to Infanta, 179; death, 180
Anastasius II, Pope, 72
André II of Hungary, 42
Antoninus, Marcus Aurelius, persecutes Christians, 20
Arbués, Pedro, appointed Inquisitor of Aragon, 163; assassinated, 164; sanctified, 166
Arians, 21, 23
Aridius, 70
Arius, Founder of Arianism, 21
Arnalt, Hernan Nuñez, 113
Arnaud, Guillem, 46, 56
Arnauld, Abbot of Citeaux, 28
Attila, 69, 70
Augustine, St., 20, 21
Aurelian, Roman servant of Clovis I, 70, 71
Autos de fé, 135, 147, 149, 155, 159, 162, 163, 165, 178
Azevedo, Diego d', Bishop of Osma, in South of France, 24, 25; sent on Embassy for Alfonso IX, 34, 35

Baker, Reverend J., 142, 143
Baldj, 78
Baldwin II of Jerusalem, 52
Barberi, Filippo de', Inquisitor of Sicily, 111
Barca, Hamilcar, 67, 68
Bartholomew, St., Massacre, 55/56
Bartholomew of Trent on St. Dominic, 34
Bazan Martin de, Bishop of Osma, 34
Beatriz of Portugal, 102
Beaumonts, 94, 96
Becket, Thomas a', murder of, 26

185

THE GROWTH OF THE
SPANISH INQUISITION

NOTE

In order to avoid footnotes, sources and references are given in the text.

My very special thanks are due to the librarians of Kensington Public Library who have worked so hard and patiently to procure rare books for me, and thus have aided me considerably in my research.

CONTENTS

ILLUSTRATIONS

ACKNOWLEDGMENTS

Illustrations nos. 1, 2 & 4 are reproduced by permission of the
Trustees of the British Museum; nos. 6 & 7 are from Radio Times
Hulton Picture Library; the remaining illustrations are from the
Mansell Collection.

PRINCIPAL WORKS CONSULTED

Acton, John Emerich Edward Dalberg, First Baron Acton, D.C.L., LL.D. Edited with an introduction by John Neville Figgis, M.A., and Reginald Vere Laurence, M.A. *The History of Freedom and Other Essays* (1907).

Adams, Nicholson B. *The Heritage of Spain: An Introduction to Spanish Civilization* (1949).

Alberti, L. de, and Chapman, A. B. Wallis, D.Sc. (Econ.), Edited by. *English Merchants and the Spanish Inquisition in the Canaries*. Extracts from the Archives in possession of the Most Hon. The Marquess of Bute (1912).

Aradi, Zsolt. *The Popes* (1956).

Aubrey, William Hickman Smith. *History of England*.

Bainton, Roland H. *The Reformation of the 16th Century* (1953).

Bainton, Roland H. *The Travail of Religious Liberty* (1953).

Baker, The Rev. J., M.A. *The History of the Inquisition as it subsists in the Kingdoms of Spain, Portugal, etc., and in both the Indies to this day* (1734).

Berdyaev, Nicolas. With a Commentary and Notes by Alan A. Spears. Translated by Alan A. Spears and Victor B. Kanter. *Christianity and Anti-Semitism* (1952).

Bertrand, Louis of the Académie Française and Sir Charles Petrie, Bt., M.A., F.R.Hist.S. *The History of Spain* (1934).

Bury, J. B. With an Epilogue by Blackham, H. J. *A History of Freedom of Thought* (1952).

Butterfield, Herbert. *Christianity in European History* (1951).

Cary-Elwes, Columbia, Monk of Ampleforth. With a Preface by Professor Arnold Toynbee. *Law, Liberty and Love* (1949).

Creighton, M., D.D. *Persecution and Tolerance* (1895).

Dawson, Christopher. *Religion and the Rise of Western Culture* (1950).

Deanesly, M., M.A. *A History of the Medieval Church 590-1500* (1925).

Giffard, William Alva. *The Story of the Faith*. A Survey of Christian History for the Undogmatic (1946).

Gordon, Janet. *The Spanish Inquisition: Its Heroes and Martyrs* (1898).

Gowen, Herbert H., D.D., F.R.A.S. *A History of Religion* (1934).

Guizot, M. Translated by Robert Black, M.A. *The History of France from Earliest Times to the Year 1789* (1881).

Hope, Thomas. *Torquemada, Scourge of the Jews* (1939).

Hume, Martin A. S. Revised by Edward Armstrong. *Spain, Its Greatness and Decay* (1479-1788). Cambridge Historical Series (1931).

Lea, Henry Charles, LL.D. *A History of the Inquisition of the Middle Ages.* 3 Volumes (1901).

Lea, Henry Charles, LL.D. *A History of the Inquisition of Spain.* 4 Volumes (1907).

Lea, Henry Charles, LL.D. *Superstition and Force* (1892).

Lea, Henry Charles, LL.D. *The Inquisition in the Spanish Dependencies* (1908).

Limborch, Philip. *The History of the Inquisition as it has Subsisted in France, Italy, Spain, Portugal, Venice, Sicily, Sardinia, Milan, Poland, Flanders, etc.* (1816).

Marchant, John, and others. *A Review of the Bloody Tribunal;* or the *Horrid Cruelties of the Inquisition, as practised in Spain, Portugal, Italy, and the East and West Indies, on all those whom the Church of Rome brands with the name of Hereticks* (1770).

Maycock, A. L., M.A. With an Introduction by Father Ronald Knox. *The Inquisition from its Establishment to the Great Schism* (1926).

McKinnon, James, Ph.D., D.D., D.Th., LL.D. *Calvin and the Reformation* (1936).

McKnight, John P. *The Papacy* (1953).

Merton, Reginald. *Cardinal Ximenes and the Making of Spain* (1934).

Mortimer, R.C., M.A., B.D. *The Elements of Moral Theology* (1947).

Nickerson, Hoffman. With a Preface by Hilaire Belloc. *The Inquisition. A Political and Military Study of its Establishment* (1923).

Poole, Reginald Lane. *Illustrations of the History of Medieval Thought and Learning* (1880).

Prescott, William H. *History of the Reign of Ferdinand and Isabella the Catholic.* 2 Volumes.

Prescott, William H. *History of the Reign of Philip II, King of Spain.* 3 Volumes (1879).

Robertson, John M. *A Short History of Freethought, Ancient and Modern.* 2 Volumes (1915).

Roth, Cecil. *The Spanish Inquisition* (1937).

Rule, William Harris, D.D. *A History of the Inquisition.* 2 Volumes (1874).

Sabatini, Rafael. *Torquemada and the Spanish Inquisition* (1928).

Shewring, Walter (Translated and Introduced by). *Rich and Poor in Christian Tradition.* Writings of many centuries (1947).

Simon, Dr. Paul. Translated from the German by Meyrick Booth, Ph.D. *The Human Element in the Church of Christ* (1953).

Stephen, James Fitzjames, Q.C. *Liberty, Equality, Fraternity* (1873).

Swain, John. *The Pleasures of the Torture Chamber* (1931).

Turberville, A. S., M.C., M.A., B.Litt. *Medieval Heresy and the Inquisition* (1920).

Turberville, A. S., M.C., M.A., B.Litt. *The Spanish Inquisition* (1932).

Wiseman, F., M.A. *Roman Spain. An Introduction to the Roman Antiquities of Spain and Portugal* (1956).

The Catholic Encyclopedia: An International Work of Reference on the Constitution, Doctrine, Discipline and History of the Catholic Church. Edited by Charles G. Herbermann, Ph.D., LL.D., Edward A. Pace, Ph.D., D.D., Condé B. Pallen, Ph.D., LL.D., Thomas J. Shahan, D.D., John J. Wynne, S.J., assisted by numerous collaborators (1907).

INTRODUCTION

U NITED SPAIN was born in that fateful year of 1492—and it seemed that about its cradle were gathered all the gifts the good fairies had to offer. Its governors were those two sovereigns— Ferdinand the soldier, Isabella the administrator—both monarchs in their own right and each endowed with qualities which, even had they reigned alone, would have brought greatness to Spain.

After seven hundred years of Moorish occupation, Spain (under Isabella and Ferdinand) had driven the enemy from the land. Over the Alhambra in the last Moorish town to hold out, now flew the standard of Christian Spain.

The gifts the good fairies had to offer were glittering indeed; and perhaps the significance of the greatest of these gifts was not realized when it was handed to the sovereigns. This was the gift of a new world, which—as that of Christian Spain—must depend for its value on the use to which it was put.

Christian Spain had long been the dream of the sovereigns; this they had planned for, worked and fought for. The development of their country, from a bickering group of states with a Mussulman enemy within their midst to a united land, must have seemed little short of miraculous. When they had married in 1469, Isabella's brother Henry IV had been alive, and his daughter (had she not been almost certainly illegitimate) would have been heir to the throne of Castile. But the war of succession had been won, the Treaty of Lisbon signed in 1479 and Isabella had become Queen of Castile while Ferdinand, on the death of his father in 1479, had inherited the throne of Aragon. In twelve years the sovereigns had replaced with justice and order the anarchical rule of Isabella's father John II and her brother Henry IV; this in itself would have brought great credit to them if they had not won the additional merit of completing the reconquest. It was a record of which they could be justifiably proud.

From small states they had made one great country which had every opportunity of becoming the leading country of the world. And as if this were not enough, seemingly limitless possibilities had been laid at their feet, for on the 12th October of this glorious year a navigator who had set out on a voyage of discovery under the aegis of Isabella came upon a new land.

So far the Portuguese had been leading in nautical adventures. The Infante Henry (known as Henry the Navigator), who was the son of John I of Portugal, had already discovered the Madeira Islands and had explored the coast of Africa as far as Cape Blanco. (As his mother was a daughter of John of Gaunt one wonders whether his great love of and talent for exploration came from English forbears.)   Henry also has the distinction of being the first to use a compass in navigation.

The Spaniards, however, were not far behind their neighbours on the high seas.   They had taken possession of the Canary Islands (the Fortunate Isles); and Ferdinand and Isabella were certainly fully aware of the wealth which could come from an Empire. Certain rivalry had already sprung up between Spain and Portugal, but these differences had been settled by the Treaty of Lisbon.

There were men who dreamed of great discoveries, and among these there appeared a Genoese named Christopher Columbus.

He was of humble origin, the son, it is said, of a weaver; but he had great dreams.   He had studied mathematics at Pavia, but when he was fourteen, experiencing the call of the sea, he left Pavia to follow the life of adventure.

He continued to sail the seas until 1470 when he was in his twenties.   (It is not certain in what year he was born.   Most authorities give the date as 1446, but Bernaldez says that when he died in 1506 he was seventy—" more or less ".)   He then decided to go to Portugal.   In that country congregated the adventurous men of the world, for the Portuguese government more than any other was inclined to listen to their plans for the discovery of new land and, what was more to the point, provide ships and crews for the journey.

Columbus firmly believed that there was land beyond the Atlantic, and it was his intention to state this belief to the King of Portugal, John II, and enlist his help.

But there were numerous adventurers in Lisbon all seeking to impress the King with their plans, and Columbus found obstruction wherever he turned; he therefore decided to leave Portugal for Spain in the hope that he would win more sympathy from the Spanish sovereigns.   Thus Portugal lost the honour of sending the expedition which resulted in the most important of all land discoveries.

However, Columbus met with frustration in Spain.   He had arrived at an inopportune period, for the sovereigns were deeply concerned with the great war against the Infidel, and it is easily understood that, being thus occupied, they had little time or money to spare for what might prove to be the dream of a visionary. But Columbus discovered a friend in Fray Juan Perez de Marchena who was guardian of the Andalusian convent of La Rabida; Fray Juan was very interested in Columbus's plans, and so eloquently did the latter talk of these that Fray Juan decided to put the adventurer in touch with a man who had great influence with the Queen because he had become her confessor: Fernando de Talavera.

This was unfortunate, for Talavera was the last man to help in such an enterprise. Deeply religious, intensely bigoted, he distrusted everything that was new; he was eager to complete the conquest of the Moors and it seemed the utmost folly, in his view, to dissipate money and energy on wild schemes of exploration. He put the matter before the sovereigns—from his own angle; and as a result the Council of Salamanca, which was set up to consider it, decided that the project was "impracticable"; so Columbus, frustrated once more and feeling that he had wasted a great deal of time, prepared to leave Spain for France where he hoped for a more sympathetic hearing.

Before he left the country he paid a farewell visit to Fray Juan Perez de Marchena at the Convent of La Rabida, and there he found that Fray Juan was as disappointed as he was himself. But Fray Juan would not give up, and decided to make the journey to the Queen himself, even though she was at Santa Fé, the great camp which had been built before Granada.

As a result of this Columbus was asked to visit the Queen who would reimburse the expenses of his journey. He arrived at an important moment: Granada had capitulated.

He told the Queen that he was confident of reaching a hitherto undiscovered land. He stressed the riches of the East, which he believed he could reach by sailing westward across the Atlantic Ocean; and he did not forget to remind Isabella that, if new lands were discovered and brought under the domination of the sovereigns, they would be won for Holy Church and the Christian Faith.

The thought of great riches deeply attracted Ferdinand, and the hope of bringing pagans into the Church attracted Isabella. Ferdinand, however, was wary and inclined to listen to the arguments of Talavera. This was one of those occasions, however, when Isabella showed herself ready to act on her own responsibility. She declared that she would give Columbus what he asked, even if it were necessary to pawn her jewels to find the money.

So on the 3rd August, 1492, Columbus set sail for the unknown; on 12th October, after two months of danger on the high seas, land was sighted. America was discovered. Thus was a new world presented to newly-born united Spain.

But they were not all *good* fairies at the christening.

In March the edict expelling the Jews had been signed, and this new Spain was to be robbed of a hard-working section of the population, remarkable in their peculiar genius for creating financial prosperity wherever they lived. Here was one of the curses on the new-born infant, and one which was to have far-reaching repercussions.

And over the cradle there also loomed intolerance and bigotry; no person, high or low throughout the land, could feel completely free from fear.

The Inquisition was firmly established in Spain and showing signs of growing stronger. It threw a dark grim shadow over all the blessings which the good fairies were showering on newly-united Christian Spain.

I

THE END OF TORQUEMADA

THE EXPULSION of the Jews was the high light of Torquemada's career. From the time he had risen to power he had worked for this, and when he saw that pitiable army of refugees leaving the country which had been their home for centuries, wretchedly seeking new homes in unknown lands where they could not know what their reception would be, he must have felt that his life's work was accomplished. Spain was still not completely Christian for, as a price for the surrender of Granada, Boabdil, the last Moorish king, had asked that the Inquisition should not be set up in Granada and that the Moors living there (although subjects of Ferdinand and Isabella) should be allowed to follow their own religion; this request had been granted. And although Torquemada may have been dismayed at this leniency towards non-Christians, he was too old to begin a new campaign. He had expelled most of the Jews and only those who had been baptized were allowed to remain. The Moors must be left to his successors to deal with.

Another important event had occurred in that fateful year of 1492 which was to affect Torquemada although it happened outside Spain. Innocent VIII had died and during August a Conclave was held in Rome. There were great rivalries for the Papal throne and, after certain acts of bribery and simony on the part of wily Roderigo Borgia, he was elected Pope Alexander VI.

Alexander was a man of tremendous energy and it may have been that he was not pleased by the immense power the Inquisition was wielding in Spain for, in the hands of Torquemada, it had freed itself from the influence of Rome.

Moreover, many of the persecuted were wealthy people, and their friends and relations, although they dared not raise their voices at home against the Inquisition (for to do so would immediately bring them into its power), sent out complaints in other directions; and to whom could these complaints be more advantageously addressed than to Pope Alexander who was already showing his disapproval of Torquemada?

As for Torquemada, he was widely increasing the powers of the Inquisition, so that the civil courts were actually coming under the jurisdiction of the Holy Office. Any magistrate who did not conform with Torquemada's wishes was judged tainted with heresy and forced to perform certain minor—but public—penances.

Alexander had already issued a decree directed against Torquemada, in which he stated that the Inquisition had no right to proceed against priests unless they first obtained the sanction of the Pope.

Torquemada, under the protection of his doting sovereigns, was ready to flout the Pope if need be; but he was making many enemies, not only among the magistrates but among the prelates.

In the Vatican, Alexander was alert. Pleasure-loving, seemingly lenient as he was, he was yet not the man to allow any to flout him with impunity and escape.

Torquemada had brought about the exodus of the Jews, but that did not mean he had abandoned his persecutions of these unfortunate people. Although it is very probable that he himself had Jewish blood (through his paternal grandmother) he continued suspicious of others who had it.

One of these was Juan Arias Davila, who was Bishop of Segovia. The Bishop's grandfather had been a Jew, and although his grandson had risen in the Church to such high rank, Torquemada set his inquisitors to pry into the past of his long-dead grandfather, although Juan Arias Davila at this time was himself an old man.

By dint of the usual examination and terrorizing of witnesses it was " discovered " that the grandfather of the Bishop of Segovia had been guilty of celebrating the rites of his old religion although he had been baptized into the Christian Faith.

Now the usual action should be taken: The bones of the dead man dug up, put into the *sanbenito*, taken to the *quemadero* and publicly burned. That was not all; his family could not expect to continue in prosperity. Their lands and goods would be confiscated and they themselves robbed of their offices.

Davila was aware of the slight tension between Torquemada and Alexander, and he therefore wisely appealed to Alexander.

Alexander's response was to remind Torquemada that when prelates were to be charged with sins against the Church the matter must be undertaken by an Apostolic Court.

Davila then set out for Rome where he was received with great kindness by the Pope; his case was put before a court called together by Alexander, the charge was found to be false, and Alexander gave the Bishop a post in the retinue of his nephew, Cardinal Borgia of Monreale, who was about to set out for Naples to attend the coronation of Alfonso II.

This was a snub for Torquemada; but he brought forward charges against another Bishop, and in this case he was more successful. This victim was Pedro de Aranda, Bishop of Calahorra. The case against him was that his father, a New Christian, had committed the sin of turning back to the Law of Moses. Aranda, like Davila, went to Rome and was received there with that gracious charm which was an essential part of Alexander's personality. He was found innocent at the court set up by Alexander, and favours were showered upon him—no doubt as a further snub to Torquemada.

But Torquemada was a man of great power and he would not meekly suffer two such defeats. A further charge of personal Judaizing was brought against Aranda, and this time there were witnesses to bring forward evidence against him, so that the Pontifical Court could not fail to find him guilty. As a result, he was denuded of his benefices and imprisoned in Sant' Angelo. He died there after a few years' incarceration.

But these two bishops, during their sojourns in Rome, had carried many complaints against Torquemada to Alexander, and the Pope made up his mind that Torquemada should not much longer hold the post of Grand Inquisitor in Spain.

It was typical of Alexander that, while he planned to rob Torquemada of his office, he should maintain an illusion of great friendliness towards him. He decided to play upon the most obvious reason for the resignation of the Inquisitor-General.

Torquemada was an old man, he said (Alexander was sixty, but he looked upon himself as a superman), and the great tasks which the Inquisitor-General took upon himself were too much for him. Greatly did Alexander cherish Tomás de Torquemada who had laboured long for the glory of the Faith, but he had decided to appoint four helpers who would take over some of his more irksome duties, and thus, now that he had greater need of rest, he would be able to enjoy it.

Alexander, wily as ever, did not intend those whom he had chosen for the new appointments to be in any way inferior to Torquemada; their power should equal his; to have referred to them as " assistants " was merely an example of that diplomatic tact which had sustained Alexander through his dangerous career.

Two of the four " assistants " appointed by Alexander (Martin

Ponce de Leon, Archbishop of Messina, and Don Francisco Sanchez de la Fuente, Bishop of Avila) assumed office with Torquemada, so that instead of there being one supreme head of the Inquisition there were now three in command; moreover, Alexander forthwith addressed all communications concerning the Inquisition to the Bishop of Avila.

This was a great blow to Torquemada's pride, and there can be no doubt that, had he been in better health, he would have bitterly opposed interference from Rome. But although Alexander had succeeded in reducing Torquemada's title of Inquisitor-General to one of mere courtesy, he was far from the scene of Torquemada's activities and did not realize the extent of the power which the Prior of the Holy Cross held over the sovereigns and the people of Spain.

Torquemada had made the Inquisition what it was; he was so much a part of it that no interference from outside—however powerful—could dislodge him.

The new Inquisitors, confident of their power, made a new rule that they themselves should control the disposal of goods which had been confiscated from heretics instead of, as hitherto, turning it over to the treasury.

This ruling naturally incurred the immediate wrath of Ferdinand, whose chief interest in the Inquisition was the riches it poured into his ever hungry coffers.

He at once appealed to Alexander, and Alexander, eager to keep peace with the Spanish sovereigns, immediately gave orders to the Inquisitors to desist from the new practices.

*   *   *

Torquemada had another and more formidable adversary than Alexander. In 1496 he was so feeble in health that he could no longer remain at Court. One of his chief ailments was the gout (generally supposed to be the result of rich living, so that it seemed an odd quirk of fate that this ascetic man should be so afflicted) and he retired to the monastery he had built at Avila.

In spite of the fact that he was absent from Court he was not forgotten by Isabella who always held him in great affection and respect, and she and Ferdinand visited him at the monastery, which left no doubt in the minds of all that he stood as high in favour as he had ever done, and that the Pope's sly efforts to oust him had not been entirely successful.

During the last year of Torquemada's life the sovereigns suffered a great tragedy. Isabella loved all her children dearly, but the

only son was naturally of especial importance to his parents.   This
was the Infante Juan who at eighteen years of age had been married
to the Princess Margaret, the daughter of the Emperor Maximilian;
and it was arranged that Margaret's brother (Archduke Philip, son
and heir of Maximilian) should marry Juana, second daughter of
Isabella and Ferdinand.   A few months later another marriage was
arranged; this was for the Infanta Catalina (known in English
history as Catherine of Aragon) with Arthur, Prince of Wales, son
of Henry VII of England.

Isabella's and Ferdinand's was indeed a tragic family.

Juan, the sovereigns' heir, during the celebrations of his marriage
in Salamanca fell into a fever; Ferdinand hastened to his bedside
to find his son—who was not quite twenty years of age—resigned
to death.

Deeply concerned as to the effect this would have on Isabella
who had always been a particularly fond parent, Ferdinand dared
not break the news immediately, so caused several despatches to be
sent to her, each preparing her for worse news to come.

There was general mourning throughout Spain at the death of
the Prince of the Asturias; and hopes were centred on Juan's young
wife, Margaret, who was pregnant.

But ill-fortune had already set in for the family.   Margaret gave
birth to a still-born child; and the heir to the throne of Spain was
now Isabella (the sovereigns' eldest daughter) who had, much
against her will, taken for her second husband Emanuel, King of
Portugal.   One of the conditions she had made before agreeing to
the match was that Emanuel should expel all Jews from his
dominion where many had taken refuge after the great exodus from
Spain.   Was this inspired by her parents, who in their turn had
been inspired by Torquemada?

Emanuel, however, who was noted for his enlightened views,
was very reluctant to bring in this measure which his intelligence
told him was both harsh and foolish; but so eager was he for the
match that he eventually consented.

The second daughter of Isabella and Ferdinand, Juana, who had
married the ambitious Archduke Philip, was already noted for her
eccentric manners; and it was a great grief to Isabella and
Ferdinand when, inspired by her husband, she took the title of
Princess of Castile thus implying that she considered herself heiress
to the crown of Spain.

Isabella and Ferdinand then decided that their eldest daughter,
Isabella of Portugal, should with her husband come at once to
Castile that she might be publicly acclaimed as the heiress to her

parents' crowns. They came in the spring of the year 1498. Young Isabella was pregnant, but her condition gave little cause for rejoicing for it seemed scarcely possible that she could have a satisfactory confinement.

The death of Juan hung over the family, and Isabella told her parents that she felt certain she could not survive the birth of her child.

She died in her mother's arms an hour after her son Miguel was born. Miguel himself died before he was two years old.

Now the next in succession to the throne was the eccentric Juana, much, there can be no doubt, to the satisfaction of her ambitious husband Archduke Philip.

Juana was to become insane, and the tragic history of Catalina, who was brought to England to marry Prince Arthur, and on his death married Prince Henry (who became Henry VIII) and was superseded in his affections by Anne Boleyn, is well known.

But in the year 1498 the sovereigns were mourning the deaths oι Juan and Isabella; and it is a sign of the affection and respect they felt for Torquemada that they requested that the body of the Infante should be taken to Avila and buried there.

Perhaps an even greater sign of the favour in which the sovereigns held Torquemada was illustrated by the fact that, when it was necessary to send an embassy to England to negotiate for the marriage of Prince Arthur and Catalina, the arrangements for this embassy were put into the hands of the Inquisitor-General.

Torquemada, ever mindful of his beloved child, the Inquisition, sought to turn the occasion to advantage; he chose his embassy with care and sent with it a personal message to the King of England.

England was one of those countries into which the Inquisition had not entered, except on one isolated occasion (the persecution of the Templars by Edward II); that strip of Channel had been a barrier between the self-contained island and the rest of Europe, but now that a match was proposed between England and Spain, Torquemada was determined to take advantage of the situation, as he had (presumably) through the marriage of Isabella and Emanuel in Portugal by insisting on the exile of the Jews.

Henry VII was quite ready to make promises to further the match which he greatly desired. His shrewd mind would have been fully aware of the rising power of Spain; he was notorious for his miserly nature and naturally eager for the rich dowry which Catalina would bring to England.

The request, which reached him through Torquemada, was that none who sought refuge from the Holy Office should be given it in England.

Torquemada's ambassador reported that Henry put both hands on his breast and swore an oath that he would persecute any heretic or Jew in his dominions to whom the Spanish authorities called his attention.

This compliance of the English sovereign must have brought a certain consolation to Torquemada, who would at this time have been feeling bitterly resentful towards Rome. Alexander had shown (as clearly as the suave Pontiff could) his lack of friendliness towards the Inquisitor-General; in addition he had shown a lack of respect for the methods of Torquemada in the *auto de fé* which was held in July 1498, in St. Peter's Square, when a leniency had been shown towards heretics in direct contrast to the severe measures imposed by Torquemada's instructions. Torquemada had urged his sovereigns to protest to the Pontiff on account of the leniency displayed; to which Alexander blithely responded that he had forbidden the penitents to return to Spain without the permission of the sovereigns—implying thereby (still preserving that delightfully suave and most diplomatic manner) that what happened to them was no concern of Spain's. With such a man reigning in Rome, it was small wonder that Torquemada wished to make other allies, even as far afield as the island off the coast of Europe where the unpredictable Tudor dynasty had come into being.

So racked with pain was Torquemada during the last few years of his life that it might seem that a malicious fate was forcing him to suffer a little of the torment he had caused to be inflicted on so many. But if his body was reduced to inactivity, this was not the case with his mind.

Five months before his death he summoned the chief Inquisitors to Avila, and there he made known to them a further set of instructions which he had prepared for the procedure of the Inquisition.

This was the fourth set of instructions which Torquemada had produced, the others having been issued in 1484, 1485 and 1488. This last set, issued in May 1498, consisted of sixteen articles, the gist of which was:—

1. Two Inquisitors were to be appointed to each court, and one of these must be a jurist, the other a theologian. They must not proceed separately to sentence a person to prison or to the torture; nor must they, except jointly, publish names of witnesses.

2. Officers of the Inquisition were not to be allowed to carry weapons in those places where the carrying of weapons was forbidden.

3. No person must be arrested unless there was good proof of

guilt, and trials should be conducted with all possible speed, not (as had been the case in the affair of La Guardia) delayed in order to acquire damning evidence.

4. Actions against the dead should be conducted with promptitude, for delay caused great suffering to the children of such people, who were not allowed to marry while their parents' cases were *sub judice*.

5. Penances should not depend on the state of the Inquisition's exchequer, as had happened in the past.   (When the Inquisition's funds were falling low, penances were increased.)

6. Corporal penance and imprisonment could not be excused on payment of fines; and only Inquisitors-General could give permission to discard the *sanbenito* and relieve children of the burden of their parents' sins.

7. Inquisitors must take great care in allowing reconciliation to those who confessed their sins *after* arrest, for when it was considered how long the Inquisition had been in operation, it would be seen that their sins had been committed out of sheer disobedience to the law, of which they must have been fully aware.

8. The Inquisition must severely and publicly prosecute all false witnesses.

9. In no tribunal should there be people who were related to each other, not only by blood but by course of business, such as masters or servants.

The remaining seven articles are concerned with matters of procedure and administration, such as the need for secrecy, the punishment of notaries who betray information, the setting up of courts of the Inquisition in territory as yet unexplored by them, and so on.

These were the last instructions of Torquemada, and on a casual examination it would appear that the spirit of the Grand Inquisitor had grown more kindly in his pain-racked body. But he was mainly concerned with the more efficient working of the Inquisition, and when the clauses are examined more closely they seem less kindly and certainly very revealing.

For instance when, as in Clause 3, Torquemada states that no person shall be arrested unless there is good proof of guilt, this means—as it always did—that people could be arrested providing the Inquisition consider there was sufficient proof. Their methods in the torture chambers with their *suspending* instead of *stopping* torture, and thus making it legal to pursue their hideous work, lay them open to suspicion in this respect. When names slipped from the mouths of men and women who were being submitted to the

most acute agony in the torture chambers, it was considered sufficient proof and reason for arrest; so this clause, which sounds so
kindly, is after all almost meaningless.

Clause 4 declares that actions against deceased persons should be
conducted with great promptitude, that the children may not
suffer. This again sounds as though a certain humanity was
creeping into the mind of the Inquisitor-General. But at this time
the corpse of almost every wealthy *converso* had been gruesomely
exhumed and submitted to the faggots, and his wealth confiscated
by the Inquisition.

The very fact that it should be necessary to warn against adjusting
fines to the state of the exchequer gives a clear indication that
nefarious practices had been pursued hitherto.

The article which states that false witnesses should be punished
is also open to question. How could it be proved that a person
had borne false witness when it was one of the laws of the Inquisition
that the accused should not know who had accused them? The
Inquisition had its own ideas of false witnesses, and these were not
those who bore witness against the accused; they were those who
denied knowledge of heresy in accused people whom the Inquisitors
wished to condemn.

Yet it would seem at first glance that, in his last weeks on Earth,
Torquemada had endeavoured to soften the harshness he had
brought into being. He may have given the impression that he
had done this, but his last Instructions smack of hypocrisy; one
wonders whether he—who was so much the spirit of the Inquisition—
was unconsciously deceiving himself. The Inquisition was his
passion, his creation; he loved it tenderly; it was harsh, bitterly
cruel, yet perhaps this man who saw himself as right, and all those
who disagreed with him in the smallest detail wrong (not only
wrong but wicked and undeserving of life) believed that the harshness was necessary. Yet how strange it is that, being on the point
of death, he should have produced this set of Instructions which, on
the surface (and the surface only) appear to show a glint of compassion—though perhaps that is too strong a word to use in connection with Torquemada. It is also characteristic. It remains in the
tradition of that very spirit which created the Inquisition—
arrogance, brutality, and an almost clinical cruelty, all carefully
clothed in self-righteous anger and hypocrisy.

After completing the sixteen articles, Torquemada issued certain
rules which the officers of the Inquisition were commanded to follow.

In these he laid down that no person was to visit prisoners of the
Holy Office except those who brought them their food, and that

such visitors must swear to preserve secrecy; examination of all the food which was taken to the prisoner must be made in order to search for any messages which some persons might have sought to convey to them. All officials must swear to remain silent concerning anything they had seen or heard within the prisons of the Inquisition. Should suspects be found guiltless and their goods restored, these goods must be restored in their full value at the time of confiscation; but any debts owed by the prisoners should be paid by the Inquisitors without consulting them.

If any property of condemned men had passed into other hands action should be taken to recover it.

Property confiscated from the condemned was to be sold after one month, but the receivers were not allowed to buy it; if they did so, and their fault was discovered, they would be fined as much as 100 ducats and, worse still, threatened with excommunication.

Inquisitors were bound to serve the Inquisition faithfully and were bound on oath to preserve secrecy; no gifts were to be accepted from prisoners, and if any were discovered breaking this law they would be subject to a heavy fine of as much as 100,000 maravidis and discharged from their Inquisitorial duties; and any who were aware that such a gift had been received by another and did not betray him would suffer a similar punishment.

It was further stressed that Inquisitors should never in any circumstances be alone with prisoners. They must never accept hospitality from New Christians but must pay for all they had; and all officers must hold only one post in the Inquisition and consequently receive only one salary.

There can be no doubt, when considering these new rules of Torquemada's, that he was aware of certain evil practices which were being carried on among the officers of the Inquisition, and these would naturally be deplored by a man such as Torquemada. Yet, because he was eager to prevent his servants from taking bribes, because he wished to institute in the Inquisition a mode of conduct which he could persuade himself was justice, this does not excuse him. Torquemada in those last weeks of his life, while suffering great bodily pain, was as eager as he had ever been to drive those who disagreed with him, through torture and fire, to salvation—according to the laws of the Church as laid down by himself.

These last instructions of Torquemada were a gesture to show the world that he and he alone remained supreme head of the Inquisition in Spain. Indomitable, he was in fiery action to the last. In May 1498 he issued his instructions; in July 1498 he, through the sovereigns, protested to Alexander VI concerning the famous *auto de fé* held in the square before St. Peter's; and when the Pope's reply, which was a direct snub to the *Spanish* Inquisition, was received, Torquemada was dying.

On the 16th September, 1498, he died; he was buried in the chapel of the monastery which he himself had built. A simple stone above his tomb bore the inscription:

HIC JACET REVERENDUS P. F. THOMAS DE TURRE-CREMATA
PRIOR SANCTAE CRUCIS, INQUISITOR GENERALIS
HUJUS DOMUS FUNDATOR. OBIT ANNO DOMINI
MCDLXLVIII, DIE XVI SEPTEMBRIS.

It is impossible to stress too much the great effect this man had on Spanish history. He had succeeded in releasing Spain from Papal influence; he had played the biggest part in forming this great and independent nation. He has been called the Saviour of Spain; it is interesting to contemplate that his greatest effort, which was the setting up of the Inquisition, was to contribute so largely to the downfall of that country.

His life presents—more than most others—the most striking contrasts, so that while to many he is the Light of Spain and the saviour of his country, to many more he is one of the cruellest bigots who ever lived. Strangely enough both these assessments have some truth in them. The unification of Spain and its rise to temporal power were in a large measure due to him; and the Spanish Inquisition, founded on his instructions, played a significant part in bringing about the destruction of Spain's greatness.

Those Catholic writers who seek to excuse his cruelty insist that there have been gross exaggerations as to the number of people who were burned at the stake during his rule. There may have been exaggerations by Protestant writers, but one cannot help feeling that the Catholics have been overwhelmingly modest with their figures. Llorente states that between 1483 and 1498, while Torquemada was in command, 8,800 were burned at the stake and 96,504 suffered less severe penalties. Some historians put the figures at 10,000 burned by fire. Michael Ott, writing in the *Catholic Encyclopedia*, tells us that " the purity of the Christian Faith was in danger " and that the action of Torquemada was necessary to preserve Spain. He also states that only 2,000 were burned between the years 1481 and 1504, when Isabella died.

Perhaps the figures of Llorente can be treated with greater respect than those which appear excessively high or low. Many *autos* took place between 1483 and 1498, and many people suffered the supreme penalty; moreover Llorente was working from the records of the Inquisition itself and it appears that he writes with calm integrity, allowing for occasional lapses into righteous anger, which any normal person would feel against great cruelty.

Philip II, whose admiration for Torquemada can be well understood—for there is much which is similar in their natures—had the remains of the Inquisitor-General removed from their humble grave and re-interred in a place of honour in the Cathedral.

They were taken from this resting-place in 1836, when the tomb was rifled, and were then scattered.

Thus Torquemada, who had caused suffering to so many, died in bodily misery; and he, who had caused many to be taken from their graves that their remains might be humiliated, had the same treatment accorded to his bones.

2

THE RISE OF XIMENES

IF THERE was another person during the reign of Isabella and Ferdinand who had as great an effect on Spain's history as Torquemada that person was surely Cardinal Ximenes; and it is an interesting fact that these two men—the former a Dominican, the latter a Franciscan and both Inquisitors-General—should be of such similar characters. Though perhaps this is to be expected, for Ferdinand, Isabella and the newly-born Spain could make use of such men; and it was doubtless for this reason that Torquemada and Ximenes did more than any others to set the new course and carry Spain along the journey she was to take.

Ximenes (Gonzalo Ximenes de Cisneros) was born in Torrelaguna, a small village close to Madrid, in the year 1436, and as in the case of Torquemada it was during his later life that he did the work which was to give him a place in history.

He was thirty-seven when he came into such conflict with the Primate of Spain, Carillo, Archbishop of Toledo, that he leaped into prominence.

Carillo, who was an uncle of the Marquis of Villena, a favourite of John II, had in his turn played a certain part in the politics of Castile, for he was a prelate who was more suited to the battlefield than to the Church. A strong man, he was excessively proud; his friendship was important to the peace of the monarch, and his enmity was to be feared. Poor weak Henry IV was to discover this to his cost when Carillo, with the help of the disgruntled Villena, sought to depose him and set up his young half-brother Alfonso in his place. Later, on the death of Alfonso, he had given his support to Isabella, but since he was a man ever on the look-out for slights which would impair his dignity, he eventually began to plot against Isabella; and he rode into battle side by side with Alfonso of Portugal who had come to fight for the crown of Castile on behalf of Henry's illegitimate daughter, La Beltraneja, whom he (Alfonso) planned to marry and with whom he hoped to share the throne.

When the Portuguese armies were beaten Carillo was forced to sue for pardon, which was granted by the victorious Isabella in exchange for a large portion of his estates.

After such disasters Carillo was forced to retire to Alcalá de Henares, where he spent his remaining years in the study of alchemy, which he pursued so earnestly that he dissipated a large part of his fortunes. There he died and was succeeded as Primate of Spain by Pedro Gonzalez de Mendoza, who had long been a rival.

Mendoza was the fourth son of the Marquis de Santillana; he was extremely talented and not content to work only within the limits of the Church. Like Carillo, he wished to take a place in politics; and even during the reign of Henry IV he sought to ingratiate himself with Isabella. It may have been that his foresight assured him that Isabella would one day be the Queen of Castile and that it would be wise to throw in his lot with her. If this were so he was certainly proved to be right.

The character of Mendoza was in striking contrast to that of Ximenes and Torquemada; he was a lover of luxury, and the pomp and magnificence of high office appealed greatly to him. He had not allowed his position in the Church to interfere with those carnal pleasures in which he indulged so freely, and he was the father of several illegitimate children.

The Cardinal's nature was tolerant. This is shown by an occasion when a priest, in his presence, was bold enough to deliver a sermon on the morals of high churchmen, which was clearly aimed at Mendoza. The Cardinal's followers wished to punish the preacher for his insolence, but Mendoza declared that all preachers had a right to state their views, and would not allow the priest to be touched. He himself sent him a gift of game, accompanied by a large sum of money, as reward for his boldness. But although Mendoza recognized the preacher's right to state his opinions, he claimed the right to live according to his own desires; and the words of warning delivered from the pulpit had no effect on his way of living.

When Carillo died and Mendoza succeeded him as Archbishop of Toledo he found greater scope for action in that field which had always attracted him: politics.

His pleasure-loving easy-going nature made him oppose the new laws which Torquemada wished to introduce into the Inquisition, and it was due in some measure to him that the delay occurred between the sanction of Sixtus IV and the setting up of the Inquisition in Spain, much to the irritation of Ojeda and Torquemada.

It was Mendoza who prepared the Catechism (*Catecismo de la Doctrina Cristiana*) in an attempt to stave off the introduction of the new Inquisition.

Events moved in favour of Torquemada and Ojeda, and Mendoza could do nothing but join with Torquemada and appoint Juan de San Martin and Miguel Morillo as the Inquisitors of Seville. Mendoza—more interested in matters of state than of the Church —played such a big part in politics that he became known at Court as The Third King of Spain; and when the armies were before Granada, Mendoza was there at the head of a detachment of troops; and he was with the sovereigns when they entered the fallen city.

It was Mendoza who supported Christopher Columbus when he was seeking Isabella's help in fitting him out for his voyage of discovery, and who was largely responsible for turning the Queen's opinion in the explorer's favour.

Cultured, aristocratic and greatly talented, the Cardinal continued to hold favour until his death; and when he was dying Isabella ordered that the Court move near to Guadalaxara, where he lay, that she might visit him frequently and in person.

As Mendoza lay on his death-bed Isabella discussed with him the difficult task of appointing his successor; and Mendoza warned her emphatically against selecting him from the nobility. Archbishops of Toledo were the Primates of Spain and, calling attention to the arrogance of his predecessor, Carillo, Mendoza pointed out the danger of appointing a member of the nobility who had a powerful family and riches behind him.

It was at this time that Mendoza suggested that the man best suited to the post was the Queen's confessor, Fray Gonzalo Ximenes de Cisneros.

* * *

Ximenes came from a family which, although in the past it may have been affluent, was, at the time of his birth, in humble circumstances. When he came to fame an illustrious ancestry was provided for him by those who thought it was necessary that he should have it, but it is not possible to say how much truth there is in legends such as that of a maternal ancestor, de la Torre, who was a famous duellist of the tenth century and who eventually restored Madrid to the Castilians.

He was destined for the priesthood at a very early age and accordingly was sent first to Salamanca and then to Alcalá de Henares where he studied canon and civil law.

The family was poor and he had two brothers, John and Bernardín, whose future must be thought of; therefore it was decided that Gonzalo would have a better chance of advancement in Rome; and he accordingly set out for that city.

He stayed there for five years, and nothing is known of his progress there except that he practised as an advocate; and when his father died he decided he should return to his home, but he must have distinguished himself by his service in Rome because, when he left, he was given a Papal Bull (*expectative*) which offered him the first benefice of value to fall vacant; and as his native village of Torrelaguna was in Toledo, he chose Toledo; and it was his choice of Toledo which was to bring him into conflict with Carillo.

It was some years after his return when the Archpriest of Uzeda died and the vacancy occurred; Ximenes immediately took possession of it. Not that it was an important benefice; it was, however, situated in that spot where Ximenes had chosen to live, and with the Papal permission in his pocket he felt himself justified in taking it.

The Sovereigns had always resented Papal interference in their country, and the arrogant Carillo, Archbishop of Toledo, was furious, not only on account of the Pope's high-handed behaviour but because he, Carillo, had promised the benefice to a friend. He therefore demanded that Ximenes abandon the benefice without delay. This Ximenes refused to do, and as a result Carillo descended on him in fury; and since he refused to leave his post he was removed by force and imprisoned in the fortress of Uzeda. There, Carillo believed he would realize the folly of setting himself against the high officials of the Church in Spain and learn to understand that Papal influence could do little to extricate him from the predicament in which he found himself.

Ximenes however remained obstinate and continued to assert that the benefice was his, since it had been granted by Pope Paul II.

The furious Carillo then removed him from Uzeda to Santorcaz, which was a fortress used to imprison recalcitrant members of the Church. Carillo kept him in this prison for six years and then suddenly released him. Ximenes' release is said to have been brought about by the intervention of Carillo's niece, the Countess of Buendia, although why this lady should have interested herself in the priest is not known. However, released he was, and realizing that he could hope for little in Toledo where Carillo held sway he found a vacancy in Sigüenza and became a chaplain there. In this post he had his first stroke of good fortune, for Mendoza was then Bishop of Sigüenza.

Mendoza recognized the unusual intellectual powers of the chaplain immediately—and it was possible that he was interested in a man who had stood up so valiantly to his, Mendoza's, great rival, Carillo; however Mendoza selected Ximenes for special favours and very quickly made him Vicar General of the diocese.

Mendoza shortly afterwards became Archbishop of Seville, and Ximenes carried on in Sigüenza; he became noted not only for his ecclesiastical learning and skill but for his business ability, and when the Count of Cifuentes was taken prisoner by the Moors he asked that Ximenes might be allowed to look after his estates, which were in the diocese.

Ximenes was now on the road to fortune, but stern priest that he was, following devotedly in the footsteps of Torquemada, he had no wish for secular triumphs, and he decided to enter the most austere of all monastic orders, the Observatine Franciscans.

When St. Francis died there had been a division of opinion in the order he had founded. Many of his followers believed that they should adhere strictly to the rules laid down by St. Francis; but many others, finding these too rigorous and seeing little virtue in torturing their bodies and suffering hardship and discomfort, insisted that it was enough to live in their monastery and pray at certain times. Therefore there was a split and the two sects decided to go their own ways. It was with the Observatines, who lived the rigorous life, that Ximenes chose to live.

So he entered the Convent of San Juan de los Reyes at Toledo. This had been newly erected as a result of a vow which Ferdinand and Isabella had made during the siege of Granada; and here Ximenes gave himself fervently to the life of austerity. He abandoned the name he had been given at his birth—Gonzalo—and took that of the founder of the Order, Francisco. He refused to sleep in a bed and chose the floor with a plank for his pillow. He constantly suffered the discomfort of the hair-shirt, and vied with St. Francis himself in the privations to which he subjected his body.

His fame began to spread, and many rich and powerful people invited him to become their confessor or to advise them on their spiritual problems; so finding himself beset on all sides by wordly matters he begged his superiors for permission to go into retreat.

As a result he set out for Our Lady of Castañar a convent which was so called because of the forest of chestnut trees in the midst of which it was situated. Within the convent there was great privacy; but Ximenes yearned for the life of a hermit and, again with the permission of his superiors, he went out into the forest to live in complete solitude. He built himself a hut—rough and so small that it was only big enough to contain his person, and here he lived on bread and water for days at a time and in all weathers. He spent hours on his knees in the forest; and it is said that his fellow Franciscans sometimes came upon him in a trance lying on the ground or in a kneeling posture.

It seems that during the years Ximenes spent in the solitude of the forest he was seeking self-knowledge. He would appear to have been a man of deeper spiritual conscience than Torquemada. Ximenes was aware of the ambition which was strong within him. A man of the Church he wished to be, but he also possessed a great desire for power. It may have been that he found it more difficult to deceive himself than Torquemada had. He had been given the Papal Bull almost certainly at his own request. Why should he have asked for it if he had not hopes of rising in his profession; and why should he have insisted on taking it when Carillo had sought to withhold it? Why had he in the first place gone to Rome? Because there was more chance of advancement there. This all points to ambition. And the reason Ximenes fled from his growing power in Sigüenza could have been because he was discovering within himself an overwhelming love of that power.

He was clearly being pulled in two directions—towards obscurity and sanctity such as he felt he could achieve in the convent of Our Lady of Castañar and towards ambition which he knew could be satisfied because of his undoubted talents. He had come to know Mendoza, Bishop of Sigüenza, soon to be Archbishop of Seville and shortly after that to aspire to the highest place of all, the Archbishopric of Toledo, and he would have seen in his benefactor a man such as he himself might easily become. Might it not have been because of this that he shut himself away in the convent and the lonely hut in the forest so that he might purge himself of all wordly desires and increase that spirituality after which he was straining?

He spent three years of acute austerity and meditation at Our Lady of Castañar, and at the end of that time his superiors decided that there was work he could do for the Order in the Convent of Salzeda, where he was made Superior. In his new role he insisted on continuing in his humility and himself undertook menial tasks such as sweeping the floors. Like Torquemada he was by nature arrogant and possessed of great pride. Unlike Torquemada he was aware of these characteristics and continually sought to repress them.

He was at Salzeda in that fateful year 1492; and with the conquest of Granada Isabella bestowed the title Archbishop of Granada on her confessor, Fray Fernando de Talavera; thus Isabella found herself in need of a confessor, and asked the advice of Mendoza as to

whom she should appoint. Mendoza, at that time Archbishop of
Toledo, and Primate of Spain—a post which he had held since the
death of Carillo ten years before—immediately thought of Ximenes.
Mendoza believed that Ximenes was too brilliant to spend his
life in a convent; there was no need, because he was a Franciscan,
to cut himself off from affairs of state. Mendoza had never allowed
his connection with the Church to shut him off from politics. He
was fully aware that the Queen's confessor had a double part to
play. It had been thus with Talavera and Torquemada before
him. Ximenes was a man who could be trusted to look after
Isabella's secular problems as well as her soul.

As a result of Mendoza's recommendation Isabella sent for
Ximenes and, knowing a great deal about the man through what
she had heard from Mendoza, she did not at first tell him why she
had sent for him. She was impressed by his calm manners; and
his wasted body and pallid looks bore witness to his saintly habits.

She thereupon decided that he should take Talavera's place, and
must have been astonished when Ximenes received the news with
dismay.

His new post meant that his prospects were excellent; as Queen's
confessor he would have every opportunity of gaining influence over
her, but Ximenes had no wish to rise in the world outside his convent
and he made it a condition of accepting the Queen's offer that he
should be able to retire there when his presence was not required at
Court.

*   *   *

It was not long before Isabella was putting the utmost trust in
her confessor.

Two years later Ximenes was made Provincial of the Franciscan
Order in Castile, and this gave him the opportunity he needed to
act against the Conventuals, that branch of the Franciscans whose
members had not followed in the footsteps of their founder but had
sought the less rigorous life.

He continued to live in the utmost austerity and, when he went
about the country visiting the various Franciscan monasteries in
accordance with his new role, he always travelled on foot in abject
humility, begging his way as he went. Often he would be accompanied by Fray Francisco Ruiz who was his faithful friend (according
to some records, his nephew) and whom he subsequently made
Bishop of Avila.

Ximenes made complaints to the Queen about the manner in
which the Conventuals lived. Many of them had large estates

where they enjoyed great splendour and indulged in amorous adventure.

Isabella was sympathetic, and prevailed upon the Pope (Alexander VI) to issue a Bull which would give Ximenes permission to introduce the reforms he sought. Ximenes got to work with that zeal which he was later to use in the service of the Inquisition, and those monks who would not fall into line were expelled from their monasteries.

Shortly after this work was begun Mendoza became very ill and it appeared that the highest post in Spain under the King and Queen was about to fall vacant; for not only did the Archbishopric of Toledo carry with it the post of Primate but also that of the Grand Chancellorship of Castile (thus providing temporal as well as spiritual power).

Greatly impressed by the high moral character of her confessor and having heard him recommended from the dying lips of a man whose judgment she had always trusted, Isabella was inclined to nominate Ximenes for the post.

Ferdinand however had a candidate. This was his illegitimate son Alfonso, whom he had made Archbishop of Saragossa when the boy was six years old.

Isabella was a woman who believed firmly in the sanctity of the family; she was exceedingly jealous where her husband was concerned, and the lusty Ferdinand had given her cause enough for such jealousy. Yet, had she believed the choice of young Alfonso to have been a wise one, she might have granted her husband's request. Mendoza had recommended Ximenes and he had also warned her against choosing one who had powerful family connections.

Isabella could be very firm; and one imagines her conveying to her wayward husband, who not only was unfaithful enough to have a son by another woman two years after his marriage to Isabella, but bold enough to ask his wife for favours for that son, that she and she alone was mistress of Castile and would herself decide all important matters such as this one.

She therefore sent to Alexander VI asking him to confirm her nomination of Ximenes as Archbishop of Toledo, and when the Papal Bull arrived she summoned Ximenes to her presence.

It was Good Friday of the year 1495, and she allowed Ximenes to hear her confession before she handed him the Bull which had arrived from the Vatican.

It was addressed: " To our venerable son, Francisco Ximenes de Cisneros, Archbishop-elect of Toledo."

When Ximenes read those words he was astounded, for it was the first intimation he had had that he was being considered for the honour. One wonders what his true feelings were when he realized what was being offered to him. He must have felt that the devil was showing him the kingdoms of the world. His first reaction was the need to escape—which might be an indication of the greatness of the temptation. He dropped the letter, murmured that there had been a mistake and, before the Queen could speak, rushed out of her presence in a manner which must have bordered on *lèse-majesté*.

Isabella was not displeased. She could assess the worth of this man and she had learned to trust him. As he did not return she sent servants after him to command him to come to her presence.

When Ximenes came back Isabella argued with him, but again and again he refused the honour, declaring himself to be unfit for and unworthy of it.

For six months he held out against his advisers and the Queen's desire, but when another Bull arrived from the Vatican, commanding him to take the appointment which the Church had sanctioned, he gave in.

He was then sixty years old.

On October 11th of that year, 1495, he was consecrated at Tarazona, became Archbishop of Toledo, Chancellor of Castile and Primate of Spain; and from that day for the next twenty-two years he retained his high office and was thus able to escape but rarely from the world of affairs into the seclusion of his hermit's hut.

3

THE POWER OF XIMENES

THE ARDOUR with which Ximenes pursued those defaulters among the Franciscans gave a clue to how much more zealous he would be in the extirpation of heretics.

He had subdued his own flesh to such an extent that he could have little sympathy for the suffering of others. Pain and even life on Earth would seem to him of little account; the sole purpose in being on Earth, in the estimation of such men as he, was to prepare for the life hereafter. Happiness to these men was in itself a sin— laughter, gaiety, pleasure were the handmaidens of the devil, and to enjoy them oneself or to allow them to others savoured of mortal sin. In place of happiness they put self-righteousness, contentment with their own state, their certainty of a place in heaven. Arrogance was the key to their character, and men such as Torquemada and Ximenes contained more of this characteristic than those such as the Borgia Pope himself, who made no secret of their love of worldly pomp and pleasure.

Following the tolerant Mendoza it was natural that Ximenes should quickly become unpopular. The nobles were disconcerted that a man of humble origin should have been chosen to fill the highest position under the Sovereigns; the Conventuals already had their grudge against him; and there must surely have been that suspicion of him amongst countless others which is certain to rest upon one who, by his austere conduct and ultra-pious habits, sets himself apart from his fellow men.

The facts that Ximenes could not be reached through bribes, and did not care whom he offended, did not endear him to the Court. His wasted frame and gaunt figure would have been a continual reminder to others of their own self-indulgence. Saints cannot expect to be popular amongst sinners. And although some of us today, looking back on the picture over almost five hundred years, see quite clearly that Ximenes was no saint, he might have appeared so to those who could not look—as we can—beyond the outward performance. Today many people would define a saint as one who had acquired the gift of self-effacement and self-sacrifice; we are not inclined to attach the label to those who, by submitting their bodies to privation here on Earth, imagine they are preparing it for a state of glorification in a life to come. Their motive is entirely selfish, and selfishness and saintliness cannot go hand in hand. And as to some of us it appears that these medieval saints never seemed to be content with harming their own bodies but continually sought to lead others to their own brand of salvation by torturing them, we question their claim to sainthood.

In addition to the rancour, irritation and envy which Ximenes aroused in so many about him, there was also the resentment of Ferdinand himself who, naturally enough, could not forget that this man had been preferred to his own son; it would have been asking too much of a man like Ferdinand to give wholehearted support to the new Primate. Ximenes may not have helped their relationship by never swerving from his loyalty to the King, for there must have been times when the more human Ferdinand would have welcomed a little resentment of certain slights he himself could not resist offering the new Archbishop of Toledo.

Ximenes was determined to pursue what he believed to be the righteous path, and he made this very clear from the beginning. Mendoza had appointed his brother, Pedro Hurtado de Mendoza, to be Governor of Cazorla. This governorship was one of great prestige and with it went a considerable fortune. As the Cardinal had been responsible for the rise to power of Ximenes it seemed natural that Ximenes should show his gratitude in his behaviour towards the Mendoza family, and naturally enough all expected the new Archbishop to confirm the young Mendoza's appointment.

The Mendoza family and their friends did not hesitate, when Ximenes seemed in no hurry to assure the young Mendoza that his appointment was secure, to remind the Archbishop of all the great Cardinal had done for him. Ximenes was on his mettle, declaring that he neither sought favours nor gave them. As Archbishop of Toledo he considered himself free to act in accordance with his own conscience, and if he were not so, he would have no hesitation in resigning immediately.

There was consternation throughout the Mendoza family. As for Isabella, she looked on with approval at the conduct of her new Archbishop.

However, Ximenes did not mean to withhold the rich post from the brother of his friend, but merely to show that he gave no favours.

Shortly afterwards, he took an opportunity of meeting the young Mendoza at a public function, where he greeted him as Governor of Cazorla. Thus he proclaimed that he had selected the man whom he believed most suited to the post, and that the appointment had nothing to do with friendship.

In a world where nepotism was so flagrantly practised by the heads of the Church, this new attitude was particularly astonishing. It brought consternation to many, but those who profited by it or in spite of it (such as Pedro Hurtado de Mendoza) applauded it, and the young Mendoza became as ardent a supporter of Ximenes as his brother had been.

It is interesting to look at Ximenes' relationship with his own brother. Bernardín had joined the Franciscan Order and Ximenes had made him a steward in his own household. One wonders how the appointment fitted in with Ximenes' rigorous determination to eschew nepotism, for Bernardín, judging from his conduct, was certainly not worthy of the honour bestowed on him.

Ximenes probably felt that he had a duty to this young brother and gave him the post that he might keep his eye on him. Often he lectured the younger man on his lack of virtue, and again and again Bernardín left his brother's household for his monastery, preferring the life there to living perpetually under the eye of austerity. Bernardín's conduct became so tiresome that he imprisoned him for a few months; afterwards however, he took him back to his role of steward.

Bernardín, feigning repentance, felt none and, when Ximenes was ill, he, professing to speak on behalf of his brother, prevailed upon an ecclesiastical court to give a judgment which was unjust. Ximenes, who was very angry, sent for his brother in order to rebuke him; but looking at that wraith of a man lying feebly on his pillows Bernardín lost his head; he might be morally weak, but he was physically strong. He pushed his brother back onto his pillows and, taking one from under him, pressed it down over Ximenes' face. Had not the attention of one of the servants been attracted by the scuffle, Ximenes might have been murdered by his brother.

Ximenes sent Bernardín back to his monastery, gave him a small pension, and never saw him again. His conduct towards his own brother was certainly more lenient than it was towards others.

His unpopularity persisted and it was stronger than ever amongst the Franciscans, who had expected favours to fall into their laps when one of their number was elevated to such high office. Those whom he took into his household found that they were no better off than they had been in their monasteries, for as Ximenes himself accepted no bribes, he certainly would not allow those who served him to do so.

Several of them sent a deputation to the General of their Order in Rome, and as a result the General came to Isabella with a complaint against the new Archbishop. He happened to belong to the Conventuals and was angered by the monastic reforms which Ximenes was trying to bring about.

In Isabella's presence this man ranted against Ximenes to whom he referred as an upstart without noble blood in his veins, a hypocrite whose assumed piety cloaked his ambition. He demanded that the Queen remove him at once from his high office.

Was he mad, demanded Isabella, or did he not realize to whom he was speaking?

The General, furious beyond discretion, cried out that he was fully aware whom he addressed. She was Isabella, Queen of Castile—a mere handful of dust, as he himself was. With that he hurried from the Queen's presence.

The visit of the General did nothing whatever to turn Isabella's loyalty from her new Archbishop. She was determined to support him whenever possible and to protect him from his enemies— even from such a powerful one as her own husband, Ferdinand— for she felt she understood what underlay their enmity towards him.

Now that Ximenes had become so powerful it would seem that his attitude had undergone a change. He had been reluctant to assume that power; now it was his, he was even more reluctant to relinquish any part of it.

When those who were alarmed at his increasing reforms decided to send an emissary to the Pope to complain about him, Ximenes was determined to intercept the messenger. The man chosen for this delicate task was a certain Albornoz, and as soon as Ximenes heard he had set out, the Archbishop sent one of his men to the coast to arrest him. Ximenes' man arrived too late, for Albornoz had already set sail for Italy; however the official also took ship and arrived on the coast of Italy before Albornoz who, on touching Italian soil, was arrested and brought back as a prisoner of state. He was put in prison where he remained for nearly two years— time enough to meditate on the folly of seeking to work against the powerful Archbishop of Toledo.

Ximenes' energetic conduct in the matter showed quite clearly how determined he was to keep his power. No doubt he believed, as Torquemada had believed, that he could use that power to the glory of God. It is impossible for us to decide—as indeed it may have been for Ximenes himself—how much this power was desired for the glorification of the man himself.

Complaints however did reach Alexander in Rome. The new Archbishop brought no dignity to his office, it was said. He walked about in garments patched by himself. The high office had lost prestige since those days when it had been held by that aristocrat, the Cardinal Mendoza.

Alexander, that lover of gaiety and pomp, magnificence and splendour, could well understand the irritation Ximenes must be causing.

According to Alvaro Gomez de Castro, who was born in 1515, (2 years before the death of Ximenes) and who provides the main source of information concerning him, Alexander wrote in the following strain to the Archbishop: " Dear Brother, the Holy and Universal Church, as you are aware, like heavenly Jerusalem, has many and diverse adornments. It is wrong to seek them too vehemently, and it is also wrong to reject them with contempt. Each state has certain conditions which are suited to it, and which please God and are therefore to be praised. All—and especially prelates—should eschew arrogance by too much display, and superstition by too much humility. In both cases the Church may be weakened. We advise and urge you to live according to the rank which you hold; the Holy Father has raised you from humble state to that of Archbishop, and although you should live in your conscience according to the rules of God (and this we applaud) in your external life you should maintain the dignity of your rank."

Such admonition, diplomatically couched as it was, was a command; and, coming from such a quarter, one which Ximenes could not ignore. Thereafter he wore the brilliant garments of his rank, but always under them was the rough vest of the Franciscan, and beneath that the hair shirt. These he mended with his own hands. He set up an elaborate bed in his chamber, but beneath this was the pallet on which he lay each night.

He was determined to live as the hermit had lived in the forest about Our Lady of Castañar; but, in place of the hermit who sought solitude that he might meditate and come to greater spiritual understanding, there was growing the reformer.

*   *   *

When the town of Granada had surrendered to the Christian Armies which were laying siege to it, the last Moorish King, Boabdil (who has been often condemned for his weakness) secured very favourable terms for the Moors. These terms related mainly to religion, and in them it was set out that the people of Granada were to keep their mosques and be allowed to follow their own religion.

These terms had been strictly adhered to for the eight years which followed the surrender of the city, and as a result peace reigned in Granada.

Isabella had no wish to make trouble; Ferdinand was rarely concerned with religion unless such concern could bring material benefits. He was in favour of the Inquisition mainly because it brought large revenues to the exchequer.

At the time of the fall of Granada Isabella had appointed two men to look after the affairs of the city. One of these was a member of the Mendoza family, the Count of Tendilla, and the other was Talavera, who was made Archbishop of Granada.

The Count of Tendilla had been made alcayde and captain-general of Granada on its fall and was in charge of the civil administration; Talavera, who had been Bishop of Avila, had been given the archiepiscopal See of Granada at the same time.

Tendilla, a wise man and one who was not intolerant for his time, was a good choice on the part of Isabella and Ferdinand. Talavera, who was of humble origin and had been a Hieronymite monk in the monastery of Santa Maria del Prado for twenty years before he became the Queen's confessor, was learned and modest, although something of a bigot. But both Tendilla and Talavera, being aware of the conditions made at the time of the surrender, were determined to carry them out for the honour of Spain; and thus during almost eight years since the Moorish capital had come under the domination of Ferdinand and Isabella, harmonious conditions had prevailed within the city.

Ximenes however could not tolerate the thought of the Infidels' following their own religion within the kingdom; and when the Court travelled to Granada, and Ximenes went with it, he determined to convert the Moors to Christianity. Thus a situation was arising very similar to that which had brought disaster to the Jews who had become New Christians. The place of the Jews in the tragedy about to be enacted was to be taken by the Moors.

Since the expulsion of the Jews in 1492, the Inquisition had been busy, and every Jew in Spain was suspect for, by the very nature of the exodus, he must be a *converso*. Torquemada's last instructions, issued in 1498—only a year before the journey of Ximenes to Granada—showed clearly that the Inquisition was in need of reform. Mussulmans were outside its scope since they could not be persecuted for heresy; therefore if the Inquisition needed more victims, here was an untapped source waiting for it. If the Mussulmans were forced to baptism they would be as vulnerable as the converted Jews; they could be smelt out for following old Moorish customs as the Jews had been for following theirs. Quite clearly there must have been many enthusiastic supporters of the Inquisition who were eager to force baptism on the Moors.

When Ximenes came into Granada he questioned Talavera on the state of affairs there and was eager that more should be done to bring about the conversion of the Moors. When the Court moved on to Seville he stayed behind. Isabella and Ferdinand however reminded him of the treaty which had been made before Granada and, knowing the zeal of their Primate, impressed on him the need to give no offence to the Moors.

Talavera had learnt Arabic and had had certain books translated into that language in the hope of bringing about greater under-standing between Mussulmans and Christians. Both he and Mendoza had not spared themselves in trying to convert the Moors to Christianity. But their methods, Ximenes insisted, were not active enough. He himself would set about the reformation of the city.

He began by inviting many of the *alfaquis* to meet him; he pre-sented them with gifts of rich silk and red hats, for the Moors delighted to adorn themselves with fine clothes; he then began to lecture them on the superiority of the Christian religion. The Moors, no doubt delighted with the red hats and bales of silk, wished to please the kind bringer of gifts, and many did as he asked and accepted baptism. Many more came to the meeting place, for they had heard of the rich presents which were being given away; and indeed Ximenes is said to have impoverished himself by the amount of gifts he was obliged to bestow.

There were however many wise men among the Moors who were growing uneasy. They did not forget the existence of the Inquisition. They had arranged that it should not enter Granada; nor could it if the Moors had remained Mussulmans and the Spanish Sovereigns had kept faith. They saw that this was the beginning of trouble. They were not, it was true, being forced to accept baptism; but this fiery Archbishop of Toledo, with his eloquence and gifts, was perhaps not strictly carrying out the spirit of the contract. Day after day men and women were being coerced into accepting the Christian Faith; they did not seem to be aware of what could happen to those who were baptized and then, perhaps innocently, reverted in any way to their own faith.

The shadow of that grim monster, the Inquisition, had been kept so far from Granada, that these people did not realize, as they joyously set their new red hats on their heads, that they were opening the gates of the city to a force, the evil power of which they could not begin to understand until they had experienced it.

One of the Moors, a learned *alfaquis* named Zegri, who was regarded with great respect by his countrymen, came to see Ximenes and was unimpressed by all the gifts and eloquence. Losing patience with him and realizing that if he could convert him he would bring hundreds more to baptism (and if he did not the *alfaquis* might influence his flock against Christianity), Ximenes made him a prisoner and told the official who took him away to take such measures as would bring Zegri out of his ignorance.

Zegri was submitted to rigorous confinement, was made to fast and kept in fetters; and after a period of this treatment he declared that Allah had visited him in a vision and commanded him to become a Christian.

As Ximenes had expected, the example set by Zegri was followed by hundreds of the Moors of Granada, for tension, which had not been there before the coming of Ximenes, had crept into the city.

Ximenes was acting contrary to the Treaty of Granada for his bigotry had come between him and his sense of justice. He could see nothing wrong in breaking a treaty if as a result he could force the citizens of Granada into submission. He determined to destroy the Moslem Faith in Spain. At this time he was as fanatical as Torquemada had ever been concerning the Jews. He knew that the learned members of the Moorish population were deeply disturbed by what was going on; they had built up during their years in Spain a great literature; and literature is naturally feared by all tyrants. Ximenes decided that no writings in Arabic should exist in the city of Granada, and he sent out an order that all books, manuscripts and any forms of Arabic writing were to be brought out and placed in piles in the great squares of the city.

The making of books had been perfected by the Spanish Arabs as by no other people in Europe; they could produce magnificent bindings, and illustrated beautifully. The books were of the greatest value, yet that did not save them.

Ximenes received the books and from them selected three hundred which dealt with medical science, in which the Moors excelled; these he preserved for the university of Alcalá, which he was building, for since they did not deal with religion they were considered to be untainted.

The rest—thousands of them—he caused to be burned, irrespective of their value, and their religious significance to the Moors.

As the smoke rose upwards it would have seemed that here was a

grim warning to the people of Granada. Their first *auto de fé*.
On this occasion it was books which were burned. There would
be other occasions when human flesh would take the place of books.
And the man who had commanded the burning of books and was
presiding over the melancholy scene, was the Inquisitor-General.

Fortunately many people had not given up their books, and
some were smuggled out of the country; but the loss was felt in the
centuries to come and, being deprived of their literature, the Arabs
were robbed of their culture; and this became apparent in the years
ahead.

It was not only Moors who looked on at this distressing scene
with dismay and disgust; men such as Tendilla and Talavera
warned Ximenes that he was going too far; they reminded him of
the treaty, and that those who had been forced to receive baptism
could not be true Christians. Ximenes had an answer to that.
Temporal matters might be served by mildness, he retorted, not so
the saving of souls. Unbelievers should be forced to accept salvation
if they would not accept it willingly; and at such a time when
Mohammedanism was shaken to its roots, he should relentlessly
pursue the course he had taken.

Perhaps he was also thinking of that organization which knew
very well how to deal with those who became converted and relapsed
into the old evil ways. Torquemada had shown the way with the
Jews; Ximenes would show the way with the Moors.

It was not to be expected that the Moors could stand placidly
by and watch with equanimity the destruction of their national
culture; and when Ximenes sent three of his servants into the
Albaycin (that section of the city which was inhabited solely by the
Moorish population) they were received with a sullenness which
was ominous. These men had been assiduous in the service of their
master and had worked with him in his proselytizing. A quarrel
was picked with them and, as a result, two of Ximenes' servants
were assassinated; the other managed to escape.

Now the fury of the Moors was aroused and they were determined
to drive from their city those who had interfered so disastrously
with their peace. The leaders of the insurrection went through the
streets calling all the servants of Allah to take arms. In a very
short time the whole of the Albaycin was ready for action.

An avenging party made its way into the city to that palace
where Ximenes was lodged. The servants of Ximenes were alarmed
for his safety, for they knew how deeply he was abhorred for his
actions, and begged him to escape at once to the Alhambra where
the Count of Tendilla (whose liberal and tolerant rule had made the

Arabs regard him as their friend) could, if any could, save him from
the fury of the mob.

Ximenes however was no coward. His conduct had brought
about this insurrection and he was ready to take the consequences.
Perhaps the hermit of Our Lady of Castañar believed that the
martyr's crown was about to descend upon his head, and welcomed
it. He would see great virtue in his conduct, which had brought
unhappiness to many Mussulmans, for he was undoubtedly possessed
of that blind faith which made him see his own bigotry as virtue
to be rewarded in heaven by his God who, made in his own image,
would be as arrogant a bigot, as indifferent to the suffering of others,
as he was himself.

He would not, he declared, think of his own safety, for so many
of the true faith were putting theirs in danger.

His palace was a strong one, and his guards capable of its defence;
moreover a message had been conveyed to the Count of Tendilla
who made with all haste to succour Ximenes. The sight of the
Count, who had won the trust of the Moors, at the head of a strong
contingent, was enough to send the Moors back to the Albaycin.

However, the Moorish blood was up. They were not going to
submit willingly to further persecution; and although they returned
to their quarters in the city they were still in a mood of rebellion;
their purpose was to drive Ximenes out of their city.

The situation was saved by those two who had the confidence
of the anxious Mussulmans—Tendilla and Talavera—and they, with
great bravery, went into the Albaycin, into the heart of the revolt,
to attempt to make peace. First came Talavera with a few of his
servants, all of them unarmed; his chaplain led the way, carrying the
cross before him.

As the crowds saw these brave men coming among them, they
ceased to shout for vengeance on the Christian meddlers. The
Moors were great respecters of courage, an attribute which they
themselves possessed in no small measure, and as they had never
known injustice from Talavera and had never taken exception to
his persuasions to bring them into the Christian Faith, they were
ready to listen to him.

Following Talavera came Tendilla, riding among them with a
small escort of his soldiers. As he took off his hat and threw it into
the crowd a great cry of pleasure went up, for this was a sign that he
came in peace.

The Moors were ready to listen to these two men whom they
trusted.

Tendilla explained that if they persisted in their revolt they would come into conflict with the Spanish Sovereigns, and they had only to consider the power possessed by Isabella and Ferdinand to realize that they could not possibly stand against them. Let them lay down their arms, let them return peacefully to their work; he would go to the Sovereigns and ask that they might be pardoned for their insurrection; and he felt sure that he would win that pardon. As a sign of his good faith he would leave his own wife and son as hostages in the Albaycin.

To this the Moors agreed, and the insurrection was over.

Some Catholic historians have sought to depict the Moors as untrustworthy barbarians because they did not believe in the Christian story. Yet Tendilla, who knew them very well indeed, could leave his wife and child as hostages. This is merely one incident which points to the integrity of the Moors. It is doubly significant that at the time when Ximenes was so flagrantly breaking the Contract of Granada, Tendilla could trust the Moorish rebels with his wife and son.

There seemed to be one desire among fanatical Christians; this was to force others to believe as they believed. How this aim was to be achieved seemed of little importance to them. This is the essence of the spirit which first established the Inquisition and caused it to flourish.

*   *   *

Ximenes realized that news would very quickly reach Isabella and Ferdinand in Seville of what was happening in Granada, and he was anxious that they should hear his account of the proceedings before they heard any other.

This seems to point to the fact that Ximenes at this stage of his career was very eager indeed to keep the power which had fallen into his hands. He had come a long way from the forest of Our Lady of Castañar. Perhaps he had begun to deceive himself, had begun to argue with the hermit within him: It is my duty to the Faith to remain in power that I may thus bring others to see the glory of God. However, Ximenes certainly seemed eager to keep the good opinion of Isabella and Ferdinand, to which, at the time of his appointment to the Archbishopric of Toledo he had seemed indifferent.

He therefore hastily wrote his account and sent the fleetest of his negro slaves with it to the Court at Seville. Unfortunately for Ximenes his slave lingered on the way. Perhaps certain enemies of Ximenes lured the man to a tavern and there made him drink more than was good for him and his mission. The fact was that the slave

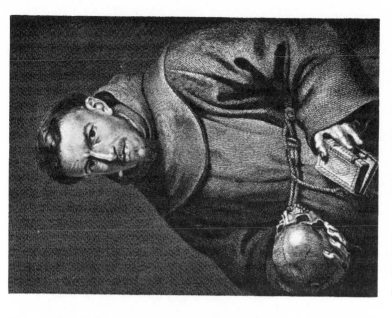

Cardinal Ximenes, Primate of Spain, in the habit of a Franciscan friar (from a print in the British Museum)

Christopher Columbus, Genoese navigator, and discoverer of the New World (from a print in the British Museum)

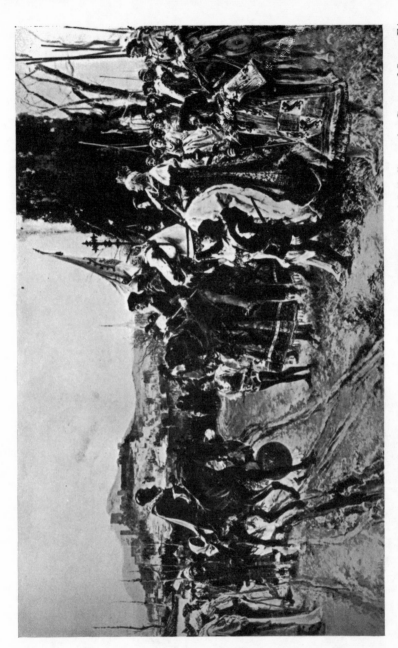

The capitulation of Granada by the last Moorish king, Boabdil, to Ferdinand and Isabella at the Camp of Santa Fé (from a painting by Pradilla)

became intoxicated and, while he lingered in his drunken stupor, others reached Seville with the news.

Isabella was deeply distressed. She had been anxious that the Treaty should be observed for she wanted no trouble in Granada which had lived so peacefully since it had come under her domination. One can imagine Ferdinand's dismay secretly tinged with satisfaction. It is reputed that he was overheard saying triumphantly to the Queen: " Ha, Señora! We are paying dear for your friend, the Archbishop! See what his rash acts are costing us! We have lost, in a matter of hours, that for which we fought over many years! "

How much better, Ferdinand implied, to have given the post to my son, a man of breeding, of royal blood, a man who would know how to carry his power and position; you must now see the folly of giving the highest post in Spain to a man of the people!

Isabella, knowing nothing of the drunken slave, could not understand why there was no news from Ximenes, and she wrote to him sternly.

When Ximenes received Isabella's letter he left at once for Seville.

There must have been great power in Ximenes. Perhaps that indifference to the good opinion of the Sovereigns (for even if it were not entirely genuine, it would seem so) convinced them of his piety.

Yes, he assured them, he and he alone was responsible for the revolt in Granada. Yes, he had acted on his own initiative without asking permission of the Sovereigns.

Perhaps the Sovereigns were reminded of that occasion when Torquemada had come to them; then Ferdinand and Isabella had been inclined to allow the Jews to remain in Spain on the payment of 30,000 ducats, but Torquemada had cried: " Judas Iscariot sold his Master for thirty pieces of silver; you would do so for thirty thousand."

Surely that indifference to royalty, so rarely encountered, must have given the impression of complete honesty. And as with Torquemada, so with Ximenes. The King and Queen were confronted by that countenance, pallid and wasted from fasting—such undeniable evidence of the life of privation; they would have been impressed—particularly Isabella—by the obvious piety of this man. He had acted without their consent, declared Ximenes, because he knew that had he asked for it, it might well have been refused.

This arrogance would seem to them sincerity, and they assured themselves that they were in the presence of a most unusual man. Thus he swayed them by his eloquence, his zeal for the faith and his seeming indifference to worldly benefits; and when he saw that the Sovereigns had become so impressed by his argument that they had ceased to blame him, he began to advise them as to the punishment which should be meted out to the Moors.

They had been guilty of treason but the Sovereigns must show mercy; let them offer the Moors baptism or exile. This was the way to create an all-Catholic Spain.

*   *   *

As a result of the insurrection, many of the Moors left Spain, and many more accepted baptism. Approximately 50,000 became " Christians " at this time. They were known as *Moriscos*.

Talavera wished to have the Bible translated into Arabic that the new converts might understand the Faith into which they had been forced. Ximenes was against this; and how typical is this reasoning of him and his kind. No, said Ximenes, the Gospels were not to be given to the ignorant. The Bible should remain a mystery to them; they would have more respect for what they did not understand!

The revolt in Granada had far-reaching effects.

In the Alpujarras, that range of mountains which runs to the sea between Granada and Almería, there were many Moorish villages; the people who inhabited them lived a less civilized life than those who inhabited the towns, and were wild by nature.

News of what had happened in Granada reached them; they understood that many of their race had been forced to leave the homes which had been theirs for centuries and that many more had been forced to baptism. They anticipated that those methods of coercion, which had brought about the existing state of affairs in Granada, would soon be applied to the villages of the Alpujarras.

They therefore gathered together an army and sought to defend themselves against Christian intrusion. They tried to show their determination by attacking Christian towns.

Tendilla decided that this rebellion must be quashed before it was allowed to grow. Fortunately for him there was in Granada at that time one of the most famous of Spanish soldiers, Gonsalvo de Cordova, who was to be known as the " Great Captain ", and into this man's hands Tendilla put the task of defeating the mountain dwellers.

Gonsalvo de Cordova first turned his attention to the fortified town of Huejar; this presented great difficulty, for the Moors had dug trenches in the fields which surrounded it and, as Gonsalvo's cavalry advanced, they sank into them while the Moors from the walls of the city attacked. However, there can be no doubt of Gonsalvo's military genius, and in spite of this difficult start he had soon captured Huejar where little mercy was shown. The majority of the men were slain by the sword while the women and children were taken into slavery.

The wild men of the mountains were far from subdued by the terrible fate of Huejar. Ferdinand himself took the field against them and after some difficulty captured the town of Lanjaron, approaching it by surprise after traversing the dangerous mountains. Its inhabitants were submitted to the same treatment as those of Huejar.

After the capture of this town the Moors sued for peace, which Ferdinand granted for the surrender of their arms with certain fortresses and a payment of fifty thousand ducats. Missionaries were immediately sent into the Alpujarras villages that the conversions to Christianity might go on. Many of these people realized that there was no choice left to them and, following the example of the Moors of Granada, they submitted to baptism.

There were however some Moors who were determined to fight for their faith, and there was a further insurrection in the mountains known as the Sierra Vermeja (the Red Sierra, so called on account of the colour of the rocks) which lie between Ronda and Gibraltar. Here Alonso de Aguilar, the elder brother of Gonsalvo de Cordova, the Great Captain, went into action with his son Don Pedro de Cordova.

This family were noted for their bravery and military skill, but in this battle Don Pedro was wounded (and was carried protesting from the battlefield on his father's orders) while Alonso himself lost his life in personal conflict with the great Arab fighter, Feri de Ben Estepar.

Here also fell Francisco Ramirez, Ferdinand's great engineer whose use of gunpowder had been so effective before Granada.

The Christians were defeated, and Ferdinand led a strong body of men from Ronda, determined to avenge the fallen. The Moors however realized that their victory could only be a local one and that, ranged against them, was the whole might of Spain. They sued for peace.

Ferdinand, furious as he was by the defeat his men had suffered, passionately called out for vengeance; but Ferdinand was a shrewd ruler; he realized that further fighting could only result in loss on his side as well as that of his enemies, and he decided to grant the peace for which the Moors were asking.

He gave the Moors the now familiar choice. They could be

baptized into the Christian Faith or leave the country. He himself would provide the transport they needed at the price of ten doblas of gold for each person.

Some Moors emigrated; many stayed behind and were baptized. It must have been very difficult for these people. For eight centuries Spain had been their home, and now it could be theirs no longer, unless they professed to give up the beliefs in which they and their ancestors had been brought up, and accept a Faith which was alien to them.

It is said that many more would have left the country if they could have found the money to pay for their passage.

In the year 1502, Isabella and Ferdinand issued a *pragmática* in which they declared that it was the duty of all Castilians to drive the enemies of the Faith from the land; and all Moors, who had not received baptism and who lived in the kingdoms of Castile and Léon, must leave the country; no male over the age of fourteen must stay, nor must females over the age of twelve; they were given until April to leave (the *pragmática* was published in February); they would be allowed to sell their property but, as in the case of the Jews, they might not take gold or silver out of the country!

It was apparent that the only course open to many thousands was baptism.

It was ten years since Granada had capitulated, and ten years since the signing of the treaty. Ximenes' action, in first of all so tormenting the Moors that they revolted, and then advising the breaking of the treaty as a punishment for the revolt, brings no credit to him. His conduct in this affair shows him to be as devoid of Christian charity as his prototype, Tomás de Torquemada; it was the existence of men such as these that made it possible for the Inquisition to flourish in Spain.

The *Moriscos* had appeared. Baptized as Christians, they could no longer keep aloof from the Inquisition. Since its establishment in Castile under the instructions of Torquemada it had dealt severely with the *Marranos*; now here was a fresh source of victims hitherto untapped; the Inquisition was eagerly awaiting the *Moriscos*.

4

DEZA AND LUCERO, INQUISITORS

WHEN TORQUEMADA died, his place as Inquisitor-General was taken by Diego de Deza. Deza was born at Toro and like Ximenes' his origins were humble. When he was young he became a Dominican and soon called attention to himself by the devout life he led and his aptitude for learning. His superiors brought him to the notice of Ferdinand and Isabella, and he was called to the Court where he was made tutor to the Infante Juan.

This naturally gave him great influence, and he eventually became Archbishop of Seville. He must have been a man of extraordinary talents to have risen so far from lowly beginnings; and in addition to other honours, Ferdinand appointed him his confessor, and the Sovereigns placed great trust in him.

It was Deza who, at the time when Columbus was seeking the help of the Sovereigns in his enterprise, threw in the weight of his influence with that of Cardinal Mendoza on the side of the adventurer, and was certainly in some part responsible for the favours shown to Columbus.

It was a pity that a man of such undoubted talents should have dissipated them in the service of the Inquisition; for, following on Torquemada, Deza undoubtedly felt that he must emulate the master, and during his term of office the cruelties of the Inquisition increased.

The bigotry of Deza is displayed in his dealings with the scholar, Elio Antonio de Nebrija.

Isabella had long realized the importance of culture to her people and she had lifted the *alcavala* (a tax of ten per cent) on all books coming into the country. Torquemada in 1490 burned hundreds of Jewish books and later, at an *auto de fé* in Salamanca, as many as six thousand Jewish volumes were sent up in flames. Ximenes acted similarly, as already mentioned, with Arabic volumes in Granada.

Anyone discovering heresy in books was in duty bound to take them, within a week of its discovery, to his bishop or the inquisitor for his district.   It was stated that there was no penalty for failing to deliver such a book into the hands of authority (and here again was one of the inquisitorial quibbles), although any who failéd to do so laid themselves open to violent suspicion of harbouring heretical tendencies; and such must almost certainly render examination by the Inquisitors necessary.   Anyone who wrote a book tainted with heresy was, naturally, a self-confessed heretic.   Any who possessed such a book was merely a suspect.

By the year 1502, Isabella and Ferdinand began to realize the enormous power of literature, and they decreed that no book should be printed in Spain or imported into that country without a licence; and before it received this it should be submitted to a thorough examination.   In Ciudad Real and Valladolid the president judges of the royal courts were appointed censors; in almost every other town this duty fell to archbishops and bishops.   Booksellers and printers were asked to look after the cost of these operations!   If any printer or bookseller attempted to circulate a book which had not passed through the censorship, that book was confiscated and burned publicly, while the bookseller and printer concerned were no longer allowed to carry on in their business.

This was a civic law and outside the jurisdiction of the Inquisition; but the Inquisitors, greedy for power, and feeling that the censorship of books came within the range of their duties, found means of making this matter one of their concerns, for it was a fact that secular officers were less zealous in such duties than were the men of the Church.

It was thus that Deza came into conflict with Elio Antonio de Nebrija.

Ximenes was preparing his Complutensian Polyglot Bible, a work which took fifteen years to complete.   It was written in four languages (Latin, Greek, Hebrew and Aramaic) and Ximenes had engaged several collaborators to help him with the work, one of whom was the scholar, Elio Antonio de Nebrija, who, in the course of his labours, corrected certain errors in the Vulgate, that Latin version of the Bible which was, two hundred years after its completion, generally accepted in the Western Christian Church.

Deza saw a reason here to attack Nebrija whom he said was guilty of sacrilege because he dared to tamper with the Scriptures. He had, declared Deza, dared to presume that the rules of grammar were more important than the orthodox faith.

" What slavery is this! " wrote Nebrija.   " What iniquitous domination which prevents, by violence, a man from speaking as he feels, even though he does not interfere in the least with religion. It is not permitted to write even if one is alone within four walls. It is not permitted to examine and investigate for the discovery of truth, if a man allows a word to escape him."

(Rule & Bibliotheca Hispanica A., art. Antonius).

Ximenes, powerful Archbishop of Toledo that he was, could not entirely save his collaborator from the fiery Deza; and Nebrija, known as one of the greatest of Spanish scholars was forced to retire from the work, although Ximenes was able to save him from greater calamity; and instead of this learned man's being wakened by night with the sound of the *alguazils* at his doorstep and dragged into the gloomy prisons of the Inquisition, he was merely required to abandon that work for which he possessed a rare skill very difficult to replace.

Ximenes must have been deeply frustrated. His Polyglot Bible, like the university of Alcalá which he founded, was a very dear project; but although he could save his friend from more violent persecution he could not bring him out of exile, where he remained until Deza was replaced in his office as Inquisitor-General by Ximenes himself. When this occurred the scholar was brought out of retirement and once more set to work on the Bible.

Ximenes is said to have begged his collaborators to lose no time in this great work, for if he were to die they would lose their patron; and if any of them died he would be made desolate, for he valued their work more than all the riches and honours the world could bestow on him.

This incident gives a strong clue to the character of Diego de Deza, the man who replaced Torquemada at the head of the Inquisition.

One of Deza's first actions on being invested with the office of Inquisitor-General was directed against certain Jews who, homesick for the country in which they and their ancestors had lived, returned after the great exodus of 1492. The Jews pretended to be new-comers to the country and when they were arrested declared that their great desire was to embrace the Christian Faith.

The new Inquisitor-General took stern action against them and an Edict was issued which declared that all Jews and Jewesses who entered Spain should be punished by death, and that their property should pass to the state.

There must be no failure to carry out the strict laws against them; only those Jews who, before entering the country had already made known their desire to return and be converted and who went before a notary with witnesses and publicly became Christians, would be allowed to stay. If any came into the country and failed to carry out these instructions they must immediately suffer confiscation of their property and death.

In spite of all the suffering which members of their race had endured, some Jews did return to Spain, notwithstanding the fact that by becoming New Christians they placed themselves within the grasp of the Inquisition.

In the year 1500 Deza produced a Constitution in seven articles. These were:

1. There should be examination of every town and village in which the Inquisition had not yet been set up.

2. All persons should be reminded yet again in no uncertain terms of their duty to pass on to the authorities any information they might discover concerning the suspicious conduct of family, friends and acquaintances.

3. There should be a search for books, and all persons mentioned in such a way as to place them under suspicion should be arrested.

4. Those who committed blasphemy and such minor sins should not be brought before the Inquisition, for these were not worthy of its attention which should be directed with greater force against heretics.

5. When a person had been vindicated it should be necessary for two witnesses to swear responsibility for the vindicated person's orthodoxy.

6. Those who had been vehemently suspected, and abjured, should swear solemnly to have no more communication with heretics but to inform against them.

7. Those who abjured after conviction of heresy should also swear to have no more intercourse with heretics and to inform against them.

Although there was nothing very new in these seven articles this was a sign that Diego de Deza intended to get to work with vigour and there followed Deza's election a reign of terror which exceeded even that endured under Torquemada; and this reached its zenith in Cordova where the most venomously cruel of Inquisitors, Lucero, was established.

Diego Rodríguez Lucero was given the name of Tenebrero—agent of darkness—and he soon had the whole of Cordova reduced to a state of terror.

He was a man who was already in high favour with the Sovereigns who had bestowed upon him a canonry in Cadiz; and the number of heretics whom he brought to judgment was so large that both Isabella and Ferdinand complimented him upon this. They were grateful for the large sums which were flowing into the treasury through the work of this man.

Lucero had no compunction in the methods he used. Torture was liberally applied to the prisoners for the sole purpose of incriminating more and more people. Lucero's great desire was to have the prisons of Cordova overflowing, while the possessions of these unfortunate people were taken from them to swell the treasury of the Inquisition and State and win for the Inquisitor of Cordova the thanks of his grateful Sovereigns.

A letter in the Archivo de Simancas tells how two men, Alfonso Fernández Herrero and Fernando de Cordova escaped from the purge and sought refuge in Portugal. Without asking royal permission to do so, Lucero immediately despatched *alguazils* to bring them back.

This was against international law and Emanuel was naturally furious at the high-handed conduct of the Inquisitor. He refused to relinquish the two men who had sought refuge in his country unless he was given a detailed account of their sins.

Lucero, assured of his Sovereigns' support, immediately appealed to them with the result that Emanuel was asked out of the affection he bore Isabella and Ferdinand to give up the two wanted men. He was gently reminded that he must lay no impediment in the path of the Holy Office and that by doing so he was working against the glory of God.

The people of Cordova were naturally deeply disturbed to have such a man in such a position in their city. And not only were the ordinary citizens disturbed; the authorities were also growing uneasy. There is an account of a clash between the mayor of Cordova and Lucero. The mayor showed his contempt for Lucero and the Inquisition in a public square of the town during an auction of confiscated property. The mayor was hastily removed and put into prison. The sentence which was passed on him was a harsh one. He was dismissed from his office for life and was not to fulfil any other public position. He was to be banished from Cordova, which he must prepare to leave in a week.

Thus Lucero showed the people of Cordova what happened to those who sought to flout him.

Complimented by the Sovereigns on his zeal, Lucero became more and more zealous. More arrests were made without reason and many noblemen and even good churchmen—if they happened to be Old Christians—were hustled into jail. The machines of torture were working constantly. Lucero was eager to incriminate as many people of wealth as possible; no one knew in what direction the next attack would be made. There were stories of plots to establish Judaism in Cordova and overthrow the Catholic Church throughout the land. No man, woman or child in the city of Cordova was safe.

This was a state of affairs which could not be tolerated.

* * *

Meanwhile events of historical importance had been taking place in Spain.

Isabella was drawing very near to the end of her life. The calamitous misfortunes of her family had given her great cause for anxiety; and these misfortunes undoubtedly hastened her end.

The Infante Juan was dead, and he died without giving Spain an heir; her beloved daughter Isabella, Queen of Portugal, had quickly followed him; but perhaps the greatest misfortune of all was the growing insanity of her daughter Juana, who was now heir to the throne of Castile.

Juana's strange conduct was causing comment wherever she went; and this was worsened by the fact that her husband known as Philip the Handsome, was notoriously unfaithful to Juana who doted on him and was given to frantic displays of jealousy.

Accounts of these outbursts must have brought humiliation to Isabella; particularly as, after one of them, Philip had declared his intention of never again having intercourse with his wife. This was an occasion when the fickle Philip became enamoured of one of Juana's ladies and, according to his custom, made no secret of his preference. This particular young woman was noted for her beautiful golden hair which Philip particularly admired.

Juana, driven into one of her mad rages by her jealousy, had the woman brought to her, bound her hand and foot and caused her hair to be sheared.

When Philip saw what had happened he announced his intention to cut himself off from his wife.

The effect of such scandal on the pious Isabella can well be imagined. It was fortunate however that Philip and Juana already had two sons, both born before she showed signs of insanity. One of these was Charles, born on 24th February, 1500, and to achieve great fame as the Emperor Charles V of Austria, and I of Spain; and the other was Ferdinand, born on the 10th March in 1503.

Those last months of Isabella's life must have been indeed uneasy when she contemplated the crown which she must leave behind, and thought of her ambitious husband and son-in-law, her grandsons—one in his cradle, the other only just out of it—and her poor mad daughter Juana the heiress of Castile.

In the midst of all this trouble Ferdinand caught a fever and Isabella was very anxious on her husband's behalf. This anxiety, coupled with her melancholy over her daughter Juana, weakened Isabella considerably and she became very depressed over Ferdinand's illness and refused to believe the doctors when they assured her that the illness was far from fatal and that Ferdinand would recover.

Ferdinand did recover, but Isabella herself had contracted the fever and, in her case, there was less resilience to fight against it.

Her condition grew weaker and it became apparent to all about the Court—including Isabella herself—that she was near to death.

She was always conscious of her duties and received ambassadors whilst being unable to rise from her bed; and she continued to conduct state business, sick as she was.

In October of that year 1504 she began to prepare that elaborate and revealing document: her will.

In this she asked that her body be taken to the Franciscan monastery of Santa Isabella in the Alhambra and there buried with the utmost simplicity; but should Ferdinand on his death prefer a more elaborate tomb in a different spot, then her body should be taken from its humble resting place and laid beside that of her husband. This was to be a sign that in life they had been united, and in death were not divided.

She then went on to donate certain sums to charity and to arrange that all her debts should be discharged within a year; she stressed to her successors the importance of maintaining the integrity of the kingdom and retaining control of Gibraltar.

The crown of Castile she settled on her daughter Juana—as Queen Proprietor—and on Juana's husband, Archduke Philip, together with much advice.

She then wrote of the government of the realm in the absence of Juana or at such other times as she should be incapable of ruling. She therefore appointed her husband Ferdinand as Regent until the time when her grandson Charles should be of an age to rule.

There were other bequests, and the two main executors were Ferdinand and Ximenes.

On the 26th of November 1504, only three days after the execution of her will, she died.

* * *

Ferdinand resigned the crown of Castile and in the great square at Toledo the new rulers were proclaimed. Juana and Philip were at this time in Flanders and, in accordance with the terms of Isabella's will, Ferdinand took up the regency.

The Castilians however were not pleased to see an Aragonese ruling over them even as Regent. They had accepted Ferdinand during the life of Isabella because they had looked upon him merely as the husband of their Queen; it was a different matter when he was ruling without her. Certain lords, among them Juan Pacheco, Marquis of Villena, and the Duke of Najara, corresponded with Archduke Philip and persuaded him to demand complete supremacy in Castile and that Ferdinand should retire to Aragon.

Ferdinand's reply to this was a contemptuous refusal and a demand to know how Philip thought he could govern a people like the Spaniards when he knew so little of them. Ferdinand did however advise him that it would be advantageous if he and Juana came to Castile to show themselves to the people.

Meanwhile Ferdinand's enemies grew in number. Philip, it was understood, was generous, and Ferdinand's parsimonious ways had been long deplored.

Juana, who was being treated badly by her husband, wrote a letter in which she stated her belief that her father should be allowed to continue to rule Castile. The secretary to whom Juana had entrusted this letter was betrayed and sent to a dungeon. Philip, furious with his wife, put her under guard and kept her a prisoner in conditions which increased her wildness.

To add to his troubles Ferdinand discovered that Philip, with the help of his father, the Emperor Maximilian, was attempting to win the confidence of Gonsalvo de Cordova, the great Captain who was in command of Naples, with a view to annexing Naples as a dependency of Castile. Ferdinand had always been shrewd and he now saw that the only way of combating the claims of Philip and Maximilian was to win the French to his side; Louis XII, who had his eyes on Naples, had been delighted by the conflict between Ferdinand and his son-in-law; he was however a little disturbed to contemplate the enormous inheritance which would eventually come to Philip. It seemed that not only would Castile but the whole of Spain eventually fall into his hands, with Austria, Flanders and Burgundy, in addition to those rich lands which, since the discovery of America, had become appendages of Spain.

Ferdinand was fully aware of this, and he decided to take that step which never failed to bring two countries closer together. It was but a short time since the death of Isabella, but Ferdinand was ready to contemplate a French marriage.

Accordingly it was decided that he should marry Germaine de Foix, who was the daughter of a sister of Louis XII; her grandmother was that Leonora who had poisoned her sister Blanche for the throne of Navarre (see *The Rise of the Spanish Inquisition*).

To Germaine Louis resigned his claims to Naples, and it was part of her dowry that these should be secured to her and her heirs. A treaty of alliance and commerce was made between the two sovereigns, and Ferdinand was to pay one million gold ducats in ten yearly instalments to defray the expenses Louis had incurred during the Neapolitan war. (Prescott's *History of the Reign of Ferdinand and Isabella*). Ferdinand came badly out of the agreement; he must have missed the sound good sense of Isabella and he was no doubt disconcerted to feel that he must seek help from France against his own son-in-law.

Now that Ferdinand had a powerful ally in his father-in-law, Philip appeared to be a little more accommodating. In the Concord of Salamanca, which was signed on November 24th, 1505, it was agreed that Castile should be governed in the names of Ferdinand, Philip and Juana, but that Ferdinand should have one half of the revenues.

Ferdinand could congratulate himself that his new alliance had given Philip reason to pause and consider before continuing his high-handed policy; but on the 8th January, 1506, Philip left Zealand intending to visit Spain.

Storm drove him to England where he and Juana were received in great friendliness by Henry VII. They were taken to Windsor where they were entertained for three months. They returned to Spain on the 28th April, only six weeks after the marriage of Ferdinand and Germaine had taken place.

Arriving in Spain Philip had with him three thousand German soldiers; and a larger number of Spaniards hastened to place themselves under his command. Philip then announced that he was no longer agreeable to the Concord of Salamanca and was determined that he and his wife alone should rule Castile.

Ferdinand was now to realize to the full the power which he had enjoyed through Isabella. The French marriage had not endeared him even to those who supported his claims; and the diplomatic skill of Ximenes could gain nothing for Ferdinand's cause.

At length it was decided that Ferdinand and Philip should meet in a field near Puebla de Senabria on the boundary of Leon and Galicia.

Philip came surrounded by his soldiers, archers and light cavalry, making a glittering display. Ferdinand came attended only by two hundred gentlemen who were weaponless.

The two kings dismounted and went to a house attended only by their most trusted advisers: Philip by Juan Manual and Ferdinand by Ximenes. Philip knew how strong his position was; and Ferdinand was forced to agree that Juana and Philip should be the sole sovereigns of Castile; he also agreed that his daughter was incapable of ruling, and made a declaration that he would help Philip in every way in the government of Castile, although he stated that he made these concessions under protest and solely to prevent civil war; he would continue to consider his claims to the regency valid and he would, as soon as he was in a position to do so, seek to bring Juana from the captivity which her husband had imposed upon her.

Ferdinand returned to Aragon, and Philip went to Valladolid to receive the homage due to him as ruler of Castile. It was necessary to bring Juana from her captivity that she might appear with him; and this he did, though much against his will. Juana accompanied him dressed in garments of mourning; and at Valladolid they received the oath of allegiance to Juana as Queen, to Philip as her consort, and to their elder son, young Charles, who was recognized as Juana's heir.

Philip now took control; all the high places at his Court went to the Flemish; if the people had had cause to complain of Ferdinand's parsimonious ways they now had greater cause to regret Philip's extravagance.

Ximenes, in his position as Primate of Spain, remonstrated with Philip, who at this stage dared show nothing but respect for this important man, but quite clearly he was seeking ways of escaping from his influence.

Meanwhile the people were disturbed not only by Philips' extravagance and his lechery, but by the humiliating position into which he had forced his wife who was the true Queen of Castile.

It was at this time that events in Cordova, which was suffering from the Inquisitor Lucero, came to a head.

*　　*　　*

Many members of the prominent families of Cordova had been arrested and were imprisoned in the dungeons of the Inquisition; others had been brought before the tribunal for listening to the preacher Membreque, and over one hundred of them were burned alive.

Lucero was even worse than his predecessor, Doctor Guiral, Dean of Guadix, who had been sent from Cordova to Avila in 1499. He had been suspected of nefarious practices and at length the

Inquisitor-General had had to take action against him. His case—as that of Lucero—is very interesting because it gives an indication of what was happening behind the carefully guarded walls of the Inquisition, and consequently a light is shone into places which Inquisitors had been at such pains to keep in darkness.

It was discovered that Guiral had made as much as 150,000 *maravedis* by selling " exemptions " to victims. This meant that on payment of a certain sum, arranged between them, to the dishonest Inquisitor, a man or woman who had been sentenced to wear the *sanbenito*, was excused from doing so. Guiral had not kept his hands off confiscated property, and in this way, among other treasures he was the possessor of ninety-three very valuable pearls. He imposed fines on all whom he accused of withholding confiscated property and was not too proud to collect a few ducats from his humblest servants. He entered into negotiations with *Conversos* accepting large sums in exchange for allowing them to evade confiscation of the whole of their property. This business man was eventually arrested and brought to trial (Archivo de Simancas). The result of his trial is not known, but his misdeeds could not have been taken very seriously to heart because when Lucero took his place he behaved with equal dishonesty and much more cruelty.

Perhaps he was allowed to continue unmolested because although he looked after his own interests he was not blind to those of his masters, and during his term of office treasure flowed into the coffers of the Inquisition and the State.

One of his accomplices—very wisely chosen by Lucero—was Juan Róiz de Calcena, who, for inquisitorial purposes, was Ferdinand's secretary. He took his cut of the profits and made sure that excellent accounts of Inquisitor Lucero of Cordova reached the ears of Ferdinand.

In 1507 the Captain Gonzalo de Avora wrote a letter to the royal secretary Almazan in which he discusses the methods of the Inquisition. He says that these methods were such that they defamed the kingdom and destroyed without justice a great part of it, slaying and robbing, violating maidens and wives—and all this brought great dishonour to the Christian religion (Lea).

However, Ferdinand stood firmly behind Lucero because Lucero's accomplice was Calcena, who was always at hand to give Ferdinand a good account of his friend.

Lucero had in one of his prisons a man named Diego de Algiciras. Lucero only had to imply that he wanted evidence against such and such a *converso* and Diego de Algiciras would willingly give what was asked. So useful was this man that he was often borrowed by the tribunal of Jaen to help them out when they needed to bring about arrests of the wealthy.

Torture was, of course, freely applied to obtain the required evidence, but it was useful to have a man on hand, eager and willing to supply it, and for five years Lucero made use of this man's services.   Many unsavoury details came to light at this time, such as imprisoning a young girl of fifteen, stripping her and whipping her until she was ready to inform against her mother.   There is no doubt that with such men as Lucero at its head the affairs of the Inquisition were at their most despicable.

The apprehensive people of Cordova appealed to Deza to make an enquiry into Lucero's methods of conducting the Inquisition, but Deza was evasive.   The people realized that it was useless to try to put their case before Ferdinand because Calcena would either not allow any such appeal to reach him or would poison his mind in advance against those who complained.   But there were Philip and Juana who might be more ready to listen.   Philip was antagonistic towards the Inquisition; he had accepted bribes from the *Conversos* and the hopes of the people of Cordova were high.   It seemed that he was prepared to give them justice, in which case there would certainly be an enquiry into the behaviour of Lucero.

Lucero, perhaps to make a diversion, then produced allegations against Talavera, Isabella's favourite whom she had made Archbishop of Granada.   Lucero would not have dared do this while Isabella lived; but now he reminded the people that Talavera had a Jewish taint in his blood.

Talavera had a great reputation for sanctity; he had given generously to charity during his life and had few possessions of his own; he was beloved by the people, particularly the Moors of Granada who had learned to trust him.

It seemed incredible that such a pious man could have been accused of Judaizing; but naturally Lucero had his own methods of finding witnesses.   He had one—a Jewish woman who had declared she was a prophetess—who had already suffered acutely under torture and it was only necessary to threaten her with more unless she supplied the required evidence against Talavera for her to say exactly what was required.   Talavera's nephew, his nieces, his sisters and his servants were all arrested, but before Talavera himself could be taken up it was necessary to get permission from the Pope to do so; this was sent for.

Before it arrived, Juana and Philip had returned to Spain, and the hopes of the *Conversos* were raised once more.   Ferdinand left for Naples and Philip, having locked up his wife on account of her

Philip I of Castile, husband of Juana, and son-in-law of Ferdinand and Isabella

The insane Juana of Castile, with the coffin containing the embalmed body of her husband (from a painting by Pradilla)

insanity, set about ruling the land. So it now seemed possible to bring Lucero to justice. An enquiry was to be made and the wicked and wily Inquisitor, terrified of what might come to light, hastily arranged that all his prisoners should immediately be hustled to an *auto de fé* where they should perish at the stake. Orders from Philip came in time to prevent this.

Unfortunately for the suffering people of Spain at this juncture Philip was taken suddenly ill; it is said that he caught cold after playing a strenuous ball game; he developed a fever, and six days after he first became ill he died.

There are various versions of the cause of his death. His physicians are blamed for being unskilful and neglecting to bleed him in time. The many draughts of cold water which he is said to have drunk when he was overheated from his game are blamed. There were, of course, the usual suggestions that he was poisoned; and according to Bergenroth it was generally accepted at the time that this was the true cause of his death and that Ferdinand's envoy to Philip was the murderer. Ferdinand would certainly have had a motive for removing his troublesome son-in-law.

One of the physicians, who was present at the death, Dr. Parra, wrote to Ferdinand that after playing this violent ball game for several hours Philip had cooled himself off too suddenly and thus caught a chill. This was followed by fever and the spitting of blood. Cupping glasses and purgatives were administered, and when he was bled the blood was " thick and bad ". Philip grew very weak, found it difficult to speak, and then fell into unconsciousness. He was afflicted with sweating which brought out black spots on his body.

Prescott takes the view that, since Parra wrote such a letter to Ferdinand, and in view of the symptoms he described, this points to a natural death.

Yet Philip was a healthy twenty-eight, and it seems strange that a man so young should have died merely because he became overheated in a ball game and drank cold water afterwards, particularly when there were those who would find the world so much more tolerable without him.

With the death of Philip, Deza, the Inquisitor-General, immediately stepped back into office and restored Lucero to his.

The latter determined to make up for lost time by letting loose his wrath on all those who had endeavoured to put an end to his career, and the terror in Cordova was intensified. His accusations were more reckless than ever; the prisons were again full to overflowing.

But such a state of affairs could not continue. Two of the nobles of the city, the Marquis of Priego and the Count of Cabra, were ready to help the people to revolt. Priego, was particularly eager because he knew that Lucero was about to arrest him. Complaints were laid before Padre Fray Francisco de Cuesta of the Convent of La Merced who declared that Lucero was guilty and should be arrested and his property should be confiscated.

The people assembled to make the arrest. They forced their way into the alcázar which was the headquarters of the Inquisition, set the prisoners free, but looked in vain for Lucero who, having heard that they were on the way, had taken refuge in flight.

Deza, however, immediately gave an order that all those who had revolted in Cordova against the rule of Lucero should be prosecuted, and sent his nephew Pedro Juárez de Deza to carry out this order.

Lucero resumed full command and those prisoners who had been freed—including Talavera and his family—were once more arrested.

As for Talavera, by the time the testimony against him was admitted to be false, he had suffered so much from the rigours of imprisonment and anxieties on account of his family, that he did not live to enjoy his freedom.

*   *   *

Ferdinand was now ruling as Regent—his daughter being too unstable to wear the crown, and his grandson Charles too young—and with Ximenes at his elbow, he was forced to the decision that he must take action against the demoniacal inquisitors who seemed to want to outdo Torquemada in their cruelty.

There are some who hint that Ximenes had his eyes on Deza's position, and this may have been so since he became Inquisitor-General after Deza vacated the office, but Ximenes was a just man who would deplore the shame men like Deza and Lucero were bringing to the Holy Office.

Deza was asked to resign; but Lucero could not be allowed to escape so gracefully. His sins had been too flagrant.

He was to stand for trial, accused of forcing people to give false testimony against others. Julius II appointed an apostolic judge to try the case and on October 17th, 1507, it was decreed that Lucero should be put into prison.

Nothing however was done; and Peter Martyr, who was recording at the time and on whom we rely for this information, declares that the Supreme Council were in league with Lucero, and that the usual examination of documents and witnesses, calculated to last for a very long time, took place.

At length Lucero was arrested and taken in chains to Burgos. There Ximenes gathered together a committee headed by himself to try the case.

Ximenes, for all his harshness, was determined to be just, and hundreds of those who had been imprisoned by Lucero were set free, for it was proved that many of the accusations brought against them were groundless. Lucero was found guilty of injustice and harshness, but he was not punished on account of the thousands whom he had condemned to the stake and who had suffered the fiery death at his orders. He was merely required to retire from his post and live at Almería where he continued with his duties as *maestrescuela*, a teacher of the clergy. (Rule).

Llorente states that during Deza's term of office 2,592 people were burned alive, 896 burnt in effigy, and 34,952 were imprisoned and lost all their wordly goods.

These figures can only be approximate; and it is possible that a proportion of the 2,592 were strangled as the fires were lighted, so that they may not have been burned alive. All the same, these numbers are very shocking when it is considered that Deza's reign of office extended only from Torquemada's death in 1498 to 1507.

But the rising in Cordova had shown the rulers both in Spain and in Rome that the Inquisition was in danger if men such as Deza and Lucero were put at its head.

Ferdinand therefore nominated a new Inquisitor-General for Castile, and the Pope, Julius II, confirmed this appointment.

As a result Ximenes became Inquisitor-General of Castile, and at this time Ferdinand secured from Julius a Cardinal's hat for his minister.

Ximenes, Cardinal and Primate of Spain and Inquisitor-General of Castile, had reached the zenith of power, for he had climbed as high as it was possible for any man to climb in the Catholic Church of Spain.

He had come a long way from the hermit's hut in the forest about Our Lady of Castañar.

5

XIMENES—INQUISITOR-GENERAL

No sooner had Ximenes taken his place as head of the Inquisition than he felt less enthusiastic concerning those reforms which previously he had felt to be necessary. He burned with zeal; he was as eager for an all-Catholic Spain as Torquemada had been; and realizing immediately that the Inquisition could be used in the service of the State, his plan was not to diminish its powers but to increase them.

As Cardinal of Spain—an honour rarely bestowed—he was second only to the Pope in the Roman Catholic Church. Politically he was second to his King; and now that he had been nominated Inquisitor-General of Castile, the administration of the Inquisition was largely in his hands.

He divided Castile into ten sections for the purposes of the Inquisition, and at the head of each section he set an Inquisitor of his choice.

In spite of his severity, he did attempt to be just, and he did aim to set right a great many anomalies which had crept into the Inquisition under the rule of Deza and Lucero.

One of the projects near to the heart of Ximenes, and ranking perhaps with that of the founding of the University of Alcalá and the compiling of the Polyglot Bible, was the desire to capture the Holy Land for Christianity and banish the Infidel from its soil.

He had, before the death of Philip, endeavoured to make an alliance between Spain, England and Portugal. These three countries were bound together by family ties, for Emanuel of Portugal was the husband of Maria, the third daughter of Isabella and Ferdinand (she had married Emanuel after the death of his first wife, her sister Isabella who had died in childbirth). England was bound to Spain by the marriage of Catalina, the youngest daughter of Isabella and Ferdinand, with Arthur Prince of Wales; in 1509, after Arthur's death, she was to marry his brother Henry VIII.

Ximenes believed that these three countries jointly could undertake a glorious campaign in the Holy Land; however the uncertainty of Ferdinand's position, the death of Philip and the insanity of Juana obliged him to shelve this project.

Ferdinand had been urged to show himself to his subjects in Naples and had in September 1506 set out on the voyage. He had been made anxious concerning his viceroy in Naples, Gonsalvo de Cordova, the Great Captain and brilliant soldier who had aroused the envy of many who sought to discredit him with his sovereign. It was during Ferdinand's journey that news reached him of the death of his son-in-law Philip. Ferdinand absent, Philip dead, and Juana mad! Here was a situation which might have caused grave disorder through the land had not the primacy been in the capable hands of Ximenes.

With admirable energy and foresight on the day before Philip's death (when it was obvious that the young man might not live) Ximenes called together a council, with himself at the head, which was to form a regency until Ferdinand's return.

There were seven members of the council: the Duke of Infantado, the Duke of Nájara (both of whom had opposed Ferdinand), the Grand Constable and the Admiral of Castile (both of whom stood firmly behind the King) and two Flemish lords. By his choice of council (with himself at its head) Ximenes displayed his determination to be just; and in this he also showed his wisdom, for the country was in a ferment and it was largely due to the skilful handling of matters by the Primate that revolution was avoided at this juncture. Ferdinand must have been once more reminded of Isabella's wisdom when she had insisted on bestowing the Archbishopric of Toledo on a man who had no great family connections to make demands upon him and was well known for his honesty of purpose (misguided though it might sometimes be).

Ferdinand did not immediately return. He was shrewd enough to understand that his presence in Castile might not have a soothing effect on a situation full of dangers; moreover he could fully trust Ximenes.

Meanwhile Henry VII of England was looking for a wife. He had hoped for Margaret, who was the widow of the young Infante Juan, son of Isabella and Ferdinand, and negotiations for their marriage were about to be brought to a conclusion when Margaret declared that in no circumstances would she marry the old King of England. Henry then turned his eyes to Spain. Juana, mad as she was, was Queen of Castile, and Henry was eager to cement the alliance with Spain.

He therefore let it be known through his daughter-in-law Catalina, that when Juana and Philip had been shipwrecked and forced to land in England he had fallen in love with Juana. There was, of course, only one thing with which Henry was capable of falling in love: wealth. He was very eager for this match.

Catalina was also eager for the marriage. She must have felt very unhappy in England; her husband was dead and her position uncertain; so that the thought of having her own sister living as Queen in the same country must have been very comforting.

Ferdinand himself wrote that, although he did not know whether his daughter would be willing to marry, he would sooner see her married to Henry VII of England than to any other prince in Christendom; he adds however: " more particularly on the terms of the treaty which the King of England is willing to sign with me ".

In Ferdinand and Henry were to be found two of the most parsimonious of monarchs, so there was no doubt that had the terms been advantageous enough for both, they would have done all in their power to bring about the match.

To Ferdinand such a marriage seemed infinitely desirable. It would mean that Juana would go to England and while she was there he would remain Regent of Castile until his grandson Charles was old enough to rule; and as Charles was not yet seven years old, that would be a very long time.

The English, he was assured, were willing that he should remain Regent of Castile. As for the madness of Juana, the English could not see that that should provide a deterrent to the marriage, for it was clear that whatever Juana's mental state happened to be she was capable of bearing children.

While all these suggestions for her remarriage were in progress Juana was giving more definite signs of madness. In spite of the fact that Philip had treated her as badly as he possibly could—first by his infidelity and then by imprisoning her—she had been deeply enamoured of him. It is often suggested that it was due to her possessive absorption with her handsome husband that Juana's unbalanced mind toppled over into insanity.

Dr. Parra reported that during Philip's last illness Juana was constantly at his bedside and herself took charge of the nursing. However, when he died she gave way to her grief to such an extent and in such an eccentric manner that any who had previously doubted that she was insane no longer did so.

She did not weep, but shut herself into a dark room and sat as though she were a statue, her head resting on her hand; she appeared to be in a coma.

She had had the body of her husband embalmed and the coffin was taken wherever she went; each night it was set up in a position so that she could see it from her window, and she would sit staring at it, never shedding a tear; it is said that she did not shed a tear after she discovered Philip's intrigue with the Flemish woman whose hair she cut off.

At the end of the year she decided to bury Philip in Granada. The coffin was placed on a carriage of great magnificence which was drawn by four horses, and a procession in which were nobles and men of the Church left Burgos on the 20th December on the way to Granada. They were forced to travel by night, for Juana declared that she as a widow, " the sun of whose soul had been extinguished ", should never expose herself to the light of day. At every halting-place the coffin was taken to a church or a monastery where it remained throughout the day, and where a funeral service was held as though Philip had just died. Juana set a bodyguard about the coffin, her aim being to protect it from women. She continued to be jealous of women; and on one occasion, when the coffin was placed in a nunnery, she was furious because she had thought the place was a monastery. Even when he was dead she would not allow Philip to be surrounded by women, so she ordered that the coffin be removed at once. It was taken from the grounds of the nunnery to a field some distance away. Juana's madness, which had been so aggravated by her passionate jealousy of Philip the Handsome, must have been very obvious to her companions on that night, for she insisted that the coffin be unsealed that she might examine the relics and touch them. She had to assure herself that those women at the nunnery had not sought to rob her of any part of him.

She and her party encamped in the field with the coffin; it must have been a wild and macabre scene with the mad Queen urging her servants to open the coffin by the light of torches which were continually extinguished by the howling wind.

Yet Juana had her lucid moments. Before embarking on the journey with her husband's remains she had snapped her fingers at all Philip's favourites who had profited so much since they came with him to Spain. She revoked all grants made since the death of her mother; and she stubbornly refused to recall her father.

Mad as she was, she seemed to understand at times that she was the Queen.

She continued however on the grim journey to Granada, wearing clothes that were dark, dirty and tattered; and when Ferdinand returned to Spain in August 1507 she, in the company of Ximenes, met him at Tortoles.

Ferdinand was horrified at the sight of his daughter for he scarcely recognized her in her wild state; but he persuaded her to give up her travelling by night from place to place in that melancholy cortège; and as a result she went to the Castle of Tordesillas taking the coffin with her. Philip was later buried in the monastery of Santa Clara which adjoined the palace of Tordesillas; thus Juana could from her window look on the tomb of her husband.

Juana, Queen of Castile in name only, remained in the palace for forty-seven years never leaving it.

The remains of Philip were eventually removed to Granada and placed in the Cathedral Church; Juana was placed beside her husband and a sepulchre was built for them by their son Charles V near that of Ferdinand and Isabella.

Juana's madness has been the subject of some controversy. Bergenroth brings forward an interesting theory, and Bergenroth is a writer who made such intensive researches into the history of Spain that his theories are well worth consideration. He was born in 1813, son of a Prussian magistrate, and in his youth was appointed to the post of assessor to the court of Cologne; he also worked in other German towns. Being involved in revolutionary movements he found it necessary to leave his native land, and went to California— a very different place in those days of the 1850's from what it is today. He became head of a gang of adventurers, narrowly escaped death, and continued to live dangerously until he suddenly became homesick for Europe.

He returned to Europe to write historical works—first in London and then in Spain. He went to Simancas, a Castilian village not far from Valladolid where he knew there was an enormous source of hitherto untapped information, for the archives had been kept in this village since the time of Philip II.

He stayed there for eight years and eventually died of typhus, which he had no hope of evading in the squalid little village. But during his stay there he selected documents, collected them, deciphered them, and eventually edited three volumes of the Calendar of State Papers.

Bergenroth states that the story of Juana's madness must be discarded. He believed that she was sane until the very end of her life when, after so many years of imprisonment, her reason deserted her, as might happen to most people who had been subjected to such treatment. She was kept a prisoner, says Bergenroth, for the benefit of the three rulers of Spain: Ferdinand, Philip and Charles.

Ferdinand was eager to make it known that she was insane so that he might rule as Regent; he did not wish her to die, but merely to be out of the way, for her death could avail him nothing. If she died her son Charles would be the King of Castile, and Ferdinand's position would be no better.

As for Philip, if Juana had died he would have had no claim whatsoever to the throne of Castile; it was therefore to his interest to keep her alive but powerless. How could he be better served than by her " madness " ?

It was in the interest of these two ambitious men that she should continue to live, while being judged unable to rule.

Charles, says Herr Bergenroth, wished his mother to be out of the way that he might reign alone, so it was to his advantage to support the theory of madness.

Prescott, discussing this theory of Bergenroth, finds it " ludicrous ", and he points out that had she died Ferdinand's position would not have changed; he could still have hoped for the regency until Charles was of age. Philip had he lived also might have ruled in the place of his son until Charles grew up.

Bergenroth does not seem to have taken into consideration the fact that Juana was mad at times and sane at others; and that there were occasions when, had Juana wished, she could have asserted her rights yet did not do so.

On considering all the available evidence there seems to be very little doubt that Juana was indeed periodically mad and that Ferdinand, Philip and Charles must be exonerated from the charge of imprisoning Juana merely for their own advantage.

* * *

Since the Moors had been driven from Spain there had been frequent raids on the coast by Moorish pirates who had set up their headquarters in various ports on the north coast of Africa. One of these ports was Mazalquivir, a mere two or three miles from Oran, almost opposite Carthagena.

Ximenes who, during the uncertainty in Castile, had been forced to abandon his grandiose schemes for the capture of the Holy Land, was determined to make a start on his grand project. If he could take Mazalquivir, Oran would be his next objective, and Oran was a considerable port, the chief market for the trade of the Levant with a population of some twenty thousand. Its capture would, Ximenes was sure, strike a strong blow for Christendom.

Ximenes approached Ferdinand, pointing out the advantages to Spain of the capture of Mazalquivir. Ferdinand agreed on this but he regretted he had no money for the enterprise, whereupon Ximenes offered to provide funds from his own revenues.

Ximenes was prepared to find this, for he had made up his mind that Mazalquivir was to be the first step in the capture of the Holy Land; so preparations were made—Ferdinand being eager to suppress Moorish piracy, Ximenes eager to suppress the Infidel or to make Christians of them.

The expedition was successful and, after a hard struggle which lasted for fifty days, the port was captured for Christian Spain. This was on September 13th, 1505.

Ximenes was delighted, but it was at this point that internal affairs in Spain began to be so complicated and dangerous, that further plans for extending Christianity had to be postponed.

Later however, in 1509, when Ximenes had become a Cardinal and Grand-Inquisitor, he was eager to continue with his conquests, and his objective was the important town of Oran.

Ximenes knew that he would be expected to finance this expedition, as he had the previous one, and was prepared to advance the money.   This he did; he must have been a very rich man, for the building of the University of Alcalá was a continual strain on his resources yet he did not suspend this.   The project was reviewed with great interest throughout Castile; not because a man of the Church had appeared to become a Generalissimo of the armies (previous Archbishops of Toledo, Mendoza and Carillo, had ridden into battle) but because many believed they saw in it a state of friction between Ferdinand and Ximenes.   Ximenes was a man of the utmost importance; he had actually been Regent during the absence of Ferdinand; and Ferdinand, aware as he was of the brilliance of Ximenes, could never forget that he had been chosen by Isabella to fill a post which Ferdinand had greatly desired for his own bastard son.

It was now said that Ximenes' motive in the Oran adventure was to get Ferdinand out of the country so that he might again occupy the position of Regent.

Whether Ferdinand himself believed this, we do not know, but it is suggested that he put forward the idea that Ximenes should lead the expedition.   Yet it appears to be a fact that Ximenes had determined from the first to lead the expedition himself.

Ximenes must have aroused an irritation in Ferdinand, perhaps because he was Archbishop of Toledo, perhaps because of that self-righteousness of Ximenes, a very irritating quality to a man of Ferdinand's nature who, while he declared himself to be a firm adherent of the Catholic Church, had been guilty of many sins which would be shocking to a man such as Ximenes.   However, from the beginning it seems that Ferdinand—although he would derive great advantages from the success of the expedition—was determined to put obstacles in its way.

For instance, the expedition needed a military leader who must be the finest soldier available, and there was one who was ideal for the post. This was Gonsalvo de Cordova, the Great Captain. Ximenes wished this man to take command, but Ferdinand, who had doubted the Captain's loyalty during his vice-regency in Naples, refused to allow the Great Captain to lead the expedition, and threatened to cancel it unless another man was chosen.

So in place of the Great Captain, Ximenes was obliged to take Count Pedro Navarro, a choice which was to prove to be a bad one from his point of view.

Many of the nobles then became sceptical of the whole affair and asked each other what success could come of a project when a monk set out to fight the battles of Spain and the greatest soldier in the country was left at home to count his beads like a hermit.

It was on the 16th of May, 1509, that the Fleet set out for Mazalquivir. When they landed, Ximenes on his mule rode along beside the soldiers, a friar in the Franciscan costume riding before him, carrying the huge silver cross.

Trouble broke out between Ximenes and Navarro before the battle. Navarro wished the troops to rest before going into action, but Ximenes answered that the battle was to be one between Jesus Christ and the false prophet Mohammed, and the sooner it was begun the better.

The soldiers, weary from the march, were naturally more ready to support Navarro than Ximenes, but the latter then addressed them with all his fiery eloquence, reminding them of the raids which had taken place along the Spanish coast and the many Spaniards who had been abducted and taken off to slavery—and who could say what torture and misery? He did not forget, however, to stress the wealth of their enemies and the booty which awaited capture. Then, because he himself was not interested in booty but in the souls of the Infidel, he went on to remind them— and perhaps the recording angel—that he came at the peril of his life in the service of the Faith.

The fleet bombarded the town, and the sea mist was of the utmost help to the Spaniards. Ximenes remained at Mazalquivir praying, while the soldiers went into action. In a few hours Oran had surrendered.

The conduct of the victorious soldiers was brutal. It is ironical to consider that they had marched forward under the sign of the cross. Murder, rape and pillage were hideously practised in the streets of Oran, and it was not until the men were weary of blood-shed, bloated with food and drunk with wine, stolen from the inns and houses, that they ceased inflicting these horrors on the unfortunate population of Oran.   Then they lay snoring in the squares among the mutilated and the dead.

Four thousand Moors were said to have been slaughtered on that day, and between five and eight thousand made prisoners. Christian losses were said to have been slight.

Ximenes came in great joy to take official possession of the city, declaring that the victory was due to Christ.   It was said that the day was fading as the battle began, but that a miracle took place and the sun stood still for several hours to allow the Christians to complete the slaughter.   Four eye-witnesses bear testimony to the miracle.   Prescott, commenting on it, says that it was an even greater miracle that the standing-still of the sun should have escaped the notice of Europe, where it must have been as evident as it was at Oran.   The universal silence concerning this strange behaviour of the sun is certainly odd, but what seems equally remarkable is that these men could have looked on Oran and all the misery and suffering which had been inflicted on it, and tell themselves that their loving Father had made the sun stand still in order that it might be brought about.

Ximenes is said to have murmured: " *Non nobis, Domine, non nobis,*" as he blessed the army; but he was disturbed when he saw the corpses of men, women and children piled high in the streets. Navarro, we are told, reminded him that they were only Infidels. To which Ximenes replied, it was true that they were Infidels, but at the same time they were people who might have been made into Christians.

When one considers the means employed to make these people " Christians ", one wonders whether they were not after all fortunate to have fallen in the streets of Oran.

Ximenes now dreamed of setting the banner of the cross over every Moslem city, turning the inhabitants to Christianity, and introducing the Inquisition throughout all the dependencies of Spain.

However friction occurred between himself and Navarro, who told him that it was impossible for an army to prosper under a divided rule.   He, Navarro, was the military man; Oran was captured, and Ximenes should return home; for fighting was for soldiers, not for monks.

Ximenes was not the man to avoid such conflict, and there is no doubt that he would not have gone back to Spain but for a certain letter which fell into his hands.   Whether Navarro *allowed* this letter to be seen by the Cardinal is not known, but it is very possible. In it the King asked Navarro to do all in his power to keep Ximenes in Africa. " Make use of him and his money ", wrote Ferdinand. " Keep him busy at Oran and, if there is no new enterprise to absorb his interest, invent something."

This letter had the effect Navarro would have desired—supposing he had allowed it to fall into Ximenes' hands—and the Cardinal, fearful of what Ferdinand was doing in Spain, decided that he must return with all speed to what after all had first claim on his duty. He therefore declared that he was too old a man to endure the heat of the African summer, and on the 22nd of May he embarked for Spain.

Ferdinand made a great show of pleasure on receiving him, but Ximenes set no store by such pageantry, particularly as he had good reason to distrust the King's sincerity. So as soon as possible he made haste to Alcalá with his servants, certain gold and silver which had been taken from the mosques of Oran, and some Arab books for the university he was founding at Alcalá.

Ferdinand, delighted with the success of Oran, did not need the persuasion of Ximenes to continue with the African campaign. Consequently Navarro took Bugia in January 1510; and during the early months of that year, Algiers, Tennis, and Tremecen, together with several other towns, were captured by the Spaniards. In July Tripoli fell to Navarro; but in August he suffered a serious defeat in the Island of Gelves, and during this battle four thousand Spaniards were either killed or taken prisoner.

This put an end to the African campaign, and although Ximenes' dream of carrying Christianity to the Holy Land was not realized, the operations had brought several very important towns into the Spanish net.

As for the Count of Navarro, he was a professional soldier and, when his services were no longer required in Africa, he went to Italy and was engaged in the wars there. He was captured by the French; Ferdinand, who was too fond of money to part with it in ransoms for his subjects, left Navarro to suffer in captivity, a fact which so infuriated the count that he offered his services to France, at the same time renouncing his allegiance to the King who had deserted him when he so desperately needed help.

Unfortunately for him, during a battle he was captured by the Spaniards and imprisoned at Castel Nuovo in Naples. He died there, by whose hand it is not certain. The gossipy Brantôme suggests that Charles V had him murdered; others believe he committed suicide.

Ximenes, back in Spain, ordered that agricultural labourers be brought home from Africa to deal with the harvest; he visited the families, in his diocese, whose members had been lost in battle or were still serving in Africa. He comforted them not only with words. The Cardinal's exchequer must have been considerably depleted, and it was no simple matter to get Ferdinand to repay him the money which had been lent for the campaign.

One of the clauses in the agreement which had been arranged between Ferdinand and Ximenes when the money had been advanced was that the loan should be repaid when the military operation was over, or that Oran should be joined to the See of Toledo which could then recover, over a certain number of years, from the great drain on its finances.

Ferdinand was against both methods of repayment. Those in whom the Cardinal had aroused a great deal of envy pointed out to the King that Ximenes had gained much from operations in Oran. Not only had he brought home rich booty but he had gained great glory; let that suffice.

Ximenes (as shown when he insisted on taking the benefice of Uzeda) was a man who could insist on his rights; and Ferdinand was unable to find a way out of his difficulties. Always at his worst when money was demanded of him, Ferdinand sent one of his servants to the Palace of Alcalá to make a valuation of all the booty Ximenes had brought home from Oran, that this might be set against the amount he had lent the King.

All that was found in the palace was a few carpets—the rest of the booty had not come into Ximenes' private possession; however, the value of these carpets was set against the sum Ferdinand owed.

Ferdinand was still anxious to see his son, the illegitimate Alfonso of Aragon made Archbishop of Toledo; and he chose this time to ask Ximenes if he would change Sees with Alfonso.

Ximenes was horrified, not only because he knew that Ferdinand's sole desire to appoint the young men was because he was his son, and this smacked of that flagrant nepotism which Ximenes had always declared he deplored, but because Alfonso was wordly in the extreme and quite unfitted for the post of Primate.

Moreover Ximenes himself (whether or not he had convinced himself, and with good reason, that he was one of the few men in the kingdom wise enough for the post) was determined not to give it up.

He declared that he would allow no such barter with the dignities of the Church. If the King should suggest such an exchange to him again he would give up the Archbishopric and return to that cell from which Queen Isabella had taken him.

*   *   *

On returning to Spain Ximenes gave his attention to the Inquisition against which a charge had been brought to the effect that when comely women were taken into the Holy Houses on charges of heresy they were often violated by the Inquisitors.

Ximenes was naturally horrified at such scandal and decreed that any who were found guilty of these outrages should be sentenced to death. William Harris Rule, D.D., states that none was put to death for this crime because none was convicted; and none could be convicted because none was prosecuted. " Neither," he continues, " did the abomination cease." Rule is of course fiercely anti-Catholic; and it is almost certain that had Ximenes found any of his Inquisitors guilty of rape (no matter who they were) he would have had them put to death.

We have an interesting sidelight on Ximenes's attitude towards women. He was sternly chaste; but that was not enough, for there were such evil rumours afloat concerning the clergy (often with good reason), and Ximenes was surrounded by men who would with the utmost willingness misconstrue any act of his which gave them an opportunity of doing so. Therefore, for the sake of the Church, Ximenes was determined to avoid any chance of scandal touching him.

When he went on his journeys he travelled without money and in the utmost humility, relying upon the hospitality of those who were prepared to give it. On one occasion, the Duchess of Maqueda, knowing he was passing her house, invited him to put up there for the night; she added that she herself would be absent but her servants would look after him. She knew full well that had she, a beautiful woman, not told him she would be absent he would have considered it unwise to accept the invitation.

However, the Duchess, who wished to talk with Ximenes on religion, had not left the house; she remained in hiding while her servants looked after Ximenes; and then, when he was preparing to retire for the night she came into the room.

Ximenes was angry; he rose, told the Duchess that she had deceived him, and that if she had anything to say to him the confessional was the place in which to say it.

Late as it was he walked out of the house.

One cannot help wondering whether such drastic behaviour was due to a certain temptation. If Ximenes had felt no interest whatever in the woman surely he could have taken a more gracious departure.

His attitude towards the *Beata* of Piedrahita is revealing, and an indication of the superstition of the day; it also throws an interesting light on the complexities of the human character. Here was a man, without doubt of great intellect, yet capable of childish reasoning (as shown in his campaign against the Mussulmans in Granada and Oran) and of amazing superstition, as shown in the case of the *Beata*. But perhaps the first instance is more surprising, for his conduct in Granada grew out of an injustice which was not to be expected from a man of high principles, while the blind faith of Ximenes which is such a part of his nature and was shared by many intellectuals had grown out of superstition.

In the year 1509 the devout woman (or *Beata*) of a small village in the diocese of Avila called attention to herself by her conduct. She was a peasant woman and someone had apparently trained her in mysticism, for she was capable of fasting for long periods of time. When she was a girl she had taken to the Dominican habit, and she became known for her sanctity. Mysticism was beginning to be practised in Spain and, according to Francisco de Villalobos, who wrote in 1498 and was physician to Ferdinand, many mystics came from Italy and were called *Aluminados*; they claimed to have special powers which enabled them to see into the future, and that visions appeared to them in which coming events were revealed. Villalobos declared that the *Aluminados* should be driven from all houses and kept without food, that they should be put into prison or scourged from the towns.

However there were many people who were impressed by the prophecies of these people, and Ximenes was apparently one of them, for in 1493, when he went to Gibraltar in his capacity of Provincial of the Franciscans, he wished to cross to Africa as a Christian missionary, which would have meant certain death. A *Beata* spoke with him, told him that she had had a vision of his greatness and the good he could bring to both the state and the Church; she advised him against rashly throwing away his life; and Ximenes had listened to her and followed her advice.

Now came the *Beata* of Piedrahita with her extraordinary stories. She declared that she was the Bride of Christ and that there was physical contact between them. She went into trances, and lay on the ground arms outstretched, so that her body had the form of a cross. There were times when she assured her listeners that she *was* Christ. She talked with Christ and the Virgin as though they were with her—she speaking for all of them; and often her listeners heard conversations such as this when the *Beata* was passing through a church doorway: " The bride of my dear Son should go before me." That was supposed to be the Virgin Mary speaking. The *Beata* would reply: " But if you had not borne Christ I could not have been His bride; the mother of my husband should have the greater honour."

It was all very impressive and the *Beata* through long practice was able to go without food and to endure great privations.

There were many people who were shocked by the woman's revelations of the intimacies she enjoyed with Christ, and these demanded that she be brought before the Inquisition, as surely blasphemy such as hers was the worst sort of heresy.

The case was so important that it was brought before the Inquisitor-General himself. Ximenes having questioned the woman declared that she was truly wise and saintly. However, there were still many who were not satisfied, and demanded that the matter be brought to the notice of the Holy See.

Julius II, who had succeeded Pius III in 1503, sent Giovanni Ruffo of Friuli and the Bishops of Burgos and Vich to examine the *Beata*, with a command that if they should find the woman to be guilty of fraud she should be punished with the utmost severity, but in such a manner as to subdue the scandal.

The *Beata* was discharged, and it was assumed that a decision had been made in her favour. Llorente however states that she was later taken before the Inquisition but escaped through the favour of Ferdinand and Ximenes.

The case of the *Beata* of Piedrahita gave rise to a new assumption; this was that those who gave themselves up to prayer and fasting could be filled with divine spirit which would manifest itself in trances and a gift of prophecy. Naturally enough there were others who wished to attain notoriety in the manner in which the *Beata* had.

There is one recorded instance (Lea in his *Religious History of Spain*, who quotes Vicente de la Fuente's *Historia Eclesiástica de España*) of a Franciscan friar of Ocaña. The custodian of the Franciscan province of Castile reported this case to the Inquisitor-General. It appeared that the friar declared that after much prayer and fasting he had been rewarded by a vision, in which God had appeared and told him that he had been selected to beget a race of prophets on numerous holy women. These prophets would reform the world.

This was too much even for the superstitious to accept, and the unfortunate friar was taken to a dungeon and there given such " active treatment " that it was not long before he was made to see that the visions (if any) he had experienced had come not from God but from the devil.

*   *   *

At the Cortes of Aragon in the year 1510, complaints were made against the Inquisition when it was stated that the Inquisitors were seeking to take over civic administration of justice. They intruded into all courts on the pretext that religious laws had been broken; they were adding to the number of their officials and, as these were exempt from taxation, the country was being deprived of more and more revenue. Any man who tried to point out the error of their ways—whatever his rank—was penalized even to the extent of excommunication. Ferdinand, who was presiding over the Cortes on this occasion, was asked to limit the power of Inquisitors and restore the laws and rights of the people of Aragon.

Ferdinand promised to look into these matters; but the Inquisition was powerful and there were two years of procrastination before certain amendments were made.

State affairs occupied the mind of the Inquisitor-General to a great degree. The league of Cambrai had been signed by Louis XII, Ferdinand, the Emperor Maximilian and the Pope; Venice had been attacked and defeated. Ferdinand had quarrelled with his one-time ally, Louis, and sought to make Pope Julius and Henry VIII of England his allies against the French King. Henry VIII had already married Catalina, widow of his brother, Prince Arthur, and was prepared to follow the advice of his father-in-law Ferdinand, which he received through his wife, for at that time Henry did not regard Catalina with the disgust he was to feel in later years.

Louis, realizing that Ferdinand was preparing to strike against him, attacked first; he invaded Papal territory, took Bologna in May of 1511 and planned to elect a new Pope in place of Julius whom he accused of bringing war to Europe, breaking promises and simony (that accusation which could often be applied with truth to Popes).

Julius called on Ferdinand for help; and Ferdinand withdrew his forces from Africa preparing for a campaign in Italy against the French. As for Ximenes, he was eager to protect Julius who had made him a Cardinal, and was ready to hand over a large sum of money towards the defence of the Pope.

Fighting began at the end of 1511, and the French under Gaston de Foix, Duc de Nemours (whose sister was Ferdinand's wife, Germaine) won some quick victories in the north of Italy. Ferdinand and his allies were disconcerted; but quite suddenly Gaston de Foix was killed in battle and the French, so disturbed by this fact, withdrew from Italy in June 1512.

Ferdinand had made Naples secure for Spain, and then turned his attention to Navarre. The Queen of Navarre at this time was Catherine who was a granddaughter of Ferdinand's half-sister Leonora, and Ferdinand had once tried to annex Navarre by peaceful methods when he had endeavoured to arrange a match between his son, the Infante Juan, and Catherine. This had failed, largely through the machinations of Catherine's mother who, being French, insisted that her daughter should marry Jean d'Albret, a Frenchman.

Spain's hostility to France gave Ferdinand the opportunity he needed and before the year was out he was master of Navarre; and in these great plans Ximenes was close beside his master, but he did not relax his grip on the Inquisition.

In 1515 the Cortes of Toledo, as had that of Aragon, asked that the Inquisitors should be prohibited from interfering in secular courts, and this was granted by the King, for neither Ferdinand nor Ximenes wished for an outbreak of rioting. Ximenes contented himself with setting up the Inquisition in Oran and making plans to send out his Inquisitors to the New World.

The New Christians, who were being persecuted so cruelly, believed that if the names of those who bore witness against them were published, they would have a greater chance to prove their evidence false. But the wicked law of the Inquisition which demanded secrecy in the tribunal, was one of its strongest weapons and it was clear that if it were abandoned it would not be so easy to " prove " persons guilty of heresy.

The New Christians, knowing this and knowing also that the King's love of money was one of his strongest characteristics, offered Ferdinand 600,000 ducats if he would rescind that law and order that the names of witnesses should be published.

Ferdinand, as ever finding the impulse to take money irresistible, was on the point of agreeing; there was however, the Inquisitor-General close at hand. He put down a large sum of money which, if it was not as great as that offered by the New Christians, was enough to turn the King from granting their request.

Ximenes was certain that the Inquisition was necessary to Spain and, if he desired to put a stop to the evil practices of certain of its officers, he was determined not to relax any of the harshness meted out to its victims.

In fact Ximenes shows clearly (as at Granada where he had no compunction in breaking his country's solemn treaty) that where the extirpation of heretics was concerned he was without conscience or humane feelings. He must have realized that the appalling injustice imposed on victims by the secrecy of the tribunal was barbarically cruel; but what did he care for that? To his fanatical mind all that mattered was that heretics should die; and if, by some evil chance, those who were not heretics suffered in the process, he would reason as others had reasoned before him: If they died the fiery death they had nothing to fear. God would know them for members of the Catholic Church when they arrived in heaven, and for that reason their place there would be ready for them.

Ximenes did not fear death or discomfort; therefore he had no sympathy to spare for others who suffered that fear.

*   *   *

In the year 1515 Ferdinand's health began to fail; he was suffering from a very bad heart and dropsy. There were times when he was unable to walk and had to be carried from place to place in a litter. He was sixty-three but he still hunted when he felt well enough to do so. In December he was staying with the Duke of Alva near Placencia, and on leaving him he travelled through Andalusia until he became so ill that he was forced to rest at the village of Madrigalejo near Truxillo.

Ferdinand was very suspicious of the presence of Adrian of Utrecht, who was chief adviser to his grandson Charles and who, he rightly suspected, was there because he, Ferdinand, was not expected to live, and at such a time it was necessary to have one who was devoted to Charles' interest close at hand.

There was some anxiety in the kingdom, for Charles, the heir, was a boy of only sixteen who had been brought up in Flanders in the care of his aunt Margaret, the sister of his father Philip the Handsome, who was also the widow of his uncle the Infante Juan.

Charles' brother Ferdinand was three years his junior, and Ferdinand was the favourite of the King. This was natural enough, for the boy who was his namesake had been brought up as a Spaniard, whereas Charles was looked upon as a foreigner in Spain.

*   *   *

In spite of Ferdinand's determination not to accept the approach of death it was necessary that his affairs should be in order, and although he refused to have Adrian of Utrecht admitted to his presence because, as he said, the man had come to see him die, there came a time when his doctors could no longer keep the truth from him.

Ferdinand had made a will in 1512, and in this he had appointed young Ferdinand Regent of Castile and Aragon during his brother Charles' absence. He also left to his namesake the grand mastership of the military Orders of Alcántara, Santiago and Calatrava.

That was more than three years ago, yet young Ferdinand was still only thirteen years old, and the counsellors felt it incumbent upon themselves to point out to the dying Sovereign that such an arrangement was impossible. A boy of thirteen could not possibly be accepted as Regent of Spain.   There was, Ferdinand was advised, only one man who should be given the post: Ximenes.

Ferdinand was silent and turned his face away from those present. It must still have rankled that Isabella had chosen this man of humble origins and raised him up above Ferdinand's own son, to be the " third King of Spain " as Mendoza had never been.   Yet Ferdinand knew that he was dying; he knew that his beloved grandson could never shoulder all the responsibilities which would fall to him; he was also fully aware of the stern qualities of Ximenes and the needs of the country which he loved.

He therefore slowly nodded his head and said that they were right, for Ximenes was an honest man, who had no family to push forward into high places; Ximenes would be a grateful man, always remembering that he owed his good fortune to Queen Isabella, and would therefore act to the best of his power in the interests of her young grandsons.

His advisers then assured him that he was wrong to separate the grandmasterships of the military orders from the crown, for Isabella had incorporated these with the crown to the great advantage of the country.

Ferdinand wept, and muttered that his grandson would be poor indeed; to which his advisers answered that Ferdinand would be the brother of the King, and what better good fortune could he possess than that?

The succession was therefore fixed upon Juana and her heirs, and Ximenes was to be Regent of Castile until Charles came to Spain. Ferdinand did manage to leave the governing of Aragon, until the return of Charles, to his illegitimate son, the Archbishop of Saragossa, which must have delighted him for he had certainly schemed earnestly, and had boldly faced the disapproval of Isabella to win favours for that young man.

He died in the early morning of the 23rd January, 1516, and his body was laid beside that of Isabella in the Alhambra.   On the completion of the Metropolitan Church they were both taken there, where Charles eventually caused a white marble mausoleum to be built.

*   *   *

For the second time Ximenes was Regent of Castile.   From the beginning of the Regency he came up against opposition, for Adrian of Utrecht declared that Charles intended to appoint *him* Regent. Ximenes was not the man to give way lightly, and eventually an arrangement was made that he and Adrian should share the Regency until Charles' further instructions should arrive.   Charles was no doubt advised about the superior capabilities of Ximenes for very soon instructions did arrive from him to the effect that the Cardinal was to have full authority; but at the same time the young Prince made it very clear that he had the utmost confidence in Adrian; and since Adrian was a man who wished to keep the peace, Ximenes allowed him to remain within his counsels so that it appeared that the Regency continued in their joint hands.

Charles then announced his desire to be crowned King. This was difficult, for Juana, though living almost a prisoner in Tordesillas, was still Queen.

The suggestion was strongly opposed, not only by Ximenes but by the royal council. Sixteen-year-old Charles however was determined to have his way.

If he took his advice, Ximenes wrote, he would not, out of respect for his mother, persist in his conduct.

But Charles was ready to take no one's advice on this point; he wanted to be called King and he was determined he would be; and realizing that nothing else would satisfy him Ximenes ordered banners to be set up containing the words: *Real, real real, por el Rey Don Carlos nuestro Señor*.

The people of Spain were somewhat unenthusiastic because they considered that the son was being disloyal to his unfortunate mother.

However, Charles had his way, as he was to have it so often in the future.

Ximenes at this time was eighty years old and his vigour and courage were astonishing. There was almost certain to be trouble at such a time and in such circumstances, and undoubtedly there would have been but for the strong hand of the Cardinal.

Ferdinand, beloved of his grandfather, a favourite of Ximenes, had expected to be placed at least equal with his brother in his grandfather's will; and there were many at his little court to cluster about him and seek to make a revolution. His elder brother, who could not even speak Spanish and who was under the influence of his paternal grandfather, the Emperor Maximilian, would not understand the customs of Spain; it was only to be expected that there were many who would have preferred to see the younger brother—every inch a Spaniard—on the throne; and one day when Ferdinand was hunting and met a hermit in the forest who pretended to be a wise man and assured him that he would one day be King of Castile, the boy was ready to take his stand at the head of a revolt.

But Ximenes was at hand. However fond he was of the boy who had been brought up at Alcalá, he did not forget his duty. He may never have seen Charles, but Charles was the true heir to the throne, and Ximenes was going to keep that throne for him until he returned to Spain.

Therefore he decided to set the Court in the centre of Spain where he could be within easy reach of any district in which trouble might arise. He chose Madrid—in his own diocese of Toledo—and from that day the town assumed a new importance in Spain.

Ximenes' attention was continually focused on young Ferdinand and he never allowed the boy to make long journeys from Madrid. He was determined that Castile and Aragon should remain united, and if, as some hoped, Aragon were given to Ferdinand and Castile to Charles, Spain would have taken a step backwards in her history to those days before the country had been united by the two great Sovereigns. Therefore Ximenes was determined to save Spain for the young man whom he had never seen and to curb the ambitions of that other youth for whom he must have had some real affection.

So this man, at that great age, ruled Castile as Regent for Charles who on his part was Regent for his mad mother; and in addition to these onerous state duties he did not forget that he was Grand-Inquisitor of Castile.

During his term of office the harshness of the Inquisitors had not abated in the least; Ximenes was as determined as any of his predecessors to wipe out heresy.

The New Christians, now that Spain had a new King who was not imbued with Spanish ideas and had been brought up among the Flemish, let their hopes rise. Surely such a King would not show the same favour for the Inquisition as his grandfather had. They therefore renewed an offer which they had once made to Ferdinand —and how near Ferdinand had been to accepting it —to pay a large sum of money to Charles if he would introduce fresh legislation into the Inquisition. They asked once more that the rule of secrecy might be abolished and that those who were accused might have an opportunity of facing those who had given evidence against them, as was the custom in civic courts.

Charles was ready to accede to this request, but Ximenes was as fierce in its denunciation with Charles as he had been with Ferdinand.

If a person were to be confronted with the one he accused of heresy, demanded Ximenes, who would be willing to be an informer?

The practice must never be introduced. Ximenes foresaw a dearth of victims if it were.

Ximenes won the day. Charles was ready to accept the advice

of his counsellors; he was only sixteen but already aware of his great responsibilities and his ignorance of the country which he was called upon to rule.

Prescott points out that Charles " showed a facility to be directed by those around him in early years, which gave little augury of the greatness to which he afterwards rose".   But surely this willingness to be directed is a certain augury of the greatness to come, for Charles even at sixteen was wise enough to be aware of his own ignorance.

It was twenty months after Ferdinand's death when Charles came to Spain.   Ximenes by this time was failing in health.   Pope Leo X hearing of his condition, wrote to him reminding him that he was past eighty years of age and that he should allow himself more comfort.   He should not sleep in the coarse garment of the Franciscans and should have a bed to replace his pallet.   Leo ordered him to take more comfort, for his services to the Church could be replaced by no other.

Ximenes was quite indignant when he read this letter, crying out that he had worn the Franciscan habit for the greater part of his life, and was now ordered to give it up.   It is certain that he disobeyed this command of Leo's.

When he knew that Charles had landed in Spain his spirits rose so much that it appeared to those about him that he had regained his great energy and would live for many years.

On the 26th of September he went to the monastery of La Aguilera not far from Aranda, and in early October he was well enough to say Mass and take supper with the monks.   Charles had made no great haste to meet his Regent, and news was brought to Ximenes that he intended to visit Aragon before coming to Castile.

Charles' Flemish followers who hoped to rule him were anxious that he should not meet Ximenes, for they were certain that the powerful personality of the old man would have a deep and abiding effect on their young King; and Charles, according to some chroniclers, was prevailed upon to write to Ximenes that famous letter, amazing in its ingratitude, which has been said to have broken the heart of Ximenes and hastened his death.

It is not absolutely certain that the letter was written, although there is mention of it by all contemporary sources.

In it Charles was reputed to have thanked Ximenes for his services as Regent and named a place where they could meet that Ximenes should give him counsel; when he had done this Ximenes was to leave Court for his diocese and there live in retirement, seeking from Heaven the rewards which Heaven alone could give.

This was all the new King had to say to the man who had served his grandfather and grandmother faithfully and to whom the present peaceful state of the country was due.

It is difficult to imagine the heart of Ximenes being broken, as some writers suggest. At the same time this must have been a bitter blow to him, for Charles could not have stated more clearly that he had no further need for his services.

Ximenes died in his house at Roa to which he had gone in order to be near the new King. His death took place, only a few days after he received the letter dismissing him, on November 8th, 1517, when he was eighty-one years old.

His last words, we are told, were: *In te, Domine, speravi.*

*   *   *

Ximenes was one of those men whose mingling love of austerity and harshness made the Spanish Inquisition what it was. Without his piety he could not have commanded respect; without his harshness he would have reformed the cruel laws of the institution. But although he believed in justice and was eager to rectify the guilty conduct of his inquisitors he was as eager as any who had gone before him to maintain the harshness of treatment towards heretics. There is no doubt, of course, of his good intentions. He was certain that he wanted nothing for himself. As a statesman he worked for the State and as a churchman for the Church. Would he have been a greater man if he had suffered from the human foibles of, say a man like Mendoza? He would certainly have been a more lovable one.

One can respect Ximenes (taking into consideration his times and, in understanding that cruel bigotry, forgive it) but one cannot feel any affection for him.

He was clearly a brilliant man; there is no doubt that the work he did for his country was admirable. He really did intend to suppress nepotism, that persistent failing of his day (and of our own) when an important office was given to a man not because he was fitted for it, but because of the influence he had been able to command. Yet he had a softness for his own family. Bernardín got off very lightly after attempting to murder him; and Juana de Cisneros the daughter of Juan, his brother, was the object of his interest and attention. Juana, being the niece of the rich and powerful Ximenes was a good *partie* and there were many noblemen of Castile who were eager to marry her. Gonzalo Mendoza, the nephew of the Duke of Infantado, was one, and on this match Ximenes smiled, until he discovered that the Duke's motive in arranging the marriage was to take Gonzalo's estates from him and give them to his own son, for, he reasoned, the husband of the niece of rich Cardinal Ximenes would be wealthy enough.

Ximenes then, instead of smiling, frowned on the match. Gonzalo and his niece were too young for marriage, he said; and this was true, for the prospective bride and bridegroom were eleven and thirteen respectively; however their very youthful state had not troubled the Cardinal until he had discovered the intentions of Infantado to rob the boy of his estates.

Later a more satisfactory match was arranged for Juana with Alonso, son of the Count of Corunna.

So, in spite of Ximenes' horror of nepotism he was not averse to arranging affairs to the advantage of his family.

He never sought to hide the fact of his humble origins; indeed, he so frequently alluded to them that once again he might be considered to lay himself open to the accusation of pride—pride in his great rise to power from such humble beginnings. So mixed were his motives that it is not easy to know the man.

There is a story that on one occasion a preacher attacked those churchmen who flaunted their extravagance before the world in fine garments. Ximenes was at this time wearing an ermine robe and the discourse was directed against him. He could not however resist taking the preacher aside and showing him, beneath the rich ermine, the patched and threadbare Franciscan robe.

Why should Ximenes have bothered to show this man the coarse habit? What did it matter what such a man thought of him? But the pride of Ximenes was great and his humility was so bound up in pride that it is often difficult to separate the two.

The story goes on that beneath *his* coarse monk's habit the sanctimonious preacher was wearing fine linen.

On the death of Ximenes a box was found among his possessions which contained the needles and thread with which he was accustomed to darn his habit; but why there should have been great virtue in this it is difficult to see. Surely a man such as Ximenes could have been better employed in the service of his fellow men than with needle and thread.

As a matter of fact his time was often occupied with other matters, matters which brought upon his head the reproof of the generations to come; I refer to his activities with the Inquisition.

In 1516, he, eager to carry the work of proselytizing in lands beyond Spain, appointed Juan de Quevedo Bishop of Cuba and made him the first Inquisitor in those lands.

A case against Juan de Covarrubias, who had died, was brought to his notice during those last months of his life. The penalty was the digging up of Juan de Covarrubias' bones, decking them out in the *sanbenito* and giving them to the flames. But this man had been a friend of Pope Leo's, who sought to defend him from the infamy of public burning and save his estates for his family.

Ximenes, however, was determined to punish heresy which had been proved by his Inquisitors; and there was conflict between Leo and Ximenes when the latter received that important letter from young Charles; Ximenes died with the case of Juan de Covarrubias still unsettled.

He is praised by many who declare him worthy of sainthood. But reflect for a moment on an account of the numbers of his victims: 3,564 burnt at the stake; 1,232 burnt in effigy; and penitents who suffered from confiscation of worldly goods and other punishments, 48,059.

These figures may not be exactly accurate; but let us suppose they were somewhere near the truth.

Fifty-two-thousand people is a large number; one can be sure that every one of these would be very doubtful of the claim of Ximenes' admirers that the latter was a saint.

What can we really know of this man? Not a great deal. We can though be sure of this: under his guidance the Inquisition firmly planted by Torquemada became that sturdy growth which was so firmly rooted in Spanish soil that it was able to exist through the seventeenth and eighteenth centuries and into the nineteenth.

6

MARRANOS AND MORISCOS

FROM 1507 there were separate Inquisitions of Castile and Aragon; and when Ximenes was appointed Inquisitor-General of Castile, Juan Enguera, Bishop of Vich, became Inquisitor-General of Aragon. In 1513 he was followed by Luis Mercader, Bishop of Tortosa, on whose death in 1516 Fray Juan Pedro de Poul, Dominican Provincial of Aragon, took over his post. Fray Juan however died in the same year and was succeeded by Adrian of Utrecht, Cardinal and Bishop of Tortosa.

After the death of Ximenes the Inquisitions of Castile and Aragon were united and Adrian of Utrecht became Inquisitor-General of both Castile and Aragon, and continued to hold this post until 1522 when he was elected to the Papacy.

Up to this time the victims of the Inquisition had been mostly the Marranos and the Moriscos, but eight days before the death of Ximenes Martin Luther had nailed his theses to a church door in Wittenburg and in addition to Jews and Moors, who had been baptized and were suspected of returning to the faith of their fathers victims were to be discovered among those who embraced Lutheranism.

Although there had been a general exodus of Jews in 1492, this unfortunate race still provided the majority of victims for *autos de fé*. Many of these came into the country from Portugal where, on their expulsion from Spain, they had settled in 1492. However when Isabella, daughter of Isabella and Ferdinand, married Emanuel, King of Portugal, she had declared she would not set foot in Portugal until Emanuel had sworn to follow the example set by her parents and expel from his territory all those Jews who would not embrace Christianity. Emanuel had foreseen the stupidity of following this policy but he had given way, for a match between Spain and Portugal could have succeeded in uniting the peninsula under one crown, and that crown could fall to the heirs of himself and Isabella.

Emanuel, however, not wishing to lose a valuable section of his subjects, sought to convert the Jews to Christianity; he used bribery and force. His confessor, Jorje Vogado, urged him to take very stern measures, and he ordered that all Jews who refused baptism must leave the country, except children of under fourteen who were taken from their parents to be forcibly baptized. Emanuel hoped that many parents, realizing that they would lose their children if they left the country, would accept baptism as the only alternative, and thus remain.

This decree caused great anguish to many families and some even killed their children rather than let them fall into the hands of the Christians.

When those Jews who had remained loyal to their own religion were preparing to leave the country, Emanuel sent preachers among them in a last effort to convert them; and when this failed, he imprisoned them until the time limit for departure had been reached. Then he offered them slavery or baptism. They were driven to the churches and, if they refused baptism, attempts were made to force it upon them with threats of torture, or torture itself. Thus in Portugal there were living many Jews who were called Christians; they had been given Portuguese names, but many of them had in secret reverted to their old Jewish names and gave them to their children.

In Portugal, as in Spain, the Jewish community began to prosper financially and thus aroused the envy of the people among whom they lived. There were outcries against them and pogroms occurred; yet still they prospered and multiplied.

It was a source of great irritation to the people of Portugal that King Emanuel, having forced Christianity upon the Jews who remained in Portugal, had given them some concessions. In 1497 he had promised them that they should be immune from the Inquisition for twenty years. He had also promised that all accusations of Judaism should be brought within twenty days of the alleged acts having been committed and that the trial should take place in accordance with the secular law. This meant that any charged would be brought face to face with their accusers—a concession which New Christians in Spain had long and in vain sought to establish, even offering large sums to their sovereigns in exchange for it. In Portugal the property of a condemned man was not confiscated as in Spain but was allowed to be enjoyed by his heirs.

The promise that they should not be treated as a separate race in the kingdom, given at the same time, was broken two years after it was made, when a law was introduced forbidding them to leave Portugal without permission, or to sell their lands.

In 1506 there occurred the terrible massacre of Lisbon. This began when one of the New Christians entered a Dominican church at Eastertide. He happened to glance at a crucifix, which was reputed to have magical powers, and lightly express his doubts of its holiness.

The mob, always envious of the prosperity of the race, was ready to wreak its malice. The unfortunate New Christian was seized by the hair and dragged from the church into the street. In a very short time he was torn to pieces by the " Christian " mob.

That however did not satisfy them. They formed into a procession, and the Dominicans (eager to set up the Inquisition in Portugal) urged them to take vengeance on these New Christians who had accepted baptism and who, they were sure, practised Judaism in secret. The mob needed little urging. They thronged the streets, entering the houses of the New Christians, robbing, murdering and committing every atrocity they could conceive. The massacre continued for three days and nights, and would not have ended then had it not been impossible to find more victims. Thus several thousands were killed because of a careless remark of one man. But the mob was still ready to be roused, ever watchful, determined, since the King had promised the New Christians leniency and there was no Inquisition established in their kingdom, to take the law into its own hands.

After the massacre certain hardships were abolished and New Christians were allowed to trade, and leave or come into the country as they desired.

In 1512 the exemption from persecution was extended to 1534, but in 1515 Emanuel did consider setting up the Inquisition in Portugal. He tackled this matter half-heartedly however, and when certain difficulties arose he allowed it to drop.

This was great good fortune for the New Christians who continued to prosper and, as they had in Spain, marry into noble families and even take up posts in the Church itself. Spanish Jews seeking refuge from the rigours of the Inquisition naturally found their way to Portugal.

This state of affairs lasted during the reign of Emanuel, but when John III, who followed him, married Catalina, the sister of Charles V, in 1525, greater pressure was brought to bear on this twenty-year-old King to set up the Inquisition in Portugal.

Clement VII agreed to absolve the King from his promise not

to set up the Inquisition until the term agreed to had expired, and sent Fray Diogo da Silva as Inquisitor to Lisbon.

The arrival of Diogo in Lisbon gave rise to an outcry among the New Christians who sent an emissary to Rome—Duarte da Paz, a New Christian of great wealth and persuasive powers. Meanwhile Clement died, and Paul III who succeeded him at first hesitated but later agreed to set up the Inquisition in Portugal. Thus in 1536 it was established there; the New Christians in spite of their wealth and power had managed only to delay it for a few years.

The first Lisbon *auto de fé* took place on September 20th, 1540; others were to follow. Thus it was that many New Christians of Portugal thought to better their lot by slipping across the border into Spain and settling down in obscurity.

Later to be a Portuguese Jew living in Spain was to rouse immediate suspicion; thus even after the great exodus there were many *Marranos* to supply victims for the Inquisition.

* * *

It was hardly to be expected that the Moors who had been forced to accept baptism should have been any more free from the suspicion of reverting to their old religion than were the Jews.

The zealous officers of the Inquisition needed victims, and the *Moriscos* provided as productive a source as did the *Marranos*.

In 1526 certain descendants of the old Kings of Granada, approached Charles and asked his help against the officials of Granada who ill-treated them and their kind in direct opposition to the treaty which had been signed at the time of the surrender of Granada.

This step was the worst the *Moriscos* could have taken, for the commission, which Charles had set up to look into these matters and which was led by the Bishop of Guadiz, reported to Charles that the attention of the Inquisition should immediately be turned on Granada.

In spite of past promises the Inquisition was installed in that town. The familiar pattern began to take shape, beginning with the term of grace for all those who would come forward voluntarily to confess their heresy.

People were now urged to commence spying on one another. It was not necessary for *Moriscos* to perform actions which obviously proclaimed them to be Mohammedans, such as observing the fast of Ramadan, or circumcising their children, praying with faces turned to the East or indulging in baths; they could be condemned for abstaining from the eating of pork and the drinking of wine, or for staining their nails with henna, or singing Moorish songs, dancing Moorish dances, refusing to eat animals which had died a natural death, or even because of the way they slaughtered animals for food.

These customs were listed for the use of Inquisitors and those who must spy for them.

New laws were made for the *Moriscos*. They must leave their doors open when they were celebrating weddings or on feast days, so that at any moment a spy could mingle with them to discover if they were following any custom which would make it necessary for them to be brought before the Inquisitors. There must be no wearing of Moorish garments; Arabic must not be taught or used; at every birth a Christian midwife must be in attendance.

These new laws sent shudders of alarm through the *Morisco* population; they had the terrible example of the Jews before them. They called together their leading citizens and it was agreed to offer Charles 80,000 ducats if he would withdraw the edict.

There was now no Torquemada nor Ximenes to lash the King to scorn, and Charles accepted the money, and suspended the edict " during his pleasure ". There was however a tax called *farda* which must be paid for the wearing of Moorish garments or the use of Arabic. This brought in a sum of 20,000 ducats to the treasury.

But the Inquisition was established in Granada and the first *auto de fé* was held in that city in May 1529.

On this occasion a proclamation was made in which it was explained that the Lord Inquisitors Apostolic of the city had determined to celebrate an Act of Faith in honour and reverence of Jesus Christ for the exaltation of the Holy Catholic Faith and Evangelical Law and the extirpation of heresies.

A recorder of the times (an official of the Inquisition whom Rule quotes in Vol. 1 of the *History of the Inquisition* from *Auto General de la Fé Exaltacion de Su estándarte catolico, etc.*) reports that the pious population of Granada heard this publication with breathless attention, and welcomed it with Catholic demonstrations of ardent religion, their eyes being " covered " with " liquid sparkles of tenderness " as they came out very reverently to listen.

By the time the great day arrived the population must have been in a suitable state of excitement. Rule gives a list of the chief actors in the drama (Vol. I. *History of the Inquisition*). They are as follows:

 1 Heretical *alumbrado*. (Blasphemous hypocrite)
 1 Forger of passports in the Name of the Inquisition

3 Bigamists

3 Witches

33 Jews who had been baptized but who had been discovered practising Judaism

22 Jewesses accused of the same

2 Mohammedans

7 Effigies of Judaizers who had escaped (Men)

10 Effigies of Judaizers who had escaped (Women)

1 Effigy of a Mohammedan who had done likewise

These were all penitents who would be required to become reconciled to the Church and suffer some penalty—severe enough, but not death at the stake.

Six Jews however were in the party under this sentence, and the people of Granada were to have their first smell of burning human flesh.

The six condemned to the flames were three men and three women. Five of them lost heart at the sight of the faggots and were garrotted before the flames consumed their bodies; but one man held out to the end and as a consequence suffered the terrible penalty.

This was Rafael Gomez. The chronicler records of this brave man: " Thus died that infinitely miserable Hebrew and, giving his being to the ashes, delivered his unhappy name to the mute horror of time, and his sacrilegious memory to the eternal night of oblivion."

In this first *auto de fé* it is interesting to note that only two Mohammedans figured, and one effigy, presumably for minor offences since they were not among those condemned to death.

The *Moriscos* of Granada, full of alarm, pointed out this fact to the authorities of the Inquisition, declaring that the Inquisition could find so little against *Moriscos* that it should therefore be withdrawn from those quarters in which the population consisted almost entirely of converted Moors.

This was an unfortunate suggestion, for the officials of the Inquisition were determined not to be withdrawn or suspended. They had worked hard to set their feet on the soil of Granada, and there they intended to remain. It had never been difficult for them to find charges against *Marranos*—why should it be against *Moriscos*?

The *Moriscos* responded, as the *Marranos* had done, with further offers of money to the King as bribes in order that they might live in peace. Charles, a practical man, was always ready to accept these offers, and because of this the *Moriscos* were able to buy their peace.

During the reign of Charles they were able to ward off disaster by these bribes; and it was only when Charles' son, Philip II, came to the throne that they found at the head of the State one who was immune from bribery and an even more fanatical supporter of the Inquisition than his great-grandmother, Isabella, had been.

It was after the accession of Philip, therefore, that the *Moriscos* provided so many victims for the Inquisition.

7

MARTIN LUTHER

AT THAT time when the Catholic Church through the Inquisition was fighting so desperately to retain supremacy in all lands, there arose in Europe its greatest menace.

For several years before Martin Luther pinned his famous theses to the door of the Wittenburg church there had been certain rumblings throughout the Christian world which showed the dissatisfaction of many people with the existing ecclesiastical doctrines.

So often when people consider the Inquisition at work they imagine Protestants being tortured and burned at the stake by Catholics; but it is a fact that the number of Protestants who became victims of the Inquisition was small compared with that of the Jews and the Moors.

For as long as the Inquisition existed the Jews suffered from it; but Protestantism in Spain itself was of shorter duration; and was almost eliminated in forty years.

The Reformation could be said to have begun in the early part of the sixteenth century, about one hundred years after the Council of Constance which put an end to the Great Schism of the West and elected Martin V Pope—and incidentally passed the death sentence on Huss and Jerome of Prague. By the sixteenth century learning had spread through the printed word and was no longer confined to members of the clergy; and when such as Reuchlin, Melanchthon and Erasmus sent forth their works into the world, food for thought was given to a great number of people. Erasmus, the most famous of these, while perhaps not himself a great reformer, certainly did more than any other to prepare the minds of men for the acceptance of the Reformation.

His satires on the vices practised in the Church were far more effective than fulminating would have been; and thus it was that he prepared the way for Martin Luther.

Pope Leo X wished to raise money; and he chose the by no means original method of doing so by the sale of Indulgences. He might announce that he wished to use the money so gained for holy purposes such as a war against the Infidel or the rebuilding of St. Peter's in Rome, but when he received the money he could use it for whatever purposes he needed it most.

Popes who had practised these somewhat dishonest methods in earlier days had not had to contend with the more enlightened population of the early sixteenth century.

Sir Thomas More (in *Utopia*) and Erasmus (in *Christian Prince*) had both condemned unfair taxation. In *Praise of Folly* Erasmus had even gone so far as to refer to the criminal habit of bestowing false pardons. Yet it was typical of the rather timid nature of Erasmus, who was no fiery reformer such as Martin Luther but a man who preferred to remain in the background, lightly pointing out anomalies and prodding others to act, that he should add that he did not include Indulgences in his criticism unless they were false, it being no affair of his to dispute the rights of the Pope. He did, however, go on to say that people who relied on pardons were encouraged to commit crimes.

However, the writings of these men were enough to set the people wondering whether pardons granted simply because the Pope was in need of money, even for a holy war or the building of a cathedral, had any value.

The amount realized from Indulgences did not all find its way to Rome, for a " commission " was granted to the sovereigns in whose lands the pardons were sold. There can be no doubt that this was a painful necessity as far as Rome was concerned, but it is certain that without such a system it would not have been easy to raise the money.

When John Tetzel, the Dominican friar, who had won fame by the clever way in which he was able to dispose of Indulgences, was appointed by Leo X to raise the money for St. Peter's by further sales, Charles V was able to raise a loan of 175,000 ducats on what he hoped to draw from the sales in his territory.

Tetzel passed through Germany in great pomp. When he and his associates came to a city, he would send on his deputy to announce his coming. The deputy would present himself at the house of the magistrate with the words: " The Grace of God and of the Holy Father is at your gates."

Immediately the church bells would peal and the whole town would turn out to greet them, from the highest dignitaries of the churches to the smallest of the children; all carried tapers, and the processions would be escorted to the church.

At the head of this procession was the Pope's " Bull of Grace ", which was carried on a cushion made of velvet and cloth of gold. Immediately behind the cushion came the bearer of the great red cross followed by men swinging censers.

When they reached the church it was Tetzel's duty to mount the pulpit; and almost like a barker at a fair he would begin to extol the virtues of Indulgences.

They were the most precious of all God's gifts. The cross which his supporters carried was a symbol of the cross on which Christ had been crucified, and as a blessed symbol had all the holiness of that other cross. If they paid him they should have pardons, not only for the sins they had committed, but for the sins they intended to commit.

He compared himself with St. Peter. He would not change places, he declared, for he, by the sale of Indulgences, had saved more souls even than St. Peter had by his preaching.

There were Indulgences for all sins. Even the most violent sin conceivable could be pardoned, providing the sinner was ready to pay in accordance with the enormity of the sin.

Indulgences could also be bought for the dead. Let them reflect. Was there some loved one who at this moment was writhing in hell fire? And they had the power to save that loved one from further torment by purchasing for him an Indulgence! " For twelve groats you can deliver your father from purgatory. What fate do you think will await *you* when you die if you neglect to make this sacrifice? "

Did they not understand that God had ceased to reign and had given all his powers to the Holy Father? Thus could the Pope give them eternal salvation—if they bought their Indulgences.

Tetzel was a business man. He had his tariff. Royalty and heads of the Church paid twenty-five ducats for an ordinary Indulgence. Counts and barons paid ten. Others paid according to the reduced scale of their incomes. But the price naturally rose in proportion to the size of the sin. Polygamists received absolution for six ducats; murderers paid eight ducats; those guilty of witchcraft, two; and so on.

Tetzel arrived at Juterbock four miles from Wittenburg; and in Wittenburg was the man who was ready to sweep away the old Church and found a new one.

*   *   *

In the year 1483, in the little town of Eisleben in Saxony, Martin Luther was born. His family was poor but his father, John Luther, believed in the advantages of learning and wished his son Martin to have a better chance than he himself had had. Therefore when Martin was fourteen he was sent to the Franciscan school at Magdeburg. Here Martin suffered great hardships. The teachers were cruel, and he was timid; moreover he was one of the poorest of the scholars and was often forced to beg his bread. Martin tells a story of how one Christmas he and some other poor scholars went out to sing carols in the hope of earning a little food. A farmer hearing their singing called to them, but his voice sounded harsh to the boys, and so accustomed were they to ill-treatment by their masters that they ran away, and only when the farmer ran after them, calling them to come into the farm where they would be fed, did they stop and enjoy his hospitality.

It was this timid boy who was to shake the Western hemisphere with his doctrines and who was capable of the great courage necessary to such a reformer.

When he passed from Magdeburg to a school at Eisenach he once again went carol-singing and it was thus that he was seen by Ursula, the kindly wife of Conrad Cotta, who noticed his hungry looks and how poorly he was clad—and perhaps she saw some light in his face which she recognized as potential greatness, for not only did she give him food on that occasion but she insisted that he lodge in her house, free of charge.

This was a great opportunity for Martin, who now need not concern himself with feeding and clothing his body and could give himself entirely to his studies. He loved music and learned to play the lute and the flute; he composed music, and it is significant that this music should take the form of martial hymns such as *Ein feste Burg ist unser Gott* and *Komm Heil'ger Geist, Herre Gott*.

When he was eighteen Luther was sent to the university oₓ Erfurt to study law, and here it was soon recognized that he was exceptionally clever. It is said of him that he spent all his spare time in the library of the university and one day whilst there he discovered the Bible. He had never before seen a Bible and was surprised to find how much it contained of which he had never heard. He had always believed that what he had heard read in churches comprised the entire Bible.

He went back and back again to the library and always to the Bible.

Luther obtained degrees of Master of Arts and Doctor in Philosophy, but he did not, as had been intended, take up law; instead when he was nearly twenty-two years of age he entered a religious order: the convent of St. Augustine in Erfurt.

The family was furious; it must have been a great blow after the sacrifices both they and their son had made to acquire an education; they could not see into the future.

In his convent he practised those privations which were considered necessary to produce sanctity, and learned to go for days without food or drink. One day, having carried abstinence from food and drink too far, he was discovered in his cell in a state of unconsciousness.

He was eventually appointed teacher of physics and dialectics at the university of Wittenburg, where he learned Greek and Hebrew in order to enable himself to make a closer study of the Bible. He lectured on the Bible, and crowds came to hear him; and later the title of Doctor of Divinity was bestowed upon him.

It was when Tetzel was in the neighbourhood of Wittenburg that Luther's indignation became so great that he could no longer remain silent.

He expressed his indignation when people came to him and told him that they could sin as much as they liked because they had just purchased an Indulgence and their salvation was therefore assured. He declared that there could be no forgiveness of sins without full repentance and the determination not to sin again.

Tetzel, furious at the interference, denounced Luther.

Then on the 31st October, 1517, one day before the festival or the Elector's new church of All Saints, when many pilgrims were gathered there in the hope of acquiring Indulgences, Luther walked up to the church door and nailed on the posts his list of ninety-five Theses which were an outcry against the sale of Indulgences.

Those who had come to buy their salvation were astonished to read:

" When our Lord and Master Jesus Christ says ' repent ', he means that the whole life of believers on Earth should be a constant repentance."

" The Pope is unable and desires not to remit any other penalty than that which he had imposed of his own good pleasure, or comformably to the canons i.e. the papal ordinances."

" They preach mere human follies who maintain that, as soon as the money rattles in the strong box, the soul flies out of purgatory."

" Those who fancy themselves sure of salvation by Indulgences will go to perdition along with those who teach them so."

" We should teach Christians that he who gives to the poor, or lends to the needy, does better than he who buys an Indulgence."

"The Indulgence of the Pope cannot take away the smallest deadly sin, as far as regards the guilt of the offence."

" The bishops pastors and theologians who permit such things to be told to the people, will have to render an account of them."

" This shameless preaching, these impudent commendations of Indulgences, make it difficult for the learned to defend the dignity and honour of the Pope against the calumnies of the preachers, and the subtle and crafty questions of the common people."

In a very short time first Germany then Europe was talking about these Theses of Martin Luther.   Leo X was not inclined to take them seriously.   Tetzel however was furious at this attempt to stop the money rattling into the strong box.   He announced that Martin Luther should be burned at the stake; and he had a scaffold erected on which he publicly burned Luther's Theses in place of his body.

In 1518 Luther appeared at Augsburg to answer charges brought against him, and conducted himself with such courage and skill that it was impossible for the Papal authorities to bring a case against him.

By 1520 a Papal Bull forbade any country to accept the teachings of Luther.

The Reformation had begun, and those followers of Martin Luther were to provide a fresh supply of victims for the Inquisition.

8

THE PROTESTANTS OF VALLADOLID AND SEVILLE

T HERE ARE some countries which could not be nationally Protestant, and others which could not be nationally Catholic. The Germans and the English are natural Protestants (it is due to the character of the people) while the French, Italians and Spaniards are natural Catholics. The emotional, almost sensuous, ritual of the Catholic Church is more suited to the Latin than the Nordic races. For this reason there was never any great danger of Lutheranism gaining a hold in Spain.

However in April 1521, Adrian of Utrecht, the Inquisitor-General, sent out a command that all Lutheran books in Spain be seized.

There must have been some demand for these books for in 1524 a ship, which came from Holland and was bound for Valencia, was captured and brought into San Sebastian. Lutheran books were discovered among the cargo and publicly burned. Venetian ships also brought books into Granada; these were seized and burned and the captain and crews of the ships imprisoned.

In 1528 a Ghent painter—Cornelius—was brought before a tribunal for denying the heresy of Luther and existence of purgatory, and declaring that no good purpose was served by confession.

Cornelius was no martyr, and was quickly made to assure the council that he had been drunk when he had made such fantastic statements and that, although when he was in Flanders he may have listened to such foolish talk, now that he was in Spain he fully realized its error. He was not burned at the stake, but merely sentenced to perpetual imprisonment.

Hugo de Celso, a doctor of Burgundy, was another Lutheran who tried to introduce his beliefs into Spain. He was tried at Toledo and was later burned at the stake.

Another would-be reformer, Melchor de Württemburg, came to Valencia to do what he believed was his duty. He went through the streets, on a preaching mission, urging all whom he saw to repent, for the world was on the point of destruction. He told his hearers that he had travelled to Germany to confer with the Lutherans and consider whether their doctrines held the answer of which mankind was in need. The mention of Lutheranism made authority prick up its ears, and Melchor was brought before a tribunal. His wild stories of the end of the world were not, it was decided, the result of deadly sin; it was only if he was tainted with the dreaded Lutheranism that he would be considered worthy of the flames. Melchor quickly denied all belief in Lutheranism and consequently escaped with a whipping.

An early Protestant martyr in Spain was Francisco de San Roman of Burgos. In his youth he visited the Netherlands on business, and while there he became an adherent of Lutheranism. He was clearly a very earnest man for he quickly felt it to be his duty to convert Charles V himself and, nothing daunted by the enormity of this task, made an attempt to accomplish it. He bearded Charles at Ratisbon and for his pains was made a prisoner and sent to Spain that the Inquisition might deal with him.

There, since he refused to revert to the Catholic Church he was condemned to the flames; and in the *quemadero* suffered the additional torment of having his body pierced with swords by those spectators who had congregated for the pleasure of seeing a man burned alive.

There were two danger spots to the Catholic Church in Spain from Protestantism in the middle sixteenth century: one of these was in Seville and the other in Valladolid.

The community in Seville had been founded by Doctor Juan Gil known as Dr. Egidio who was a canon-magistral of Seville Cathedral. During his lifetime he was accused of Lutheran tendencies and as a result was sentenced to a term of imprisonment in the Castle of Triana. When he was released he travelled to Valladolid and there exchanged views with others of the Reformed Faith. Fortunately for Dr. Egidio he died before there was any great outcry against Protestants.

When Dr. Egidio died his place in the magistral canonry was taken by Doctor Constantino Ponce de la Fuente, a man who had acted as confessor and chaplain to Charles.

The Prior of the Geronimite house of San Isidro, Maestro García Arias, known as Doctor Blanco, was an important man who had also become interested in Lutheran ideas. He was in a position of influence, for the brethren under his command rather naturally began to share their Superior's interest in the reformed religion and thus the numbers of converts began to swell.

Francisco de Zafra, another influential churchman who was able to bring in many converts, also joined the group, which now began to have among its members people from every walk of life. There was Don Juan Ponce de Leon who was related to the Dukes of Arcos; at the other end of the scale were two brothers who were rag-pickers, Francisco and Antonio Cardenas.

Such activities could not be allowed to go on undisturbed and it was not long before the Inquisition received secret information concerning the Geronimites of San Isidro. The fact that an investigation was pending was somehow conveyed to certain of the monks, who, knowing full well the methods of the Inquisitors, were not going to fall into their hands if they could help it.

Therefore some of them slipped away. Two who did so were Cassiodoro de Reina and Cipriano de Valera. That they escaped was fortunate because both these men achieved fame by their writings: Cassiodoro became head of the Protestant Church, Spanish and French, in Frankfurt, Antwerp and London. He translated the Bible into the Castilian tongue (which has been reprinted and circulated in modern times). Cipriano de Valera wrote *Los dos Tratados del Papa y de la Misa* which was published in London in the year 1588 and again in 1599, and was reprinted once more in 1851 and contained in his work *Reformistas antiguos Españoles*. He also translated the *Institutio* of Calbin. (Lea).

But the flight of these men only served to increase suspicions, and the writings of Doctor Constantino Ponce de la Fuente were seized by the Inquisition. As a result some of his books which had been in circulation for many years were condemned to be confiscated.

A pastor of Geneva named Juan Pérez de Pineda had in the meantime been preparing books on Lutheranism which he wished to send into Spain, and there was one very brave convert who undertook to see that they were delivered. This was Julianillo Hernández. He was a Spanish deacon of a Lutheran church in Germany and he was evidently seeking martyrdom in undertaking such a task. He was a little man and as a result he became known as Julianillo *el chico*. He equipped himself as a muleteer and made his journeys between France and Spain, carrying goods among which were hidden the books he wished to smuggle into Spain.

In July 1557 he arrived in Seville and, not daring to go into the city, waited outside its walls for Don Juan Ponce de Leon to come to him and collect them.

A fatal mistake occurred during one of these expeditions. The books were delivered to those who it was known could be trusted, but it appeared that a staunch Catholic priest possessed the same name as one of the reformers and he received the books intended for his namesake. The Catholic priest lost no time in getting into touch with the Inquisition.

The mistake was discovered almost as soon as it had been made and Julianillo and Don Juan lost no time in leaving Seville.

But the mischief was done. Arrests were numerous; moreover both Don Juan and Julianillo were captured before they could leave Spain.

Then began the slow and painful task of collecting information, which was conducted with that formality so beloved of the Inquisition, and the prisons were soon full to overflowing.

Eventually even Doctor Constantino and Dr. Blanco were languishing in the prisons of the Inquisition.

* * *

While all this was happening in Seville the Inquisition had had news of that other little colony in Valladolid. The head of this group was Don Carlos de Seso, reputed son of the Bishop of Piacenza who had become a Reformist. He quickly made converts; among these was the Bachiller Antonio de Herrezuelo and his wife Leonor de Cisneros. Another was Juan Sánchez who became so wildly zealous that he was a danger to his friends. He had been a favourite preacher of Charles' who had taken him with him to Germany and it may have been during one of these visits that he had become a member of the Reformed Faith.

When Sánchez came to Valladolid he entered the household of Doña Catalina de Hortega and converted her. Pedro de Cazalla, the parish priest, had become an ardent Reformist, and he, with his sisters Doña Beatriz and Doña Costanza de Vivero, and his brothers Agustin de Cazalla and Francisco and Juan de Vivero, conducted meetings in the house of their mother Leonor de Vivero.

It was impossible for this state of affairs to exist for many months without discovery. The people had been taught by the Inquisition that the only way in which they could escape suspicion was to spy for the Church. One of the converts was Doña Ana Enríquez, a daughter of the Marchioness of Alcañizes; and a certain Christóbal de Padilla, who was her steward, evidently talked too much. He was arrested and the group, realizing that they could place little reliance on his discretion, were deeply alarmed.

Escape was almost impossible for already the Inquisition was alert; some however attempted it. The only one to achieve it was Sánchez, but a year later he was caught and brought back to trial.

The Inquisitor-General at this time was Valdés, Archbishop of Seville. Valdés looked upon this discovery of Protestants in Valladolid and Seville as an excellent opportunity. He badly needed not only the distraction this would offer to the people, but to show the King how important was his own position in the land. He was on the verge of disgrace and this affair seemed as though it might have the effect of setting him back in favour.

The King, Philip II, was at war and urgently needed money; he called on his subjects for this and, as the King was in Flanders, the Princess Juana, Philip's sister, who was then Governor of the Kingdom, demanded 100,000 ducats as Valdés' contribution.

Valdés was not prepared to pay, and this brought a reproof from Charles V now in retirement at Yuste. Valdés however, while knowing that by refusing the royal request he was placing himself in jeopardy, could not bear to part with his money, first declaring that he had none, then that money obtained from priests for the purpose of war would prove unlucky, and that all Philip needed was God's help, not that of his priests.

Philip meanwhile sent instructions that Valdés was to be banished from Court although he might be given an opportunity to retire of his own accord.

Thus, with the discovery of Protestants in Seville and Valladolid, Valdés no doubt felt that he had a chance to show how useful he could be to the State and keep both his money and his position. He therefore set about working up a scare. He arranged that stories of hair-raising orgies, which were reputed to have taken place in the houses of the reformers, should be circulated throughout the country.

Meanwhile Juana, the mad Queen, died and Princess Juana, as Governor of the Kingdom, commanded Valdés to convey her body to Granada. This Valdés refused to do. The burial could wait, he said; he had work of the utmost importance to perform in Seville and Valladolid.

The discovery of the Protestants completely changed the attitude of Charles and Philip towards Valdés, as the Inquisitor-General had known it would. Instead of being asked to leave the Court he was now commanded to stay.

Charles in Yuste, close to death, was deeply disturbed. He wrote to Juana—and a copy of the letter was sent to Philip in Flanders—assuring her that there should be no leniency shown to Protestants, who could grow into a great menace to the country.

The results of the investigations were the notorious *autos de fé* of Valladolid and Seville.

* * *

The first of these took place on Trinity Sunday, May 21st, 1559; and in this suffered the first of the Valladolid prisoners.

Valdés, determined to make a great show of his own importance through the Inquisition, had the *auto* proclaimed fifteen days before it was to take place; and he put armed guards on the prisons because, he let it be known, so great was the Lutheran menace that he feared an uprising to free the prisoners.

The day before that fixed for the *auto* there took place the ceremony which consisted of carrying a bush to the *quemadero*. Officials left the Palace of the Inquisition and when they reached the square of the town a banner was unfurled; on this was inscribed an order forbidding any person to carry arms from that moment until the *auto* was at end, and ordering that no one should ride through the streets either on horseback or in a carriage while the procession passed.

After the procession of the bush came that of the Green Cross. Then the friars of the neighbourhood, who had assembled at the prison of the Inquisition, emerged with the *alguazils* and other officials, all carrying white tapers.   In the centre of the procession was a bier covered by a pall.   The men chanted as they walked to the square where the ceremonies of the next day would take place. There the scaffold would already have been erected, and on this scaffold was the altar.   Then the pall would be lifted from the bier to disclose the Green Cross draped in black veiling.   It was erected on the altar, and the Dominicans in the party then kept watch during the night while the rest of those who had made up the procession went home.

The next day was that of the great occasion.   The victims were assembled, their heads and beards closely shaved, some in coarse black coats and trousers without shoes or stockings, most in the *sanbenito*.

The *auto* of Trinity Sunday 1559 was one of special note, not only because in it some of the Valladolid Protestants suffered, but because it was the first in Spain to be attended by Royalty.   Princess Juana, sister of Philip II, who was governing the country during her brother's absence, was present and with her was the Prince, Philip's son, Don Carlos.

The presence of these two made it a very glittering occasion, for with the Royal party came many of the courtiers, and galleries of great magnificence were set up.

The procession of victims was headed by the dead body of Leonor de Vivero.   Fortunately for this woman she had died during the trials, but under torture several people had said that she had entertained Lutheran opinions and had allowed her house to be used for meetings of Lutherans.   Therefore her body was dug up, arrayed in the *sanbenito*, the *caroza* set upon her head, and she was carried through the streets to the *quemadero* where she was publicly burned.

The house which had been used for the meeting place was burned to the ground and a pillar set up inscribed with words to the effect that during the pontificate of Paul IV and the reign of Philip II, the Holy Office of the Inquisition condemned the house of Pedro de Cazalla and his wife, Leonor de Vivero, to be razed to the ground since in it the Lutherans had assembled to hold meetings against the Holy Catholic Faith and the Church of Rome, May 21st, 1559.

Another victim was Leonor's son, Doctor Agustin de Cazalla, who was Canon of Salamanca. He had denied a leaning towards Lutheranism but under the rigours of the torture chamber he had broken down and confessed, begging for the opportunity to be reconciled to the Catholic Church. The Inquisitors, having no intention of sparing his life, allowed him to hope that this might be done, assuring him that for his soul's sake he must confess more and give more information concerning other people who had been involved in the community of Protestants. When he said that he could give no more information he was brutally told that he was to die on the next day. He therefore prepared himself to die, saying that he must do so without falsehood on his lips, and only by uttering falsehoods of the worst kind could he implicate others.

His brother, Francisco de Vivero, was also a priest, being a curate of Hormigos. Like his brother he denied that he was Lutheran until submitted to the torture, when he broke down and confessed, imploring reconciliation with the Church.

During the reading of the sermon in the great square the two brothers were placed side by side on two of the highest seats reserved for those who were considered to be guilty of the greatest heresy; and there they sat while the sermon, of one hour's duration, was delivered by Melchor Cano. The oath to protect and aid the Inquisition was roared out by the spectators, and the crowd then took up the cry " To the death! " The two priests were put upon asses and thus conveyed to the Plaza de la Puerta del Campo, the *quemadero* of the occasion, and there they were burned, both preferring to deny Lutheranism for the sake of strangulation before death.

Their sister, Doña Beatriz de Vivero, who had been tortured, was also strangled and burned.

Alfonso Perez, a Master in Theology, Christóbal de Ocampo, a Knight of the Order of St. John and Almoner of the Grand Prior of Castile and Leon, and Christóbal de Padilla were all strangled first and then given to the flames.

Another who suffered was Juan Garcia, a silversmith. It was his wife who had discovered where he was meeting his fellow Lutherans and had betrayed him to the Inquisition. He was strangled and thrown to the flames; she was awarded a pension—as a good child of Holy Church.

Juana Blasquez, a servant of the Marchioness of Alcañizes, Catalina Roman and Isabel de Estrada, the last a *beata*, were all strangled first and burned afterwards. Perez de Herrera, a magistrate, and Gonzalo Baez, a Portuguese, were other victims dying in the same way.

The true martyr on this occasion was the Licentiate Antonio Herrezuelo, and the story of him and his young wife is a particularly pathetic one.

This advocate from Toro was a braver man than any of his friends. When he had accepted the Lutheran doctrines he had accepted them for life, and no fear of physical torture could shake him. He had recently married a young and beautiful girl, Leonor de Cisneros, and together they had studied the new ideas and discussed them earnestly. They both came to the conclusion that Lutheranism was the true religion.

Leonor however, twenty-three years old, with plans for a happy future in her mind, was seized by the *alguazils*, separated from her husband and dragged to the " Holy House " for questioning. She was submitted to all the gruesome stages of torture devised by the founders of the Inquisition and when she—so young, so full of life— was shown those hideous instruments which could ruin a young woman's beauty in a very short time, could maim her for life and submit her to the most hideous pain conceivable, she gave way and agreed that she had listened to Lutheran ideas and implored to be reconciled to the Church.

For this she was saved from the *brasero* and preserved for perpetual imprisonment in the *casa de la penitencia*.

Meanwhile her young husband was determined to remain true to his faith. He refused to implore forgiveness; he accepted Lutheranism as the true religion, he declared, and he was ready to die for his belief. He was therefore condemned to the flames without the blessing of strangulation before burning.

On the way to the *quemadero*, his friends urged him to save himself from the hideous death of being burned alive; it was of no avail. He sang hymns as he was paraded through the streets and quoted passages from the Bible. Nothing annoyed the mob more than a show of such courage in the face of the most hideous of deaths. Naturally it shook their belief in their own righteousness. How

Two old prints showing the application of torture under the supervision of the Inquisition

The Emperor Charles V of Austria and I of Spain, elder son of Philip and Juana
(from a painting by Hans von Schwaz, in the National Museum of Naples)

could a man go almost joyfully to die for his beliefs if those beliefs came from the devil? Therefore, because they were shaken and filled with certain self-doubts, they wished to vilify the martyr. Antonio Herrezuelo's journey to the *quemadero* was a very painful one for him.

Since he insisted on singing hymns and quoting the Scriptures the painful gag was put into his mouth. Even so, he presented such a calm face to the crowd that he only succeeded in infuriating them. As the faggots were about to be lighted, one of the soldiers, so maddened by the calm of the martyr, thrust his halberd into the victim's stomach; but this brutal act was not enough to kill him and put him out of his misery, it merely increased his pain.

All this Antonio Herrezuelo bore with fanatical calm, showing that to die for his faith was a glorious experience.

Meanwhile Leonor remained in the house of the penitents, for ten years in a state of terrible remorse. With the passing of each day life became more intolerable and eventually Leonor knew that she could not endure to live in her present state. There seemed to be only one course open to her; she must follow her husband. She therefore confessed that she was a relapsed heretic, knowing that there was only one punishment for such: death by burning. She was tried again and condemned to the flames.

Even now, if she implored reconciliation at the last moment, she might be strangled before the faggots were ignited. But this time Leonor was determined to die as her husband had died. There was no recantation. She was burned alive on September 28th, 1568, nearly ten years after the death of her husband.

On this first of the famous *autos de fé* of 1559, fourteen people had been condemned to the flames. Sixteen others had been found guilty of minor offences—some to be sent to the galleys to endure a number of years, perhaps a lifetime, of humiliating toil and frequent applications of the lash; some to be stripped to the waist and paraded through the streets, whipped as they went; others to stand in the squares that the self-righteous mob might heap upon them any indignity they cared to.

This *auto de fé* is remembered, not only because in it suffered some of the first of the Protestant martyrs, but because Princess Juana and Don Carlos, Prince of the Asturias, had been present and had been required to swear allegiance to the Inquisition.

There is no doubt that Don Carlos did this with an ill grace. It may have been that he felt it to be a great indignity for the heir to the throne to swear an oath of fidelity to any, even the Inquisition; and poor crippled Don Carlos was deeply conscious of his dignity.

It may have been that at this *auto de fé* his sympathy with the Protestants, which was to bring a great deal of inconvenience in the future to himself and others, was born.

*   *   *

The second *auto de fé* was held at Seville on September 24th, 1559. This was another of those grand occasions and three days before it people began to gather in the town.   The setting was as magnificent as it had been at Valladolid and the Duchess of Bejar brought a party of friends to view the spectacle.   She had a very special interest because her kinsman, Juan Ponce de Leon, was to be burned, and she longed to see this done.

Don Juan Ponce de Leon was the most distinguished of the victims on that day.   He had been an ardent Protestant and he had never thought that he would be taken to the *quemadero*, always believing that his family connections and his wealth would save him from such a fate.   It must have been a bitter disappointment to find that his influence availed him nothing, apart from bringing the Duchess to the show.

Although there was no royalty present on this occasion the great crowds which had been assembling and the presence of the Duchess, and of course the fact that Lutherans were to be burned, made it an outstanding *auto*.

Don Juan Ponce de Leon, the aristocrat, had, when he realized that the Inquisition was on the track of his Lutheran community, been one of those to escape; he had made some progress but as he had been on the point of embarking for England the officers of the Inquisition had caught up with him.   Chains were put about his arms and legs, an iron cap was placed over his head and shoulders, and attached to this cap was a loop which went into his mouth and held his tongue down.   In this painful condition he was brought back to Seville.

He was a brave man however and was determined to remain true to the religion he had adopted.   Torture could not make him swerve and he was abandoned to the secular arm.   When he was brought to the *quemadero* the gag still remained in his mouth distorting it horribly, and a recorded description says that the appearance he presented was so grotesque that he seemed scarcely human.   No doubt the noble Duchess enjoyed the spectacle.

On this occasion twenty-one people were condemned to the flames, and eighteen to do penance.   There was one effigy which was condemned to the flames.   This was that of Francisco de Zafra. Francisco, a presbyter of the parish church of St. Vincent of Seville, was a man of great learning and skilfully he had managed to hide his interest in Lutheranism. But he was foolish enough to entertain in his house a *beata* who soon discovered a great deal about his ideas and the people whom he was meeting in order to discuss them. This *beata* became hysterical, and Francisco de Zafra put her under restraint, an action which so enraged the woman that as soon as she was free she went to the Inquisition and told them of Zafra's interest in Lutheranism. She gave the Inquisitors lists of names; and when Zafra was questioned, he insisted that the woman was mad; but meanwhile with their accustomed zeal, the Inquisitors had made many arrests, had shown their prisoners the persuasive machines in their secret chambers, and very soon they were on the way to uncovering the greatest Protestant heresy as yet heard of in Spain.

Zafra was arrested; fortunately for him so numerous were the prisoners that there were not enough prisons to contain them and insecure ones had to be used. Into one of the latter Zafra was put, and in a very short time he had escaped. It was for this reason that his effigy, not his person, was taken to the *quemadero* on that tragic September day in Seville.

Several people died bravely on that day. There were Don Gonzaler, a great preacher, and his two sisters. He had been tortured with the utmost severity, but nothing could make him deny his faith. He was condemned with his sisters to be burned alive and, when the fires were lighted, instead of asking the mercy of strangulation in exchange for recantation, these three brave people sang together: " Hold not thy peace, O God of my praise; for the mouth of the wicked and the mouth of the deceitful are opened against me; they have spoken against me with a lying tongue."

Rule says these three people died in the faith of Christ and of His Holy Gospel; by which he means that they died in the Protestant Faith. Whether they accepted one dogma and refused another seems unimportant compared with the overwhelming and admirable courage with which they were able to face the fire, sacrificing their lives for the right to their own opinions.

Fray Christóbal de Arellano and his two brothers also went as martyrs to the flames. Fray Garcia de Arias, an elder monk of the monastery of San Isidro of Seville, was another martyr. Christóbal de Losada, who had practised as a physician in Seville, and Fernando de San Juan who was a schoolmaster, also were burned alive.

Morcillo, a monk of the monastery of San Isidro, was less brave. At the last moment he wavered and received strangulation before his flesh was consumed.

Another victim was Doña Maria de Bohorqués, who was nearly

twenty-one years of age. She was the illegitimate daughter of a nobleman of Seville and had been well educated.

She was arrested, and calmly admitted her interest in the new ideas, but would not mention the names of others. She was taken to the torture chambers and there put to the torture, and in a weak moment she admitted that her sister Juana, although aware of her interest in Lutheran doctrines, had not protested nor tried to turn her away from them. When she was taken to the *quemadero* and the iron was placed about her neck at the stake, she was ordered to recite the creed. She obeyed, but her manner of doing so betrayed her adherence to Lutheranism, and afraid of so much courage, her tormentors strangled her. One feels relieved that she received this small mercy.

The Inquisitors lost no time in arresting Maria's sister Juana for, they insisted, had she been a good Catholic not only would she have reproved her sister for her heretical leanings but she would have reported her to the Inquisition. Juana was pregnant at this time and, with a show of great magnanimity, the Inquisitors did not torture her. They waited until her child was born, and eight days later took it from her; after another week she was taken down to the torture chambers. These wicked men were able to devise especial torture for a woman recently recovered from childbirth, and in addition to their usual cruel practices they passed cords about her breasts gradually tightening them until they cut into the flesh hoping that in her anguish she could be induced to betray her husband and her friends. Her ribs were crushed in the process and her poor mangled body was taken back to its dungeon. Mercifully she died within a week.

*   *   *

The most famous of all the *autos* of this year was the one which took place on October 8th. This is notorious because Philip II himself took part in it.

A contemporary recorder, a Flemish official, states that there were two hundred thousand spectators. This was another of the Protestant *autos*, for there were among the victims only one relaxed Morisco, one Judaizer reconciled to the Church and two other penitents convicted of minor offences, while there were no less than twenty-six Protestants.

Philip had made a vow when he had come near to shipwreck. His fleet had begun to founder within sight of Laredo, and then he had solemnly declared that if God would save him and his ships he would, as a reward for the Deity, take the utmost vengeance on the heretics in Spain. Philip came safely out of the adventure and lost no time in keeping his vow.

With the King came his son, Don Carlos, Prince of the Asturias, and his sister Juana—in the cases of the two last this was their second *auto* of recent date. Philip's presence naturally brought out many other great personages, and the *auto* was attended by the Prince of Parma, the Archbishop of Seville and among other high prelates the Bishops of Palencia and Zamora. Ambassadors from France and Rome represented those places and thus gave their implicit approval of the fierce attack on the new religion.

The sermon was preached by the Bishop of Cuenca; and this occasion was made even more remarkable because during it Philip took the oath of allegiance to the Inquisition. This he did in all humility with bared head and ungloved hand, drawing his sword and brandishing it as he swore.

The most distinguished of the victims on this day was Don Carlos de Seso who was forty-three years of age and had spent many years in the service of the Emperor Charles. He was recognized as one of the leading Lutherans and was certainly a very brave man, for on the day before he was to die—and it does not need a great deal of imagination to picture the state of mind of people, who had been weakened by torture, suddenly to learn that the last terrible ordeal was immediately before them—he asked for pen and paper and when it was given him wrote a full confession of his faith; he affirmed that the doctrine of the Catholic Church was not the true faith and that the one in which he was fully prepared to die was the living faith.

Such men were disconcerting. They must have presented a noble sight on their way to the *quemadero*, an alarming inspiration to those watchers in the crowd. For this reason men like de Seso were burdened with the additional torment of the gag.

De Seso had been so acutely tortured that he was unable to stand whilst listening to his sentence, and it was necessary for two *alguazils* to stand on either side of him and hold him up. One story is that this brave man, when the gag was removed from his mouth, found himself not far from the Royal gallery. He lifted his burning fanatical eyes to the cold blue ones of Philip and asked him how he could allow such horrors to take place within his kingdom; to this the King, burning with righteous indignation against heretics, having within the hour, in the face of the world, declared his determination to support the Inquisition with heart, mind and soul, replied: " I would myself bring the wood to burn my own son if he were guilty of heresy as you are."

It is not difficult to picture that dramatic scene: Philip, cold as he ever was, so certain that he had God on his side; the maimed martyr; and the glowering cripple who was already aware of his father's dissatisfaction with him and already learning to hate him.

De Seso is reputed to have shown no fear of the flames and to have told the crowd that if he had had time he would have convinced them that they should follow his example. But as this would not be allowed, he continued, he begged his tormentors to light up the fire as quickly as they could, for he was ready and eager for it.

And this was the case, for when the faggots had been lighted and the rope which bound him to the stake had burned through, eagerly he threw himself into the heart of the fire.

There was only one other martyr on that occasion; this was Juan Sánchez who had escaped to Flanders. Like de Seso he called for more and more fire and seemed to revel in his agonies.

The other victims took advantage of the rule to be reconciled to the Church of Rome, and for this they received the mercy of strangulation before death. One woman did manage to commit suicide by cutting her throat with a pair of scissors. The Inquisition took revenge on her by burning her effigy.

* * *

There took place another *auto de fé* in Seville on December 22nd, 1560, and at this suffered many of the Protestants who had been gathered into the Inquisition's net when the enquiries had started in Seville and Valladolid.

On this occasion thirteen people were burned with three effigies, and thirty-four were condemned to penances.

The effigies were those of Dr. Juan Gil (Egidio) and Dr. Constantino Ponce de la Fuente. The first had died a natural death but Doctor Constantino had not been so fortunate. He was arrested and put into a dungeon which was so small that it was impossible for him to move, and there he was kept until he died of dysentery. He is reputed to have exclaimed: " Oh my God, were there no Scythians, no cannibals, nor beings even more cruel than these in whose power You could have left me rather than to have made me the prisoner of these barbarians? "

The bodies of these two were brought from the grave to be burned with their effigies on December 22nd, 1560.

One of the victims on this occasion was that Julianillo Hernández, who had been living peaceably in Frankfurt and had brought the books to Spain in the hope of introducing Lutheranism to that country. He was an exceptionally brave man and during his three years in prison had been submitted to the vilest tortures, yet never had he betrayed any of his friends. He had shown the utmost defiance towards his jailors and is reputed to have chanted, after they had left him in his cell:

> " *Vencidos van los Frailes, vencidos van;*
> *Corridos van los lobos, corridos van.*"
> " *There go the friars, there they run!*
> *There go the wolves, the wolves are gone.*"

This bold chanting voice, heard in the corridors of the grim prison, struck chords of new hope in many fainting hearts.   It was men like the little Julianillo Hernández who were the greatest danger to the Inquisition.

Naturally he was brought gagged to the *auto* but, when at the last moments the gag was removed and he was besought to implore reconciliation with the Catholic Church and thus escape burning alive, he reproved them for making such suggestions; and stretching out for a burning faggot he held it near his head that he might be consumed the quicker.

This *auto de fé* is made more interesting by the fact that among the victims were a Frenchman and two Englishmen.

A little is known of the case of one of these Englishmen who appears in the records as Nicolas Bertoun (presumably Nicholas Burton).

Burton was a Londoner who sailed the seas and had often called at Spanish ports in the course of business.   About two years before this *auto* took place he had landed at Cadiz and there he had talked too freely of his beliefs, for he was arrested by an *alguazil* and brought before the Inquisition.   Naturally when he was arrested his ship and all her cargo were confiscated; it is probable that this rich booty was one of the main reasons for Burton's arrest.

He was not told on what grounds he was imprisoned, but he was kept in a dungeon for two years.

Meanwhile the owners of his ship were eager to recover their property, and they despatched another Englishman, John Frampton, to Spain in order to discover what had happened to Burton.   Every obstacle was put in Frampton's way and eventually he himself was arrested on the charge of having a heretical book in his luggage.

Frampton was tortured and, not being able to withstand this form of persuasion—as Burton was—he agreed to become a Catholic. Frampton was sentenced to more than a year's imprisonment, and all his possessions were confiscated; he was to wear the *sanbenito* for a year and was never to leave Spain. Meanwhile Burton was condemned to the flames and was burned alive.

Nothing is known of William Brook, except that he was a sailor from Southampton, nor of the Frenchman Barthélemi Fabienne, except that they were also burned at the stake.

In the next *auto* which took place on April 26th, 1562, there were forty-nine victims who were Lutherans, and twenty-one of these were foreigners.   In October at another *auto* there were thirty-nine Lutherans.   These numbers were not great when compared with those of the Marranos and the Moriscos, the reason being that Lutheranism did not take a firm hold on Spain, and the risings in Valladolid and Seville were the only ones of any note.

But the *auto de fé* was becoming a common spectacle throughout the country, no more unusual than a bull-fight and having very much the same appeal to public taste.

9

ARCHBISHOP CARRANZA

O NE OF the most important victims of the Inquisition during
the Protestant persecution was Bartolomé de Carranza y Miranda,
Archbishop of Toledo and Primate of Spain.

His case is an indication of the insecurity of every man in Spain
during that era.

It seems incredible that a man of such high position, of such
influence and importance, could be dragged so low; but such was
the power of the Inquisition.

Carranza was born in the year 1503 at Miranda de Arga in
the kingdom of Navarre. His parents were of noble status and
when he was fifteen he was sent first to the university of Alcalá,
and later to the college of St. Balbinia, to study philosophy.

When he was eighteen years old he took his vows in the Dominican
Order and went to study at the College of San Gregorio at
Valladolid.

Carranza was however a man of deep intellect and he was not
one to curb his tongue. During his lectures he spoke more freely
than was actually safe for any man, and he was not without his
enemies.

Before he had passed his twenty-seventh birthday he could
have been in serious trouble. A Dominican, one of the lecturers
of the college, went to the Inquisition concerning Carranza and
told the officials that his colleague harboured unhealthy notions.
He had actually stated that the power of the Pope and Church
were limited, and the only salvation was to be attained through
Jesus Christ.

The Inquisitors considered this information and, for some reason
known only to themselves, decided to do nothing about it. But
such information was never lost; it was treasured, stored away in
the archives for future reference.

Meanwhile another accuser appeared. This was a Dominican,

Juan de Villamartin, who informed the Inquisition that Carranza was a great admirer of Erasmus and had often, in his lectures, defended those works of the scholar which had attacked confession and penance as ordained by the Catholic Church.

This was also docketed and put away.

Carranza began to climb to prominence. He was made a professor of Arts and junior professor of Theology, and in 1534 the great honour, not only of chief professor, but that of consulter of the tribunal of Valladolid was given to him. He even became Theologian Qualificator or Examiner of the Holy Office of the Inquisition of Valladolid, and in this role often acted.

In 1540 he was sent to Rome to represent his Order to the General Chapter, and there was given a doctorate by Paul III and with it a licence to examine and prohibit the introduction into Spain of heretical literature.

He was now well known through the country as a man destined for a very high place; and in 1542 was offered the See of Cuzco in the American Dependencies, but this he refused. In 1544 he was present on the first occasion when a Lutheran was burned. This was San Roman who died the martyr's death demanding of all those who watched him whether they did not envy him his happiness in dying for the true faith.

Perhaps Carranza never forgot this man.

He continued to rise. In 1545 the Emperor Charles selected him to go to the Council of Trent as one of the theologians, and while at Trent he showed himself to be the firmest possible supporter of the Catholic Church. At the same time however, he published a book—a very dangerous thing to do—the purpose of which was to reform the Bishops' custom of absenting themselves from their Sees, Carranza being assured that a Bishop could only do his best work if he lived in his diocese. This touched a lot of the Bishops in a vulnerable spot, and once again there was a flutter among Carranza's enemies. This time however they had grown in proportion to his fame. He was a very distinguished man and he had many enemies who would be only too eager at the appropriate moment to bring about his downfall.

In 1548 Charles offered him the post of confessor to Philip—one of tremendous influence, particularly with a man as religiously minded as Philip. Carranza refused this, as he did the See of the Canaries which was offered to him in 1550.

At that time he became Provincial of his Order in Castile and a year later was sent to join the Council of Trent, which had once again been convoked.

On returning to Spain he went back to San Gregorio at Valladolid. Meanwhile historical events were moving towards him.

Philip was about to contract a marriage with Mary Tudor, and he called upon Carranza to accompany him to England.

* * *

During the reign of Philip II the Inquisition grew to a new magnitude. Not one of Spain's monarchs was a more ardent supporter of this Institution than Philip, and there can be no doubt that it is due to his zeal that during his reign it came into its heyday.

Philip was every inch a Spaniard, as Charles, his father could never have been. Charles spent a very small proportion of his life in Spain and his sympathy and understanding always remained with the people of the Netherlands. He had been born in Flanders; he spoke the language of that country as he could never learn to speak Spanish; but it was more than a language which separated him from the people of Spain. He was German, and it is as the Emperor Charles V of Germany rather than Charles I of Spain that he is known.

How different it was with Philip! From that May day in 1527 when he was born in the Valladolid Palace he was a Spaniard and his upbringing accentuated this. He might have been named Philip after his grandfather Philip the Handsome, son of Emperor Maximilian, but there was little of the Hapsburg in this young man.

Philip was carefully instructed by his professors—Juan Martinez Siliceo to look after his academic life, and Juan de Zuñiga to teach him how to excel in sport. Zuñiga might be outspoken and not the man to mince his words even to the heir to the throne, but Siliceo was certainly not going to risk offending his pupil. It is typical of Philip's solemn nature that he was no more angered by Zuñiga's outspokenness than he was ready to take advantage of the accommodating nature of his professor.

It is clear that in Philip Spain was to have a very serious-minded King.

Philip was twelve years old when his mother died (May 1st, 1539). The Emperor at this time was not quite forty, Isabella his wife was thirty-six. Charles however did not marry again. He was deeply engaged in wars away from Spain and he had his heir in Philip. Isabella had borne Charles two other sons but both of these had died of epilepsy when they were very young; and Philip, in spite of being small, seemed to be healthy. In any case there was no second marriage.

Charles was determined to train his son at a very early age for the greatness which was to come to him, for this pale-eyed boy would be heir to half the world one day.

When the boy was only sixteen Charles took him into his confidence with regard to his method of government; there were warnings to beware of the hypocrisy of statesmen, and Charles often discussed with his son the most important of these men, who would be Philip's advisers, dissecting their characters with a great deal of analytical skill, and some malice, for his son's enlightenment. In 1543 when Philip was but sixteen the Emperor left Spain, appointign Philip Regent during his absence. The Emperor could be sure that Philip would, no matter at what cost to himself, do his duty. Charles often wished that his son was a little gayer in personality, but he could not have had a more dutiful boy.

The royal families of Spain and Portugal had become closely related by continual intermarrying and, in November 1543, Philip married the Princess Maria of Portugal, his young cousin. She was five months younger than Philip and Philip was pleased with the match. He was not the kind of boy to have had a great deal to do with women and was prepared to be a good husband to little Maria.

Married life was short-lived however. In less than two years, on July 8th, 1545, Maria gave birth to a son. This was the notorious and ill-fated Don Carlos. Three days after the birth of Carlos, Maria died. Thus the young husband had become a young widower; it was true he had a son, but if he could have seen into the future he would have known that it would have been better to have no son rather than Carlos.

It was difficult for Charles to make the Flemings love his heir. The quiet, serious young man was so different from those noisy, pleasure-loving people, and so different from his father, that Charles often despaired of the relationship which must ensue between Philip and a very large proportion of his subjects.

Philip, of course, could not remain for ever unmarried, and the prospect of a bride for him occupied both the minds of himself and his father to a large extent.

There came the summer of 1553 and the death of Edward VI of England. Edward was succeeded by his half-sister Mary, daughter of Catalina of Aragon, aunt of the Emperor Charles. There seemed possibilities here of an alliance with England, for surely Mary, with her connections with the Spanish House, would be very ready to consider her Spanish kinsman with favour.

Moreover religious affairs had undergone a great change in

England. Henry VIII had broken with the Pope and had abolished the monasteries. England had remained Catholic but not Papist. Yet during the reign of young King Edward VI there had been a welcome for the new Lutheran ideas in England and Protestantism became the recognized religion of the country.

Charles and Philip would say that fortunately the previous reign had been short, the King too young, for this to have had a great effect upon the people, and now on the throne was the daughter of their own Catalina of Aragon, as ardent a Catholic as her mother.

There is an interesting account of England of this day, which was given by the Venetian Giovanni Micheli. It was the custom of Venetian merchants at that time to visit foreign countries, assess their wealth and come back to their native Venice where they would read an account of their travels to the Doge and Senate.

London, declared Micheli, was one of the greatest cities in Europe and its population, including its suburbs, about one hundred and eighty thousand. England was strong enough to hold off any invasion in spite of a small navy; its army was strong, particularly in bowmen, in which art all Englishmen were trained from early days. There were no taxes on wine, beer and salt, nor on cloth— a great difference this, when compared with other countries in Europe whose people were crippled by taxation. The entire revenue was rarely more than two hundred thousand pounds. The royal will was law and rarely was the parliament summoned.

As for the Queen, she was thirty-six years of age and had been handsome in her youth. Unfortunately she suffered much from disease, and this had left its mark upon her countenance. She was clever, spoke many languages and was less frivolous than her half-sister Elizabeth. She was determined to bring the Catholic Faith back to England and had been heard to say that she would lose ten crowns rather than imperil her soul.

Mary, now that she was Queen of England, was turning her eyes towards Spain. When she had been a child of six, the Emperor Charles had visited England and had been persuaded by Mary's mother to enter into an agreement to marry the little girl. The disparity in their ages, however, was too great, and Charles too impatient a man to wait as long as he would have to wait for Mary.

Charles now determined to secure the English crown for Philip and accordingly wrote to Mary telling her that, since he himself had become infirm and elderly, he could not suggest marrying her himself. Therefore he offered her the person most dear to him: his son Philip.

After some coquetry on Mary's part the marriage treaty was drawn up.

This laid down that Philip should respect the existing laws and not interfere with the rights and liberties of Englishmen; that the power of conferring titles and offices, should remain with the Queen. Foreigners to the English were not to be given office. If there should be male issue of the marriage, that son was to be heir to the English crown, and to Spanish possessions in the Low Countries and Burgundy. Should Don Carlos die, any son Philip should have by Mary should also inherit Spain and her dependencies. The Queen was not to be forced to leave England unless she desired to do so. If Mary should die, Philip was to claim no right in the government of the country.

In spite of this treaty, which was very favourable from the English point of view, there was a great outcry in London when its contents were made public; and there was much dissatisfaction throughout the country, the chief insurrection being that under the leadership of Sir Thomas Wyatt.

Meanwhile Philip made ready to leave Spain for England. The Regency was left in the hands of the Princess Juana, Philip's sister who was eight years his junior. Don Carlos, already showing himself to be a menace to his father's peace, was left in the charge of his preceptor, Luis de Vives.

Philip set sail for England on the 11th July, 1554, and with him were all the highest ranking gentlemen of the Castilian nobility —men such as Ruy Gomez the Prince of Eboli and the Duke of Alva. And as one of Philip's intentions while in England was to bring England back to the Church, with him sailed the man whom he and his father had considered the most suitable for this task: Bartolomé de Carranza.

*   *   *

Arrived in England Carranza became the associate of Cardinal Pole, and Philip let Mary know that he wished his Archbishop to be one of her chief advisers in her great task of re-establishing the Catholic Faith in her domain. Carranza was soon deeply resented by the English, who nicknamed him the Black Friar, partly because of his dark complexion and partly because of his Dominican robes.

Carranza, accustomed to the methods employed in Spain against heretics, was, according to many of his biographers, largely responsible for the Marian persecutions which culminated in the Smithfield fires. So unpopular did he become that several attempts were made on his life; he survived them all.

In September 1555, Philip, heartily tired of Mary and eager to escape from her cloying affection, joined his father in Flanders. However, he left Carranza in England, strongly advising Mary to keep him as her chief religious adviser; and Mary, who was eager to keep her husband's favour at all costs, agreed to do this.

When Mary came to the throne it was stated that "Her Grace's conscience is stayed in the matter of religion, yet she meaneth graciously not to compel or strain other men's consciences otherwise than God shall (as she trusted) put in their hearts a persuasion of the truth that she is in, through the opening of His word unto them by godly virtuous and learned preachers."

On the surface this sounds as though she intended to be lenient, but there is a hint of a threat in the words; she herself has the truth, she implies (always a dangerous assumption), and her learned preachers are going to put before her people the same truth.

Mary's true intention very soon became obvious. Certain laws which had been passed during the reign of her half-brother were repealed; one of these was the Act of Uniformity which allowed priests to marry. Those who had been teaching the Reformed Faith found themselves in prison—Latimer, Cranmer, Ridley and Hooper among them.

A petition had been drawn up, acknowledging the misconduct of England in breaking away from the Papal rule, and on the 30th November, 1554, with Mary and Philip on their knees in a ceremony which can only be called humiliating to the monarchy of England, that country was received back into the Apostolic fold.

In the following January (1555) a solemn procession took place in the streets of London to celebrate the re-conversion to Rome and the acceptance of the Pope's authority. This was led by the children of Grey Friars (Christ's Hospital) and of St. Paul's schools; one hundred and sixty priests carried ninety crosses singing the Roman service as they walked. Eight Bishops were in the parade, with them Bonner himself, now come into his own after his years in the wilderness. In the streets that night there were bonfires; it was not very long before the people of London were to see bonfires of another nature.

The first court which was set up to deal with heresy was in the church of St. Mary Overy, presided over by Gardiner, Bonner, Tonstal and three priests.

Hooper was brought before this tribunal after having withstood eighteen months imprisonment in the filthy Fleet Prison. Another, one John Rogers, who was Canon of St. Paul's, stood on trial with him. Rogers had done a great deal of work on translating the Bible into English and was thus, in the opinion of men such as Bonner and Gardiner, guilty of heresy. He was a very bold man and when he was condemned, for he refused to recant, he asked that he might take a last farewell of his wife and children. Since he was a priest, Gardiner retorted, he had no wife, and then this self-rightous man went on to refer to Mrs. Rogers and the children in the coarsest possible terms.

For six days Rogers and Hooper were kept in Newgate, and at the end of that time Rogers was taken to Smithfield. In the crowds he saw his wife with their children (eleven of them—and one a baby in arms) waiting for a last glimpse of him. He did not falter and when he was offered a pardon if he would accept the Catholic Faith, he answered that what he had preached he would seal with his blood. " Thou art a heretic ", the sheriff told him, to which Rogers replied: " That will be known when the last day comes." " I will never pray for you," the sheriff said. " But I will pray for you," replied Rogers. And when the fires were lighted he appeared to bathe his body in them most joyfully.

Hooper was taken to Gloucester and burned near the Cathedral. He too was offered pardon if he would recant; and he too refused it. He suffered dreadfully, for the faggots were sparse and green and would not burn easily and the fire only reached the lower part of his body because of the direction in which the wind blew. He called for more and more fire, and at length gunpowder was brought. He suffered the most acute agony for three quarters of an hour, and it is recorded that in the crowds who watched him die, there was much weeping and lamentation.

It is gratifying to note that the spectators of these scenes in England were very different from those blood-crazed fanatics of the *quemadero*.

Philip was wise enough to realize that the English did not take as naturally to this sport of burning heretics as did his own people, and it was he who suggested that they should not offer too many such spectacles to the people of England. The day after the burning of Hooper he caused a sermon to be preached in which the practice of burning heretics alive was condemned. But the lull was short-lived. After five weeks a weaver was burned in Smithfield, and a short while after others followed.

Mary by this time was experiencing one of those distressing false pregnancies, and she believed that the more heretics she burned the

Queen Mary I of England (from a painting by Antonio Moro in the Prado
Gallery, Madrid)

Philip II of Spain (from a painting by Coello)

more likely God would be to make her fruitful! Therefore she was eager to continue with the persecutions.

Latimer and Ridley were burned. Latimer was fortunate—he died quickly—but Ridley suffered acutely for, as in the case of Hooper, he was not given enough faggots and one of his legs was completely destroyed by the fire before the rest of his body was touched.

Cranmer met his death in 1556, and before he went to the stake refused to recant and told of the shame he felt because, in his fear of death he had committed the ignominious action of signing a recantation. He thereupon renounced the Pope and the Catholic Church and when he was at the stake, we are told, he was seen to hold in the flames to be first consumed that right hand which had signed the recantation.

It is impossible to state with accuracy the numbers who, during the Marian persecutions, died by fire, torture or through being shut away in insanitary prisons.

There is the usual wrangling between Catholic and Protestant recorders when it comes to figures. Catholics declare that many of the victims were condemned as traitors and not for their religious beliefs. Protestants on the other hand are inclined to swell the numbers of martyrs.

One estimate is that of Dr. Lingard, which is: " in the space of four years almost two hundred people perished in the flames for their religious opinions".

Maitland in his *Essays on the Reformation* gives the number as two hundred and seventy-seven, but some omissions from his list have been discovered. The total number must have been somewhere in the region of three hundred.

This is horrifying, yet, after a consideration of the Spanish Inquisition, it seems almost insignificant. It is interesting to note that there were very few persecutions in the north of England, probably due to the fact that the northern dioceses were far from the seat of government. London had the largest number, forty-three people having met their deaths at Smithfield; at Canterbury forty-one died; Colchester had twenty-three. But apart from those burned at the stake many died in prison and many were tortured to death; and although these figures may seem comparatively small, this period was one of the darkest through which our country has ever passed; the reason is that, owing to the Spanish marriage, for a few years our skies were darkened by the shadow of the Inquisition. Had Mary lived there is no doubt that Philip would have induced her to set up the Inquisition in this country, and that Mary herself would have been delighted to do so. Whether or not the people would have stood quietly by and allowed this to happen is a matter for conjecture.

I like to think that it could not have happened here, that the less excitable English, the less fanatical English, would never have allowed their fellow countrymen to be persecuted as were the inhabitants of Spain.

It is a fact that they did not gather in their thousands to watch a burning; they did not make a festival of it; the spirit shown at the Smithfield fires and those of Canterbury, Coventry, Lewes and other places was in no way similar to that at the *autos de fé* of Seville and Valladolid. The Spaniards willingly chanted their oath of allegiance to the Inquisition; they shouted abuse at the victims; they applauded their soldiers who ran their halberds through bodies already broken by torture, destined for the fire. But the English sullenly watched the fires; and in later years when the cry of " No Popery " echoed through the land, they showed they had not forgotten.

It was Carranza's boast that during the three years he was in England he had either burned, brought back to the Church or driven out of the country thirty thousand heretics.

Perhaps his zeal caused him to exaggerate a little; however, the fact remains that he played a large part in the Marian persecutions.

*   *   *

While he was in England Carranza had, by order of Cardinal Pole, who was the Papal Legate, helped the Queen in establishing the Catholic religion in the Universities and had drawn up the canons which were to be passed in a National Council. He had been particularly active in the condemnation of Thomas Cranmer; and in 1557 he joined Philip in Flanders to report on what was happening in England. While he was in Flanders he was still burning with fanatical zeal against heretics and seized a large number of books to which he gave a ceremonial burning.

When the Archbishop of Toledo died Philip decided to honour Carranza by bestowing this office upon him. It was the highest honour of the Church and with it went the Primacy of Spain. Carranza was not eager to accept. He had written a book, which was being printed in Antwerp, and this seemed of greater importance to him than any honour; as it turned out it was certainly to be so, but not in the way Carranza had hoped.

Philip however insisted on his accepting the Archbishopric, and

Pope Paul IV during Carranza's preconisation in Rome dispensed with many of the usual formalities which involved an examination of the past life of the man under review, for he said Carranza was well known to him as a man devoted to the Catholic Church and one who had done it good service in England and Flanders as well as Spain.

Carranza was now at the height of his power; and his enemies had been increasing with the years. There were many who remembered how, at the Council of Trent, he had spoken against Bishops who did not live in their dioceses, and had even published a treatise on this subject. These envious people gathered together and discussed the rise of Carranza, asking one another whether there had not in the past been certain heretical statements attributed to him.

One of Carranza's foremost enemies was the Inquisitor-General Valdés. As Archbishop of Toledo, Carranza was beyond his control, for Carranza was supreme in the Church in Spain and if Valdés wished to arrest him on a charge of heresy he could not do so without the consent of the Pope.

Philip sent Carranza to Yuste to consult Charles on certain matters and when the Archbishop arrived at the Emperor's retreat he found Charles very weak indeed.

During his stay at Yuste Charles sought religious comfort from the Archbishop, and Carranza, who had recently come from countries such as England and Flanders where the Reformed religion was the accepted one, seems to have used expressions which were used in that Faith. His enemies were on the watch for every word he uttered, every gesture he made.

Juan de Regla who was the Emperor's confessor was very jealous because his master had chosen to turn to the Archbishop for comfort, and when at this bedside Carranza read a psalm and followed it with the words: " Your Majesty may have full confidence; for there is not, nor hath been, any sin which the blood of Jesus hath not sufficed to efface," these words were construed as being the expression of reformed thought and were remembered against him. Charles died and Carranza's methods of administering the last rites were noted and criticized.

Regla, Valdés, Melchor Cano, and Pedro de Castro, the Bishop of Cuenca, were all on the watch now. It was not usually difficult for the Inquisition to substantiate a charge of heresy when it decided to bring one.

The great chance came with the publication of Carranza's book *Commentaries on the Christian Catechism.*

Valdés bought a large number of copies of the book which he distributed with the instructions that a thorough search was to be made with a view to discovering heretical phrases. If anything were discovered, there must for a time be secrecy, but thorough notes should be made and kept.

It was at this time that the prisons of the Inquisition were filling with the Lutherans of Valladolid and Seville. If Valdés needed evidence against any man in Spain he had so many victims in his power that it was almost certain he could find what he wanted. These poor men and women had only to be taken to the torture chambers and put on the hoist or the rack where physical sufferings were so intense that they were ready to do or say anything that was required to buy a little respite from pain.

Thus from the torture chambers came further damning evidence against Archbishop Carranza.

There was one thing Valdés could do, and that was apply to the Pope telling him that Carranza was vehemently suspected of heresy, and to ask for permission to place him in the hands of the Inquisition.

The Dean of Oviedo, who was a nephew of Valdés, was sent to the Pope to obtain the desired permission. The Pope had been a friend of Carranza's; he disliked the Spaniards and had referred to them as the scum of the Earth, adding that although they were now in possession of certain parts of Italy, a short while before they had been known in that country only as cooks. Even so, he was not eager to run into any trouble by defending Carranza, and all he did was delay matters a little.

Meanwhile news reached Carranza that his book was under suspicion. This aroused his alarm, which was indeed natural, and he wrote to Sancho López de Otalora who was a member of the Supreme Council that he was prepared to withdraw the book. If Valdés had really been concerned with preventing the spread of possible heresy this action of Carranza's should have satisfied him; but Valdés' great desire was to make Carranza a prisoner of the Inquisition and to bring about his disgrace and downfall.

Meanwhile Paul IV died and Pius IV was elected; the latter confirmed the necessary permission, and Dean Valdés of Oviedo returned to Inquisitor Valdés in triumph.

When Philip heard that the man, whom he and his father had chosen to honour, was to be arrested on a charge of suspected heresy and brought before the Inquisition, he did nothing to save him. Philip had proved himself to be quite without sentiment even towards those who thought themselves to be his friends; and any lapse into heresy was in his eyes the greatest of sins. He was told that in addition to the suspicion attached to Carranza's works, many of the imprisoned Lutherans of Valladolid and Seville had testified against him. All Philip asked was that, since Carranza was Archbishop of Toledo and Primate of Spain, his arrest should take place without disturbing his dignity.

He then wrote to his sister Juana, who was once more Governess of Spain during his absence from the country, and told her that he wished her to summon Carranza to Court on some pretext; that when he was there he might, with the utmost decorum, be taken into custody.

The Princess accordingly wrote to the Archbishop telling him that he must come with all speed to Valladolid where he was summoned to wait the return to Spain of His Majesty the King.

This message was conveyed to him by Rodrigo de Castro who was a brother of Pedro de Castro, a man who had determined on Carranza's downfall; he was so eager to see Carranza arrested that he carried the message to Carranza's palace at Alcalá de Henares with such speed that when he arrived he was quite exhausted and had to rest a few days before he was able to go on.

* * *

Carranza was completely duped by the summons, and immediately arranged for special prayers to be said for the safe arrival of the King; at the same time he must have remembered the suspicions which his book had aroused, and he arranged not to leave until de Castro was sufficiently recovered to accompany him.

A few days after the arrival of de Castro, another visitor appeared. This was Diego Ramírez who had come to announce an Edict of Faith.

The proclamation was celebrated in the Church of San Francisco, and Carranza himself preached the sermon, telling the people that they must obey the Edict and, if they suspected any person of heresy, they must come forward and denounce that person.

It was noted that in the Edict there was on this occasion no mention of heresy in books; and this had probably been eliminated out of respect for the Archbishop.

Carranza was no doubt beginning to grow uneasy. From the moment his book had been under suspicion he could not have felt free from apprehension; he as much as anyone knew the methods of the Inquisition; he probably guessed that it was solely because of his position that he had been allowed to remain a free man.

He now seemed eager to delay the departure to Valladolid. He probably felt that if he could wait until Philip was in Spain he would have the support of a man on whose justice he could rely. He therefore, before leaving Alcalá, arranged to hold confirmations at various places through which he was to pass, so great was his desire to postpone the arrival at his destination.

At Fuente del Saz a monk, who was a professor of a college of Alcalá, came to Carranza and told him that rumours were circulating in Valladolid that there was a plot to arrest him and take him before the tribunal of the Inquisition; this monk advised him to return at once to Alcalá or to make with all speed to Valladolid, for in the quiet little villages on the road between these two places it would be a simple matter for the *alguazils* to descend upon him by stealth one night and carry him off to prison and he might never be seen again.

Carranza replied to this that his friend had been listening to wild stories. He had been summoned to Valladolid by the Princess Juana to await the King who was on his way home. How could he be under suspicion of heresy? Had he not recently come from England where he had led the campaign against heretics?

Valdés was eager to make the arrest. He was afraid that Carranza would reach Valladolid and that Philip himself might arrive there. If Carranza had a chance of putting his case before the King it was quite possible that he would free himself from suspicion. Valdés was determined that Carranza must not have that opportunity.

When Carranza reached Torrelaguna on Sunday, August 20th, 1559, there waiting for him was Fray Pedro de Soto who was full of dire warnings. Carranza was in imminent danger, he warned, for his friend, Luis de la Croz, had already been arrested in Valladolid. Carranza asked on what charge, and when told he replied: " Then accordingly, they will make me a heretic!"

Disaster was nearer than he realized. The *alguazils* were gathering in stealth in Torrelaguna. Cebrian, chief *alguazil* of the Council of the Inquisition, was in one of the hostels of the town, staying in bed by day and emerging only at night, that his presence might not be suspected. On Tuesday 22nd, a hundred men were stationed within a short distance of Torrelaguna ready to close in for the arrest.

On Sunday the 27th Rodrigo de Castro took supper with the Archbishop; then, declaring that he was very tired, he left him and went to the house in which he was staying to make sure that his assistants were in readiness. He then returned to the house in which the Archbishop was lodging, and seeking out the landlord told him that he was about to give orders in the name of the Holy Office which must be obeyed to the letter. The trembling landlord readily assured de Castro that he, like all subjects of the King, was the willing slave of the Inquisition. That was good; he was to leave all the doors of his house unbarred that night.

During the night de Castro with several assistants entered the house in which the Archbishop lay and mounted the stairs, pausing outside that ante-room where the friar who served Carranza was sleeping. They knocked on the door. " Who calls? " asked the friar, starting up from his bed. " Open to the Holy Office," was the answer. It was the summons which none dared disobey.

The door was opened and they walked through the ante-room to that where the Archbishop lay. " Who is there? " asked the Archbishop in alarm. There came the dreaded answer: " The Holy Office."

Rodrigo de Castro entered and called to the leading *alguazil* to do his duty. " Most illustratious Señor," said the *alguazil*, " the Holy Office commands me to make you its prisoner." He then read the order from the Inquisitor-General and the Council. Carranza pointed out that even the Inquisitor-General had no power to arrest the Primate of Spain. Whereupon the brief from the Pope was produced; and thus Carranza knew that his doom had come upon him.

* * *

He was taken from the town by night, and all the inhabitants were warned that they were not to look from their windows until the dawn; nor must they leave their houses; and when the miserable cortège reached Valladolid, Carranza was lodged in the house of Pedro González de Leon just outside the walls of the city.

The arrest had been carried out in the utmost secrecy, and many were afraid to mention the Archbishop's name. Some were imprisoned for talking of him and suggesting that he had been taken by the Holy Office. The whole affair was, as it was meant to be, wrapped in that secrecy so beloved by the Inquisition.

Carranza was not treated as badly as most prisoners who came into the prisons of the Inquisition. According to Llorente he was allowed an attendant, Fray Alonso de Utrilla, and a page, Jorje Gómez Muñoz de Carracosa. The party of three were given two rooms; this might imply some comfort, but the windows were shuttered and all light and air kept out; and the trio was not allowed to move out of these rooms for any reason whatsoever. This meant that the stench became poisonous and the Archbishop very soon succumbed to an illness which brought him near to death. A doctor who was allowed to see him said that the windows must be opened from time to time, but the Supreme Council of the Inquisition would not allow this, though they agreed that a small grating in the door might remain open if a guard were posted outside.

He was put under the charge of Diego González, who was one of the Valladolid Inquisitors, a miserable man, delighting in contemplating the wretched squalor to which a man who had once borne the highest title in Spain was reduced. He did little to help him, suppressing Carranza's correspondence with the Suprema when he though fit, spying on him and misconstruing his actions in his reports.

It was considered inadvisable to take Carranza to the headquarters of the Inquisition to face his judges; therefore Valdés, with the Supreme Council, came to the Archbishop's prison; and here Carranza, with a great show of courage accused the Inquisitor-General of having brought him to this pass, not because he suspected him of heresy, but because he was envious of his rise to power. Carranza and his friends felt their only hope to be in having the case tried in Rome, and this was what they were working for. Pius IV however, who might have been a friend to Carranza, was very eager not to offend Philip, and here again was one of those controversies between sovereign and Pope when each was more concerned with political advantage than the justice of the case under review.

Philip, who was never quick to act, waited a year before selecting new judges; and all this time the Inquisition and Philip were enjoying the enormous wealth of the Archbishopric of Toledo, and poor Carranza was languishing in his noisome jail.

In March of 1561 Philip appointed Gaspar Zuñiga, Archbishop of Santiago, as chief judge—a man known to be hostile to Carranza. Carranza however was allowed to choose two lawyers to defend him, and he selected Martin de Azpilcueta and Alonso Delgado.

Thus, it was two years after Carranza's arrest that his trial began. Carranza announced that during his two years' imprisonment he had continually tried to discover the reason for his arrest. He should, of course, have realized that he was in the hands of the Inquisition and it was the rule of this institution that prisoners should be kept in the dark as to their sins.

He was presented with thirty-one articles, to each of which he was to give a spontaneous answer. He realized then that the Inquisitors had combed his past life, from the time when he was a boy, in an endeavour to discover anything he had said or written which could be construed as heresy.

Another year passed while his case was being considered. Pius IV fretted in Rome. It was an offence against the dignity of the Church, he declared, to keep the Archbishop of Toledo so long a prisoner. He demanded that, if they could not bring the case to an end in Spain, there was one course open to them: transfer it to Rome to be settled.

In the midst of the wrangle between Spain and Rome Pius IV died, and in January 1566 St. Pius V was elected to the Papal chair.

St. Pius V was a strong man. He was the son of an Italian peasant and was clearly a man of very exceptional ability to have arrived at the highest office in the Church from his humble beginnings. He was a man of great energy determined to persecute heretics with all his strength, but at the same time he deplored the subversive methods which had been employed to this end. He was disturbed by the prolongation of the trial of the Archbishop of Toledo, and no sooner had he attained his office than he demanded the removal of Valdés from the office of Grand Inquisitor and that Carranza should be sent to Rome there to be tried by a tribunal which the Pope himself would set up.

Valdés was naturally furious, not only at the thought of handing his enemy over to the Pope, but also that it should be suggested that he himself should be dismissed. He sought to persuade Philip to stand out against Pope Pius V as he had against Pius IV; but the fifth Pius was a strong man; and when Philip countered with his usual hesitancy the new Pope thundered back that excommunication awaited those who flouted Papal authority. Philip decided on obedience. Valdés was dismissed from his post, and Carranza was taken from those two foul rooms, where he had existed for seven years, and sent under guard to Carthagena.

The Archbishop, who had been a healthy man when he was arrested, was now unable to walk and had to be carried in a litter.

When he reached Carthagena he remained there for four months during which time the Inquisitors refused to hand over to the Papal nuncio those papers dealing with the case. But eventually he left Carthagena and in May 1567 arrived at Civita Vecchia. He reached Rome a few days later and there he was made a prisoner in Castel Sant' Angelo.

Though still a prisoner, he found his new lodging was quite different from the old one. Here he could take exercise and enjoy the beautiful views from the windows. His health began to improve a little.

But the Pope seemed in no greater hurry to settle the fate of this long-suffering man than had the Spaniards, for he decided that all the papers must first be translated into Italian—a task which took the whole of what was left of that year to perform.

Further delays occurred by the discovery that the Spanish Inquisitors had not handed over all the papers; these had to be acquired and translated. The works of Carranza which were under discussion must also be translated into Italian; a year slipped away.

The Pope had set up a committee of seventeen consulters, four of whom were Spaniards who had been trying the case in Spain; they met once a week with the Pope as President.

The Pope now prepared his verdict. He had found the accusations of Valdés not proven; he commanded that the book, the publication of which had started the trouble, was to be given back to Carranza that he might translate it into Latin and have an opportunity of explaining those passages which had caused all the concern.

Pius believed that Philip would be delighted with this verdict. He had misunderstood Philip's true motives. Philip was filled with cold fury. He considered it an insult; as for the Inquisitors they too were incensed.

Unfortunately for Carranza, Pius V died (May 1572), only a few weeks after his ambassador arrived in Spain with the verdict, and Philip and the Inquisitors were ready to see in this death the hand of God which was, they believed, so firmly set against heretics.

They recorded their pleasure. The death of a man who had been willing to compromise the honour of the Spanish Inquisition for the sake of a Dominican monk could not be regarded as a great loss to Holy Church. On the other hand the death of such a Pope was a boon to the Inquisition.

The new Pope, Gregory XIII, was not such a bold man as his predecessor; he did not wish to antagonize a monarch of the stature of Philip II. Philip wished for the condemnation of Carranza in order to preserve what he considered to be the honour of Spain and the Inquisition. Gregory XIII was ready to do all in his power to oblige. He therefore took action against those bishops and theologians who had found no heresy in Carranza's works; they were threatened that they themselves might be suspected of heresy unless of course they were clever enough to discover new heresies in those written words.

In our period of partial freedom of speech, writing and the expression of opinion, it is easy to condemn these people, but one must remember that they had full knowledge not only of the terrible dungeons of the Inquisitions, those gloomy chambers of pain, but of the prolonged suffering of the Archbishop Carranza himself, if they had need to remind themselves of how the mighty could be brought low. One of these men was the Archbishop of Granada who was noted for his piety and would in a more lenient age have won great respect. But he was an old man; he could not be expected to view with equanimity all the horrors that the Inquisition was capable of forcing upon him. He was one of those, who, to save himself, discovered new heresies in the works of Carranza.

As a result, where sixty-eight of the propositions set out in Carranza's Catechism had been judged tainted with heresy, now there were two hundred and seventy-three.

Another two years passed and still the trial dragged on; and at length in April 1576 there assembled in the Hall of Constantine, the Pope, cardinals, prelates and counsellors to pronounce sentence. Carranza was brought before them.

Thus came this poor old man, quite devoid of all hope after seventeen years of imprisonment. He was now approaching seventy-three years of age, and when misfortune had first fallen upon him he had been but fifty-six. He came to stand before the Pope, bareheaded, bent double with infirmity, trembling with senility and certainly apprehension.

The Pope then announced that:

Carranza was vehemently suspected of certain errors and would be required to abjure them.

He was to be suspended and removed from the administration of his church for five years, and to await the pleasure of the Pope and the Holy See before he was allowed to regain any of his lost dignities.

During that time he was to retire to a monastery which had been chosen for him in Orvieto; and he must not leave this monastery without the consent of the Pope and the Holy See.

The Pope proposed to appoint an administrator of the church of Toledo; and all its riches accumulated since the day of the Archbishop's arrest and during his suspension, would be taken for the use of the Church, after the expenses such as pensions and debts had been dealt with.

A thousand crowns from this vast wealth should be set aside each month for the maintenance of the Archbishop.

Penances would be imposed upon him.

It was prohibited for any to possess, read or print his Cathechism.

So ended the trial which had been prolonged for seventeen years

* * *

The captain of the guard conducted Carranza to the Dominican monastery of Santa Maria sopra Minerva. The first of his penances was to visit seven churches on the Saturday of Easter week. Gregory, having passed the sentence to please Philip and the Spanish Inquisition then seemed to be worried by his conscience. He offered Carranza his own litter and horses.   He also offered him a letter in which he set out his esteem for the ex-Archbishop and wrote of his concern for his future.   Both these offers Carranza refused with the utmost dignity.   However, he began his penance and visited the seven churches; and when he did so, the people turned out in crowds to follow him from church to church and show him the sympathy they felt for his sufferings, and their refusal to believe in his guilt: some consolation, though a poor one for the suffering of years.

In a few days he became very ill, and hearing of his plight Gregory immediately sent him absolution and exemption from further penances.

Knowing that his end could not be far off, Carranza sent for his secretaries and before them made a solemn declaration that he had never swerved from the true faith.

He died on May 2nd, 1576.

His death was considered a little mysterious and therefore an autopsy was ordered.   Slight ulcers were discovered in the kidneys and gall-bladder, but there was no whisper that he had died of poison.   His death, though, is not without suspicion.   It may have been that the long arm of the Spanish Inquisition had caught him and hustled him to his death.   His popularity as seen when he visited the seven churches must have been alarming to those who might have felt that his return to Toledo was not an impossibility.

However seventeen years of terrible uncertainty and horror, lived partly in noisome prisons, could easily have brought an old man to his death.

Philip would never have tolerated his return, and Gregory could have used Carranza in his intrigues against Spain.   There would have been many people—Philip among them—who must have determined that Carranza must never return to Spain; and these people were such as did not hesitate to administer a dose of poison to those who stood in their way.

But if we are uncertain as to how Carranza died, we are by no means so concerning the long imprisonment; and his case is one of the most oustanding in the annals of the Inquisition because it gives us such an indication of what could happen to the highest in the land, not because of their religious opinions, but on account of envy.

It is hard to believe that any of Carranza's accusers ever thought him guilty of heresy. His zealous persecution of Cranmer and his kind in England showed him to be a staunch supporter of the Catholic Church. As for his writings, it is often possible to misconstrue words when the desire to do so is acute enough.

His case is so interesting because it showed how powerful was the Inquisition in Spain, how unwise and dangerous it was for a man to possess great wealth and standing, and so arouse the enmity of his fellows.

Carranza's story must have been a warning to every man in Spain. Now surely they must have realized the nature of this monster which they had nourished in their midst.

The terrible example of Carranza showed that in Spain no man, no matter how rich or influential he might be, was safe from the Spanish Inquisition.

10

WITCHCRAFT AND THE INQUISITION

I HAVE often heard the opinion expressed by Catholics that the Inquisition was a necessity because witchcraft was growing at an alarming rate throughout Europe, and that the Holy Office was set up as a deterrent.

It is rather strange that this reason should be given, for those countries in which trials for witchcraft were predominant were not those where the Inquisition flourished; although it was one of the duties of Inquisitors to examine those suspected of witchcraft.

There is a widely held opinion that witchcraft was actually a relic of paganism. It was not a form of heresy, but had its very roots in the religion which had flourished before the spread of Christianity, and at the Sabbats—those weird midnight gatherings to which witches were supposed to ride on their broomsticks, taking with them their familiars, usually in the shape of cats—were practised the fertility rites.

The wild dances, performed in the nude, were calculated to stimulate sexual desire, a very understandable procedure when life was held cheap and it was advisable continually to replenish the population. At these ceremonies we hear of the presence of the Horned God, usually in the shape of a goat, who was supposed to be Satan; this horned creature usually selected the most desirable of the females for his mate during the orgy; and it is possible that he may have been the most enterprising member of the group who had disguised himself as a goat. All the ceremonies of the Sabbat, it seems, were calculated to produce sexual abandon; for instance the nature of the dances, the abandoning of clothes, and the sign of allegiance to the Horned God which was to kiss him beneath his tail.

It is no easy matter to supplant one religion by another. It appears that the new religion has been accepted; people are baptized, quote creeds, say prayers and declare themselves believers, but old superstitions cling.

Christianity appeared to have been accepted, but men still worshipped the sun and trees; they still clung to the old charms which would provide lovers, babies, good fortune for themselves and bad for their enemies.

According to the Venerable Bede, King Redwald who lived in the seventh century kept two altars in his temple; one to placate the Christian God, the other for the pagan gods. Clovis the King of the Franks, when attacking the Allemannians at Tolbiac, was contemplating becoming a Christian and offered to do so if the God of his Christian wife, Clotilde, would give him the victory; but he did not forget to pray to the old gods at the same time. Too much was at stake to risk offending any gods; and superstitious man could not imagine a god who had not all the pride, envy and vindictiveness of man himself.

Witchcraft comes to us from the Palaeolithic age and has stayed with us even until the present day. Some ten years ago a woman living in Cornwall visited a doctor friend of mine and, when all doors had been closed and certain precautions taken against the powers of witchcraft, she told him that her neighbour had " overlooked her baby " and she feared the worst.

It is small wonder that in the thirteenth century such beliefs were rife and had a strong grip on a certain section of the population even as late as the nineteenth.

*   *   *

It was when a worship of the devil was discovered in witchcraft that it was seen as heresy, and then the Inquisition stepped in, in order to suppress it.

Those who were suspected of witchcraft often seemed to have had a great desire for confession and revelled in recounting the stories of their sins: they talked freely of their adventures at the Sabbats and of their familiars and devils with whom they enjoyed sexual intercourse. They seemed to suffer from hysteria and really believed the fantastic stories they told. Torture and hideous death was the lot of many; thousands were burned alive; and that death alone not being considered bad enough for them many suffered also by having their flesh first torn by red hot pincers; and the fires which burned them were slow fires. In France it was a custom to seize the children of witches, strip them and beat them with rods round the town while their parents were burned alive. One French commentator, himself a judge who had been guilty of passing this inhumane sentence on innocent children, deplored the fact that this was all that happened to them (except of course that they lived the rest of their lives under suspicion and were likely to be tried for witchcraft at any time).

In order to stamp out witchcraft the Church and State stood firmly together, and witches were judged by both episcopal and secular courts. In 1437 Eugenius IV was urging Inquisitors throughout Europe to display greater zeal in bringing witches to judgment.

With the appearance of Jacob Sprenger's *Malleus Maleficarum*, Hammer of Witches, in 1489, witchcraft increased. The publication of the book meant that people were more deeply aware of witchcraft and that many were eager to dabble in it; the authorities looked for witches and they were determined to find what they sought.

Jacob Sprenger was a fanatic; he had acted as Inquisitor in Germany where, Innocent VIII declared in his Bull of 1484, witches abounded and endeavoured to seduce the good people of those lands to follow their malignant lead.

There was a theory at this time that those who worked for the suppression of witchcraft were protected by God and could not be harmed by witches and their familiars, or the demons who were sent from hell to help them. A holy relic worn on the body served as protection, it was believed; and witches grew pale and fled if a victim made the sign of the cross in their presence. Sprenger declared that he and his colleagues, during witch-hunts, had often been confronted by devils in some animal form. They had never been harmed by them, however, because they were employed in God's service.

This, however, did not always appear to be effective for Sprenger states that witches often bewitched their judges while they were in the act of sentencing them; and during a burning in the Black Forest a witch, at the moment when her executioner was lighting the faggots at her feet, blew into his face telling him that he should be rewarded for what he had done that day. Immediately he was afflicted by leprosy and was dead within a few days, we are told.

Such stories inflamed the imagination, and as Sprenger's superstitious legends were accepted as truth, the whole world was ready to believe that witchcraft was the cult of the devil.

But, asked some, if God was all-powerful, how was it that the devil was able to give such power to his followers? The explanation was a rather feeble one. It was this: God sometimes allowed Satan a certain amount of power which enabled him to raise a storm or kill people and animals, but Satan could only work within the limits God allowed him. God sometimes allowed him to create illusions in which men believed. There were no such things as riding on broomsticks to Sabbats; this was all part of the illusions which God allowed the mischievous Satan to create; and incubi and succubi were unable to make children.

But the judgment was that witches, in worshipping Satan, committed heresy and should be put to death.

The more witchcraft was talked of, the more zealous the Inquisitors became in their endeavours to stamp it out.

Witches flourished in Germany and Italy in very large numbers, and in the hundred years or so which followed the fifteenth century the cult began to multiply alarmingly.

During the fifteenth century a witch was occasionally burned alive; later they were burned by the hundred. We hear that, in the town of Ravensburg at the end of the fifteenth century, forty-eight witches were burned in five years; there is an account from Geneva a few years later of five hundred burning in three months; and in Savoy eight hundred were condemned together.

In 1586 the winter was a very cold one on the banks of the Rhine, and the cold weather continued into the summer with lamentable results to the harvest. Because there was at this time a witchcraft craze in progress, witchcraft was judged to be the reason for the unusual weather. As a result one hundred and eighteen women and two men were imprisoned and hideously tortured until they confessed to having tampered with the elements; they were burned alive. And so extraordinary was the fascination of witchcraft that these people must have believed that they were responsible for the weather, since they declared even on their way to their deaths, that had they not been arrested they would have continued with their plots and all the corn would have been destroyed together with all the fruits.

It seems that a great deal of physical torture and even hideously prolonged death, were considered a fair price to pay for the assumed possession of such extraordinary powers.

One supporter of the Inquisition records that from the beginning of the fifteenth century and for the next hundred and fifty years the Inquisition burned at least thirty thousand witches; and thus the world must thank the Holy Office, for had these witches been allowed to live they would have destroyed the world.

One wonders what the people were expected to think of the all-powerful God, who was said to allow Satan his powers for some perverse and unaccountable reason.

*   *   *

So from the fifteenth to the nineteenth century there were outbreaks of witchcraft in Europe. The more it was talked of, the more persecutions there were.   It appeared to have a fatal fascination for women more than for men; it is perhaps explained by the fact that these people were obsessed by the desire to call attention to themselves.   Many of them were old, ugly, poor and of no account; and when they heard the constant talk of witchcraft and saw the fear it inspired in so many people, they must have realized that they too could acquire power over their fellow men and women; that it was power presumed to be derived from Satan, that it could bring them to hideous torture and death seemed of small account.   When they became known as witches they acquired power, and their dull and very boring lives were lifted out of their monotony.   There have always been people who are ready to risk their lives to escape from boredom.

In 1484 Innocent VIII put witches into a different category from that in which they had till this time existed, with his Bull *Summis desiderantes*.   Calixtus III, Pius II, Alexander VI, Julius II, Leo X, Adrian VI and Clement VII all lifted their voices against the cult and declared that it was the duty of the Church to exterminate witches.

Strangely enough there were fewer witches in Spain than in other European countries.   This may have been due to the fact that the Spanish Inquisition acted against them, and there was a deep-rooted dread in Spain of falling into the hands of that secret organization which was so powerful that even the most sensation-crazy would-be witch would pause to consider before laying herself—or himself—open to prosecution.

Witchcraft had been prevalent in France, and that district of Spain which was most infected by the cult was the adjoining mountainous one of the Pyrenees.

One of the first cases of witchcraft dealt with by the Inquisition was that of Gracia la Valle who was burned alive in Saragossa in 1498.

There does not appear to be another case until 1499 when Maria Biesa was burned; and when one considers what was going on in other parts of Europe it seems that witchcraft had scarcely touched Spain.   Llorente states that in the Biscay area more than thirty witches were burned in 1507; and there are accounts of rigorous efforts in 1517 against witches in Catalonia.

In 1522 an Edict of Grace was presented to all witches in the area of Jaca and Ribagorza.   They were given six months in which to come forward and confess their sins.   What is so extraordinary is that the Spanish Inquisition should show such leniency towards witches when in Northern Italy, where there seemed an unlimited supply of witches, they were being burned by the thousand.

Perhaps the answer is that the Spanish Inquisition was not entirely convinced that witchcraft was a heresy; many of the Inquisitors had insisted that it was impossible for women to fly through the air on broomsticks, and that those women who confessed that this was what they did were suffering from delusions. That these delusions were the result of communication with the devil they did not doubt, and they were of the opinion that any who had intercourse with the devil were only fit for the torture and the stake; but at the same time there was a divided opinion as regarded witches and this may have induced a certain leniency towards them. Another point—and perhaps this is the real reason—witches were for the most part poor old women with no possessions. One of the great incentives to prosecutions—as is seen in the case of Archbishop Carranza—was the hope of confiscating the wealth of the victim. Poor old women had nothing to bring to the coffers of the Inquisition. Was this the real reason why the Suprema was comparatively lenient towards them? And so perverse is human nature that the fewer prosecutions the less the interest in witchcraft; when interest was lacking, there was not the same urge among these poor women to tell fantastic stories about their adventures with the devil.

However in 1528 the Inquisitor-General, Alfonso Manrique, gave orders to one of his Inquisitors, Sancho de Carranza de Miranda, to make a very detailed enquiry into the spread of witchcraft in Calahorra and to punish any witches discovered with the utmost severity, for reports had reached him that the harvests were being affected to an alarming degree in that district, and that many young children had been killed. Even so Edicts of Grace were published and the Supreme Council urged caution and moderation, for it was so difficult to arrive at the truth in these cases of witchcraft where women, suspected of consorting with the Devil, only had to be brought before an examiner to indulge in the wildest aberrations which it was felt could not be true.

Moreover Inquisitors were told that they must verify the truth of accusations before making arrests. Such leniency is hardly credible. How different the treatment of witches from that of *Marranos, Moriscos* and Lutherans Surely this luke-warm attitude *must* have had its roots in the small amount of profit to be obtained from persecuting witches.

* * *

When there was a scare in Navarre in the year 1538, Inquisitor Valdeolitas was sent to investigate, but his instructions were to ignore the hysterical demands of the population and make certain, before he arrested a single witch, that he had good reason for doing so.   He was to explain to the people that bad harvests came in places where there were no witches and were not necessarily the result of the powers given by Satan to evil women.

An example of the Inquisitorial attitude is given in the case of Anastasia Soriana, the twenty-eight-year-old wife of a peasant, who presented herself before the tribunal which had been set up at Murcia and declared that she had had a carnal relationship with a devil.   She was told to go home as she was suffering from delusions.

Where else but in Spain could this have happened in the year 1584?

But the woman was obsessed by the idea.   Clearly she wished to be the paramour of a demon, for she presented herself once more to the tribunal—this time at Toledo—and told the same story. Once again she was told she was suffering from delusions and sent home.

In 1591 three women were arrested in Cazar.   These were Catalina Matheo, Joanna Izquierda and Olalla Sobrina.   It appeared that the deaths of several children had occurred in their village; the women were tortured, and under torture Catalina made a confession.

She said that Olalla had come to her some years before and talked of the delights of sexual intercourse with demons.   Would Catalina like to be provided with a demon-lover?   Catalina was fascinated by the idea, and one night she was asked by the third woman, Joanna Izquierda, to visit her house.   When she arrived, Olalla was present and they had not been there very long when an extraordinary being arrived in the form of a goat.   They stripped and danced with the goat until they were roused to a frenzy; the orgy continued far into the night and Catalina was introduced to the delights of intercourse with a demon.   Later, for a little diversion— so said Catalina—they left the house and flew through the night to the home of a newly born infant.   This they suffocated; and afterwards they all flew back again.

Olalla when tortured told nothing however, and when Catalina's story was put to her she emphatically denied it.   Joanna also withstood torture, but she could not resist boasting of her exploits to the wife of her jailor.

She told this woman that witches and demons had come to her house and, after anointing her body, carried her to a Sabbat by force.   There were generally assumed to be two ways of attending a Sabbat: one was by flying there, usually on a broomstick; the other by anointing the body with oil and rubbing it in until a stupor was produced; then the anointed one was conveyed there by supernatural forces. When she reached the Sabbat, Joanna told the jailor's wife, she had seen Olalla and Catalina there; they had all kissed the Horned God under the tail, danced the wild dances and indulged in the orgy which followed.

When the women were taken before the Tribunal of the Inquisition, Catalina admitted that what she had said was false; she declared that she had said it on account of the severity of the torture. Neither Joanna nor Olalla broke down under the further torture which they had to endure.

These women really escaped very lightly. Catalina, who had confessed (that she had done so under torture was ignored), had to appear at an *auto de fé* where she received two hundred lashes. The other two women merely appeared at the *auto* to make their confessions; and no further penance was imposed upon them.

It is safe to say that only in Spain and in no other country in the world at this time would these women have escaped so lightly. It is almost certain that anywhere else they would have been hanged or burned alive, and that witch hunts would have been started as always happened after a burning. People would believe when misfortune overtook them that witchcraft was working against them and would seek to find the witches. As a result of this leniency which took place in 1591, there were no more cases of witchcraft in the area for almost twenty years.

The Supreme Council of the Inquisition most certainly protected many people from charges of witchcraft. The people and the secular courts would have liked to see more witchcraft trials. They provided an entertainment, and from time to time many sought to work up a scare. The orgies which were reputed to take place at the Sabbats were discussed at great length; no abomination was too vile to be suggested. Sexual adventure was of course the most discussed—the prowess of the Devil himself and the succubi and incubi he provided for those who were faithful to him. That was not all. Witches were said to dig up corpses and eat them at their Sabbat feasts. They were reputed to find the blood of children very delectable; and the bones of new-born infants were needed for their spells and potions.

Yet the Suprema insisted that it was easy to be deceived by charges of witchcraft, and all information, it was decided, should be sent to the Council for investigation. In 1555 when many people were arrested on suspicion of witchcraft in the Guipúzcoa area, the Suprema reproved the tribunal and expressed fear that many innocent people might be involved.   An order was issued that no more arrests were to be made without first submitting all details to the Suprema.

In this tale of terrible suffering which the Inquisition brought to Spain it is very pleasant to be able to record something in its favour; and perhaps it is rather churlish to look for the motives which prompted such action.   Let it be said however that the action of the Inquisition in Spain towards witchcraft was such that it stopped the development of the cult which spread throughout the rest of Europe.   By refusing to take witchcraft seriously, the Inquisition destroyed the desire of many people to indulge in it.   Consequently Spain remained comparatively free from witchcraft and all its attendant horrors which prevailed in Europe from the fifteenth to the nineteenth century.

Even in Britain—usually so much more moderate than other European countries—the total number of witches done to death is in the neighbourhood of thirty thousand (at least a quarter of this number were executed in Scotland).

Here then is some good performed by the Inquisition; a very small credit to set in the balance sheet against the overwhelming evil—but still, it is something, and there is no doubt that many old women in Spain avoided torture and hideous death because of the existence of the Spanish Inquisition.

II

MYSTICS AND THE INQUISITION

I T W A S inevitable that this race of Spaniards, made up of Iberians, Tartesians, Phoenicians, Romans, Visigoths, Arabs and others, should be possessed of a strong streak of mysticism.

With the setting up of the Inquisition and the expulsion of first the Jews then the Moors, there was born in the people a religious fervour. The Inquisition had taught them that it was their duty to spy for the sake of the Church. It was more than a duty: It was a sin not to report any enemy of the Church.

Periodically these people saw the green cross, draped in black, carried in solemn procession to the city squares; they heard the bells of the prisons tolling and saw the prisoners, arrayed in hideous *sanbenitos*, emerge; they saw men and women who had been tortured so cruelly that they could not stand and had to be carried to the place of execution; they saw the penances which were imposed; men and women whipped through the streets; and they saw the faggots lighted at the feet of living men and women.

All this was treated as though it were a sacred duty—a ceremony for Sundays and Saints-days. It was not to be wondered at that in such a country there should be an emotional uprising, a preoccupation with mysticism.

As there were those who professed to be witches in league with the Devil, there were those who declared themselves to be singularly blessed, to have communication with Christ or the Virgin Mary. These people ran a risk of being proved impostors; but like the witches, they found the temporary glory of setting themselves apart from their fellow men well worth the risk.

Hence throughout Spain there appeared many *beatas* or devout women, all of whom claimed to have been sanctified in some way. They were admired and respected by the population, who were ready to believe in them. Even a man as intellectual as Cardinal Ximenes himself was ready to accept certain *beatas* as holy women, as he showed when he turned back from a visit to Gibraltar on the advice of one, and by his support of the *Beata* of Piedrahita.

After the death of Santa Teresa many wished to follow her example, but there was a time during the life of this saint when she was in danger of being accused as an impostor.

People believed that they could attain the desired state by submitting the body to privations and thus subduing the flesh and increasing the power of the spirit.   Devotees of this cult tried to deprive themselves of sleep and even whipped themselves, inflicting painful wounds in order to keep themselves awake.   Hair shirts were common and the wearing of them taken as a matter of course. It is almost certain that these people were in a state bordering on hysteria; sleepless, half starved, they would be a prey to delusions; and it is very possible that many of them believed the fantastic stories of their adventures which they told were true.

Santa Teresa explains her union with God by saying it was a form of ecstasy or trance, during which the soul leaves the body.

" I do not see God with the eyes of my soul," she writes, " yet I know Him with a strange certainty."

She tells us that at Easter 1579, at the time when she was founding the Barefooted Carmelities, she was uncertain concerning this new order and prayed for guidance; the result was a vision of Christ who gave her what she needed.

When Teresa died one of her followers, Catalina de Jesus, declared that she had visions of Teresa who told her what to do with regard to the Order; this was bound to lead to difficulties, for when another of Teresa's followers wished to work along different lines it was easy for her to have—or imagine she had—a vision of Teresa confirming what *she* wished.

Mysticism was clearly a dangerous weapon in the hands of those who were not necessarily unscrupulous but merely hysterical. When conversations with Christ and the Virgin Mary were not considered an impossibility, what a simple matter it was for some highly strung man or woman, whose body had not only been ill-nourished but tormented, to imagine that he was admitted to one of these conversations!   And how simple for those who were entirely unscrupulous to invent fantastic adventures with the Deity, to pass on " His Orders " and thus get what was wanted.

Zapata gives an indication of how easy it was at this time to dupe the people.   The story he tells is of a company of travellers who moved about the country, stopping at various inns during their journey.

There were thirteen of these men—a significant number—and

it was their custom to arrive at an inn where one of the thirteen would approach the innkeeper and tell him that he was greatly honoured, for his guests that night were Christ and his twelve disciples.

The innkeeper, superstitious, his mind full of the wonderful adventures of the *beatas* and saints, would believe what he was told.

He would call to his staff to produce a meal—a meal such as they had never produced before; bowls of water would be brought out that the feet of " Christ " and the " disciples " might be washed.

The company would accept the attentions, allow their feet to be washed, and would partake of the supper; then one of the " disciples " would summon the innkeeper to the table and tell him that Christ asked that he should confess his sins. The poor innkeeper would probably fall on his knees, remembering all the little sins he had committed (usually cheating his customers), really believing that the silent man at the head of the table to whom the rest of the company showed such veneration, was Christ and therefore was aware of every little squalid act.

After the confession judgment would be passed. The innkeeper would be told to bring out all the money he possessed, and warned that it would be dangerous to hold any back for he was in the presence of the Omnipotent, Omniscient Being. When the money was brought forth it would be divided into portions. There would be a little for the innkeeper, that portion which had been, according to the " disciples ", honestly earned. A certain amount would also go back to the innkeeper to pay for the supper just eaten; it was tainted money, pointed out the " disciples ", but the fact that it had bought a supper for " Christ " removed the taint. As for the rest of it—the far larger part—that was to go where it belonged— to the devil.

The charade was well staged, for at that precise moment the door of the inn would open and in would come a figure wearing horns and hoofs.

" Take your own!" the " disciples " would cry; and " Satan " would swoop on the money and disappear with it.

It was an interesting and well thought out little scene, with " Christ " and the " disciples " appearing to take nothing for themselves; of course when they left the inn they caught up with " Satan " and there was a general share-out.

The little act went on for some time, the simple country people believing in it. Eventually some bold spirit declared himself dissatisfied and asked that the company of fourteen be arrested at that moment when " Satan " flew in to take the money.

Thus a discomfited master, his band of disciples and the visiting Satan were all taken before the authorities. Satan shorn of horns and hoofs proved to be an ordinary man, and the identity of the remaining thirteen was soon established.

The result: fourteen criminals were publicly whipped and sent to the galleys. (From *Miscelánea de Zapata*).

But that such a fraud could have taken place is an indication of the receptive state of mind of the people of Spain at this time.

*   *   *

Mysticism did not give the Church any great cause for anxiety until the coming of Lutheranism. To watch a great split in the Christian Church and to see another Church spring up to exist side by side with the Catholic one, a Church which threatened to become equally powerful, filled all serious-minded Catholics with alarm. They must be on the alert for all who diverged from orthodox thought. Thus they turned their attention to the mystics.

The task before the Inquisition was an extremely difficult one. Mystics declared that they committed no sin against the Church; they lived holy lives and it was thus they obtained their communion with God, the Father, Son, Holy Ghost and the Virgin Mary.

The Inquisition realized that if they accused these people and brought them before their tribunals they could bring ridicule upon themselves, for mystics of the past had been canonized.

But many mystics were straining away from the orthodox Church and thus in this age of Reformation, they were becoming highly dangerous. Those who diverged from orthodoxy were known as *Alumbrados* (the Spanish version of the Italian *Illuminati*) and it was the Inquisition's duty to suppress them, at the same time employing the greatest caution. The fact that many of the mystics were impostors (*Embusteros*) was helpful.

What the Inquisition was compelled to do was differentiate between the orthodox mystic (who could do no harm and might eventually become a saint) and the *Alumbrado*, who either sought or was suspected of seeking to introduce new ideas which, because of this person's holy reputation (she or he having been believed to be in communication with the saints and the Deity and thus having the information straight from the source of all wisdom), might have an alarming effect on a great number of people.

Edicts of Faith began to be issued which were to lead to the detection of *Alumbrados*.

Their sin was that they preached the all-importance of mental prayer and the uselessness of oral prayer, and that those who wished to aspire to holiness should do nothing but meditate on holiness. They were reputed to speak against marriage and to declare that only their particular sect was the right one (one would have thought this failing common enough among all sects and unnecessary to be stated). They went into trances and declared that this was the outward sign of their state of grace, and that they possessed the Holy Ghost. They declared that there was no need for those who had reached this state of spiritual glory to close his or her eyes at the elevation of the Host or even to reverence images and listen to sermons.

All this was error in the eyes of the Church for these people were flagrantly denying certain laws laid down by the Church. Thus they were guilty of heresy, and it was the duty of the Inquisition to extirpate heretics.

* * *

One of the most well-known *beatas* and one whose case gives a very good example of the working of the Inquisition in this field, is that of Francisca Hernandez.

Francisca was undoubtedly an individualist; she wished for all the honour and prestige which came the way of holy women, but she was not very keen on suffering all the privations which were usually necessary to call attention to a state of holiness.

It is a tribute at least to her originality that she managed to attract attention without these practices.

She did not enter one of the religious orders—as so many did who had gone before and were to come after her; she did not wear the unbecoming habit of a nun; she lived in comfort in a house provided for her by her followers; and she had two maids to look after her comforts. She was visited by many admirers of her holiness, and she had a preference for masculine admirers; her bed was reputed to be a soft one and she did not always sleep in it alone; and far from starving herself she was very fond of her food, and there is a story that she once, in an unholy outburst, slapped the face of one of her maids because she had overcooked the dinner.

She was illiterate, but it was said that she was capable of performing miracles; people believed that she had the power of healing; and articles which had been in her possession were eagerly sought by her followers as holy relics.

The attention of the Inquisition was turned upon her, and she was brought up for questioning. The Inquisitor-General—at that time Adrian of Utrecht, for it must have been about 1518—himself saw her. Judging a *beata* was a very delicate matter. If she were condemned, her followers would be enraged, and these women always seemed to inspire their followers with great devotion; on the other hand she might be proved to be sincere; *beatas* and holy women of the past who had had strange visions and performed miracles had been canonized. Adrian was an ambitious man; he had no wish to put it on record that he had condemned a woman who subsequently became a saint.

Therefore he acted warily. He decided that Francisca should not be punished in any way. He also had to consider however the possibility that later she might be proved to be an impostor. In that case he would not wish it to be said that she had been brought before him and he had found her innocent.

A very difficult position! Adrian therefore ordered that although she was discharged, a watch should be kept on her by the Inquisition.

Francisca must have been a very clever woman, for she certainly impressed Adrian. When he was elected Pope Adrian VI in 1522, he remembered Francisca and asked for her intercession with God and the saints for himself and the Church.

For some years after her first encounter with the Inquisition Francisca was left in peace, living in her comfortable house, waited on by her maids, receiving her masculine admirers, performing her miracles and so on.

She was undoubtedly a very fascinating woman and a very handsome one; and among the men who admired her so ardently was a certain Francisco Ortiz.

Ortiz was of the Franciscan Order, a young man who had already made his mark as a great preacher. The Order expected great things from him and there was enthusiastic interest in his career.

He had heard of Francisca and was very eager to meet her. He was nineteen years old when he endeavoured to bring about this meeting but it did not take place until six years later. He, being a friar, could not visit a woman without the consent of his Superior, and this was denied him.

This was the year 1523, and by that time his reputation had grown. Charles the Emperor had shown a special interest in him for when he was speaking the churches were full. There were some of course to listen suspiciously to what this young man said; every preacher of brilliance must encounter a certain amount of suspicion, for after all when so many people flocked to hear him, his influence was great. Never had the Catholic Church felt itself to be in such jeopardy as it was at this time, with the Reformation breaking out all over Europe.

Charles however was so impressed by the young man's ability that he offered him the post of Court preacher. Although Francisco Ortiz had not met Francisca Hernandez there had been communication between them; and before he accepted a post of such eminence he asked her advice. She warned him against it, and because of this he refused it.

The fact that Francisca could have such influence over a great preacher such as Ortiz alarmed the Inquisition, and the Superior of the Franciscan monastery to which Ortiz belonged implored the Inquisitor-General to curtail the activities of this woman.

When Adrian of Utrecht had been elected Pope, Alfonso Manrique, the Cardinal and Archbishop of Seville, had been appointed Inquisitor-General in his place. Manrique was not so impressed by Francisca as Adrian had been, and he thought it would be a good plan if she was ordered to retire to a convent. He therefore suggested that she should be received into Santa Isabel; but the Superior of this convent was immediately alarmed at the thought of having such a disturbing element in her convent, and refused to receive Francisca.

Francisca however did leave Valladolid and, when she did so, Ortiz joined her at Castillo Tejeriego.

That he should have disobeyed the order of his superior was considered decidedly shocking and he was ordered to return to the monastery and never to see or have any communication with Francisca again.

Ortiz answered this command by declaring that Francisca was the beloved of God, and it was more important to obey the orders of God than even those of the Superior of his monastery.

The Inquisition was more concerned over Ortiz than over Francisca, because he was such a remarkable preacher and the Church had urgent need of such men. Therefore it was agreed that Francisca should be once more arrested, it being assumed that if she could be proved to be an impostor, Ortiz would cease to be her devoted admirer.

It was arranged that Fransica should be arrested after Easter of the year 1529. Ortiz was expected to preach during Holy Week, and it was thought very necessary that he should not be disturbed at this time; for this reason it was decided to postpone the arrest.

News reached Ortiz of what was afoot and he visited Manrique imploring him to leave Francisca in peace. Manrique replied firmly that Ortiz himself had better take care, for his connection with Francisca brought him under suspicion; and it was solely due to the fact that he was such a popular preacher that he was being allowed his freedom.

Francisca was accordingly arrested after Easter and was put under guard, not in a prison but in a private house, so careful were the Inquisitors not to make a false step. But when Ortiz, hearing of her arrest, hurried to her, she was immediately removed to the secret prison of the Inquisition.

Ortiz then did a very foolish thing. He was so enamoured of Francisca that he thought of nothing but securing her immediate release through popular protest.

On April 6th he was to preach in the Franciscan Church and, as usual on those occasions when he graced the pulpit, the church was full to overflowing. He was certainly very brave, for he was fully aware of the power of the Inquisition. Obedience to God, he said, was more important than obedience to man. He did not pretend to be a prophet but he was certain that God would inflict great punishment on those who had committed the sin of arresting the beloved of God, Francisca Hernandez.

This was a direct insult and challenge to the Inquisitor-General and there was an immediate outcry against Ortiz, who was pulled down from the pulpit and hurried to a nearby house. There he was left some hours before he was taken to the prison of the Inquisition.

A wild fanaticism possessed Ortiz; he had criticized the dreaded Inquisition in public and he could not expect to escape its vengeance. He declared that he cared nothing for the Inquisition; he only cared for Francisca. He would found a new society for the honour of God and Truth, and if necessary this would work in opposition to the Holy Office. He would not retract a word of his sermon.

When he heard that he was accused of unbecoming love for Francisca he declared that she, being the bride of Christ, was as God himself and however much love he bore her could not be too much. He went on to say that it mattered not if one fasted or feasted, or how one lived, as long as there was love of God in one's life. He pointed out—a very dangerous thing to do—how the doctrines of the Church had changed from time to time and how what was considered right at one time was wrong at another.

There are no records of Francisca's trial, although her name is mentioned in connection with other trials; and it would appear from these that she was easily persuaded to give evidence against former friends.

As usual in the affairs of the Inquisition the formalities were many and the delays considerable; thus in 1532, Francisca was still a prisoner of the Inquisition, although by this time she was no longer in the *carceles secretas* but was living in a private house and was allowed to have a maid to wait on her.

It may have been that the Inquisition was loath to punish one who had a reputation for sanctity; or it may have been that they found her a useful witness against many people; but the fact remains that the Inquisition dealt leniently with Francisca.

And when one compares the treatment of Ortiz with that of *Marranos, Moriscos* and Lutherans one is amazed at the tolerance displayed in this instance by the Inquisition.

It must be remembered that Ortiz had actually dared criticize the Inquisitor-General, behaviour which would have meant certain death to any who was considered a heretic. Ortiz however was put in prison and whilst there Luis Coronel, a secretary of the Inquisitor-General, was sent to him to try to make him retract his recent statements.

He refused however and, being sure that he was possessed of the glory of God, he stoically endured imprisonment, not omitting during that time to undergo the privations of a man determined to live the spiritual life. He gave up eating meat, slept on a plank, and wore his hair shirt continually.

Ortiz had been too popular a man for the Inquisition to treat him like any common heretic. Even the Princess Juana asked for his release. This was when his brother Doctor Pedro Ortiz was to be sent to Rome on a royal commission, and it seemed to Juana that it was unfitting that the brother of a man who was engaged on such a mission should be a prisoner.

The commission undertaken by Doctor Pedro Ortiz was a very important one, for at this time Henry VIII, having become enamoured of Anne Boleyn, was seeking to prove that his marriage to Catalina of Aragon was no true marriage. As a result of this there was a great stir of activity in England, Spain and Rome.

But the Inquisitor-General could not allow insults to be hurled at him and the Holy Office and be ignored, and even the request of Princess Juana did not bring about the release of Ortiz.

Eventually after several years of imprisonment the influence of Francisca Hernandez seemed to weaken, and Ortiz was prepared to acknowledge his errors.

As a result he was sentenced to do penance for vehement suspicion of heresy. He walked in a procession, carrying a lighted taper, to the cathedral where he heard his sentence. For two more years he would remain in a cell, which he must not leave, in the convent of Torrelaguna; for five years he must not perform the functions of a priest; he must perform certain penances at regular intervals; he was not to communicate in any way whatsoever with Francisca Hernandez nor live within five miles of her.

If he disobeyed any of these rules he would at once be condemned to the stake, where he would meet the fate of a relapsed heretic.

The Inquisition believed that he could do great good for the Church if his mind were purged of all unorthodox ideas and heresies; and at the end of his sentence they wished him to resume his preaching.

However, Ortiz could not after all his years of imprisonment tear himself away from the life he had lived in his cell at Torrelaguna. There he became renowned for his sanctity; he apparently had no more desire to get into touch with Francisca; all he wished for was to lead the life of a recluse.   Perhaps his encounter with the Inquisition had taught him that it was the safest way.

However he remained at Torrelaguna until he died in the year 1546.

The Inquisition had certainly shown great leniency towards these two people.

*   *   *

Another interesting case is that of Magdalena de la Cruz who appeared on the scene some time before the famous Francisca Hernandez.

Magdalena was born somewhere about 1487, at that time when the interest in mysticism was beginning to grow in Spain.   It was small wonder that many aspiring young girls, seeing what happened to those who declared they were imbued with especial holiness, should wish to share in the triumph.

Magdalena let it be believed that when she was four years old she had her first vision of the Virgin, who gave her a detailed account of the life and death of Christ.   Precocious Magdalena immediately believed that she would like to follow in the Master's footsteps and, since there was no one at hand ready to crucify her, she decided to perform the act herself.   Before however she got so far as nailing herself to the cross she fell and broke her ribs. Although she had failed in this attempt, for one so young to have made it was considered to be a sign of future holiness.

Magdalena told many stories about her childhood adventures— how once she had run away from home and was suddenly carried through the air back to her bedroom; how she had once heard that the Sacrament was being taken to a dying man and, wishing to see it pass her father's house, she had been unable to do so because there was no window in her room. Suddenly, and miraculously, she discovered a crack in the wall and through this she saw the Sacrament. It was said that whenever the Sacrament passed a house in which was Magdalena, the wall opened that she might see it pass.

She was clearly a hysterical and precocious little girl who was absolutely certain what she intended to do in life. She was going to be a *Beata*; and she set about acquiring a reputation for sanctity.

When she was seventeen she went into the Convent of Santa Isobel de los Angeles at Cordova. There she delighted her fellow nuns with her trances and miracles. She declared that there was a spirit who was constantly at her side.

She was an adept at producing miracles; she was of such a hysterical nature that she was able to produce certain physical reactions which were the delight of her fellow nuns.

There is a story that she wished to experience all that the Virgin Mary had experienced in giving birth to Christ, and that she told the nuns that her spiritual guardian had promised her that she should do this.

Strangely enough her body began to swell and on Christmas Day she was found seated in her cell holding what appeared to be a baby in her arms. The child was hidden by the hair which hung from her head but which was not really her own hair—presumably a wig she had acquired to guard the child from too curious eyes.

It must have been very exciting to have such a person in the convent, for there were no dull moments with Magdalena around.

That she should develop that commonplace manifestation of holiness, the stigmata, was inevitable.

Her reputation of course grew, and the most miraculous happenings were accredited to her. The sick believed that a touch from her was enough to cure them; sailors prayed to her to intercede for them when storms beset them; ladies who were about to bear children asked her blessings. Before the birth of Philip II, his mother, the Empress Isabella sent his layette to the convent that Magdalena might bless it. Even the Pope asked Magdalena to use her special influence with the Deity for the sake of the Church.

Magdalena was at the height of her power. She became Prioress of the convent; this was very good for the convent, as gifts of great magnificence were constantly being showered on the holy woman, and Magdalena took nothing for herself but gave everything to the convent.

A rumour went round that she lived on nothing but the Eucharist. One of those who doubted her very extraordinary stories suggested that since she lived without food she would have no hesitation in allowing herself to be shut up in a cell where none could reach her, and thus prove that she could exist without food and drink.

Magdalena stayed for two days and nights in this cell, and when she was nearly exhausted she managed to escape—no doubt with the help of some of the nuns. She declared then that St. Francis and St. Anthony had come to her aid and had removed her from the cell.

So this attempt to prove her a fraud merely redounded to her credit.

But Magdalena was unlucky. In the year 1543, nearly forty years after she had first entered the convent, she became very ill. So sick was she that her physicians were sure she could not live, and she was warned to prepare for the end.

She then confessed that she had deceived them all, that her miracles had been fakes and that she had been possessed not by holy spirits but by evil ones. She begged forgiveness for her sins.

It was very unfortunate for Magdalena, because she did not die; and when she recovered there was only one thing to be done: the Inquisition must step in.

Magdalena was certainly a hysterical woman; she undoubtedly believed that she had been possessed. She told the Inquisitors that a demon had taken possession of her when she was a child. She admitted that she had invented many of the miracles and had used her skill to delude people into accepting them as truth.

She was condemned to appear at an *auto* in the Cathedral of Cordova and there recount her sins in detail; she was forced to stand on the scaffold, a gag in her mouth, a lighted taper in her hand and a rope round her neck, while she listened to her sentence.

Once again the Inquisition was lenient. Her sentence was that she must live in perpetual retirement and each day for a year she must perform her penance; she was not to receive the sacrament for three years.

Thus Magdalena outlived her glory; she then began to live a life of spirituality and, by 1560 when she died, she had lived for several years in quiet seclusion, serene, dutiful to the laws of the convent—in fact the hysterical self-advertising woman had become a model of humility.

*   *   *

The effect of a case such as that of Magdalena de la Cruz was to deter other women from following a like course. Quite understandably, while all Spain was talking of the way in which Magdalena had deceived thousands, they were unlikely to be duped by the extraordinary adventures of some other bright girl.

Maria de la Visitacion was Portuguese; but Portugal was at this time under the control of Philip II.

She was eleven when she went into the convent of La Anunziata in Lisbon. By the time she was sixteen she was having visions of Christ, and so convincing was she that by the time she was twenty-seven she was made Prioress of the convent.

News of her fame spread through Portugal and Spain and was even carried to Rome.

It was said that when she was praying she would often be lifted from her knees and appear to float upwards. She also declared that she had a vision of Christ suffering on the cross; fire came from his side and touched hers. There was a mark on her side to prove this, and on Fridays it bled, giving her a great deal of pain. On her hands the stigmata appeared in the form of nail holes, and each Thursday she suffered from a pain in the head which she said was like a crown of thorns pressing into her skin. Then it was discovered that her brow was punctured as though by thorns and from these punctures blood flowed.

It was her habit to place pieces of cloth against the wound in her side and these became marked with spots of blood—five of them arranged in the form of a cross. Naturally these pieces of linen were considered relics of the utmost holiness. Even the Pope received one.

Maria however was not content with being merely a holy woman. So much adulation came her way that she wished to play a bigger role in her country's affairs.

Portugal was restive under the rule of Philip, and when certain Portuguese decided to revolt against the Spanish yoke they sought the advice of Maria. Maria immediately became an ardent supporter of the plot, which was eventually betrayed.

Since she had dabbled in politics she had become a woman of political importance who could not be ignored, and the Inquisition was anxious to prove her an impostor, for only thus could they rob her of her influence and power.

A deputation visited her convent, but before seeing Maria they interviewed several of the nuns; it did not take the subtle Inquisitors long to draw what they wanted from the frightened women, who were ready to admit that Maria had been playing certain tricks on those who were foolish enough to be duped by them.

Then Maria was sent for. She was warned that she must tell

the truth. She persisted that she had always told the truth and that any who had spoken against her had lied.

The Inquisitors declared their desire to see the stigmata, and when it was shown to them they pinioned Maria, sent for hot water and with vigorous application were able to wash away the painted marks.

When Maria saw that she was exposed she fell sobbing at the feet of the Inquisitors, begged for mercy, and told them that she would make a full confession.

She explained that she had painted the stigmata on her hands; the wounds in her side and on her forehead had been self-inflicted; the blood-stained linen was carefully prepared before it was pressed to her side and produced by sleight of hand; she was evidently something of a conjuror, and she had many tricks at her finger-tips.

She was more harshly sentenced than Magdalena de la Cruz had been and was condemned to perpetual imprisonment in a Dominican convent. Every Wednesday and Friday she was to be whipped during the chanting of a Miserere; on Wednesdays and Fridays she was to have nothing but bread and water; every time she entered the refectory she was to repeat her crimes to the nuns, and she was to take her meals on the floor and afterwards lie across the doorway so that when the nuns went out they could walk over her body. She was not to speak to anybody without first obtaining permission.

So Maria de la Visitacion passed the rest of her days and as she was only thirty-two years old when she was sentenced her punishment was a severe one. We are told that she accepted it with stoicism and grew truly pious.

The Inquisition was certainly more severe with Maria than with others of her kind, which leads to the conclusion that her case was meant to be a dire warning to any would-be holy women who sought to interfere in politics.

*   *   *

The case of Doña Teresa de Silva is another which throws light on the methods of the Inquisition.

When Teresa was twenty-two her confessor and spiritual guardian was Fray Francisco García Calderón. Teresa had been an invalid for some years and was clearly an hysterical person. She was one of those girls who wished to call attention to herself by the difference between her life and that of others around her; and the only way to do this was to stress her spirituality. It was not long before miracles were being attributed to her.

She entered a Benedictine Order and was elected Abbess. Calderón was made confessor or spiritual father of the convent.

The situation in which a man was a frequent visitor to a convent had its effect on the women enclosed therein—rather naturally many were hysterical types, and the first sign that all was not well occurred when one of the nuns began throwing the images about. A doctor was sent for. He declared that she was not insane but possessed by a devil. Calderón then set about the task of exorcism but without success. The nun remained " possessed " and, after watching her unaccountable behaviour, two other nuns began to imitate her.

Teresa was horrified, and to her dismay she found herself becoming hysterical in exactly the same way as the nuns. Calderón sought to exorcise her, but his efforts were in vain; and the sickness, or whatever it was, began to spread through the convent until all the nuns—except five—were acting in this most extraordinary manner, throwing themselves as well as the sacred images about the convent and uttering such obscenities that all were sure that wicked devils were in possession of their bodies, for the nuns could not possibly understand the words they uttered.

This state of affairs persisted for three years and gradually scandal began to attach itself to the convent. There was something basically wrong, people said; and this was an outward manifestation of that wrongness. Was this connected with Calderón's presence in the convent? It was strange that a man should be allowed to make so free with nuns—and he a priest.

A one-time friend of Calderón (but a friend no longer) named Fray Alonso de Leon thought it was high time the Inquisition took a hand; and he reported the strange manifestations at the convent to his Inquisitor and expressed his belief that some heresy was being committed to produce such a result.

Calderón, being warned that the Inquisition was about to make an investigation, decided to leave hastily for France. This he attempted, but he was seized by the *alguazils* before he could make good his escape.

Teresa and her nuns were taken from their convent and brought to the *carceles secretas* at Toledo.

Calderón was brought before the tribunal. He would admit to no wrong-doing. He was then taken to the torture chambers, first shown the dreaded instruments, then stripped and finally submitted to the most extreme torture. He was a brave man. He assured the Inquisitors that there had been no wrong-doing at the convent; the nuns had been truly possessed by demons.

The hysterical nuns however lacked his calm; placed in solitude and never allowed to forget the threat of torture, they were ready to say what was required of them.

Thus on the 27th of April, 1630, an *auto particular* took place in the hall of the Holy House at Toledo.

Calderón was brought forward and a list of his sins was read to him. He was charged with being an *Alumbrado*. It was recalled against him that years before he had lived in an immoral relationship with a young girl whom he had caused to be treated as a *beata*, and whom when she died he had buried as though she were a saint, leaving a place for his own grave beside her, and trying to make the world believe that she had performed many miracles. He had declared that to suffer from demoniac possession was a sign of God's approval; he was also accused of trying to reform the Church and planning to make himself Pope. Other charges were brought against him, such as trying to persuade a young woman that if she would submit to him he could give her a child who would one day be Pope.

Even under the cruellest torture he had refused to admit to these crimes, and this, in the eyes of the Inquisition, increased his guilt.

His punishment was to be taken to Valladolid where he should go to a convent of his Order, and there his crimes would be enumerated while a circular whipping took place; which meant that all the monks present surrounded him and delivered blows; then he was to be taken to another convent where he would again suffer the circular beating. He was to be imprisoned for life in a cell and never allowed to perform the functions of a priest; he must fast three days every week and only be allowed to receive the Sacrament at Christmas, Easter and Pentecost.

As for Doña Teresa, she was sent to another convent for four years; the nuns were to be separated and sent to different convents.

Seven years later Teresa appealed against her sentence, and the Supreme Council of the Inquisition agreed to reconsider it. Teresa won her case. She was released from her sentence, as were all the nuns.

No one seemed in the least anxious about poor Calderón. Perhaps by this time he had died of shame, loneliness, fasting and circular scourging.

*   *   *

The methods of the Inquisition grew more severe against mystics as time passed. Torture was freely used to extort confessions, but this did not prevent *beatas* appearing in large numbers.

Thousands of women developed the stigmata on their hands, so that this phenomenon ceased to excite a great deal of attention. Men and women, wishing for the prestige which came from holiness, were not always ready to live the life of privation to achieve this. New doctrines appeared. There was the case of Juan de Jesus who declared himself unaware of carnal desires; he only knew the demands of his spirit. Thus he was able to indulge those desires for he insisted that they were quite unimportant, and whether indulged or not it did not matter. He even went so far as to announce that he had had a revelation in which he had been shown that all women who gave themselves—and alms—to him would be certain of salvation.

The Inquisition eventually caught him. He was not punished with real severity. He was given a hundred lashes and confined for the rest of his days to a convent where he was to work hard for his bread.

There is no doubt that many of these men and women believed— or half-believed—the fantastic stories they caused to be circulated about themselves. Today they would be given psychiatrical treatment; and because they would not be in an enviable position few would wish to emulate them and work themselves up into a fervour of hysteria until they reached this state of half-belief. But what a temptation it was in sixteenth-, seventeenth-, eighteenth- and nineteenth-century Spain. Any obscure little girl could call attention to herself, could receive—if only temporarily—the adulation of the multitude, by painting the stigmata on her hands or even wounding herself with a sharp knife. The slight inconvenience must have seemed well worth while since as a result she was lifted from boredom and obscurity to fame and adulation.

Cases of mystics are recorded from the early fifteenth century to the very end of the Inquisition in the nineteenth. The case of Maria de los Dolores López gives an indication as to how the Inquisition had changed during three centuries. The trial of Beata Dolores took place in 1779; and at this time the Inquisition was growing near to its twilight hour.

Beata Dolores had left home at the age of twelve to live in the house of her confessor. Precocious and sensuous she quickly became the Confessor's mistress.

Dolores was full of wiles. She pretended that she was blind, and the fact that she could read, write and do exquisite embroidery was considered a miracle.

When the Confessor who had been her lover died, Dolores was well equipped to look after herself. Thousands flocked to see the blind woman who was aware of what went on about her as though she could see.   She held long conversations with her guardian angel; and this way of life proved very profitable for those who visited her brought gifts of great value; and her fame spread.

She could not however live long without masculine companionship and took another confessor.   This man very quickly realized that he was to fill a double role—that of confessor and lover.

Dolores must have been a very attractive woman and the confessor, having recovered from his first shock of surprise, succumbed.

Unfortunately for Dolores, this man was possessed of a conscience, and to relieve this he went before the tribunal of Seville and confessed their relationship.

As a result the confessor was sent to a convent where he was to live in rigid seclusion.   Beata Dolores was brought before the tribunal.

She assured the Inquisitors that, since she was four years old, she had been in communication with the Virgin Mary and had been married to Christ in Heaven.

She would have been given some light sentence had she not insisted on defending her sensuality with the doctrine called Molinist after Miguel de Molinos.   The theme of this was that what appeared to be evil to ordinary mortals was not so if condoned by God. She maintained that the relationship which she had enjoyed with her men friends had in no way offended Christ and the Virgin and therefore was not evil.   This was, of course, in direct contrast to the teaching of the Church and could only come under the heading of heresy.

Dolores however refused to accept the Church's view and clung to her own, so giving the Inquisition no alternative but to brand her as a heretic.   There was only one penalty for such heresy: burning at the stake.

However, with the Inquisition in twilight at this time, 1781, burnings were not so frequent nor so popular as they had once been, and efforts were made to make Dolores turn from her heresy and be received into the Church.

Dolores was a strange woman.   She must have believed in herself, for knowing that a fiery death awaited her, she refused as stubbornly as had the earlier martyrs.

There was no help for it; she was conducted to the *auto de fé*; and it was necesary to put a gag in her mouth, for she insisted on shouting her dangerous views to the crowd.   But the sight of the faggots ready to be kindled broke her spirit as no amount of talking could do. Dolores broke down, confessed, and was strangled before the wood at her feet was set alight.

*　*　*

Thus in its treatment of mystics, the Spanish Inquisition appears to have behaved with admirable restraint and even mercy, although, naturally, in these more enlightened days, floggings and solitary confinement seem harsh enough punishment to be meted out to those who are suffering from unbalanced minds. There is no doubt that many of the so-called mystics were clever impostors and these too were treated with a leniency which was amazing considering the times.

It was upon the Jews, Moors and Lutherans that the Inquisitors vented their demoniacal fury; and in the sixteenth century when fanatical Philip was desirous of setting it up in every country over which he had control, the growth of the Spanish Inquisition continued and reached its hideous heyday.

INDEX

Adrian VI, Pope (Adrian of Utrecht), Presence at Ferdinand's death, 84; rivalry with Ximenes 85; works with Ximenes 86; Inquisitor-General and Pope, 92; decree concerning Lutheran books, 105; against witches, 146; attitude to Francisca Hernandez, 155, 156, 157

Aguilar, Alonso de, in action at Sierra Vermeja, 51

Albornoz, mission to Italy, 41

Albret, Jean d', marriage of, 83

Alcañizes, Marchioness of, connection with Protestantism, 108, 112

Alexander VI (Roderigo Borgia), elected Pope, 17; conflict with Torquemada, 18, 19, 20, 23, 27; confirms nomination of Ximenes, 36; love of pleasure, 38; reproves Ximenes, 42; against witches, 146

Alfonso (Brother of Isabella) set up as King, 29

Alfonso, Archbishop of Saragossa (Illegitimate son of Ferdinand), Ferdinand seeks to make him Archbishop of Toledo 36; Ferdinand again tries, 78; temporary Governor of Aragon, 85

Alfonso II of Naples, Coronation, 19

Alfonso, King of Portugal, Invades Castile, 29

Algiciras, Diego de, gives evidence, 63/64

Almazan, 63

Alva, Don Fadrique de Toledo, Duke of, entertains Ferdinand, 84

Alva, Don Fernando Alvarez de Toledo, Duke of, Goes to England with Philip, 126

Aranda, Pedro de (Bishop of Calahorra), charges against him, 19

Arellano, Fray Christóbal, martyred, 115

Arias, Maestro García (Doctor Blanco), his Lutheranism, 106, imprisoned, 108; martyred, 115

Arthur, Prince of Wales, marriage arranged, 21, 22, 68; death, 82

Avora, Captain Gonzalo de, discusses methods of Inquisition, 63

Azpilcueta, Martin de, chosen to defend Carranza, 136

Baez, Gonzalo, victim of Inquisition, 112

Beata, of Avila, 80

Beata of Gibraltar, 80

Beata, of Piedrahita, attitude of Ximenes towards, 79; her claims, 80, 81, 152

Bede, Venerable, 143

Bejar, Duchess of, her cruelty, 114

Beltraneja, La, 29, 30

Bergenroth, Gustav Adolph, theory on death of Philip, 65; career, 72; theory on Juana, 73

Bernaldez, 14

Bertoun (or Burton), Nicholas, victim of Inquisition, 119/120

Biesa, Maria, burned for witchcraft, 146

Blanche, daughter of John II of Aragon, poisoned, 61

Blasquez, Juana, 112

Boabdil, Sultan of Granada, surrender of, 17, 42

Bohorqués, Juana de, torture and death of, 116

Bohorqués, Maria de, torture and death of, 115, 116

Boleyn, Anne, 22, 159

Bonner, Bishop of London, presides over court to deal with heresy, 127, 128

Borgia, Cardinal of Monreale, 19

Brantôme, suggestion regarding Navarro's death, 77

Brook, William, victim of Inquisition, 120

Buendia, Countess of, intervention on behalf of Ximenes, 32

Burgos, Bishop of, examined *Beata* of Piedrahita, 81

Cabra, Count of, helps revolt in Cordova, 66

Calcena, Juan Róiz de, secretary to Ferdinand, 63; influence of, 64

Calderón, Fray Francisco García, connection with Teresa de Silva, 164; tried and tortured, 165; sentenced, 166

Calixtus III, against witchcraft, 146

Cano, Melchor, delivers sermon at *auto*, 111; spies on Carranza, 131

Cardenas, Antonio, converted to Lutheranism, 107

Cardenas, Francisco, converted to Lutheranism, 107

Carillo Alfonso, Archbishop of Toledo, seeks to depose Henry IV, 29; death, 30; arrogance, 31, 32, 33, 34, 35; military nature, 74

Carlos, Don (Son of Philip II), present at *auto*, 110; required to swear

THE END OF THE
SPANISH INQUISITION

NOTE

In order to avoid footnotes, sources and references are given in the text.

My very special thanks are due to the librarians of Kensington Public Library who have worked so hard and patiently to procure rare books for me, and thus have aided me considerably in my research.

CONTENTS

ILLUSTRATIONS

RULERS OF SPAIN FROM THE RISE OF THE SPANISH INQUISITION TO ITS SUPPRESSION

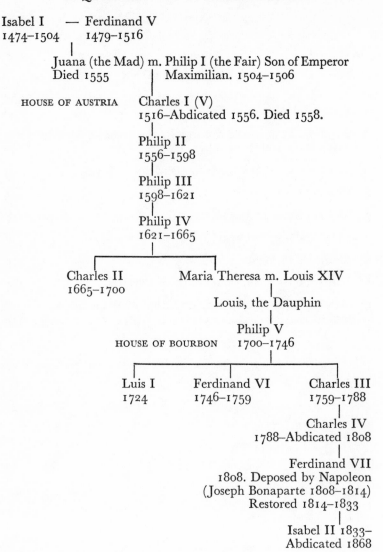

Isabel I   —   Ferdinand V
1474–1504   1479–1516
|
Juana (the Mad) m. Philip I (the Fair) Son of Emperor
Died 1555   Maximilian. 1504–1506

HOUSE OF AUSTRIA   Charles I (V)
1516–Abdicated 1556. Died 1558.
|
Philip II
1556–1598
|
Philip III
1598–1621
|
Philip IV
1621–1665
|

Charles II   Maria Theresa m. Louis XIV
1665–1700
Louis, the Dauphin
|
Philip V
HOUSE OF BOURBON   1700–1746

Luis I   Ferdinand VI   Charles III
1724   1746–1759   1759–1788
|
Charles IV
1788–Abdicated 1808
|
Ferdinand VII
1808. Deposed by Napoleon
(Joseph Bonaparte 1808–1814)
Restored 1814–1833
|
Isabel II 1833–
Abdicated 1868

PRINCIPAL WORKS CONSULTED

Acton, John Emerich Edward Dalberg, First Baron Acton, D.C.L., LL.D., Edited with an introduction by John Neville Figgis, M.A., and Reginald Vere Laurence, M.A. *The History of Freedom and Other Essays* (1907).

Adams, Nicholson B. *The Heritage of Spain: An Introduction to Spanish Civilization* (1949).

Alberti, L. de, and Chapman, A. B. Wallis, D.Sc. (Econ.) (Edited by). *English Merchants and the Spanish Inquisition in the Canaries.* Extracts from the Archives in the Possession of the Most Hon. The Marquess of Bute (1912).

Aradi, Zsolt. *The Popes* (1956).

Aubrey, William Hickman Smith. *The National and Domestic History of England.*

Bainton, Roland H. *The Reformation of the 16th Century* (1953).

Bainton, Roland H. *The Travail of Religious Liberty* (1953).

Baker, The Rev. J., M.A. (Compiled and Translated by). *The History of the Inquisition as it subsists in the Kingdoms of Spain, Portugal, etc., and in both the Indies to this day* (1734).

Berdyaev, Nicolas. With a Commentary and Notes by Alan A. Spears. Translated by Alan A. Spears and Victor B. Kanter. *Christianity and Anti-Semitism* (1952).

Bertrand, Louis and Sir Charles Petrie, M.A., F.R.Hist.S. *The History of Spain* (1934).

Bury, J. B. with an Epilogue by H. J. Blackham. *A History of Freedom of Thought* (1952).

Butterfield, Herbert. *Christianity in European History* (1951).

Cary-Elwes, Columbia, Monk of Ampleforth. With a preface by Professor Arnold Toynbee. *Law, Liberty and Love* (1949).

Creighton, M., D.D. Oxon. and Cam. *Persecution and Tolerance* (1895).

Dawson, Christopher. *Religion and the Rise of Western Culture* (1950).

Deanesly, M., M.A. *A History of the Medieval Church 590-1500* (1925).

Gifford, William Alva. *The Story of the Faith. A survey of Christian History for the Undogmatic* (1946).

9

Gordon, Janet. *The Spanish Inquisition* (1898).

Gowen, Herbert H., D.D., F.R.A.S. *A History of Religion* (1934).

Guizot, M. Translated by Robert Black, M.A. *The History of France* (1881).

Hume, Martin A. S. Revised by Edward Armstrong. *Spain: Its Greatness and Decay (1479-1788) Cambridge Historical Series* (1931).

Hume, Martin A. S. *The Court of Philip IV. Spain in Decadence* (1907).

Hume, Martin A. S. *Queens of Old Spain* (1906).

Lea, Henry Charles, LL.D. *A History of the Inquisition of the Middle Ages.* 3 Volumes (1887).

Lea, Henry Charles, LL.D. *A History of the Inquisition of Spain.* 4 Volumes (1908).

Lea, Henry Charles, LL.D. *Chapters from the Religious History of Spain connected with the Inquisition* (1890).

Lea, Henry Charles, LL.D. *Superstition and Force* (1892).

Lea, Henry Charles, LL.D. *The Inquisition in the Spanish Dependencies* (1908).

Limborch, Philip. *The History of the Inquisition* (1816).

Marañón, Gregorio, Translated from the Spanish by Charles David Ley. *Antonio Pérez "Spanish Traitor"* (1954).

Marchant, John, and others. *A review of the Bloody Tribunal; or the Horrid Cruelties of the Inquisition as practised in Spain, Portugal, Italy and the East and West Indies* (1770).

Maycock, A. L., M.A. With an Introduction by Father Ronald Knox. *The Inquisition from its Establishment to the Great Schism* (1926).

McKinnon, James, Ph.D., D.D., D.Th., LL.D. *Calvin and the Reformation* (1936).

McKnight, John P. *The Papacy* (1953).

Mortimer, R. C., M.A., B.D. *The Elements of Moral Theology* (1947).

Nickerson, Hoffman. With a Preface by Hilaire Belloc. *The Inquisition. A Political and Military Study of its Establishment* (1923).

Presscott, William H. *History of the Reign of Ferdinand and Isabella the Catholic.* 2 Volumes.

Presscott, William H. *History of the Reign of Philip II, King of Spain.* 3 Volumes (1873).

Poole, Reginald Lane. *Illustrations of the History of Medieval Thought and Learning* (1880).

Robertson, John M. *A Short History of Freethought Ancient and Modern.* 2 Volumes (1915).

Roth, Cecil. *The Spanish Inquisition* (1937).

Rule, William Harris, D.D. *History of the Inquisition.* 2 Volumes (1874).

Shewring, Walter. (Translated and Introduced by) *Rich and Poor in Christian Tradition. Writings of many centuries* (1947).

Simon, Dr. Paul, Translated from the German by Meyrick Booth, Ph.D. *The Human Element in the Church of Christ* (1953).

Stephen, James Fitzjames, Q.C. *Liberty, Equality, Fraternity* (1873).

Swain, John. *The Pleasures of the Torture Chamber* (1931).

Turberville, A. S., M.C., M.A., B.Litt. *The Spanish Inquisition* (1932).

Turberville, A. S., M.C., M.A., B.Litt. *Medieval Heresy and the Inquisition* (1920).

Wiseman, F. J., M.A. *Roman Spain. An introduction to the Roman Antiquities of Spain and Portugal* (1956).

The Catholic Encyclopedia: An International Work of Reference on the Constitution, Doctrine, Discipline and History of the Catholic Church. Edited by Charles G. Herbermann, Ph.D., LL.D.; Edward A. Pace, Ph.D., D.D.; Condé B. Pallen, Ph.D., LL.D.; Thomas J. Shahan, D.D.; John J. Wynne, S.J. Assisted by numerous collaborators (1907).

I

THE COUNCIL OF BLOOD

DURING THE second half of the sixteenth century Spain was ruled by the most notorious of all her kings—Philip II—and partly because the country had reached a certain stage in her development, partly because of the character of the strange man who sat upon the throne, the Inquisition flourished to such an extent that it dominated the country.

Philip was the most powerful sovereign in the world, but the burdens which had been laid upon his slender shoulders were too much for him, and his eventual failure was due to an absence of imagination and the inspired genius necessary in a great ruler, not to any lack of conscientious devotion to duty.

There was no monarch in the world who had a higher sense of duty; it was no fault of his that his mind worked slowly and that he was constantly finding himself a move behind his opponents. His father had taught him to govern; he continued to follow his father's methods, although Emperor Charles would have been the first to point out that other times demanded other methods. Philip, lord of half the world, suspicious of all, unlovable, secretive and above all bigoted, was not a strong enough man to fill the role of most powerful monarch in the world.

He was determined to establish the Catholic Faith in all countries under his dominion; and there was no country which suffered more agony, on account of this desire of his, than the Low Countries.

This tortured land which was, unfortunately for its people, under Spanish rule, clearly desired to be a Protestant country; and it is not in Spain that the Protestants were persecuted so bitterly (for Protestantism had never had a very firm hold in that country) but in the Netherlands.

The Emperor Charles, born in Flanders, was more Fleming than Spaniard; yet he was guilty of trying to force Catholicism on a people who were prepared vigorously to reject it.

Strangely enough Charles, presiding over the Diet of Worms,

had, when Martin Luther stood before it, been instrumental in bringing about the latter's escape. It is true that Luther had been given a safe conduct, but that was no guarantee of safety; it was not difficult to find means of wriggling out of promises. However Luther had been allowed to state his beliefs and escape.

Charles later regretted this and thirty years after the event, at the time when he was abdicating in favour of Philip, he actually stated that he had committed a grave error by not allowing Luther to be sent to the stake.

However he set about rectifying that so-called error very soon after he had made it; as it was in his power to fight Lutheranism in the Netherlands, he did so with enthusiasm.

An edict was proclaimed forbidding the people of the Netherlands to publish Lutheran books, and the penalties for disobeying this rule were very severe indeed. In 1522 Charles appointed Councillor Francis Van der Hulst of Brabant to be Inquisitor-General of the Netherlands. Van der Hulst, like many before him, practised such cruelties that had he not escaped in time he would have paid with his life.

It was necessary, after the rule of Van der Hulst, to suspend inquisitorial activities for a while, but Charles was determined to destroy Lutheranism in the Netherlands. We find him fiercely demanding the death penalty for all heretics, by "the sword, the ditch and fire".

These orders were carried out. It mattered not what nationality the victim, it was only necessary for him to be a Protestant to be submitted to the utmost cruelty.

Our own William Tyndale, whose great crime was that he had translated the New Testament into English, was one of them. He had been exiled by Henry VIII and worked in great poverty in Antwerp. He longed to return to England but Henry refused him permission to do so. In the year 1535 he was lodging at the house of Thomas Poyntz, an English merchant who was very interested in the Lutheran theory. Unfortunately, he was betrayed to the authorities as a dangerous heretic and consequently was arrested and taken to Vilvorde, a strong castle-fortress near Brussels, where he was kept for fourteen months.

He had friends in England and Thomas Poyntz was working busily on his behalf. This man went to England and begged Cromwell to intercede for their countryman. Poor Poyntz, not only were his efforts in vain, but he himself was arrested and imprisoned for heresy. But he was more fortunate than Tyndale and succeeded in escaping.

Meanwhile Tyndale remained in prison, calm, very ready if

necessary to wear the martyr's crown. He believed firmly that the Bible was for the use of all, and he was ready to die to give it to the people. He was known among the little band of exiles as a man of great virtue. Each Monday he visited all those exiles who were in need, and out of his small wealth aided them to the best of his ability; on Saturdays he acted in the same way towards any destitute people he found in the streets of Antwerp. This benevolence was made possible by those merchants of this city who, sharing his views and being determined to uphold the Protestant Faith, clubbed together to make him an allowance. We are told that the whole of this allowance was devoted to the needs of others.

It was this man who, on the 6th of October, 1536, was taken from his dungeon to the stake. He showed no fear but quietly awaited his fate, and he is reputed to have said as the ropes were bound about him: "Lord! Open the eyes of the King of England!" Rule, in his *History of the Inquisition,* writes that he was burned alive; other historians state that he was strangled before the faggots were lighted. Rule, being fiercely Protestant, is inclined to paint the Catholics in as dark colours as possible.

In 1522 the Augustinian Friars of Antwerp declared their belief in Lutheranism. Several of them were burned alive, singing psalms until the smoke choked them. One was tied in a sack and thrown into the Scheldt.

These terrible sentences did not deter the noble people of the Netherlands. They welcomed the Lutheran ideas and, once they had accepted them, could not be turned from them. As the years passed and Philip took the place of his father, persecution became more fierce, and it was the custom to burn the men and bury the women, alive.

But Rule records several accounts of horrible punishment under Charles. In 1524 a sailor, who went aloft in a ship lying at anchor in the port of Antwerp and preached Lutheranism to the crowds who gathered on the shore to listen to him, was arrested, handed to the secular arm, put into a sack and thrown into the river.

Several priests were burned alive because they believed the new ideas and had married. There is one account of a family of six— father, mother, two daughters and two sons-in-law—who were all burned alive together because they had accepted Lutheranism.

One of the most cruel practices was to take women who were about to give birth to children and burn them at the stake during the birth. This, says Rule, was the fate of several women in Holland.

The people of the Netherlands seemed to be inspired rather than deterred by these horrific sights. It may have been that they found Protestantism a religion suited to the national character; it may have been that they were a people who had for years learned to make their own decisions. They had always discussed new ideas and, if need be, criticized their rulers. They were not a people to lie down meekly and accept a certain doctrine because their rulers had decided they should.

The soil of Flanders was to be saturated with the blood of martyrs in the years to come when the Spanish Inquisition in all its fury was set up in that freedom-loving land. Even at the time of Charles's retirement to Yuste it is calculated that his victims had numbered between 50,000 and 100,000. In retirement at Yuste and reviewing the situation he wrote that he wanted to establish the Spanish Inquisition in the Netherlands that he might prevent heresy spreading from Germany, France and England. He had come to the conclusion that all who had fallen into heresy should be condemned to suffer death by fire and their heirs the confiscation of their property. He admits that the people were outraged by the severity of this treatment, but insists that he was compelled out of necessity to act as he had.

And when Charles decided that he had done with the world and would end his life in retirement at the monastery of Yuste, he handed over his crown to his son Philip.

The Netherlands had suffered mildly compared with what was to come.

*   *   *

When the Inquisition was set up in the Netherlands the resentment of the people was intense. How different these Netherlanders were from the people of Aragon who, at the time of the assassination of the Inquisitor Pedro Arbués, instead of making a stand beside those who had risen in revolt called for their blood.

These people of the Netherlands were determined to fight for the right to worship God as they pleased. Discontent reigned in the land and the more rowdy elements of the population seized the opportunity to show their disapproval. Thus in August of 1566, three hundred people, clubs and axes in their hands, entered the churches in the neighbourhood of St. Omer and set about demolishing those images so beloved by the Catholic community. From St. Omer they went to Ypres where they attacked the Cathedral. Menin, Comines, Valenciennes, Tournay and finally Antwerp were dealt with in their turn.

News of what was happening spread through the country, and riots broke out in big towns such as Rotterdam and Haarlem and, when the soldiers were called upon to take up arms against the rioters, they refused to do so.

It was naturally the uneducated mob who took part in these riots; they went into the pulpits and mimicked the Catholic priests; they put on their robes and made obscene gestures; they placed the images of the saints against wooden stakes and set fire to them. Valuable books were burned; and it was calculated that the damage done to Antwerp Cathedral alone was about four hundred thousand ducats.

When news of the rioting reached Brussels the Regent of the Netherlands declared that the country must be defended against those who sought to destroy its religion.

This Regent was Margaret, Duchess of Parma, who was an illegitimate daughter of Emperor Charles, and therefore half-sister to Philip. Her mother had been Margaret Vander Gheenst who when she was seventeen had caught the roving eye of the Emperor. The fruit of this liaison was brought up by Charles's aunt, who was herself then Regent of the Netherlands. Charles however, as he showed later in the case of Don John of Austria, was not one to forget his children, illegitimate though they might be; and Margaret was royally educated. When she was twelve she married Alessandro de'Medici; fortunately for her Alessandro died a year after the marriage.

Later she married Ottavio Farnese, a grandson of Paul III, and Charles benignly bestowed upon her the Duchies of Parma and Placentia as a dowry, doubtless to make up for the fact that, although Margaret was then a young woman, her new bridegroom was a child of twelve.

In 1559, when Margaret was thirty-eight, she became Regent of the Netherlands, an office bestowed on her by her half-brother, Philip II of Spain.

There was however much opposition from the noblemen of the Netherlands to the threatened curtailment of religious liberty; and the three most prominent of these were Egmont, Hoorne and Orange. And of these three it was William of Orange who became one of the great figures of history.

He was born at Dillemburg in Nassau on the 25th of April, 1533, of Lutheran parents, and in his early days he was educated in that faith. This did not please Emperor Charles, so when the boy was twelve years old he took him from his parents that he might be brought up by his, Charles's, sister Mary, as a Catholic.

William was so outstandingly intelligent that the Emperor was attracted by him, and when he was fifteen he took him into his own household as one of his pages. Charles came to have a great affection for William and entrusted him with many delicate missions; at the famous abdication ceremony it was on William's shoulder that he leaned; and he asked Philip to make use of the services of this brilliant young man and see that adequate rewards came his way.

There can be no doubt that Charles regretted that William was not his own son; his attitude to William would doubtless have been different had he been able to look into the future and see in William the great leader who was, in time, virtually to free his suffering country from Spanish tyranny.

William in his turn had a great respect for Charles. The Flemings revered their Emperor for, harsh though he could sometimes be, they felt that he was one of them. It was when Philip—so essentially a Spaniard—stepped into his shoes that they showed their resentment.

William married Anne of Egmont, daughter of the Count of Büren, when he was eighteen; she died a few years after the marriage and he then made an alliance with Anne of Saxony, a rich heiress and an earnest Lutheran, which caused consternation to Philip, who had by that time taken his father's place. This marriage broke up after thirteen years, when Anne returned to Germany. The fact that it was most unsatisfactory may explain why William was inclined to indulge in amorous adventures.

In spite of his love of gaiety and courtly manners he was far from free and easy in his behaviour; he was known as "William the Silent", for he spoke little, although when he did so he could be very eloquent. His perfect manners and gallantries enhanced his popularity with his fellow countrymen; and the fact that he never allowed his tongue to betray him was a great advantage in his political life. William the Silent was very adequately endowed with the qualities necessary to the great leader he was to become.

There was one other quality he possessed—perhaps the finest of them all. He was vehemently against persecution and earnestly supported the right of all men to worship as they pleased.

It was said of him by a contemporary writer that he was known as a Catholic among Catholics and a Lutheran among Lutherans; and it may have been that in his great fight against Spanish tyranny he became a Protestant; but what William the Silent really fought for was the freedom of his people.

Had he been a bigot it is doubtful whether he would have been such a fine leader. Philip's eventual failure was in a large measure due to his bigotry; and it is interesting to compare his failure and that of his wife, Mary I of England (another bigot), with the success of Elizabeth I, a queen who may in secret have murmured "A plague on both your houses", while in public she could give the impression of being the friend of all.

Meanwhile in Spain Philip was kept informed of what was happening in the Netherlands. "By the soul of my father," he is reputed to have said, "this shall cost them dear." He kept his word.

The time had come, Orange knew, either to fight or to flee, and as he was not in a position to do the former, being a wise man he left the Netherlands. The rebels were brought to order and Margaret restored temporary peace to the land. She was not however prepared to forgive those who had risen against Catholicism, and she inflicted terrible punishment on the offenders. She sent her troops across the country and wherever they discovered those of the reformed faith meeting together, they rode among them deliberately trampling them under the horse's hoofs, shooting them or taking them to execution. In many cases there was no trial; those suspected of the slightest interest in the reformed faith were hung up on gibbets; and all over the countryside these gruesome spectacles were to be seen.

Meanwhile Philip had decided to send the Duke of Alva into the Netherlands at the head of the army; and the blood bath was about to begin.

This very successful general was already noted for his harshness even before he came to the Netherlands; and what his coming was to mean to that persecuted land was clear when he wrote to Philip that his aim was to have every man feeling that at any hour of the day or night his house might fall about his ears.

As soon as he arrived in the Netherlands he established his garrisons in the important towns. The soldiers were given great licence and there is no need to state the nature of the cruelty and indignities heaped upon the inhabitants. Contemporary writers tell us that the oppression of the Spaniards was great and that anyone who possessed something which the Spaniards desired was immediately accused of heresy so that what was coveted might be confiscated.

The people were filled with panic and many left the country by stealth, taking with them all they possibly could.

Egmont and Hoorne were arrested. William of Orange had shown his astuteness by leaving the country. Cardinal Granvelle, whose experiences in the Netherlands make it clear that he knew what he was talking about, said when he heard of the arrests of Egmont and Hoorne: "But have they drawn the Silent One into the net?" And when he was told that Orange had escaped, he answered: "Then if they have not caught Orange, they have caught nothing."

Alva's first task was to call together a tribunal which was to be invested with extraordinary powers and was to investigate the recent riots and bring those responsible to justice. It was called the Council of His Excellency and was made up of twelve judges;

one of these was the notorious Juan de Vargas, a vicious man capable of great cruelty. The Council was called by the people of the Netherlands: "The Council of Blood."

The persecution began; the great need was to bring victims before the Council of Blood. So the familiar methods were used. Husbands and wives were induced by threats to inform against each other, as were children against their parents; if they would not do so, they were introduced to the rack and the hoist and those other devilish persuaders. Those who were suspected and remained in hiding had their names posted up in the streets, and criers paraded the towns shouting that they were wanted and that any who knew where they were and did not inform against them were themselves suspect. On the night of Ash Wednesday, 1568, five hundred people were arrested in Brussels in the middle of the night, dragged from their beds to prison—all to be condemned to death.

A common enough sight in the streets was that of people being seized, pinioned and dragged away. If the victims were poor they were hanged without delay.

Some were beheaded, many were hanged; others were burned alive at the stake. "Condemned to die" was the order of the day; the method was left to the judges who were often the uneducated and mercilessly cruel soldiers. It was understood that any man or woman who was a steadfast Lutheran merited the more terrible death by fire.

One exceptionally cruel practice was to burn the tip of the tongue with a red-hot iron. The swollen tongue was then compressed between two plates of metal which were screwed tightly together. The sufferer was taken to the scaffold where he—or she— was to be hanged or burned alive. In acute pain it was very probable that the victim would be unable to suppress his groans which, with his swollen tongue between the pieces of metal, would sound like some strange language. This was intended to add to the amusement of the spectators.

Alva and his lieutenant, Vargas, appear to have enjoyed exercising their cruelty on these people. Vargas is reputed to have shouted when awakened from sleep: "To the gallows! To the gallows!" Words which when awake he used so frequently. As for Alva, in his letters to Philip he gives an impression of licking his lips over his achievements. "I am going to arrest some of the richest and worst offenders, and bring them to a pecuniary composition." "I have reiterated the sentence again and again, for they torment me with their inquiries whether in this or that case it might not be commuted to banishment. They weary me of my life with their importunities." These comments are revealing, betraying as they do Alva's cynical attitude towards the misery he was bringing to thousands and an almost fiendish delight that it was in his power to do so.

Again we have an example of the stupidity of the bigots. The cities were being deserted and the Netherlands was fast losing that prosperity which its flourishing merchants had brought to it before the Inquisition was introduced into its midst. Thousands escaped into Germany where a refuge was gladly given to them.

Margaret had abdicated. She believed that the leaders of the revolt should have been punished, but she considered this attack on the people to be foolish as well as cruel. She went to Parma and there lived in comparative obscurity until her son Alexander Farnese became Governor of the Netherlands, when she was at his side.

De Thou asserts that Philip, aware of the criticism of many countries, sought to justify the action which Alva was taking in the Netherlands, and put the case before the Inquisition in Madrid.

The tribunal's verdict was that all who were guilty of heresy, apostasy or sedition, and those who, declaring themselves to be good Catholics, had done nothing to bring heretics to justice, were guilty of treason both to Church and State. The penalty for such crimes was well known; and as the people of the Netherlands, with very few exceptions, had committed this crime, they were all condemned to death, and their property was to be confiscated. That they might serve as an example to all in the future they were to have no hope of grace whatever.

Prescott doubts the authenticity of this story, although he admits that it has been repeated many times by writers to whom it does not occur to distrust it. He says: "Not that anything can be too monstrous to be believed of the Inquisition. But it is not easy to believe that a sagacious prince like Philip II, however willing he might be to shelter himself under the mantle of the Holy Office, could have lent himself to an act as impolitic as it was absurd." *(History of the Reign of Philip II.)*

When the Emperor Maximilian protested to Philip and asked him to put an end to persecution in the Netherlands, Philip replied: "What I have done has been for the repose of the Provinces, and for the defence of the Catholic Faith. Nor would I do otherwise than I have done, though I should risk the sovereignty of the Netherlands—no, though the world should fall around me in ruins." *(Correspondence of Philip II.)*

Thus spoke the bigot, and it is gratifying to record that his conduct was to set his empire tottering. Even at this stage the exiles from their country were rallying round the man to whom they looked to save them. At Dillemburg William the Silent was making plans.

There were two unsuccessful expeditions, one led by the nobleman Hoogstraten and the other by Villers, but at Heyligerlee, Louis of Nassau (brave brother of William the Silent) won a victory over Alva's forces. This was wonderful news for the suffering people, and Alva's fury was boundless. The Counts Egmont and Hoorne were beheaded; and William and his brother Louis were sentenced to perpetual banishment, and their estates were to be confiscated.

It was impossible, of course, to carry out the threat to exterminate the entire nation, but Alva's tyranny and the execution of great leaders like Egmont and Hoorne, did for a time appear to have the effect of subduing the people. So that three years after Alva's arrival in Flanders he felt justified in proclaiming a free pardon for all those Flemings who would now become faithful subjects of Philip II.

According to Hume *(Spain: its greatness and decay)* it was not religion which made the Flemings revolt against the Spanish yoke so much as their love of money. Philip had levied the *alcabala* on all sales and purchases; this was ten per cent which went to the treasury. It was the merchants who had made Flanders wealthy, and they were not prepared to see business deteriorate because of such a tax.

Philip had been accustomed to draw on the Flemish bankers for loans; they now declared that, owing to the conditions imposed upon trade, they were bankrupt and could no longer supply the King with money. Philip at this stage began to question the wisdom of Alva's rule. Protests were coming in from all over the world; and, perhaps most important of all, Alva had his enemies in Madrid, the chief of whom was Antonio Pérez who was later to figure in one of the most dramatic cases connected with the Inquisition.

In 1573 Alva was recalled to Spain, a disgraced man who had failed in his mission, which was to subdue the Netherlands and make the people docile vassals of Spain. We are told that his disgrace almost "broke Alva's heart"—an inadequate punishment for the misery he had brought to thousands.

His place was taken by Don Luis de Requesens y Zuñiga whose orders were to pursue a more conciliatory course.

Protestants were persecuted in the Netherlands with greater ferocity and with more frequency than anywhere else, for in this case the Inquisition was working against an entire nation; and in Spain Protestantism, apart from the two outbreaks at Seville and Valladolid, was rare.

It is not known how many people suffered during Alva's command. It was, naturally, impossible to eliminate the entire nation of some 3,000,000; but Alva is reputed to have boasted that, during his term in the Netherlands, he was responsible for the death of 18,600 people, and that about 60,000 left the country in order to escape him and his bloody-minded assistants.

2

ENGLISH CAPTIVES OF THE INQUISITION

It is not surprising that, when the Spanish fleet sailed against England in 1588, the country rose with a mighty determination and, lacking the great galleons, and the finer military equipment of the would-be conqueror, struck the first great blow which was to shatter a mighty empire.

The English knew that the intention was to set up the Inquisition in their land. They were aware that English sailors who had fallen into the hands of the Inquisition had been tortured and murdered for their faith. The fact that some humble sailor—who might have been a friend or relation—had been brutally murdered, was enough to bring home to them the menace which threatened them.

There was danger of falling into the hands of Spaniards when sailing the seas or trading in the towns of Spain. A chance word, a book which was carried, might bring a charge of heresy. There would be the arrest, the imprisonment and the hopelessness of being far from home with no help at hand so that the torture chambers and burning at the stake would very possibly be the outcome.

English merchants in 1576 brought a petition to the Queen, protesting against the treatment received in Spain; and later the behaviour of the Inquisition towards English merchants and sailors was the cause of much diplomatic activity; but the Holy Office was adamant. Those who did not adhere strictly to the Catholic Faith were heretics whatever their nationality and therefore worthy only of death.

The Catholic Church was desperately afraid of Lutheranism. The power of the new Church could not fail to be appreciated and it was fast becoming the most formidable rival Catholics had ever known. It has been said that but for the Inquisition the Catholic Faith could not have survived, that for this reason the former was necessary and its cruelties must be forgotten. Determined to keep Protestantism from Spain the government placed the harbours

24

under the control of the Inquisition. One of the rules, quickly brought into force by the Holy Office, was that ships coming into harbours should be searched and, if any heretical book were found, the crew was to be taken before the tribunal.

This rule had been established during the reign of Henry VIII, but Henry was not the man to stand aside and see his sailors treated in such a way; he immediately protested to the Emperor Charles who, at that time wishing to remain on good terms with the King of England, withdrew the rule.

Philip was different from his father. There were times when his bigotry could carry him beyond the realm of reason. Under Philip, if an English Bible or Prayer Book were found in the possession of an English sailor he was arrested, brought before the tribunal and perhaps sentenced to a term at the galleys if he denied his own religion; and if he did not deny it, it was the stake for him in a "fool's coat"—the English ironical term for the *sanbenito*.

In the year 1565 twenty-six English subjects were burned at the stake in Spain, and ten times as many were lying imprisoned awaiting a similar fate. Sir John Smith was sent on a special mission to Philip to make complaint about this, but the mission was unsuccessful.

This seizing of Englishmen was not confined to Spain alone; for Spain was in possession of a large part of the world, and every sailor who left his native land was in danger not only from the elements and chances of fights at sea but—most dreaded of all—the Spanish Inquisition.

*   *   *

At an *auto de fé* in the Canaries (which, though discovered in 1402 by a Norman sailor, Jean de Bethencourt, had eventually fallen into the possession of Castile) an Englishman, George Gaspar, appeared in the year 1587.

He had been arrested on suspicion of heresy and taken to a prison in Tenerife, and whilst there had been seen to turn his back on the crucifix as he knelt in prayer. On being asked why he did this, he replied that he addressed his prayers to God and not to images. This was asking for trouble and it was not denied him.

He was taken before the tribunal, where he admitted that he was a Protestant, and then cruelly tortured; but nothing could make him deny the faith in which he had been brought up. He was a self-confessed heretic, quite impenitent, and there was only one course open to the Inquisitors. He was handed to the secular arm and condemned to be burned at the stake.

George Gaspar was undoubtedly a very brave man, but he was

determined to avoid that agonizing death at the stake; at the same time he was equally determined not to deny his faith. He had managed to hide a knife in his prison and, when he heard that the terrible sentence had been passed on him, he plunged this into his stomach.

Unfortunately for him he did not die of the wound, and the Inquisitors piously declared that it was the will of God that this wicked man should not escape his just punishment on Earth. He was dying, it was true, but there was still time to let him feel the fire. He had to be taken to the *quemadero* on a litter and the flames hastily lighted, so that he might die in the utmost agony.

Even if prisoners escaped burning at the stake, other punishments were inflicted which must have been almost as hard to bear. There was one man, whose case is recorded under the name of John Reman (presumably Raymond), who was an English sailor and had been brought before the tribunal of the Holy Office in the Canaries. He was imprisoned and whilst there was discovered discussing Lutheran theories with other prisoners. He was immediately brought before the tribunal, vigorously questioned and taken down to the gloomy torture chambers. He was racked so cruelly that he was ready to admit anything that was asked of him and, declaring his wish for reconciliation with the Church of Rome, escaped death. He was "pardoned" but his punishment was to be two hundred strokes of the lash and ten years in the galleys. When one imagines the prolonged hell of the galleys, quick burning at the stake seems almost preferable.

At the same *auto* there appeared the crew of the ship *Prima Rosa* which had been taken by the Spanish. This crew consisted of eleven Englishmen and one Fleming. They were imprisoned and tortured, and all, with the exception of one who died while in prison (no doubt due to the hardship imposed upon him), declared themselves converted to the Catholic Faith. They were "forgiven" but their punishment was a hundred lashes and sentences to the galleys.

It was particularly infuriating to Englishmen to know that the oars of the Spanish ships were in many cases manned by their own countrymen.

A cousin of Sir Francis Drake, John Drake, was arrested in South America after a shipwreck; he was obliged to appear at an *auto de fé* as a penitent, which must have been excessively galling for Sir Francis.

In 1594, one year before the death of Sir John Hawkins, his son Richard became a prisoner after an action at San Matteo. Many of his crew were, without trial, sentenced to the galleys, but

Richard with some of his senior officers was taken to Lima, there to be brought before the Inquisition. None of them, it is recorded, was so firmly Protestant as to be burned at the stake; and in his book, *The Spanish Inquisition*, Cecil Roth points out that the member of this party who stood most firm in his faith, and was consequently sentenced to perpetual imprisonment, was named Leigh, as was the famous character in *Westward Ho!* So perhaps it was the records of this particular case which fired the inspiration of Charles Kingsley.

*   *   *

William Gardiner, a Bristol man, came before the Lisbon Inquisition in the reign of Edward VI. He was, we are told, "Honestly brought up and by nature given to gravity." He was a small man but very handsome and "in no part so excellent as in the inward qualities of his mind".

He was employed by a merchant whose business connexions were in Spain and Portugal; and when William was twenty-six he was sent by his employer to Lisbon to complete some transactions.

There were several Englishmen living in Lisbon, and these were Protestants. William made their acquaintance on his arrival and spent a great deal of time in their company.

On the 1st of September, 1552, a royal marriage took place in Lisbon, the King's son marrying a Spanish princess, and William, who had mingled with the crowd sightseeing, for the first time in his life saw Mass celebrated. He watched incredulously while the Host was elevated and the people knelt, and it seemed to him like a pagan rite. As he left the crowds and went silently to his lodging, he came to the conclusion that he must point out to all those people that, in behaving as they did and bowing down to images, they were giving way to superstition.

He was so concerned about all this that he felt he must do something. He knew that public protest would almost certainly mean painful death for him, yet he felt himself forced to act.

The festivities of the wedding continued, and when Mass was again celebrated, he found a place near the altar; when the King himself entered the church and Mass began, William took a Testament from his pocket and began to read it. The Host elevated, the people fell to their knees, but William merely sat reading his Testament. Then suddenly he ran to the Cardinal who was officiating and, snatching the Host from him, he threw it to the ground and stamped on it.

There was consternation which for the first few seconds showed itself in silence; then the people fell on William and would have torn him to pieces, if the King had not commanded that he should be released. His was a case for the Holy Office.

The King then approached William and asked why he had done this.

William explained that he was an Englishman in this country on business, and went on to say that when he witnessed such idolatry he could not endure it.

He was handed over to the Inquisition, and his English friends were arrested, also. Before the tribunal he talked freely of religion and his fearlessness astonished all who came into contact with him.

He was submitted to torture. The Portuguese were more brutal than the Spanish yet less disciplined. Behind the Inquisition in Spain was a fierce determination to wipe out heresy; in studying the methods used in Portugal it often seems that the Inquisitors did not care so much whether heretics were reconciled to the Church of Rome as that a spectacle was provided for the people. In Spain any criticism levelled at the Inquisition would bring the critics to immediate examination and almost inevitable death; in Portugal, however, possible changes in the methods of the Inquisition were openly discussed. Yet for all their carelessness the Portuguese appear to have been what would seem impossible: that is, more cruel than their neighbours in the Iberian Peninsula.

William Gardiner suffered many kinds of torture. One of these was to have a ball forced down his throat, then violently jerked up; this was repeated again and again until he was in a state of collapse. But whatever tortures they applied or threatened, William remained adamant and declared that if he had the chance he would behave in exactly the same way as he had in the cathedral.

His tormentors lost their patience with him. When they cut off the right hand which had seized the Host and thrown it to the ground, William seemed to delight in his suffering, for he picked up the bleeding right hand with his left and kissed it.

He was then taken out into the streets that the large crowd of spectators might enjoy his further sufferings. In the market place his left hand was cut off. He was then set upon a donkey and carried to the river's edge where the stake was set up. But this was no ordinary stake which had been prepared for the man who had insulted the Host. Attached to it was a rope and pulley; and when the faggots at its foot were lighted William was hoisted above the flames and lowered into them. Up and down he went, so that his agony might be protracted and that the people might see him slowly roasted to death.

All the time he was suffering this indescribable agony he was answering the people who called to him, and quoting psalms and passages from the Bible. "When Christ ceases to be your Advocate," he is reputed to have said, "then will I pray the Virgin Mary to be mine."

He continued thus until the rope was burned through and his body fell into the flames. (Rule's *History of the Inquisition*.)

*   *   *

The case of Isaac Martin is more often quoted, perhaps because he escaped from the Inquisition and published his own account of what happened to him.

Isaac Martin arrived in Malaga in the year 1714 with his wife and four children; and when he landed and his goods were searched at the Custom House, a Bible and certain books of devotion were discovered in his baggage. These were confiscated because, he was told, they must be examined to see whether they contained anything against the Holy Catholic Faith.

He lost the books and after two or three months' residence in the city he was summoned to appear before a court where he was accused of being a Jew; because his name was Isaac and one of his children was called Abraham this was reckoned to be very suspicious. Several of his neighbours were brought up for questioning and they all agreed—no doubt because it was expected of them —that he was a heretic. His position was a very dangerous one, for he was liable at any time to be seized by the Inquisition as a heretic; and if he were practising Judaism his position was even more dangerous, for Jews were not allowed to live in Spain or Portugal unless they became Catholics.

For four years nothing happened, but the Inquisitorial eye had not ceased to watch Mr. Martin. An Irish priest, he tells us, made his life intolerable by calling continually upon him in order to make him turn Catholic. Isaac could see that there was to be no peace at Malaga and planned to sell up and return to England.

His friends shook their heads warningly over this, because they knew that if he attempted to move he would be seized by the Inquisition which, while it allowed him a little licence—as a cat will a mouse—would not allow him to escape altogether.

One night, when he and his family had retired, there was a knocking on his door, and before opening it he saw from a window that several people were standing there. He asked what they wanted at such an hour and was told that they wished to come in. "Come back in the morning," replied Isaac; "I do not open my doors at such an hour." They broke open the door and, to his horror, Isaac recognized the dreaded *alguazils* and the priests and familiars of the Inquisition.

Bewildered he asked what they wanted and was told that their business was with the master of the house. "I am the man," Isaac answered, and was told to get his cloak and come with them. Isaac then said that he was an Englishman and that the Inquisition had nothing to do with him. He said that if they had anything to say to him they could say it after he had given notice to his Consul which as an Englishman he was entitled to do.

They shook their heads. Apparently he knew little of the methods of the Inquisition. Meanwhile his wife and children, hearing the commotion, came to see what was wrong. Terrified they clung to him and implored the officers of the Inquisition for mercy. Such scenes were of course too familiar to these men to have any effect on them. Isaac was dragged away to prison, and his wife and children turned out of the house that it might be searched for incriminating evidence.

The poor woman and her children had nowhere to go; and their terror at finding husband and father taken from them and themselves turned into the streets at night can well be imagined. Fortunately a kind friend took them in, and the keys of the house were not returned to Mrs. Martin until five days later when, returning to her home, she found all the family's possessions had been taken away, and there was nothing there, as Martin says in his account, but "the bare walls".

After four days in prison, Isaac was told that he was to go before the Inquisition at Granada. He begged to be allowed to see his family before he went, but this was forbidden. He was fettered and set on a mule, and thus he left Malaga while the people gathered about him calling out that as a Jew and an English heretic he deserved to be burned.

As Isaac was fettered and the mule on which he rode was loaded, riding was difficult; as the fetters hurt the mule's neck the animal took the first opportunity to throw its rider and Isaac was pitched upon a rock. His back was almost broken so that he had to be lifted back on to the mule, and thus very painfully journeyed to Velez-Malaga.

Here he had a stroke of good fortune, for an English merchant who knew him well saw his arrival and insisted that a doctor should dress his wounds. This was a great comfort to Isaac who was able to ask his friend to look after his family and, if he were murdered by the Inquisition, to see that they were able to get back to England. This the friend promised to do and it was suggested that coach or chaise be procured to take Isaac into Granada as he was in such pain; but his guard said that this was impossible as only a mule could be used on the rough roads. The friend provided mules and provisions and all the comforts he could think of, and Isaac and he took a sorrowful farewell for they were fully aware of the fate of those who fell into the hands of the Inquisition.

Isaac records that it took three days to travel the seventy-two miles from Malaga to Granada, and that his physical agony was only exceeded by his mental torture.

When they reached Granada he and his guard put up at an inn, for it was day-time and, writes Isaac, they put nobody in the prison of the Inquisition by daylight. He was allowed to write to his wife, but he says that his wife did not receive the letter, and the purpose in suggesting he should write it was doubtless that he would in some way incriminate himself.

As soon as night fell he was taken to prison and put in a dungeon. His jailer asked him what his religion was and, on Isaac's answering that he was a Protestant, he was told that he was then no Christian. He was warned that he must be very quiet in his cell and not speak, whistle or sing; and if he heard anyone cry out or make any noise he must remain silent. Any sound from him would be rewarded by two hundred lashes.

He was given some bread, a little wine and half a dozen walnuts and told to undress and go to bed. It was very cold in the cell, the floor being bricked and the walls two or three feet thick. In one of these walls was a hole a foot long and five inches broad, but owing to the thickness of the walls little light came in.

In the morning Isaac was told to dress and get his provisions. He was given half a pound of mutton, two pounds of bread, some kidney beans and some raisins, with a pint of wine and two pounds of charcoal.

In his cell he had an earthen stove, some earthen plates and a few pitchers; he had a wooden spoon but no knife, fork nor table. He also had a broom with which to sweep the floor.

He was told that the food was to last him three days and then he would be given more. A doctor was allowed to visit him, for the pain in his back was acute, and he was bled and given oil for his back and allowed to stay in his bed.

He was eventually taken to an audience and describes the room in which were two men, "one sitting between two crucifixes, the other on his left with pen, ink and paper". He was bidden to seat himself upon a stool provided for this purpose.

Asked if he could speak Spanish, he told them that he could, and was questioned concerning his religion. He was a Protestant, he said; and he was then questioned about his birth—in London— and his religion. He was then told that he had been brought up in the dark but that he might enlighten himself if he desired to do so.

When he was asked if he did not worship the Virgin Mary and the saints he replied that he believed the Virgin Mary was the mother of Jesus Christ carnally, and that the saints were happy, but he did not worship them. He worshipped God in three Persons and nothing else.

The Inquisitor then said that it was a pity England had left the true Faith and fallen into heresy. Once the country had produced great saints; now it produced nothing but schisms and heresies. When Isaac said that he believed England was producing men as good as it ever had he was promptly told to hold his tongue.

The audience over—it had lasted an hour—Isaac was told that his case was not hopeless and could be remedied; and a week later he was again taken before the Inquisitors, more questions were asked and when this audience was over he was returned to his dungeon; after that there were many other audiences.

The Inquisitors cajoled and threatened. Isaac quotes them as saying: "You have been brought up in heresy; it is a pity. You were all good people and good Christians in England till Henry VIII came; and that was your first loss. Then came Queen Elizabeth, and she was a very wicked woman; that everybody knows; and here of late you have had one that you call King William; he had no religion; what he aimed at was to get the Crown; and so you have been led away."

Again and again Isaac was taken back to his dungeon, and again and again he was brought before the Inquisitors. This was the well-known pattern of wearing down the victim; at the audiences he was questioned and cross-questioned, and reminded that there were means of saving the souls of heretics. These dark hints at torture filled Isaac with apprehension, for his state by this time was very weak, suffering as he had for so long the rigours of prison life and the continual anxiety as to the fate of his family.

During four months Isaac was subjected to fifteen audiences. He was then moved to another dungeon which pleased him at first because it was lighter than the one he had left and he was able to hear a cock crow in the morning and some dogs bark. It must have been wonderful to feel again this contact—small as it was—with the outside world. Moreover in the first dungeon he often heard other prisoners groaning in agony and he presumed that they had been suffering under the hands of the torturers. However the new dungeon, he tells us, was infested with bugs which made sleep impossible during the night.

Twenty-six weeks after he had come to the prison he was taken from the cell with some ceremony, having first been blindfolded. He was led to a chamber and there stripped of his clothes. All this time he was in mental agony, because he believed he was about to be tortured; but it turned out that all this meant was an examination to discover whether he had been circumcised. This was typical of Inquisitorial methods, for these men were well aware of the efficacy of mental torture.

As he had not been circumcised, Isaac hoped this would count in his favour; and so it seemed, for a month after this, one of his jailers came to him and told him he was to be released. He thought this was a further torment and begged the man not to make such jests, but he was assured it was no jest and that the barber was coming to make him presentable. Isaac was so overcome that he could only cry weakly.

When he was ready he was taken to an audience chamber where many people waited, all dressed in ceremonial robes; a rope was put about Isaac's neck and he was made to kneel. He was told: "Your case has been seen and examined; go along with these gentlemen. You shall soon be released."

He was taken to a church, in a procession of about forty people, and set on an altar facing the pulpit. A priest mounted the pulpit, carrying papers in his hand, and read out an account of Isaac's misdeeds. "The Holy Inquisition had done what she could in admonishing me to embrace the Holy Faith of the Church of Rome, without which no man could be saved," wrote Martin. "But I was such a pernicious heretic that I would not hearken to the salvation of my soul, and that the Holy Tribunal had found me a great enemy to the Holy Faith." The priest went on to say that for the crimes which Isaac had committed the Lords of the Holy Office had ordered him to be banished out of their Christian dominions upon pain of two hundred lashes and five years in the galleys if ever he returned to "these Christian parts"; and having made this pronouncement he gave the order that Isaac was to receive two hundred lashes, which should be applied in the streets of the city.

After this ceremony Isaac was taken back to his dungeon where he was told that if he changed his religion he would escape the lashes. His answer was that he had endured so much that he would suffer this little more.

Next day the executioner came with ropes and a whip, and Isaac was told to take off coat, waistcoat, wig and cravat. His body was put through a collar which was fixed about his waist, hands tied together, and a rope placed round his neck. He was then led into the streets where great crowds had assembled to see the punishment bestowed on an English heretic. The priest read his sentence, ending with the words: "And so let it be executed." He was put on an ass and led through the streets, the executioner whipping him with a scourge made of leather thongs as they went, while the people threw refuse at him, crying out that he was an English heretic and no Christian.

Isaac, who was no coward, spoke to the people asking them what country he was in, and when they said he was in a Christian country, he retorted that such conduct was surely not that of Christians, and that they behaved as did the people of Barbary. This sobered the people and made many of them so ashamed that the pelting was considerably diminished.

When the whipping was over, Isaac was taken back to his dungeon and there he asked for brandy with which to bathe his back. This was supplied by his not unkindly jailer; but he was in great pain for some time and unable to lie on his back; but this did not trouble him as much as his anxiety as to when he was to be allowed to leave.

After a fortnight he was told that he was to be taken to Malaga, there to await a heretic ship. He was once more warned that he was never to return to Spain; to which, naturally enough, he retorted that he had no wish ever again to set foot on Spanish soil.

He was told then that he must take an oath that he would keep secret what had happened to him, and not reveal anything of what he had seen or heard during his incarceration by the Holy Office. (An oath which Isaac felt justified in ignoring. Indeed he may well have felt it his duty to warn Englishmen of the calamities which could overtake the visitor to Spain.)

In Malaga he was fettered and put in the common jail. His wife came to see him, and he told her to make immediate arrangements to get him aboard a ship.

At last he was on an English ship, but a few hours after he went aboard, war was declared between England and Spain, and the ship was taken by the Spaniards and all in her put into prison.

Poor Isaac must have felt that he would never escape, but an official of the Inquisition came to him and told him that as they had ordered that he should not be allowed to stay in Spain, out of Spain he would go, for he was not fit to live in a Christian country. The prisoners were told that Isaac Martin was a dangerous man, being a heretic, and that none of them must have any communication whatsoever with him.

Isaac eventually went on board a vessel from Hamburg and waited for his wife who was trying to get back some of their possessions of which they had been robbed. But Isaac was told that they were very foolish to hope for this or to make any requests, for although Isaac and his family had suffered great hardship, when they considered the cases of others, they must realize that they had been very fortunate; Isaac, being such a stubborn Protestant, might so easily have been burned at the stake.

As the Inquisition had threatened to take one of his children to be brought up in the Catholic Faith (and Mrs. Martin had hurriedly had the child smuggled to England) Isaac made her hastily bring the rest aboard. Meanwhile, she was given a little of what had been stolen from her, although, says Isaac, "they gave out that they had returned us everything."

So Isaac Martin came home to England. He ends his narrative with the statement that several bishops and clergymen advised him to publish his narrative and that he is "following their advice".

Isaac's story makes pitiable reading but in view of what happened to so many at the hands of the Inquisition, there is no doubt that he escaped very lightly.

How fortunate he was that this happened in the early eighteenth century! Under Philip II Isaac would have suffered hideous torture and almost certainly have been burned at the stake. He would never have lived to tell the tale and give us such a comprehensive picture of the methods of the Inquisition.

* * *

In his account of his trial and sufferings Isaac Martin gives a description of the Inquisition of Granada, and as it is a particularly vivid one, I will give a brief paraphrase of it here.

The Inquisition, he says, is like a palace until you open the doors of the dungeons.

Built after the style of a convent it had galleries all round it, and the Inquisitors had their apartments in the building. The dungeons were on the ground floor and "up one pair of stairs and two pair of stairs". They were fifteen feet long and ten feet broad, and there were two doors to each dungeon; they numbered about a hundred and the prisoners did not share them. Twice a week the prisoners were let out to collect their allowance of food and "throw out their dirt". He gives an account of the provisions allowed him, and they seem at this time to have been fairly adequate. Isaac states that he grew very lean but remained in good health.

Prisoners were not allowed books, pen, ink or paper, and however long they were incarcerated were forbidden to receive letters from their families. They must not hear sermons or Mass, and if they prayed they must do so inaudibly; if they were heard they were chastised.

The chief of the prisons of the Inquisition was situated in Madrid; and this was the headquarters, for all prisons in other parts of the country must give an account of their affairs to that one in Madrid.

The Holy Tribunal of Granada was (continued Isaac Martin) almost as large as our upper House of Parliament, and in it hung some very fine pictures. There was also an altar and a throne of red velvet. The Inquisitors sat in decorative arm-chairs which were placed before a large gold-embroidered crucifix, on the right of which was the triple crown and beneath it the cross keys; on the left was a naked sword, and under it the King's arms.

The table was covered with red velvet, and on this table stood a gilded crucifix two feet in height. The secretary sat at the end of the table and the prisoner on a stool before the crucifixes. (From *A Review of the Bloody Tribunal; or the Horrid Cruelties of the Inquisition,* by John Marchant and others.)

As Isaac Martin was brought into this chamber some fifteen times, it would seem that his description is likely to be an accurate one.

*   *   *

From Limborch we hear of the fate of an English woman in Lisbon. She was Elizabeth Vasconellos who was born in Devonshire to the wife of a certain John Chester. When she was eleven years old her uncle, David Morgan, of Cork, who was a doctor, decided to settle in Jamaica. He arranged that he should take Elizabeth with him and treat her as his own daughter.

This was in the year 1685, and as their ship neared Jamaica it was attacked by two Turkish ships. There was a fight during which David Morgan was killed. The ship managed to elude the Turks and put into Madeira, but without her uncle the young girl did not know what to do, for she was penniless in a strange land; fortunately a merchant named Bedford, hearing of her plight, took her into his household as a servant, and here she remained for eleven years.

In 1696 she was married to Cordoza de Vasconellos who was a doctor living in the island.

For eight years she lived happily; then her husband had to leave her to visit Brazil, and while he was away she became very ill. She had always been a Protestant, but during her illness the sacrament had been given her, although she knew nothing about it; on her recovery she was told of this and assured that consequently she had changed her religion and must now acknowledge herself as a Catholic.

This she refused to do, whereupon she was made a prisoner and after nine months was sent to Lisbon to appear before the Inquisition.

Everything she possessed was taken from her and she was put into a cell about five feet square and there left for more than nine months.

During the first week or so she was given only bread and water and wet straw to lie on. When she was taken before the Inquisitors she declared that she had been brought up as a Protestant and that she would remain in that religion. They told her that she had accepted the Roman Faith, and if she denied it she would be sent to the stake.

She was then sent back to her cell, and a month later was again brought before the Inquisitors. Persisting that she was a Protestant she was stripped to the waist and whipped with knotted cords.

Fifteen days later she was once more taken before the Inquisitors. A crucifix was set up and she was commanded to go down on her knees and worship it, and when she refused to do this was told that she would be burned alive at the next *auto de fé*.

Again she was sent back to her cell, and a month later was brought up for re-examination. This time a more severe punishment was inflicted. Her breast was burned to the bone with a red-hot iron in three places. She was returned to her cell with no ointments or bandages to help ease the pain of her wounds.

When a month later she was brought before the Inquisitors who demanded that she accept the Catholic Faith or burn, she answered boldly that she was English and a Protestant and she doubted not that she would be protected if her condition was known to the English who lived in Lisbon. She was ready for the stake but not to renounce her religion.

She was told that any English heretics living in Lisbon would be damned, and since she seemed eager for the fire she should taste it before she was called upon to face the great ordeal.

She was put into a chair and her legs and arms were bound. A doctor was brought in that he might warn her tormentors how far they could go without killing her. Then her left foot was bared and an iron slipper, which had been made red hot, was brought in. Her foot was put into this and when the flesh had burned to the bone and she lay unconscious, the doctor ordered that the torture be stopped for her life was in danger. So she was taken back to her cell.

Later she was yet again brought before the Inquisitors and her back laid bare while she was savagely whipped. She was threatened with more terrible tortures than had yet been inflicted, and told that if she would sign a paper they would set before her she would be given her liberty.

Now in a state of mental daze produced by so much physical agony Elizabeth signed and gained her liberty. She was told that she would be wise to avoid English heretics; and all her goods which had been taken from her were kept by the Inquisition. She was then turned adrift "destitute of relief", goes on the account, "but what she received from the help and compassion of charitable Christians."

It is comforting to know that there were a few of these living in Lisbon at that time.

Elizabeth's deposition of what happened to her is witnessed by John Milner and Joseph Wilcocks, and is dated Lisbon, 8 January, 1707. (*History of the Inquisition*, Philip Limborch.)

* * *

In Mexico towards the end of the sixteenth century many English Protestants fell into Spanish hands and were tried by the Holy Office. Some met their deaths at the stake.

Philip II set up the Inquisition in Mexico (1569–70) because, he said, he wished to "free the land which had been made evil by Jews and heretics".

In 1568 one of Sir John Hawkins's ships, engaged in the slave traffic, was involved in a fight at San Juan de Ulloa, and a party of his men lost their ship and were forced to the land. They lived there in peace for three years, until the coming of the Inquisitors. Then the hunt began for the Englishmen, who were caught and brought before the tribunal. They were beaten through the streets to the applause of the spectators and many of them were sent to Seville that the Holy Office there might deal with them. Seven of them escaped, but the rest of the party who had broken jail were recaptured. Some were burned, others were sent to the galleys.

* * *

It was because Englishmen and women roaming the world were often brought before the Inquisition and subjected to torture and death that the Holy Office was known throughout England as the great enemy of Protestants. This was so, of course; but many people forgot the sufferings already endured by Jews and Moors, which were even greater than those inflicted on Protestants.

Through the years men and women from many countries were brought before the Spanish Inquisition, in spite of fierce protests from the nations involved.

Oliver Cromwell demanded liberty of conscience for Englishmen in Spain that they might worship God as they pleased in their private houses and that there should be freedom of trade with Spanish possessions. For these concessions he offered alliance with Spain against France. But his offer was declined, the Spanish Ambassador replying in amazement that Cromwell, in asking such concessions, asked for "his master's two eyes".

This state of affairs continued, much to the detriment of Spanish prosperity. Thus through the years accounts continued to reach England of the sufferings inflicted by the "Dogs of the Inquisition" on English Protestants.

3

POLITICAL USE OF THE INQUISITION BY PHILIP II. THE CASE OF PÉREZ

Philip II had made it clear that he did not intend to use the Inquisition as a political weapon; he was determined—as fiercely as his great-grandmother, Isabella the Catholic, had been—to maintain a Catholic Spain. It is difficult to sort out Philip's motives; he could deceive himself and tell himself that he was determined to save the souls of his subjects for God, when he was at heart concerned to keep them loyal to the crown.

Apologists for the Inquisition are delighted to tell us that it was a political instrument used by the State. Thus they exonerate the Church from association with this much hated institution; and it must be admitted that those in authority were ready enough to use the Inquisition in a political issue, if the opportunity arrived.

Continually in Spain the Inquisition threatened to become a weapon in the hands of the Sovereigns; it brought great financial gain to the exchequer. Philip received through the Inquisition all the galley slaves he needed to man his vessels because "condemned to the galleys" was one of the most frequent minor penalties.

In fairness to the *Spanish* Inquisition it must be said that it was not put to political service as frequently as the Inquisition in other countries had been. The case of the Templars springs to mind as one of the most flagrant examples of a monarch's using the Inquisition for political purposes. Philip of Spain could never be so blatantly dishonest as his namesake of France had been in the barbarous affair of the Templars.

In the case of Joan of Arc, whose death was of paramount importance to the English, it had been necessary to call in the aid of the Inquisition in order that she should be brought to the flames. Joan had been taken prisoner by the Bâtard de Vendôme, a follower of Jean de Luxembourg who was second-in-command to the Duke of Burgundy. Joan, as a valuable prisoner, would have been worth a very big ransom, for it was the custom for those who greatly desired a particular prisoner to offer a large sum to the captor; and as Joan was calculated to be worth more than five hundred fighting men, the ransom would have been very high indeed. But the English were in a state of near bankruptcy and of even greater fear that the French would provide the ransom money and take the prize. They were eager to have her condemned as a sorceress—for they believed she was one—and for this she could be judged by the Church. According to the law, sorcery was one of the crimes which came under the jurisdiction of the Inquisition; and shortly after her arrest Martin Billon who was Vicar of the Inquisitor of France demanded that she be surrendered to the tribunal.

This was France in the fifteenth century, and Philip the Fair had, more than a hundred years ago, clipped Inquisitorial power so that Jean de Luxembourg, who was very reluctant to hand over the prize, made no haste to do so.

It was then that Pierre Cauchon, Bishop of Beauvais, who, although French, supported the English, was told that since Joan had been captured in his diocese he must, in his episcopal role, demand that she be delivered to him for trial; and once again the surrender of Joan was demanded on a charge of idolatry, sorcery and other matters concerned with the faith. However a large sum had to be raised before Joan was handed over, and the Regent, Bedford, was obliged to impose a special tax in order to raise it.

Joan was forced to stand trial as a heretic and eventually was sent to the stake wearing a paper crown on which was written: Heretic, Relapsed, Apostate, Idolator.

The *Spanish* Inquisition was never so blatantly used for political ends. Archbishop Carranza aroused the enmity of his political enemies and thus suffered unjust imprisonment, but his case cannot be compared with those of Joan of Arc or the Templars, those victims of the medieval Inquisition.

*　　*　　*

There is, however, a notorious case in the records of the Spanish Inquisition in which it was used to bring a man to disaster, not because of his heresy but because of political scheming. I refer to that of Antonio Pérez.

Concerning this case there is a mystery which has never been satisfactorily cleared up; and as there is a possibility that it may have touched Philip, not only politically, but emotionally, it possesses a romantic appeal which no doubt accounts for its having become one of those cases which are resurrected from time to time by various writers who seek to provide the solution. There is, though, another reason why the case of Antonio Pérez is significant in the history of the Inquisition: this is because of the effect it produced in Aragon.

One theory is that Antonio Pérez was the illegitimate son of Gonzalo Pérez, a cleric, who was in the service of both the Emperor Charles and Philip. There is some disagreement about the date of Antonio's birth. Many writers give it as 1534, but Gregorio Marañón insists that it was 1540. The date has little significance, for whether Antonio was six years older or six years younger would have made no difference to his fate.

His mother was Doña Juana de Escobar, a young woman of Madrid. It was not certain whether she was a married woman— and that again is unimportant.

What was of the utmost importance was that Gonzalo, having been ordained, could not marry, and therefore a son provided a certain embarrassment. Antonio was sent to the country to be brought up, and Gonzalo, who visited him frequently, must have been very proud of him, because he was exceptionally handsome and intelligent. He was known as Gonzalo's nephew and was legitimatized by Emperor Charles in 1542, although this fact was kept secret for many years. That part of the country in which Antonio was brought up was Val de Concha in the district of Pastrana, and Pastrana was in the heart of the estate of Ruy Gómez de Silva, the Prince of Éboli, favourite of the King and one of the most important men in Spain; thus was Antonio brought to the notice of the Prince and Princess of Éboli.

Another theory is that Antonio was the son of Ruy Gómez. It was said, when Antonio was on trial, that he visited the household of Ruy Gómez with great frequency and in that house was treated as a member of the family. In appearance Antonio resembled Ruy Gómez more than Gonzalo Pérez, for Antonio was short of stature, very handsome, slender and lithe, and possessed of a great power to charm. All these qualities were possessed by Ruy Gómez, while Gonzalo Pérez was thickset and completely lacked that suave charm.

Moreover the great interest and favour shown by Ruy Gómez for the young man might indicate that he had a very special reason to seek his advancement.

But Antonio himself never made any reference to the possibility. He is quoted as saying, when Ruy died in 1573, that he felt his death deeply for Ruy Gómez was to him as a father. But surely a very common expression such as this could have naturally been said about one who had been such a good friend to him, as Ruy undoubtedly was. Moreover he referred to Gonzalo Pérez as "my father and master"; and all through his life he appears to have shown the utmost love and reverence for him.

So, the life of Antonio Pérez began in mystery.

Gonzalo Pérez—and perhaps Ruy Gómez—apparently determined that the young Antonio should be given the best possible education, and he was sent to universities in Spain, Flanders and Italy; in addition to this Gonzalo himself gave the boy tuition. He was clearly destined for a high place in state affairs.

When his education was complete, there were Gonzalo and Ruy Gómez ready to see him launched. Ruy Gómez no doubt saw in him a useful adherent to his own party which was in direct opposition to that of the Duke of Alva, for Gómez, suave, polished and humane, was the natural enemy of the bloodthirsty soldier and persuaded the King to a peaceful policy, whereas Alva fervently believed in fire and the sword.

Antonio, the protégé, was brought to the notice of Philip who was attracted by the young man, and when in 1566 Gonzalo died, it seemed natural that Antonio, who had now had a certain amount of experience under Gonzalo and Ruy Gómez, should take his father's position as one of the King's secretaries.

But meanwhile Antonio had been sowing a few wild oats; and Philip could be prim. There was a young girl at Court, Doña Juana de Coello; she was neither rich nor beautiful, but she became enamoured of the handsome Antonio who was at this time indulging rather freely in love affairs. Juana was no doubt one of many and when she became pregnant and marriage was desirable, Antonio drew back. If he was amorous, he was also ambitious, and there is no doubt that, as the protégé of a man of such power as Ruy Gómez, his prospects were so brilliant that a dazzling match was not an impossibility. He refused to marry Juana and the child was born.

Ruy Gómez disapproved of this callous behaviour; Philip did so even more strongly. Juana was a lady of the Court, and Philip abhorred scandal. So when the name of Pérez was laid before him as successor to his father, the King retorted that he expected those who shared his secrets to present a virtuous front to the world.

In view of such disapproval in high places Antonio consented to marry Juana who was to prove such a noble woman and such a devoted wife to him in his misfortunes.

Thus at twenty-eight Antonio took on the office of Secretary, and from the beginning he won the King's favour. Of all his secretaries Philip selected him for special favours. Moreover he worked very hard; he was determined to succeed, and very soon mastered state matters to a degree which was a continual delight to Philip. He had acquired the art of subtle flattery; he paid flowery compliments and made even the humblest with whom he came into contact feel that he was aware of them.

Antonio Pérez was possibly of Jewish extraction and there was in his nature a love of ostentation. He was highly intelligent, he had the King's favour, and on the death of Ruy Gómez he was on the way to becoming the most important minister in the kingdom; it is understandable perhaps that he should have wished to flaunt his wealth and power.

In the year 1575 he rented one of the most magnificent houses in Madrid in the Plaza del Cordón. He filled it with valuable pictures and exquisite furniture; his servants were dressed in rich materials and were taught to behave not as lackeys but as gentlemen, so that his guests were uncertain of their status. Even the horse he rode was perfumed.

But eventually he decided that the mansion in the Plaza del Cordón must be merely his office, and he built another just outside Madrid. In this new house the beds were of silver; and on his own bed he had silver angels fixed and the words "Antonio Pérez sleepeth: enter softly" inscribed there. It was said that he possessed the most magnificent house in the whole of Spain. Ostentatiously he named it La Casilla (the Cottage).

It was not possible for a man to reach such eminence, and to make such displays, without arousing the enmity of many. For all his suave charm, Antonio's enemies began to spring up all about him.

He needed a great deal of money to live in the style which was so dear to him. As Secretary of State his income was 200,000 maravedís a year and he received another 100,000 as Secretary of Castile besides a warrant for 150,000. This was wealth, but he needed even greater wealth and so he found other means of increasing his income. He was not the first to accept presents for the good he could bring to those who wished to make use of his influence; but it was sometimes necessary for him to pay others for services required.

He was a gambler; his debts were huge; but he continued to live like a Prince and in much more lavish style than that affected by the hermit-like King.

Antonio's position was dangerous; moreover he had come under the influence of his patron's widow, the Princess of Éboli.

*　　*　　*

Ana Mendoza y de la Cerda Princess of Éboli was a member of the famous Mendoza family, a great-granddaughter of Pedro González de Mendoza, Archbishop of Toledo, who in the reign of Ferdinand and Isabella had played a part in shaping Spain's destiny and had been known as "the Third King of Spain". The Archbishop's position in the Church had not prevented his having several children, and one of these was Diego who was born to a lady-in-waiting who came to Castile from Portugal with Juana, the wife of Henry IV. Eventually after a glorious military career Diego married Ana de la Cerda the granddaughter of the Duke of Medinaceli. The son of this marriage married Catalina de Silva, sister of the Count of Cifuentes, and their daughter was Ana who was to marry Ruy Gómez and become the Princess of Éboli.

In 1552 when Ana was twelve years old a marriage was arranged for her with the Portuguese Prince who was then thirty-six. The marriage was, however, not consummated until Ana was nineteen.

After they had lived together as husband and wife for fourteen years, during which Ana had borne Ruy six children (and had had four miscarriages) Ruy died. He was fifty-seven, Ana thirty-three, and she already had a reputation for immorality and lust for power. Ruy's gentle strength and excessive charm, it has been said, kept her subdued during his lifetime; but she is reputed to have shared in his councils and had a firm place in his political life. It was hardly likely that a woman such as Ana would be content to be relegated to obscurity on the death of her husband.

Ana is one of the most intriguing figures of the sixteenth century. As there had been an accident when she was quite a young girl during a fencing match with a page, and she was never seen in public without a silk shade over her right eye, it is extraordinary that she should have been considered such a beauty. Perhaps it was her personality, her charm and vivacity which were so attractive. Yet according to some accounts she was a very difficult woman, and Ruy had greater trouble keeping her in order than he did in managing the affairs of the country. The Count of Luna said that Éboli "covered up a thousand trespasses of that irate and terrible woman". And St. Teresa, who was entertained by the Ébolis at Pastrana, writes that Ana caused her a great deal of trouble which the mildness of the Prince put right.

But when the Prince died and Ana no longer felt his guiding hand, there was certain to be trouble at Pastrana. Ana, determined to call attention to herself, on the very day that he died made up her mind that she would enter a convent. Imperious as ever she did not wait to consider this move but left that very evening for the Monastery of Pastrana, wearing the habit of the Discalced Carmelites, riding through Pastrana in an open cart that the whole neighbourhood might be aware of what she was doing. The people stared in astonishment to see their Princess, usually so sumptuously clad, dressed in a nun's habit. That was what Ana wanted; her gestures appear to be dramatic in the extreme. But though it might have been interesting for the countryfolk to see their Princess thus, it was very disconcerting for the Prioress, Mother Santo Domingo, who, we are told, wrung her hands and cried out that there would be trouble in her house when the Princess entered it.

She was right. Ana had brought two servants with her and for a day or so she obeyed the rules, but then her imperious nature revolted. She refused to speak through the grille and wished to summon people to her cell when she wanted to speak to them; and eventually she retired to apartments at the bottom of the garden and had a door made to open on to the street, so that she could be in contact with the outside world.

St. Teresa was angry and threatened to remove the nuns from this convent; and eventually Philip ordered Ana to return to her family and estates for, he said: "She is more obliged to do that than be a nun."

Ana was certainly not going to live in seclusion at Pastrana. She looked for a new outlet for her tremendous vitality, and she found it in Antonio Pérez, who, on the death of Ruy Gómez, was perhaps the King's most favoured minister.

Popular legend has it that they became lovers; and this seems a reasonable supposition when the reputations of both these people are considered. Antonio was the hero of many amorous adventures; Ana has been accused of having many lovers. There was undoubtedly a partnership between these two; surely it was, besides a political one, a sexual one.

Consider the lusty Ana still young at the age of thirty-three. It is almost certain that she would have looked for a lover, and because she wished to use Antonio as a means of regaining the power which had been hers while Ruy lived, that did not mean that she would not take him as a lover. Ana was a woman of the world and, if she wished to lead Antonio by the nose, she would have been aware how much more easily she could do this if there were a sexual bond between them.

Gregorio Marañón, who prefers the theory that there was no love affair, says that the story of this intrigue has spread because "the public loves history to be as like a Vaudeville as possible", and that "when historians give themselves free reign, serial story writers are left absolutely nowhere!"

Yet when all the known facts are considered it seems that a sexual-political intrigue is far more likely to be correct than a merely political one; and that in this case the Vaudeville, and far more interesting, situation is the true one.

However, no one denies that an intimate relationship of some sort grew up between Antonio Pérez and the Princess of Éboli.

*   *   *

Meanwhile Don John of Austria had been sent to the Netherlands as Viceroy in an effort to placate that turbulent country which had suffered so much under the rule of Alva.

Don John was a wise choice. He resembled his father, the Emperor Charles, more than Philip did; he was fresh from the victory of Lepanto (1571) and was greatly admired throughout the world.

Don John had been born in Ratisbon in 1547, the result of a love affair between Emperor Charles and a beautiful Flemish girl. In his early years John had lived the life of a village boy, educated somewhat scrappily by the village priest. When he was seven years old he had been sent to the household of Luis Quixada, a steward of Charles's household. Charles did not forget him, and commanded Philip to look after his half-brother, which Philip, always a stickler for duty, tried hard to do.

There is a pretty story of their first meeting which had been arranged to take place in a wood. There for the first time Don John beheld the King, his half-brother. Philip is reputed to have taken John in his arms and told him that he was descended from a great man and that the Emperor Charles, "now in glory", was the father of them both. Philip decorated him with the insignia of the Golden Fleece, and buckled a sword to the boy's side, after conferring a knighthood upon him. The peasant had become a prince.

Don John lived up to his romantic beginnings. He grew to be handsome and charming. Tall and fair he was a great soldier, excelled at the jousts, and was attractive, kindly and beloved. He was, naturally, not without ambition.

Philip, by nature suspicious, must have been somewhat wary of a young man such as Don John. Prince Carlos, Philip's son and heir to the throne, had died in mysterious circumstances, and it was possible that Don John had his eye on the crown. Respected and loved, he would have been a welcome heir. He was regarded as a hero, for after Lepanto he had conquered Tunis. There was one thing he greatly desired and which Philip stubbornly refused to grant; Don John wished to be known as "Highness", which would have been tantamount to the cancellation of his illegitimacy.

When Don John had taken Tunis, Philip had ordered him to dismantle the bastion La Goleta and set up the son of Muley-Hacem as King. Don John, however, disobeyed the King's orders and instead left a garrison in the fortress, hoping, so it was believed, that one day he himself would be the ruler of Tunis.

When some months later La Goleta and Tunis were lost by Spain, Don John was blamed, and so for the first time in his young and successful life Don John had suffered defeat.

But when he went to Madrid Philip received him with kindness.

Perhaps Philip found it easier to be kind to the handsome young man who came less triumphantly than usual; and the next year, on the death of Luis de Requesens, he sent him as Governor to Flanders. Don John took with him as his secretary Juan de Escobedo, a man who, like Pérez, had been a protégé of the Prince of Éboli.

Don John did all in his power to win the Netherlands to his side by following a more gentle policy than his predecessors. William the Silent however had already determined to free his country of the "Spanish vermin", and there was war.

Don John laboured under great difficulties; he was surrounded by spies who, fully aware of the suspicion with which Philip regarded his half-brother, reported every thoughtless word of the young Prince. Don John began to realize that he had been given a hopeless task and that he, whose efforts had always been so glamorously successful, was now heading for failure. He longed to leave the Netherlands, and he wrote to Pérez suggesting that as the King did not enjoy the best of health and the heir to the throne was but a child, would it not be a good thing if he returned to Madrid and helped to shoulder the responsibilities of the crown.

This, to the suspicious eyes of Philip, seemed dangerous thinking; and Pérez did not hesitate to show Philip the confidential letters from Don John. Pérez was at this time eager to be friendly with John while he continually made Philip aware of his own loyalty. If by any chance John's dreams were realized Antonio Pérez wished to stand as high with him as he had with Philip.

Meanwhile John needed funds to continue in Flanders, and he dispatched Juan de Escobedo to Madrid to explain to the King his desperate need.

Pérez had warned the King that Escobedo's mission to raise money was a blind, and that he had actually come in order to stir up revolt in Castile in favour of Don John against Philip. Philip thereupon gave Pérez secret orders to have Escobedo put out of the way.

Pérez decided on poison, which would be simple as Escobedo was a frequent guest at his house. He thereupon called in the services of three of his servants: Diego Martinez, his steward, Pedro de la Exa, his astrologer, and Roderigo de Morgado, his squire. Another who was drawn into the conspiracy was Antonio Enriquez, a page of Pérez, who was to play the important part of mixing the poison into Escobedo's wine.

The poison was put into the wine as planned, but either it lacked the expected potency or Escobedo was able to throw off the effects, for the next day he was as well as he had ever been.

Again he was invited to dine, and again he was given the poison. This time he was very ill. An attempt to finish what had been begun was carried out by an accomplice in Escobedo's own kitchens, and more poison was put into the soup. Escobedo however took one sip and, tasting something strange, grew suspicious; he called one of his dogs to him, gave him the soup and shortly afterwards his fears were confirmed by the death of the dog. One of his slaves was hanged on suspicion.

Meanwhile, according to the most popular—and most likely—version of this story, Escobedo discovered the relationship between Pérez and the Princess of Éboli. He had been so devoted to Ruy Gómez that he was very shocked, and he threatened to tell the King of the intrigue between the pair.

There was a reason why the thought of Philip's hearing of the intrigue alarmed both the Princess and Antonio Pérez. The King had been a great friend of the Ébolis and many people believed that he was the lover of the Princess; some say that he aspired to make her his mistress and failed. Others state that Ruy Gómez had been a complaisant husband and had even arranged the love affair between the King and his wife in order to retain his influence at Court. It has even been said that the King confided in Antonio Pérez regarding his unrequited passion for the Princess at that time when Pérez was her successful lover.

Whichever version is true, there is no doubt that Philip had a great interest in the Princess and that, when Escobedo threatened to tell the King what he had discovered, she and Antonio Pérez decided that Escobedo must die without delay.

Poison was unreliable, so Pérez sent his page, Antonio Enriquez, to Catalonia for a special kind of dagger, and it was arranged that Escobedo should be waylaid in the streets of Madrid by a band of assassins when Miguel, brother of Antonio Enriquez, should strike the fatal blow. The steward, Diego Martinez, brought in two assassins from Aragon, and added to these was Gil de Mesa, a devotee of Pérez, and two others.

It is difficult to understand why it should have been necessary to call in so many to accomplish one murder; and it seems that in doing so, Pérez was being unnecessarily reckless. It may have been that having made more than one unsuccessful attempt he was going to be certain that should one man fail to strike the fatal blow, others would be on hand to do so. However, the fact remains that on 31st March, 1578, Escobedo was killed in a street of Madrid.

It was not long before there were rumours that Pérez had instigated the murder, and Mateo Vázquez, a fellow secretary of Pérez, who was jealous of the latter's influence with Philip and

Ferdinand Alvarez of Toledo, Duke of Alva.
Portrait by Dirck Barentys in the Rijksmuseum, Amsterdam

Arrest of Egmont and Hoorne by the Duke of Alva in Brussels on 10th September, 1567. An etching by the sixteenth-century engraver Franz von Hogenberg who was himself a Protestant and had to flee from the Spanish

determined to oust him from his favoured position, went to Philip and told him of these rumours.

The Princess, when she heard what Mateo Vázquez had done, could not restrain her fury, and she declared that the interfering secretary should share the fate of Escobedo. This did not help matters, and Philip, who preferred to work in the dark, was growing very uneasy.

He must tread warily, for it was on his orders that Pérez had arranged for Escobedo's murder; but if he had been deceived and Escobedo was removed, not because of his intrigues with Don John, but because he had threatened to carry to the King tales of the intrigue between Pérez and the Princess, this was a very different matter. Such deceit, such profligacy, roused Philip's cold and implacable anger.

At the end of the year Don John died suddenly in camp near Namur. He is said to have died of spotted fever, though many believed that a dose of poison had carried him off. He was very young; he had been full of vigour; it was true that disappointments in Flanders had depressed him; but was such depression enough to carry off a healthy young man? The general verdict is that he died of the fever, which would not be difficult to contract while in camp. But his death did follow suspiciously close on that of Escobedo, and with it were removed Philip's fears of one who might have become a rival.

Meanwhile Escobedo's wife implored the King to bring her husband's murderer to justice; and Philip, who after all had commanded that the murder should take place, falsely promised her that justice should be done.

The Princess of Éboli, now growing terrified of the rumours concerning herself and Pérez, which she knew must have reached the King, herself begged an audience of Philip. Philip's answer to her was characteristic of him; he assured the Princess, for whom he had once had such a great affection, that he would never forsake her (adding ominously) as long as she deserved his protection.

Philip had to act and there can be no doubt that after months of hesitancy he decided to sacrifice Pérez. First he had to replace him, and he recalled Cardinal Granvelle who was living in retirement in Rome. Granvelle reached the Escorial on 29th July, 1579, and as soon as Philip knew that the Cardinal was at hand, he ordered the arrest of Pérez and the Princess of Éboli.

The Princess was imprisoned for nearly two years, after which she was allowed to return to Pastrana; but she was not permitted to live in freedom and was again taken to a prison where she remained until she died in 1592—the punishment for having deceived and humiliated Philip II of Spain.

With Pérez under restraint it was important to Philip to retrieve those papers which would incriminate him in the murder of Escobedo and which he knew must be among the secretary's possessions. At this point Juana de Coello, wife of Pérez, began to show the stuff of which she was made. Realizing that, if she gave up the documents and they were destroyed, her husband could be convicted of murder for his own ends, she stubbornly refused to relinquish them, even when threatened with imprisonment and starvation. Pérez, however, hearing of her plight, wrote to her ordering her to deliver up the papers; he had, with accustomed astuteness, provided for this situation and had already extracted those documents which incriminated the King, and had deposited them in a secret place.

As in all such situations which arose in Spain, time seemed unimportant. The Princess and Pérez continued in prison while Philip was making up his mind how he should act. Ten years after the arrest the friends of Pérez raised twenty thousand ducats which the Escobedo family agreed to accept in return for calling off the case for the prosecution. But Philip did not easily forget and, while prepared to wait for many years, he was determined to have his revenge in the end.

In February 1590, Pérez was put on the rack and at the eighth turn of the *cordeles* he confessed that he had arranged the murder of Escobedo, but that he had done so at the order of the King.

After the torture Antonio Pérez was so ill that his wife was allowed to visit him. This courageous woman arranged an escape (knowing that by doing so she would place herself in the utmost jeopardy) and Pérez was enabled to reach Aragon. He had a special reason for this: he was Aragonese, and the old law of Aragon was that the Court of Justicia could protect its oppressed people against the King himself, if the need arose.

The time was propitious because Aragon was insisting that its Viceroy should be of Aragonese descent, and Philip was contesting this.

Philip, made furious by the escape of Pérez and the part his wife had played in it, ordered that Juana and her children be immediately arrested. This was done and they were sent to prison where they remained for nine years—until after the death of Philip. Nor was he going to allow Pérez to elude him. He gave orders that he should be brought back to Castile.

Taking no chances Pérez made with all speed to the Convent of St. Peter's at Calatayud where he placed himself in sanctuary. Pérez had been accompanied in his escape by Gil de Mesa, who was to prove a faithful friend to the end of his life. It was Gil de

Mesa who, in the disguise of a groom, had had horses waiting for him when he had escaped from his prison. Now realizing that Philip's men would have little respect for the sanctuary of the convent, Gil de Mesa went with all speed to Saragossa, where he claimed for Pérez, the *manifestacion* which would assure him of the protection of the Justicia of Aragon even though the King himself came against him.

Since the Aragonese were at this time determined to cling to their independence, Gil de Mesa was successful in his appeal, and many of the noblemen and officials arrived at the convent in order to escort Pérez to Saragossa, and lodge him in the prison there, the *cárcel de los manifestados*, for his own safety.

Prisoners who were taken there were not under the immediate authority of the King but were judged by the Chief Justice of Aragon. They could not be tortured or taken from the prison except after a fair trial in public court. This was one of their ancient privileges to which the Aragonese were determined to cling.

Philip, cautious as ever, now hesitated once more. He openly accused Pérez not only of the murder but of forging state documents and revealing state secrets. Pérez replied that he had documents in his possession which could prove that he had acted on orders from the King, and Philip temporarily abandoned the prosecution.

Philip could see that, owing to the cunning of Pérez and conditions in Aragon, if he were not careful the man would escape him, and it was at this juncture that the King, realizing that Pérez while at large could betray many secrets, decided to call in the Inquisition. Had he been accustomed to using the Inquisition for political means he would have called in this most powerful of all instruments much earlier in the case; but it can be clearly seen that it was only when he found it impossible to proceed with the case by any other means that he decided to make use of it.

It was now necessary to bring a charge of heresy against Pérez, which was not easy, for Pérez was by no means a religious man and therefore he had never acted in any way which could be called other than orthodox.

The Count of Almenara, who had been sent to Aragon by Philip to deal with the differences between the Justicia and the sovereign, was put in charge of the case and told to find the necessary evidence to bring Pérez to the notice of the Inquisition.

Almenara bribed Diego Bustamente, an old servant of Pérez, who then declared that he had heard his master blaspheme, for he had said that if God slept during his trial and did not perform a miracle in his favour he would lose his faith. He was reported as saying that if God the Father put any obstacle in his way he would cut off His nose.

These words were clearly spoken with the utmost lightness but the Inquisitors worked hard on them and the result was that they were declared blasphemous, scandalous and impious and, inasmuch as Pérez had declared his belief that God had a body, they were heretical.

The *alguazils* and all the dreaded officials of the Holy Office were sent to make the arrest; but the jailer refused to hand over his prisoner even to the Inquisition unless he had permission from the Justicia to do so. The officials of the Inquisition were forced to leave; they wrote to the jailer threatening him with excommunication and a fine of a thousand ducats for daring to obstruct the Inquisition. The jailer merely sent this communication to the Chief Justice, Juan de la Naza, who, seeing that the order came from the dreaded Holy Office, decided to take the safe course and obey. Pérez was then conducted to the prison of the Inquisition.

Pérez however, aware of what was happening, had already sent word to his friends in Aragon. The Inquisition was resented there and its high-handed action in taking a man from their prison could be construed as a deliberate slight and insult to an old custom. The friends of Pérez went into the streets, crying out that the liberty of Aragon was at stake; and men poured out of the houses and marched to Almenara's house, because they felt that he, who was in Aragon on the King's business, was at the root of this attempt to curtail their liberty.

Almenara was attacked and, although he was rescued from the mob, he died of his wounds two weeks after the incident.

While one section of the mob was attacking Almenara, another was marching to the Aljafería, the old Moorish castle, which was the headquarters of the Inquisition. They threatened to set fire to the place and would have done so if the Inquisitors, knowing themselves worsted, had not agreed to hand over Pérez. He was then taken in triumph back to his old quarters.

Pérez was too wise to feel complacent; he knew that the people of Aragon could not stand out against the forces of the King which would surely be sent to subdue them; he knew that if he remained in Spain the Inquisition would in time make him its prisoner.

He procured a file with which he worked on the bars of his window, and was ready for escape one dark night, but was betrayed by Juan de Besante whom he had believed he could trust. He was in despair, knowing full well what his fate would be at the hands of the Holy Office.

Arrangements were made to remove him, and the *alguazils*, with all the officials of the Inquisition who, determined not to be foiled again, brought with them a band of three thousand armed men, came to the prison to take him.

The carriage which was to take Pérez to the dungeons of the Aljafería was waiting and he was about to be fettered, when a crowd of rioters led by that most faithful of friends, Gil de Mesa, arrived and, shouting slogans about the liberty of Aragon, stormed into the prison, pushed aside the Inquisitors and set them running for their lives, while Pérez was seized and carried to a near-by house where horses were waiting. He made his way to Saragossa and there attempted to cross the frontier, but this was heavily guarded and he was forced to hide in the house of a friend until plans could be made for him to leave the country.

Philip meanwhile had dispatched an army under Alphonso de Vargas to punish the rebellious Aragonese. Philip, shrewd statesman that he was, recognized the opportunity this affair had given him of suppressing the old customs of Aragon which limited the sovereign's power. He was also determined to impress on these people that it was a grave offence to show opposition to the Holy Office.

Pérez seems to have had a charmed life, for he was given refuge in Navarre by Catherine, Princess of Béarn, sister of the King of France, Henri IV. When Philip's men arrived in Béarn and asked that the prisoner should be handed to them, Catherine refused to relinquish him, and, since Philip had no wish for trouble with Navarre, he was not inclined to resort to force.

During his stay in Béarn, Pérez published two accounts of his own life which further angered the King; and many attempts were made to lure him back to Spain. But Pérez was fully aware of what his fate would be if he were such a fool as to return; and from Béarn he went to England where he was made much of by Philip's greatest enemy, Elizabeth I of England. After England he visited Paris and although attempts were made on his life he continued to survive. Philip died before he did, and although he knew that Philip's son, Philip III, would have allowed him to return to his native land in peace, Pérez believed that the Spanish Inquisition would never forget or forgive one who had flouted it.

Nevertheless in 1611 he was persuaded by the Bishop of the Canaries, who was General of the Franciscans, that if he were to return to Spain and offer himself to the Inquisition, after a mock trial he would be given his liberty. Pérez, tired of the wandering life, nostalgic and longing now to see his children and the wife who had done so much for him, wrote to the Bishop and told him that as soon as his safe-conduct arrived he would leave for Spain.

He sent to his wife a petition, in which he described his sufferings, and asked her to pass it to the Supreme Council. This she did; but perhaps because the Inquisition moved ponderously as it ever did, Pérez died before the safe-conduct was given him.

He had spent twenty years banished from his country.

His case is notable not because it resembles a romantic adventure story but because of its effect on the history of Aragon.

The Justicia, who had been in office only three months and who was but twenty-seven years old, was publicly beheaded as a result of the rising, and at an *auto de fé* on 29th April, 1592, many of those who had taken leading parts in the disturbances appeared. Six of these people were relaxed and the rest sentenced either to exile from Aragon or to the galleys.

Philip had taken an oath that the constitution of Aragon should be respected, and he dared not openly break his word; but the Aragonese had seen Philip's soldiers in their towns, they had seen the power of the Inquisition extended, and they knew that they would be most unwise to show opposition to the will of the King.

*   *   *

Another occasion when Philip used the Inquisition for political ends was in the case of Jeanne of Navarre. He commanded that the Inquisition should prepare a case against her—no difficult matter since Jeanne was an ardent Huguenot—and that she should be captured and brought before the tribunal of Saragossa. Had this been effected, Jeanne would undoubtedly have been burned at the stake as a heretic; which would have been very advantageous to Philip's designs on Navarre.

The account of Philip's invoking the Inquisition in the case of his son, Don Carlos, is not so reliable; and the death of the young Prince is wrapped in mystery.

If he were murdered by his father, it is very possible that Philip did instruct Inquisitor-General Espinosa to prepare a case against him. It would be in keeping with Philip's character to find an adequate excuse for the removal of a son whose existence was becoming intolerable to him, and who, in the opinion of Catholic Spain, deserved death more than a heretic.

Wild, stormy Carlos had been a source of trouble not only to his father but to all those about him for many years. Philip, sternly devoted to duty, must have suffered great anxieties when he thought of his crown's passing to such a man. Carlos had already attacked Cardinal Espinosa (the Inquisitor-General) because he had banished from Madrid an actor whom Carlos favoured. The attacks of Carlos were always violent, and he had drawn his sword and would have killed Espinosa had he not been prevented in time. "A little priest to dare oppose me!" he is reputed to have said. If Philip did call in Espinosa to prepare a case of heresy against his son, there can be little doubt that the Cardinal would have gone to work with a will.

Carlos had greatly desired to go to the Netherlands as Governor, and had openly shown his sympathy with the Flemings. He put forward schemes for pacifying these people which may have shown the Inquisition that if ever he came to the throne there would be stormy times ahead. When he heard that Alva was to be sent he tried to stab him.

Carlos was obviously tottering on the edge of madness. His hatred for his father grew to such an extent that he made no effort to hide it. The fact that Philip had married Elisabeth of France, the daughter of Henri Deux and Catherine de'Medici, inflamed that hatred, for Elisabeth had at one time been promised to Carlos. When the beautiful young Princess arrived in Spain, Carlos is said to have fallen in love with her; and naturally many scandalous stories were circulated about them.

But it was when the foolish young man planned to murder his father, and confessed to his prior what he was about to do, that the climax was reached.

How could Philip allow this madman to reach the throne? Carlos was arrested and kept a prisoner, and Philip is reputed to have said that the reason for his imprisonment was not his misconduct or lack of respect towards his father, but that the measure rested upon another foundation and must be adopted in order that Philip might satisfy his obligations to God and the people. This would seem as though the theory that Carlos was arrested on account of his heresy might be true.

Also Pius V, after reading a letter from Philip concerning the arrest of Carlos, is said to have remarked to the Spanish Ambassador that the preservation of Christian Spain was dependent upon Philip's living for many years and having a successor who would tread in his footsteps. Philip's words to Carlos de Seso at the Valladolid *auto de fé* will be remembered. When de Seso asked him how he could endure to see his subjects so persecuted, he answered that he would carry the faggots for his own son if he were a heretic.

Those who support this theory say that that trial would naturally have been conducted in secrecy and the Prince could have been condemned to death. It is understandable that the heir to the throne could not take part in an *auto de fé*; therefore it was decided to poison him.

He died at the age of twenty-three and, although it was given out that quartan fever was the cause of death, most contemporary writers attributed it to poison.

De Thou states that Carlos was condemned by the Inquisitors

and that subsequently poison was put into his broth. Others also assert that he was condemned by the Inquisition and poisoned.

We cannot be sure but, if the Inquisition did try Carlos and condemn him, this would be a case of the Inquisition's being used for political purposes, for there was no doubt that it was politically important to keep Carlos from inheriting the throne.

4

THE MOORISH TRAGEDY

PHILIP DIED in September 1598 after a long and painful illness, and was succeeded by his son, Philip III. Although the power of the great Spanish Empire was beginning to crack, Philip II had succeeded in making Spain even more uniformly Catholic than it had been during the reign of his father.

Philip III was lazy and good tempered, the kind of king who was almost certain to be easily swayed by his favourites; and it was during his reign that there took place that event which was to prove so calamitous to the prosperity of Spain: the expulsion of the Moors.

When Philip III inherited the crown the exchequer was in a sadly depleted condition. Trade had been adversely affected by the *alcabala*, that tax which was levied on sales and purchases; and it was realized that the people could not be made to pay what they did not possess.

The third Philip was not a prudent man as his father had been; Philip II had lived like a hermit, had dressed in sombre fashion and had eschewed ostentation of any sort; not so his son. Philip III loved magnificence and when he travelled through the country-side to meet his bride, in spite of the country's poverty, the splendour of his equipage was compared with the brilliant displays which had been seen in the days of the Emperor.

The bride was Margaret of Austria, and before his death Philip II had also arranged a marriage between his daughter Isabella and the Archduke Albert. Margaret and Albert had travelled through Italy with the utmost magnificence, and the marriages had been celebrated by proxy at Ferrara by Clement VIII.

After his marriage Philip and Margaret travelled to Aragon where he, in his easy-going way, granted amnesty to those prisoners who had been arrested during the recent risings in Aragon. The people of Aragon, who had been so crushed and had seen the soldiers in their towns and the Inquisition more powerful than ever, were enthusiastic in their welcome of the new king. They ventured to ask Philip to abolish the Inquisition, but even Philip realized that he could not go as far as that, and his answer to that request was very evasive.

The position of the Moriscos was becoming more and more precarious. It had been decreed that however slight the suspicion of heresy they incurred, it should be treated as vehement and even if there was but a single witness against them, they must be sent to the galleys for three years or more, whereas in the case of victims who were not Moriscos, if the evidence against them was given by a single witness, they had a slight chance of acquittal and a very good one of having the examination suspended.

Moriscos who did not confess under torture and could not therefore be condemned to the stake were nevertheless punished with whippings and fines.

In the year 1594, of ninety-six Moriscos who underwent torture, fifty-three came through without confessing. This was a great number and might imply that the Moriscos were capable of suffering in silence; but there are suggestions that some torturers would, providing the bribe offered was large enough, modify the torment. In 1604 a torturer was brought to trial for accepting bribes from Moriscos. This may have had something to do with the ability of many Moriscos to endure the torture.

The Archbishop of Ribera was eager that the Moriscos should be expelled from Spain, as it was impossible to kill them all. They were becoming the most persecuted sect in Spain and, according to a Toledo record from 1575 to 1610, while there were one hundred and seventy-four Marranos and forty-seven Protestants among the victims of the Inquisition, there were one hundred and ninety Moriscos.

In 1563 Guerrero, Archbishop of Granada, had visited Pius IV whom he told that his flock in Granada called themselves Christians but were such in name only; and later, on returning to Spain, he begged Philip to rid Spain of Moriscos. Philip sent Guerrero's complaint to a special council of the Inquisition, and it was decided that the Moors must be forced to be Christians in fact. The old edict of 1526 was revived. The people were forbidden to speak or write Arabic; the doors of the houses were to be kept open during feast-days and marriages, as well as on Fridays; the use of henna was forbidden; baths, public and private, were to be destroyed, and so on.

These rules were accepted with a very bad grace by the Moors; and when it was learned that children between the ages of three and fifteen were to be taken from their parents to be brought up in the Christian Faith and to speak Castilian, the anxiety among the Moorish population grew fast; for although the Moors looked on with apprehension while their precious baths were destroyed they were more than angry at the prospect of losing their children.

In spite of the fact that they would be pitting their small strength against the might of Spain, the Moors prepared to fight for their freedom. They believed they could raise a hundred thousand men and that they would be supported by their kinsmen of Africa.

A rising was planned for Holy Thursday, 18th April, 1568, but their intention was betrayed so that it was necessary to postpone the date; and it was not until 23rd December that it took place.

Captain-General Mondéjar, a grandson of Count Tendilla, who had been put in charge of Granada by Isabella and Ferdinand at the time of the Re-conquest, had constantly warned Philip and the Inquisitor-General Espinosa that the revolt planned by the Moriscos would be on a large scale, and he had asked for reinforcements. Espinosa refused to recognize his need and thus, when the revolt came, Mondéjar was not very well prepared to combat it.

Yet he dealt vigorously with the insurgents and by February he had crushed the revolt; but those who were clamouring for the extinction of the Moors saw here a chance to accomplish this. Granada was not easily subdued, and the Moors, no doubt feeling their position to be desperate indeed, set up their standard in the mountains of the Alpujarras and in a short time the entire kingdom of Granada was ready for war.

Philip appointed his bastard half-brother Don John to command the army. Don John was then little more than a boy and his experience was not great.

This war was carried on with the utmost cruelty. Men were massacred by the thousand, and the women and children captured that they might be sold as slaves. It is said that the soldiers set out on their expeditions, not to fight a battle, but to hunt for slaves. These soldiers, not content with wreaking their inhumanity upon the Moors, even attacked the villages through which they passed, robbing and murdering as they went.

After the battle of Galera two thousand Moors were discovered, huddled together in a square; they cried out for mercy as Don John's men approached, but these Christian warriors knew no mercy. The Moors were shot in spite of their entreaties; and four hundred women and children who were discovered in the town were treated in the same way. Don John had ordered that not a living soul in Galera should be spared, because the Spaniards had suffered more loss than he had anticipated in the town's capture.

For this gallant exploit the Pope hailed Don John as the Champion of Christendom. Philip was pleased and gave thanks to Our Lady of Guadaloupe for the glorious victory.

Pedro de Deza, who was a member of the Suprema and had been appointed president of the Chancellory of Granada, now desired to move the population of Granada to the mountains in the north of Spain.

This plan was to be put into practice in 1569. The men were divided into groups, their hands tied with ropes, and marched off under guard. The women were allowed to remain for a while that they might first sell what they could of their household goods. On the road to the north many died of starvation; many were killed by robbers; and others were taken to be sold as slaves.

This method was applied to town after town as they fell into the hands of the Spaniards.

The suffering of the Moors was so great that it wrung pity from Don John who wrote to Ruy Gómez that many Moorish families who had been deported from the district of Guadix had met on the road such a blizzard that members of families had lost each other; and that it was difficult to imagine anything more to be pitied than the depopulation of a kingdom.

Strangely even the Moors, like the Jews, as soon as they were allowed to settle in any place began to prosper. Whereas the Jews had possessed a financial wizardry, the Moors by their energetic labour, in particular on the land, began to cast off their poverty. Again as with the Jews it may have been that the hatred of the people towards the race was based more on envy of their prosperity than on the differences in their religions.

It was feared that within a few years these people who had been robbed of their privileges and allowed, as a great concession, to settle in certain districts, would soon by their industry make themselves masters of the land and employ those very natives who had graciously consented to receive them as an inferior people. Complaints were put forward that they never went to war, that they did not enter the church but were devoted solely to their work; and, because they were prepared to work harder for less wages than the Spaniards, employers of labour preferred them to the latter.

The character of the Moors can be assessed when it is considered that they were able to grow to prosperity in spite of the rigorous laws against them: they were to be flogged if they left the districts to which they had been sent, and not only flogged but sent for a term to the galleys; they were forbidden to observe their Moorish customs and there were harsh penalties for possessing Arabic books; yet this industrious people, in spite of these restrictions, began to rise to prosperity.

It is inconceivable that the laws imposed upon them should always have been obeyed; and there must have been a smouldering resentment against the people who had treated them so badly. Certain Moriscos became bandits; others, who had become rich, offered Philip a bribe of thirty thousand ducats if he would allow them to carry arms. Philip, considering the state of the treasury, was unable to resist this offer and, in a certain district the Moors soon began to live much as they pleased, and if any of their number were caught and brought for trial, there were irresistible bribes waiting for their accusers.

*   *   *

In 1608 the Moriscos of Valencia were in touch with Muley Cidan, who was a pretender to the throne of Morocco. They promised him two hundred thousand men if he would bring twenty thousand to Spain and join with them against the Spaniards.

When this plot was discovered it filled the King, Philip III, and his Court with alarm and schemes were put forward for ridding Spain of the troublesome Moors.

The fact that Muley Cidan did not wish to be embroiled in the troubles of the Moors in Spain did not prevent the King and his counsellors from continuing to think of ridding the country of the Moors. They had become a menace. They plotted with the corsairs of Barbary and when Henri Quatre was planning an attack on Spain he believed with reason that he could rely on the help of the Moors.

In 1609 it was decided to banish all Moors from Spain beginning with the troublesome district of Valencia, and in August of that year Don Agustin de Mexia was sent to Valencia to carry out the expulsion. Ribera, who had been one of the chief agitators for the expulsion, had realized what disaster would be wrought in the districts of Aragon and Valencia if the Moors were driven out; he had at last understood that where the Moors were allowed to continue with their industrious lives there was prosperity, and although he wished to expel them from other parts of Spain he desired to keep them in his own districts of Valencia and Aragon where, he maintained, they could be controlled. Therefore when Agustin de Mexia arrived in Valencia, Ribera suggested that he should join with him and put it to the King that Valencia and Aragon be left in peace and the expulsion begin in Andalusia.

This appeal was ignored and by September sixty-two galleys and fourteen galleons brought some eight thousand troops to the area.

The order was given that the Moors were to confine themselves to their houses for three days to await instructions; anyone failing to do so would suffer death. They were then ordered to leave at once for the port to which they were directed. They were allowed to take with them as much as they could carry and their destination was Barbary.

The Spanish inhabitants of the area made immediate protest, for how, they demanded, were the sugar and rice crops to be saved if all the workers were deported. Who was going to irrigate the canals, a task which the Moors had always so expertly handled? It was necessary even for the most fanatical to consider this problem, and eventually it was decided that six per cent of the Moriscos should be allowed to remain.

Those to stay were selected in this way: Those who for two years had observed no Moorish customs; all children of under four, and children under six whose fathers were Old Christians, might stay with their father, and if the mother was a Morisco she might stay also; but if the father was a Morisco he must go, and if the mother was an Old Christian she was to stay and keep the children with her.

This splitting of families produced great anguish, and it was immediately necessary to bring in a stern penalty for giving shelter to those who had been ordered to go: six years in the galleys.

The Moors, who had at first been resentful and ready to do battle, suddenly seemed to understand that there was no hope in resisting. They decided that they would all go—even the selected six per cent who, although they had been offering bribes to be allowed to stay, were soon being offered bribes by the other side to stay.

The only bribe they would accept was freedom to follow their own religion. So desperate was one owner of a sugar plantation— the Duke of Gandía—that he went so far as to ask if this concession could be granted. The answer was that even the King had no power to allow such a concession; so the Duke, in desperation, was forced to contemplate the ruin of his sugar crop. There were many others in the district who were in a similar position.

This was a case of history's repeating itself; in this instance the Moors were playing the tragic role which more than a hundred years before had been taken by the Jews. They were selling their rich possessions and getting scarcely anything for them, just as years before the Jews had bartered a vineyard for a piece of cloth.

When the first shock was over some of the Moors did not seem heart-broken at the prospect of leaving Spain. No doubt they thought of the Inquisition which had continually threatened their lives, and dreamed of following their own religion openly; moreover they were an industrious people and they knew that wherever they were able to settle they would soon begin to prosper.

But there were some who resisted. Between fifteen and twenty-five thousand of them could not bear to leave the land where their ancestors had lived for so many centuries, and they sought refuge in the mountains. They were not allowed to remain in their sanctuary, but were rounded up and thousands of them massacred; the remnant, suffering from starvation, offered themselves up to the authorities for transportation to Africa. Few of them reached the ports, for the barbarous soldiers robbed and murdered most of the men and took the women and children to sell as slaves.

While the Moors of Valencia were being expelled, preparations for exodus were taking place in other districts. Aragon, Catalonia, Murcia and Val de Ricote followed, until in 1615 the plan for deportation had been completely carried out.

It is impossible to say how many people were driven from their homes in this great exodus. Records vary from 300,000 to 3,000,000. Llorente suggests 1,000,000, but many statisticians have declared this to be exaggerated. The fact remains that many thousands suffered; and for the purpose of creating an all-Catholic Spain, that country, determined to destroy its prosperity, drove from its borders a very valuable section of its population. The rich agricultural country became as a desert; the system of irrigation was neglected so that where there had been prosperous farms there were ruined farmhouses and infertile land.

The Inquisition had however lost one rich source of victims, although naturally Moriscos appeared now and then in the *autos de fé*. Many people had retained their Moorish slaves of whom, owing to the custom of selling captured people into slavery, there were many.

As late as May 1728 forty-five Moors appeared in an *auto*; and in October of that year there were another twenty-eight. In 1769 the Inquisition discovered that a mosque had been set up by Moors who secretly worshipped there. But from 1780 to 1820 there is no case of a Morisco's being brought before the tribunal of the Holy Office. (Lea, from the *Archives of Valencia*.)

Thus the Inquisition was triumphant. It had rid the country of a race which, having been forced to baptism, was likely to lapse into heresy. Bigotry was once more served at the expense of reason.

5

THE INQUISITION IN MEXICO

WHEN ISABELLA had financed voyages of discovery she had proclaimed—and believed this to be so—that her motive in doing so was to spread the Catholic Faith all over the world; and there can be no doubt that Philip II shared his great-grandmother's sentiments in this respect, although many of the adventurers who set out on these voyages appeared to be more interested in the richness of the booty to be won than in the saving of souls.

As was to be expected, among those who set out from Spain to populate the new world were many Jews who, despairing of ever being able to live in peace in Spain, sought refuge elsewhere. There was an effort to prevent Jews from sharing in these ventures, but Ferdinand was always open to bribes, and a law was made that for a price—twenty thousand ducats—any merchant could go to the colonies and trade there for two years. Emperor Charles repealed the law, but after some negotiations it was revived—and the price was raised to eighty thousand ducats.

Before the Inquisition was set up in the Spanish possessions a very costly method of bringing heretics to trial was practised. The case of Pedro de Leon, which occurred in 1515, gives a good illustration of this. Pedro with his family had gone to Hispañola where they hoped to live in peace beyond the shadow of the Holy Office. They were mistaken, for the Inquisitor-General of Seville sent one of his officials to bring them back to Spain. Orders were given that a ship was to be provided for this purpose, and any other escaping heretics were to be returned at the same time. How much less costly and how much simpler it would be to have the Inquisitors on the spot!

The Emperor Charles was very much aware of this, and in 1519 Cardinal Adrian was appointed Inquisitor-General of the Indies with the Bishop of Puerto Rico, Alfonso Manso, and Pedro de Cordova, a Dominican monk, as Inquisitors.

These were followed by Martin de Valencia who went to Mexico with a dozen men of the Franciscan Order to which he belonged.

Cruelties of the Spaniards in Haarlem, 13th July, 1573.
From the etching by Franz von Hogenberg

PAR ANT. V. LEEST A. MAIN. DOR.

D. IOAN. AB AVSTRIA:
FR. PHILIPPI REGIS HISP. CATHOLICI.

Don John of Austria. Engraving by Anthony van Leest

Others followed, but little is known of their activities until the century had grown old, and then we hear of Lutherans being burned and suffering lighter penances, and a woman's being reconciled to the Church after having made a pact with the Devil.

There is an account (Lea, *Inquisition in the Spanish Dependencies*) of a Flemish painter, Simon Pereyns, who, in conversation with a fellow artist, happened to state that fornication was not a sin; his friend argued with him about this but Pereyns persisted in defending his assertion.

But later, on sober consideration, he considered it prudent to present himself to the tribunal and confess what he had said, for he believed that by reporting himself he would attract less suspicion than if someone denounced him. Moreover it was frequently said that sexual intercourse between the unmarried was no sin, and in Spain at this time the Inquisition was attempting to correct this popular belief. In 1559 at an *auto de fé* in Seville there were twelve cases of people who had made this same statement; some suffered whippings and others were sentenced to parade in the *vergüenza* (public whipping through the streets, stripped to the waist).

Later, in 1562, there were twenty-five such cases, all forced to appear at the *auto* wearing nothing but shirts, and carrying candles; some were beaten, others heavily fined; and most of them were gagged, presumably to remind them that they should have kept their mouths shut.

Even as late as 1818 there is an account of one lieutenant accusing another before the Valencia tribunal of saying there was no sin in fornication.

Simon Pereyns no doubt thought that he would escape with a light reprimand, but he was mistaken. He was put into prison and, when the artist to whom he had stated his views was questioned, he remembered that Pereyns had said that he found the painting of portraits more interesting as well as more profitable than painting holy images. This was considered as a remark tinged with heresy, and Pereyns was tortured. He was put on the rack and given three turns of the *cordeles*, and in addition was made to suffer the water torture to the extent of three jars.

He endured all this without confessing to heresy, but he was not given his freedom. Instead he was called upon to pay the cost of his trial and to paint an altar piece for the church, which should be a picture of Our Lady of Merced.

Those who stood in judgment in Mexico at that time were not officials of the Holy Office but merely ecclesiastical courts which must submit any extraordinary evidence to Spain to be considered by the Holy Office there.

It was in January of 1569 that it was arranged to set up the

Inquisition proper in the Spanish Dependencies, and as this matter proceeded in the usual dilitary way it was not until a year later, 3rd January, 1570, that Doctor Moya de Contreras was informed by Espinosa that he had been selected as Inquisitor-General for Mexico.

To be banished from Spain on such a mission might not seem very agreeable, and Moya de Contreras (who at first declined to accept the post) was told that it was to be only of short duration and that for his services he would be awarded the Archbishopric of Mexico. He was more or less forced to accept, and it became the custom, when appointing his successors, to indicate that some great honour would be given after a few years' service in Mexico —a necessary inducement.

Contreras did not reach Mexico City until September 1571; and when he did so ceremonies and spectacles were arranged that the population might realize the importance of what was happening.

Contreras was conducted to the church with great pomp and, after the sermon, letters from Philip II were read aloud to the crowds assembled, explaining the dangers of heresy and that the Inquisitors had come to Mexico in order to prevent the spread of this evil, and how all who were discovered to be concerned in its growth would be brought before the Inquisition to answer for their sins.

An Edict of Faith was then read, accompanied by the usual threats and promises, and all present were commanded to raise their right hands and swear to accept and obey the Inquisition. The Edict of Faith soon began to have the desired effect, and the prisons were filled with those suspected of heresy. Contreras appointed an *alguazil*-mayor of the city, a receiver of confiscations, an *alcaide* of the secret prison and other officials.

The first Mexican *auto de fé* was held on 28th February, 1574, and was performed with as much solemnity as though it were taking place in one of the large Spanish towns. Two weeks before the fixed date, drummers and trumpeters paraded the city and the announcements were made. People crowded into the city from the outlying neighbourhood and we are told that there were some seventy or eighty victims—thirty-six of whom were Lutherans, mostly English sailors.

Contreras retired from his position in 1573, for the promise to make him Archbishop of Mexico was kept; and he was followed by Bonilla who in turn became Archbishop of Mexico on Contreras's return to Spain, and Bonilla was followed by Alonso Granero de Avalos.

An incident concerning Granero gives a clear illustration of his character and indicates the fear which must have haunted all who came into contact with the Inquisitors.

Granero was in the habit of selecting people at random and fining them in order to pay his expenses; and when a notary, Rodrigo de Evora, wrote some verses, stressing the habits of the Inquisitor-General, which fell into his possession, the unlucky man was arrested on Granero's orders and put into prison.

His feet and hands were chained and he was afterwards put on the rack where he was so severely treated that his joints were dislocated. He was then condemned to appear at an *auto de fé* where his punishment was proclaimed to be three hundred lashes and six years in the galleys. His property was confiscated by Granero who kept it for himself.

This was one of the men who were charged with the spiritual guidance of Mexico.

One of the most cruel of the Inquisitors was Alonso de Peralta who took office in 1594; no sooner had he arrived in Mexico than the activity of the Inquisition increased; *autos de fé* took place more frequently, and more people were condemned to be burned. One victim, Luis de Carvajal, said that he hoped he would not have to look on Peralta's face, for the mere sight of him "made his flesh creep". (Lea's *The Inquisition in the Spanish Dependencies* from Adler.)

This Luis de Carvajal was a man of some position and his crime was that he had not denounced his sisters who had been found guilty of heresy. For this he was robbed of his offices and later tortured and burned in the *auto* of 1596.

* * *

The best way to understand how the Inquisition worked in Mexico is to look at some of the recorded cases, and one of the most interesting is that of an Irishman, William Lamport or Guillen Lombardo de Guzman. He aroused the interest of the Inquisition when he made a startling claim. At the time Philip IV was on the throne, and Lamport said that although his mother was an Irish woman he was an illegitimate son of Philip III and therefore half-brother to the reigning king.

It was said of him that he planned a rising in Mexico in order that it might break away from Spain, and that in such an event Mexico's ruler should be the illegitimate son of Philip III.

The Inquisition had not arrested him on this charge however, but had not found it difficult to bring him to trial on one which was within its jurisdiction. In order to assure the success of his treasonable schemes, it was said, he had consulted sorcerers and astrologers; which was, of course, a crime against the Church.

Whether or not Lamport was the son of Philip III is not known, but the account he gave of his life appeared to have verisimilitude. He said that he had been born in England where he lived for twelve years; young as he was he had written a pamphlet directed at the King, and for this reason had been forced to leave the country. He had adventures in various parts of the world and, so he said, had been received by Philip himself, who had given him the title of Marquis and instructions to take over the viceroyalty from the present Viceroy. The papers he showed, purporting to come from Philip, were discovered to be forged, but at the same time Lamport was very knowledgeable concerning the Court and, although he was put in prison—where he remained for seventeen years—orders came from the Suprema in Spain that he was to be treated with consideration and, if he wished it, to be given a companion to share his cell.

He was provided with one, and very soon he had induced the man to share in a very elaborate plan for escape. Like all Lamport's plans it was worked out in detail, and in theory seemed flawless. This plan might have worked, but it seems that during his long confinement Lamport's mind had become unbalanced and on the night fixed for the escape, instead of making off to some safe place, he lingered in the town posting his writings in prominent places and trying to persuade a man to take a letter to the viceroy in which he demanded the arrest of the Inquisitors.

Eventually, after hours had been wasted, he hid himself, for as it was now daylight he had little hope of getting far away; and he was very soon recaptured.

When he was put into a well-guarded cell and fettered, he asked for pen and paper and, in view of the orders that he should receive special treatment, these were given to him. He then wrote a vitriolic attack on the Inquisition, after which he was not allowed to have paper, so he wrote on the sheets of his bed.

As time passed he became more and more unbalanced in his mind, and in 1659 he was condemned to the flames for sorcery, heresy and plotting rebellion.

Because he had written against the Inquisition a special punishment was ordained for him, and he was conducted to the *auto de fé* with the painful gag in his mouth and, while his sentence was read, he was hung up by his right arm and thus hanging had to listen to his sentence.

He was to have been burned alive but, as the flames were lighted, he threw himself against the iron ring about his throat with such repeated violence that he killed himself.

When the Suprema heard what had happened to him, and that the Mexican Inquisition had acted without orders from Spain, they were very angry. Why the Suprema should have been so concerned for the life of Lamport has never been discovered; but it makes one wonder whether there might have been a grain of truth in the story of his royal birth. (Lea, *The Inquisition in the Spanish Dependencies*.)

* * *

Among others who suffered at the same time as Lamport was an old man named Sebastian Alvárez who had declared he was Christ. For this he was condemned to be burned alive; when he reached the *quemadero* however he "confessed" and was given the mercy of strangulation as the fires were lighted.

Francisco López de Aponte was, in the same *auto*, accused of sorcery as well as heresy. He was pronounced to be sane and therefore fit for punishment, and when he was cruelly tortured he bore his suffering with such fortitude that it appeared he was insensible to pain. It semed certain, to his tormentors, that he was in league with the Devil who had given him this special power. Every part of his body was then shaved and a careful search made for the mark which would proclaim him a witch. He was again tortured and once more bore all that was inflicted with great calm; he was condemned to be burned alive. In his cell on the last night of his life he is reputed to have told the priest, who was urging him to become reconciled and so escape the hideous death by burning, that there was no God, no Heaven and no hell; there was only birth and death. He attended the *auto* in the same impassive state in which he had endured the torture, and without a groan stood still while the flames consumed his body.

Pedro García de Arias was a pedlar who had written three books, uneducated though he was, which were said to contain heresy. García had been whipped through the streets and was condemned to be burned at the stake. He declared that he had been misjudged but would not ask for mercy. But he changed his mind at the end when he saw the faggots about to be lighted. He was strangled before his body was burned; and the books which he had written were tied about his neck so that they might burn with his body. (Lea.)

* * *

Louis Ramé was a Frenchman who suffered at the hands of the Inquisition; and the Rev. J. Baker, M.A., in his collection of writings under the title of *The History of the Inquisition as it subsists in the Kingdoms of Spain etc. to this Day* gives what is purported to be Ramé's own account.

He was a sailor and had had a very adventurous life even before he fell into the hands of the Inquisition. He became captain of a cargo ship which carried wine and brandy from Rochelle to Nantes and pilchards from Port Louis to Barcelona.

When war broke out between France and Holland he served for a while in the navy, and later, at Rochelle, married a widow with four children.

He could not spend his life at Rochelle however, and after three months he sailed for Fagal, Cayenne, and Martinico. Whilst on this voyage he was captured by a privateer who took his ship and set him ashore. He found a ship to carry him home, but this ship met disaster, sprung a leak and sank. Ramé and some others managed to scramble into a boat and drifted for five days, during which time they were without food or drink. They landed at Puerto Rico and after having feasted on oranges and water went in search of provisions for the boat. They found these, but the man who supplied them thought it necessary to warn the Governor of their presence and they were put under guard. They remained prisoners of the Governor for sixteen months.

Into the harbour came the Spanish ship S. Lawrence, and Ramé was taken aboard and carried to Vera Cruz. He was given a little money from the "Charity Box which the King of Spain allows for poor Prisoners" and was told that he might go ashore and find work. He did this and became journeyman to a baker.

He did this work for some months, and then one night a Dutchman who lived in the baker's house became very ill, and a priest who visited him tried, while he was in a weak state, to make a Catholic of him. All the Dutchman could reply to the priest's earnest admonition to change his faith was that he did not understand.

The priest then remembered that there was a much-travelled Frenchman in the house who could probably speak the Dutchman's language; and Ramé was sent for and told to act as interpreter. This Ramé refused to do for, he said, he was himself a Protestant and would not allow the dying man, who was only half conscious of what was happening, to be perverted from his religion.

He was then told that *his* religion had been composed by "ill persons and for to please libertines" and that the Pope was the Vicar of Jesus Christ.

"To which I answered [writes Ramé] that I had never heard our ministers preach anything else but the gospel, with strict orders to follow what our Saviour had commanded us, and that as to the Pope, I acknowledge him not as Vicar of Jesus Christ."

This was courting danger, but on the 17th of December, 1678,

Ramé committed an even more reckless action. He met the Holy Sacrament being carried through the streets, and refused to kneel to it.

He was arrested, taken as a prisoner to the house of a certain Don Pedro Estrada, and kept there on very small rations for two weeks with his feet fixed in stocks.

He was then put in irons and taken to the prison of the Inquisition and brought before the Inquisitors. Asked why he had not knelt to the Holy Sacrament, he said that he had read in the Holy Scriptures that idolatry was forbidden. He was then asked to abjure the Protestant Faith and on refusing was threatened with burning at the stake.

He was taken back to his cell and there he saw no one but his jailer, who said to him each morning and evening when he entered the cell: "Praised be the Holy Sacrament of the Altar." To this Ramé was obliged to answer or be accused of insolence, so he retaliated with: "Praised be our Lord Jesus Christ," or "Praised be God." The Fiscal, who Ramé tells us was "a sort of Judge" visited him every Saturday for five months and tried to convert him to Catholicism.

Suddenly the food which was given him began to have a strange effect upon him. He was very ill and his mind wandered. After three months of this he was again brought before the tribunal, when he was accused of not paying the respect to the Sacrament which was due to it, and denying that the Pope was the Vicar of Jesus Christ; and when he was asked why he did not pray to the saints, he replied that Jesus had said: "Come unto me all ye that are heavy laden and I shall give you rest."

The Inquisitor, furious, cried out that he should be given the torture, ordinary and extraordinary, to which Ramé boldly answered that the torture they had already inflicted ought to satisfy them.

Back to his cell he was taken, to be visited every Saturday for three months by the Fiscal, who urged him to give up his religion. The drugged food was again administered and Ramé reduced to such a state of depression that he contemplated suicide. He was a strong-minded man and realized the state into which he was falling; so, as a desperate antidote, he made a harp by taking some of the boards from his bed and unpicking a pair of silk stockings. He unravelled more stockings and made a cap; and he found a way of making needles out of the boards of his bed.

After two years he was taken before the Tribunal again, and this time he found waiting for him, instead of the Inquisitor and Fiscal, a "great many Ecclesiastics and lawyers".

A Jesuit then told him before them all that God had chosen

this opportunity to open his eyes, and had brought him to the Inquisition in order that his soul might be saved; he quoted the Parable of the Vineyard and how God had sent to seek for labourers in the morning, noon, and evening.

Ramé answered that he had read that Jesus Christ called the people to his preaching and never made use of secret prisons and fetters.

The ecclesiastics began to talk disparagingly of the Protestant religion and how it had been invented by Calvin who was a very "ill man", to which Ramé retorted that he knew nothing of the religion of Calvin, for his own religion was that of Christ.

He was told that he was blind and rebellious to the will of God and was asked to choose, out of four men who were presented to him, an advocate who would defend him in his trial. He asked them how one of their men could defend him when he acted against their will and pleasure, and said that he would rely on his Saviour, Jesus Christ.

He was, however, forced to accept one, who immediately began to urge him to become a Catholic!

He was then returned to his cell. Each Saturday he was visited by an Inquisitor, Don Juan de Miel, and, he writes, when he was asked how he did, he generally answered that he did as well as any man could in such a place. And when the Inquisitor asked if he wanted anything, he replied: "I want the patience of Job, the virtue of Joseph, the wisdom of Solomon, the resolution of Tobit, the repentance of David, justice from your tribunal and a quick expedition."

He was kept in prison for another two years and was again made ill by the food which was given him, before he was taken before the Tribunal and sentenced to banishment from the kingdom of New-Spain; consequently he was put into the royal prison.

This royal prison was the old palace of Montezuma who had been Emperor of Mexico, and here Ramé's sentence was read to him, and he was asked to swear to tell nothing of what had happened to him at the hands of the Inquisition, and warned that if he did so he would be awarded two hundred lashes.

Ramé tells us that his reply was that, while he would undertake to say nothing whilst he was in the dominions of the King of Spain, when he returned to France it would be necessary to explain what had been happening to him. This they appeared to accept.

He was taken to another prison where he was fed well for a week, so that his health recovered and he regained his sight which he had almost lost; after that he was returned to the royal prison and, when he had been there a short while, he was sent to a village a few miles from Mexico City; and in this village he was set to work manufacturing cloth with criminals.

Among the workers was a man named Thomas. Ramé forgot his surname, but he knew that he came from Plymouth, so presumably he was a sailor who had fallen into the hands of the Inquisition. To save himself Thomas had become a Catholic, and as a penance was sent to work at the cloth factory. Thomas, having been taken into the Catholic Church, was sent' to the Tribunal to give an account of the ceremony, and Ramé wrote a letter to the Tribunal which he persuaded Thomas to deliver. In it he reminded them that they had said he should be deported.

He had a reply that he must present a petition to the President of Criminal Affairs; this he did, and as a result he was taken back to prison and fettered; thus he remained for six more months.

He was then taken from prison and put on a mule which was to carry him to Vera Cruz. The animal was vicious and heavily loaded, and Ramé believed that the authorities intended that he should have a serious accident.

Arriving at Vera Cruz he was put into prison, but he met with a little good fortune there, for a man, for whom he had once worked in Vera Cruz, had heard of his sufferings and sent him food, gave him money to buy what he needed, and visited him twice a week.

Eventually he was taken to the quay and put aboard a ship for Havana which, after a stormy passage, he reached.

Here he was again put in prison, where he remained for another six months, being fed very badly, all the time being pestered to change his religion. When a captured Dutch ship, which had been renamed the *St. Joseph* by the Spaniards, came into the harbour, he was put aboard, but as the ship could not sail immediately owing to the wind, Ramé was put into the stocks until she did.

After two months at sea they reached Cadiz, but Ramé was not allowed to go ashore and was still kept a close prisoner. He was later taken to Seville where he was once more imprisoned, and for six weeks he had scarcely anything to eat; only the English prisoners fared well for there were English merchants in the city who sent food for them.

When at length Ramé was sentenced to serve the King of Spain in Cadiz at whatever work the Governor of the city should find for him, he protested and demanded that his case should be set before the Tribunal of Madrid.

By this time many might have despaired of ever escaping but Ramé did not give up; he sent petitions to Madrid and managed to get a letter to his wife, and a French friend in Seville worked hard for him but without result. But eventually with the help of ambassadors and other Frenchmen in Spain, Ramé was released, turned out of prison without money and ordered to leave the country, but was given no means of doing so.

Fortunately for him, his French friends came to his aid, money was provided, and a ship was found, *The Loyalty of London,* which took him to England.

He arrived in England on 18th August, 1685.

He ends his account with the poignant words: "God be praised; I was thought dead, but I am living."

*   *   *

In his account Louis Ramé provides some interesting sidelights on incidents which he saw during his imprisonment. He tells of how in Holy Week people went to church in masks and whipped their own naked backs as they passed through the streets. These whippings were often so severe that the whipped backs were covered with blood. In procession they carried an image which represented Christ and another which represented the Virgin Mary. Masked men dressed in brilliant colours with tails affixed to their backs made gestures before the images. These men represented Jews who the people believed were born with tails because they had descended from those Jews who had crucified Christ.

He tells too that when he was in the prison of Vera Cruz, one hundred and eight buccaneers were captured, among whom were fourteen officers who were brought to the prison in which Ramé was kept. They were Protestants and therefore condemned to the stake.

When they were taken to the *quemadero* five of them suffered the fire, but the remaining nine declared their desire to become Catholics. They were brought back to the prison, allowed to wash, and all given clean shirts, feasted and told to choose god-fathers. They were given plenty to drink, and were very merry because they believed they had come near to death and had saved their lives. Ramé tells us that he was invited to this dinner, and that his beard amused the newly-shaven men who called him "Papas", a name, says Ramé, given to "grave old learned men". Ramé was allowed to shave his beard and everybody was very merry.

But, as soon as the feast was over, the new Catholics were hurried out to a place of execution where they were to be strangled.

Eight of the nine died, but the ninth, named John Morgan, was very fortunate. The rope about his neck broke, and when a new one was tried that broke also. There was a third attempt, which ended in failure; then were the executioners overcome with dread. John Morgan was pardoned, for all believed that he was a true convert and that it was the will of the Virgin Mary that he should not die.

Ramé also writes that on his journey from Vera Cruz to Mexico he saw near Mexico City a hot spring which flowed from the mountains. The legend was that the Virgin Mary appeared at this spot to an Indian who went to the Archbishop to explain that he had seen the Virgin and that she had told him of the spring; but the Archbishop did not believe his talk of visions.

Once again the Virgin Mary appeared to the Indian and insisted that he go to the Archbishop and tell him of the existence of the spring; the Indian replied that the Archbishop would not listen to him, whereupon the Virgin gathered some roses from where before that moment there had been no roses and put them inside the Indian's blanket which he wore as a cloak.

The Archbishop changed his mind when he saw the flowers, and a chapel was built on the spot where the encounter was supposed to have taken place.

Below the mountain was built a magnificent church in which were gold and silver lamps and pearls and emeralds which Ramé estimated must have been worth something in the region of a million pieces of eight. The name of the church was Our Lady of Guadalupa, and those who did not go there every Saturday were not considered to be good Christians and were in danger of being regarded with suspicion. Crutches lay about the entrance to the church. They had belonged, Ramé tells us, to people who were said to have come as cripples and had been cured by the Virgin.

* * *

There are three Inquisitors of the Mexican Tribunal who are remembered for their special cruelty. It is known that they even went so far as to request the Supreme Council in Spain for permission to relax ten prisoners who had asked for reconciliation to the Church.

There was a prisoner, Doña Catalina de Campos, who became very ill in prison and begged these Inquisitors to give her some comfort; she declared that she had always been a good Catholic and would continue so to be; the cell in which she was lodged was particularly noisome, being overrun with vermin.

The answer of the Inquisitors to this request was to send the woman back to her cell. A few days later she was found dead, her body gnawed by rats.

The names of these three were Juan Saenz de Mañozca,

Francisco de Estrada y Esvobedo and Bernabé de la Higuera y Amarilla. (Lea, *The Inquisition in the Spanish Dependencies.*)

Another very sad case is that of Gabriel de Granada, a boy, thirteen years old, whose trial (or process—the Inquisitorial description) took place from 1642 to 1645.

This boy was arrested on suspicion of being an "Observer of the Law of Moses" and when he was prevailed upon to testify against over a hundred people, including all the members of his family, he told the Inquisitors how his mother had initiated him into the Law of Moses and had told him that it was the true religion. His mother eventually starved herself to death in her cell, presumably in order to avoid a more frightful death; other members of the family and their friends also suffered.

As for Gabriel himself, he was told that he would be pardoned for his crimes because he had shown contrition and repentance and had begged forgiveness from God. This he had done, of course, by betraying to indescribable misery those who had been good to him—but that was what was required of a "good" Catholic by the Inquisition.

God, he was told, did not desire the death of the sinner but that he should be converted and live, and therefore was to be admitted to reconciliation.

He was to go forth to the *auto* with other penitents "without waist-band and bonnet and with a penitential habit of yellow cloth with two red bars in the form of St. Andrew's Cross, and carrying a green wax candle in his hands, where this our sentence shall be read to him, and publicly abjure his said errors which before us he hath confessed and all species whatsoever of heresy and apostasy".

Gabriel was condemned to wear over his clothes the *sanbenito* for a year while he was kept a prisoner, and every Sunday and feast day he was to go to hear high Mass, and on Saturdays he was to go in pilgrimage to the church where he was to recite the paternoster five times and the Ave Maria, Creed and *Salve Regina*. He was to confess and receive the Sacrament at Christmas, Epiphany and Easter every year of his life and was to be banished from the West Indies and from Seville, Madrid and the King's Court.

He was to leave Vera Cruz as soon as possible and present himself at the Tribunal of the Holy Office in Seville, where he would be told where to go to work out the rest of his sentence. He was never to hold any public or honourable office either ecclesiastical or secular; he was to wear neither gold, silver, pearls, nor precious stones, nor silk camelot nor fine cloth; nor was he to travel on horseback nor carry arms.

This was the sentence on the boy who had betrayed his family and friends. (*Trial of Gabriel de Granada*. Translated from the original by David Fergusson in the Publications of the American Jewish Historical Society.)

*   *   *

Sebastian Domingo was a negro slave and sixty years of age when he fell into the hands of the Inquisition. His wife had been sold separately and his owner, fearing that he might attempt to escape in order to join his wife, insisted on his marrying another woman.

The Inquisition stepped in and he was arrested for bigamy and incarcerated in the Inquisition of La Puebla de los Angeles.

So many people had been taken into this prison that, no doubt because Sebastian's offence was not one of heresy and probably because he was the sort of man who would make a good servant, he was put to work in the prison.

All servants of the Inquisition were sworn to secrecy and not allowed to have communication with the prisoners. It might have been that Sebastian was an ignorant man and did not understand these rules; however he spoke to a male prisoner through his grating and agreed to take a note to this man's wife. When the wife received the letter she was so delighted and grateful to Sebastian that she rather naturally offered him some money—which he accepted.

There were of course spies everywhere in the prison and the prisoner's wife was herself soon a prisoner—her offence being that she had received a letter from her husband. As for Sebastian, he was accused of two crimes: first taking a letter from a prisoner to his wife, and then receiving a reward for doing so.

Poor Sebastian was sentenced to two hundred lashes and six years in the galleys in Spain, but if he could not go to Spain (and the Inquisitors knew some reason why he could not) he was to be sold for a hundred dollars, which should go into the exchequer of the Holy Office.

The sale must, of course, be only for a certain time, for Sebastian belonged to the master whom he had been serving at the time of his arrest. The Inquisition decided they would sell him for ten years and in case he should die under the lashes, and thus the money be lost to the Inquisition, he was to be forgiven the lashes.

This was done, for the Inquisitors did not consider that by selling a slave who belonged to someone else they were committing a fraud. But no doubt they assured themselves that as it was done in the name of the Inquisition, that exonerated them from blame.

*   *   *

It is very interesting to compare these harsh punishments with those inflicted on priests.

The prevailing sin among priests was that of solicitation, and the punishment for this naturally fell within the scope of the Inquisition.

This seduction of women who came to confess their sins was known as *solicitatio ad turpia* and had given great trouble to the Church ever since there had been confession. Many priests—condemned to celibacy—found temptation irresistible when they had young women kneeling at their feet, confessing their sins, real or concocted. In the middle of the sixteenth century the box with the grille was invented, but there were many cases of solicitation after that.

In 1558 Archbishop Guerrero of Granada called the Pope's attention to this recurring sin and asked that measures be taken to suppress it. Solicitation came under the jurisdiction of the Inquisition when it was agreed that anyone who committed this sin could not be perfect in his faith.

Priests were usually treated with great leniency by their fellow priests, and in 1626 Urban VIII was asking all Archbishops to warn priests of their responsibilities. Little attention was paid to his words, and when these philandering confessors were discovered they were given the lightest possible sentences.

It was suggested that there should be two witnesses against a priest before he could be accused, and as the offence would by its very nature be rarely committed in the presence of a third party this was making denial easy for the priest. But even this was considered harsh, and it was suggested that a priest should be found guilty of four offences before he was sentenced.

Paul IV instructed the Inquisition in the Spanish Dominions to deal with priests who were accused of solicitation; but even when a priest was found guilty he did not appear in the public *autos de fé*, unless of course he was to lose his orders. He was conducted to a room and there, behind closed doors and in the presence of a few priests, his sentence was declared to him.

There was, as can well be imagined, less restraint among the priests in such lands as Mexico than among those in Spain. It was generally believed by numbers of the settlers that while there might be some sin in seducing a Spanish girl this was not the case with the Indians. (The natives of Mexico did not come under the jurisdiction of the Inquisition, for the settlers believed that they were not intelligent enough to understand religion, and so were left to the care of the Bishops who were almost certain to be more gentle than the Holy Office.)

Consider the case of Fray Juan de Saldaña which was brought

to light in 1583. Saldaña had attempted to seduce an Indian girl, and when she refused him he had had her arrested and flogged, threatening to repeat the floggings until she accepted his attentions. The girl finally agreed.

Saldaña held a high position in his Franciscan Order and, although only thirty-three years of age, was guardian of the Convent of Suchipila. The convent soon became a happy hunting-ground for this amorous Franciscan, and during confession he seduced three sisters in turn.

He made no secret of his behaviour—rather did he boast of his prowess. He said that he had not only seduced Spanish girls but Indians, and not only in the convent but wherever he heard confessions.

His friends thought it advisable to warn him, and reminded him that such conduct could bring him before the Tribunal of the Inquisition. He merely laughed at the warnings, and retorted that the only punishment which would be meted out for such offences as he had committed would be a dozen strokes of the discipline and a year's suspension from his guardianship of the convent—which of course was a small price to pay for the fun he was having.

The Inquisition could not remain blind to the vices of such a blatant sinner, and he was eventually brought before the Tribunal. Blithely he confessed his sins, and it almost seems that he was as ready to boast of his exploits to the Inquisitors as he had to others. Yes, he had seduced several Spanish women during confession, as well as seven Indians. He admitted that previously he had been prevented from confessing Spanish women because of similar offences but, as guardian of the convent, he had naturally been the confessor.

His sentence was that he should be whipped "during the space of a *miserere*", deprived of the opportunity of hearing confessions, suspended from his order for six years, retired to a convent for two and then banished from Guadalajara for six years. (David Fergusson.)

Presumably when that time had elapsed he might continue with his activities. It is astonishing to recall that hideous tortures and burning alive were inflicted on people for not eating pork, for staining their nails with henna, or for praying to Christ instead of the Virgin Mary.

*　　*　　*

The case of Fray Juan de Saldaña is by no means an isolated one. There were numerous cases of solicitation, and not only in Mexico but in other dependencies and Spain itself. And in all such the penalties were astonishingly light when compared with those inflicted for other crimes.

In 1619 the Mexican Inquisitors stated in a letter to the Supreme Council that solicitation occurred very frequently in their part of the world and that it was regarded by many as trivial.

Lea suggested that the punishment for solicitation became less severe as time passed, and cites the case of Fray Francisco Diego de Zarate as an instance of this.

Fray Francisco was a Franciscan and President of the Mission of Santa Maria de los Angeles of Rio Blanca, and therefore a man of some standing.

He was brought before the Tribunal on charges of solicitation in the year 1721, when a hundred and twenty-six cases of solicitation were proved against him in respect of fifty-six women. It was said that he never failed to attempt the seduction of any woman who came to him to confess.

He might have gone on indefinitely, but he eventually tried to seduce a woman who was determined to resist him. He was equally determined not to be resisted. He declared that if she did not become his mistress he would have her and her family banished from Rio Blanca.

The woman went away and told all her friends what the priest had tried and failed to do and how he proposed to punish her and her family because she had resisted him. There was such a scandal that it was impossible for the Inquisition to ignore, and thus Fray Francisco was arrested and brought before the Tribunal of the Holy Office.

He was then accused of seducing numerous women. He appears to have been a little hurt because according to his reckoning he had seduced far more than appeared on the Inquisitors' list. He therefore corrected this, having been in a better position to keep the score.

The sentence was that he should receive a circular discipline, that he should never hear confession again, and should be deprived of his high office in his Order. He was to refrain from celebrating Mass for six months and spend two years in seclusion in a convent; and the first year he was to spend in a cell, living on bread and water (only on Fridays and Saturdays though) and he should have the last place in the choir and at the refectory.

It may be that even these sentences were not carried out, for in 1666 a letter was written to the Supreme Council in which it was stated that certain sentences on frailes had been rescinded.

*   *   *

William Harris Rule, in his *History of the Inquisition, Volume II*, states that information he has acquired makes it possible for him to remind us of another punishment which was used by the Inquisition in Mexico. This is known as "Walling up" and consists of building four walls about a living person, giving that person just enough room to stand or sit, and leaving them thus to die.

He tells us that when the Inquisition came to an end, part of an old palace, which had been the headquarters, fell into the hands of the Rev. Dr. William Butler, a Missionary of the Methodist Episcopal Church. Realizing that he was in possession of part of what had once housed the Inquisitor-General of Mexico, Dr. Butler was very eager to examine his property in the hope of discovering relics of the Inquisition.

In the basement was a long gallery and, when he had the paving stones removed, he found about two hundred skeletons. They lay side by side, "shoulder to foot and foot to shoulder alternately".

The bones were removed and the stones relaid. There is no suggestion from the Rev. Dr. Butler nor from William Harris Rule, D.D., that these were not the skeletons of people who had died natural deaths, but it does seem strange that they should have been buried in this manner.

Another discovery was made.

The inside of the main wall was for a large part unbroken by any windows or doors, and on examination it was seen that in places the bricks had been broken away and small spaces were revealed—chambers (or cupboards) in which a person of average size could barely stand upright. Dr. Butler, intrigued by this discovery, had the rest of the wall tapped, and in four places it was found to be hollow. The bricks were removed and the skeletons of four bodies were discovered—three men and a woman. The woman was lying down, and at her feet was that which was presumed to have been a child.

These remains were taken to the museum in the city of Mexico, "where," said William Harris Rule, writing in 1874, "they may still now be seen."

He goes on to say that these niches must have been left in the wall when it was built—for the purpose of walling up. None of the four walls about these small closets let in light or air, and there was naturally no possibility of passing food to those incarcerated therein.

The four bodies which were found were dressed alike, and it is to be presumed that this was the regulation dress for those who were to die this way. It may have been, suggests Rule, that the treatment of men and women was slightly different and that the longer and lower cavities were provided for women, who were allowed the privilege of dying in a recumbent position.

The heads of all four had been shaved, the arms bent at the elbows and bound; and there were fetters about the ankles.

One of the bodies was seated on a stone in his niche. This may have been due to the fact that he had been so violently tortured that it was impossible for him to stand.

When these bodies were discovered, the flesh was not entirely decayed, and this leads Rule to the conjecture that they had been walled up only a few years before the discovery. He submits that this ghastly form of death-dealing may have been adopted because the power of the Inquisition was fast waning in the nineteenth century and the people, becoming more enlightened and consequently more humane, would no longer tolerate the sight of human beings burning at the stake. Therefore this horrible method of murder was conceived and used by the men of the Holy Office because it could be carried out secretly within the precincts of the Holy House itself.

It must be said however that it is not absolutely certain that these walled-up people were the victims of the Inquisition. Yet they were discovered in the old palace which was the headquarters of the Inquisition, and the fact that they must have been put there in that century is very strong circumstantial evidence in favour of the belief that this hideous form of murder was used by the Inquisition in Mexico.

6

PERU

THE INQUISITION was established in Peru in 1570, when Servan de Cerezuela came to Lima to set up the tribunal. Before this date the power to judge heresy was in the hands of the Bishops and, as had been the case in other countries since the earliest days, there was antagonism between the Bishops and officials of the Inquisition; and in 1584 the Inquisitor of Peru, Ulloa, complained bitterly to the Supreme Council in Spain of the secret action of the Bishops in writing disparagingly of him to the King. The Bishops had every good reason to do this; but even if they had not, it seems certain that the antagonism towards the Inquisition was natural, for with its coming it usurped much of their power.

Ulloa was preceded by Servan de Cerezuela, who was selected by Inquisitor-General Espinosa in 1569 to go to Peru, in the same manner as Doctor Moya de Contreras had been selected for Mexico. He was instructed to make ready to leave at once, and with him were to sail the Viceroy, Francisco de Toledo, and another Inquisitor, Dr. Andrés de Bustamente.

They sailed in March 1569 but by June, when they had reached Nombre de Dios, their money had run out, and it was necessary to raise more. Meanwhile Andrés de Bustamente died.

During the delay Cerezuela tried a few cases, and when he reached Panama the Viceroy and the judges were commanded to take the oath of allegiance to the Inquisition.

Cerezuela arrived at Lima on the 28th of November.

The usual pattern was followed: the ceremonies to inspire and terrify the people, the recital of the Edict of Faith which was followed by numerous denunciations and arrests; and by 15th November, 1573, the first *auto de fé* was held.

Cerezuela was not a popular Inquisitor; there were continual complaints of his inexperience, and it was very quickly felt that he should be replaced. Consequently Antonio Gutiérrez de Ulloa arrived to take over in March 1571, and it could not have been long before it was realized that the incompetence of Cerezuela was preferable to the villainies of Ulloa.

The latter was soon engaged in amours, and even went so far as to keep a permanent mistress whom he allowed to influence him in his judgments.

He wandered the streets at night (not in his Inquisitorial robes but dressed as a gay gallant) in search of adventures, was engaged in many a brawl and enjoyed the company of prostitutes. When he was caught, *in flagrante delicto*, by a husband, he assumed the role of Inquisitor, informing the husband of what could happen to him if he fell into the hands of the Inquisition— which he would certainly do if he sought to criticize the conduct of Inquisitor Ulloa.

Another husband, in similar circumstances, was bolder; he murdered his wife and threatened Ulloa, in spite of the fact that he was Inquisitor. This was the cause of great scandal.

Money interested him as much as women; he had an interest in the quicksilver mines in Guancavelica, and a great deal of money which should have gone to the Treasury of Spain found its way into his pocket.

So many complaints about this man reached the Supreme Council that it was decided to send a *visitador* to Lima to discover the truth. This man, Juan Ruiz de Prado, was given all the authority he needed to prosecute any member of the Inquisition in Peru.

The Viceroy, Villar, who had been largely instrumental in calling in the services of Prado, expected him to be his ally, but when he arrived Prado seemed more inclined to form a friendship with Ulloa, the very man whose actions he had come to investigate.

At the time of Prado's coming Sir Francis Drake's cousin, John Drake, and Richard Farrel were wrecked in the River Plate, and as they were heretics they were brought before the Inquisition. The capture of two such men seemed, in the Viceroy's opinion, to offer an unusually good opportunity for discovering the whereabouts of English shipping, and he wanted them brought to him for questioning. Ulloa, however, insisted that they were the prisoners of the Inquisition and that he could not release Drake and Farrel without express orders from the Suprema in Spain. As this would take about a year to obtain, Villar pointed out the folly of the decision, for he needed the information immediately.

Then came the alarm (unfounded) that the English ships were sighted, and Villar called up all men available to defend Callao against the English. Both Ulloa and Prado, making sure that the offices of the Inquisition were protected, gave orders that the men were not to obey Villar.

Exasperated, Villar pointed out that the men would be defending the Inquisition as well as the city.

But Ulloa and Prado had their way; together they rendered the Viceroy powerless and took charge of the city. Villar realized the uselessness of attempting to govern when the Inquisition was more powerful than the state.

Prado at this time was determined to stand by Ulloa, and when a man from whom Ulloa had borrowed a great deal of money asked for its return and, not getting it, produced a writ against the Inquisitor, it was Prado who had the poor man arrested, suspended from his benefice (he was a priest), and sentenced to four years' confinement, during which he was so maltreated that he died.

The friendship between Prado and Ulloa suddenly ceased; and from that time the end of Ulloa's pleasant way of life was in sight. Prado seemed suddenly to remember the reason he had been sent to Peru and set about examining all the evidence which had been accumulating against the man who had until now been his friend; and as a result he drew up 216 charges against Ulloa.

He discovered the scandals concerning many women, and how Ulloa had taken control of the quicksilver mines by reminding all other bidders that he was at the head of the Inquisition and that they could guess what would happen to them if they bid against him; as a result he and his brother and a friend had been granted concessions at a much lower price than the other bidders had offered.

Ulloa then began to inquire into the peccadilloes of Prado, that he might expose them. He accused him of shady financial dealings.

The Suprema in Spain sent orders to both men. Prado was to leave Peru at once and return to Spain; 118 of the 216 charges against Ulloa were accepted, and he was to be suspended from his office for five years, pay a fine, and return to Spain for a reprimand by the Inquisitor-General.

Prado had proposed some reforms and, when the Supreme Council studied these, it was decided that it might be a good thing to try some of them. Prado was therefore instructed not to leave Peru, but by the time the order came he had already sailed for Spain in accordance with the original instructions.

Ulloa in the meantime was in no hurry to obey the summons to return to Spain. The Licentiate, Antonio Ordóñez y Flores, arrived on 4th February, 1594, to take Ulloa's place, and then Ulloa began his very slow journey across the country. He still behaved as though he were Inquisitor, and terrified the people in the villages through which he passed.

An example of his behaviour is given by Diego Vanegas who was the son of the judge of the Contratacion of Seville.

Ulloa had stopped at Cuzco and was lodging with Francisco de Loaysa. One of the latter's servants boasted in the presence of Vanegas and his friends, who were talking together in the public square, that staying in his master's house was the Inquisitor, Ulloa, whose power exceeded that of anybody in Peru. He then began to tell a story which illustrated the power of Ulloa, and Vanegas lightly remarked that he and his friends were not really interested and did not wish to hear any more.

Vanegas was arrested and taken before Ulloa, who called some twenty of his men and told them to kill this man who had spoken disparagingly of the Inquisition and its Inquisitors. The men would have obeyed and Vanegas would have lost his life if Doña Mariana de Loaysa had not begged them to refrain from killing a man in her house. Ulloa, susceptible to the pleas of some women, agreed to spare the life of Vanegas and ordered that he should be given five hundred lashes. On further protests from Doña Mariana, Ulloa agreed that there should be only two hundred, but on the lady's further protests against violence he said that Vanegas should be banished.

When Ulloa left Cuzco word reached him that Vanegas, who was in bed recovering from the beating which had been given him, had declared his intention of going to Spain that he might report in person the ill conduct of Ulloa. Furious, Ulloa sent some of his men back to Cuzco to arrest Vanegas, who was dragged from his bed and taken to prison, where he remained for four months. After that he was sentenced to serve for three years as a soldier on the frontier or in the galleys.

Vanegas managed to escape, and went to Lima where he saw the Viceroy, explained what had happened and was given permission to go to Spain to make a complaint against Ulloa. (Lea.)

Ulloa meanwhile had no intention of going to Spain to be reprimanded, so he complained of ill health and his inability to travel. Perhaps there was some truth in this, for he died in Lima in 1597, nearly three years after the Suprema had accepted the charges against him.

*   *   *

Peru was unfortunate in her Inquisitors, and although Ulloa may have been one of the most villainous, those who followed him were not noted for their virtues. When it is realized that these men were kings in their territory, that they had the power to excommunicate, that they could stand in judgment and only the Suprema, far away in Spain, could call them to account for their actions, it is perhaps understandable.

The Inquisition had been set up in the Spanish colonies to protect them from Protestant infiltration, but there was little for it to do in this respect, although some of the victims who appeared at the *autos de fé* were sailors who had been shipwrecked or taken prisoner at sea.

In 1581 and 1587 two Flemings, Jan Bernal and Miguel del Pilar were arrested, accused of being Protestants and were both burned alive; and in the first *auto de fé* (1573) two Protestants appeared, Joan Bautista and Mateo Salado. But these were few, and after 1587 another does not appear until 1625.

The Inquisition found itself more concerned with Jews, for many of this race had come to the colonies in the hope of making their fortunes as well as finding a haven where they would be safe from the persecution of the old country. So many opportunities did the Jews see in these new and as yet unexploited lands, that they overcame all the difficulties which were put in their way and many emigrated. Thus they provided the Inquisition with the victims it sought.

In 1626 one of the most interesting of the cases against a Jew began, although it did not end until 1639, a typical example of the circumlocution at Inquisitorial trials. This concerned a Francisco Maldonado de Silva, who was a greatly respected surgeon in Concepcion de Chile, and of Portuguese origin.

Francisco had been brought up as a Catholic, for his father had been a prisoner of the Inquisition which had allowed him to become reconciled to the Church and ordered him to bring up his children—Francisco, Isabel and another girl—as Christians.

When Francisco was eighteen he read the *Scrutinium Scripturarum*, a book which had been written by one of the greatest Jewish teachers, Rabbi Selemoh Ha-Levi, who was converted to Catholicism in 1390 and became Pablo de Santa Maria. He was later Regent of Spain and Bishop of Cartagena and Burgos. This book was supposed to be written to help Jews to become Catholics but it had the reverse effect upon Francisco.

He spoke to his father about these doubts, and his father's advice was that he should study the Bible, and at the same time he gave him some instruction in the Law of Moses.

It was not long before Francisco decided that he would accept the Jewish Faith and no other, although he kept this a secret, and his mother, two sisters, and even his wife had no idea that he had reverted to the faith of his fathers.

The family appear to have been an affectionate one and

Francisco was particularly fond of his sister Isabel (who was about two years younger than he was). This must have been the case because it was to Isabel that he eventually confided the news of his conversion. She was at this time thirty-three years of age, and, it seems, a devout Catholic, for when she heard her brother's confession she was thrown into an agony of uncertainty.

Again and again she had been taught the duty of a good Catholic: there was no loyalty to be set against that due to the Church.

First she told her confessor, and this gave rise to further misery, for her confessor informed her that the only way she could expiate the sin of listening to her brother, was by denouncing him to the Inquisition.

Isabel wrestled with her love for her brother and her fear of eternal damnation, and eventually fear was the conqueror. As a result Francisco was arrested and brought before the Tribunal. He was firm in his resolve to cling to the Law of Moses, and efforts to make him return to the Catholic Church failed.

His wretchedness must have equalled that of his sister, for he knew that no one was aware that he had changed his religion, except Isabel, and that she was the one who had betrayed him.

Boldly he admitted to the Tribunal that he was a Jew and that he intended to die in that faith; with the result that he was branded a relaxed heretic and sentenced to death at the stake.

Life in prison had weakened him and he was very ill. He asked that instead of his ration of bread he should be given maize husks. This was done, and he made a rope which enabled him to escape from his room and visit other Jewish prisoners.

During the years he spent in prison he made two books out of scraps of paper, pens from egg-shells and ink from charcoal.

It was thirteen years before he was finally brought out of prison and burned alive. The books he had made were hung about his neck and burned with him. (Lea and *Publications of the American Jewish Historical Society.*)

* * *

The *auto de fé* at which Francisco Maldonado de Silva was burned was the most important that had yet been held in Peru, because on this occasion suffered many Jews who had been rounded up in what was called the *"complicidad grande"*.

At this time there were many Jews in Peru, and their presence was being felt, for they were beginning to control the commerce of the country. Envy brought them to the notice of the Inquisition, and in 1636 almost a hundred had been arrested, and had there been bigger prisons available there would have been more arrests.

These prisoners were almost all wealthy men and in some cases they brought great temptation to their jailers. There is a recorded case of one, Bartolomé de Pradeda, on whom suspicion fell because he suddenly began acquiring a great deal of property. The matter was investigated, and the discovery was made that Bartolomé's wealth had been acquired in exchange for certain favours.

The Inquisition was never really very severe with its own; bribery, solicitation—such sins were venial in their eyes compared with heresy. So Bartolomé was merely dismissed; but the temptation proved too great for his successor and he too soon followed Bartolomé into retirement, as did *his* successor and two others who came after him. The Inquisitors by that time had realized the need for a little more severity, and two of the three last, who did not hold very high positions in the Inquisition, were punished—one sent to the galleys, the other to do penance in an *auto*.

The treatment of prisoners concerned in the *complicidad grande* was very severe. A twenty-seven-year-old woman, Murcia de Luna, died under torture; her sister, Isabel de Luna, aged eighteen, was stripped to the waist and given a hundred lashes in the streets with her mother who was treated in the same manner. A boy of eighteen, Enrique Jorge Tavares, refused to confess, though cruelly tortured, and was so ill-used that he became insane.

One very rich man, Manuel Bautista Pérez, who was the foremost merchant in Lima, was burned alive. He had made himself a leader of a group, and meetings had been held in his house. The owner of silver mines and plantations, he was a great prize, and his carriage alone brought in the sum of 3,400 pesos. His attempt to commit suicide was unsuccessful and he went bravely to his death.

Another victim of this purge was Antonio Cordero who was a merchant's clerk. Another merchant denounced him to the Inquisition, so this may have been a case of business rivalry. The merchant, de Salazar, reported to the Inquisition that he had gone into the shop of which Cordero was in charge and had been told by Cordero that customers were not served on Saturdays. He also declared that he had on a certain Friday seen Cordero at a meal in the shop and asked him why he did not eat bacon; to which Cordero was alleged to have replied that his father and grandfather had never eaten bacon, so neither would he.

The Inquisition decided to arrest him on suspicion and sent

one of their familiars into the shop as though he were a customer. The familiar then forced Cordero into a room behind the shop and locked him in; after dark Cordero was conducted to the secret prison of the Inquisition.

It was not generally known that he had been made a prisoner, so secretly was the arrest made, and it was believed that Cordero, knowing the Inquisition was on his trail, had fled from the city.

Cordero was tortured and implicated others, so that because a man refused to eat bacon and serve a customer on a Saturday, the lives of many people were either lost or ruined.

*   *   *

Another source of supply was the great body of mystics; and, as the people of Peru were as ready to accept miraculous wonders as the people of Spain, there appeared many *beatas* and holy men, and some of these encountered the suspicions of the Inquisition.

One of the most notorious of these *beatas* flourished in the 1560s. Her name was María Pizarro, and she declared that she had had a visitation from the Angel Gabriel, and that the Immaculate Conception had been revealed to her.

Among her admirers were two Jesuits who had been sent to Peru as missionaries; one of these men was Gerónimo Ruiz Portillo and the other Padre Luis López; the highly-respected Professor of Theology, Fray Francisco de la Cruz, was also among her admirers.

María was evidently a hysterical subject and believed that she was in contact with the Devil. The trouble started when one of her admirers, a Dominican, Fray Alonso Gasco, confessed that he had in his possession certain objects which had been blessed by the Devil.

As a result María was arrested and, when she was in prison and no doubt thought her end was near, she made her confession. She said that in the first place the Jesuit Padre Luis López had seduced her and that afterwards she was invited by the Devil to become his succubus, which she did.

Later she changed her confession and said that she had lied concerning López. She died before she could be brought to trial.

The denunciation of María Pizarro meant that many of her supporters were brought under suspicion, and among these was the Professor of Theology, Francisco de la Cruz. Under examination he persisted that he had believed María's revelations had come from the Angel Gabriel and that the doctrines which María had preached were true ones.

Many of these women who sought to set themselves apart from

their fellows by their intimacy with the Trinity, the Virgin Mary, the angels and saints, followed this way of life because they enjoyed the limelight. Moreover it was an easy and very interesting method of earning a livelihood, for the woman—or man—who was endowed with such special powers was treated with the utmost respect by almost all, and rich gifts and presents frequently came their way. Some of them dedicated themselves to a life of privation, but others wished to live full and sensuous lives; they wished to indulge in amorous relations with the opposite sex; and because of this they were obliged to formulate a new doctrine, which was that there was no sin in making love and therefore priests and holy women could indulge in it as freely as they wished.

De la Cruz, who upheld these beliefs—and even went so far as to teach them—was clearly in the eyes of the Inquisition guilty of heresy.

By a married woman he had had a son who strutted about the city boasting that he was the Son of God. This child was captured by the Inquisitors and shipped to Panama where he was put into stern hands to be brought up in a fitting manner.

Meanwhile de la Cruz was taken to prison, tortured and finally condemned to the stake. It is believed that he asked for reconciliation at the last moment and was strangled.

Padre Luis López was a bold man. He dared to say that de la Cruz had been ill-treated by the Inquisition, since he was clearly insane. For this he was arrested. The case against him was that he had seduced María Pizarro in the first place, that he was guilty of solicitation on many occasions, and that he had actually written a pamphlet to the effect that Philip II had no right to take possession of Peru.

The last charge was treason and outside the scope of the Inquisition which had only to deal with the criticism of itself, the seduction of María, and the solicitation.

López confessed that he had seduced women in the confessional, and he was given a scourging during the space of two *misereres*, imprisoned, and then sent to Spain. I can find no record of what happened to him there.

*   *   *

So the persecution continued to the detriment of Peru's prosperity. In 1813 the Inquisition was suppressed, but in 1814 it was established once more, only to be finally suppressed in 1820.

The number of cases dealt with by the Inquisition in Peru seems astonishingly small. Henry Charles Lea quotes Teodoro Marino as stating that 3,000 were tried in the 250 years of its existence. His researches though (Lea points out), which were exhaustive, enabled him to name only 1,474 cases.

If Lea is right and there were even fewer cases than Marino believed, the folly of establishing the Inquisition is even more obvious. It flourished at enormous expense; it had an adverse effect on the trade of the country; but even if these figures are accepted, for every one man who was brought before the Tribunal thousands feared to be taken there. So that if physical torture was carried out on comparatively few people the whole nation could never have felt entirely at ease. For how could they be sure when, in the darkness of the night, there would not come that ominous knocking on the door?

7

NAPLES

When Ferdinand conquered Naples the Papal Inquisition had previously been set up there by Charles of Anjou, and after the Aragonese robbed the House of Anjou of its possession, the Inquisition was allowed to remain as long as its members understood that it was second in importance to the crown. For this reason it languished.

When Ferdinand appeared on the scene, Pope Julius II was endeavouring to establish an Inquisition which should be under the wing of the Papacy. This was naturally not to Ferdinand's taste and he planned to introduce the Spanish Inquisition into Naples.

All preparations for doing this were made, but Ferdinand's object was not achieved. There is no detailed information as to why this should have been so; but it was probably due to the fact that there was great opposition in Naples; and because the inhabitants were known for their fiery dispositions, Ferdinand was too wise to force the Inquisition on them as soon as he had acquired dominion over them.

Ferdinand contented himself by persecuting the Jews in Naples. The Neapolitans, however, did not hate the Jews as the Spaniards had, and the persecutions began in a leisurely manner; the order of expulsion was not entirely carried out until 1540, when the Emperor Charles was in command. Large numbers of these Jews found their way to Turkey; but the exodus, like those which took place from Spain, resulted in great misfortune for thousands. There were the usual slaughterings and misery; and many were captured and sold into slavery. François Premier showed kindness to them, for when many of them appeared in Marseilles he allowed them to settle in the Levant without making any charge for this—which was a very generous act, since the French exchequer, like most, was in need of constant replenishment. This expulsion was followed by the usual disadvantages, and in Naples prosperity was undermined.

In the early fourteenth century the Waldenses had settled in the mountains of Calabria and Apulia; they cultivated the land, made it prosperous and lived peaceably for more than 200 years. When the Inquisition grew to power its eye was turned on these people, and Charles V was told that he should not allow them to continue in heresy. Charles was less interested in making trouble among an industrious section of the community on the grounds of religion than his son was to be, and little was done about these people.

But by 1560 the Waldenses were once more attracting attention and Rome sent an Inquisitor, Valerio Malvicino da Piazenza, to San Sisto, La Guardia and Montalto to study the beliefs of the people. Valerio ordered them to accept the Catholic Faith, which they refused to do. San Sisto was first dealt with, for the population had taken up arms. San Sisto itself was burned, the men were slaughtered, and the women and children submitted to brutal outrage.

Many of the inhabitants of La Guardia and Montalto, who had also revolted, were sent before a tribunal. They were tortured, and there followed an *auto de fé* on 11th June, 1561.

A letter exists which was written on the day of this *auto de fé* by an observer who was a Catholic (Lea, *The Inquisition in the Spanish Dependencies*). The victims were led one by one into the open, their eyes covered by a blood-spattered bandage which had been used by the previous victim. In the public square their throats were cut, their bodies quartered and the fragments affixed to poles which had been set up from one end of Calabria to the other. This observer writes as though the sight shocked him deeply, but another faithful Catholic who witnessed the scene wrote that the sight was one to inspire the heretic with fear while it confirmed the believer in his faith. It is easy to understand the former statement, but why the brutality of a sect should make its doctrines more convincing it is difficult to see. Eighty-eight people were treated in this way and seven, who had not broken down under violent torture and had refused to relinquish their beliefs, were burned alive. A hundred elderly women were condemned to death; and the total number of casualties on this occasion was calculated to be 1,600. How the rest died we cannot be sure, but it seems likely that they suffered in the same brutal way.

A reward of ten crowns per person was offered for the return of those who sought to escape, and this brought in men and women in their hundreds. From Rome came instructions that the *auto* of 1561 had been conducted in too brutal a fashion and liberation was advised. It appears that this advice was not accepted; more prisoners were sent to the galleys and the five leaders of the revolt were burned alive after their bodies had been covered with pitch that their sufferings might be increased. All children under fifteen were taken from their parents and put with Catholic families.

The Inquisition was more stern with La Guardia than it had been with San Sisto, because San Sisto had been guilty of a revolt against authority, whereas La Guardia was entirely heretic. Many of the inhabitants went to the stake, many were sentenced to the galleys, and the entire community were condemned to wear the *sanbenito* and to hear Mass thus garbed every day. No more than six people were allowed to meet together and their native speech was to be replaced by Italian.

The Waldenses who lived in the Apulia district were treated less harshly. The more obstinate went to the stake and some to the galleys, but the majority of the population became reconciled and the conditions imposed upon them were apparently acceptable. It may have been that both sides had realized the folly of what had happened in Calabria, where the land had been laid waste and there had been so much death and destruction.

This was the work of the Papal Inquisition; and although in the case of the Waldenses it had acted in as barbarous a manner as the Spanish Inquisition, it grew milder as the years passed, until its suppression in the eighteenth century.

8

SICILY

THE SPANISH INQUISITION was established in Sicily in 1487. Sicily, of course, in the fifteenth century, belonged to Aragon; and until Torquemada, then Inquisitor-General of Aragon, sent his Inquisitor to the island it had been under the supervision of the Papal Inquisition. This had become too lax for the zealous Torquemada to tolerate and, on 18th August, 1487, the island celebrated the introduction of the Spanish Inquisition by an *auto de fé*.

Torquemada's Inquisition was mainly concerned with the destruction of the Jews, and this unfortunate race was driven from Sicily at the time of the great exodus of 1492.

The people of Sicily found the Spanish Inquisition more zealous and more severe than the Papal Inquisition, and they grew restive. By 1516—at the time of Ferdinand's death—they were ready to rise against the Viceroy, Hugo de Moncada and the Inquisitor, Melchor Cervera, who had arrived two years before with strict instructions from Torquemada to obey in every detail the rules which he had laid down.

The barbarous rule of the Viceroy had reduced the islanders to great poverty, for he had cornered the wheat production and exported it, thus bringing starvation to Sicily. He was afraid, when he heard of Ferdinand's death, that he would be removed from his office, for he knew that the people would clamour for his dismissal; so he sought to withhold the news from the Sicilians, but it leaked out and the mob attacked his palace. The Viceroy, in the disguise of a lackey, managed to escape, and sailed across to Messina.

Having lost the Viceroy the people turned to the Inquisitor, Melchor Cervera, whom they had grown to hate. Cervera was not so fortunate as the Viceroy, Hugo de Moncada, had been, and would have been torn to pieces if he had not, to protect himself, grasped and held aloft a consecrated Host in a monstrance; and although he was jeered at by the people, they were superstitious enough to regard him as immune from their attack while he held such an object. Thus he too was able to find a ship and escape.

The mob then turned its attention to the prison of the Inquisition, stormed the building, freed the prisoners and scattered the records.

After that three years elapsed during which the Inquisition ceased to exist in Sicily.

The case of Cervera was examined, but as usual the Inquisition was lenient with its servants, and in 1519 he was sent back to the island.

During the following five or six years *autos de fé* were celebrated at the rate of approximately one a year, but the numbers executed were not large, perhaps on account of the small population.

The numbers of those who suffered death at the stake are given as: in 1519, 5; 1520, 5; 1521, 1; 1524, 5; 1525, 5; 1526, 5.

Inquisitors outside Spain appear to be more often accused of bribery and corruption than those living close to the alert eyes of the Suprema. Inquisitors took bribes called "presents" from so many people that it was noticed that while many were sentenced to the galleys they did not all go there; and others who were condemned to wear the *sanbenito* escaped doing so. It was not very difficult to divert funds, which should have gone to the Inquisition, into the pockets of individual Inquisitors; and there were continual complaints.

The Inquisition continued active however after the Treaty of Utrecht (1713) when Sicily passed to Savoy; but even then the Inquisition which ruled Sicily continued to be the Spanish Inquisition.

Five years later Savoy exchanged Sicily for Sardinia, and the island fell into the hands of Austria. The Emperor of Austria was not content to allow the Inquisition to be ruled by the Suprema in Spain and, although it remained fundamentally the *Spanish* Inquisition, a supreme council was created in Vienna. The Emperor ordered that there should be a very special *auto* to celebrate the change, and this took place at Palermo on 6th April, 1724.

In 1734 Charles III reconquered Sicily, but by this time the Holy Office was past its zenith, and it was in the eighteenth century that it was suppressed.

Lea, quoting Franchina, who was writing in 1744, says that, in less than 300 years, 201 men and women had been burned alive in Sicily on orders from the Holy Office.

9

SARDINIA

As Sardinia was a dominion of Aragon, the Inquisition was introduced there about the year 1492, with Micer Sancho Maria as Inquisitor. He remained there in this post until 1497 when he was sent to Sicily and was replaced by Gabriel Cardona.

Cardona was soon involved in a quarrel with the Lieutenant-General and Archbishop of Cagliari because he had imprisoned a man—Domingo de Santa Cruz—who they believed should have been left unmolested. The Lieutenant-General and Archbishop, using force, released Santa Cruz, and this was the cause of numerous angry communications between Ferdinand and Sardinia, for Ferdinand was anxious to see the Inquisition supreme over the state.

However it was not long before Cardona was relieved of his post, and the Bishop of Bonavalle took his place. It may have been that Cardona had asked to be allowed to leave Sardinia, for he was certainly in danger of losing his life. The Inquisition was received in Sardinia, as in almost every other country in Europe —certainly by the people, at least—with the utmost suspicion; and Cardona's assistant, Miguel Fonte, who was known as the "receiver", because it was his duty to deal with confiscated property, had been set upon in Cagliari, and although he had not died immediately and he was taken back to Spain, he very shortly afterwards died of his wounds in Barcelona.

After his assassination it was not easy to find another willing to take the post he had vacated. The dangers of such an unpopular position were fully realized, and it was some months afterwards when Juan López arrived in Sardinia in the role of receiver.

During its early days the Inquisition in Sardinia seemed to be directed mainly against the *conversos*; but its history is one of disputes and wrangling with the Bishops who, as had happened so many times before, were not pleased to see the authority they had enjoyed pass to the Inquisitors.

Again, as happened before, when the Inquisition moved

away from headquarters its officials had a tendency to become more and more corrupt. Unnecessary officials were appointed, and the expenditure was prodigious.

In 1580 Philip II asked Gregory XIII for financial help. This request was not granted. In the reign of Philip III the financial condition of the Inquisition in Sardinia was even more needy. It became difficult to induce people to accept positions in Sardinia, not only on account of the climate but because the remuneration was so small.

In 1718 Sardinia passed into the hands of the Duke of Savoy, and with the cessation of Spanish control the Inquisition ceased to be, and the Bishops resumed the power to condemn people for heresy. The House of Savoy had never taken kindly to the Inquisition, which was a menace to secular power; and as it was a rule of the Church that churchmen could not condemn but must hand over prisoners to the secular arm to be sentenced, persecution for heresy appears to have disappeared in Sardinia during the second half of the eighteenth century.

10

MILAN

MILAN CAME into Spanish possession in 1529 by the Treaty of Cambrai, and because it became a refuge for those whose opinions differed from the orthodox Catholic Church it received the attention of the Papal Inquisition. But up to the time when it came under Spanish dominion the Inquisition had grown lax. This naturally did not please Philip II who sought to replace the old Inquisition by that more virile version The Spanish Inquisition.

He proposed sending Gaspar Cervantes, who had had a great deal of experience in Spain and who had been made Archbishop of Messina, to begin operations. Cervantes was not eager for the appointment, and the Pope was in no hurry to give his assent.

Meanwhile the people of Milan, hearing what was proposed, became apprehensive—more than that, they began to show that, if any attempt were made to set up the Spanish Inquisition in Milan, they would make trouble.

Philip was eager that there should not be revolt in his possessions and, realizing that the people of Milan had determined not to accept the Spanish Inquisition, he sought to temporize, and made it known to them that he had had no intention of setting up that Inquisition in Milan as it existed in Spain, but had only meant to give them an Inquisitor of experience who would look after them with greater care than they had been accustomed to.

Philip had failed to establish the Spanish Inquisition in Milan.

In 1560 Pius IV made his nephew, Cardinal Carlo Borromeo, Archbishop of Milan, a position which gave him power over the whole of Lombardy. The Cardinal went to work with great zeal in the extirpation of heresy, so that it is very doubtful whether, in escaping the Spanish Inquisition, the people of Milan were as lucky as they had believed they would be.

II

CANARY ISLANDS

In the Canary Islands the Spanish Inquisition was established in 1505 when the Inquisitor-General, Deza, sent Bartolomé López Tribaldos there as Inquisitor (whose power was not great as it was decided that all matters of importance should be referred back to Seville).

At first it languished and was even temporarily suspended, until Espinosa, Inquisitor-General, realizing that by limiting its power it had been crippled, decided to revive it by making it independent of Seville, and appointed the energetic Diego Ortiz de Fúnez to put new life into it.

Fúnez had not been long in the Canaries before he was able to arrange an *auto*. This *auto* attracted such crowds from other islands that the spectators were said to be twice as many as the entire population of Grand Canary. Juan Felipe, one of the victims, who was a Morisco and a rich trader of Lanzarote, discovering that he was about to be arrested, took ship with his family and other *Moriscos* and escaped to Morocco where he was able to give a great deal of information about Inquisitorial methods in the Canaries.

The rule of Fúnez however was soon giving cause for complaint, and a *visitador* was sent out to investigate him. The two became friends and worked together planning *autos*, but at the same time the *visitador* did not hesitate to bring charges against Fúnez. It was the old story. There were so many temptations for these men who had such power and who were far from the centre of authority. Fúnez was accused of allowing Inquisitorial funds to find their way into his own pocket, of carrying on a profitable trade with the Moors of Barbary, of accepting presents; in fact he was accused of all the usual crimes of which a man in his position was likely to be guilty. But returning to Spain he appears to have given a good account of himself at Madrid.

Many English and Dutch sailors were brought before the Tribunal, with many more *conversos* who had escaped to the

101

islands from Spain in the hope of finding a refuge where they could live in peace. *Moriscos* were also persecuted but, strangely enough, there were more cases of blasphemy, sorcery and solicitation in the confessional than of heresy.

There was one case of solicitation which is of particular interest because in this present decade there has been a similar case in France. In 1747 Fray Bartolomé Bello seduced a young girl named Maria Cabral González. Maria became pregnant and a child was born. This the girl took to the priest, her lover, who first baptized it and then strangled it.

As the sentences for solicitation were so light it is not surprising that this crime appears so frequently in the records; and it is only logical to presume that, for every case which came to light, there must have been several which were never heard of, for many women would be very reluctant to come forward and denounce their confessors, particularly if they had submitted. Out of twenty-two men who were brought before the Tribunal in the nineteen months between 1706 and 1708 seven were charged with solicitation (Lea). It is a large proportion.

The Inquisition was suppressed in the Canaries in 1813, and the people were so overjoyed that all the *sanbenitos* which had been hanging in the churches were taken out to the *patios* and publicly burned.

Rejoicing was a little premature, for on 17th August, 1814, a decree was issued which set up the Inquisition again.

But in 1820 it was suppressed for ever, and the Inquisitors left everything and set out for Spain. No respect was paid to the archives, which was a great pity, for they were taken by anyone who cared to do so, with the result that many interesting records are lost to posterity.

12

PORTUGAL

In the year 1580 Portugal was conquered by Philip II, and this meant that its Inquisition came under the zealous eyes of the conqueror. Philip immediately wished to bring the Inquisition of Portugal under the jurisdiction of the Inquisitor-General of Spain, but this the Pope, Gregory XIII, refused to allow; even so, the activities of the Inquisition increased and between 1581 and 1600 fifty *autos de fé* were held.

Now that the two countries were joined under one ruler, many Jews who had been living in Portugal decided to slip into Spain which, as a much richer country, could give them more scope in their enterprises. Ninety thousand of them had taken refuge in Portugal after the exodus of 1492. John II had allowed them to stay on payment of large sums of money, but their stay was to have been temporary. Many Jews however had become Christians in order to be allowed to remain; and it was these people who now returned to Spain.

By the end of the sixteenth century, after some twenty years of Spanish domination, Portugal had become very impoverished. Rich merchants had left Lisbon, so that the once busy city was almost deserted; only 200 remained of the country's 700 ships, and the harvests were poor. The people blamed the Jews for this. Early in the century, at Easter 1506, the terrible Lisbon massacre had taken place—that rising against the Jews which continued for three days and nights and in which several thousands lost their lives.

The Inquisition of Portugal was even more notorious for its cruelty than that of Spain, but there was one man who, in the seventeenth century, sought to make reforms. This was Antonio Vieyra, a Jesuit, who came back to Portugal from South America in the year 1661 and was shocked by what he saw.

He was brought up in Bahia and educated at the Jesuit school, and although his parents (according to Rule, who refers to the Jesuits as "an ill-reputed company") did not intend him to become a Jesuit he was weaned from his parents by the Society.

When he was thirty-three John IV gave him a position as preacher in the chapel-royal; and because he was exceptionally brilliant, and the King presumably felt that he was wasted merely as a preacher, he was sent on certain diplomatic missions and in this capacity did the King's work in Holland, France, England, and Rome.

He then became a missionary and went to Brazil, but after a while the Portuguese authorities there decided to expel the Jesuit missionaries, and Vieyra returned to Lisbon where he was given a post at Court. He had his enemies in Lisbon and was forced to leave for Coimbra; but not content with his banishment these enemies sought to destroy him, and the simplest way of doing this was to bring a charge of heresy against him.

His sermons were noted and everything he said was sifted for a sentence that could be called heretical.

By October 1665 he was in the prison of the Inquisition.

It was held against him that he condemned examination of heresies and had declared that it would be well for the kingdom if the names of informers and witnesses were made known to the New Christians who were accused of Judaism. He had also expressed the desire that Jews should be allowed to take public offices, and that, provided they did not attack Christians, they should be allowed to worship as they pleased.

He had also expressed sympathy for the victims of the Inquisition and had published writings concerning their sufferings.

He had recorded the case of a certain Maria da Conceição who had been arrested by the Inquisition on a charge of Judaizing. She had been put on the rack and, after she had been cruelly treated there, she finally "confessed" as the torturers wished her to; when she was able to use her limbs she was taken before the examiners and asked to ratify her confession. Very boldly she spoke up. Torture had driven her to say what she did not mean; she retracted her confession. She was again tortured, again confessed, and later again refused to confirm what she had said on the rack. She told the Inquisitors that, even though under torture she had said what they demanded of her, as soon as she was taken from the torture chamber she would tell the truth. She was racked a third time, and this time she did not confess.

The furious Inquisitors condemned her to be whipped through the streets of Lisbon and then to be banished to the west coast of Africa.

Vieyra had also written vivid descriptions of the prisons of the Inquisition in which he states it was customary to put five people in a cell nine feet by eleven, and in which the vessels were only changed once a week, and the only light and air which penetrated this foul place came through a narrow slit in the ceiling.

Such a man was dangerous to the Inquisition, but he was a highly-respected member of the Society of Jesus; therefore the Inquisition could not treat him as they would some poor *Marrano*, *Morisco* or Protestant far from home.

His sentence was that he should be deprived of the authority to preach and sent to a college or house of Jesuits which the Holy Office would select; he should be unable to leave this particular college without first obtaining the consent of the Inquisition.

It was decided that he should be taken to the Jesuit House at Perroso which had been chosen for him, but the decision was changed and he was sent to the house of the Cotovia in Lisbon.

About this time the Jesuits were instrumental in helping the Queen Mother, Doña Luisa, to depose Alfonso VI and set Pedro IV on the throne, so the Jesuits were in high favour with the new king. Vieyra was released, and left Lisbon for Rome.

From Rome he made an attack on the Inquisition; he wrote that the Portuguese Inquisition had become a tribunal which robbed men of their fortunes and their lives and could not tell the difference between guilt and innocence, that while it proclaimed its piety, it was guilty of injustice and cruelty.

This was very heartening to the New Christians who had great hopes of bringing the Inquisition in Portugal more in line with that of Rome.

In 1671 there was a general attack on the New Christians in Lisbon. The trouble started when it was stated that some wafers had been stolen from a church. This may have been falsely rumoured and the wafers may not have been stolen at all. However, the Inquisitors decided to use the occasion for a fresh attack on the New Christians.

They were arrested in hundreds and submitted to the most cruel forms of torture. But the people were becoming more enlightened as time was passing; many of the more educated were horrified at what was happening, and made a petition to the King imploring him to stop this wave of terror.

The King, too much in awe of the Inquisition even at this date to interfere, did refer the matter to Rome. Meanwhile the thief was discovered not to be a New Christian but an old one. But the Inquisitors would not release their prisoners, and stated that they meant to hold them for further questioning.

Pope Clement X asked the Inquisitors to send him records of a few trials so that he might judge the manner in which they were conducted. They had to be threatened with excommunication before they would forward two cases.

The King then asked the Pope to study the rules of the Inquisition as it was carried out in Portugal, and make reforms. Nothing was gained however. It was difficult to act from a distance and the Inquisitors were at this stage very powerful. Yet there must have been a certain comfort, to those living in constant fear, to know that people—in high places—were concerned to win justice for them.

13

GOA

It was St. Francis Xavier who urged the King of Portugal to set up the Inquisition in the Portuguese possession of Goa. He had noticed that "Jewish perfidy" was daily spreading in the countries of east India which were subject to the crown of Portugal, and implored the King to set up the Holy Office there as the only remedy. Thus he wrote in November 1545.

When Portugal had taken possession of Goa in 1510, a bishopric had been established and the usual methods of converting the population were applied. Children were taken from their parents and brought up as Catholics, and there were many forcible baptisms.

Although St. Francis Xavier's plea was not answered, by 1560 Aleixo Diaz Falcäo was sent to Goa as Inquisitor, and the tribunal he formed became known as one of the most merciless in the Christian world.

To repeat the processes of establishment and to give accounts of procedure would become boring because they were much the same as in other instances; I think though that the best pictures of the Inquisition come from those people who actually experienced it and lived to tell the tale.

We have a good picture of the Inquisition of Goa from the Frenchman, Monsieur Dellon, who wrote his own account of his adventures in his book *Relation de L'Inquisition de Goa* (Paris 1688).

Monsieur Dellon, a traveller in India, was staying for a time at Damaun on the north-west coast of Hindustan. He was paying attention to a certain woman, but unfortunately for him the governor of the place and a priest had designs on the same woman. Presumably French gallantries were about to succeed, and this so angered the other two suitors that they decided to do something about it.

Dellon had been careless in his conversation. No doubt he thought that as a Frenchman he had nothing to fear from the

Inquisition (this happened in the 1670s) and he had freely stated his scorn for some Catholic beliefs.

The priest happened to be secretary of the Inquisition at Damaun; so that it was not difficult for the two unsuccessful suitors to conspire together to get Dellon arrested.

To the Frenchman's surprise and dismay he was seized one night and conveyed to a prison where he was forced to exist with the lowest possible criminals; and here he was left for four months.

At the end of that time he was put into irons and taken aboard ship, which stopped at Bacaim for a short stay, during which they were lodged in noisome prisons and then taken on to Goa.

The Archbishop arranged that the prisoners should be kept in his own prison until they could be taken to that of the Inquisition. Dellon wrote of it that it was the most filthy, dark and horrible he ever saw, and he doubted whether there was a prison more shocking anywhere. It was a kind of cave in which there was no light but that which came through a little hole, and the stench was terrible.

Eventually he was loaded with irons and taken to the Prison of the Inquisition. There his irons were taken off and he was at length summoned to an audience.

In the room which was known as the Board of the Holy Office sat the Grand Inquisitor of the Indies at the end of a huge table which was set upon a dais. This was in the centre of the room, and at the end of it was a large cross which reached almost from floor to ceiling. Close to the crucifix a notary was seated on a stool.

Dellon was asked by the Inquisitor whether he knew why he had been arrested, and he told his story, to which the Inquisitor, Francisco Delgado Ematos, listened. Then he rang a bell and the prisoner was taken away and stripped of all his possessions. His hair was cropped to his head. His imprisonment in the Holy House had begun.

He gives us a good description of the institution in Goa during the seventeenth century, and wrote that the building was large and grand, that there were three gates in front and that prisoners entered by the central one, when they mounted a great staircase and entered the hall. The servants of the Inquisition used the side gates which led to their apartments in the building. There was another building at the rear of the main one and in this were the cells, which opened into galleries. The lower-floor cells were tiny and there was no way of letting in the light, while the upper cells were much more comfortable, being high and vaulted, each having a small window.

The prisoners were each given an earthen pot in which to wash, and another pot for other purposes which was emptied once in four days. They had three meals a day and there were doctors on the premises to attend to the sick. Any who died were unceremoniously buried in the precincts of the building, and if they were considered to be guilty of heresy their bones would be dug up to be burned at the next *auto de fé*.

Any prisoner who spoke, groaned, or even sighed was immediately and severely beaten.

Every two months an Inquisitor and notary visited the prisoner to ask if he was being well looked after. It was wise to answer in the affirmative. Dellon had been told that if he desired an audience he had only to ask for it; yet again and again he implored that he might be given one. This was the formality of the Inquisition which was the same at Goa as in Spain or Portugal.

At length he obtained his audience, was once more asked if he knew the reason of his arrest, and repeated what he believed he had said at Damaun. The Inquisitor replied that he had been wise to accuse himself, and asked him in the name of Jesus Christ to complete his self-accusation that he might reap the benefit of the tenderness and mercy which the Tribunal always showed towards those who confessed without being forced to do so.

These were ominous words and meant to strike terror into the heart of the prisoner; and after they had been delivered Dellon was taken back to his cell to brood on them.

After a fortnight there was another audience when he was again asked if he knew the reason for his arrest. He was then told to repeat the Paternoster, Hail Mary, the Creed and Commandments of God, the Commandments of the Church and *Salve Regina*. All this Dellon was able to do in such a manner that even they could find no fault with it. Then came the warning: In the name of Jesus Christ he must confess more.

Fearing what was in store, Dellon tried to commit suicide by starvation. Finding this unsuccessful he invented more confessions and asked for another audience. But what he had to tell was not enough and he was sent back to his cell once more.

He pretended to be ill and a doctor ordered that he be bled. He tore off the bandages hoping to bleed to death; but again he was unsuccessful.

The priest who had been sent to confess him was a kindly Franciscan, and when Dellon confided his terrors to him, the monk arranged that he should have a companion in his cell. As a result a negro, who was in prison on a charge of sorcery, was sent to keep him company, and life became more tolerable, but eventually the negro was removed.

Once more he attempted to commit suicide, was discovered by his jailers, and his life saved. After this he was put into irons, but so desperate did he become that he threw himself about in a frenzy and it was necessary to take off his irons to prevent him from doing himself further injury.

He saw men and women taken past his cell to and from the torture chambers; he heard their groans, saw them bloodstained and crippled. Presumably this was a form of mental torture, a reminder that this fate was probably in store for *him*.

One Sunday in January 1676, when he offered his dirty linen to the jailer to be washed, he was alarmed to hear the jailer say that he did not want it. He then heard the bells ringing and, guessing that there would be an *auto de fé* next day, was convinced that he would be taken to the stake and burned to death.

The next morning a vest and a pair of trousers were brought to him, and barefoot he was taken from his cell to a large hall, lit only by a few lamps and ominously gloomy, where he found other prisoners—about 200 in all—and they were all commanded to sit in a gallery.

Among one section of the prisoners priests moved; quite clearly they were urging these miserable people to confess and become reconciled to the Church that they might receive the "mercy" of strangulation before the flames consumed their bodies.

Dellon had been taken to this room at two o'clock in the morning and after he had been there for two hours refreshment was offered in the form of bread and figs. When Dellon, who had rarely felt less like eating, refused the food, he was advised to take it and put it in his pocket for he would be hungry before he returned.

The last phrase seemed to him revealing and he guessed that he was not destined to suffer at the stake that day.

Immediately before dawn the cathedral bell began to toll and the people crowded into the streets as the prisoners were led out.

They were marched to the Church of St. Francis and by the time they arrived Dellon's feet were sore and bleeding from the flinty stones which had been scattered about to cause suffering to the barefooted prisoners. As the heat was intense, the *auto* was not to be celebrated out of doors but to take place in the church.

There the Grand Inquisitor and the Viceroy were seated in state and on the altar was the crucifix between huge silver candlesticks.

The sermon was preached by the Provincial of the Augustinians and Dellon has noted his comparison of the Inquisition with Noah's Ark which, said the preacher, received all sorts of wild beasts and sent them out tame.

The crimes of each prisoner were enumerated and the sentences read. Dellon's crimes were that he had doubted whether images should be adored and had referred to an ivory crucifix as a piece of ivory. He had criticized the Inquisition and spoken of it with contempt; he had maintained the invalidity of baptism and he was accused of "ill intention" towards the Faith. For these crimes he was to lose all his property; he was to be banished from India and to serve five years in the Portuguese galleys with additional penances which the Inquisitors would decide upon.

There were two people of whom the Inquisition had washed its hands, and these two—a man and a woman—were to be taken out to the *quemadero,* the Campo Santa Lazaro near the river, to be burned, together with effigies of some prisoners who had died.

Dellon was taken to Lisbon where he was put to work with convicts; eventually some of his own countrymen secured his release.

*   *   *

Rule gives an account of how an English Anglican cleric, Dr. Claudius Buchanan, visited Goa in the year 1808, and much to his surprise was entertained by Friar Joseph à Doloribus who was an Inquisitor of high standing in the Tribunal.

By this time the Inquisition was far less powerful than it had been in the days when Dellon had been its victim, and *autos de fé* were no longer held in public, sentences being carried out within the walls of the prison.

Dr. Buchanan, who was a writer as well as a priest, accepted the hospitality offered by the Inquisitor, for he believed that he might discover, through him, something of the secret working of the Inquisition, which he could make known to the world.

Friar Joseph, refusing to acknowledge the Anglican orders of his visitor, expressed his interest in his literary work; but Dr. Buchanan insisted on discussing the Inquisition. He gave the Inquisitor Dellon's book, *Relation de l'Inquisition de Goa,* which had been translated into Portuguese. When Friar Joseph had read the book he declared it to be quite untrue, but Dr. Buchanan was not to be put off so easily, and he asked Friar Joseph to mark the passages which were lies; and he told the Inquisitor that he had other books in his possession which confirmed Dellon's statements.

Friar Joseph eventually admitted that Dellon's descriptions of the prison were true, but that he had misunderstood the motives of the Inquisition and had written without charity of Holy Church.

Dr. Buchanan then made a request. Could he not see the

building of the Inquisition? He was writing a book about India, and he could not do this adequately without some reference to the Inquisition. Perhaps there was a slight threat in the doctor's words. Perhaps he implied: If I am not allowed to see what I want, I must presume that there is some reason for keeping it from me. British prestige in India was high, and the Inquisitor was in a quandary. Reluctantly he agreed to show his guest the building of the Inquisition.

Dr. Buchanan was accordingly taken to the great hall which had been described by Dellon, and there he met several of the officials and familiars who, he thought, seemed silent, severe, and embarrassed.

When he had examined the hall he asked to see the dungeons and the prisoners. That could not be, he was told. But, declared Dr. Buchanan, unless he saw the prisoners he would be obliged to believe that Dellon's descriptions were true, and that the Inquisitors were hiding something. If prisoners were treated well, as Friar Joseph suggested, would it not be wise to let a writer see them, that he might explain this to the world? He wanted to see the two hundred dungeons which were ten feet square, and which had been described by those men who had been imprisoned in them and lived to describe them. Dr. Buchanan added ominously that he wished to see if there were any British subjects among them for whom it might be his duty to seek protection. He wanted to see the torture chambers and to discover what method of punishment was used within the secret prison to replace that of the *auto de fé*. And, added the doctor, if he were not allowed to discover these things, naturally he must presume the worst.

The Inquisitor had nothing to say, and intimated that he had no more time to spare for Dr. Buchanan.

Dr. Buchanan then thanked him for his hospitality, and begged him to answer one question. This was: How many prisoners were there in the cells? The Inquisitor replied that it was a question he could not answer.

In 1774 the Tribunal was abolished and re-established in 1779, and in 1812, when Dr. Buchanan's *Christian Researches in Asia* appeared, it was still in existence; but it was finally suppressed in 1812.

14

OLIVARES

With the coming of the Bourbon dynasty to Spain it was inevitable that the Inquisition should slide down that swift decline to eventual impotence. Louis XIV had summed up his attitude in the famous words *"L'état c'est moi"*.

This was the Bourbon policy; and the Bourbon Kings of Spain intended that it should apply in Spain as in France; and as the Inquisition was an institution which had for so long proved itself to be even more powerful than the state it must be reduced to second place.

It seems extraordinary that the country which had once been the richest in the world should have made such a rapid decline, that it should have been ready to accept the Bourbons, and that the Inquisition, which by its secret methods had amassed such power, should have begun its slow recession.

But a glance at the history of the country, from the end of the reign of the second Philip to the end of that of the fourth, will give an idea of how this state of affairs came about.

The character of Philip II has been frequently examined in these pages; and when on his death-bed he contemplated the coming reign with apprehension and said of his son Philip that he feared his favourites would rule him, Philip's foresight had not deceived him.

Philip II had had a simple faith. As long as he could satisfy his conscience he was at peace; if the results of his actions were disastrous, in his absolute belief in divine control, he could say, "That is the will of God." Perhaps this was a reason why, in the battle of wits with Elizabeth I, he was the loser.

Philip III was not a fool but he was weak and, as his father had prophesied, in the hands of his favourites. Because of his weakness it was natural that the Inquisition should become even more powerful; but the times were changing, the people were becoming more enlightened, as was inevitable with the passing of time. As the Inquisition grew more powerful, so the nation appeared to be more devout—it had to do so to avoid the attention of the Inquisitors. Yet it was a surface devoutness, a matter of expediency; and the awakening to reality was beginning to set in.

Under Philip III the prosperity of the nation declined. The people were starving; the cloth-weaving industry was being ruined by the *alcabala*; the King's chief minister and favourite, the Duke of Lerma, had tampered with the currency; and all the time such extravagance was maintained at the Court as had never been indulged in during the reign of Philip II.

On the day when Philip IV was born the *Moriscos* had staged their rising; the King had discovered that they were guilty of plotting against Spain with Henry IV of France, with the Duke of Savoy, Elizabeth I, and with the King of Fez. They had been expelled from the country with the result that an industrious section of the population had been lost, the farmlands had become derelict and the irrigation system was no longer working.

In spite of signs of ruin, the King continued in his extravagant policy; and the people were taxed still further to pay for the lavish ceremonies in which the favourites delighted; and the King sought to ease his conscience by building convents.

But Philip III was not entirely stupid and was fully aware of the state to which the country was reduced. Early in 1619 he caused reports to be drawn up that he might have full understanding of the poverty which had overtaken his people; the results shocked him so profoundly that he called a halt to extravagance. He was not yet forty but he had little desire for life. He was clever enough to know that his rule had brought Spain to the state to which she had come. His great concern was to repent in time, that his soul might be saved; and to show that his repentance was genuine he sought to instil into his son the need to govern with wisdom and make a better job of kingship than his father had.

The favourites who had circulated about Philip III were aware of his delicate state of health, which was not helped by the remorse which had now come to him.

They considered the heir who, it seemed to them, would soon mount the throne and look for favourites of his own; the Duke of Lerma's enemies sought to place new favourites about the Infante, and one of these was Gaspar de Guzman, Count of Olivares, a young man of twenty-eight.

Olivares became a gentleman of the chamber to the Infante, and immediately began to exert a great influence over him. Philip, not yet fourteen, pale and sandy haired, was in awe of the handsome, domineering Olivares who began to form the boy's character as he wished it to be. At first young Philip had been a little resentful of Olivares, but the Count soon won the boy's respect and friendship, and then proceeded to arrange his household.

Olivares chose the Infante's servants who were all his own supporters; talked to the boy about the affairs of the country and instilled in him a desire to rule with greater success than his father had; and in every way prepared to become the power behind the throne on the death of Philip III, which it was clear at this stage could not be long delayed.

In 1612 the King's eldest daughter Ana was betrothed to Louis XIII of France, and the young Infante Philip to Isabel of Bourbon, eldest daughter of Henri Quatre.

The ceremonies that attended these betrothals and the entry of Isabel into Spain were extravagant in the extreme. In July 1619 the King and his son made a ceremonial visit to Portugal where the young fourteen-year-old boy, magnificent in white satin covered with gold and jewels and in black velvet shoulder cape, received the homage of the Portuguese who took their oaths to accept him as their ruler on the death of his father; then he in turn took his oath that he would respect their rights.

On this journey Olivares accompanied his Prince, for it was believed that the King's low state of health might prevent his ever returning to Madrid.

In November 1620, Olivares, who had encouraged the Infante in sexual adventure, decided that the married life of the boy and his young bride should commence; at this time Philip was fifteen and a half, and the couple started married life in the palace of Pardo under the eyes of Olivares.

Meanwhile the King's health was deteriorating rapidly and, although he occasionally made slight recovery, he was close to death. He was full of remorse for what he conceived to be an evil life since he was convinced that he had been an unworthy ruler; and he was hysterical, imploring his confessors to plead on his account with the saints; he was terrified of death; and on one occasion when he was very ill indeed the dead body of Saint Isadore of Madrid was brought to him that he might hold the corpse in his arms. When this was done and the King's health improved, all were sure that this was due to the presence of the dead body in his bed; but a few months after that brief recovery he was dying and this time nothing could save him.

Terrified of the vengeance which he felt would be waiting for him on his death, he sent for his son—now sixteen years old. He implored him to learn his lesson from his father's life; above all things he begged him to keep Spain absolutely Catholic and to see that his sister Mariia made a Catholic alliance (Charles, Prince of Wales, afterwards the ill-fated Charles I, was angling for Maria at this time).

This was the hour for which Olivares had been waiting. His young Infante was now Philip IV.

*   *   *

The new King was of a generous nature and kindly; in his youth he was less devoted to religion than his father had been and more fond of sensual pleasures. In public he conducted himself with the solemnity demanded of Spanish monarchs, but in private he was very gay and even witty; and the friends whose company he most delighted in were writers, actors, musicians and painters. He was later to become one of the greatest royal patrons of art.

His sensuality however governed all his feelings and he was unable to escape from it; and as he, like his father, was troubled by a conscience, he would suffer greatly after those debauches which, at the time he indulged in them, he was unable to resist.

His wife, Isabel, was charming and pretty, and Philip was delighted with her; but this did not prevent his continuing with ex-marital love affairs, for this indulgence, even at his early age, had become a habit. As for Isabel, she was the daughter of Marie de'Medici and the gallant Henri Quatre who has been said to have had more mistresses than any other king of France, even including François Premier. There was the inevitable scandal; and, although Philip found it impossible to be a faithful husband, he was very jealous of his wife.

It was very shortly after the wedding that the King showed his jealousy in the well-known incident concerning Don Juan de Tassis, the Count of Villa Mediana. It will be remembered that the Count was reputed to have ridden into the arena, during the jousts, his device being a mass of those silver coins known as *reals* (or royals). Above them were inscribed the words *My loves are*——. His ardent glances were directed towards the Queen and the meaning read into his actions was that he was attempting to win her favours. This was probably deliberately meant to discountenance the young King, because at that time Villa Mediana was seeking to win the affection of Francisca de Tavara who was one of Philip's mistresses.

He succeeded, however, in annoying the King, and the Queen did not help when she murmured to the King that Villa Mediana aimed well. Philip is reputed to have snapped ominously: "Yes—and he aims too high!"

A few months later another scene took place in which the gallant Count played a prominent part. Philip was enamoured of the play and Isabel shared his enthusiasm. To celebrate the King's seventeenth birthday a tent theatre was erected outdoors and the comedy *La Gloria de Niquea* was to be played for his entertainment, Queen Isabel herself taking a part.

During the play the stage curtain caught fire and Philip hastened to the back of the tent to see if Isabel were safe. The tent by that time was ablaze and, when Philip came upon his wife, he found her half fainting in the arms of Villa Mediana.

The gossips declared that the bold Count had staged the fire so that he might gallantly rescue the Queen.

These stories are said to be fabrications of over-imaginative writers, and historian Martin Hume is careful to state that some of them depend on the "untrustworthy evidence" of the French writer Madame d'Aulnoy; but there is no doubt that the final scene in the drama did take place.

Four months after the burning of the tent, one night when Villa Mediana was driving home, his coach passed under the arch of the Calle Mayor and as it did so a masked figure appeared and shot a bolt from a cross-bow at him. The aim was very accurate and Villa Mediana was pierced through the heart. Villa Mediana staggered out of the coach and was drawing his sword when he fell dying on the cobbles.

The King was suspected of having instigated this murder.

* * *

Both Philip and Isabel shared a love of pleasure. Philip would rise in the morning to find Olivares at his side instructing him in the affairs which had to be attended to that day; he was only too delighted to leave them in the hands of this man who, many said, was the true king of Spain.

If Philip and his Queen were fond of lavish spectacles and encouraged the theatre, they never forgot their duty to the Catholic Church and many of the spectacles they arranged, or which were arranged for them, were religious ceremonies.

This was an atmosphere in which the Inquisition flourished.

The first child, a princess, had been prematurely born in 1621, and had died; and the second, Margarita Maria, died a month after her birth; but before that, a lavish ceremony had been arranged to celebrate her birth and baptism.

The hysterical atmosphere of devotion will be understood when the affair of Reynard de Peralta is recalled.

This French pedlar wandered into the church of the Augustinian Monastery of St. Philip at that time when it was crowded with sightseers and worshippers who had come to give thanks for the birth of the baby Infanta.

Imagine Madrid at this time of celebration. The excitement would be intense, the bells ringing, the crowds jostling each other in the streets and particularly in the *Mentidero* (Liars' Walk) where actors, authors and those down on their luck assembled to exchange and recite satirical verse about the Court. At noon the angelus would call the hungry writers and their friends who would assemble at the gates of the monastery where bread and soup were given them; eagerly they would eat and talk endlessly of the hope the young King had given men of their profession.

And suddenly Reynard de Peralta walked into the church and made his gesture. He knelt at the altar and we are told that he insulted the Holy Mystery, which was tantamount to a denial of the Immaculate Conception.

Peralta was seized and dragged before the Tribunal of the Inquisition.

There was only one end for such a man; he was found guilty of heresy and handed to the secular arm for punishment. He repented in time and was reconciled, thus earning the mercy of strangulation before his body was burned.

But the hysteria which ran through Madrid after this event gives an indication as to why the Inquisition was in full flower.

The Church had been defiled, and Madrid was plunged in mourning on this account. More ceremonies were hastily devised, not brilliant, colourful displays, but processions marched through the streets carrying the cross draped in black crêpe; and in these processions walked men and women, bare-backed, flagellating themselves and each other, presumably in the hope of placating the Virgin Mary for the insult which had been paid to her by the heretic pedlar.

The churches were hung with black crêpe and for a whole week no plays were to be performed, and prostitutes were forbidden to ply their trade.

Madrid gave itself up to this religious hysteria during that week which was to have been devoted to festivity.

This was characteristic; side by side with profligacy and wanton extravagance was this ostentatious piety.

Two theatres had been built in Madrid; they were not in the least like the theatres which were to flourish in London under Charles II. They were situated in courtyards surrounded by houses; and the houses belonged to the owners of the theatre and formed part of it. At one end of the courtyard was a stage covered by tiled eaves; and there was an awning over the seats which were set up in the courtyard. Men occupied these seats, and the women used an enclosed space, not unlike a gallery, on the cobbles, which was given the name of *cazuela* (stewpan). In the houses, watching from the windows were the nobility. These two theatres became notorious for the intrigues which were carried on in the houses, where the most adventurous had all the opportunities they sought.

The Queen was very gay and often, to amuse her, fights would be started among the common people in the courtyard seats, and there was one occasion, so it is reported, when snakes were let loose in one of these courtyards so that the Queen could be amused by the panic of the people.

But the most exciting spectacle of all to the people of this time was the *auto de fé*, and the Inquisition was ready to provide the people with the amusement they demanded.

Philip and Isabel were present at the *auto* of 4th July, 1624; and because of this almost the whole Court attended also. Balconies had to be fitted up and hung with silks and velvet; and a special stage was erected. Because this was a royal occasion the stage was crowded with high officials of the Supreme Council, as well as those from the Inquisition of Toledo and the Town Council of Madrid.

The evening before the day of the *auto* the procession left the Convent of Doña Maria de Aragon carrying the great green cross in accordance with the usual custom, but on this day the bearer of the cross was the Constable of Castile, and the Admiral of Castile was entrusted with the tassels of the banner.

Early next morning Philip and Isabel left the palace with the Court for the balconies, and as soon as they were seated the procession began.

Many of the victims on this occasion were Jews who, it was said, had been in the habit of meeting in a house in the Calle de las Infantas in order to practise the rites of the Law of Moses and to insult Christians by flogging a crucifix.

The Inquisitor-General administered the oath to Philip to keep the purity of the Church inviolate at no matter what cost; and this oath was afterwards repeated by the members of the council. The King's confessor preached his sermon, the sentences were read; and at three o'clock in the afternoon, when all these ceremonies were concluded, the prisoners were led to their punishment—seven of them condemned to be burned alive in the *quemadero*.

There can be little doubt that while Philip and his Queen proved their devotion to the Church by showing themselves at scenes like this, they believed that they were expiating their sins, and since they could be so pious their little frivolities were of no account.

This was the spirit in which the Inquisition flourished; and the nation followed the example set by the Court.

*   *   *

Olivares was determined to lead the King. No one was allowed to enter the royal bedchamber before he did; he himself drew the curtains and stood beside the King whilst he dressed, never allowing Philip to put on a garment which had not passed through his hands.

He was nearly twenty years older than Philip and Philip took his advice on all matters. Olivares was not a man who was out to gain wealth and power merely for his own gratification; he wished to make the country strong and if his policies eventually failed it was because of a lack of unity in Spain. The Aragonese stood aloof, as did the Catalans; as though they had been separate states. Portugal was a conquered country and had never given real allegiance to Spain. Such a lack of unity brought Olivares, good statesman though he was, face to face with insurmountable difficulties which were eventually to give his enemies the chance they needed.

He was determined that he and he alone should lead the King, and each morning when he entered the royal bedchamber to draw the curtains, his pockets would be stuffed with state papers, and documents would even be stuck in the band of his hat, which caused a great deal of amusement to the Court who wondered how the pleasure-loving King could tolerate such a reminder of business at an early hour in the morning when he was sleeping off the effects of last night's junketings.

However, Olivares remained supreme in those early years of the reign, and his power even over the Inquisition is apparent in the rather comic affair of the *Golilla*.

During the reign of Philip III enormous ruffs had become fashionable. Some of these were quite ridiculous, and efforts had been made to change the fashion and to bring back the Walloon collar into general use. This flat collar which fell on to the shoulders was very plain after the glorious ruffs, and the people rejected it; their grounds for doing so were that it was greatly favoured by the Flemings and therefore the collar was connected with heresy in the minds of the people.

Then a tailor of the Calle Mayor invented a new collar. This was made of cardboard which was covered with cloth to match the doublet and lined with silk. Heated irons and shellac applied to the cardboard enabled the tailor to make it into a most graceful shape which bent outwards where it reached the chin and showed the beautiful silk lining.

When he had completed the collar the tailor took it to the King, who was delighted with it; and the tailor considering this patronage from the King, believed he had made his fortune with the *Golilla*, which was the name given to the new collar. No doubt the tailor had his rivals—those makers of ruffs and Walloons—who realized that his success would mean their failure, and it was very easy to trump up a charge against him. How did he achieve that wondrous sweeping curve? He had some devilish machine for doing it, and it was sorcery because, it was said, while the irons were applied he must mutter incantations to his master, the Devil.

Very soon someone had informed the Inquisition, and the tailor was brought before the Tribunal, on a charge of sorcery. The Inquisition ordered that all the goods should be taken from his shop and burned before his door.

Fortunately for the tailor he had supplied the collars to the King, and he sent frantic messages to Olivares begging his help.

Olivares, who no doubt had decided to adopt the *Golilla* which did not have to be washed and lasted for about a year, was annoyed; he summoned the Inquisitors to his presence, jeered at their stupidity and ordered the immediate release of the tailor.

As the tailor was released and allowed to continue making collars, it is clear that Olivares was the most powerful man in Spain. In a very short time *Golillas* were being generally worn there and in other countries; in France they were less popular, the French considering them somewhat inelegant and inventing the jabot and the lace cravat to replace them.

In 1634, when the finances of Spain were very low indeed, Olivares began negotiations with Jews in the Levant and Africa, and granted licences for certain of them to return to Spain. He explained that they should have a district in Madrid assigned to them, for he believed that they could bring financial prosperity back to the country.

Again he shows how powerful was his position, since he dared make such a suggestion; but, touched on such a vulnerable spot, the Inquisition roused itself and demanded the dismissal of Olivares, for, it was said, if such a man were allowed to make his wild dreams actualities, the Faith of Spain would be ruined.

Philip, under the sway of Olivares as he was, was nevertheless subservient to the Inquisition; like his father he was from time to time worried by his conscience and feared what was waiting for him on the other side of death.

This time the Inquisition won, regarding the Jews.

On another occasion Olivares demanded to see records of certain cases with which the Inquisition was dealing. This the

Inquisitor-General, at this time Sotomayor, refused to allow; but Olivares became threatening and Sotomayor was forced to comply. Sotomayor melodramatically laid the papers at the foot of a crucifix, hoping to appeal to the superstition in Olivares. But Olivares was unimpressed by such gestures; he seized the papers, burned them and freed the prisoners whom they concerned.

It was said that one of Olivares's projects was to abolish the Inquisition altogether, and that he would seize an opportunity of advising the King to this course. But Philip was the kind of man who clung to religion; to indulge in religious ceremonies, after an extravagant debauch, comforted him. He felt that whatever the state of Spain, she was still a Catholic country. He would never have consented to the abolition of the Inquisition, the iron rule of which kept the country Catholic.

The Inquisition, naturally, did not forget the man who had done so much to perturb it.

*   *   *

Olivares had his worries. In 1627 Philip fell ill and it was believed that he could not live. His baby daughter had died and the Queen was pregnant, but Olivares was uncertain of the Queen's ability to bear a child who would live. Carlos, the elder of the King's two brothers (the other, Fernando, had been made a cardinal), was no friend of Olivares.

While the King lay in this desperate state, his bedchamber full of old bones and other relics which had been brought in the hope of saving him, plots were going on to oust Olivares from his position.

But this time the King recovered and Olivares had the pleasure of discomfiting his enemies.

Philip's conscience troubled him greatly at such times. He was worried about the life he had led. He had had thirty illegitimate children—perhaps more—and some of these had received great honours. The most favoured was Don John of Austria, a very handsome boy on whom Philip doted, for, as happened so often in royal houses, while he failed to get a legitimate heir, his bastards were healthy and handsome—and Don John was the healthiest and most handsome of them all.

Moreover Philip had been deeply in love with the boy's mother, Maria Calderon, who was a sixteen-year-old actress when Philip first saw her. The King, watching her from the *aposento* (one of those rooms of the houses which looked on the courtyard of the theatre) decided to make her his mistress. Maria was a very virtuous girl, and remained faithful to the King; she looked forward to the day when the King should cease to desire her, for it was a custom that a king's mistress should have no other lover and that when the affair was over she should retire to a convent. When Don John was born, Maria begged to be allowed to go into a convent; and Philip, who was deeply in love with her, tried to dissuade her from this; but eventually he gave way to her pleadings, made her an abbess, and remained devoted to her son.

In October 1629, six months after the birth of Don John, Philip's legitimate son was born: Baltasar Carlos, Infante of Spain and heir to the throne.

*   *   *

Olivares had succeeded in winning the enmity of the Queen, for, since he undertook to pander to the King's pleasures, this was almost inevitable. Moreover, he excluded her from political matters. Therefore, while continuing in the King's good graces, the minister was accumulating a large number of enemies in high places, and the Queen's position was strengthened as young Baltasar Carlos appeared to be growing into a healthy boy.

A quarrel arose between the Inquisition and the judges of the Court; and some minor officials on both sides were imprisoned by the authorities on the opposing side. Lawlessness broke out in the capital and there was war with France. Everything that went wrong was blamed on Olivares.

But Olivares was still strong; and when the nobleman, Lujanes, made a scene in the royal chapel by kneeling before the King and imploring him to rid himself of Olivares, although poor Lujanes was declared to be mad he was imprisoned and when he died mysteriously a few days later it was generally believed that the minister had arranged for him to be poisoned.

Lujanes was not the only one who protested against the minister; the people in the streets cried out that he must go.

Olivares gained more enemies when he brought to the Court a young man of twenty-eight whom he acknowledged as his son. This young man was now known as Enrique Felipe de Guzman, and previously had been brought up by a Madrid government official. Enrique Felipe was by no means attractive, and was in fact somewhat crude in manners; before he had been brought to Court and acknowledged by Olivares, he had married, but this was declared invalid as Olivares wanted a grander marriage for his son. Philip was induced to bestow honours upon him, and Olivares demanded for him the daughter of the Duke of Frias, Constable of Castile—and the Duke agreed to the demand, being afraid to do otherwise.

But although he was still master at Court, the people were

murmuring against Olivares. He needed money to face the French; the Portuguese had escaped from Spanish domination; the currency had been debased; many people were in prisons in Madrid because they had either refused to pay or could not pay the taxes demanded of them; and for all these misfortunes the people blamed Olivares. They said that he had advised the King to legitimize Don John of Austria, merely because he wished to bring his own illegitimate son to Court and have him legitimized.

Olivares now had too many powerful enemies; the Queen, his rivals at Court, the people and the Inquisition.

The Spanish on sea and land were being beaten and the French were already on Spanish soil. Philip roused himself from his pleasure-loving existence and determined to put himself at the head of his troops. Olivares opposed this, but Philip, at last, decided to act against the advice of the minister who had dominated him so long. The Queen became Regent and Olivares was no favourite of the Queen. He joined the King but he was beginning to see that his hold on the monarch was slackening.

The Queen was successful in raising money and plate for the war, and the people were enthusiastically on her side; moreover certain members of Olivares's own family were now turning against him because he had legitimized Enrique Felipe, and thus their chances of profit from their influential relative were lessened.

Philip's army was defeated by Marshall de la Motte before Lerida in 1642, and Philip was told that unless he changed his counsels he would lose his crown. When Philip returned to Madrid the Queen took their son, Baltasar Carlos, to him and implored him to cast off Olivares, if not for his own sake for that of the child. His old foster-mother, Ana de Guevara, waylaid him as he left the Queen and implored him to rid himself of Olivares. She reminded the King that Olivares had banished her and that she had only been able to return to the Court during his absence, for the sad fact was that Olivares wished to banish from the King's side all whom he loved, because he feared they might impair his own influence. The King was deeply moved by this and wrote to Olivares, telling him that he gave him leave to retire. Olivares could not believe that he was dismissed, but he was to discover that at last his enemies had separated him from the King. Philip went to the Escorial for two or three days so that he might not see the departure of the man who had been his intimate friend and counsellor for twenty-two years.

It has been suggested that the secret methods of the Inquisition were used to bring about Olivares's downfall, and that even when the ex-minister was living in obscurity there were those who sought to put an end to his life. As for Philip, he was a man of some sentiment, and he often thought of recalling Olivares; this would have aroused revolt, Philip knew, for he was constantly being urged that death should have been the reward of his ex-minister.

The people were demanding his head, and the Inquisition would not have forgotten that he had once tried to destroy it; it may have been that it considered it could never allow such a man to continue to live.

The King must have come very near to granting the requests for vengeance on Olivares, for when the latter wrote to him asking to be allowed to end his exile, Philip answered that he must reign and his son must be crowned King of Aragon; yet he was afraid that this might not be unless he delivered the head of Olivares to the people.

This letter unnerved Olivares, and it is reported that on receiving it he went mad and died. This event took place on 22nd July, 1645, over two years after his dismissal.

15

THE INQUISITION UNDER PHILIP IV

ALL THIS time the Inquisition had been working as zealously as ever, the mental climate of the country suiting its unhealthy growth. The King, that conscience-stricken sensualist, was typical of his country's mood; and it was as though he believed that the poverty of the people and the disastrous relations with other countries could be hidden by this flaunting show of piety, these lavish ceremonies which were conducted with such pomp in the streets and had their hideous climax in the *quemadero*.

After the dismissal of Olivares the King desperately tried to reform his ways. He was beginning to believe that his conduct had brought his country's fortunes to this present state and he grew maudlin in his repentance.

It was at this time that he met Sor Maria de Agreda. He was travelling with Don Luis de Haro (the nephew of Olivares whom since the fall of the latter he had made one of his chief ministers, for Don Luis had turned against his uncle when he had brought forward Enrique Felipe and had him legitimized), when they visited the Convent of the Immaculate Conception at Agreda.

Sor Maria was the abbess; a woman of about forty at this time, she had written many mystical books and the King was eager to meet her; when he did so he was so impressed by her wisdom that he and she became lifelong friends.

He wrote to her regularly, consulting her on all matters. One letter of his begins by pointing out that he has left a wide margin so that she can comment on his remarks, and he tells her that the contents of the letter are for her eyes alone.

Six hundred letters passed between Sor Maria and the King during the twenty-two years of this strange friendship; she was Philip's chief adviser until she died in 1655; Philip himself died four months later.

Sor Maria was noted for her piety and the revelations which were reputed to have come to her; she was said to be in constant communication with God, the Virgin, and the angels.

When the Cortes of Aragon made complaints to Philip concerning the Inquisition, which was hated in Aragon to a greater extent than in Castile (for in Aragon the Inquisition was at its most powerful), Philip was perplexed. As one minister had said, the Inquisition was to Philip as one of his eyes; he felt that while he upheld it and it provided him with spectacular *autos de fé* he could feel that he had upheld the Faith of Spain and that if misfortune had come to him it must be through the will of God. Yet he feared a rising in Aragon which could cost him his crown.

On this occasion he did not ask the advice of his ministers but of the nun, Sor Maria. In spite of her mysticism she must have had a shrewd mind, and there is no doubt that she had a deep affection for the King. When he told her that he must preserve the Faith of Spain at all costs and therefore would support the Inquisition with all his might, she begged him to think again and consider what revolt in Aragon would mean at this stage of the country's fortunes. Catalonia was in revolt; what if the Aragonese joined the Catalonians? What would happen then to the unity of Spain?

As a result the officials of the Aragonese Inquisition lost many of their privileges; and this was apparent when the murder of Inquisitor Lazaeta occurred.

Inquisitor Lazaeta was having a love affair with a married woman in San Anton. The woman's husband, Miguel Choved, discovering this, prepared to trap the lovers, and told his wife that he was going on a journey. Choved's wife arranged that her lover should visit her after dark, which he did; the Inquisitor's coach was left in a near-by street and he went to the house to which some time later Choved came back. Lazaeta's coachman grew restive when his master did not return, and going in search of him found his dead body lying on the cobbles of a near-by alley. Both the Choveds disappeared, but a servant, Francisco Arnal, was arrested by the Inquisition for having helped to commit the murder.

The court of Justicia, however, intervened and there was trouble between the ecclesiastical and secular courts. The Supreme Council then declared that it would be better to remove the Tribunal from Aragon than that it should be submitted to such humiliation. This was a clear indication of how the new laws had reduced the power of the Inquisition in Aragon.

In 1644 the Queen was suffering from erysipelas and some form of choleraic attack. She died in October. Only two children survived her—the heir, Baltasar Carlos, and Maria Teresa. The King was filled with grief, for in spite of his infidelities he had had a great affection for his pleasure-loving Queen whose character had not been unlike his own. Letters to Sor Maria continued to be written, when he implored her to intercede for him with the saints that he might overcome his misfortunes. Philip mourned for the poverty he saw in his country and wept for the misery of his people; yet at the same time he did little to curb his own extravagance. It was comforting to believe that everything that happened was due to the will of God; yet at the same time his conscience worried him; but that was soothed by the signs of piety in the punishment meted out to heretics in the great *autos de fé*.

Sor Maria wrote that he must purge Madrid of its sin. She heard that men and women promenaded in the Liars' Walk, and that their dress, conversation, and manners were far from becoming, and most unsuitable for subjects of this Catholic country.

Philip, becoming more and more under the spell of this nun, tried to carry out her advice and, much to the people's dismay and astonishment (for Philip had been a devotee of them), the theatres were closed. It is only fair to say that Sor Maria advised Philip to look closely into the system of the press-gang which, in seizing men to fight, caused great hardship to their families; and that her counsel was often followed to the good of the country.

In 1646 Baltasar Carlos began to suffer from tertian fever, and Philip was overcome with fear at this threat to the life of his heir. He wrote to Sor Maria that if he did not believe that his troubles were sent as warnings from Heaven, in order that he might prepare for the salvation of his soul, he could not endure them.

Baltasar Carlos was betrothed to Mariana of Austria, but later that year he succumbed to the fevers, and Philip's grief at the death of his beloved son was great. He became listless and left the governing of the country to his favourites, which distressed Sor Maria who told him she had had a vision of Baltasar Carlos who informed her that he was grieved to see his father surrounded by men who sought their own advantage rather than that of the nation. (At the time of the Queen's death Sor Maria had said she had had a vision of the Queen who had expressed her distress at the manners of the women of Madrid.)

Philip answered her with more spirit than usual, pointing out that it was necessary for a king to employ ministers. He did not shirk his duty, he insisted, for he was constantly at his desk, his pen in his hand.

"A Visit from the Inquisitors."
Engraving by J. Godfrey after the picture by D. W. Wynfield

"The Unholy Tribunal." Nineteenth-century engraving

Philip IV in prayer. The portrait in the Prado Gallery,
Madrid, attributed to Velasquez

Sor Maria replied by urging him to take up arms once more against the French who had been defeated at Lerida.

The death of Baltasar Carlos had aroused anxieties concerning the succession, and the King, who was only forty-two, was urged by his ministers to marry again. They eyed the ambitious Don John of Austria with some misgiving, for he would not readily be accepted as king. Philip had one legitimate child—a daughter aged eight, Maria Teresa, who was eventually to marry Louis XIV. In 1649 Philip married his niece Mariana (the daughter of his sister, Maria). She was fifteen at the time of the marriage, and for a time Philip was absorbed in this union. He had been writing to Sor Maria explaining how hard he had tried not to indulge in amorous intrigues, and how the habit of a lifetime had been too much for him. Now he declared he would reform; he would never stray from the virtuous life; he would devote himself to his young wife, and he prayed that before long the union would be blessed with an heir—which was after all, the sole reason for its having taken place.

Philip soon tired of this child-wife and resumed the old habits, but in 1651 a daughter was born. This was Margaret Maria (whose portrait is to be seen in Velasquez's *The Maids of Honour*). To Philip Mariana was a child more suited to be the companion of his daughter, Maria Teresa, and he often referred to her as "my niece" as though he had forgotten that she was also his wife and the Queen of Spain. Mariana grew homesick when she realized that the King had lost interest in her, and then she must have found the etiquette of the Spanish Court stifling. An example of Spanish formality is given by the conduct of young Maria Teresa at the christening ceremonies of Margaret Maria. Taking off her gloves, Maria Teresa dropped a very valuable diamond bracelet, but when a woman, in the crowd pressing about her, picked it up and handed it to her, she refused it, for it was a matter of etiquette that no royal person must take anything direct from a commoner. Hastily officials signed to the woman that she might keep the bracelet, so there was one person on that occasion who must have been very thankful for the formality of Spanish court manners. (Hume from Florez's *Reinas Catolicas*.)

Mariana bore other girls who died soon after their birth, and Philip—and the country—despaired of a male heir, but eventually in 1657, a boy was born, and named Philip Prosper.

Three years later Philip's daughter, Maria Teresa, was married to Philip's nephew, *le Roi Soleil* (one of the results of a peace between the two countries); but Philip was still beset by anxieties, for the heir was proving to be a sickly little fellow and there was little hope of his reaching manhood. He died in November 1661; and Philip wrote to Sor Maria that he saw he had offended God and was being punished for his sins.

His health declined. He suffered, among other things, from gallstones, and when Sor Maria begged him to take care of his health he answered that he asked nothing but that God's will be done. Now that he felt himself to be growing near to his end his conscience was even more active; and because he was not blindly foolish he realized that his indolence and love of pleasure had had an adverse effect on the fortunes of Spain.

Ambitious Louis XIV was a dangerous neighbour; Mariana was already thinking of the time after Philip's death when she would be a power in the land. She had borne him another son, a very delicate boy, whose jaw was malformed so that he could not speak clearly, and who was obviously mentally deficient. But he was the heir to the throne and, while he lived and his mother could occupy the regency, her position would be a powerful one. Thus was the dying Philip aware of the desire for power which had been stirred within his niece-wife. Sor Maria had recently died and he was without her guidance.

In June 1665 the Spanish suffered great defeat at the hands of the Portuguese who had been helped by the English since the marriage of Charles II of England to Catherine of Braganza; men and equipment had been lost and Philip had no means of providing more.

Dying Philip looked back over his life and saw to what a pass his great Empire had been reduced since the great days of Emperor Charles and Philip II—great-grandfather and grandfather. He believed that this was God's revenge for all those nights of revelling and illegitimate children, of the number of whom he was uncertain.

He fell into such a mood of melancholy that many believed he was bewitched. There was a rumour that the Inquisitor-General had been trying to free the King from the spell, and that the evil forces had brought about his death for this reason. Many of the writers and artists at the Court laughed at these ideas and insisted that the ailments of the body had produced these symptoms; but the men of the Church insisted that Satan was responsible for the King's maladies, and the new Inquisitor-General, with the help of his confessor, went through the King's collection of relics, because they feared some evil charm might have been put among them.

In the Dominican monastery of the Atocha a book on witchcraft and some pictures of the King, in which pins had been stuck, were burned with solemnity.

Neither these remedies nor those of the physicians were effective, and on the 17th of September, 1665, Philip IV died.

*   *   *

It was during this reign that the Inquisition reached those heights of power which it was never to touch again; and the reason for this is seen in the character of the King which was reflected in the nature of the Court, which in its turn had its effect upon the mood of the people.

The King was weak but he longed to be good; and he saw in strict adherence to what he thought of as religious duty, the neutralizer of pleasure. He indulged in his debauches, but he supported the Inquisition; he committed his sins but he could confess and be given his penance, and all was well.

Thus the Inquisition was as his "right eye" to him; his weak indecisive policy, his reliance on favourites, had brought low the temporal power of his country; but he had determined that that quality on which Philip II had insisted (the unity of faith) should be kept intact.

There was one quality in this King, though, the importance of which had not been seen during his reign. He had made of Madrid a great artistic centre, surrounding himself with writers and painters. He had found one of his greatest pleasures in the work of Velasquez in whose studio he had passed many pleasant hours. Thus he had brought into the country an element which was to make itself felt.

A new age of enlightenment was coming to Spain; and in that atmosphere the Inquisition would find its way made less easy; it would have to fight for its survival.

16

THE CASE OF VILLANUEVA

THROUGHOUT THE history of the Inquisition there are many instances of trouble between the sovereigns of countries and the Papacy, the Pope being eager to retain control of ecclesiastical trials, the sovereigns determined that they should reign supreme in their lands. One of the most interesting and important examples which occurred during the reign of Philip IV is that of Gerónimo de Villanueva.

Gerónimo de Villanueva was Marquis of Villalba, an ancient Aragonese family. Olivares had favoured him—and consequently so had Philip—and he held many offices under the Crown.

Villanueva had been involved in the case of Teresa de Silva and the nuns of San Placido. It will be remembered that many of the nuns in the convent, including Teresa, their abbess, were reputed to be possessed by demons and indulged in the wildest conduct. Villanueva with the family of Teresa de Silva had supplied the money to found the convent of La Encarnacion Bedita de San Placido and had appointed Fray Francisco Garcia de Calderon as confessor. Calderon was denounced to the Inquisition in time and tried at Toledo, while the nuns were arrested and made to confess what the Inquisitors wished them to, with the result that Calderon was judged to be guilty of teaching heresy and of being an *alumbrado*. He was sentenced to perpetual imprisonment, Teresa was sent to a convent for four years, and the nuns placed in different convents.

Villanueva could not remain aloof from the scandals which had touched San Placido and Calderon. The house in which he lived adjoined the convent and he had spent a great deal of time there. During Calderon's trial it had leaked out that witnesses had actually seen him, his head on Teresa's lap, in most affectionate manner, while she hunted for lice in his head.

It was recalled that the revelations of Teresa and her nuns had concerned the future glory of the convent, Calderon and Villanueva. They had prophesied that Calderon would become Pope, reign for thirty-three years, and reform the world with the help of Villanueva.

The Inquisition decided that he was either guilty of practising heresy or of condoning it, but since Villanueva was a favourite of Olivares, who at that time ruled the King, the Inquisition was wary of bringing an accusation against him.

Yet Villanueva was fully aware of the power of the Holy Office and although Olivares and the King might wish to protect him, he knew that the latter was fanatically behind the Inquisition; so Villanueva presented himself to one of the chief Inquisitors, Antonio de Sotomayor, who later that year was to become Inquisitor-General, admitting that he had put his confidence mistakenly in Calderon, and that if he had sinned against the Church in doing so he was prepared to do penance.

While Villanueva was eager not to offend the Inquisition because of the King's regard for the institution, the Inquisition was eager not to offend *him* because of his standing with the King and Olivares, and he was proclaimed not guilty and a certificate was given to him accordingly.

Having secured his own acquittal he decided to work on behalf of the nuns that they might return to the convent. This would be a difficult matter, for if he could prove the nuns innocent that was tantamount to proving the Inquisition guilty of false judgment. However, Villanueva was shrewd and clever and although it took some time to make a case for the nuns he did this. They were, he insisted, innocent; they had done nothing but obey Calderon who had been set above them as their spiritual adviser. Was it wrong to obey a spiritual adviser? Nine judges were appointed to try the case again. Pressure from Villanueva, and possibly Olivares, made the nine judges eager to give the desired verdict; but they were again anxious not to offend the Inquisition. Their verdict was that the nuns were innocent, but the judges added that had they been asked to consider the evidence which had been laid before that tribunal they also would have pronounced them guilty.

Words were carefully chosen, gestures were very graceful; the fact remained that Calderon became the scapegoat and the nuns returned to San Placido.

But the Inquisition had a long memory and it was scarcely likely that it felt very pleased with Villanueva. He had come safely out of the case of the possessed nuns because he had influential friends at Court, but once those friends were removed, it would not be necessary to treat him with such leniency. The storm was growing about Olivares and, if that minister fell from grace, the Inquisition need not have the same fear of reopening the case against Villanueva, for they often reopened cases when it was expedient to do so.

St. Pius V had laid down the rule that acquittals for heresy should not be held *res judicata* and permanent, whoever pronounced them. The moment might not be propitious, but the Inquisition would continue to remain alert. Villanueva was a rich man and therefore a worthy prey; he had won a case against the Inquisition when he had re-established his nuns; it may have been that the Inquisition had its eyes on an even greater prize— Olivares, for there is an opinion that the Inquisition was behind the downfall of Philip's favourite minister. If Villanueva fell into the hands of the Inquisition, it would certainly be easy to discover evidence against Olivares. Therefore the Inquisition was waiting to bring Villanueva into its web.

There is a story of a scandal in which Villanueva, the King, and the nuns of San Placido were concerned.

As has been said, Villanueva's house was next door to the convent in the Calle de Madera, and he was a frequent visitor to the convent. He had also, with Olivares, helped to arrange the King's love affairs; and after the rehabilitation of the nuns he discovered one of them to be an exceptionally beautiful young woman, and told the King about her.

Philip, ever amorous, was captivated by the prospect of seducing a beautiful nun, and Villanueva, who had done so much for the convent with his money and influence, was able to take the disguised King inside the convent walls.

The nun however had taken her vows and the King could only speak to her through the grille, she declaring that they could not meet in any other way. The King grew impatient, and Olivares and Villanueva, always ready to appease his desires, no doubt to keep him from meddling too much in state affairs, determined that his passion for the beautiful nun should be consummated.

Villanueva begged the nun to renounce her vows, and so that no time should be wasted, Philip growing more impatient as though for fear his conscience would begin to trouble him before the affair was completed, Villanueva set workmen making a passage from his cellars to the convent, so that, once the nun was ready, the King could visit her with the greatest ease whenever he wished.

The nun, however, in a moment of panic confessed to the abbess, Teresa, what was about to happen, and Teresa begged Villanueva to reconsider what he was doing and what would happen to him and the convent if it were discovered. Villanueva merely laughed at her. This adventure concerned the King; none, not even the Inquisition, would dare criticize what he did.

The passage was ready, the plans were made, and the nun was

to be waiting for the King in that cloister which was now connected by the passage with the house next door.

The King, led by Villanueva, arrived in the cloister, to find it in gloom, except at that spot where tapers lighted a bier. Stretched out on this bier was the beautiful nun, in her hands a crucifix.

This dramatic gesture was typical of the hysterical Teresa, who had sought to deter the King presumably by the implication that the nun would better be dead than become his mistress.

Philip, whose superstitious fears were never far away and whose conscience was always stalking him, so we are told, shivered at the sight of the woman on the bier and made with all speed through the secret passage to Villanueva's house.

According to the story, however, his desire was stronger than either superstition or conscience, and later the affair continued in less dramatic but more comfortable circumstances.

The affairs of kings have always been of great interest to their subjects, and it was not long before it was known that the King had a new mistress; and the Inquisition discovered that she was one of the nuns of San Placido—that convent which had been re-established after the tribunal had ordered that it should be disbanded and its inmates scattered.

It was a delicate matter since the King himself was so vitally concerned, but the Inquisitor-General, Sotomayor, who was Philip's confessor (and it had been thought by the King and Olivares, completely in the latter's power) was obliged to remonstrate with the King on his behaviour and to try to appeal to his conscience that he might stop visiting the nun; in which case it might be possible to bring a charge against Villanueva.

Olivares by this time was deeply conscious of powerful enemies all about him, and he felt the Inquisitor-General to be one of them, since he had dared remonstrate with the King.

An opportunity came to rid themselves of Sotomayor, and Olivares and the King took it. Although Philip usually gave his full support to the Inquisition he had on occasions stood out against it. Aragon had asked that all officials of the tribunals should be men of Aragon, and Philip had promised that he would use his influence with the Inquisition that this should be so. As a consequence he made several appointments which did not meet with the approval of the Inquisition and there was a certain controversy. The result of this was that, when a high position in the Tribunal was to be filled, a list of three names must be submitted to Philip that he might select from them; thus both King and Inquisition would, in a way, have a say in the selection. The Supreme Council had agreed to this but Sotomayor was not entirely satisfied.

For this reason (officially at least) he was made an offer. He must resign his position as Inquisitor-General and leave for Cordova when he would be given 12,000 ducats a year; if he failed to do this he would be dismissed his office and banished from Spain. He might make his choice. It is obvious what Sotomayor's choice was.

When the Pope expressed his desire to examine the case of Villanueva, the Inquisition prepared to forward all the documents concerning him to Rome, and selected as their messenger a certain Paredes.

Olivares and the King determined that these papers should never fall into the Pope's hands if they could help it; they prevented Paredes leaving immediately and one of the Court painters did several sketches of him; these were hastily dispatched to Philip's agents in the coast towns of Italy through which Paredes would have to pass on his way to Rome. With the sketches went orders that Paredes was to be kidnapped immediately he was sighted in Italy.

The plan succeeded, and no sooner had the messenger landed at Genoa than he was seized and imprisoned in the castle of Ovo at Naples. Poor man, because he had been selected as the Inquisition's messenger he was to spend the rest of his life—fifteen years —in prison there.

The papers he had been carrying with him were taken back to Olivares who, as soon as they were in his hands, took them to the King; they were destroyed in Philip's private apartment.

Sotomayor was followed as Inquisitor-General by Diego de Arce y Reynoso, Bishop of Plasencia, who wrote to the Pope asking his views on the case, but as the messenger and the documents had vanished there was no proof against Villanueva.

The disgrace of Olivares followed shortly and, with this favourite out of the way, Villanueva was no longer so secure. The Inquisition had a long memory and was determined to take him in the end.

Philip was in a state of melancholy; the affair with the nun had long petered out, and the King had no doubt overcome the worrying of his conscience concerning this and was probably engaged in another. Spain was in a desperate plight; three disastrous wars had imperilled her status, and now Philip had been deprived of the minister whom he had trusted to govern the kingdom for the last twenty years. The Inquisition felt that this was the moment to strike at Villanueva and it began with the Convent of San Placido.

A letter was drawn up to be signed by Philip, in which it was stated that the King was greatly concerned about the affair of the possessed nuns which had never been satisfactorily cleared up.

Philip's signature on this was obtained without any difficulty and, as a result, Inquisitors visited the convent for the purpose of building up a new case against Villanueva.

There were fresh papers which indicated that Villanueva had been accustomed to writing down the words of the demons which came from the mouths of the nuns, that he had fervently believed in the existence of the demons, and dabbled in astrology. This was heresy against the Church, and the Inquisition felt itself justified in acting.

The chose their time carefully and waited until the King was away on the campaign in Catalonia.

At two o'clock in the afternoon at siesta time, two Inquisitors, Ortiz and Calaya, called on Villanueva, took him out to a coach, which was waiting, forced him inside and were quickly driven with him through the quiet streets out to Toledo.

Villanueva was put in a cell in which was a little cot; there he was kept in solitude, and Philip at that time could have had no notion of what had happened, for secret dispatches continued to arrive for Villanueva which had to be dealt with by others; but when Philip was informed of the arrest and was told that it had been carried out in the service of the Faith, so subservient was he to the Inquisition, so eager to placate his God with his piety, that he did nothing to save Villanueva, declaring that he only lived to preserve the Holy Catholic Faith in his country.

The arrest caused apprehension in many quarters. The country was in danger and the Inquisition had arrested one of its principal ministers. Villanueva had been a very influential man and, if he had enemies, he also had friends. The kingdom of Aragon expressed its disapproval of the Inquisition's action, and it was said that a man of such a great family, which had for years served the state well, should have been treated with more dignity and imprisoned in a private house, if it was necessary to imprison him at all.

Philip, however, conscience-stricken by the weight of his peccadilloes—no doubt thinking of the nun on the bier—remained silent to the pleas, and gave his support to the Inquisition.

Villanueva, suffering from acute mental strain, became very ill and was allowed to have one of his servants to look after him; but when Philip returned to Madrid on account of the Queen's illness, he did nothing to help his old favourite.

Villanueva's trial lingered on according to the usual custom, and it was not until two years after his arrest that he was tried and sentenced.

He was found to be suspected of heresy, though not vehemently, and in February 1647 he was called to an audience chamber to hear his sentence. He was reprimanded for his conduct and warned that it must never occur again; he was to have nothing more to do with the nuns of San Placido and was never again to live in the house next door to the convent, but was to be banished for three years from Madrid and Toledo and twenty leagues around them.

Considering the fate of so many, this seems a light sentence; but it must be remembered that Villanueva had been one of the most important ministers in the country, and his career was ruined; he had suffered more than three years' imprisonment, and his family who were disgraced with him worked indefatigably to secure a remission of the sentence. His two brothers and one sister were all in important positions in the country (Ana had become abbess of San Placido, and one brother was a proctor, the other a Justíca). The Inquisition, however, was deaf to these appeals.

When Villanueva heard his sentence he was enraged, and in a frenzy of anger he shouted accusations at his judges; as a result he was taken back to his cell and later put in a secret prison where he was treated with much harshness.

He had been commanded to abjure *de levi* and this he refused to do until he was warned that failure to comply meant that he would be handed to the secular arm to be condemned to the stake.

Agustin, the Justíca, worked hard for his brother and applied to Rome; Philip also appealed to the Pope pointing out that if he used his influence on Villanueva's behalf after the Inquisition had sentenced him, this would be harmful to the Catholic Faith; but Joseph Navarro, who had been sent to Rome by Agustin, was able, in spite of the protests of Philip's ambassador, to obtain Papal permission for an appeal.

Villanueva, hearing what was happening and realizing that the Pope was far away and he was at the mercy of Philip and the Inquisition, wrote to Philip telling him that although Papal permission had been granted for an appeal against his sentence he was ready to forgo this if it was the will of the King. The Inquisitor-General meanwhile refused to accept the Papal brief. This was one of the most notorious differences between the Papacy and the Inquisition in Spain.

The King and the Inquisitor-General were ready to plunge into conflict with the Pope—Innocent X—but a junta of six of the leading statesmen of Spain summed up their views of the case; and even those who were not on the side of Villanueva decided that, in view of the present ferment in Naples which might lead to revolt, it would be very unwise to arouse the Pope's anger against Spain, for then Spanish possessions in Italy might be in real danger.

Had it not been for the views of this junta, Villanueva would undoubtedly have been persecuted further.

Innocent was furious at the manner in which his brief had been treated, and threatened Arce, the Inquisitor-General, with excommunication and dismissal from his post. Arce wrote placatingly to Innocent telling him that Villanueva had been treated with justice and even kindness and that it was necessary for the Inquisition to have great power, for heresy was spreading throughout the country in an alarming fashion. He asked that the Pope should allow the Supreme Council to deal with the case.

Innocent however was determined to obtain obedience and appointed bishops to try the case. None was very eager for the task, fearing the power of the Inquisition, but at last the Bishop of Avila accepted. However Villanueva, growing more and more fearful of the storm which his case was arousing, did not appear before Avila to have the case reconsidered. But the Pope was not prepared to let the matter drop. This was more than the case of one man justly or unjustly accused by the Inquisition; it was a recurrence of the old fight. The Pope was demanding supremacy for the Papacy, while the Spanish Inquisition and the King of Spain were seeking independence of Rome.

The wrangle continued, and letters went back and forth between Madrid and Rome, both sides manœuvring for position, and Villanueva, the cause of it all, wishing to escape and live in peace. Inquisitor-General Arce was fervently advising the King to resist the Pope, knowing that if he did not he himself would be the one to suffer, while Philip's statesmen were urging caution. Preparations for war with Italy were begun, and all ships from Italy coming into Spanish ports were subjected to close scrutiny, for Philip had forgotten that he did not possess the strength of Emperor Charles and Philip II which would have enabled him to defy the Pope.

Innocent threatened to abolish the Spanish Inquisition; Arce retorted that God would never allow it. But Philip by this time was beginning to understand his danger. Arce, seeing this and thinking only of his own, implored Philip for the sake of the Holy Catholic Faith, not to yield. But Philip decided to take the advice of the junta.

Innocent then suggested that Arce should retire to his See of Plasencia, since it was many years since he had been there; this was tantamount to commanding him to resign his position of Inquisitor-General, and Arce was both incensed and terrified. His reply was to relinquish the bishopric of Plasencia.

But the Pope was winning the battle. Philip could see that he had no alternative but to send to Rome what documents remained concerning Villanueva's case, and doing so, begged the Pope not to open the case, for if he did so he was humiliating not only the King but the Spanish Inquisition.

Innocent was however not so much interested in the case of Villanueva as in establishing his supremacy over Spain. He had no wish to consider the matter and announced his intention of passing it over to certain bishops.

The affair dragged on inconclusively because the fate of Villanueva was important to neither side, and in July 1653 Villanueva died.

The wrangle between the Papacy and Spain continued even after Villanueva's death into the reign of Alexander VII.

17

CHARLES THE BEWITCHED

When Philip's near-imbecile son, Charles II, came to the throne it appeared that everything of Spain was on the decline except the Inquisition. To all outward appearances that remained as powerful as ever, and in 1680, fifteen years after the death of Philip IV, one of the greatest *autos de fé* ever seen was celebrated in the Plaza Mayor of Madrid. Charles and his Queen honoured the occasion with their presence and 105 people were brought out of their prisons to receive their sentences. Outside the gate of Fuencarral, the *quemadero* of the occasion, the bonfire was 60 feet square and 7 feet high.

So the Inquisition was in its full glory while the country was in a desperate state. The expulsion of Jews and Moors had depopulated Spain to an extent which was alarming; excessive taxation had impoverished the people; and foreigners were snatching the trade which had once been Spain's.

The King had been a poor creature from birth and could not provide the country with an heir. He had been four years old when his father died, and his mother, whom Philip had appointed to be Regent during his son's minority, had proved herself to be a woman determined on acquiring power.

Mariana was an Austrian and her aim was to strengthen alliances with her own kinsmen and the friendship with France which was being made possible by the marriage of Maria Teresa and Louis XIV.

Although Mariana had declared, when she took over the Regency, that she would not allow favourites to govern the kingdom, she had soon arranged special favours for her confessor, Father Juan Everardo Nithard; and before long he was not only given a place on the Regency Council but was made Inquisitor-General.

Trouble was inevitable considering the circumstances: a child-king, a Regent who was a foreigner and favoured foreigners such as Nithard, a country weak from the effects of taxation and wars, and a handsome young hero in Philip's illegitimate son by the actress, Maria Calderon—Don John of Austria.

Like his famous namesake he could not entirely avert his eyes from the crown; he sought to control the government and it was not long before he was taking sides against the Queen and her favourite Nithard.

Don John had a real grievance against the Queen and Nithard when Malladas, one of his intimate friends, was arrested by the Queen's orders for no apparent reason, except that he was a friend of Don John and therefore presumed to be an enemy. Malladas was strangled in prison a few hours after his arrest, having had no trial and not even knowing the reason for his arrest.

Don John could not be expected to accept such conduct without protest, and when he made known his disapproval he was told to leave Court.

More of his friends were arrested and rumours of plots against the Queen were circulated. An order for Don John's arrest was issued, but he did not wait for it to be carried out; he escaped to Barcelona and was there received with acclaim.

Now the country was ready to take sides and—as Don John was young, handsome and something of a hero, and Nithard was German—the late King's illegitimate son found himself at the head of the more popular party.

The Queen tried to placate her late husband's son, but Don John stated that the only way to a reconciliation was for her to dismiss Nithard; and with the army which had gathered about him he marched to Madrid.

The country was behind Don John in his demand, and the Queen saw that the only way in which she could save herself was to dismiss her favourite.

Nithard went to Rome where he stayed until his death in 1681 and, as the country was then more sympathetic towards the Queen, Don John realized that he should not go too far. There was a compromise, and Don John was made Viceroy of Aragon.

In spite of her declaration that the reign of favourites was over in Spain, no sooner had Nithard disappeared into exile than Mariana began showering honours on Valenzuela. Here was a man of great ambition, determined to rule the country and its Queen Regent. Young Charles did not count, of course; he was too delicate to have received a proper education, and up to the age of ten had been treated as though he were a baby. He was completely under the domination of his mother whom it suited that he should remain powerless to govern.

The energetic Valenzuela proved himself so useful to the

Queen that he was not only managing affairs of state but had also found a place for himself in her bed. Mariana's grateful appreciation was apparent in the titles she bestowed on him, and he was fast becoming the most powerful man in Spain, so that all those who wished for advancement knew they must please him.

Such a man must inevitably arouse enmity, and there was Don John with his jealous eyes on the throne and on his young half-brother who was now fifteen, that age when, it had been ordained in the will of Philip IV, he should come of age.

Don John and his partisans tried to persuade Charles to sign an order commanding Don John to return to Madrid. Not only was Don John to be recalled but to be made first minister. But Valenzuela heard what was happening before this order was signed, and the Queen, who had always governed her son, was able to prevent his putting his signature to the order; so Don John's schemes for ruling through the King and thus displacing Valenzuela, who ruled through the Queen, failed; and it was Valenzuela who remained Prime Minister, taking up residence in the palace.

Meanwhile the condition of the people in Madrid was growing worse. Letters written at the time state that it was not uncommon to see people dying of starvation in the streets. In Philip II's time the population had been about 400,000; it was at this time about 200,000; and Madrid was typical of other towns. The starvation of the people was due to loss of that agricultural land which it had been the Moors' special talent to cultivate. Trade, which had flourished largely on account of the Jewish population, had been taken by other countries.

Countries in trouble look for a scapegoat, and Valenzuela was chosen by the people on this occasion. Charles was induced to escape from the influence of his mother and her lover, and in January 1677 he left the palace and from a distance, with counsellors who were the enemies of Mariana and her lover, he ordered his mother to remain a prisoner there. Meanwhile Don John marched towards the capital, where he was received with joy. He gave his terms for undertaking the government of the country—which were that the Queen was to leave the capital for Toledo, and Valenzuela be arrested and banished from the country. These terms were agreed on and Valenzuela, after a short imprisonment, was sent to the Philippines and later went to Mexico where he remained until his death.

But Spain under Don John's dictatorship was no happier than it had been under that of the Queen Regent. Conceited, eager that all should remember his royal blood, Don John was more concerned in keeping the Queen Mother a prisoner than in righting the ills of Spain. He gave his time to the discussion of etiquette and whether or not French fashions should be adopted, while Louis XIV was conducting a successful campaign against Catalonia and waging war in Flanders. The people were asking themselves why they had revolted against the Queen Regent in favour of Don John, when under his rule the condition of the country had gone from bad to worse.

The peace of Nimeguen was signed in 1648 and a marriage was arranged between Charles and Princess Marie Louise of Orléans, the daughter of the French King's brother and Henrietta, sister of Charles II of England.

This was a direct blow at the Queen Mother who had hoped for a union between the King and a member of her own family. It is surprising that she should have wished for such a match, with the example of her son before her. Charles, with a tongue so large that his speech was unintelligible, and a chin so ill-shaped that his food had to consist mainly of slops because he could not chew, who had been carried about as a baby until he was ten years old, was the result of Hapsburg marrying Hapsburg. However, if Mariana realized this, it did not perturb her, for she was only concerned with the power she could bring to her Austrian family; but realizing that she could do nothing but accept the French marriage, she did this with as good a grace as possible; and the beautiful, rather giddy French princess, who had been brought up at the most glittering Court in Europe, came to Spain as the bride of a creature who was almost a degenerate.

It may have been that had Don John lived he would have been defeated by the Queen Mother's supporters. He died in September 1679. Fever and the ague were said to be the causes of death, but there were the usual rumours of poison; for, said the Queen Mother's enemies, she was determined to remove the man who had taken her place.

Charles was delighted with his gay bride; naturally she was less delighted, and there was great scandal when she insisted on introducing French manners to the Court. She snapped her fingers at Spanish solemnity, smiled, and even laughed in public; she insisted on behaving as she had at Versailles, introduced new comedies which were played at Court, ate and drank too freely and was ready to smile and converse with the common people.

The royal *ménage* must have been incongruous with its gay and carefree Queen and its King who was incapable of speaking intelligibly and who indulged in childish pleasures such as running wildly through the rooms of the palace from one balcony to another, quite purposelessly, as a very young child might.

Mariana was back in power, but she still had to contend with

Gaspar de Guzman, Count-Duke of Olivares. Detail of the equestrian
portrait by Velasquez in the Prado Gallery, Madrid

Old prints depicting the methods of the Inquisition to purify the souls of (*left*) and
obtain repentance from (*right*) its victims

the maudlin devotion of Charles for his beautiful wife. As for Marie Louise, she had selected two favourites who scarcely ever left her and advised her in all things. These were Madame Quintin, a widow who had married an equerry in Marie Louise's French suite, and the equerry, Viremont himself. Those who wished to remove them from the Queen, tried to do so by bringing an accusation of immorality against them, but the Queen defended them so fiercely to the King that they were allowed to remain at Court.

An elaborate scheme was then devised for proving that they had tried to poison the King; and Charles, always terrified of poison, insisted that they be removed. Marie Louise's enemies whispered to the King that she had been involved in the plot, and thus brought about the end of her influence with Charles.

There was no child of this marriage, and in 1689, only ten years after her arrival in Spain, Marie Louise died, believed by many to have been poisoned.

* * *

Before the year was out Charles was married to Mary Anne of Neuburg, daughter of the Elector Palatine. The new wife proved to be eager for power, and a party was formed of which she was the head and which had the support of the Queen Mother.

There were no children of this marriage and it was now obvious that Charles was impotent; therefore the succession to the Spanish throne was the subject of much speculation throughout Europe.

Wily Louis XIV was scheming to bring Spain under the influence of France. He was a grandson of Philip III and had married a daughter of Philip IV. Emperor Leopold was also a grandson of Philip III and had married a daughter of Philip IV. Both Louis and Leopold therefore kept alert eyes on Spain.

Mariana died in 1696 and Charles's health was failing lamentably. Terrified of being poisoned, he suspected his Queen of wishing him out of the way. He realized the difference between the flighty French princess who had been his first wife, and the scheming German who was his second; and he must have longed for the old days. Queen Mary Anne was determined that the succession should go to the son of the Emperor and was at great pains to keep from the King's side any who might influence him in favour of the French.

The battle continued over the dying King, who, although not yet forty, was suffering from senile decay; his wits were quite unable to cope with the intrigue, and the jostling for position continued.

The King's confessor, Father Matilla, had been procured for

him by the Queen, and he influenced the King to such an extent that it seemed the German faction must be triumphant. But there was in the King's entourage a nobleman named Count Benavente, who became the secret tool of the French faction. One night Benavente secretly brought the Archbishop of Portocarrero to the King's private apartments, and to him Charles was induced to confess his fears of his wife. The Archbishop and Benavente then decided that the King must be rescued and that the first move would be to banish the confessor, Matilla, from the King's side, and appoint a new one, favourable to the French faction.

Matilla was replaced by Froilan Díaz, and within a few days Matilla had mysteriously died.

Froilan Díaz discovered that in the convent of Cangas some of the nuns were said to be possessed by demons, and he believed—a belief which was generally accepted—that during the ceremony of exorcism, when the demons were terrified of being banished from the bodies they were inhabiting, they could be forced to reveal facts which were outside the knowledge of ordinary people.

Díaz suggested that the demons in the nuns of Cangas might be made to tell the reason for the King's illness, for if the cause were known, the cure could more easily follow.

It had long been thought that the King had been bewitched and that was the reason for his ill-health. The Supreme Council of the Inquisition had even discussed taking steps to discover whether this was due to sorcery, but had done nothing.

In 1695 the Inquisitor-General, Valladares, had died and been succeeded by Juan Tomás de Rocaberti, Archbishop of Valencia; and the King in secret consulted Rocaberti, asking him to discover whether there was any truth in the theory that he had been bewitched.

Rocaberti put the King's request to the Suprema which still considered the matter highly dangerous. During the last reign the Inquisition had lost a little ground. Philip IV had been its devoted slave, but he had at the same time encouraged the writers at his Court, and ideas had begun to simmer in the minds of Spaniards. When complaints had been made concerning the Inquisition a commission had been set up to look into its activities, and this had been composed of fearless men who had boldly announced that the Inquisition, far from contributing to the good of the nation, was often a danger to it. In view of this the Inquisition was wary.

Froilan Díaz as King's confessor had a seat on the Suprema and he asked Rocaberti to help him discover whether Charles was bewitched. This Rocaberti promised to do, and he himself visited Cangas where he wrote the names of the King and Queen on paper which he enclosed in his doublet. He then had one of the possessed nuns brought to him and demanded to know whether either of the people whose names were written on the paper in his doublet had been bewitched.

The "demon" replied: Yes, one of the people had been bewitched. It was the King. When he was fourteen, on 3rd April, 1675, his mother had given him a cup of chocolate; in this cup was a spell made from certain parts of a dead man's body, and its object was to render the King impotent and so feeble in mind that he would be unable to govern the kingdom.

Could the King escape from the spell? was the next question. Yes, was the answer. He must be separated from his Queen, anointed with oil which had been blessed, and subjected to constant purging.

For a whole year the Inquisitor-General and Díaz tried to extract more information from the demons, but they—or the nuns —were mischievous. First they said he had not been bewitched at all, and they were only amusing themselves in saying that he had been. Then they said that he had been bewitched on a second occasion in 1694.

Poor Charles was anointed, purged and exorcized—all of which operations, far from improving his health, made it deteriorate.

Meanwhile another candidate for the Spanish throne had appeared in the field. This was the Electoral Prince of Bavaria, grandson of Empress Margaret, Philip IV's younger daughter, who had been the first wife of the Emperor Leopold.

Louis XIV was anxious, for it appeared that this last candidate might be the most favoured, and he slyly proposed that the Spanish crown should be divided among the three pretenders. This caused grave concern, as Louis knew it would: one of the greatest fears of all who cared for the good of Spain was to see it divided as it had been before the days of Ferdinand and Isabella. Oddly enough the Prince of Bavaria, who was only six years old, died mysteriously, so once more there were only two contestants in the field.

The Queen was fuming. Separated from her husband, her power was clipped, and she could see the French faction gaining all the ground that she had lost; and when she heard that the demons had said Charles had been bewitched a second time, in 1694, she was more than furious, she was alarmed, for this, she knew, was intended as a direct thrust against herself.

Four weeks after she had heard of this second bewitching Rocaberti died in suspicious circumstances, and the Queen did all in her power to have one of her men, Fray Antonio Folch de

Cardona, appointed Inquisitor-General. But Charles was now highly suspicious of his Queen and determined to get to the bottom of his bewitchment. He therefore ignored the Queen's proposal and appointed Cardinal Alonso Fernandez de Cordova y Aguilar, who swore he would pursue the matter vigorously until he had sifted the truth and could lay it before the King.

Poor Aguilar! He had taken on a more dangerous task than he could have realized. He became ill and in a few days he was dead. His death coincided with the confirmation from Rome of his appointment.

By this time the King was growing very feeble and the Queen had regained some of her old power—enough for her to appoint the next Inquisitor-General, who was Balthasar de Mendoza y Sandoval. She had determined on the downfall of Díaz and those who had sought to involve her in this tale of demons and spells; Mendoza's reward was to be a cardinal's hat.

As a result an exorcizer, Fray Tenda, was arrested and during his examination he described what had happened at Cangas, involving Díaz, who was then questioned. Díaz answered that he had acted on instructions from Rocaberti at the request of the King, and that he could answer no question without the King's consent. Mendoza then asked for the King's consent to bring a charge against Díaz. The King's mind was now so bemused that it was easy for the Queen to persuade him to give his consent.

Díaz was ordered by Mendoza to go to the Dominican convent in Valladolid, and set out to do this, but before reaching Valladolid he decided that he would escape the Inquisition by seeking refuge in Rome. But Mendoza ordered his arrest, and he was brought back and put in the secret prison at Murcia.

Eventually Díaz was brought to Madrid and imprisoned in the Dominican house of Nuestra Señora de Atocha. Here he remained for four years, after which time he was found suspect of heresy.

His case developed into another of those long-drawn-out wrangles between the Pope and the Suprema, while the prisoner in his dungeon was disregarded.

However Díaz was reinstated in the Supreme Council after the death of Charles, and was rewarded with the See of Avila, for all that he had suffered; but the Pope, Clement XI, refused confirmation of the appointment because the Inquisition had failed to show him the papers concerning the case, and he was not sure of the justice of the acquittal. The new King, Philip V, would not allow anyone else to accept the See and it remained vacant until after the death of Díaz.

*   *   *

As Charles's death grew nearer the wrangling over the succession became more intense. The Pope came out on the side of the French, and Louis XIV intimated that if an attempt were made to put the Archduke on the throne he would oppose it with force.

Poor Charles, surrounded by holy relics, pestered on all sides, made a will in which he stated that his heir was to be Philip of Anjou.

The Queen immediately used her powers to persuade him to change his mind, with such persistence that Charles then said that the throne of Spain should go to the Archduke, but no alteration was made in the will.

Charles the Bewitched died in November 1700, aged thirty-nine, and it is said that he looked like a man of eighty. Thus ingloriously had lived and died the last Hapsburg king of Spain.

Philip of Anjou, to be Philip V of Spain, began the new dynasty; the Bourbons had arrived. Handsome, virile, seventeen years of age, he had the powerful King of France behind him. The French Ambassador was given a seat on the Council—a concession, insisted Louis XIV, which must be granted to all future ambassadors—the Austrian faction was banished from power, and the Queen retired to Toledo.

To welcome the new King of Spain an *auto de fé* was arranged in his honour. To the astonishment of all, Philip declined the invitation to attend.

This was a sign of things to come. Spain would change under the rule of the Bourbons.

18

THE INQUISITION AND THE BOURBONS

PHILIP'S SLIGHT to the Inquisition did not mean that he objected to it on humanitarian grounds. He had been brought up in the reflection of *le Roi Soleil,* and therefore believed that there could be only one head of a state: its King. Philip made this clear from the beginning, and the Inquisition was immediately put into a different position from that which it had occupied during preceding reigns.

Philip was entirely French; Louis XIV had impressed on him before he left for Spain never to forget that he was a Frenchman, and in this at least he obeyed his grandfather. He was young and thoughtless and it was not long before the high places about the throne were filled by Frenchmen; French fashions were introduced and the name Austrian became a term of abuse to be hurled at any who criticized that which was French.

It was hardly likely, after there had been such controversy concerning Philip's claim to the throne, that he would be allowed to enjoy it in peace. The Emperor was furious; Queen Mary Anne, supported by the Inquisitor-General, let it be known that Charles II had changed his mind about his heir—on his deathbed—and had nominated the Archduke as future King of Spain. What Philip's accession meant to the bloated power of Louis XIV was at the root of. much dissatisfaction. William III of England was furious with Louis for regarding James II as still King of England. Thus began the War of Succession which was to drag on until 1714; and it was not until that year that Philip could truly call himself King of Spain.

He did win the applause of his people by placing himself at the head of his soldiers and himself leading them into battle— a kingly habit to remind the Spaniards of the Emperor Charles.

His bride was Marie Louise, the daughter of Victor Amadeus of Savoy. She was only fourteen, and as soon as Philip saw her he fell in love with her and was to prove an uxorious husband.

As the girl was so young, Louis XIV, aided by Madame de

Maintenon, sent with her as her counsellor a clever old woman, Anne Marie de la Trémouille, who was known in France as La Princesse des Ursins because she was the widow of Flavio Orsini, Duke of Bracciano. The task assigned to her by Louis and Madame de Maintenon was to establish her influence over the King and his bride, and obey the instructions which would reach her from Versailles. This the Princesse did very successfully. By Marie Louise, Philip had four children one of whom was that Luis in whose favour he abdicated, and another Ferdinand VI.

Philip fought with great gallantry which won him the respect of his people, but the War of Succession was long and there were many victories for the enemy. Philip had against him the genius of Marlborough who scored successes over the Spaniards in the Netherlands and distinguished himself at Blenheim, Ramillies, Oudenarde and Malplaquet; and when the league between Holland, Denmark, Austria, Prussia and England was formed he began to develop that melancholy hypochondria which was a feature of his later life and which was to dim all the bright hopes which the coming of a virile young man had raised in the hearts of so many Spaniards.

In 1714 Philip was at peace with the world—apart of course from the Emperor, who would never accept him as King of Spain. Flanders had been lost in the struggle but Flanders had always been an uncertain blessing.

Marie Louise died that year and Philip was very unhappy. The Princesse des Ursins, however, continued to advise him, and during that time of mourning she was the only one whom he seemed to want near him. When he left the Court for the Palace of Medina Celi and the Princesse was lodged in a near-by monastery, in order that she might be at his instant call, the monks were asked to leave and a connecting passage was made between the monastery and the palace so that they could be in constant communication. So much did he rely on her that it was said he might marry her, even though she was old enough to have been his grandmother.

Instead he married Elizabeth Farnese, who was niece and step-daughter of the Duke of Parma. The Princesse approved of this match. Elizabeth had been brought up simply, and she believed the girl would be easily subdued; such a marriage, the Princesse told Louis XIV, would enable Philip to regain his power in Italy.

The Princesse was soon to discover her mistake. Elizabeth may have been brought up simply, but she was ambitious and arrogant in the extreme. The truth was quickly disclosed to her for Elizabeth did not hurry to meet the King on her arrival in Spain, and delayed unnecessarily during the journey, in the

Princesse's view. As soon as they met the Princesse delivered a mild reproach at which Elizabeth cried out imperiously that she would not be insulted by that old fool, who was to leave her presence at once.

Elizabeth made it clear that there was no room at her Court for the old Princesse who was put in a coach an hour after their meeting, dressed as she was for the Court ceremony, not having been given time to change, and on a wintry night was driven out of Spain... a reward for thirteen years' devoted service to the King and his first wife!

Philip was very soon in the power of this new one who continued to rule him throughout his life. By Elizabeth he had six children and their mother schemed ambitiously, trying to jostle them into the highest positions.

By 1724, Philip became more melancholy than ever; he was convinced that he was ill, and was perpetually watching for new symptoms. His wife was his constant companion, advising him on all state matters; his days were spent in talking with her, in prayer and discussion of his ailments.

In January 1724 he announced to the world that he had become too infirm to rule, and that he was about to abdicate in favour of his eldest son Luis. He himself would retire to the Palace of St. Ildefonsa de la Granja which he had built after the manner of Versailles, whence he could gaze towards France, and there he would live in obscurity with his wife to nurse him.

He wrote a letter to Luis in which he gave him his advice with such a religious fervour as might have belonged to Philip II. Luis was to maintain the Faith throughout the land. He was to give his support to the Inquisition, which had preserved Catholicism in Spain and kept out heresy so that Spain was the most purely Catholic country in the world.

Philip had changed from the virile young man who had come to the throne nearly twenty-five years before. Overtaken by religious mania and melancholia he shut his eyes to the fact that industry in Spain had almost come to a standstill, partly because of the expulsion of Jews and Moors whose financial genius and industry would have saved it, partly because of the absurd *alcabalas* which imposed a tax so severe that Spanish manufacturers could not compete with those abroad. He could not have realized the growing power of England, which was almost entirely heretic and was on the way to building up an Empire which was to be even greater than the Spanish one had been in its prime. All over Europe new ideas were springing up, men were discussing reforms, not only in religion, but in economics. Such ideas were barred from Spanish territory and would continue to be so while the Inquisition held sway. Yet this state of affairs Philip, in his condition of religious melancholy, believed must persist—as long as the Inquisition realized that it was second to the monarchy.

Luis, who had been born in Spain, pleased the Spaniards; he was young, handsome and amiable, and soon earned the name of Luis the Well-beloved; but seven months after his accession he caught smallpox and died, and as the next son, Ferdinand, was only eleven, there was nothing for Philip to do but reassume the crown.

Philip obviously did not fulfil the promise he had brought with him to Spain. Had he been a stronger man, less ready to be influenced by his wives, it is possible that the power of the Inquisition might have been decidedly crippled during his reign. He came from France, the most intellectual Court in Europe; his manners were French; his ideas were French; he had been well primed in his duties by Louis XIV—not that he always followed his grandfather's advice.

He believed that he, as King, should give encouragement to the arts, and that he should bring the men and women of his country in line, intellectually, with those across the Pyrenees. There must therefore be a literature; but a literature to be of any use must be a free literature, and how was it possible for such to survive in a country dominated by the Inquisition? He founded the National Library, the Academies of Languages, History, and Medicine, and the Seminary of the Nobles. But the censorship remained, and a great many of those ideas which were circulating in other parts of Europe were kept out of Spain.

Moreover Philip was not strong enough to bring any great change to Spain, as seen in the affair of Belando and Giudice.

He had broken off relationship with Rome because in 1709, during the War of Succession, Clement XI had recognized the Archduke Charles as King of Spain; and as a result Philip dismissed the nuncio and stopped money being sent to Rome. The old quarrel between Papacy and monarchy had broken out again, and in this the Inquisitor-General, Francesco Giudice, became involved. He was dismissed and banished.

Belando wrote a history of the times—giving a truthful account of this affair—which was to be dedicated to Philip and his Queen. The King and Queen read the history and accepted the dedication, but when that which Belando had written was brought to the notice of the Inquisition the book was seized by them on account of its exposure of the Giudice affair.

Belando was brought before the Tribunal and even when he offered to eliminate the offending passages, the offer was ignored and he was put into prison. Later he was sent to a convent where he was to spend the rest of his life, and was ordered to produce no more books.

This was in direct defiance of that freedom which was to produce a worthy literature, but the King allowed this to happen because by this time, 1744, he was too overcome by his religious mania to move in the matter.

This happened two years before his death. He had for some time believed he was near death, expressing even more abnormal interest in the minor ailments of his body than was habitual with him. His religious mania had grown to such an extent that there were periods towards the end of his life when he was considered to be insane; had he been a stronger man, had he not been so ready to be influenced by his wives and their favourites, he might have done a great deal more than he did for the country he ruled. His intentions had been of the best; his weak good nature, his absorption with his health and his superstitious fear of the after-life had come between him and greatness.

On 9th July, 1746, Philip had an apoplectic fit and died. He had left the country a little better than he had found it. Although the Inquisition had worked incessantly during his reign and the brutalities had continued, a few new ideas had penetrated from a more enlightened country. The long and costly War of Succession, with which Philip's reign had begun, had more than anything else prevented his being the great ruler he might have been; his second wife's rabid ambition for her children had been another factor against him; but the weakness in his own character was more responsible than anything else. Yet with the coming of the first of the Bourbons, it seems that a little light was being shed on that tragic country; and in spite of the fact that the Inquisition still appeared to be a great power in the land, its foundations were beginning to tremble.

Although the Inquisition had been working as zealously as ever during the reign of the first Bourbon, perhaps on account of that sovereign's attitude the ceremonies had not been conducted with that fierce publicity which had been a feature of past *autos*. Hume in his *Spain; its Greatness and Decay* says that during the reign of Philip there were 782 *autos,* and that 14,000 people were sentenced. Edward Armstrong however, who revised Hume's history, says that Hume has taken his figures from Llorente, whom Edward Armstrong does not trust. Quoting Lea he says that there are authentic statistics only for the years between 1721 and 1727. During these years 77 people were burned in actuality and 74 in effigy; 811 were penanced; thus making the figures for the actual records 962 while those given by Llorente were 1785.

Whatever the figures, there is enough evidence to show that, during the reign of Philip, the Inquisition continued to work with accustomed zeal.

* * *

Ferdinand VI was of a kindly nature; this must have been the case because he was magnanimous towards his stepmother, Elizabeth Farnese, who had intrigued against him in the hope of securing the throne for her own son Charles. He was more eager than his father to bring culture to Spain and, like his father, he was ruled by his wife, Queen Barbara. They both wished to live a peaceful family life, free from the cares of state, and it was largely due to them that Spain remained aloof during the War of Independence when both France and England sought to draw her into the quarrel. Ferdinand was prudent, a true lover of peace, and under his rule prosperity began to return slowly to Spain, for during his reign the strength of the Spanish fleet increased considerably and there was no longer bankruptcy in the treasury.

Unfortunately in August 1758 Queen Barbara died, and the King's grief was so intense that he shut himself away in complete solitude, and there were periods when he lost his reason. He died in August 1759, exactly a year after Barbara's death.

The change, which his thirteen years of rule had brought about, was apparent. Scholars were now finding their way into Spain, visiting the academies which had been set up by the Bourbon kings; this inevitably brought about a new age of enlightenment and, most important of all, the position of the Inquisition was subtly changing, for people were looking askance at an institution which had brought terror into many lives over many generations. With the spread of culture, a certain amount of superstition was bound to disappear. As fewer people were brought before the tribunals there were no longer the large-scale confiscations; salaries of Inquisitors could not be increased and the cost of living had risen considerably. There was no longer the same desire to accept posts within the Inquisition. Thus it was necessary to employ people of lower standing who were less eager to do their work than their predecessors had been. Inevitably the great fear and respect in which the Inquisition had been held began to diminish.

* * *

Charles III, returning from Naples over which he had been ruling as King of the Two Sicilies, took the throne on the death of his half-brother Ferdinand; and in Charles III the Spaniards had the most intelligent of the Bourbons.

Charles was a patron of arts, even more determined than his father and brother to bring culture to Spain; he was equally determined to be ruler of the country and was less respectful to the Inquisition than any preceding monarch had ever been. Yet he did not seek to suppress the Inquisition, and is reputed to have given his reason as this: "The Spaniards want to keep it and it gives me no trouble." He had in fact made sure that it should give him no trouble, for in 1768 he had imposed new rules on censorship and later had taken from it the power to judge crimes other than heresy that it might not interfere with the secular courts. In that year 1768 it was decided that the King was the patron of the Inquisition and therefore possessed the *rights* of patronage. As patron the King should prevent violence and extortion.

But during the last years of Charles's reign the Inquisition discovered a new form of heresy, in the new ideas which, for all its vigilance, it could not prevent from seeping into the country from across the border.

Some of the King's most important ministers were suspected, but so had times changed that the Inquisitors had no power to arrest such men on suspicion. To do so they would need the King's consent and these men were too important to the King to be handed to the Inquisition merely because they held certain opinions.

Although they dared not touch men of influence they sought to make an example of men of lesser importance as in the case of Dr. Luis Castelanos of Cadiz who was a philosopher and an agnostic. He was brought before the Tribunal and sentenced to confiscation and abjuration, to wear a *sanbenito* and to serve ten years in a hospital at Oran.

But the most important case of this time is that of Pablo Olavide, who had been a lawyer and judge of Lima. During the terrible earthquake of 1746 he had worked with such skill and courage that he had been put in charge of the treasures which had been brought out of the ruins, and was trusted to restore their belongings to people who could bring satisfactory claims. Out of that which he believed could not be claimed he built a church and a theatre; but naturally there were some disgruntled people who accused him of cheating, and as a result he was imprisoned for a while and made to pay certain sums of money.

After that he left Lima, married a rich woman and travelled to Europe. Arriving in France, he found the atmosphere of a country tottering on the brink of revolution extremely interesting, and he quickly became the friend of Voltaire and Rousseau.

Imbued with their ideas of bettering the conditions of the

starving multitude he returned to Spain. Although he was a philosopher he was—as is seen by his activities at the time of the earthquake—a practical man, and he soon made a plan of action.

There were in the country great tracts of land which was useless except for sheep-grazing and was used by a band of people called the *Mesta* who owned sheep which wandered from place to place grazing on this uncultivated land—the *baldios* as it was called. They had secured the right to use this land and to prevent its being cultivated.

It had for some time been realized that this land could be put to useful service, and it was decided to bring into the country German and Swiss Catholics to cultivate the waste land. Olavide was made superintendent of the colony and governor of Seville.

This was to bring him many enemies, not only among the *Mesta* who hated him for spoiling their grazing grounds, but among the friars who had accompanied the colonists, for Olavide had become imbued with ideas from France, liberal ideas which seemed like heresy to the bigoted priests.

The charges brought against him were that, when calamity threatened, he did not pray but used practical means to avert it; he did not order that bells should be rung when storms rose; he supported the Copernican statement that the sun was the centre of the solar system, which it was against the command of the Church to believe.

In earlier days Olavide would have quickly been a prisoner of the Inquisition, but with the changing times caution was needed; and it was necessary to obtain royal permission before an arrest could be made.

This consent was given—very probably because the King realized that the ideas, which Olavide held and which he was no doubt circulating, were those of his friends Voltaire and Rousseau and, although he could not yet see the disaster this was to bring to his relations in Versailles, Charles was clever enough to scent danger in them.

Olavide was arrested in November 1776 and for two years nothing was heard of him. Meanwhile many witnesses were brought before the Tribunal in order to build up a case against him, and at length one hundred and sixty-six possible charges were drawn up. Olavide admitted that he had talked freely, but he denied that he was not a Catholic.

The Inquisition would have preferred him to be paraded in a public *auto de fé* as a warning to others who might be dabbling in new ideas. Yet again here is an example of their waning power. Instructions came from Rome that the *auto* should not be a public one, so it was held in an outer court of the Inquisition of

Madrid without the banners and trumpetings of the past, and instead of the hysterical crowd, a mere sixty spectators—all of high rank and many of whom had already been flirting with the new ideas.

Olavide dressed in black serge and holding an unlighted torch in his hand was commanded to march three times round the court, although he was excused from wearing the *sanbenito* and rope round his neck.

He was then obliged to listen to a recital of his crimes which lasted for three hours; he cried out that it was wrong to say he had lost his faith. These interruptions were ignored. As a great favour he was allowed to sit on a bench while his sentence was read to him.

Under Philip II it would have been the stake for him; in these more enlightened days he was given a less severe sentence, but it was none the less a very harsh one—so harsh that when Olavide heard it he fell from his bench in a faint.

He was accused of being a heretic and a bad member of Holy Church; therefore he must be reconciled and suffer confiscation of his goods; he was to be banished, for as long as he lived, from Madrid, nor must he come within forty leagues of the city, all royal residences, Andalusia, Lima and the colonies of Sierra Morena which he had recently governed. For eight years he was to suffer strict imprisonment in a convent, where he would occupy a cell and take orders from a confessor who would be appointed to him by the Inquisition. He was never to ride on horseback again, or wear jewels, gold, silver, diamonds or pearls or any precious stones. His garments must never be made of silk or fine wool, but always of coarse serge.

Two years after the sentence was passed he became so ill in his prison that he was allowed to leave it for a short respite, and he then escaped to France. It is said that many at Court were aware of his intended flight and were sympathetic towards him. The Inquisition, however, demanded that he be brought back to serve his sentence, and Olavide thought it safer to go to Geneva.

He returned to Paris when the revolution broke out but doubtless found it different from what he had anticipated; indeed he himself narrowly escaped death by the guillotine; and no doubt realizing that revolution in practice was very different from revolution in theory he wrote his *The Gospel Triumphant; or the Converted Philosopher*, which so impressed the Inquisitors that they graciously allowed him to return to his native land.

He died in 1804, a disillusioned man, it is said.

The case of Olavide was considered by the Inquisition to have been an important one because it provided a lesson to many who were dabbling in the new ideas. It was for this reason that many suspected of harbouring them were invited to see Olavide condemned; and one of these, Don Felipe Samaniego, who was Archdeacon of Pampeluna, confessed immediately that he had read literature concerning the new ideas; and during an investigation of his case suspicion was levied at many of the King's ministers. These cases, however, remained suspended on the grounds that only one witness had been found to testify against the accused. This clearly indicates the waning power of the Inquisition which in the past had never failed to find terrified witnesses ready to testify against those whom it was desired to prosecute.

The end of the Inquisition was in sight, although it was to continue for some years. In spite of war which overshadowed the reign of Charles III, he left Spain a richer country than he found her. The population had increased considerably, taxation had diminished although revenues had increased. Spain began to be famous for the leather of Seville and Cordova, for the cotton-velvet of Avila, for the glass of La Granja, and the porcelain of Buen Retiro. Agriculture revived, the coinage was reformed; marshes were drained and arid lands irrigated; canals and roads were built. If the monarchs who succeeded Charles III had been of his calibre there would have been every chance of Spain's rising to become a great power once more.

Charles III died in December 1788; he was seventy-three years of age, but the temperate life he had lived had preserved his strength and vigour; the twenty-nine years, during which this intelligent and just king had ruled, were indeed a boon to the long-suffering country.

19

DECLINE AND FALL

Unfortunately Charles IV was very different from his father, Charles III, and, while his intentions were good, he was weak, lazy and considerably under the influence of his forceful wife, Maria Luisa of Parma, who was not even faithful to him, but was, in her turn, strongly influenced by her lover, the ambitious Manuel Godoy.

As Charles IV came to the throne in 1788, the revolution was about to break over France, and since the coming of the Bourbons there had been a strong affinity between the two countries.

A censorship was imposed on all literature coming in from France, and the Inquisition began to regain some of the importance it had lost. Yet, as is seen in the case of the favourite, Manuel Godoy, it was not gaining any real strength with the passing years.

Goday's relationship with the imperious Queen was deeply resented by her son, the Prince of the Asturias, and when there was an intrigue to bring about the fall of Godoy, the Inquisition was appealed to as the most likely means of achieving this.

Godoy was accused of his immorality with women and the fact that he did not observe ordinary religious duties such as communion and confession. Inquisitor-General Francisco Antonio de Lorenzana, Archbishop of Toledo, was very wary of attacking the favourite, hesitated and would not take action unless he could first receive the permission of the Pope, Pius VI, to do so. The Archbishop Despuig of Seville, who was one of the instigators of the plot against Godoy, with his friend Cardinal Vincenti, begged the Pope to write to the Inquisitor-General reprimanding him for having failed in his duty towards such a sinner as Godoy. Napoleon, who was in Genoa, captured the messenger and the letter, and sent it to Godoy, for the Corsican adventurer was well aware of the power Godoy held in Spain and how useful he might be.

Godoy was therefore aware of the conspirators' aims, and sent them, with the Inquisitor-General, into exile.

With the French monarchy abolished and Napoleon striding across Europe, it was small wonder that the Inquisition felt its position to be growing more and more uneasy. Yet it was prodded to fresh bursts of energy by the fear of revolutionary ideas, spreading to Spain from France; and at this time it became more an instrument of the state than one for suppressing heresy; which was, at this time, its surest way of keeping itself intact.

When the French and English were at war it was necessary for Spain to take sides, and after Godoy had signed the Treaty of San Ildefonso, England declared war on Spain. The result was defeat for the Spaniards off Cape St. Vincent and the loss of Trinidad; and later the great battle of Trafalgar was fought, when Nelson destroyed both French and Spanish fleets.

When Napoleon realized that he could not beat the British by force of arms he determined to do so by economic blockade, and insisted that all European ports should be closed to British shipping. Because Portugal refused to comply, Napoleon planned to use force against her, and it was arranged that the armies of Spain and France should together conquer Portugal.

When Napoleon seized the opportunity of sending troops to Spain this naturally caused some concern in Madrid. The Prince of the Asturias had been imprisoned for taking part in the plot against Godoy and there were riots in the capital, the result of which was the desired abdication of Charles IV in favour of Fernando VII, Prince of the Asturias.

Napoleon then summoned Charles and Fernando to Bayonne where he insisted that they renounce the throne in favour of his, Napoleon's, brother Joseph.

Thus began the War of Independence, with Spain in revolt against the French. In December 1808 Madrid capitulated to Napoleon, and when the Emperor reached the city he suppressed the Inquisition because he considered it against civic authority and sovereignty, and at the same time confiscated its property.

The members of the Supreme Council escaped from Madrid in spite of the fact that Napoleon had ordered them to be imprisoned; and although they were unable to keep in communication with the Pope, they managed to set up tribunals in those parts of Spain not yet in French hands.

The Inquisitors were now more concerned with keeping their freedom than prosecuting for heresy, and Lea quotes the archives of Valencia as giving the total number of cases brought before all the tribunals in 1808 as 67; in 1809, 22; in 1810, 17; in 1811, 25; in 1812, 1; and in 1813, 6.

Stories of the barbarous conduct of the Inquisition were now circulated throughout the world. Instruments of torture, which the invading armies had discovered, were described in all their horrible detail. There is a story that the French, entering the Palace of the Inquisition at Madrid, were greeted with great courtesy by the Inquisitors and shown the building from top to bottom, being assured that the stories of brutalities were gross exaggerations. One of the French officers, after having searched in vain for the dungeons of which he had heard, had the flagstones of the great hall taken up, and there below the floor discovered the cells and torture chambers which had been described. The French were reputed to have found victims still living among the dead. It was on this occasion that soldiers were said to have discovered that instrument of torture known as the Iron Virgin— an image of the Virgin Mary the front of which was covered with sharp nails and daggers. The arms of this image could be moved to draw a victim close until the body of that victim was pierced by the nails and daggers.

The story of Napoleon's disasters is well known; and how when he turned his attention to Russia he found defeat. His brother Joseph could not hold Madrid, for Wellington had brought his military genius into the field.

Joseph was forced to return to France and the War of Independence was over. But the Napoleonic invasion of Spain had brought with it new ideas as to the constitution; previously the King had reigned supreme; now the Council of Castile governed, but without much success; and *juntas* appeared in various parts of the country.

The Church party sought to bring back the Inquisition, and there was a long and heated debate in the Cortes; and finally it was decided that the Inquisition was not compatible with the Constitution. The Church party wailed that the Catholic Faith —and Christianity itself—was at stake. But the liberals were triumphant, and their manifesto stated that the Inquisition, which had been guilty of many abuses, was responsible for the decline in the fortune of Spain. They returned the right to judge religious crimes to the bishops.

During this time Fernando had been living in exile at Valençay, virtually the prisoner of Napoleon who had allowed him to live a life of ease, giving him all the privileges he asked except to ride on horseback. Napoleon is reputed to have kept him well supplied with handsome women, for Fernando was very fond of them; and for these benefits Fernando had been ready to obey Napoleon.

Fernando now returned to Madrid, and everywhere he was

greeted with jubilation, for the people believed that with the coming of the King their troubles were at an end.

* * *

The people of Spain did not know their King. Idle, debauched, he was treacherous and quite incapable of the great task which lay before him. In the first place he wished to return to absolute monarchy and was not prepared to be guided by the Cortes.

He declared that he would not accept the new constitution and that any who upheld it were guilty of treason, the reward of which was death. Tyranny returned; arrests were made; and those who opposed the King's will were imprisoned and tortured; and on 21st July, 1814, Fernando declared that the Holy Office should be revived, and Xavier de Mier y Campillo, Bishop of Almería, became Inquisitor-General.

* * *

Fernando might believe he could return to the old despotic days, but liberalism had come to Spain and it was not easily suppressed. During the next years revolution was continually threatening to break out, and in 1820 Rafael de Riego, the commander of a battalion of the Asturias, incited his men to rebellion. Revolution swept through Spain and everywhere men and women were declaring their desire for the return to the constitutional method of government.

Fernando, the coward, readily took the oath to the Constitution when he saw that he could do nothing else; and after that the bells rang for three nights, and the people stormed the prisons of the Inquisition and set prisoners free. Fernando did as he was commanded and issued an order abolishing the Inquisition.

Those who were determined to uphold the Inquisition watched the revolution with trepidation, knowing that should it prove entirely successful the days of the Holy Office were numbered.

The new government was not successful in maintaining peace throughout the country, and Spain was in chaos. The King, although still recognized as King, was a captive, and the French, under Louis XIV's nephew, the Duc d'Angoulême, chose the opportunity to invade on pretext of restoring the monarchy.

The French campaign was successful inasmuch as Fernando was restored to his kingdom. One of his first acts was to restore the conditions which were existing before 1820, and which included the re-establishment of the Inquisition. His next was to give full vent to his vindictiveness, and the prisons were full of his enemies who were maltreated in every conceivable way.

The Fren'ch however were opposed to the return of the Inquisition, and Fernando, whose great desire was to be an absolute monarch, was uncertain whether the Inquisition might not curb his ambitions; he realized also that to restore an Institution which was being universally condemned throughout Europe would be an unwise act.

The bishops continued with the work of the Inquisition under the name of *juntas de fé*; they used similar methods to those used by the Inquisitors, and these were even more to be feared than the Inquisition itself had been in later years because there was no Supreme Council to keep an eye on what was going on. Yet there were still many who clamoured for the return of the Inquisition.

On 26th July, 1826, Cayetano Ripoll, a schoolmaster of Rizaffa, met his death. During the war he had been made a prisoner and taken to France where he had become interested in new ideas, and had turned from Christianity to Deism. He had lived very simply, following the teaching of Christ, sharing everything he had with others. He believed that it was not necessary to go to Mass, and all that mattered was that people should do to others as they would be done by.

It was reported to the Inquisition that he and his scholars used the ejaculation "Praise be to God" instead of *"Ave Maria purissima"*, that he did not insist on his scholars going to Mass and kneeling to the Viaticum. It was also brought against him that the only religious teaching he deemed necessary was the keeping of the Ten Commandments.

He was arrested in 1824 and kept in prison for two years, during which time attempts were made to force him to admit his errors. This he refused to do.

The Tribunal and the *junta de fé* finally judged him to be a heretic, and he was sentenced to be hanged and burned. He was duly hanged, but owing to the changed opinion of these times the burning was to be a matter of form, and the body of the schoolmaster was merely put into a barrel which had flames painted upon it. In this barrel he was buried in unconsecrated ground.

The execution of this truly pious schoolmaster was discussed throughout Europe, and there were shocked comments on the barbarities still practised in Spain.

The schoolmaster of Rizaffa has become famous for being the last victim executed for heresy.

In 1833 Fernando VII died and, as he himself said, the cork was removed from the fermenting and surcharged bottle of Spain. The following year the Inquisition was finally suppressed.

The *juntas de fé* continued to exist, but the old Inquisitorial customs had no place in the modern world, and in 1835 the Regent, Queen Cristina, commanded that they should be immediately abolished. With this order that Institution, which had brought so much misery to countless thousands and had played a leading part in the destruction of a mighty empire, was no more. The fire of Torquemada, the piety of Isabella, the cupidity of Ferdinand, the zeal of Ximenes, the bigotry of Philip II, had contributed to its monstrous power, but now it was dead—brought to its ignoble end by the enlightenment of a new era.

INQUISITORS-GENERAL FROM THE RISE OF THE SPANISH INQUISITION TO ITS SUPPRESSION

Tomás de Torquemada, 1483–98.
Miguel de Morillo shared Inquisitor-Generalship in 1491.

In 1494 the following additional Inquisitors-General were appointed:
Martin Ponce de Leon, Archbishop of Messina. Died 1500.
Iñigo Manrique, Bishop of Córdova. Died 1496.
Francisco Sánchez de la Fuente, Bishop of Avila. Died 1498.
Alonso Suárez de Fuentelsaz, Bishop of Jaen. Resigned 1504. Died 1520.

Appointed in 1498:
Diego Deza, Archbishop of Seville. Appointed for Castile, Leon and Granada. In 1499 appointed for all Spain. Resigned 1507. Died 1523.

Inquisitions of Castile and Aragon separated.

Castile
Francisco Ximenes de Cisneros, Cardinal and Archbishop of Toledo, 1507–17.

Aragon
Juan Enguera, Bishop of Vich and Lérida, 1507–13.
Luis Mercader, Bishop of Tortosa, 1513–16.
Juan Pedro de Poul, commissioned 1516, died 1516.
Adrian of Utrecht, Cardinal and Bishop of Tortosa, appointed 1516.

The Inquisitions of Castile and Aragon were then united.

Adrian of Utrecht was Inquisitor-General until he was elected to the Papacy, 1522.
Alfonso Manrique, Cardinal and Archbishop of Seville, 1523–38.
Juan Pardo de Tavera, Cardinal and Archbishop of Toledo, 1539–45.
Francisco García de Loaysa, Archbishop of Seville, February 1546–April 1546.

Fernando Valdés, Archbishop of Seville, 1547. Resigned 1566, died 1568.

Diego Espinosa, Cardinal and Bishop of Sigüenza, 1566–72.

Pedro Ponce de Leon y Córdova, Bishop of Plasencia, appointed 1572. His brief arrived after his death, 1573.

Gaspar de Quiroga, Cardinal and Archbishop of Toledo, 1573–94.

Gerónimo Manrique de Lara, Bishop of Avila, August to November 1595.

Pedro de Portocarrero, Bishop of Cuenca, 1596. Resigned 1599. Died 1600.

Fernando Niño de Guevara, Cardinal and Archbishop of Seville, 1599. Resigned 1602. Died 1609.

Juan de Zuñiga, Bishop of Cartagena, July to December 1602.

Juan Bautista Acevedo, 1603–8.

Bernardo de Sandoval y Roxas, Cardinal and Archbishop of Toledo, 1608–18.

Luis de Aliaga, 1619. Resigned 1621. Died 1626.

Andrés Pacheco, Bishop of Cuenca, 1622–26.

Antonio de Zapata, Cardinal and Archbishop of Burgos, 1627. Resigned 1632. Died 1635.

Antonio de Sotomayor, Archbishop of Damascus, 1632. Resigned 1643. Died 1648.

Diego de Arce y Reynoso, Bishop of Plasencia, 1643–65.

Pascual de Aragon, Archbishop of Toledo, 1665.

Juan Everardo Nithard, 1666. Banished 1669. Died 1681.

Diego Sarmiento de Valladares, Bishop of Plasencia, 1669–95.

Juan Tomás de Rocaberti, Archbishop of Valencia, 1695–99.

Alfonso Fernández de Cordova y Aguilar. Died September 1699 before his brief arrived.

Balthasar de Mendoza y Sandoval, Bishop of Segovia, 1699. Resigned 1705. Died 1727.

Vidal Marin, Bishop of Ceuta 1705–9.

Antonio Ybañez de la Riva-Herrer, Archbishop of Saragossa 1709–10.

Francesco Giudice, 1711. Resigned 1716. Died 1725.

Felipe Antonio Gil de Taboada. Appointed 1715 but did not serve.

Josef de Molines. Appointed 1717 while in Rome. Died in Milan on way home to his appointment.

Juan de Arzamendi. Died without serving.

Diego de Astorga y Cespedes, Bishop of Barcelona, 1720. Resigned 1720. Died 1724.

Juan de Camargo, Bishop of Pampeluna, 1720–33.

Andrés de Orbe y Larreategui, Archbishop of Valencia, 1733–40.

Manuel Isidro Manrique de Lara, Archbishop of Santiago, 1742–6.

Francisco Pérez de Prado y Cuesta, Bishop of Teruel, 1746–55.

Manuel Quintano Bonifaz, Archbishop of Pharsalia, 1755. Resigned 1774. Died 1775.

Felipe Beltran, Bishop of Salamanca, 1775–83.

Agustin Rubin de Cevallos, Bishop of Jaen, 1784–93.

Manuel Abad y la Sierra, Archbishop of Selimbria, 1793. Resigned 1794. Died 1806.

Francisco Antonio de Lorenzana, Archbishop of Toledo, 1794. Resigned 1797. Died 1804.

Ramon Josef de Arce y Reynoso, Archbishop of Saragossa, 1798. Resigned 1808. Died 1814.

Xavier Mier y Campillo, Bishop of Almería, 1814–18.

Gerónimo Castellon y Salas, Bishop of Tarazona. 1818–34. The last Inquisitor-General.

INDEX

Acevedo, Juan Bautista, years as Inquisitor-General, 168

Adler, views on Alonso de Peralta, 67

Adrian, Cardinal, appointed Inquisitor-General of Indies, 64

Agreda, Sor Maria de, relationship with King, 126; King asks her advice, 127; attitude to Liars' Walk and influence over King, 128; advises him to take up arms against French, 129; death, 130

Aguilar, Cardinal Alonso Fernandez de Cordova y, appointed Inquisitor-General and death, 148, 168

Albert, Archduke, marriage, 57

Alexander VII, conflict with Spain, 140

Alfonso VI of Portugal, plot to depose him, 105

Aliaga, Luis de, as Inquisitor-General, resignation and death, 168

Almenara, Count of, put in charge of Pérez case, 51; attacked by Moors, 52

Alva, Duke of, sent to Netherlands and calls Council of Blood, 19, 20; cruelty and cynicism, 20, 21; disgraced and recalled, 22; his victims, 23; opposition to Ruy Gómez, 42; sufferings under his rule, 46; attacked by Carlos, 55

Alvárez, Sebastian, victim of Inquisition, 69

Amadeus, Victor, marriage of daughter, 150

Ana, Infanta (daughter of Philip III), betrothal, 115

Angoulême, Duc de (nephew of Louis XIV), invades Spain, 163

Anne of Egmont, marriage to Orange, 18

Anne of Saxony, marriage to Orange, 18

Aponte, Francisco López de, victim of Inquisition, 69

Aragon, Pascual de, as Inquisitor-General, 168

Arbués, Pedro, his assassination, 16

Arias, Pedro García de, victim of Inquisition, 69

Armstrong, Edward, questions Hume's figures, 154

Arzamendi, Juan de, appointment and death, 168

Aulnoy, Madame d', evidence on Isabel and Philip IV, 117

Avalos, Alonso Granero de, appointed Inquisitor, 66; his cruelty, 67

Baker, Rev. J., collected writings, 69

Baltasar Carlos, Infante of Spain, birth, 123; with his mother, 124; betrothal and death, 128, 129

Barbara, Queen, marriage and death, 155

Bautista, Joan, Protestant victim of Inquisition, 87

Bavaria, Electoral Prince of, candidate for Spanish throne, 147

Bedford, Regent, imposes tax for capture of Joan of Arc, 40

Belando, writings brought to notice of Inquisition, 153

Bello, Fray Bartolomé, guilty of solicitation, 102

Beltran, Felipe, reigned as Inquisitor-General, 169

Benavente, Count, tool of French, 146

Bernal, Jan, Protestant victim of Inquisition, 87

Besante, Juan de, betrays Pérez, 52

Bethencourt, Jean de, discovers Canaries, 25

Billon, Martin, demands surrender of Joan of Arc, 40

Bonaparte, Joseph, 8; received throne of Spain, 161; forced to return to France, 162

Bonaparte, Napoleon, 8; assists Godoy against his enemies, 160; his effect on Inquisition, sends troops to Spain, gives throne to Joseph, orders members of Supreme Council to be imprisoned, 161; his defeats, his treatment of Fernando, 162

Bonavalle, Bishop of, replaces Cardona in Sardinia, 98

Bonifaz, Manuel Quintano, reigned as Inquisitor-General, resignation and death, 169

Bonilla, Archbishop of Mexico, Inquisitor-General for Mexico, 66

Borromeo, Cardinal Carlo, attacks heresy in Milan, 100

Buchanan, Dr. Claudius, visits Goa and asks to inspect prisons of Inquisition, 111, 112